Over 10 Million Copies in Print!

W9-AZQ-821

COMPREHENSIVE
CURRICULUM
of Basic Skills

GRADE

6

Math

Reading

Reading Comprehension

English

Writing

Thinking Kids™
Carson-Dellosa Publishing LLC
Greensboro, North Carolina

Thinking Kids™
Carson-Dellosa Publishing LLC
P.O. Box 35665
Greensboro, NC 27425 USA

© 2016 Carson-Dellosa Publishing LLC. Except as permitted under the United States Copyright Act, no part of this publication may be reproduced, stored, or distributed in any form or by any means (mechanically, electronically, recording, etc.) without the prior written consent of Carson-Dellosa Publishing LLC. Thinking Kids™ is an imprint of Carson-Dellosa Publishing LLC.

Printed in the USA • All rights reserved.   ISBN 978-1-4838-2415-4
02-123161151

Comprehensive Curriculum - **Grade 6**

TABLE OF CONTENTS

READING

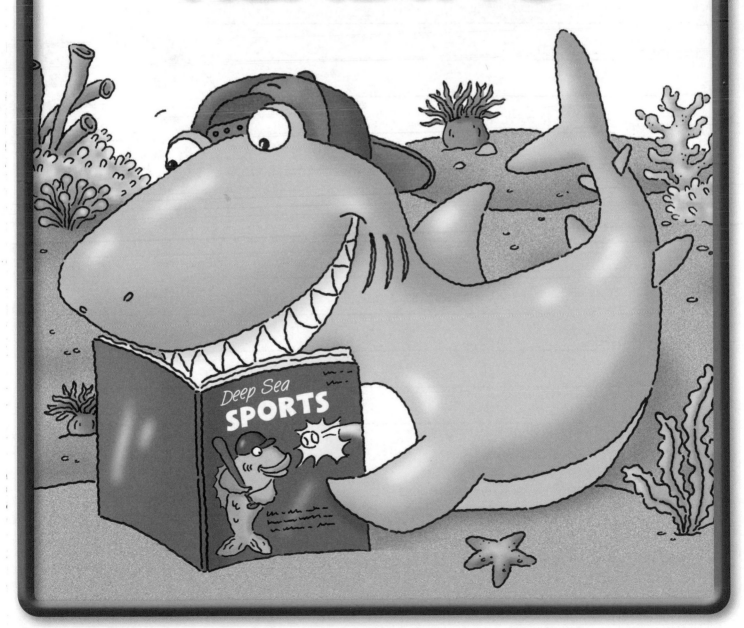

Name _____

Spelling: Words with ā

Directions: Write a sentence for each word. Use a dictionary if you are unsure of the meaning of a word.

1. favorite _____

2. gable _____

3. dangerous _____

_____

4. patient _____

_____

5. lakefront _____

_____

6. statement _____

_____

7. nation _____

_____

8. negotiated _____

9. operate _____

10. decade _____

Directions: Write the answers.

11. Which word means "a 10-year period"? _____

12. Which word means "a triangle-shaped end of a building's roof"? _____

13. Which word means "arbitrated"? _____

Spelling: Words with ē

Directions: Write a sentence for each word. Use a dictionary if you are unsure of the meaning of a word.

1. niece _My niece was_____

2. meaningful _____

3. conceited _____

4. baleen _____

5. field _____

6. disease _____

7. reactivate _____

8. peony _____

9. seafaring _____

10. theme _____

Directions: Write the answers.

11. Which word is a summer-blooming flower?
_Sunflower_____

12. Which word is a type of whale?
_Moby Dick_____

13. Which word is an illness?
_The flu_____

Spelling: Words with ī

Directions: Write a sentence for each word. Use a dictionary if you are unsure of the meaning of a word.

1. bisect _____

2. identify _____

3. frightened _____

4. glider _____

5. idol _____

6. library _____

7. pipeline _____

8. hieroglyphic _____

9. rhinoceros _____

10. silent _____

Directions: Write the answers.

11. Which word means "to be scared"?

_____

12. Which word means "to divide into two sections"?

_____

13. Which word is an animal?

_____

14. Which word is a type of ancient writing?

_____

Spelling: Words with ō

Directions: Write a sentence for each word. Use a dictionary if you are unsure of the meaning of a word.

1. clothing _____

2. slogan _____

3. total _____

4. stethoscope _____

5. voltage _____

6. stereo _____

7. protein _____

8. negotiate _____

9. locust _____

10. locomotive _____

Directions: Write the answers.

11. Which word is an insect?

_____

12. Which word means "a train"?

_____

13. Which word means "a listening device to hear the heart"?

_____

14. Which word means "to bargain"?

_____

Comprehensive Curriculum - Grade 6

Name _____

Spelling: Words with ū

Directions: Write a sentence for each word. Use a dictionary if you are unsure of the meaning of a word.

1. universe _____

2. cruise _____

3. absolute _____

4. influence _____

5. unanimous _____

6. vacuum _____

7. putrid _____

8. incubate _____

9. peruse _____

10. numerous _____

Directions: Write the answers.

11. Which word means "to read carefully"?

_____

12. Which word means "everyone is in agreement"?

_____

13. Which word means "a sea voyage taken for pleasure"?

_____

14. Which word means "to keep eggs warm until they hatch"?

_____

Name _____

Spelling: *I* Before *E*, Except After *C*

Use an **i** before **e**, except after **c**, or when **e** and **i** together sound like long **a**.

Examples:
relieve
deceive
neighbor

Exceptions: weird, foreign, height, seize

Directions: Write **C** in the blank if the word in bold is spelled correctly. Write **X** in the blank if it is spelled incorrectly. The first one has been done for you.

i before **e**,
except after **c**,
or when sounding like **a**,
as in **neighbor** and **weigh**

__C__ 1. They stopped at the crossing for the **freight** train.

__X__ 2. How much does that **wiegh**?

__C__ 3. Did you **believe** his story?

__X__ 4. He **recieved** an A on his paper!

__X__ 5. She said it was the **nieghborly** thing to do.

__C__ 6. The guards **seized** the package.

__X__ 7. That movie was **wierd**!

__X__ 8. Her **hieght** is five feet, six inches.

__C__ 9. It's not right to **deceive** others.

__X__ 10. Your answers should be **breif**.

__C__ 11. She felt a lot of **grief** when her dog died.

__X__ 12. He is still **greiving** about his loss.

__C__ 13. Did the police catch the **thief**?

__X__ 14. She was their **cheif** source of information.

__X__ 15. Can you speak a **foreign** language?

Name _____

Spelling: Words with *ie* and *ei*

Many people have trouble remembering when to use **ie** and when to use **ei**. The following rules have many exceptions, but they may be helpful to you.

Rule 1: If the two letters are pronounced like ē and are preceded by an s sound, use **ei**, as in **receive**.

Rule 2: If the two letters are pronounced like ē but are not preceded by an s sound, use **ie** as in **believe**.

Rule 3: If the two letters are pronounced like ā, use **ei** as in **eight** and **vein**.

Rule 4: If the two letters are pronounced like ī, use **ei** as in **height**.

The sound **s** could be produced by the letter **s** as in **single** or the letter **c** as in **cease**.

Directions: Write the words from the box on the lines after the spelling rule that applies.

veil	brief	deceive	belief	niece
reindeer	yield	achieve	height	neighbor
grief	ceiling	weight	vein	seize

Rule 1: _____

Rule 2: _____

Rule 3: _____

Rule 4: _____

Directions: Complete the sentences with words that have the vowel sound shown. Use each word from the box only once.

1. My next-door (ā) _____ wore a long (ā) _____ at her wedding.

2. Will the roof hold the (ā) _____ of Santa's (ā) _____ ?

3. My nephew and (ē) _____ work hard to (ē) _____ their goals.

4. I have a strong (ē) _____ they would never (ē) _____ me.

5. For a (ē) _____ moment, I thought Will would (ē) _____ the game to me.

6. The blood rushed through my (ā) _____ .

7. What is the (ī) _____ of this (ē) _____ ?

Spelling: Words with *ûr* and *ôr*

The difference between **ûr** and **ôr** is clear in the words **fur** and **for**. The **ûr** sound can be spelled **ur** as in **fur**, **our** as in **journal**, **er** as in **her**, and **ear** as in **search**.

The **ôr** sound can be spelled **or** as in **for**, **our** as in **four**, **oar** as in **soar**, and **ore** as in **more**.

Directions: Write the words from the box on the lines to match the sounds.

florist	plural	ignore	courtesy	observe
survey	research	furnish	normal	emergency
tornado	coarse	flourish	source	restore

ûr _____

_____

ôr _____

_____

Directions: Complete the sentences with words that have the sound shown. Use each word only once.

1. We all get along better when we remember to use (**ûr**) _____.

2. My brother likes flowers and wants to be a (**ôr**) _____.

3. What was the (**ôr**) _____ of the (**ûr**) _____ for your report?

4. He waved at her, but she continued to (**ôr**) _____ him.

5. For a plural subject, use a (**ûr**) _____ verb.

6. Beneath the dark clouds, a (**ôr**) _____ formed!

7. Firefighters are used to handling an (**ûr**) _____ .

8. When will they be able to (**ôr**) _____ our electricity?

9. How are you going to (**ûr**) _____ your apartment?

Spelling: Words Beginning with *Sh* and *Th*

Directions: Write a definition for each word. Use a dictionary if you are unsure of the meaning of a word.

1. shallow: _____

2. thimble: _____

3. shear: _____

4. sheriff: _____

5. thermal: _____

6. throttle: _____

7. shingle: _____

8. shabby: _____

9. thrifty: _____

10. shoreline: _____

11. threaten: _____

12. thyroid: _____

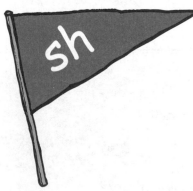

Directions: Use two of the above words in sentences.

13. _____

_____

14. _____

_____

Spelling: Words with *kw*, *ks*, and *gz* Sounds

The consonant **q** is always followed by **u** in words and is pronounced **kw**. The letter **x** can be pronounced **ks** as in **mix**. When **x** is followed by a vowel, it is usually pronounced **gz** as in **example**.

Directions: Write the words from the box on the lines to match the sounds shown.

expense	exist	aquarium	acquire	request	exact
expand	exit	quality	excellent	quantity	quiz
exhibit	squirm	expression			

kw _____

_____

ks _____

_____

gz _____

Directions: Complete the sentences with words that have the sound shown. Use words from the box only once.

1. We went to the zoo to see the fish **(gz)** _____ .

2. I didn't know its **(gz)** _____ location, so we followed the map.

3. The zoo plans to **(kw)** _____ some sharks for its

   (kw) _____ .

4. Taking care of sharks is a big **(ks)** _____ , but a number of people

   have asked the zoo to **(ks)** _____ its display of fish.

5. These people want a better **(kw)** _____ of fish, not a bigger

   (kw) _____ of them.

6. I think the zoo already has an **(ks)** _____ display.

7. Some of its rare fish no longer **(gz)** _____ in the ocean.

Name _____

Spelling: Words with Silent Letters

Some letters in words are not pronounced, like the **b** in **crumb**, the **l** in **yolk**, the **n** in **autumn**, the **g** in **design**, and the **h** in **hour**.

Directions: Write the words from the box on the lines to match the silent letters. Use a dictionary if you are unsure of the meaning or pronunciation of a word.

condemn	yolk	campaign	assign	salmon
hymn	limb	chalk	tomb	foreign
resign	column	spaghetti	rhythm	solemn

n _____

l _____

g _____

b _____

h _____

Directions: Write words from the box to complete these sentences.

1. What did the teacher (**g**) _____ for homework?

2. She put words in a (**n**) _____ on the board.

3. When she finished writing, her hands were white

   with (**l**) _____ .

4. The church choir clapped in (**h**) _____

   with the (**n**) _____ .

5. While I was cracking an egg, the (**l**) _____ slipped onto the floor.

6. Did the explorers find anything in the ancient (**b**) _____?

7. My favorite dinner of all is (**h**) _____ and meatballs.

8. Do not (**n**) _____ me for making one little mistake.

Spelling: Words with *ph* or *kn*

The letters **ph** produce the same sound as the letter **f**. When the letters **kn** are together, the **k** is silent.

Directions: Write a definition for each word. Use a dictionary if you are unsure of the meaning of a word.

1. photographer: _____

2. knowledge: _____

3. knee: _____

4. telephone: _____

5. knock: _____

6. phonics: _____

7. physician: _____

8. knife: _____

9. pharmacy: _____

10. knight: _____

11. knit: _____

12. pheasant: _____

Directions: Write the answers.

13. Which word is a place to buy medicine?

_____

14. Which word is a synonym for **doctor**?

_____

15. Which word names a bird?

_____

Spelling: Words with *gh* or *gn*

Directions: Use the clues and the words in the box to complete the crossword puzzle.

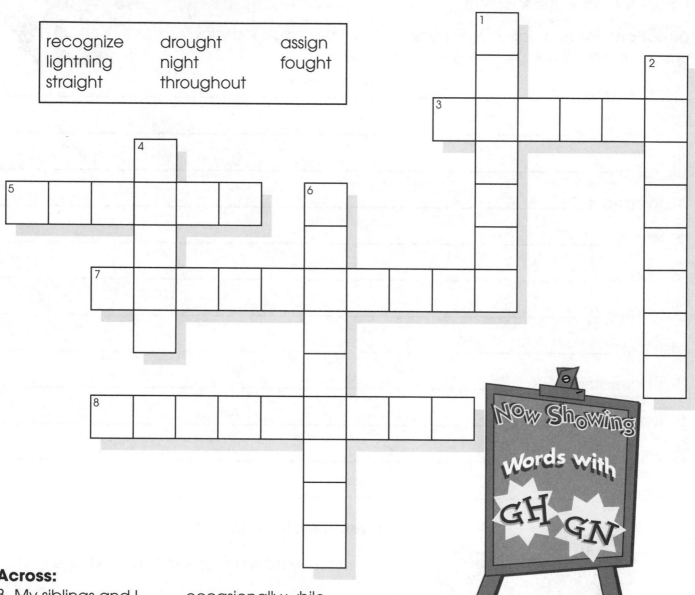

recognize	drought	assign
lightning	night	fought
straight	throughout	

Across:

3. My siblings and I _____ occasionally while growing up.
5. The teacher will _____ bus seats for the field trip.
7. _____ the storm, the rescue squads worked without stopping.
8. Do you _____ the woman you are meeting for lunch?

Down:

1. The _____ left farmers without crops.
2. My brother has _____ hair, but mine is curly.
4. Tomorrow _____, we will leave for Florida.
6. _____ struck the old barn on Walnut Hill.

Root Words

A **root word** is the common stem that gives related words their basic meanings.

Example: Separate is the root word for **separately**, **separation**, **inseparable**, and **separator**.

Directions: Identify the root word in each group of words. Look up the meaning of the root word in the dictionary, and write its definition. The first one has been done for you.

1. colorless, colorful, discolor, coloration

   Root word: _____ color _____

   Definition: ___ any coloring matter, dye, ___
   _____ pigment or paint _____

2. creator, creation, creating, creative, recreate

   Root word: _____

   Definition: _____

3. remove, movement, movable, immovable, removable

   Root word: _____

   Definition: _____

4. contentment, malcontent, discontent, discontentment

   Root word: _____

   Definition: _____

5. pleasure, displeasure, pleasing, pleasant, unpleasant

   Root word: _____

   Definition: _____

6. successor, unsuccessful, successful

   Root word: _____

   Definition: _____

Greek and Latin Roots

Many word patterns in the English language are combinations of Greek or Latin words. When you know what part of a word means, you may be able to figure out the meaning of the rest of the word. For example, if **cycle** means "circle or wheel" and **bi** means "two," then you can figure out that **bicycle** means "two wheels." **Root words** are the words that longer words are based on. For example, **duct**, which means "to lead," is the root of **conduct** or **induct**. Look at the chart below. It has several root words and their meanings on it.

Root	Meaning	Example	Definition
act	to do	interact	to act with others
aqua	water	aquatint	dyed water
auto	self	automobile	to move oneself
centi	a hundred	centennial	one hundred years

Directions: Look at each word equation below. The meaning of one part is shown in parentheses. Consult the chart of root words to find the meaning of the other part. Write the meaning in the blank. Combine the two meanings. Write the dictionary definition in the space provided.

1. react re (again) + act _____to do_____ = _____to do again_____

   Dictionary definition: To act or do again _____

2. automatic auto _____ + matic (having a mind) = _____

   Dictionary definition: _____

3. transact trans (across) + act _____ = _____

   Dictionary definition: _____

4. centimeter centi _____ + meter (meter) = _____

   Dictionary definition: _____

5. aquanaut aqua _____ + naut (sailor) = _____

   Dictionary definition: _____

Root Words

Root	Meaning	Example	Defintion
cede	to go	supercede	to go beyond
cept	seize	intercept	to seize during
duce	lead	deduce	to find the lead
fer	carry	interfere	to carry into
port	carry	transport	to carry across
spect	to look	inspect	to look in
tain	to hold	obtain	to gain by action
vene	to come	convene	to come to start

Directions: Complete the exercises below.

1. precede   pre (before) + cede _____to go_____ = _____to go before_____

   Dictionary definition: __to be, go, or come before_____

2. report   re (again) + port _____ = _____

   Dictionary definition: _____

3. intervene   inter (between) + vene _____ = _____

   Dictionary definition: _____

4. induce   in (in) + duce _____ = _____

   Dictionary definition: _____

5. retrospect   retro (backward) + spect_____ = _____

   Dictionary definition: _____

6. refer   re (again) + fer _____ = _____

   Dictionary definition: _____

7. retain   re (again) + tain _____ = _____

   Dictionary definition: _____

8. concept   con (with) + cept _____ = _____

   Dictionary definition: _____

Comprehensive Curriculum - Grade 6

Prefixes

A **prefix** is a syllable added to the beginning of a word to change its meaning. The prefix **re** means "back" or "again," as in **return**. **Pre** means "before," as in **prepare**. **Dis** means "do the opposite," as in **disappear**. **In** and **im** both mean "not," as in **impossible**. (These two prefixes also have other meanings.) **Com** and **con** both mean "with," as in **companion** and **concert**. Use **im** and **com** with words that start with **p**, **b**, or **m**. Use **in** and **con** with words that begin with a vowel or other consonants.

Directions: Match each word from the box to its definition.

disbelieve	recite	connotation	impolite	preview
impatient	distrust	configuration	prevision	incomplete
invisible	dislike	confederate	recover	compassion

1. share another's feelings ———————

2. not finished ———————

3. another meaning ———————

4. become normal again ———————

5. take away confidence ———————

6. look to the future ———————

7. arrangement of parts ———————

8. say from memory ———————

9. ally ———————

10. hate ———————

11. look at ———————

12. rude ———————

13. in a hurry ———————

14. doubt ———————

15. not seen ———————

Directions: Add the rest of the word to each prefix in these sentences. Use words from the box only once. Be sure to use the correct form of the word.

16. When he re_____ from his cold, Jeff was im_____ to get back to work.

17. Jonah stared at the ghostly figure with dis_____ and dis_____ .

18. I'd like to re_____ that poem, but my memory of it is in_____.

19. She was very im _____ during the movie pre_____.

Prefixes

A **prefix** is a syllable added to the beginning of a word that changes its meaning. The prefixes **in**, **il**, **ir**, and **im** all mean "not."

Directions: Create new words by adding **in**, **il**, **ir**, or **im** to these root words. Use a dictionary to check that the new words are correct. The first one has been done for you.

	Prefix		Root Word		New Word
1.	il	+	logical	=	illogical
2.	_____	+	literate	=	_____
3.	_____	+	patient	=	_____
4.	_____	+	probable	=	_____
5.	_____	+	reversible	=	_____
6.	_____	+	responsible	=	_____
7.	_____	+	active	=	_____
8.	_____	+	moral	=	_____
9.	_____	+	removable	=	_____
10.	_____	+	legible	=	_____
11.	_____	+	mature	=	_____
12.	_____	+	perfect	=	_____

Name _____

Prefixes

The prefixes **un** and **non** also mean "not."

Examples:
　　Unhappy means "not happy."
　　Nonproductive means "not productive."

Directions: Divide each word into its prefix and root word. The first one has been done for you.

	Prefix	Root Word
1. unappreciated	un	appreciate
2. unlikely		
3. unkempt		
4. untimely		
5. nonstop		
6. nonsense		
7. nonprofit		
8. nonresident		

Directions: Use the clues in the first sentence to complete the second sentence with one of the words from the box. The first one has been done for you.

9. She didn't reside at school. She was a __nonresident__ .

10. He couldn't stop talking. He talked _____ .

11. The company did not make a profit. It was a _____ company.

12. She was not talking sense. She was talking _____ .

13. He visited at a bad time. His visit was _____ .

14. No one appreciated his efforts. He felt _____ .

15. He did not "keep up" his hair. His hair was _____ .

16. She was not likely to come. Her coming was _____ .

Prefixes

The prefixes **co**, **col**, **com**, **con**, and **cor** mean "with" or "together." The prefixes **anti**, **contra**, and **ob** mean "against."

Directions: Write each word's prefix and root word in the space provided.

Word	Prefix	Root Word
coexist	co	exist
concurrent		
correlate		
codependent		
antigravity		
contraband		

Directions: Use the words from the chart above to complete the sentences.

1. When airplanes fly very high and then quickly drop down, they cause an

_____ effect.

2. Materials that are illegal are called _____ .

3. A dog and a cat can _____ in the same house if they get along well.

4. Events that happen at the same time are _____ .

5. When two people rely on each other, they are said to be _____ .

6. The textbook will _____ with the teacher's lectures.

Name _____

Prefixes

The prefixes **epi**, **hyper**, **over**, and **super** mean "above" or "over." The prefixes **under** and **sub** mean "under."

Directions: Write each word's prefix and root word in the space provided.

Word	Prefix	Root Word
hyperactive	hyper	active
overanxious	_____	_____
superimpose	_____	_____
epilogue	_____	_____
underestimate	_____	_____
subordinate	_____	_____

Directions: Use the words above to complete the following sentences.

1. A photographer could _____ one image on top of another.

2. The _____ of the book may tell additional information about the story.

3. All the other children settled down for the night except the boy who was _____ .

4. He could not sleep because he was _____ about the upcoming trip.

5. The company's president told his _____ to take over some of the responsibilities.

6. Just because you think you are weak, don't _____ how strong you could be.

Numerical Prefixes

Some prefixes are related to numbers. For example, in Latin **uni** means "one." The prefix **mono** means "one" in Greek. The chart below lists prefixes for numbers one through ten from both the Latin and Greek languages.

Number	Latin	Example	Greek	Example
1	uni	university	mon, mono	monopoly
2	du	duplex	di	digress
3	tri	tricycle	tri	trio
4	quad	quadrant	tetro	tetrameter
5	quin	quintuplets	penta	pentagon
6	sex	sexennial	hex	hexagon
7	sept	septuagenarian	hept	heptagon
8	oct	octopus	oct	octagon
9	nov	novena	enne	ennead (group of nine)
10	dec	decade	dec	decimal

Directions: Complete the exercises below.

1. unicycle   uni _____ + cycle (wheel) = _____

   Dictionary definition: _____

2. monogram   mono _____ + gram (writing) = _____

   Dictionary definition: _____

3. sextet   sex _____ + tet (group) = _____

   Dictionary definition: _____

4. quadrant   quad _____ + rant (part) = _____

   Dictionary definition: _____

5. decigram   dec _____ + gram (gram) = _____

   Dictionary definition: _____

Name _____

Review

Roots	Meanings	Prefixes	Meanings
fer	carry	dis	separate
graph	write	epi	upon, above
rupt	break	ex	out
tend	stretch	in	in
vade	go	trans	across

Directions: Complete the exercises below.

1. invade   in _____ + vade _____ = _____

   Dictionary definition: _____

2. disrupt   dis _____ + rupt _____ = _____

   Dictionary definition: _____

3. transfer   trans _____ + fer _____ = _____

   Dictionary definition: _____

4. extend   ex _____ + tend _____ = _____

   Dictionary definition: _____

5. epigraph   epi _____ + graph _____ = _____

   Dictionary definition: _____

Directions: The prefixes **mono** and **uni** both mean "one." Write each word's prefix and root in the space provided.

Word	Prefix	Root
monorhyme	_____	_____
monosyllable	_____	_____
unilingual	_____	_____
uniparental	_____	_____
unilateral	_____	_____

Suffixes

A **suffix** is a syllable added to the end of a root word that changes its meaning.

When a word ends in silent **e**, keep the **e** before adding a suffix beginning with a consonant.

Example: amuse + ment = amusement

Exception: argue + ment = argument

When a word ends in silent **e**, drop the **e** before adding a suffix beginning with a vowel.

Example: amuse = amusing

Exceptions: hoeing, shoeing, canoeing

Directions: Write **C** on the blank if the word in bold is spelled correctly. Write **X** in the blank if it is spelled incorrectly. The first one has been done for you.

_C_ 1. She was a woman of many **achievements**.

____ 2. He hated to hear their **arguments**.

____ 3. Do you want to go **canoing**?

____ 4. He kept **urgeing** her to eat more dessert.

____ 5. She was not good at **deceiving** others.

____ 6. He **rarely** skipped lunch.

____ 7. Would you repeat that **announcment**?

____ 8. Bicycle **safety** was very important to him.

____ 9. Their constant **argueing** got on my nerves.

____ 10. He found that **shoeing** horses was not easy.

____ 11. The sun felt hot as they were **hoeing**.

____ 12. She was so **relieveed** that she laughed.

Suffixes: Words Ending in Y

If a word ends in a vowel and **y**, keep the **y** when you add a suffix.

Example:
  bray + ed = brayed
  bray + ing = braying

Exception: lay + ed = laid

If a word ends in a consonant and **y**, change the **y** to
i when you add a suffix, unless the suffix begins with **i**.

Example:
  baby + ed = babied
  baby + ing = babying

Directions: Write **C** in the blank if the word in bold is spelled correctly.
Write **X** if it is spelled incorrectly. The first one has been done for you.

__C__ 1. She was a good student who did well at her **studies**.

_____ 2. Will you please stop **babiing** him?

_____ 3. She **layed** her purse on the couch.

_____ 4. Both the **ferrys** left on schedule.

_____ 5. Could you repeat what he was **saying**?

_____ 6. He was **triing** to do his best.

_____ 7. How many **cherries** are in this pie?

_____ 8. The cat **stayed** away for two weeks.

_____ 9. He is **saveing** all his money.

_____ 10. The lake was **muddier** than I remembered.

_____ 11. It was the **muddyest** lake I've ever seen!

_____ 12. Her mother **babied** her when she was sick.

Suffixes: Doubling Final Consonants

If a one-syllable word ends in one vowel and consonant, double the last consonant when you add a suffix that begins with a vowel.

Examples: swim + ing = swimming   big + er = bigger

Directions: Add the suffixes shown to the root words, doubling the final consonants when appropriate. The first one has been done for you.

1. brim   +   ing   =   _brimming_
2. big   +   est   =   _____
3. hop   +   ing   =   _____
4. swim   +   er   =   _____
5. thin   +   er   =   _____
6. spin   +   ing   =   _____
7. smack   +   ing   =   _____
8. sink   +   ing   =   _____
9. win   +   er   =   _____
10. thin   +   est   =   _____
11. slim   +   er   =   _____
12. slim   +   ing   =   _____
13. thread +   ing   =   _____
14. thread +   er   =   _____
15. win   +   ing   =   _____
16. sing   +   ing   =   _____
17. stop   +   ing   =   _____
18. thrill +   ing   =   _____
19. drop   +   ed   =   _____
20. mop   +   ing   =   _____

Suffixes: Doubling Final Consonants

When two-syllable words have the accent on the second syllable and end in a consonant preceded by a vowel, double the final consonant to add a suffix that begins with a vowel.

Examples: occur + ing = occurring   occur + ed = occurred

If the accent shifts to the first syllable when the suffix is added to the two-syllable root word, the final consonant is not doubled.

Example: refer + ence = reference

Directions: Say the words listed to hear where the accent falls when the suffix is added. Then, add the suffix to the root word, doubling the final consonant when appropriate. The first one has been done for you.

1. excel   +   ence   = _excellence_
2. infer   +   ing   = _____
3. regret   +   able   = _____
4. control   +   able   = _____
5. submit   +   ing   = _____
6. confer   +   ing   = _____
7. refer   +   al   = _____
8. differ   +   ing   = _____
9. compel   +   ing   = _____
10. commit   +   ed   = _____
11. regret   +   ing   = _____
12. depend   +   able   = _____
13. upset   +   ing   = _____
14. propel   +   ing   = _____
15. repel   +   ed   = _____
16. prefer   +   ing   = _____
17. prefer   +   ence   = _____
18. differ   +   ence   = _____
19. refer   +   ing   = _____
20. control   +   ing   = _____

EXCEL + ENCE = EXCELLENCE

Suffixes

A **suffix** is a syllable added to the end of a word that changes its meaning. Some suffixes change nouns into adjectives.

Examples: fool — **foolish**   nation — **national**

Other suffixes change adjectives into adverbs.

Examples: foolish — **foolishly**   national — **nationally**

Directions: Match the root words with words from the box.

personal	stylish	obviously	professional
typical	childish	practical	medical
permanently	ticklish	additional	critical
gradually	physical	musical	

1. tickle _____
2. critic _____
3. add _____
4. person _____
5. child _____

6. grade _____
7. practice _____
8. physician _____
9. permanent _____
10. medic _____

11. type _____
12. music _____
13. style _____
14. obvious _____
15. profess _____

Directions: Circle the word or words in each sentence that are a synonym for a word from the box. Write the word from the box on the line. The first one has been done for you.

16. Knowing how to cook is a (useful) skill.   _____**practical**_____

17. The lake slowly warmed up.   _____

18. Clearly, I should have stayed on the path.   _____

19. That is a fashionable outfit.   _____

20. Wanting your own way all the time is for little kids.   _____

21. Getting lost is common for me.   _____

22. My grades are a private matter.   _____

Suffixes: *ion, tion,* and *ation*

The suffixes **ion**, **tion**, and **ation** change verbs into nouns.

Examples: imitate + **ion** = imit**ation**   combine + **ation** = combin**ation**

Directions: Match each word from the box with its definition.

celebration	solution	imitation	exploration	selection
reflection	conversation	population	invitation	suggestion
combination	decoration	appreciation	definition	transportation

1. a copy   _____

2. talking   _____

3. a request   _____

4. the meaning   _____

5. a search   _____

6. mirror image   _____

7. cars, trucks   _____

8. ornament   _____

9. choice   _____

10. a party   _____

11. the answer   _____

12. people   _____

13. a joining   _____

14. new idea   _____

15. thankfulness   _____

Directions: Write the correct forms of the words in the sentences. The first one has been done for you.

16. **transport**   How are we __transporting__ our project to school?

    Did anyone arrange __transportation__ ?

17. **decorate**   Today, we are _____ the classroom.

    We brought the _____ from home.

18. **solve**   Have you _____ the problem yet?

    We need a _____ by the end of the day.

Suffixes: *ment* and *ity*

The suffixes **ment** and **ity** change verbs and some adjectives to nouns.

Examples: treat — **treatment**   able — **ability**

Directions: Circle the word or words in each sentence that are synonyms for words from the box. Write the word from the box on the line. The first one has been done for you.

equipment	responsibility	activity	
accomplishment	adjustment	ability	treatment
assignment	personality	achievement	appointment
popularity	astonishment	advertisement	curiosity

1. The workers are bringing in their (machines.)   **equipment**

2. Whose duty is it to take out the trash?   _____

3. Do you know our homework for tonight?   _____

4. I could see the surprise in his face.   _____

5. Ken is happy with his new position.   _____

6. I was filled with wondering.   _____

7. She lists one achievement in particular.   _____

8. Look at the exercise on page 16.   _____

9. The way you get along with others is part of
   your character.   _____

10. I heard that commercial a hundred times.   _____

11. Linh has a strong athletic skill.   _____

12. Jason's kindness led to his acceptance by his friends.   _____

13. I need to make a change in my schedule.   _____

14. That is quite an accomplishment!   _____

15. The doctor is trying another way to help my allergies.   _____

Suffixes: *less* and *some*

The suffix **less** means "lacking" or "without." The suffix **some** means "full" or "like."

Examples:
   Hopeless means "without hope."
   Awesome means "filled with awe."

Directions: Create new words by adding **some** or **less** to these root words. Use a dictionary to check that the new words are correct. The first one has been done for you.

Root Word		Suffix		New Word
1. heart	+	less	=	heartless
2. trouble	+	_____	=	_____
3. home	+	_____	=	_____
4. humor	+	_____	=	_____
5. awe	+	_____	=	_____
6. child	+	_____	=	_____
7. win	+	_____	=	_____

Directions: Use the clues in the first sentence to complete the second sentence with one of the words from the box. The first one has been done for you.

8. Her smile was winning and delightful. She had a _____ winsome _____ smile.

9. The mean man seemed to have no heart. He was _____

10. She never smiled or laughed. She appeared to be _____

11. The solar system fills me with awe. It is _____

12. The couple had no children. They were _____

13. He had no place to live. He was _____

14. The pet caused the family trouble. It was _____

Suffixes: *ship*, *ful*, and *ist*

Directions: Write the meaning of each word on the line. Use a dictionary if you are unsure of the meaning of a word.

1. biologist: _____

_____

2. citizenship: _____

_____

3. companionship: _____

_____

4. archaeologist: _____

5. typist: _____

6. scholarship: _____

7. doubtful: _____

8. hopeful: _____

9. dictatorship: _____

10. chemist: _____

11. principalship: _____

12. artist: _____

13. spiteful: _____

14. professorship: _____

15. geologist: _____

Suffixes: *ance* and *ence*

Directions: Write words from the box to complete the sentences. Use a dictionary if you are unsure of the meaning of a word.

performance	experience
correspondence	reliance
evidence	sequence
maintenance	absence
dependence	insurance

ance   **ence**

1. The daycare position required _____ working with children.

2. During her _____, a friend phoned each night with homework assignments.

3. My grandmother is known for her self- _____.

4. The alphabet is a _____ of 26 letters.

5. A letter to my penpal is called long distance _____.

6. The circus advertised a 2:00 P.M. _____.

7. Many people have a great _____ on calculators for math.

8. Fortunately, most homeowners in the flooded area carried _____.

9. The police gathered _____ in hopes of solving the burglary.

10. _____ of football and baseball fields requires much time and effort.

Suffixes: *ment*, *ible*, and *able*

The suffix **ment** means "the act of" or "state of." The suffixes **ible** and **able** mean "able to."

Directions: Create new words by adding **ment**, **able**, or **ible** to these root words. Use a dictionary to check that the new words are correct. The first one has been done for you.

Root Word		Suffix		New Word
1. rely	+	able	=	reliable
2. retire	+	_____	=	_____
3. sense	+	_____	=	_____
4. commit	+	_____	=	_____
5. repair	+	_____	=	_____
6. love	+	_____	=	_____
7. quote	+	_____	=	_____
8. honor	+	_____	=	_____

Directions: Use the clues in the first sentence to complete the second sentence with one of the words from the box. The first one has been done for you.

9. Everyone loved her. She was ___loveable (also lovable).___

10. He had a lot of sense. He was _____

11. She committed time to the project. She made a _____

12. He always did the right thing. His behavior was _____

13. The tire could not be fixed. It was not _____

14. They would not buy the car. The car was not _____

15. He gave the reporter good comments. His comments were _____

16. She was ready to retire. She looked forward to _____

Review

Directions: Add one of the prefixes, suffixes, or combining forms to a word in the box to complete each sentence. Use the definition in parentheses as a clue.

ian   ous   ship   an   ist   extra   trans   pre   micro   super

| friend | music | geology | sensory | America |
| paid | wave | market | atlantic | danger |

1. The _____ has a huge selection of fruits and vegetables. (large food store)

2. The first _____ flight was a remarkable feat in the history of aviation. (across the Atlantic Ocean)

3. The woman claimed that she knew the future because of her _____ capabilities. (beyond the normal senses)

4. When mailing your payment, please use the _____ envelope. (paid in advance)

5. Mrs. Johnson studied the violin for many years to become the accomplished _____ she is today. (person skilled in music)

6. The _____ oven is a modern-day convenience. (operating with extremely small electromagnetic waves)

7. Lightning is the most _____ part of a storm. (characterized by danger)

8. They raised the _____ flag over their campground in a gesture of patriotism. (belonging to America)

9. Olivia and I stick together through good times and bad times because we value our _____ . (the state of being friends)

10. Dr. Stokes is the finest _____ at the university. (one who is skilled at geology, the study of the earth's crust)

Review

Directions: Add suffixes to change these nouns into adjectives. Searching **Suffixe**

1. person_____   music_____   child_____

Directions: Add suffixes to change these adjectives into adverbs.

2. permanent_____   obvious_____   gradual_____

Directions: Add the prefix **pre**, **un**, **in**, **re**, or **con** to each word, and use the word in a sentence.

3. search _____

4. join _____

5. compatible _____

6. wrap _____

7. school _____

Directions: Add the suffix **ish**, **ment**, **ion**, **ship**, or **ful** to each word, and use the word in a sentence.

8. square _____

9. invent _____

10. force _____

11. replace _____

12. chairman _____

Directions: Add suffixes to make the noun forms of these verbs.

13. select _____   16. imitate _____

14. decorate _____   17. reflect _____

15. invite _____

Name _____

Review

Directions: Spell these silent **e** words correctly.

1. achievments _____
2. canoing _____
3. amuseing _____
4. urgeing _____

Directions: Add the suffixes to these words ending in **y**, and spell them correctly.

5. baby + ies = _____
6. stay + ed = _____

Directions: Add the suffixes, and spell these two-syllable words correctly.

7. hope + ing = _____
8. stop + ing = _____

Directions: Add the suffixes, and spell these three-syllable words correctly.

9. recur + ing = _____
10. defer + ence = _____

Directions: Spell these words correctly by inserting **ie** or **ei**.

11. h ___ ___ ght
12. ch ___ ___ f

Directions: Circle the **q** words in each row that are spelled correctly.

13. quip   qeen   qick   quit
14. qestion   equator   quiet   qart
15. squirrel   sqare   squirm   sqeak

Analyzing Words and Their Parts

A **syllable** is a word or part of a word with only one vowel sound.

Directions: Fill in the missing syllables. Use words from the box. Write the number of syllables after each word. The first one has been done for you.

expense	exist	aquarium	acquire	request
exact	expand	exit	quality	excellent
quiz	quantity	expression	exhibit	squirm

1. ex <u>c e l</u> lent (3)

2. _____ squirm ( )

3. _____ act ( )

4. _____ quiz ( )

5. aquar ___ um ( )

6. ac _____ ( )

7. quali _____ ( )

8. _____ it ( )

9. ex _____ sion ( )

10. _____ ist ( )

11. _____ quest ( )

12. ex _____ it ( )

13. _____ pense ( )

14. _____ pand ( )

15. quan _____ ty ( )

Directions: Write words that rhyme. Use the words in the box.

16. fizz _____

17. resist _____

18. fact _____

19. fence _____

20. sand _____

21. it's been sent _____

22. this is it _____

23. made for me _____

24. reflection _____

25. worm _____

26. fire _____

27. best _____

28. fit _____

A **root word** is a common stem that gives related words their basic meaning.

Directions: Write the root word for the bold word in each sentence.

29. I know **exactly** what I want. _____

30. Those shoes look **expensive**. _____

31. She didn't like my **expression** when I frowned. _____

32. We went to the train **exhibition** at the park. _____

Dividing Words into Syllables

Directions: Divide these words into syllables by putting a hyphen (-) between each syllable. The first one has done for you.

1. multiplication

   mul-ti-pli-ca-tion

2. discover

   _____

3. ultimate

   _____

4. transfer

   _____

5. continent

   _____

6. follow

   _____

7. British

   _____

8. American

   _____

9. president

   _____

10. discrimination

   _____

11. spectacular

   _____

12. commercial

   _____

13. probability

   _____

14. country

   _____

15. casual

   _____

16. political

   _____

17. wrestle

   _____

18. basketball

   _____

19. particular

   _____

20. cereal

   _____

21. picture

   _____

22. plumber

   _____

23. personal

   _____

24. sentence

   _____

Synonyms

A **synonym** is a word that means the same or nearly the same as another word. **Example: mean** and **cruel**

Directions: Circle the word or group of words in each sentence that is a synonym for a word in the box. Write the synonym from the box on the line. The first one has been done for you.

florist	courtesy	research	emergency	flourish
plural	observe	furnish	tornado	source
ignored	survey	normally	coarse	restore

1. The children seemed to (thrive) in their new school.   *flourish*

2. Her politeness made me feel welcome. _____

3. The principal came to watch our class. _____

4. Are you going to fix up that old house? _____

5. Six weeks after the disaster, the neighborhood looked as it usually did. _____

6. What was the origin of that rumor? _____

7. The cyclone destroyed two houses. _____

8. She neglected her homework. _____

9. The material had a rough feel to it. _____

10. Did you fill out the questionnaire yet? _____

Directions: Select three words from the box below. Write a sentence for each word that shows you understand the meaning of the word.

plural	flourish	source	restore	observe	furnish	research

_____

_____

_____

Antonyms

An **antonym** is a word that means the opposite of another word.

Example: hopeful and **discouraged**

Directions: Circle the word or group of words in each sentence that is an antonym for a word in the box. Write the antonym from the box on the line.

nuisance	considerate
delicate	frivolous
entrance	shiny
divide	parallel
success	valley

1. It seemed as though we'd never make it to the top of the butte. _____

2. Rosa thought the woman was rude to the store clerk. _____

3. The two streets run perpendicular to each other. _____

4. The school carnival was a total failure due to the stormy weather. _____

5. Be sure to wash this sturdy sweater with other heavy items. _____

6. The third-grade class worked hard learning to multiply. _____

7. The exit was blocked by a table. _____

8. The purchase of the coat was quite practical. _____

9. The teacher wrote that Colin was a joy to have in class. _____

10. The stone in her ring was dull and cloudy. _____

Spelling: Homophones

Homophones are words that sound the same but have different spellings and different meanings.

Examples: night and **knight**, **fair** and **fare**, not and **knot**

Directions: Complete each sentence with the correct homophone. Then, write a sentence using the other homophone. Use a dictionary if you don't know the meaning of a word. The first one has been done for you.

1. eight
   ate

   I <u>ate</u> two strawberries.

   <u>Aisha had eight strawberries.</u> _____

2. vein
   vain

   Since the newspaper printed his picture, Cam has been self-centered and

   _____ .

   _____

3. weight
   wait

   We had to _____ a long time for the show to start.

   _____

4. weigh
   way

   He always insists that we do everything his _____ .

   _____

5. seize
   seas

   The explorers charted the _____ .

   _____

6. straight
   strait

   It is sometimes difficult to draw perfectly _____ lines freehand.

   _____

7. principle
   principal

   The _____ summoned the student body to the auditorium for a special program.

   _____

8. their
   they're

   I'm sure _____ meeting us at the park rather than at home.

   _____

Vocabulary Building: Homographs

A **homograph** has the same spelling as another word but a different meaning. The two words are often different parts of speech.

Directions: Write the definition from the box for the bold word in each sentence.

con' tract	n.	an agreement to do something
con tract'	v.	to reduce in size, shrink
des' ert	n.	dry land that can support little plant and animal life
de sert'	v.	to abandon
Po' lish	adj.	of or belonging to Poland
pol' ish	v.	to smooth and brighten by rubbing
proj' ect	n.	a proposal or undertaking
pro ject'	v.	to send forth in thoughts or imagination

1. Iron is one of the metals that **contracts** as it cools.

   _____

2. You will have to sign a **contract** before I can begin work on your house.

   _____

3. The **desert** seems to come to life in the evening when the animals come out in search of food.

   _____

4. I hope you will not **desert** your friends now that they really need your support.

   _____

5. She will **polish** the stone and then use it to make a necklace.

   _____

6. My grandma is going to teach me to make an authentic **Polish** meal this weekend.

   _____

7. **Project** yourself into the world of tomorrow with this amazing invention!

   _____

8. I started this **project** on Monday, but it may be weeks before I finish it.

   _____

Vocabulary Building: Homographs

Directions: After each sentence, write the meaning of the bold word. Write another sentence using a homograph for the word.

1. The owner of the pet store tied a bright red **bow** around the puppies' necks.

Meaning: _____

Sentence: _____

2. Today, fewer pipes are made from **lead**.

Meaning: _____

Sentence: _____

3. Lia's new house is very **close** to ours.

Meaning: _____

Sentence: _____

4. Please **record** the time and day that we finished the project.

Meaning: _____

Sentence: _____

5. It takes only a **minute** to fasten your seatbelt, but it can save your life.

Meaning: _____

Sentence: _____

6. I cannot **subject** the animal to that kind of treatment.

Meaning: _____

Sentence: _____

Multiple Meanings

Directions: Use a dictionary to write the meaning of the bold word in each sentence. Be sure the meaning fits the context of the sentence and the part of speech. The first one has been done for you.

1. Rosa will **graduate** summa cum laude.

   to receive an academic degree

2. The **graduat**e looked for suitable employment.

   _____

3. The woman balanced her purse on the **counter**.

   _____

4. The boss **countered** the employee's request for a large raise.

   _____

5. Julio Mentarre will **conduct** the orchestra tonight.

   _____

6. Metal **conducts** electricity.

   _____

7. His **conduct** was questionable in that situation.

   _____

8. Please **file** these reports today.

   _____

9. The principal asked the students to leave in single **file**.

   _____

10. "Please hand me a **file**," said the woodworker to his daughter.

   _____

Vocabulary Building: Multiple Meanings

Directions: Use a dictionary to choose the correct definition for each bold word. The first one has been done for you.

1. My grandfather always has his **spectacles** perched on his nose.

   Meaning: <u>lenses worn in front of the eyes to aid vision</u>

2. The Fourth of July fireworks display was an amazing **spectacle**.

   Meaning: _____

3. We enjoy a rugged vacation, staying in a hunting **lodge** rather than a hotel.

   Meaning: _____

4. Don't let the baby have hard candy, because it could **lodge** in his throat.

   Meaning: _____

5. Termites will **bore** through the rotten wood in our basement if we don't have it replaced

   Meaning: _____

6. That television show could **bore** even a small child!

   Meaning: _____

7. Don't **resort** to lies just to get what you want!

   Meaning: _____

8. The **resort** is packed with tourists from May to September each year.

   Meaning: _____

Vocabulary Building: Multiple Meanings

Directions: Read each sentence, then write another sentence using a different meaning for the bold word.

1. The prince will **succeed** his mother as ruler of the country.

   _____

2. All through the national anthem, Johnny was singing in the wrong **key**.

   _____

3. There has been only a **trace** of rain this month.

   _____

4. I can't get involved in a **cause** in which I don't really believe.

   _____

5. It is very important to get plenty of **iron** in your diet.

   _____

6. A police officer can **issue** a warning to those disturbing the peace.

   _____

7. There is a mayoral candidate from each of the major political **parties**.

   _____

8. You can take that **stack** of newspapers to be recycled.

   _____

9. The judge will likely **sentence** the offender to a year in prison.

   _____

10. The lawyer made a **motion** to have the charges dropped.

    _____

Reading Skills: Classifying

Classifying is placing similar things into categories.

Example: January, **May**, and **October** can be classified as months.

Directions: Write a category name for each group of words.

1. accordion   clarinet   trumpet   _____
2. wasp   bumblebee   mosquito   _____
3. antique   elderly   prehistoric   _____
4. chemist   astronomer   geologist   _____
5. nest   cocoon   burrow   _____

Directions: In each row, draw an **X** through the word that does not belong. Then, write a sentence telling why it does not belong.

1. encyclopedia   atlas   novel   dictionary

   _____

2. bass   otter   tuna   trout

   _____

3. sister   grandmother   niece   uncle

   _____

4. bark   beech   dogwood   spruce

   _____

5. pebble   gravel   boulder   cement

   _____

6. spaniel   Siamese   collie   Doberman

   _____

Reading Skills: Classifying

Directions: In each row, draw an **X** through the word that does not belong. Then, write a word that belongs.

1. monkey   lion   zebra   elephant   dog   _____

2. daisies   roses   violets   ferns   pansies   _____

3. paper   pear   pencil   eraser   stapler   _____

4. sister   cousin   father   aunt   friend   _____

5. hand   mouth   shirt   foot   elbow   _____

6. shy   cry   happy   angry   sad   _____

7. puppy   dog   kitten   cub   lamb   _____

8. red   blue   color   yellow   purple   _____

9. Earth   Jupiter   Saturn   Mars   sun   _____

10. sink   bed   desk   dresser   lamp   _____

Directions: Name each category above.

1. _____   6. _____

2. _____   7. _____

3. _____   8. _____

4. _____   9. _____

5. _____   10. _____

Reading Skills: Classifying

Directions: Write three things that would belong in each category below. The first one has been done for you.

1. mammals

   ___whale___   ___horse___   ___elephant___

2. rainforest animals

   _____   _____   _____

3. capital cities

   _____   _____   _____

4. oceans

   _____   _____   _____

5. occupations

   _____   _____   _____

6. Native American tribes

   _____   _____   _____

7. wars

   _____   _____   _____

8. planets

   _____   _____   _____

9. track and field sports

   _____   _____   _____

10. famous Americans

    _____   _____   _____

Name _____

Types of Analogies

An **analogy** shows similarities, or things in common, between a pair of words. The relationships between the words in analogies usually fall into these categories:

1. **Purpose** One word in the pair shows the **purpose** of the other word (scissors: cut).

2. **Antonyms** The words are **opposites** (light: dark).

3. **Part/whole** One word in the pair is a **part**; the other is a **whole** (leg: body).

4. **Action/object** One word in the pair involves an **action** with or to an **object** (fly: airplane).

5. **Association** One word in the pair is what you think of or **associate** when you see the other (cow: milk).

6. **Object/location** One word in the pair tells the **location** of where the other word, an **object**, is found (car: garage).

7. **Cause/effect** One word in the pair tells the **cause**; the other word shows the **effect** (practice: improvement).

8. **Synonyms** The words are **synonyms** (small: tiny).

Directions: Write the relationship between the words in each pair. The first two have been done for you.

1. cow: farm   object/location
2. toe: foot   part/whole
3. watch: TV   _____
4. bank: money   _____
5. happy: unhappy   _____
6. listen: radio   _____
7. inning: ballgame   _____
8. knife: cut   _____
9. safe: dangerous   _____
10. carrots: soup   _____

Reading Skills: Fact or Opinion?

Directions: Read the paragraphs below. For each numbered sentence, write **F** for fact or **O** for opinion. Write the reason for your answer. The first one has been done for you.

(1) The two greatest poems in the history of the world are the *Iliad* and the *Odyssey*. **(2)** The *Iliad* is the story of the Trojan War; the *Odyssey* tells about the wanderings of the Greek hero Ulysses after the war. **(3)** These poems are so long that they each fill an entire book.

(4) The author of the poems, according to Greek legend, was a blind poet named Homer. **(5)** Almost nothing is known about Homer. **(6)** This indicates to me that it is possible that Homer never existed. **(7)** Maybe Homer existed but didn't write the *Iliad* and the *Odyssey*.

(8) Whether or not there was a Homer does not really matter. We have these wonderful poems, which are still being read more than 2,500 years after they were written.

1. __O__ Reason: This cannot be proven. People have different opinions about which are the greatest poems.

2. _____ Reason: _____

3. _____ Reason: _____

4. _____ Reason: _____

5. _____ Reason: _____

6. _____ Reason: _____

7. _____ Reason: _____

8. _____ Reason: _____

Chilies

Directions: Read about chilies. Find the one opinion in each passage, and write it on the lines.

Chilies are hot or sweet peppers. They are part of the "nightshade" family of plants that also includes potatoes and tomatoes. Potatoes and tomatoes taste better than chilies, though.

Opinion: _____

_____

Chilies were originally grown in Central and South America. By the 15th century, Europeans were cooking with them and drying them to use as a spice. European dishes taste better now than they did before chilies were used in them.

Opinion: _____

_____

Although it is really a Mexican recipe, every intelligent American loves *chili con carne*. It is made with spicy meat, beans, and chilies. Today, most Americans call that dish "chili."

Opinion: _____

_____

Some people think that all chilies are hot. Therefore, they never eat any of them. What a silly belief! There are many different kinds of red, yellow, and green chilies. Even red chilies can be sweet.

Opinion: _____

_____

Carol's Country Restaurant

Directions: Write in the corresponding numbered blank below whether each numbered sentence gives a fact or an opinion.

(1) I have visited Carol's Country Restaurant seven times in the past two weeks. (2) The meals there are excellent. (3) They often feature country dishes such as meatloaf, ham with scalloped potatoes, and fried chicken.

(4) Owner Carol Murphy makes wonderful vegetable soup that includes all home-grown vegetables. (5) It's simmered with egg noodles. (6) Another of my favorite dishes is Carol's chili. (7) I'm sure it is the spiciest chili this side of the Mississippi River. (8) Carol says she uses secret ingredients in all her dishes.

(9) Whether ordering a main dish or a dessert, you can't go wrong at Carol's. (10) Everything is superb.

(11) Carol's Country Restaurant is on Twig Street in Freeport. (12) Prices for main entrees range from $5.95 to $12.95.

1. _____

2. _____

3. _____

4. _____

5. _____

6. _____

7. _____

8. _____

9. _____

10. _____

11. _____

12. _____

Comprehensive Curriculum - Grade 6

Review

Directions: Write 5 sentences that are facts and 5 that are opinions.

Facts:

1. _____

_____

2. _____

_____

3. _____

_____

4. _____

_____

5. _____

_____

Opinions:

6. _____

_____

7. _____

_____

8. _____

_____

9. _____

_____

10. _____

_____

Reading Skills: Cause and Effect

A **cause** is the reason something happens. The **effect** is what happens as the result of the cause.

Directions: Read the paragraphs below. For each numbered sentence, circle the cause or causes, and underline the effect or effects. The first one has been done for you.

(1) All living things in the ocean are endangered by humans polluting the water. Pollution occurs in several ways. One way is the dumping of certain waste materials, such as garbage and sewage, into the ocean. (2) The decaying bacteria that feed on the garbage use up much of the oxygen in the surrounding water, so other creatures in the area often don't get enough.

Other substances, such as radioactive waste material, can also cause pollution. These materials are often placed in the water in securely sealed containers. (3) But after years of being exposed to the ocean water, the containers may begin to leak.

Oil is another major source of concern. (4) Oil is spilled into the ocean when tankers run aground and sink or when oil wells in the ocean cannot be capped. (5) The oil covers the gills of fish and smothers them. (6) Diving birds get the oil on their wings and are unable to fly. (7) When they clean themselves, they are often poisoned by the oil.

Rivers also can contribute to the pollution of oceans. Many rivers receive the runoff water from farmlands. (8) Fertilizers used on the farms may be carried to the ocean, where they cause a great increase in the amount of certain plants. Too much of some plants can actually be poisonous to fish.

Worse yet are the pesticides carried to the ocean. These chemicals slowly build up in shellfish and other small animals. These animals then pass the pesticides on to the larger animals that feed on them. (9) The buildup of these chemicals in the animals can make them ill or harm their young.

Name _____

Reading Skills: Cause and Effect

Directions: Read the following cause-and-effect statements. If you think the cause and effect are properly related, write **true**. If not, explain why not. The first one has been done for you.

1. The best way to make it rain is to wash your car.

   <u>It does not rain every time you wash your car.</u>

2. Getting a haircut really improved Randy's grades.

   _____

3. Michael got an A in geometry because he spent a lot of time studying.

   _____

4. Yesterday, I broke a mirror, and today, I slammed my thumb in the door.

   _____

5. Natalia isn't allowed to go to the dance tonight because she broke her curfew last weekend.

   _____

6. Emily drank a big glass of orange juice, and her headache went away.

   _____

7. The Akitas had their tree cut down because it had Dutch elm disease.

   _____

8. We can't grow vegetables in our backyard because the rabbits keep eating them.

   _____

Review

Directions: Write **fact** or **opinion** to describe each sentence.

_____ 1. Hurricanes are also known as typhoons.

_____ 2. Hurricanes are the worst natural disasters.

_____ 3. All hurricanes begin over the ocean near the equator.

_____ 4. All people are concerned about pollution.

_____ 5. Pesticides should never be used.

_____ 6. Many colonists died due to lack of food and sickness.

_____ 7. Kites are the best gift to give a child.

_____ 8. The names of Columbus's three ships were the *Niña*, the *Pinta*, and the *Santa Maria*.

Directions: If the sentence demonstrates a logical cause and effect relationship, write **yes** on the line. If the sentence is illogical, write **no**.

_____ 1. I ate fish and got sick, so all fish will make me sick.

_____ 2. The farmer began practicing crop rotation, and his crop yield improved.

_____ 3. I know how to swim, so I cannot possibly drown.

_____ 4. While learning to ski, Connor broke his leg.

_____ 5. The river overflowed its banks and caused much damage.

_____ 6. The Cincinnati Reds won 100 games last year, so they probably will this year.

_____ 7. Because I started using a new toothpaste, I will make more friends.

Name _____

Reading Skills: Personification

When an author gives an object or animal human characteristics, it is called **personification**.

Example: The dragon quickly <u>thought</u> out its next move in the attack on the village.

Thought is a human process and not associated with mythical creatures; therefore, the dragon is personified in that sentence.

Directions: In the following sentences, underline the personification.

1. The cave's gaping mouth led to internal passageways.

2. The tractor sprang to life with a turn of the key.

3. The lights blinked twice and then died.

4. Crops struggled to survive in the blistering heat, hoping for rainfall.

5. The engine of the car coughed and sputtered as if it wanted to breathe but couldn't.

6. The arrow flew through the air, eyeing its target.

7. Snowmen smile from the safety of their yards.

8. Stephanie's doll sipped tea delicately.

Directions: Write a sentence that personifies the following objects.

1. flower _____

2. stuffed animal _____

3. car _____

Reading Skills: Symbolism

Symbolism is the use of something to stand for (symbolize) something else.

Example:

The elderly woman held the pearl necklace in her wrinkled hand and thought back on her life. Many years had gone by since her husband had given her the necklace, as many years as there were pearls. Some of the pearls, she noticed, were darker than others, just as some years in her life had been darker than other years.

The pearl necklace symbolizes the life of the elderly woman. Each pearl stands for a year

in her life, and the necklace represents the many years that have passed.

_____

Directions: Write what is being symbolized in the paragraph on the lines below.

The refugees boarded the small ship with high hopes. They had to believe that their destiny was to find the New World and seek shelter there. A few dared to dream of the riches to be found. For them, the boat itself looked like a treasure chest waiting to be discovered.

_____

_____

_____

For 12-year-old Sam, the basketball court was the best place to be. In Sam's neighborhood, crime ran rampant, and the court was the one safe place for kids like Sam to play. Sam spent most nights there, practicing lay-ups, jump shots, and three-point shots. Sam worked hard because for him it wasn't just a sport, it was a golden key.

_____

_____

_____

_____

Reading Skills: Idioms

An **idiom** is a phrase that says one thing but actually means something quite different.
Example: Now that's <u>a horse of a different color</u>! There is not literally a horse of a different color. The idiom means "a different matter altogether."

Directions: Write the letter of the correct meaning for the bold words in each sentence. The first one has been done for you.

a. forgive and make up	**f.** pressed tightly together
b. fact kept secret for fear of disgrace	**g.** relatives and ancestors
c. something that dampens excitement	**h.** rudely ignored
d. get acquainted, become less formal	**i.** excessive paperwork
e. treated like royalty	**j.** people were gossiping

_g_ 1. There are a pirate and a president in our **family tree**.

_____ 2. The Rosenbergs went through a lot of **red tape** to adopt their baby.

_____ 3. Sophia gave me the **cold shoulder** when I tried to talk to her this morning.

_____ 4. The big homework assignment threw a **wet blanket** over my plans for an exciting weekend.

_____ 5. At a party, Madison likes to **break the ice** by having her guests play games.

_____ 6. **Tongues were wagging** when the principal called Luis into his office.

_____ 7. There were five people **sandwiched** into the back seat of the car.

_____ 8. It was obvious that the character in my book was hiding **a skeleton in her closet**.

_____ 9. Let's forget our past mistakes and **bury the hatchet**.

_____ 10. When the mayor came to visit our school, we **rolled out the red carpet**.

Reading Skills: Denotations and Connotations

Directions: Replace the bold word in each sentence with a word that has a more positive connotation.

Example:

shut
He **slammed** the door when he left.

The dog's energy was **uncontrollable**.

We hoped to settle our **fight** peacefully.

The mother **reprimanded** the children when people began to look at them.

The children **gossiped** at lunchtime.

The girl **scribbled** a hasty note to leave behind.

Our conversation ended **abruptly** when the phone rang.

The principal was a **severe** man.

The boy **snatched** the toy from his baby brother.

The couple **rejected** their offer of help.

Dad reminded me to clean my **disastrous** room.

Similes and Metaphors

A **simile** compares two unlike things using the word **like** or **as**.

Example: The fog was **like** a blanket around us. The fog was **as** thick **as** a blanket.

A **metaphor** compares two unlike things without using the word **like** or **as**.

Example: The fog was a blanket around us.

"The fog was thick" is not a simile or a metaphor. **Thick** is an adjective. Similes and metaphors compare two unlike things that are both nouns.

Directions: Underline the two things being compared in each sentence. Then, write **S** for simile or **M** for metaphor on the lines.

_____ 1. The florist's shop was a summer garden.

_____ 2. The towels were as rough as sandpaper.

_____ 3. The survey was a fountain of information.

_____ 4. Her courtesy was as welcome as a cool breeze on a hot day.

_____ 5. The room was like a furnace.

Directions: Use similes to complete these sentences.

6. The tornado was as dark as _____

7. His voice was like _____

8. The emergency was as unexpected as _____

9. The kittens were like _____

Directions: Use metaphors to complete these sentences.

10. To me, research was _____

11. The flourishing plants were _____

12. My observation at the hospital was _____

Vocabulary Building: Similes

A **simile** is a figure of speech comparing two things using **like** or **as**.

Example: The child was as quiet as a mouse.

Directions: Read the following paragraph. Underline the similes.

The kittens were born on a morning as cold as ice. Although it was late spring, the weather hadn't quite warmed up. There were five kittens in the litter, each quite different from its siblings. The oldest was black as deepest night. There was a calico that looked like Grandma's old quilt. One was as orange as a fall pumpkin, and another was orange and white. The runt was a black and gray tiger. She was as little as a baseball and as quick as lightning to fight for food. The kittens will soon become accepted by the other animals as members of the farm.

Directions: Using the following words, create similes of your own.

Example: piano—The piano keys tinkled like a light rain on a tin roof.

1. fire _____

_____

2. thunderstorm _____

_____

3. ocean _____

_____

4. night _____

_____

5. rainforest _____

_____

6. giraffe _____

_____

Vocabulary Building: Metaphors

A **metaphor** is a figure of speech that directly compares one thing with another.

Example: As it set, the sun was a glowing orange ball of fire.

The sun is being compared to a glowing orange ball of fire.

<u>sun</u>   <u>glowing orange ball of fire</u>

Directions: Underline the metaphor in each sentence. Then, write the two things that are being compared on the lines.

1.   The ocean, a swirling mass of anger, released its fury on the shore.

_____   _____

2.   He was a top spinning out of control.

_____   _____

3.   The heat covered the crowd, a blanket smothering them all.

_____   _____

4.   I fed my dog a steak, and it was a banquet for her senses.

_____   _____

5.   The flowers in the garden were a stained glass window.

_____   _____

Name _____

Vocabulary Building: Metaphors and Similes

Directions: Underline the metaphors in the following sentences. Then, rewrite each sentence using a simile.

1. She is a playful child, a real kitten!

   _____

2. Life today is a merry-go-round.

   _____

3. His emotions were waves washing over him.

   _____

4. His childhood was an image in a rearview mirror.

   _____

Directions: Write the meanings of the following sentences.

1. His mind was as changeable as spring weather.

   _____

2. His demand was like a clap of thunder.

   _____

3. There was joy written on the children's faces on Christmas morning.

   _____

Reading Skills: Skimming and Scanning

Skimming is reading quickly to get a general idea of what a reading selection is about. When skimming, look for headings and key words to give you an overall idea of what you are reading.

Scanning is looking for certain words to find facts or answer questions. When scanning, read or think of questions first.

Directions: Scan the paragraphs below to find the answers to the questions. Then, look for specific words that will help you locate the answers. For example, in the second question, scan for the word **smallest**.

There are many different units to measure time. Probably the smallest unit that you use is the second, and the longest unit is the year. While 100 years seems like a very long time to us, in the history of Earth, it is a smaller amount of time than one second is in a person's entire lifetime.

To describe the history of Earth, scientists use geologic time. Even a million years is a fairly short period of time in geologic time. Some scientists believe that our planet is about 4,600 million years old. Since a thousand million is a billion, Earth is believed to be 4.6 billion years old.

1. What kind of time is used to describe the history of Earth?

_____

2. For the average person, what is the smallest unit of time used?

_____

3. In millions of years, how old do some scientists believe Earth is?

_____

4. How would you express that in billions of years?

_____

The Author's Purpose

Authors write to entertain, inform, or persuade. To entertain means "to hold the attention of or to amuse someone." A fiction book about outer space entertains its reader, as does a joke book.

To inform means "to give factual information." A cookbook informs the reader of new recipes. A newspaper tells what is happening in the world.

To persuade people means "to convince them." Newspaper editorial writers try to persuade readers to accept their opinions. Doctors write health columns to persuade readers to eat nutritious foods or to exercise regularly.

Directions: Read each of the passages below. Tell whether they entertain, inform, or persuade. (They may do more than one.) Give the reasons why.

George Washington was born in a brick house near the Potomac River in Virginia on February 11, 1732. When he was 11 years old, George went to live with his half-brother, Lawrence, at Mount Vernon.

Author's Purpose: _____

Reason: _____

When George Washington was a child, he always measured and counted things. Maybe that is why he became a surveyor when he grew up. Surveyors like to measure and count things, too.

Author's Purpose: _____

Reason: _____

George Washington was the best president America has ever had. He led a new nation to independence. He made all the states feel as if they were part of the United States. All presidents should be as involved with the country as George Washington was.

Author's Purpose: _____

Reason: _____

_____

Llamas

Directions: Read each paragraph. Tell whether it informs, entertains, or persuades. One paragraph does more than one. Then, write your reason on the line below.

A llama (LAH'MAH) is a South American animal that is related to the camel. It is raised for its wool. Also, it can carry heavy loads. Some people who live near mountains in the United States train llamas to go on mountain trips. Llamas are sure-footed because they have two long toes and toenails.

Author's Purpose: _____

Reason: _____

Llamas are the best animals to have if you're planning to backpack in the mountains. They can climb easily and carry your supplies. No one should ever go for a long hiking trip in the mountains without a llama.

Author's Purpose: _____

Reason: _____

Llamas can be stubborn animals. Sometimes, they suddenly stop walking for no reason. People have to push them to get them moving again. Stubborn llamas can be frustrating when hiking up a steep mountain.

Author's Purpose: _____

Reason: _____

Greg is an 11-year-old boy who raises llamas to climb mountains. One of his llamas is named Dallas. Although there are special saddles for llamas, Greg likes to ride bareback.

Author's Purpose: _____

Reason: _____

_____

Now, use a separate sheet of paper to inform readers about llamas.

Roller Coasters

Directions: Read each paragraph, and determine the author's purpose. Then, write down your reason on the line below.

Roller coaster rides are thrilling. The cars chug up the hills and then fly down them. People scream and laugh. They clutch their seats and sometimes raise their arms above their heads.

Author's Purpose: _____

Reason: _____

The first roller coasters were giant slides made of ice in Russia. That was more than 300 years ago! The slides were about 70 feet high, and people had to climb steep ladders to reach their tops. Riders got into carts and slid down very fast. Then, they climbed the ladders again. Early roller coasters were more work than fun.

Author's Purpose: _____

Reason: _____

The first roller coaster in America was built in 1884. It cost only a nickel to ride the "Switchback Gravity Pleasure Railway" at Coney Island in New York. Roller coasters did not become very popular until the late 1920s.

Author's Purpose: _____

Reason: _____

Have you ever ridden a giant roller coaster? Some of the most famous ones in the world include the "Bizarro" at Six Flags New England; the "Intimidator 305" at Kings Dominion in Doswell, Virginia; and the "Millennium Force" at Cedar Point in Sandusky, Ohio. Roller coasters are fun because they have thrilling twists and turns. Some go very high, and some turn upside down. Everyone should go on a roller coaster at least once in his or her life.

Author's Purpose: _____

Reason: _____

_____

Now, use a separate sheet of paper to persuade people to ride roller coasters.

Review

Directions: Follow the instructions for each section.

1. Write an informative paragraph about a sport.

_____

_____

_____

_____

_____

2. Write an entertaining paragraph about the circus.

_____

_____

_____

_____

3. Write a persuasive paragraph about the desire for a later bedtime.

_____

_____

_____

_____

_____

Multiple Choice

Multiple-choice questions are frequently asked on tests. Such questions include three or four possible answers. When answering a multiple-choice question, first read the question carefully. Then, read all the answers that are offered. If you do not know the correct answer, eliminate some of the ones you know are wrong until you have only one left. Remember these points when taking multiple-choice tests:

1. Answers that contain phrases such as **all people**, **no one**, or **everybody** are probably not correct. For example, a statement such as "all children like candy" is probably not correct because it allows for no exceptions. If there is one child who does not like candy, the statement is not correct. However, if you know that more than one answer is correct and the last choice in the group is "all of the above," then that phrase is probably the correct answ

2. Answers that contain words you have never seen before probably are not correct. Teachers don't expect you to know material you haven't studied.

3. Answers that are silly usually aren't correct.

4. When two of the answers provided look nearly the same, one of them is probably correct.

5. Always check your answers if there is time.

Directions: Answer the questions about multiple-choice tests.

1. The first thing you should do during a multiple-choice test is _____

_____ .

2. When you are reading the possible answers to a multiple-choice question and you know the first one is right, should you immediately mark it without reading the

other answers? _____

Why or why not? _____

3. Write three phrases that might tell you that an answer is probably not correct.

_____

_____

_____

True/False

True/false tests include several statements. You must read each one carefully to determine if it is right or wrong. Remember these tips:

1. Watch for one word in the sentence that can change the statement's meaning from true to false or vice versa.

2. Words such as **all**, **none**, **everybody**, or **nobody** should alert you that the answer may be false. Using these words means that there are no exceptions.

3. There are usually more true answers on a test than false ones. Therefore, if you have to guess an answer, you have a better chance of answering right by marking it "true."

4. Always check your answers if there is time.

Directions: Answer the questions about true/false tests.

1. List four words that can alert you that a question is false.

   _____

2. One word in a sentence can

   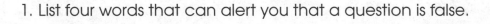

   _____ .

3. If you must guess an answer, is it wiser to guess true or false? _____

4. True/false tests are made up of several _____ .

5. Can you do well on a true/false test by only skimming each statement? _____

6. If the word **everybody** is in the statement, is the answer probably true or false? _____

7. When the word **all** appears in the statement, is the answer probably true or false? _____

8. What should you do last when taking a true/false test?

   _____

Fill in the Blank

Fill-in-the-blank tests are more difficult than true/false or multiple-choice tests. However, there may be clues in each sentence that help determine the answer. Look at this example:

The _____ of the United States serves a _____ -year term.

Can you tell that the first blank needs a person? (The answer is "president.") The second blank needs a number because it refers to years. ("Four" is the answer.) Think about these other tips for taking fill-in-the-blank tests:

1. Always plan your time wisely. Don't waste too much time on one question. Check the clock or your watch periodically when taking a test.
2. First, read through the entire test. Then, go back to the beginning and answer the questions that you know. Put a small mark beside the questions you are not sure about.
3. Go back to the questions you were not sure of or that you didn't know. Carefully read each one. Think about possible answers. If you think it could be more than one answer, try to eliminate some of the possible answers.
4. Save the most difficult questions to answer last. Don't waste time worrying if you don't know the answer to a question.
5. Sometimes, you should guess at an answer because it may be right. There are some tests, though, that deduct points if your answer is wrong, but not if it is left blank. Make sure you know how the test will be scored.
6. Review your test. Make sure you have correctly read the directions and each question. Check your answers.

Directions: Answer the questions about fill-in-the-blank tests.

1. Fill-in-the-blank tests may have _____ in each sentence that help you figure out the answer.

2. Always plan your _____ wisely when taking a test.

3. Should you try to answer a question as soon as you read it?_____

4. Should you answer the hard or easy questions first? _____

5. If you are not sure of a question, you should _____ beside it.

Matching

Matching tests have two columns of information. A word or fact from one column matches information in the other. Read these tips to help with matching tests:

1. Look at one question at a time. Start with the first word or phrase in one of the columns. Then, look at the possible answers in the other column until you find the correct one. Then, go to the next word or phrase in the first column. If you don't know the answer to one question, skip it and go back to it later.
2. If there are several words in one column and several definitions in the other column, it is often easier to read the definition first and then find the word that goes with it.
3. Carefully read the directions. Sometimes, one column on a matching test is longer than the other. Find out if there is one answer that won't be used or if an answer in the opposite column can be used twice.
4. Check your answers if there is time.

Directions: Answer the questions about matching tests.

1. Matching tests have how many columns of information?_____

2. If one column has words in it and the other column has definitions in it, which one should you look at first to make the test easier? _____

3. To eliminate confusion, you should look at _____ question at a time.

4. Do the columns on a matching test always have the same number of things in them? _____

5. Are there ever items left unmatched on a matching test?_____

6. Does it matter if you look at the right or left column of a matching test first?_____

Essays

Essay questions give you a chance to demonstrate what you have learned. They also provide the opportunity to express your opinion. Although many students think essay questions are the most difficult, they can be the most fun. Remember these tips when writing the answer to an essay question:

1. Think about the answer before you write it. Take time to organize your thoughts so that you can better express yourself.
2. Write a few notes or an outline on a piece of scrap paper or on the back of the test. This helps remind you what you want to write.
3. State your answer clearly. Don't forget to use complete sentences.
4. Review the answer before time runs out. Sometimes words are left out. It doesn't take much time to read through your essay to make sure it says what you want it to say.

Directions: Use these essay-writing tips to answer the following question in the space provided.

What is your favorite type of test? Give several reasons why.

_____

_____

_____

_____

_____

_____

_____

_____

_____

_____

Review

Directions: Complete each question about tests.

1. Four steps for writing an answer for an essay test include:

   a) _____

   b) _____

   c) _____

   d) _____

2. In a matching test, it is sometimes easier to read the _____ and then match it with a word from the opposite column.

3. One column on a _____ may be longer than the other.

4. Tests that require you to fill in the blanks may provide _____ in each statement.

5. Always _____ answers if there is time.

6. Certain words, such as **none** and **all**, should alert you that an answer may be _____ .

7. There are usually, but not always, more _____ statements on a true/false test.

8. If **everybody** or **everything** is used in one of the answers for a _____ , it is likely that that answer is not right.

9. If two possible answers for a multiple-choice question sound nearly the _____ , one of them is probably correct.

10. If two answers to a multiple-choice question appear to be correct, the answer could be one that says _____ .

READING COMPREHENSION

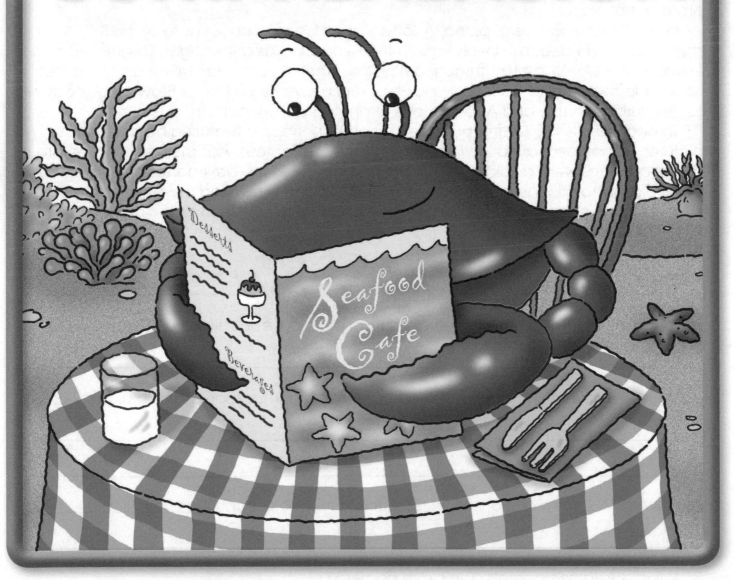

Comprehension: Ansel Adams

One the world's most well-known photographers is Ansel Adams. You may not recognize his name, but you would probably recognize his photos. Adams was known for his love of nature and his stunning black-and-white landscape photographs. Although photography ended up becoming a passion for Adams, his earlier ambitions were in a completely different area.

Ansel Adams was born in 1902 in California. He was an only child, and he grew up with a rather shy and nervous personality. He did not do particularly well in school. As a result, he learned much on his own and from tutors. As a boy, Adams discovered a love of music. For a number of years, he planned on pursuing a career as a professional pianist.

In addition to his love of piano, Adams was passionate about nature and its preservation. He became involved with the Sierra Club as a teenager. This interest in the environment would last him throughout his life. When Adams was 14, he and his parents took a trip to Yosemite National Park. His parents gave him a Kodak Brownie box camera to use during the trip, and Adams's love of photography was born.

Throughout his life, Adams published a number of books featuring his photos. His pictures of the national parks were among the most famous. Adams lived long before digital cameras were available. He spent many hours in the darkroom, working painstakingly to print an image that matched the one in his mind's eye. Adams died is 1984, but he lives on in his photographs of the natural world he loved so much.

Directions: Answers these questions about Ansel Adams.

1. For what kind of photos was Ansel Adams best known?_____

2. How was Adams's education different from a typical education?_____

_____

3. What similarities are there between a career as a photographer and a pianist?_____

_____

_____

4. How was Adams's love of nature reflected in his photography?_____

_____

5. Why did Adams's parents give him a camera?_____

Comprehension: Photography Terms

Like other good professionals, photographers make their craft look easy. Their skill—like that of the graceful ice skater—comes from years of practice. Where skaters develop a sense of balance, photographers develop an "eye" for pictures. They can make important technical decisions about photographing, or "shooting," a particular scene in the twinkling of an eye.

It's interesting to know some of the technical language that professional photographers use. "Angle of view" refers to the angle from which a photograph is taken. "Depth of field" is the distance between the nearest point and the farthest point that is in focus in a photo.

"Filling the frame" refers to the amount of space the object being photographed takes up in the picture. A close-up picture of a dog, flower, or person would fill the frame. A far-away picture would not.

Two elements that photographers work with are shutter speed and aperture. Shutter speed refers to how quickly the camera's shutter opens and closes. The longer the shutter stays open, the more light it allows in. The more quickly the shutter opens and closes, the better the photographer can capture an action shot. Shutter speed must work together with the aperture, which is the opening that controls the amount of light passing through the lens. A photographer who learns to properly balance shutter speed and aperture can take wonderful, sharp pictures that skillfully capture his or her subjects.

Directions: Answer these question about photography terms.

1. Name another term for photographing. _____

2. This is the distance between the nearest point and the farthest point that is in focus in a photo.

_____

3. What is aperture? _____

4. A close-up picture of someone's face would

   ☐ provide depth of field.   ☐ appear far away.   ☐ fill the frame.

5. Shutter speed and aperture work together.

   ☐ True   ☐ False

Comprehension: Photographing Animals

Animals are a favorite subject of many young photographers. Cats, dogs, hamsters, and other pets top the list, followed by zoo animals and the occasional lizard.

Because it's hard to get pets to sit still and "perform on command," some professional photographers refuse to photograph them. There are ways around the problem of short attention spans, however.

One way to get an appealing portrait of a cat or dog is to hold a biscuit or treat above the camera. The animal's longing look toward the food will be captured by the camera as a soulful gaze. Because it's above the camera—out of the camera's range—the treat won't appear in the picture. When you show the picture to your friends afterwards, they will be impressed by your pet's loving expression.

You can also try taking a series of good, quick shots of a pet by simply snapping several pictures right after calling its name. You'll get a different expression from your pet using this technique. Depending on your pet's disposition, the pictures will capture an inquisitive expression or possibly a look of annoyance, especially if you've awakened Rover from a nap!

Taking pictures of zoo animals requires a little more patience. After all, you can't wake up a lion! You may have to wait for a while until the animal does something interesting or moves into a position for you to get a good shot. When photographing zoo animals, don't get too close to the cages, and never tap on the glass or throw things between the bars of a cage! Concentrate on shooting some good pictures, and always respect the animals you are photographing.

Directions: Answer these questions about photographing animals.

1. Why do some professionals dislike photographing animals? _____

_____

2. Does the author suggest taking a single photo of a pet or several quick photos in a row?

Why? _____

3. To capture a pet's loving expression, hold this out of camera range. _____

4. Compared to taking pictures of pets, what does photographing zoo animals require?

_____

_____

Generalization: Taking Pictures

A **generalization** is a statement that applies to many different situations.

Directions: Read each passage, and circle the valid generalization.

1. Most people can quickly be taught to use a simple camera. However, it takes time, talent, and a good eye to learn to take professional-quality photographs. Patience is another quality that good photographers must possess. Those who photograph nature often will wait hours to get just the right light or shadow in their pictures.

   a. Anyone can learn to use a camera.

   b. Any patient person can become a good photographer.

   c. Good photographers have a good eye for pictures.

2. Photographers such as Diane Arbus, who photographed strange or odd people, also must wait for just the right picture. Many "people photographers" stake out a busy city sidewalk and study faces in the crowd. Then, they must leap up quickly and ask to take a picture or take one without being observed. Either way, it's not an easy task!

   a. Staking out a busy sidewalk is a boring task.

   b. "People photographers" must be patient people and good observers.

   c. Taking someone's photo without his or her permission is not a nice thing to do to strangers.

3. Whether the subject is nature or humans, many photographers insist that dawn is the best time to take pictures. The light is clear at this early hour, and mist may still be in the air. The mist gives these early morning photos a haunting, "other world" quality that is very appealing.

   a. Morning mist gives an unusual quality to most outdoor photographs.

   b. Photographers all agree that dawn is the best time to take pictures.

   c. Misty light is always important in taking pictures.

Comprehensive Curriculum - **Grade 6**

Generalization: Food Photography

Directions: Read each passage, and circle the valid generalization.

1. Taking good photographs of food is more difficult than it seems. Anyone can snap a photo of a bowl of soup or a basket of apples. The goal is to convey the food's best traits. If the soup is steaming hot and full of chunks of savory veggies, the photo needs to show that to the viewer. If the apples are crisp, sweet, and juicy, the photo should make the viewer want to pick one up and take a bite. A photo taken from a bad angle or with poor lighting won't make food look appealing to anyone.

   a. It is not easy to take a photo of a basket of apples.

   b. The goal of food photography is to make the food look appealing to the viewer.

   c. Only professional photographers should take photos of food.

2. Indirect daylight is the best lighting for food photography. Good light is important in making the food look appetizing. Photos of food can often look flat, with a yellowish tone to the picture. The best possible lighting is a shady spot that is surrounded by natural light. Bright, direct sunlight is too harsh. It can create shadows and bleach out bright colors and whites.

   a. No one should ever take photos of food on a bright, sunny day.

   b. Never use artificial lighting when taking photos of food.

   c. Good lighting, such as indirect daylight, is essential to taking appetizing photos of food.

3. Using props and styling the food can make a dish look much more attractive. Think of a bowl of chili. Shown on its own, it may not look very appealing. If you were to add a pretty placemat or napkin, the photo would look more interesting. Adding some cheese or a dollop of sour cream to the chili would certainly make the viewer want to dig in! A cutting board, patterned napkins, and garnishes like chopped herbs or cheese can help food look much more appealing in a photo.

   a. Props and food styling can help food appear more appealing in photos.

   b. You should always photograph chili with garnishes.

   c. The food is more important than the props and styling in a photograph.

Generalization: Choosing a Camera

Photography is an important part of American culture today. Digital cameras have made pictures incredibly easy to take. Many people have phones that can take photos, and it's also easy to share them instantly via the Internet. When it comes to buying a camera, though, there are still many options.

For the casual photographer, a point-and-shoot digital camera is a good choice. This type of camera is easy for almost anyone to use. You don't need to have a great knowledge of how cameras work or the finer points of photography. That's how these cameras got their nickname-- all you need to do is point the camera and shoot your picture. The settings are mostly automatic, and the camera makes the decisions for you. Most point-and-shoot cameras allow you to make some adjustments if you like. You can change the setting to do things like take an action shot, photograph fireworks, or take a picture of a sunny day at the beach.

For more serious photographers, a DSLR camera is a likely choice. **DSLR** stands for digital single-lens reflex. A photographer using this type of camera has much more control over the camera's settings. He or she needs to know more about photography in order to manually do what other cameras do automatically. The benefit is that the DSLR photographer can often capture things that a photographer with a point-and-shoot camera cannot. DSLR cameras tend to be quite a bit more expensive than point-and-shoot cameras. In addition, the various lenses are also expensive. Serious photographers accept the added work and expense because they can have so much more control over their photos.

Directions: Answer these questions about choosing a camera.

1. Which generalization is correct?

   a. Point-and-shoot cameras cost less than DSLR cameras.

   b. A DSLR camera is good choice for serious photographers who want to have a lot of control over the photos they take.

   c. Most of the settings are automatic in point-and-shoot cameras.

2. How are point-and-shoot cameras and DSLR cameras different from one another?

   _____

3. If you were to buy a camera, which kind would you choose? Explain why.

   _____

Comprehensive Curriculum - **Grade 6**

Review

Directions: Circle the missing word for each sentence.

1. Ansel Adams was known for his beautiful _____ photos.

   a. pianist

   b. amateur

   c. landscape

2. The distance between the nearest point and the farthest point in a photo is called the _____.

   a. graphic

   b. shooting

   c. depth of field

3. _____ refers to the angle from which a photograph is taken.

   a. Photos

   b. Angle of view

   c. Lens

4. Shutter speed refers to how quickly a camera's shutter _____.

   a. opens and closes

   b. flashes

   c. focuses

5. The _____ of the camera collects the light rays and draws them together at the center.

   a. shutter

   b. lens

   c. aperture

6. Taking a picture is often referred to as _____.

   a. shooting

   b. graphic

   c. speed

Main Idea/Recalling Details: Kites

Kites are a familiar sight on breezy fall days. They come in a great variety of sizes, colors, and designs. It is not known who invented kites, but kites have been flown since the beginning of recorded history. While today children and adults use them for recreation, throughout history kites have had other uses.

In the United States, kites have been used in weather and other scientific research experiments. Before airplanes and weather balloons, the National Weather Service had kites carry weather instruments as high as 4 miles above Earth. In addition, the United States military used kites for observing the enemy and sending messages between troops.

In other countries, kites had cultural and religious importance. The ancient Chinese flew kites over their homes to drive out evil spirits. The Chinese still enjoy kites so much that one day each year they celebrate Kites' Day.

On some Pacific islands, kites were thought to have spiritual qualities. They were believed to symbolize both sides of nature—life and death. On some Polynesian islands, kites were used as protection against evil. These kites were often shaped like birds and used as soaring messengers to the heavens. In Hawaii, kites were also used to establish land ownership. A kite was released in the air, and a claim was given for the area where it came down.

Directions: Answer these questions about kites.

1. The main idea is:

    ☐ Kites come in a great variety of sizes, colors, and designs.

    ☐ While today kites are used for recreation, throughout history they have had other uses.

2. Besides recreation, name two ways kites have been used in the United States.

    a) _____

    b) _____

3. What country celebrates a holiday called Kites' Day? _____

4. How did Hawaiians use kites to decide land ownership? _____

    _____

Comprehension: Aerodynamics

Kites are able to fly because of the principle of **aerodynamics**. Aerodynamics is the study of forces that are put into action by moving air. Three main forces work to keep a heavier-than-air kite flying—lift, gravity, and drag.

This is how it works: The flying lines, or strings, are attached to the kite to hold it at a slant. The wind pushes against the underside of the kite. At the same time, the wind rushes around the edges of the kite and "drags" some of the air from the upper side. This creates a partial vacuum there. The push of the air underneath is greater than the push of the air from the top, so the kite is held in the air. An airplane is held in the air in much the same way, except that it must keep moving rapidly to make the pressure above and below its wings different. The wind does this for the kite. In a steady airstream, a kite doesn't move backward or forward. It seems to be unaffected by gravity. This is possible because the lifting force of the wind overcomes the downward force of gravity.

If you have ever ridden a bicycle into a strong wind, you may have felt some of the forces of aerodynamics. If you held your hand out to your side, you could feel the air stream flowing around your hand. With your fingers pointed into the wind and your hand held level, there is little lift or drag. But if you raised your fingers slightly, the wind lifted your hand upwards. Raising your hand higher increases the drag and decreases the lift. Your hand is pushed downward. A kite flying in the sky is subject to these same forces.

Directions: Answer these questions about aerodynamics.

1. What is aerodynamics? _____

_____

2. What three forces are at work to hold a kite in the air?

   a)_____ b)_____ c)_____

3. An airplane is held in the air in much the same way, except that it must keep moving rapidly to keep the air above and below its wings different.

   True   False

Comprehension: Getting Your Kite to Fly

There are some basic things to know about kite flying that can help you enjoy the sport more. Here are a few of the most important ones.

First, if you have ever seen someone flying a kite in a movie, you probably saw him or her get the kite off the ground by running into the wind. However, this is not the way to launch a kite. Most beginners will find a "high-start" launch to be the easiest. For a high-start launch, have a friend stand about 100 feet away, facing into the wind. Your friend should face you and hold the kite gently. Place some tension on the flying line by pulling gently on it. With a steady breeze behind you, tug gently on the line, and the kite will rise. If your kite begins to dive, don't panic or pull on the line. Dropping the reel will cause it to spin out of control and could cause someone to be hurt. Simply let the line go slack. This usually will right the kite in midair.

For a kite that is pulling hard away from you, have a friend stand behind you and take up the slack line as you bring it in. Hand over hand, pull down the kite. It is very important to have gloves on to do this, or you may burn or cut your hands. It is recommended that you always wear gloves while kite flying.

When two kite lines get crossed, pulling may cause enough friction to cut one or both of the lines. Instead of pulling, both fliers should walk toward one another until their lines uncross as they pass.

Directions: Circle **True** or **False** for these statements about kite flying.

1. To launch a kite, run into the wind holding the kite behind you.   True   False

2. In a high-start launch, a friend stands about 100 feet away from you, holding the kite.   True   False

3. If your kite begins to dive from the sky, immediately drop the reel.   True   False

4. It is recommended that you always wear gloves when kite flying.   True   False

Recalling Details: Kite Safety Rules

Because kite flying is a relaxed, easygoing sport, it is easy to have the mistaken belief that there are no dangers involved. However, like any sport, kite flying must be approached with care. Here are some important safety rules you should always follow while kite flying:

- **Don't** fly a kite in wet or stormy weather or use wet flying line.

- **Don't** fly a kite near electrical power lines, transmission towers, or antennae. If your kite does get caught in one of these, walk away and leave it! If you must get the kite back, contact your local electric company.

- **Don't** use wire for flying line.

- **Don't** use metal for any part of the kite.

- **Don't** fly a kite near a street or in crowded areas.

- **Don't** fly a kite in a field or other area that has rocks or other objects you could trip over.

- **Don't** walk backwards without looking behind you.

- **Don't** fly a kite around trees. (If your kite does happen to get caught in a tree, let the line go slack. Sometimes the wind can work it free.)

- **Don't** fly a kite using unfamiliar equipment. A reel spinning out of control can be quite dangerous.

- **Don't** fly a kite near an airport.

- **Don't** fly a very large kite without proper guidance.

- **Do** wear protective gloves to avoid burns on your hands from rapidly unwinding line.

- **Do** use flying line that has been tested for the type and size of kite you are using.

Directions: Answer these questions about kite safety.

1. List three things you should never fly a kite around.

   a) _____ b) _____ c) _____

2. What should you do if your kite gets caught in a tree? _____

   _____

3. What material should you never use in any part of your kite? _____

Recalling Details: Aviation Pioneer

Lawrence Hargrave was born in Middlesex, England, in 1850. When he was a teenager, his family moved to Australia. There, Hargrave went to work for the Australian Stream and Navigation Company, where he spent 5 years gaining practical experience in engineering. He soon became interested in artificial flight.

Hargrave wanted to develop a stable lifting surface that could be used for flying. This goal led to his invention of the box kite, one of the seven basic models. In 1894, he carried out kite experiments along the beaches near his home. One day, in front of onlookers, he was lifted above the beach and out over the sea by four of his box kites. These experiments were very important to the development of air travel, although Hargrave has received little credit for it. In fact, because of his modesty, Hargrave failed to get a patent on his box kite. He spent more than 30 years studying flying, offering many inventions, including a rotary engine.

In 1906, Hargrave began looking for a home for his collection of nearly 200 models of kites and flying machines. After being rejected by several governments, his collection was accepted at a technological museum in Munich, Germany. Unfortunately, many of these models were destroyed during World War I.

Directions: Answer these questions about Lawrence Hargrave.

1. For what kite design was Lawrence Hargrave known? _____

2. What was Hargrave trying to create when he made this kite?

   _____

3. What was one of the inventions Hargrave contributed to aviation? _____

   _____

4. Where was Hargrave's collection of kites and flying machines finally housed?

   _____

Main Idea/Recalling Details: A Kite in History

In June 1752, Benjamin Franklin proved that lightning was a type of electricity by flying a kite with a key tied to the bottom of the line during a thunderstorm. Before his experiment, many people thought that lightning was a supernatural power.

After the success of his experiment, Franklin figured that if lightning could be drawn to a kite in a storm, it could be safely redirected into the ground by a metal rod attached to a house. His idea was met with much doubt, but lightning rods were soon seen on buildings in many of the colonies and later in Europe. During the years between 1683 and 1789, studying the universe and laws of nature was of tremendous importance. It was during this Age of Reason, as it was known, that Franklin's kite experiment gained him international fame and respect. He was elected to the Royal Society of London and the French Academy of Sciences, among other honors.

More than 20 years after his bold experiment, American patriots were enduring many hardships in their struggles for freedom from England. The colonial troops had shortages of guns, gunpowder, and food. France was sending supplies but not as much as was needed. Benjamin Franklin was chosen to go to France to persuade the French to aid the American cause. Franklin's reputation as a brilliant scientist earned him a hero's welcome there. The French people were so impressed by him that they wanted to help the colonies, even during a time when they could barely afford it. The supplies sent by the French were instrumental to the colonists in winning the war. And it all started with a kite.

Directions: Answer these questions about Ben Franklin and his historical kite.

1. The main idea is:

   ☐ A kite played a role in the American Revolution and gained a spot in history books.

   ☐ Benjamin Franklin proved that lightning was a type of electricity by flying a kite with a key tied to the bottom of the line during a storm.

2. From his kite and key experiment, what did Franklin invent? _____

3. What was the era between 1683 and 1789 known as? _____

4. Why was Franklin sent to France in 1776? _____

_____

Summarizing: Pioneers

Directions: Think about the lives and accomplishments of Ben Franklin and Lawrence Hargrave. Write one paragraph about each, summarizing what you have learned about these two men.

Ben Franklin

_____

_____

_____

_____

Lawrence Hargrave

_____

_____

_____

_____

Writing Checklist

Reread your paragraphs carefully.

☐ My paragraphs make sense.   ☐ I used correct spelling.

☐ I used correct punctuation.   ☐ My paragraphs are well-organized.

☐ I have a good opening and ending.   ☐ My paragraphs are interesting.

Review

Directions: Number in order the steps for how to launch a kite.

_____ With a steady breeze behind you, gently pull on the line.

_____ Have your friend face you and gently hold the kite.

_____ Your kite will rise.

_____ Have your friend face into the wind.

_____ Place some tension on the flying line by pulling on it.

_____ Have a friend stand about 100 feet away from you.

Directions: Write **true** or **false** for these statements about kite safety.

_____ 1. You should not use wire for flying line.

_____ 2. Fly any size kite you wish as long as you have the right flying line.

_____ 3. If your kite gets caught in a tree, let the line go slack.

_____ 4. It's okay to fly a kite in the rain.

_____ 5. You should not fly a kite in crowded areas.

_____ 6. You can use metal on your kite as long as it's not the flying line itself.

_____ 7. You don't need to wear gloves unless you're flying a very large kite.

_____ 8. You should not fly a kite around an airport.

_____ 9. If your kite gets caught in power lines, just tug the line gently until it works free.

_____ 10. The best place to fly a kite is in a large field.

Comprehension: Colonists Come to America

After Christopher Columbus voyaged to America in 1492, many people wanted to come live in the new land. During the 17th and 18th centuries, a great many Europeans, especially the English, left their countries and settled along the Atlantic Coast of North America between Florida and Canada. Some came to make a better life for themselves. Others, particularly the Pilgrims, the Puritans, and the Quakers, came for religious freedom.

A group of men who wanted gold and other riches from the new land formed the London Company. They asked the king of England for land in America and for permission to found a colony. They founded Jamestown, the first permanent English settlement in America, in 1607. They purchased ships and supplies, and located people who wanted to settle in America.

The voyage to America took about eight weeks and was very dangerous. Often, fierce winds blew the wooden ships off course. Many were wrecked. The ships were crowded and dirty. Frequently, passengers became ill, and some died. Once in America, the early settlers faced even more hardships.

Directions: Answer these questions about the colonists coming to America.

1. How long did it take colonists to travel from England to America? _____

2. Name three groups that came to America to find religious freedom.

   a) _____ b) _____ c) _____

3. Why was the London Company formed? _____

   _____

4. What was Jamestown? _____

   _____

5. Why was the voyage to America dangerous? _____

   _____

Recalling Details: Early Colonial Homes

When the first colonists landed in America, they had to find shelter quickly. Their first homes were crude bark and mud huts, log cabins, or dugouts, which were simply caves dug into the hillsides. As soon as possible, the settlers sought to replace these temporary shelters with comfortable houses.

Until the late 17th century, most of the colonial homes were simple in style. Almost all of the New England colonists—those settling in the northern areas of Massachusetts, Connecticut, Rhode Island, and New Hampshire—used wood in building their permanent homes. Some of the buildings had thatched roofs. However, they caught fire easily, and so were replaced by wooden shingles. The outside walls also were covered with wooden shingles to make the homes warmer and less drafty.

In the middle colonies—New York, Pennsylvania, New Jersey, and Delaware—the Dutch and German colonists often made brick or stone homes that were two-and-a-half or three-and-a-half stories high. Many southern colonists—those living in Virginia, Maryland, North Carolina, South Carolina, and Georgia—lived on large farms called plantations. Their homes were usually made of brick.

In the 18th century, some colonists became wealthy enough to replace their simple homes with mansions, often like those being built by the wealthy class in England. They were called Georgian houses because they were popular during the years that Kings George I, George II, and George III ruled England. Most were made of brick. They usually featured columns, ornately carved doors, and elaborate gardens.

Directions: Answer these questions about early colonial homes.

1. What were the earliest homes of the colonists?

_____

2. What were the advantages of using wooden shingles?

_____

3. What did Dutch and German colonists use to build their homes?

_____

4. What were Georgian homes?

_____

Recalling Details: The Colonial Kitchen

The most important room in the home of a colonial family was the kitchen. Sometimes it was the only room in the home. The most important element of the kitchen was the fireplace. Fire was essential to the colonists, and they were careful to keep one burning at all times. Before the man of the house went to bed, he would make sure that the fire was carefully banked so it would burn all night. In the morning, he would blow the glowing embers into flame again with a bellows. If the fire went out, one of the children would be sent to a neighbor's for hot coals. Because there were no matches, it would sometimes take a half hour to light a new fire, using flint, steel, and tinder.

The colonial kitchen, quite naturally, was centered around the fireplace. One or two large iron broilers hung over the hot coals for cooking the family meals. Above the fireplace, a large musket and powder horn were kept for protection in the event of an attack and to hunt deer and other game. Also likely to be found near the fireplace was a butter churn, where cream from the family's cow was beaten until yellow flakes of butter appeared.

The furniture in the kitchen—usually benches, a table, and chairs—were made by the man or men in the family. It was very heavy and not very comfortable. The colonial family owned few eating utensils—no forks and only a few spoons, also made by members of the family. The dishes included pewter plates, trenchers (wooden bowls with handles), and wooden mugs.

Directions: Answer these questions about the colonial kitchen.

1. What was the most important element of the colonial kitchen? _____

2. In colonial days, why was it important to keep a fire burning in the fireplace?

_____

3. Name two uses of the musket.

   a) _____   b) _____

4. Who made most of the furniture in the early colonial home?

_____

Sequencing: Spinning

Most of the colonists could not afford to buy clothes sent over from Europe. Instead, the women and girls, particularly in the New England colonies, spent much time spinning thread and weaving cloth to make their own clothing. They raised sheep for wool and grew flax for linen.

In August, the flax was ready to be harvested and made into linen thread. The plants were pulled up and allowed to dry. Then, the men pulled the seed pods from the stalks, bundled the stalks, and soaked them in a stream for about five days. The flax next had to be taken out, cleaned, and dried. To get the linen fibers from the tough bark and heavy wooden core, the stalks had to be pounded and crushed. Finally, the fibers were pulled through the teeth of a brush called a "hatchel" to comb out the short and broken fibers. The long fibers were spun into linen thread on a spinning wheel.

The spinning wheel was low, so a woman sat down to spin. First, she put flax in the hollow end of a slender stick, called the spindle, at one end of the spinning wheel. It was connected by a belt to a big wheel at the other end. The woman turned the wheel by stepping on a pedal. As it turned, the spindle also turned, twisting the flax into thread. The woman constantly dipped her fingers into water to moisten the flax and keep it from breaking. The linen thread came out through a hole in the side of the spindle. It was bleached and put away to be woven into pieces of cloth.

Directions: Number in order the steps to make linen thread from flax.

_____ The woman sat at the spinning wheel and put flax in the spindle.

_____ Seed pods were pulled from the stalks; stalks were bundled and soaked.

_____ In August, the flax was ready to be harvested and made into thread.

_____ The stalks were pounded and crushed to get the linen fibers.

_____ The thread was bleached and put away to be woven into cloth.

_____ The short fibers were separated out with a "hatchel."

_____ The woman dipped her fingers into water to moisten the flax.

_____ The long fibers were spun into linen thread on a spinning wheel.

_____ The woman turned the wheel by stepping on a pedal, twisting the flax into thread.

_____ The plants were pulled up and allowed to dry.

_____ The linen thread came out through a hole in the side of the spindle.

Recalling Details: Clothing in Colonial Times

The clothing of the colonists varied from the North to the South, accounting for the differences not only in climate, but also in the religions and ancestries of the settlers. The clothes seen most often in the early New England colonies where the Puritans settled were very plain and simple. The materials—wool and linen—were warm and sturdy.

The Puritans had strict rules about clothing. There were no bright colors, jewelry, ruffles, or lace. A Puritan woman wore a long-sleeved gray dress with a big white collar, cuffs, apron, and cap. A Puritan man wore long woolen stockings and baggy leather breeches, which were knee-length trousers. Adults and children dressed in the same style of clothing.

In the middle colonies, the clothing ranged from the simple clothing of the Quakers to the colorful, loose-fitting outfits of the Dutch colonists. Dutch women wore more colorful outfits than Puritan women, with many petticoats and fur trim. The men had silver buckles on their shoes and wore big hats decked with curling feathers.

In the southern colonies, where there were no religious restrictions against fancy clothes, wealthy men wore brightly colored breeches and coats of velvet and satin sent from England. The women's gowns also were made of rich materials and were decorated with ruffles, ribbons, and lace. The poorer people wore clothes similar to the simple dress of the New England Puritans.

Directions: Answer these questions about clothing in colonial times.

1. Why did the clothing of the colonists vary from the North to the South?

   _____

2. Why did the Puritans wear very plain clothing?

   _____

3. What was the nationality of many settlers in the middle colonies?

   _____

4. From what country did wealthy southern colonists obtain their clothing?

   _____

Recalling Details: Venn Diagrams

A **Venn diagram** is used to chart information that shows similarities and differences between two things. The outer part of each circle shows the differences. The intersecting part of the circles shows the similarities.

Example:

Basketball

Played on a court

Points scored through baskets

Five players on a team

Played with a ball

Two teams

Professional sport

Played on a diamond

Points scored through runs

Nine players on a team

Baseball

Directions: Complete the Venn diagram below. Think of at least three things to write in the outer part of each circle (differences) and at least three things to write in the intersecting part (similarities).

Colonial Kitchen   **Your Kitchen**

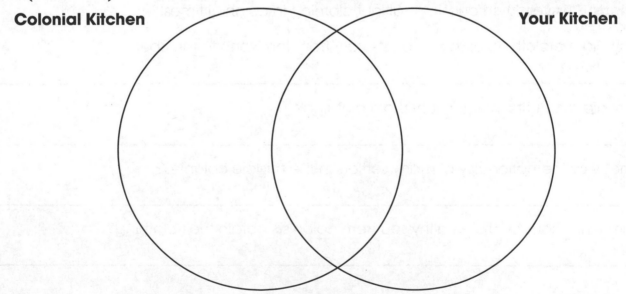

Comprehension: Colonial Schools

In early colonial days, there were no schools or teachers. Children learned what they could at home from their parents, but often their parents couldn't read or write either. Later, some women in the New England colonies began teaching in their homes. These first schools were known as "dame schools." Often the books used in these schools were not books at all, but rather "hornbooks"—flat, paddle-shaped wooden boards with the alphabet or Lord's Prayer on the front.

In 1647, a law was passed in the New England colonies requiring every town of 50 or more families to establish an elementary school. By the 1700s, one-room log schoolhouses were common. Children of all ages studied together under one strict schoolmaster. They attended school six days a week, from 7:00 or 8:00 in the morning until 4:00 or 5:00 in the afternoon. Their only textbooks were the Bible and the *New England Primer*, which contained the alphabet, spelling words, poems, and questions about the Bible.

Like the New England colonies, the middle colonies also established schools. However, there were few schools in the southern colonies, where most of the people lived on widely separated farms. Wealthy plantation owners hired private teachers from England to teach their children, but the children of poor families received no education.

Directions: Answer these questions about colonial schools.

1. What was a hornbook? _____

_____

2. What was required by the law passed in the New England colonies in 1647?

_____

_____

3. During the 1700s, what textbooks were used in the New England schools?

_____

4. Why was it hard to establish schools in the southern colonies?

_____

Compare/Contrast: Schools

Directions: Think about the differences and similarities between colonial and modern schools. Use the chart below to help organize your ideas. Then, write a paragraph discussing the similarities and a paragraph discussing the differences. The topic sentences have been written for you.

Similarities	Differences

There are several similarities between colonial schools and schools today.

_____

_____

_____

_____

Although there are similarities between colonial schools and modern schools, there are also many differences.

_____

_____

_____

_____

Comprehension: Religion in New England

Many New England colonists had come to America for religious freedom. Religion was very important to them. One of the first buildings erected in any new settlement was a church, or meetinghouse. They were generally in the center of town and were used for public meetings of all kinds. These early meetinghouses were plain, unpainted wood buildings. Later churches were larger and more elaborate. They were usually painted white and had tall, graceful bell towers rising from the roof.

Although they came to America to have freedom of worship, the Puritans thought that everyone in the colonies should worship the same way they did. Because there were so many of them, the Puritans controlled the government in much of New England. They were the only ones allowed to vote, and they passed very strict laws. Lawbreakers received harsh punishments. For example, someone caught lying might be forced to stand in the town square for hours locked in a pillory—wooden boards with holes cut in them for the head and hands. For other minor offenses, the offender was tied to a whipping post and given several lashes with a whip.

Except in cases of extreme illness, everyone in the New England colonies had to attend church on Sunday. The minister stood in a pulpit high above the pews to deliver his sermon, which could last four or five hours. The people sat on hard, straight-backed pews. In the winter, there was no heat, so church members brought foot warmers from home to use during the long services. In many churches, a "tithingman" walked up and down the aisles carrying a long stick. On one end there were feathers attached; the other end had a knob. If anyone dozed off, the tithingman would tickle him or her with the feathers. If this did not rouse the offender, he would thump them soundly with the knob.

Directions: Answer these questions about religion in the colonies.

1. The main idea is:

    ☐ Many New England colonists had come to America for religious freedom, and religion was very important to them.

    ☐ One of the first buildings erected in any new settlement was a church.

2. Which religious group exercised a lot of power in the New England colonies?

    _____

3. What was a pillory? _____

4. What was the only acceptable excuse for missing Sunday church services in the New England colonies? _____

5. What was the job of the tithingman? _____

Writing: Problem and Solution

Directions: Follow the instructions below.

1. Think of a problem the colonial Americans may have encountered. Write a paragraph about this problem. In the paragraph, be sure to state the problem, and then discuss why it would have been a problem for the colonists.

_____

_____

_____

_____

_____

_____

2. Think about a solution to the problem above. Write a paragraph outlining your ideas for the solution. Remember to state the solution to the problem and then your ideas to solve the problem.

_____

_____

_____

_____

_____

_____

Review

Many great colonists made an impact on American history. Among them was Benjamin Franklin, who left his mark as a printer, author, inventor, scientist and statesman. He has been called "the wisest American."

Franklin was born in Boston in 1706, one of 13 children in a very religious Puritan household. Although he had less than two years of formal education, his tremendous appetite for books served him well. At age 12, he became an apprentice printer at *The New England Courant* and soon began writing articles that poked fun at Boston society.

In 1723, Franklin ran away to Philadelphia, where he started his own newspaper. He was very active In the Philadelphia community. He operated a bookstore and was named postmaster. He also helped to establish a library, a fire company, a college, an insurance company, and a hospital. His well-known *Poor Richard's Almanac* was first printed in 1732.

Over the years, Franklin maintained an interest in science and mechanics, leading to such inventions as a fireplace stove and bifocal lenses. In 1752, he gained world fame with his kite-and-key experiment, which proved that lightning was a form of electricity.

Franklin was an active supporter of the colonies throughout the Revolutionary War. He helped to write and was a signer of the Declaration of Independence in 1776. In his later years, he skillfully represented America in Europe, helping to work out a peace treaty with Great Britain.

Directions: Answer these questions about Benjamin Franklin.

1. The main idea is:

   ☐ Many great colonists made an impact on American history.

   ☐ Benjamin Franklin was a great colonist who left his mark as a printer, author, inventor, scientist, and statesman.

2. How did Benjamin Franklin gain world fame? _____

3. What did Franklin sign and help to write? _____

4. Number in order the following accomplishments of Benjamin Franklin.

   _____ Served as representative of America in Europe

   _____ Began printing *Poor Richard's Almanac*

   _____ Experimented with electricity

   _____ Started his own newspaper

   _____ Helped to write and sign the Declaration of Independence

   _____ Served as apprentice printer at *The New England Courant*

Review

Directions: Match each item with its description. If necessary, review the section on colonial times.

a. hornbooks

b. 1647

c. pillory

d. Ben Franklin

e. plantations

f. 1776

g. tithingman

h. spinning wheel

i. hatchel

j. 1492

k. trenchers

l. flax

m. dame schools

_____ year Columbus sailed to America

_____ schools where New England women taught in their homes

_____ man who kept worshippers awake during Sunday services

_____ plants harvested for linen

_____ paddle-shaped wooden boards with text on them

_____ law written in this year required towns of 50 or more to establish a school

_____ punishment rack with holes for head and hands

_____ wooden bowls with handles

_____ author of *Poor Richard's Almanac*

_____ large farms in the South

_____ wooden machine used to spin wool or flax into thread

_____ used to comb out the short and broken flax fibers

_____ year Declaration of Independence was signed

Using Prior Knowledge:
Abraham Lincoln and the Civil War

Directions: Before reading about Abraham Lincoln and the Civil War in the following section, answer these questions.

1. The Civil War began because _____

_____

_____

2. Abraham Lincoln is famous today because _____

_____

_____

_____

3. What brought about the end of slavery in the United States? _____

_____

_____

4. The Gettysburg Address begins with the famous line: "Four score and seven years ago. . . . " What does this mean?

_____

_____

5. How did Abraham Lincoln die? _____

_____

_____

_____

Comprehensive Curriculum - **Grade 6**

Main Idea: The Gettysburg Address

On November 19, 1863, President Abraham Lincoln gave a short speech to dedicate a cemetery for Civil War soldiers in Gettysburg, Pennsylvania, where a famous battle was fought. He wrote five drafts of the Gettysburg Address, one of the most stirring speeches of all time.

Four score and seven years ago, our fathers brought forth on this continent a new nation, conceived in liberty, and dedicated to the proposition that all men are created equal.

Now we are engaged in a great civil war, testing whether that nation, or any nation so conceived and so dedicated, can long endure. We are met on a great battlefield of that war. We have come to dedicate a portion of that field as a final resting place for those who here gave their lives that this nation might live. It is altogether fitting and proper that we should do this.

But, in a larger sense, we cannot dedicate—we cannot consecrate—we cannot hallow—this ground. The brave men, living and dead, who struggled here have consecrated it far above our poor power to add or detract. The world will little note nor long remember what we say here, but it can never forget what they did here. It is for us the living, rather, to be dedicated to the unfinished work which they who fought here have thus far so nobly advanced. It is rather for us to be here dedicated to the great task remaining before us—that from these honored dead we take increased devotion to that cause for which they gave their last full measure of devotion—that we here highly resolve that these dead shall not have died in vain—that this nation, under God, shall have a new birth of freedom—and that government of the people, by the people, for the people shall not perish from this earth.

Directions: Answer the questions about the Gettysburg Address.

1. Circle the main idea:

   This speech will be long remembered as a tribute to those who died fighting in the Civil War.

   This speech is to honor the soldiers who gave their lives so that the nation could have freedom for all citizens.

2. What happened on the ground where the cemetery stood? _____

   _____

   _____

Comprehension: The Gettysburg Address

Directions: Use context clues or a dictionary to answer these questions about the Gettysburg Address.

1. What is the correct definition of **conceived**? _____
_____

2. What is the correct definition of **consecrate**? _____
_____

3. What is the correct definition of **hallow**? _____
_____

4. What is the correct definition of **devotion**? _____
_____

5. What is the correct definition of **resolve**? _____
_____

6. What is the correct definition of **vain**? _____
_____

7. What is the correct definition of **perish**? _____
_____

8. What is the correct definition of **civil**? _____
_____

9. In your own words, what point was President Lincoln trying to make? _____
_____
_____

Comprehension:
The Emancipation Proclamation

On September 22, 1862, a year before delivering the Gettysburg Address, President Lincoln delivered the Emancipation Proclamation, which stated that all slaves in Confederate states should be set free. Since the Confederate states had already seceded (withdrawn) from the Union, they ignored the proclamation. However, the proclamation did strengthen the North's war effort. About 200,000 black men—mostly former slaves—enlisted in the Union Army. Two years later, the 13th Amendment to the Constitution ended slavery in all parts of the United States.

I, Abraham Lincoln, do order and declare that all persons held as slaves within said designated States and parts of States are, and henceforward shall be, free; and that the Executive Government of the United States, including military and naval authorities thereof, shall recognize and maintain the freedom of said persons.

And I hereby enjoin upon the people so declared to be free to abstain from all violence, unless in necessary self-defense; and I recommend to them that, in all cases where allowed, they labor faithfully for reasonable wages.

And I further declare and make known that such persons of suitable condition will be received into the armed forces of the United States to garrison forts, positions, stations, and other places, and to man vessels of all sorts in said service.

(This is not the full text of the Emancipation Proclamation.)

Directions: Answer the questions about the Emancipation Proclamation.

1. How did the Emancipation Proclamation strengthen the North's war effort?

_____

2. Which came first, the Emancipation Proclamation or the Gettysburg Address?

_____

3. Which amendment to the Constitution grew out of the Emancipation Proclamation?

_____

4. **Secede** means to ☐ quit.   ☐ fight.   ☐ withdraw.

Comprehension:
The Emancipation Proclamation

Directions: Use context clues or a dictionary to answer these questions about the Emancipation Proclamation.

1. What is the correct definition of **designated**? _____

_____

2. What is the correct definition of **military**? _____

_____

3. What is the correct definition of **naval**? _____

_____

4. What is the correct definition of **abstain**? _____

_____

5. What is the correct definition of **suitable**? _____

_____

6. What is the correct definition of **garrison**? _____

_____

7. What is the correct definition of **vessels**? _____

_____

8. In your own words, what did the Emancipation Proclamation accomplish?

_____

_____

_____

_____

Comprehension: Lincoln and the South

Many people think that Abraham Lincoln publicly came out against slavery from the beginning of his term as president. This is not the case. Whatever his private feelings, he did not criticize slavery publicly. Fearful that the southern states would secede, or leave, the Union, he pledged to respect the southern states' rights to own slaves. He also pledged that the government would respect the southern states' runaway slave laws. These laws required all citizens to return runaway slaves to their masters.

Clearly, Lincoln did not want the country torn apart by a civil war. In the following statement, written in 1861 shortly after he became president, he made it clear that the federal government would do its best to avoid conflict with the southern states.

I hold that, in contemplation of the universal law and the Constitution, the Union of these states is perpetual. . . . No state, upon its own mere motion, can lawfully get out of the Union. . . . I shall take care, as the Constitution itself expressly enjoins upon me, that the laws of the Union be faithfully executed in all the states. . . . The power confided to me will be used to hold, occupy, and possess the property and places belonging to the government, and to collect the duties and imposts. . . .

In your hands, my dissatisfied fellow-countrymen, and not in mine, is the momentous issue of civil war. The government will not assail you. You can have no conflict without yourselves being the aggressors. You have no oath registered in heaven to destroy the government, while I shall have the most solemn one to "preserve, protect, and defend" it.

Directions: Use context clues for these definitions.

1. What is the correct definition of **assail**? _____

2. What is the correct definition of **enjoin**? _____

3. What is the correct definition of **contemplation**? _____

_____

Directions: Answer these questions about Lincoln and the southern states.

4. Lincoln is telling the southern states that the government

☐ does want a war.   ☐ doesn't want a war.   ☐ will stop a war.

5. As president, Lincoln pledged to "preserve, protect and defend"

☐ slavery.   ☐ the northern states.   ☐ the Union.

Comprehension: Away Down South in Dixie

Although many southerners disapproved of slavery, the pressure to go along with the majority who supported slavery was very strong. Many of those who thought slavery was wrong did not talk about their opinions. It was dangerous to do so!

The main reason the southern states seceded from the Union in 1861 was because they wanted to protect their right to own slaves. They also wanted to increase the number of slaves so they could increase production of cotton and other crops that slaves tended. Many Civil War monuments in the South are dedicated to a war that was described as "just and holy."

"Dixie," a song written in 1859 that is still popular in the South, sums up the attitude of many southerners. As the song lyrics show, southerners' loyalties lay not with the Union representing all the states, but with the South and the southern way of life.

Dixie

I wish I was in Dixie, Hoo-ray! Hoo-ray!
In Dixie land I'll take my stand
To live and die in Dixie.
Away, away, away down south in Dixie!
Away, away, away down south in Dixie!
(This is not the full text of the song.)

Directions: Answer these questions about southerners and "Dixie."

1. Why did southerners who disapproved of slavery keep their opinions to themselves?

   _____

   _____

2. Why did southerners want more slaves? _____

   _____

3. What are the words on some southern Civil War monuments? _____

   _____

4. What "stand" is referred to in "Dixie"?

   ☐ stand for slavery   ☐ stand against slavery   ☐ stand for cotton

Recalling Details: Abraham Lincoln

Directions: Complete the following exercises.

1. Describe two accomplishments of Abraham Lincoln. _____

_____

_____

2. Complete the time line by writing and illustrating the events.

| 1861 | 1862 | 1863 | 1864 | 1865 |

_____ _____ _____ _____ _____

_____ _____ _____ _____ _____

3. In your opinion, what could Lincoln have done differently to end the Civil War sooner?

_____

_____

_____

_____

Fact and Opinion

Directions: Read each sentence. Then, draw an **X** in the box to tell whether it is a fact or an opinion.

1. Lincoln warned the southern states that they could not legally leave the Union.

☐ Fact   ☐ Opinion

2. I believe Lincoln thought the northern states were the best because they did not have slaves.

☐ Fact   ☐ Opinion

3. I think Lincoln did the right thing, don't you?

☐ Fact   ☐ Opinion

4. The issues that sparked the Civil War were complicated and difficult ones.

☐ Fact   ☐ Opinion

5. It would take a historian to really understand them!

☐ Fact   ☐ Opinion

6. The "dissatisfied fellow-countrymen" Lincoln refers to in his statement lived in the southern states.

☐ Fact   ☐ Opinion

7. As president, Lincoln took an oath to "preserve, protect, and defend" the Union, which included all the states.

☐ Fact   ☐ Opinion

8. Lincoln did his personal best to hold the country together, but it didn't do one bit of good.

☐ Fact   ☐ Opinion

9. The Confederate States of America had already been organized in February 1861, a month before Lincoln was sworn in as president.

☐ Fact   ☐ Opinion

10. Poor Abraham Lincoln—what a crummy start to his presidency!

☐ Fact   ☐ Opinion

Using Prior Knowledge: Anthems and Songs

Directions: Before reading about anthems and songs in the following section, answer these questions.

1. How do national anthems help pull a country together? _____

_____

_____

_____

_____

2. Describe what you know about how and why "The Star-Spangled Banner" was written.

_____

_____

_____

_____

3. What is your favorite anthem or song? _____

4. What images do the words of your favorite anthem or song bring to mind? Why do you like it?

_____

_____

_____

_____

_____

_____

Comprehension: Our National Anthem

Written in 1814 by Francis Scott Key, our American national anthem is stirring, beautiful, and difficult to sing. Key wrote the song while aboard a ship off the coast of Maryland, where one long night he watched the gunfire from a British attack on America's Fort McHenry. The following morning, he wrote "The Star-Spangled Banner" when, to his great joy, he saw the American flag still flying over the fort—a sign that the Americans had not lost the battle.

The Star-Spangled Banner
Oh say, can you see, by the dawn's early light,
What so proudly we hail'd at the twilight's last gleaming?
Whose broad stripes and bright stars, thro' the perilous fight,
O'er the ramparts we watch'd were so gallantly streaming?
And the rockets' red glare, the bombs bursting in air,
Gave proof thro' the night that our flag was still there.
Oh say, does that star-spangled banner yet wave
O'er the land of the free and the home of the brave?

Oh, the shore dimly seen thro' the mists of the deep,
Where the foe's haughty host in dread silence reposes,
What is that which the breeze, o'er the towering steep,
As it fitfully blows, half conceals, half discloses?
Now it catches the gleam of the morning's first beam,
In full glory reflected, now shines on the stream:
'Tis the star-spangled banner: O, long may it wave
O'er the land of the free and the home of the brave!

Directions: Answer these questions about the first two verses of "The Star-Spangled Banner."

1. Who wrote "The Star-Spangled Banner"? _____

2. What is "The Star-Spangled Banner"? _____

3. In what year was the song written? _____

4. At what time of day was the song written? _____

5. Tell what is meant by the lines " . . . the rockets' red glare, the bombs bursting in air/Gave proof through the night that our flag was still there."

_____

_____

Comprehension: "The Star-Spangled Banner"

Directions: Use context clues or a dictionary to answer these questions about "The Star-Spangled Banner."

1. What is the correct definition of **spangled**? _____
   _____

2. What is the correct definition of **twilight**? _____
   _____

3. What is the correct definition of **ramparts**? _____
   _____

4. What is the correct definition of **gallantly**? _____
   _____

5. What is the correct definition of **haughty**? _____
   _____

6. What is the correct definition of **reposes**? _____
   _____

7. Why do you think United States citizens only sing the first verse of "The Star-Spangled Banner"?
   _____

8. What war was being fought when this song was written?
   _____

9. Have you ever heard the second verse of "The Star-Spangled Banner"? Knowing the tune, can you sing the second verse?
   _____

Comprehension: "America the Beautiful"

Written in 1895 by Katherine Lee Bates, "America the Beautiful" is another very popular patriotic song. It is so popular, in fact, that some people would like to see it replace "The Star-Spangled Banner" as the United States' national anthem. Ms. Bates was inspired to write the song while visiting Colorado, where she was struck by the splendor of the mountains. Today, "America the Beautiful" remains a tribute to our country's natural beauty.

America the Beautiful
Oh beautiful for spacious skies,
For amber waves of grain,
For purple mountains majesties
Above the fruited plain!
America! America!
God shed His grace on thee,
And crown thy good
With brotherhood
From sea to shining sea!

Directions: Use context clues or a dictionary to answer these questions about "America the Beautiful."

1. What is the correct definition of **tribute**? _____

2. What is the correct definition of **amber**? _____

   What other word might you use for **amber** in the song? _____

3. What is the singular form of **majesties**? What does it mean in the song? _____

   _____

4. "From sea to shining sea" means the oceans to the east and west of the United States. What are their names?

   _____   _____

5. Do you think "America the Beautiful" should be our national anthem? Why or why not?

   _____

   _____

Comprehension: Civil War Marching Song

When soldiers march, they sometimes sing a song to help them keep in step. One of the most famous marching songs of the Civil War was the "Battle Hymn of the Republic," written in 1861 by Julia Ward Howe. Mrs. Howe wrote the song after visiting a Union army camp in the North. The words are about how God is on the side of the soldiers.

Battle Hymn of the Republic

Mine eyes have seen the glory of the coming of the Lord,
He is trampling out the vintage where the grapes of wrath are stored,
He has loosed the fateful lightning of his terrible swift sword,
His truth is marching on.

Glory, glory hallelujah! Glory, glory hallelujah!
Glory, glory hallelujah! His truth is marching on.

I have seen him in the watchfires of a hundred circling camps,
I have builded him an altar in the evening dews and damps,
I can read his righteous sentence by the dim and flaring lamps,
His day is marching on.

Glory, glory hallelujah! Glory, glory hallelujah!
Glory, glory hallelujah! His truth is marching on.

Directions: Answer these questions about the "Battle Hymn of the Republic."

1. Who wrote the "Battle Hymn of the Republic"? _____

2. When was the song written? _____

3. What war was in progress at the time? _____

4. Why did soldiers sing while they marched? _____

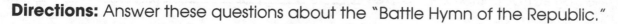

5. What marches on along with the soldiers? _____

6. What did the soldiers sing about building in the evening?

_____

Review

National anthems, work songs, and marching songs share some common characteristics. Perhaps the most important characteristic is that the words strike an emotional response in singers and listeners alike.

Have you ever sung "The Star-Spangled Banner" at a baseball game or other large public event? The next time you do, look around as you sing. You will see that Americans from all walks of life and all races sing the song proudly. The words to the national anthem help create a feeling of unity among people who may not have much in common. The same is true of the national anthems of France, England, and other countries.

Another characteristic of these types of songs is that the words are simple, the message is clear, and the tune should be easy to carry. This is not always true, of course. Many people's voices crack during the high notes of "The Star-Spangled Banner." But attempts to change the national anthem to "America the Beautiful" or another song with a simpler tune have always met with dismal failure. It may be hard to sing, but most Americans wouldn't trade it for any other tune. It's a long-held American tradition, and nearly everyone knows the words. Americans love what this song stands for. They are proud to live in a country that is the "land of the free."

Directions: Answer these questions about the characteristics of national anthems, work songs, and marching songs.

1. Explain what goes into writing a good national anthem. _____

_____

_____

2. What does our national anthem help do? _____

_____

3. What happens each time someone tries to change the national anthem to "America the Beautiful" or another song?

_____

4. Why do people stick with "The Star-Spangled Banner" as our national anthem?

_____

_____

Recalling Details: The Island Continent

Australia is the only country that fills an entire continent. It is the smallest continent in the world but the sixth largest country. Australia, called the island continent, is totally surrounded by water—the Indian Ocean on the west and south, the Pacific Ocean on the east, and the Arafura Sea, which is formed by these two oceans coming together, to the north.

The island continent is, in large part, a very dry, flat land. Yet it supports a magnificent and unusual collection of wildlife. Because of its remoteness, Australia is home to plants and animals that are not found anywhere else in the world. Besides the well-known kangaroo and koala, the strange animals of the continent include the wombat, dingo, kookaburra, emu, and, perhaps the strangest of all, the duckbill platypus.

There are many physical features of Australia that also are unique, including the central part of the country known as the Outback, which consists of three main deserts—the Great Sandy, the Gibson, and the Great Victoria. Because much of the country is desert, more than half of all Australians live in large, modern cities along the coast. There are also many people living in the small towns on the edge of the Outback, where there is plenty of grass for raising sheep and cattle. In fact, there are about five times as many sheep in Australia as there are people!

Directions: Answer these questions about Australia.

1. What are the three large bodies of water that surround Australia?

a) _____ b) _____ c) _____

2. Besides the kangaroo and the koala, name three other unusual animals found only in Australia.

a) _____ b) _____ c) _____

3. What three deserts make up the Outback?

a) _____ b) _____ c) _____

Comprehension: The Aborigines

The native, or earliest known, people of Australia are the Aborigines (ab-ur-IJ-uh-neez). They arrived on the continent from Asia more than 20,000 years ago. Before the Europeans began settling in Australia during the early 1800s, there were about 300,000 Aborigines. But the new settlers brought diseases that killed many of these native people. Today, there are only about 125,000 Aborigines living in Australia, many of whom now live in the cities.

The way of life of the Aborigines, who still live like their ancestors, is closely related to nature. They live as hunters and gatherers and do not produce crops or raise livestock. The Aborigines have no permanent settlements, only small camps near watering places. Because they live off the land, they must frequently move about in search of food. They have few belongings and little or no clothing.

Some tribes of Aborigines, especially those who live in the desert, may move 100 times in a year. They might move more than 1,000 miles on foot during that time. These tribes set up temporary homes, such as tents made of bark and igloo-like structures made of grass.

The Aborigines have no written language, but they have developed a system of hand signals. These are used during hunting when silence is necessary and during their elaborate religious ceremonies when talking is forbidden.

Directions: Circle **True** or **False** for these statements about Aborigines.

1. The Aborigines came from Europe to settle in Australia.   True   False

2. The Aborigines live as hunters and gatherers rather than as farmers.   True   False

3. The tribes move about often to find jobs.   True   False

4. The people move often to help them raise their livestock.   True   False

5. Aborigine tribes always move 200 times a year.   True   False

Main Idea/Comprehension: The Boomerang

The Aborigines have developed a few tools and weapons, including spears, flint knives, and the boomerang. The boomerang comes in different shapes and has many uses. This curved throwing stick is used for hunting, playing, digging, cutting, and even making music.

You may have seen a boomerang that, when thrown, returns to the thrower. This type of boomerang is sometimes used in duck hunting, but it is most often used as a toy and for sporting contests. It is lightweight—about three-fourths of a pound—and has a big curve in it. However, the boomerang used by the Aborigines for hunting is much heavier and is nearly straight. It does not return to its thrower.

Because of its sharp edges, the boomerang makes a good knife for skinning animals. The Aborigines also use boomerangs as digging sticks, to sharpen stone blades, to start fires, and as swords and clubs in fighting. Boomerangs sometimes are used to make music—two clapped together provide rhythmic background for dances. Some make musical sounds when they are pulled across one another.

To throw a boomerang, the thrower grasps it at one end and holds it behind his head. He throws it overhanded, adding a sharp flick of the wrist at the last moment. It is thrown into the wind to make it come back. A skillful thrower can do many tricks with his boomerang. He can make it spin in several circles, or make a figure eight in the air. He can even make it bounce on the ground several times before it soars into the air and returns.

Directions: Answer these questions about boomerangs.

1. The main idea is:

   ☐ The Aborigines have developed a few tools and weapons, including spears, flint knives, and the boomerang.

   ☐ The boomerang comes in different shapes and has many uses.

2. To make it return, the thrower tosses the boomerang

   ☐ into the wind.   ☐ against the wind.

3. List three uses for the boomerang.

   a)_____

   b)_____

   c)_____

Comprehension: The Kangaroo

Many animals found in Australia are not found anywhere else in the world. Because the island continent was separated from the rest of the world for many years, these animals developed in different ways. Many of the animals in Australia are marsupials. Marsupials are animals whose babies are born underdeveloped and are then carried in a pouch on the mother's body until they are able to care for themselves. The kangaroo is perhaps the best known of the marsupials.

There are 45 kinds of kangaroos, and they come in a variety of sizes. The smallest is the musky rat kangaroo, which is about a foot long, including its hairless tail. It weighs only a pound. The largest is the gray kangaroo, which is more than 9 feet long, counting its tail, and can weigh 200 pounds. When moving quickly, a kangaroo can leap 25 feet and move at 30 miles an hour!

A baby kangaroo, called a joey, is totally helpless at birth. It is only three-quarters of an inch long and weighs a fraction of an ounce. The newly born joey immediately crawls into its mother's pouch and remains there until it is old enough to be independent—which can be as long as eight months.

Kangaroos eat grasses and plants. They can cause problems for farmers and ranchers in Australia because they compete with cattle for pastures. During a drought, kangaroos may invade ranches and even airports looking for food.

Directions: Answer these questions about kangaroos.

1. What are marsupials? _____

   _____

2. What is the smallest kangaroo? _____

3. What is a baby kangaroo called? _____

4. Why did Australian animals develop differently from other animals? _____

   _____

Comprehension: The Koala

The koala lives in eastern Australia in the eucalyptus (you-ca-LIP-tes) forests. These slow, gentle animals hide by day, usually sleeping in the trees. They come out at night to eat. Koalas eat only certain types of eucalyptus leaves. Their entire way of life centers on this unique diet. The koala's digestive system is specially adapted for eating eucalyptus leaves. In fact, to other animals, these leaves are poisonous!

The wooly, round-eared koala looks like a cuddly teddy bear, but it is not related to any bear. It is a marsupial like the kangaroo. And, like the joey, a baby koala requires a lot of care. It will remain constantly in its mother's pouch until it is six months old. After that, a baby koala will ride piggyback on its mother for another month or two, even though it is nearly as big as she is. Koalas have few babies—only one every other year. While in her pouch, the baby koala lives on its mother's milk. After it is big enough to be on its own, the koala will almost never drink anything again.

Oddly, the mother koala's pouch is backwards—the opening is at the bottom. This leads scientists to believe that the koala once lived on the ground and walked on all fours. But at some point, the koala became a tree dweller. This makes an upside-down pouch very awkward! The babies keep from falling to the ground by holding on tightly with their mouths. The mother koala has developed strong muscles around the rim of her pouch that also help to hold the baby in.

Directions: Answer these questions about koalas.

1. What is the correct definition for **eucalyptus**?

   ☐ enormous   ☐ a type of tree   ☐ rain

2. What is the correct definition for **digestive**?

   ☐ the process in which food is absorbed in the body
   ☐ the process of finding food
   ☐ the process of tasting

3. What is the correct definition for **dweller**?

   ☐ one who climbs   ☐ one who eats   ☐ one who lives in

Comprehension: The Wombat

Another animal unique to Australia is the wombat. The wombat has characteristics in common with other animals. Like the koala, the wombat is also a marsupial with a backwards pouch. The pouch is more practical for the wombat, which lives on the ground rather than in trees. The wombat walks on all fours, so the baby is in less danger of falling out.

The wombat resembles a beaver without a tail. With its strong claws, it is an expert digger. It makes long tunnels beneath cliffs and boulders in which it sleeps all day. At night, it comes out to look for food. It has strong, beaver-like teeth to chew through the various plant roots it eats. A wombat's teeth have no roots, like a rodent's. Its teeth keep growing from the inside as they are worn down from the outside.

The wombat, which can be up to 4 feet long and weighs 60 pounds when full grown, eats only grass, plants, and roots. It is a shy, quiet, and gentle animal that would never attack. But when angered, it has a strong bite and very sharp teeth! And, while wombats don't eat or attack other animals, the many deep burrows they dig to sleep in are often dangerous to the other animals living nearby.

Directions: Answer these questions about the wombat.

1. How is the wombat similar to the koala? _____

_____

2. How is the wombat similar to the beaver? _____

_____

3. How is the wombat similar to a rodent? _____

_____

_____

Comprehension: The Duckbill Platypus

Australia's duckbill platypus is a most unusual animal. It is very strange-looking and has caused a lot of confusion for people studying it. For many years, even scientists did not know how to classify it. The platypus has webbed feet and a bill like a duck. But it doesn't have wings, has fur instead of feathers, and has four legs instead of two. The baby platypus gets milk from its mother, like a mammal, but it is hatched from a tough-skinned egg, like a reptile. A platypus also has a poisonous spur on each of its back legs that is like the tip of a viper's fangs. Scientists have put the platypus—along with another strange animal from Australia called the spiny anteater—in a special class of mammal called "monotremes."

The platypus has an amazing appetite! It has been estimated that a full-grown platypus eats about 1,200 earthworms, 50 crayfish, and numerous tadpoles and insects every day. The platypus is an excellent swimmer and diver. It dives under the water of a stream and searches the muddy bottom for food.

A mother platypus lays one or two eggs, which are very small—only about an inch long—and leathery in appearance. During the seven to 14 days it takes for the eggs to hatch, the mother never leaves them, not even to eat. The tiny platypus, which is only a half-inch long, cuts its way out of the shell with a sharp point on its bill. This point is known as an "egg tooth," and it will fall off soon after birth. (Many reptiles and birds have egg teeth, but they are unknown in other mammals.) By the time it is 4 months old, the baby platypus is about a foot long—half its adult size—and is learning how to swim and hunt.

Directions: Answer these questions about the duckbill platypus.

1. In what way is a duckbill platypus like other mammals? _____

_____

2. In what way is it like a reptile? _____

3. What other animal is in the class of mammal called "monotremes"?

_____

4. What makes up the diet of a platypus? _____

5. On what other animals would you see an "egg tooth"? _____

Recalling Details: Animals of Australia

Directions: Complete the chart with information from the selection on Australian animals.

	Gray Kangaroo	Koala	Wombat	Platypus
What are the animal's physical characteristics?				
What is the animal's habitat?				
What does the animal eat?				

Main Idea/Recalling Details: Land Down Under

Australia and New Zealand are often referred to as the "land down under." The name, made popular by American soldiers stationed there during World War II, grew out of the idea that these two countries are opposite or below Europe on the globe. While Australia and New Zealand are often linked, they are individual countries, separated by more than 1,000 miles of ocean.

Their landscapes are quite different. New Zealand is made up of two main islands, North and South Island, which are nearly covered by snowy mountains. One of the most unusual and beautiful areas of New Zealand is the volcanic region around Lake Taupo on North Island. There, you will see boiling springs, pools of steaming mud, hot-water geysers, small lakes with beds of brightly colored rocks, and waterfalls. While most of the people of New Zealand live and work in the industrialized cities, dairy farming is most important to the country's economy. New Zealanders eat a great deal of meat and butter, and they sell huge amounts to other countries.

As in Australia, many of the customs in New Zealand would be familiar to a traveler from America because the two countries were settled by British settlers hundreds of years ago. However, the native islanders have descended from Asian ancestors, so the remnants of ancient Eastern practices exist alongside the European way of life.

Directions: Answer these questions about New Zealand and Australia.

1. The main idea is:

   ☐ Australia and New Zealand are often referred to as the "land down under."

   ☐ While Australia and New Zealand are often linked, they are individual countries.

2. What is the correct definition for **landscape**?

   ☐ natural scenery and features   ☐ mountainsides   ☐ natural resources

3. What is the correct definition for **economy**?

   ☐ thrifty   ☐ money management   ☐ countryside

4. What is the nickname for Australia and New Zealand? _____

5. What business is most important to the New Zealand economy? _____

Venn Diagrams: Australia and New Zealand

Directions: Although Australia and New Zealand are close geographically to each other, they have many differences. After reading the selection, "Land Down Under," complete the following Venn diagram.

Australia   **New Zealand**

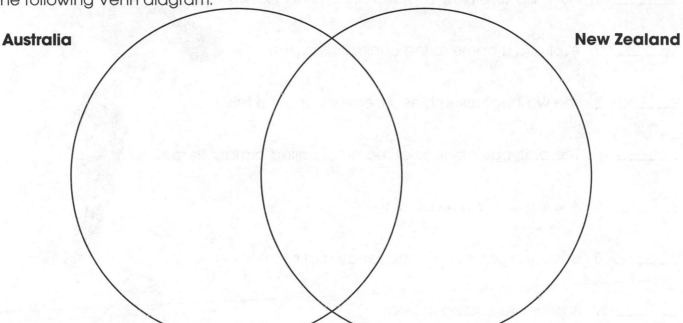

Directions: Using your knowledge of the United States and Australia, complete the following Venn diagram.

Australia   **United States**

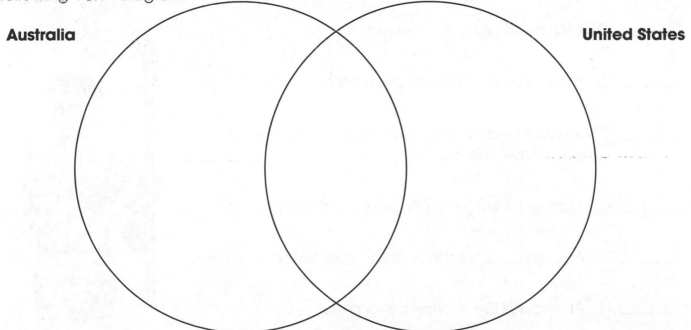

Review

Directions: Write **T** for true and **F** for false.

_____ 1. Australia and New Zealand are similar in landscape.

_____ 2. Australia is home to the duckbill platypus.

_____ 3. The wombat resembles a beaver without a tail.

_____ 4. The platypus is a special mammal called a monotreme.

_____ 5. A kangaroo is a marsupial.

_____ 6. Baby kangaroos are independent at birth.

_____ 7. Koalas are related to bears.

_____ 8. Female koalas and kangaroos both have pouches.

_____ 9. Koalas eat all types of leaves.

_____ 10. There are over 40 kinds of kangaroos.

_____ 11. The Australian Outback is located in the central part of the country.

_____ 12 Australia is known for its great number of sheep.

_____ 13. Aborigines arrived in Australia over 20,000 years ago.

_____ 14. Aborigines live in one central place.

Using Prior Knowledge: World Cities

Directions: Before reading about world cities in the following section, write one or two sentences telling what you know about each city below.

London, England _____

_____

_____

Berlin, Germany _____

_____

_____

Sydney, Australia _____

_____

_____

Cairo, Egypt _____

_____

_____

Washington, D.C., United States _____

_____

_____

Ottawa, Canada _____

_____

_____

Creative Writing: London

- London is the capital of England.
- Over 8 million people live in London.
- Among cities its size, London is the greenest city in the world.
- London is one of Europe's largest seaports.
- London has many historic sites, including Westminster Abbey, Houses of Parliament, Big Ben, and Buckingham Palace.
- Buckingham Palace is the residence of the queen of England, Queen Elizabeth II.

Directions: Using the above information, create a tourist article describing London. Do some research, and add other interesting information.

_____

_____

_____

_____

_____

When you think of England, what comes to mind?_____

_____

_____

Would you like to visit London? Why or why not? _____

_____

_____

Creative Writing: Berlin

- Berlin is the capital of Germany.
- The population of Berlin is over 3.5 million people.
- Berlin's Inland Harbor is connected to the Baltic Sea.
- Germany was once divided into East and West Germany after World War II. East Germany was Communist, and West Germany was a democracy.
- Berlin has more museums (175) than rainy days per year.
- Interesting sites in Berlin include the Brandenburg Gate, the State Opera House, Tiergarten Park, and the Philharmonic Concert Hall.

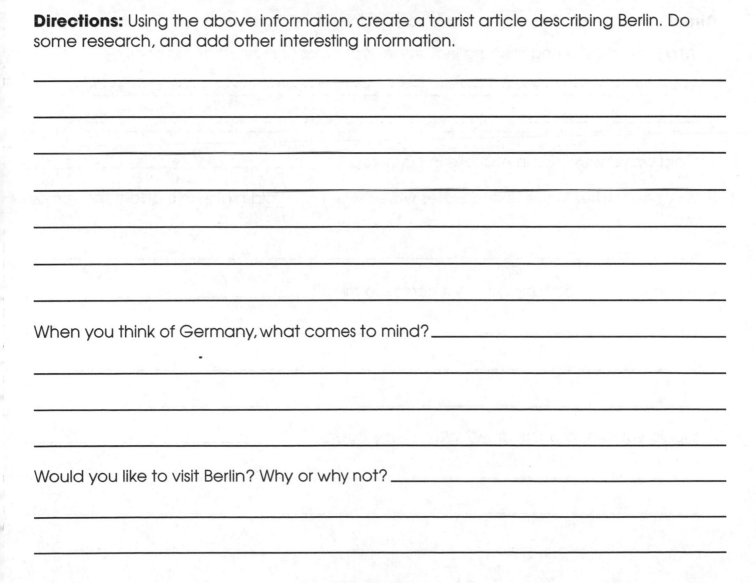

Directions: Using the above information, create a tourist article describing Berlin. Do some research, and add other interesting information.

_____

_____

_____

_____

_____

_____

_____

When you think of Germany, what comes to mind? _____

_____

_____

_____

Would you like to visit Berlin? Why or why not? _____

_____

_____

Making Inferences: Sydney

- Sydney is the capital of New South Wales, Australia.
- Manufacturing is a strong industry in Sydney. The city is also the headquarters of many large companies.
- Sydney is the major port of southeastern Australia.
- Sydney is Australia's largest city.
- The discovery of gold in 1851 increased Sydney's population. The population today is over 4.5 million people.
- Interesting sites in Sydney include the Sydney Opera House, the Sydney Harbour Bridge, and the Australia Square Tower.

Directions: Answer these questions about Sydney.

1. Why is manufacturing a strong industry in Sydney, as well as other major cities?

    Manufacturing is a strong industry in sydney because sydney is the largest city in Australia

2. Gold was discovered in Australia in what year? _Gold was discovered in Australia in 1854._

3. What two states in the United States were overrun by gold diggers at about the same time?

    _____

4. When you think of Australia, what comes to mind? _____

    _____

    _____

    _____

5. Would you like to visit Sydney? Why or why not? _____

    _____

    _____

Making Inferences: Cairo

- Cairo is the capital of Egypt.
- Cairo is the largest city of not only Egypt but also the Middle East.
- The population of Cairo is almost 8 million people.
- Cairo is the cultural center for the Islamic religion.
- Cairo is a major industrial site for Egypt.
- Cairo is a port on the Nile River near the head of the Nile delta.
- Interesting sites include the Egyptian Museum, the Sphinx, the pyramids, and the City of the Dead.

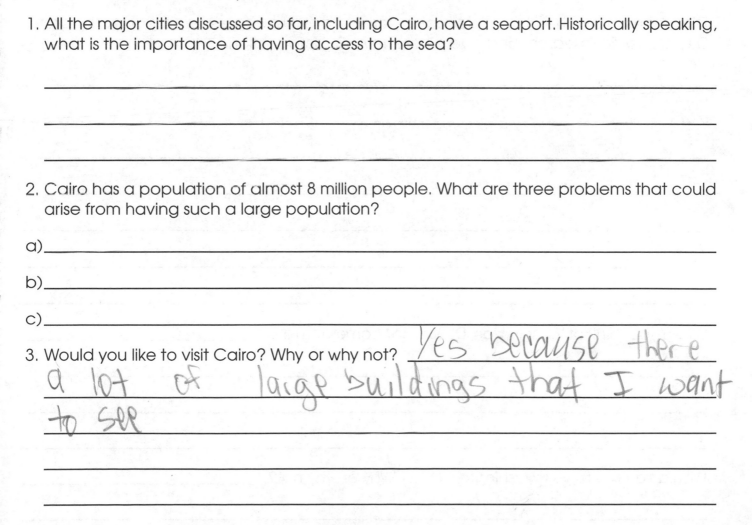

Directions: Answer these questions about Cairo.

1. All the major cities discussed so far, including Cairo, have a seaport. Historically speaking, what is the importance of having access to the sea?

   _____

   _____

   _____

2. Cairo has a population of almost 8 million people. What are three problems that could arise from having such a large population?

   a) _____

   b) _____

   c) _____

3. Would you like to visit Cairo? Why or why not? _Yes because there_
   a lot of large buildings that I want
   to see

   _____

   _____

Creative Writing: Washington, D.C.

- Washington, D.C., is the capital of the United States.
- The population of Washington, D.C., is over 600,000 people in the city itself. Many people who work in Washington, D.C., reside in suburbs of the city in Virginia and Maryland. The population of the Washington, D.C. metropolitan area is 5.4 million.
- It's no surprise that the federal government is one of the largest employers in Washington, D.C.
- The Potomac and Anacostia rivers join in Washington, D.C.
- Interesting sites include the White House, the Vietnam Veterans Memorial, the Lincoln Memorial, the Washington Monument, and the United States Capitol Building.

Directions: Using the above information, create a tourist article describing Washington, D.C. Do some research, and add other interesting information.

_____

_____

_____

_____

_____

_____

When you think of Washington, D.C., what comes to mind?_____

_____

_____

Would you like to visit Washington, D.C.? Why or why not? _____

_____

_____

Making Inferences: Ottawa

- Ottawa is the capital of Canada and is located in Ontario.
- The federal government employs most people in the city. Manufacturing is another large employer.
- The Rideau Canal connects Ottawa to Lake Ontario.
- The population of Ottawa is over 850,000 people.
- Points of interest include the Peace Tower, Parliament Buildings, the Royal Canadian Mint, and the Canadian Museum of Nature.

Directions: Answer these questions about Ottawa.

1. Who employs the most people in Ottawa, Canada? _____

2. What body of water connects Ottawa to Lake Ontario? _____

3. In order from largest to smallest, list the six cities you have read about and their populations.

_____   _____

_____   _____

_____   _____

_____   _____

_____   _____

_____   _____

4. Canada is the United States' neighbor to the north. What problems could arise due to a shared border?

_____

_____

_____

_____

_____

Compare/Contrast: Venn Diagram

A **Venn diagram** is used to chart information that shows similarities and differences between two things. You can use a Venn diagram as an organizational tool before writing a compare/contrast essay.

Directions: Review the completed Venn diagram and the compare/contrast essay below.

Ottawa

Both

Berlin

Population—more than 850,000

City has never been divided

Capital city

Inland ports connecting to larger bodies of water

Manufacturing

Population—3.5 million

City once divided

Compare/Contrast Essay

Ottawa, Canada, and Berlin, Germany, share important characteristics. Ottawa and Berlin are both capital cities in their countries. This means that both cities house the country's federal government. Ottawa has access to Lake Ontario through the Rideau Canal. Inland Harbor in Berlin provides that city's access to the Baltic Sea. Finally, both Ottawa and Berlin are sites for major manufacturing industries that help the economy.

Although Ottawa and Berlin are alike in some ways, in other ways, they are very different. The most obvious difference is in population. Ottawa has fewer than 900,000 people, while over 3.5 million reside in Berlin. Also, Berlin was once divided into East and West sections after World War II, with separate governments and facilities. Ottawa has never been divided.

Review

Directions: Using page 162 as a guide, complete the Venn diagram comparing Washington, D.C., and London, England. Then, write a two-paragraph compare/contrast essay.

Washington, D.C.   **Both**   **London, England**

Compare/Contrast Essay

_____

_____

_____

_____

_____

_____

_____

_____

_____

Review

Directions: Using page 162 as a guide, complete the Venn diagram comparing Sydney, Australia, and Cairo, Egypt. Then, write a two-paragraph compare/contrast essay.

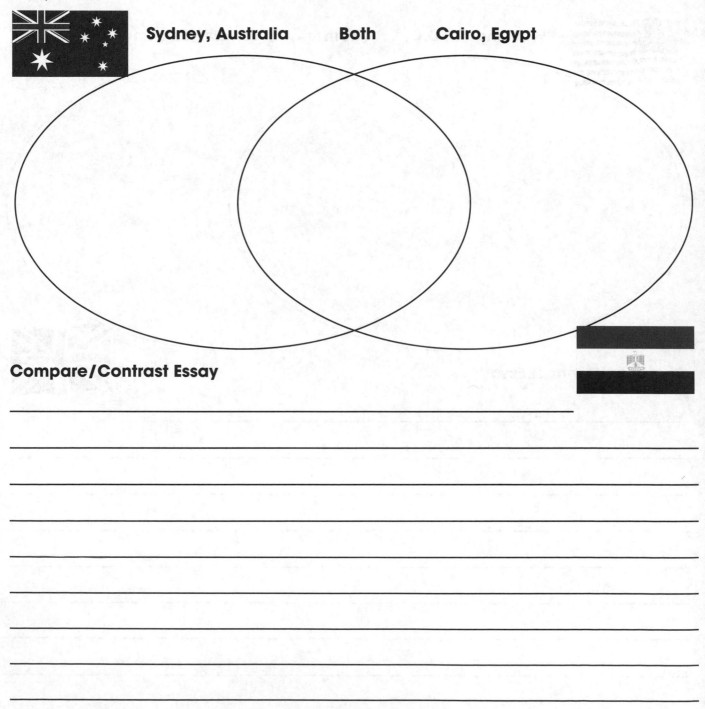

Sydney, Australia   **Both**   **Cairo, Egypt**

Compare/Contrast Essay

_____

_____

_____

_____

_____

_____

_____

_____

_____

Using Prior Knowledge: Dinosaurs

Everyone is intrigued by dinosaurs. Their size, ferocity, and sudden disappearance have fueled scientific investigations for well over a century.

Directions: Before reading about dinosaurs in the following section, answer these questions.

1. Describe what you know about meat-eating dinosaurs. _____

_____

_____

_____

_____

2. Describe what you know about plant-eating dinosaurs. _____

_____

_____

_____

_____

3. Which dinosaur most intrigues you? Why? _____

_____

_____

_____

_____

Main Idea: Small Dinosaurs

When most people think of dinosaurs, they visualize enormous creatures. Actually, there were many species of small dinosaurs—some were only the size of chickens.

Like the larger dinosaurs, the Latin names of the smaller ones usually describe the creature. A small but fast species of dinosaur was *Saltopus*, which means "leaping foot." An adult *Saltopus* weighed only about 2 pounds and grew to be approximately 2 feet long. Fossils of this dinosaur, which lived about 200 million years ago, have been found only in Scotland.

Another small dinosaur with an interesting name was *Compsognathus*, which means "pretty jaw." About the same length as *Saltopus*, *Compsognathus* weighed about three times more. It's unlikely that these two species knew one another, since *Compsognathus* remains have been found only in France and Germany.

A small dinosaur whose remains have been found in southern Africa is *Lesothosaurus*, which means "Lesotho lizard." This lizard-like dinosaur was named only partly for its appearance. The first half of its name is based on the place its remains were found— Lesotho, in southern Africa.

Directions: Answer these questions about small dinosaurs.

1. Circle the main idea:

   People who think dinosaurs were big are completely wrong.

   There are several species of small dinosaurs, some weighing only 2 pounds.

2. How much did *Saltopus* weigh? _____

3. Which dinosaur's name means "pretty jaw"?

Comprehension: Dinosaur History

Dinosaurs are so popular today that it's hard to imagine this not always being the case. The fact is, no one had any idea that dinosaurs ever existed until about 150 years ago.

In 1841, a British scientist named Richard Owen coined the term **Dinosauria** to describe several sets of recently discovered large fossil bones. **Dinosauria** is Latin for "terrible lizards," and even though some dinosaurs were similar to lizards, modern science now also links dinosaurs to birds. Today's birds are thought to be the closest relatives to the dinosaurs.

Like birds, most dinosaurs had fairly long legs that extended straight down from beneath their bodies. Because of their long legs, many dinosaurs were able to move fast. They were also able to balance themselves well. Long-legged dinosaurs, such as *Iguanodon*, needed balance to walk upright.

Iguanodon walked on its long hind legs and used its stubby front legs as arms. On the end of its arms were five hoof-like fingers, one of which functioned as a thumb. Because it had no front teeth for tearing meat, scientists believe *Iguanodon* was a plant eater. Its large, flat back teeth were useful for grinding tender plants before swallowing them.

Directions: Answer these questions about the history of dinosaurs.

1. How were dinosaurs like today's birds? _____

_____

_____

2. This man coined the term **Dinosauria**.

☐ Owen Richards   ☐ Richard Owens   ☐ Richard Owen

3. Which of these did *Iguanodon* not have?

☐ short front legs   ☐ front teeth   ☐ back teeth

4. List other ways you can think of that dinosaurs and birds are alike. _____

_____

_____

_____

Recalling Details: Dinosaur Puzzler

Directions: Use the facts you have learned about dinosaurs to complete the puzzle.

Across:

5. This dinosaur had five hoof-like fingers on its short front legs.

6. Dinosaurs with flat back teeth were ____ eaters.

9. Because of where their legs were positioned, dinosaurs had good ____.

Down:

1. Most dinosaurs had ____ legs.

2. The word **Dinosauria** means "terrible ____."

3. A bone that has been preserved for many years

4. Dinosaurs were not always as ____ as they are now.

7. Iguanodons walked on their ____ legs.

8. Richard ____ coined the term **Dinosauria**.

9. Dinosaurs are closely related to today's ____.

Comprehension: *Tyrannosaurus Rex*

One of the largest meat-eating animal ever to roam Earth was *Tyrannosaurus Rex*. **Rex** is Latin for "king," and because of its size, Tyrannosaurus certainly was at the top of the dinosaur heap. With a length of 46 feet and a weight of 7 tons, there's no doubt this dinosaur commanded respect!

Unlike smaller dinosaurs, *Tyrannosaurus* wasn't tremendously fast on its huge feet. It could stroll along at a walking speed of 2 to 3 miles an hour. Not bad, considering *Tyrannosaurus* was pulling along a body that weighed 14,000 pounds! Like other dinosaurs, *Tyrannosaurus* walked upright, probably balancing its 16-foot-long head by lifting its massive tail.

Compared to the rest of its body, *Tyrannosaurus's* front claws were tiny. Scientists aren't really sure what the claws were for, although it seems likely that they may have been used for holding food. In that case, *Tyrannosaurus* would have had to lower its massive head down to its short claws to take anything in its mouth. Maybe it just used the claws to scratch nearby itches!

Because of their low metabolism, dinosaurs did not require a lot of food for survival. Scientists speculate that *Tyrannosaurus* ate off the same huge piece of meat—usually the carcass of another dinosaur—for several weeks. What do you suppose *Tyrannosaurus* did the rest of the time?

Directions: Answer these questions about *Tyrannosaurus Rex*.

1. Why was this dinosaur called "Rex"? _____

_____

2. For what might *Tyrannosaurus Rex* have used its claws? _____

_____

3. How long was *Tyrannosaurus Rex*? _____

4. *Tyrannosaurus* weighed

☐ 10,000 lbs. ☐ 12,000 lbs. ☐ 14,000 lbs.

5. *Tyrannosaurus* ate

☐ plants. ☐ other dinosaurs. ☐ birds.

Generalization: Dinosaur Characteristics

Directions: Read each passage, and circle the valid generalization.

1. Not surprisingly, Tyrannosaurus had huge teeth in its mammoth head. They were 6 inches long! Because it was a meat eater, Tyrannosaurus's teeth were sharp. They looked like spikes! In comparison, the long-necked, plant-eating Mamenchisaurus had a tiny head and small, flat teeth.

   a. Scientists can't figure out why some dinosaurs had huge teeth.

   b. Tyrannosaurus was probably scarier looking than Mamenchisaurus.

   c. Sharp teeth would have helped Mamenchisaurus chew better.

2. Dinosaurs' names often reflect their size or some other physical trait. For example, Compsognathus means "pretty jaw." Saltopus means "leaping foot." Lesothosaurus means "lizard from Lesotho."

   a. Of the three species, Lesothosaurus was probably the fastest.

   b. Of the three species, Compsognathus was probably the fastest.

   c. Of the three species, Saltopus was probably the fastest.

3. Edmontosaurus, a huge 3-ton dinosaur, had 1,000 teeth! The teeth were cemented into chewing pads in the back of Edmontosaurus's mouth. Unlike the sharp teeth of the meat-eating Tyrannosaurus, this dinosaur's teeth were flat.

   a. Edmontosaurus did not eat meat.

   b. Edmontosaurus did not eat plants.

   c. Edmontosaurus moved very fast.

Comprehension: Dinosaur Fossils

Imagine putting together the world's largest jigsaw puzzle. That is what scientists who reassemble the fossil bones of dinosaurs must do to find out what the creatures looked like. Fossilized bones are imbedded, or stuck, in solid rock, so scientists must first get the bones out of the rocks without breaking or otherwise damaging them. This task requires enormous patience.

In addition to hammers, drills, and chisels, sound waves are used to break up the rock. The drills, which are similar to high-speed dental drills, cut through the rock very quickly. As the bones are removed, scientists begin trying to figure out how they attach to one another. Sometimes the dinosaur's skeleton was preserved just as it was when it died. This, of course, shows scientists exactly how to reassemble it. Other times, parts of bone are missing. It then becomes a guessing game to decide what goes where.

When scientists discover dinosaur fossils, it is called a "find." A particularly exciting find in 1978 occurred in Montana when, for the first time, fossilized dinosaur eggs, babies, and several nests were found. The species of dinosaur in this exciting find was Maiasaura, which means "good mother lizard." From the size of the nest, which was 23 feet, scientists speculated that the adult female Maiasaura was about the same size.

Unlike birds' nests, dinosaur nests were not made of sticks and straw. Instead, since they were land animals, nests were made of dirt hollowed out into a bowl shape. The Maiasaura's nest was 3 feet deep and held about 20 eggs.

Directions: Answer these questions about dinosaur fossils.

1. Name four tools used to remove dinosaur bones from rock. _____

_____

_____

2. What do scientists do with the bones they remove? _____

_____

3. The type of dinosaur fossils found in Montana in 1978 were

☐ Mayiasaura.　　☐ Masaura.　　☐ Maiasaura.

4. When scientists discover dinosaur fossils, it is called a

☐ found.　　☐ find.　　☐ nest.

Generalization: Plant-Eating Dinosaurs

Directions: Read each passage, and circle the valid generalization.

1. Many of the plant-eating dinosaurs belonged to a common species called Sauropods. Most Sauropods were very large. They had peg-shaped teeth, and they formed herds to search for food. They used their long necks to reach the top branches of trees, where the most tender leaves grew.

   a. Their size, teeth, and long necks made Sauropods perfectly suited to their environment.

   b. The Sauropods' peg-like teeth were not well suited to eating meat.

   c. Vegetarian dinosaurs needed short necks and sharp teeth to survive.

2. Sauropods were not the only dinosaurs that traveled in herds. Sets of different-sized fossilized dinosaur footprints discovered in Texas show that other types of dinosaurs also traveled together. The footprints—23 sets of them—were of another plant-eating dinosaur, the *Apatosaurus*.

   a. All dinosaurs traveled in herds because they needed companionship.

   b. It appears that some plant-eating dinosaurs traveled in herds.

   c. Traveling in herds offered dinosaurs protection and friendship.

3. Not all plant-eating dinosaurs were huge. The *Hypsilophodon* was only about $6\frac{1}{2}$ feet tall. It stood on its two back legs and, because of its smaller size, probably ran away from danger.

   a. The *Hypsilophodon* didn't stand a chance against bigger dinosaurs.

   b. The *Hypsilophodon* could not eat from the tops of tall trees.

   c. The *Hypsilophodon* was cowardly and always ran from danger.

Comprehension: Dinosaur Tracks

Some scientists refer to dinosaurs' fossilized tracks as "footprints in time." The tracks that survived in Texas for 120 million years had been made in sand or mud. These large footprints were of the *Apatosaurus*. The footprints were more than 3 feet across!

Although *Apatosaurus* had a long, heavy tail, there is no sign that the tail hit the ground along with the feet. Scientists speculate that the place where the tracks were found was once a riverbed, and that *Apatosaurus's* tail floated in the water and thus left no tracks. Another theory is that the dinosaur always carried its tail out behind it. This second theory is not as popular, because scientists say it's unlikely the dinosaur would consistently carry its long, heavy tail off the ground. When *Apatosaurus* rested, for example, the tail would have left its mark.

Besides Texas, fossilized tracks have been found in England, Canada, Australia, and Brazil. Some tracks have also been found in New England. The tracks discovered in Canada were quite a find! They showed a pattern made by 10 species of dinosaurs. In all, about 1,700 fossilized footprints were discovered. Maybe the scientists uncovered what millions of years ago was a dinosaur playground!

Directions: Answer these questions about dinosaur tracks.

1. Circle the main idea:

   Fossilized dinosaur tracks provide scientists with information from which to draw conclusions about dinosaur size and behavior.

   Fossilized dinosaur tracks are not very useful because so few have been found in the United States.

2. Explain how a dinosaur might have crossed a river without its tail leaving a track.

   _____

3. Name five countries where dinosaur tracks have been found. _____

   _____

4. Circle the valid generalization about dinosaur tracks.

   a. The fact that 10 species of tracks were found together proves dinosaurs were friends with others outside their groups.

   b. The fact that 10 species of tracks were found together means the dinosaurs probably gathered in that spot for water or food.

Review

Directions: Reread the following selections. Then. write the main idea of each.

Small Dinosaurs _____

_____

_____

Dinosaur History _____

_____

_____

Tyrannosaurus Rex _____

_____

_____

Dinosaur Fossils _____

_____

_____

Dinosaur Tracks _____

_____

_____

The Solar System

This section is about our solar system. It includes the sun, comparisons among the planets, each planet's physical characteristics, and each planet's moons. Before beginning this section, try to answer the following questions.

1. Name the eight planets of the solar system in order beginning with the planet closest to the sun.

   a. _____ b. _____ c. _____

   d. _____ e. _____ f. _____

   g. _____ h. _____

2. Write a distinguishing characteristic for each planet listed below.

   Earth _____

   Jupiter _____

   Saturn _____

   Mars _____

3. The study of the solar system, stars, and outer space is called

   _____ .

4. The _____ is the center of the solar system and is a star.

5. Which planet is similar in size to Earth? _____

6. Humans have landed on which outer space object? _____

7. Have humans landed on any planets? Why or why not? _____

   _____

   _____

The Sun

Directions: Read the selection. Then, answer the questions.

The Sun is the center of our solar system. It is a star that seems massive to those on Earth but is dwarfed in comparison to other giant stars farther out in the universe. It rotates on its axis just like Earth. The Sun is made up of heated gases, and it releases heat and light energy. The part of the Sun we see is called the photosphere. The chromosphere is the colored ring of gases surrounding the Sun. Solar flares often shoot out from the Sun's surface for thousands of miles. Without the Sun's warmth, life on Earth would cease to exist.

1. Define the following words.

   axis: _____

   _____

   universe: _____

   dwarfed: _____

   cease: _____

2. What effect could a solar flare have on Earth?

   _____

   _____

3. Does the Sun revolve or rotate?_____

4. Why isn't the Sun visible at night? _____

5. Why is it important never to look directly at the Sun?

   _____

   _____

Mercury

Directions: Read the selection. Then, answer the questions.

The planet Mercury is named for the Roman god Mercury who was the messenger of the gods. Ancient Greek astronomers named the heavenly bodies "planets," which means "wanderers." Mercury is the planet closest to the Sun and also the smallest of the inner planets. Because of its proximity to the Sun (nearly 36 million miles), its surface is extraordinarily hot. Mercury's solid surface is covered with craters. It rotates on its axis once every 59 days. One year on Mercury lasts 88 Earth days. Mercury has no moons or rings and has virtually no atmosphere.

1. Define the following words:

   astronomer: _____

   _____

   proximity: _____

   atmosphere: _____

   crater: _____

2. Could life survive on Mercury? Why or why not?

   _____

   _____

3. Write a three-sentence summary of the selection above.

   _____

   _____

4. Mercury's period of revolution is 88 days. How many months would that be?

   _____

Venus

Directions: Read the selection. Then, answer the questions.

Located over 67 million miles from the Sun, Venus is an incredibly hot planet. Venus is named for the Roman goddess of love and beauty. Temperatures can reach 470 degrees Celsius. Venus is close in size to Earth and is often referred to as Earth's twin. Space probes and unmanned crafts have landed on Venus and found Venus to be dust-covered and very windy. Because Venus is very bright, it is often thought of as a star. Venus has no moons or rings. Its period of rotation is 243 days, and it revolves once around the Sun in 225 days.

1. Create a Venn diagram comparing Mercury and Venus.

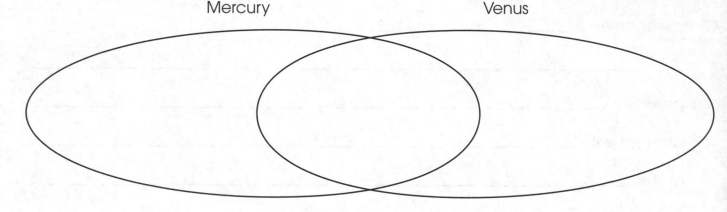

Mercury   Venus

2. Write a three-sentence summary about Venus.

_____

_____

_____

3. Approximately how far is Venus from Mercury? _____

4. If you were to design a spacecraft capable of landing on Venus, what might it require?

_____

_____

_____

Earth

Directions: Read the selection. Then, answer the questions.

Earth is the only planet with known life forms. It revolves around the Sun every $365\frac{1}{4}$ days. One rotation takes 24 hours to complete. Earth has seasons due to the tilt of its axis and its revolution. Rotation causes night and day. Earth is almost 93 million miles away from the Sun. Its surface is three-fourths water and one-fourth land mass. Earth is surrounded by gases called the atmosphere, which allows life to survive. Earth has one moon that has been explored many times.

1. Define the following word.

   mass: _____

   _____

2. Approximately how far is Earth from Venus?

   _____

3. Approximately how far Is Earth from Mercury?

   _____

4. What factors allow life to exist on Earth?

   _____

   _____

5. What causes the seasons?

   _____

6. What differences are there between Earth and the planets Mercury and Venus?

   _____

   _____

   _____

Mars

Directions: Read the selection. Then, answer the questions.

Mars is named for the god of war. It is the fourth of the inner planets. Mars is called the Red Planet and has polar caps, craters, and evidence of ancient volcanoes. Recently, space probes have landed there and given scientists information about its surface. The red color is produced by the reaction of iron-rich minerals to soil and water, which scientists believe happened long ago. Mars rotates on its axis every 24 hours, 37 minutes and is 142 million miles from the Sun. Its period of revolution is 687 days. Mars has two moons, Phobos and Deimos. Mars's identifying feature is the volcano Olympus Mons. Its temperature varies, but averages –50 degrees Celsius.

1. Define the following words.

   polar: _____

   mineral: _____

2. Name two distinguishing characteristics of Mars.

   _____

   _____

3. Could life survive on Mars? Why or why not?

   _____

   _____

   _____

4. For years, people have been interested in the possibility of Martian life. What special characteristics would life on Mars have?

   _____

   _____

   _____

   _____

Review

Directions: Follow the instructions for each question.

1. List the four inner planets.

   _____ _____ _____ _____

2. List the four outer planets.

   _____ _____ _____ _____

3. What separates the inner and outer planets?

   _____

4. Name a distinguishing feature of each planet.

   Mercury: _____

   Venus: _____

   Earth: _____

   Mars: _____

   Jupiter: _____

   Saturn: _____

   Uranus: _____

   Neptune: _____

5. List the planets in order from most moons to least.

   a) _____   e) _____

   b) _____   f) _____

   c) _____   g) _____

   d) _____   h) _____

Review

6. Which planets have rings?

_____

7. If you were in charge of the space program, what would your priorities be? Why?

_____

_____

_____

_____

8. Draw a diagram of the planets and the Sun. Be sure to depict color and the following diameter sizes.

Mercury — 3,031 mi.   Venus — 7,521 mi.   Earth — 7,926 mi.

Mars — 4,217 mi.   Jupiter — 88,730 mi.   Saturn — 74,900 mi.

Uranus — 31,763 mi.   Neptune — 30,775 mi.

Recalling Details: Earth's Atmosphere

The most important reason that life can exist on Earth is its atmosphere—the air around us. Without it, plant and animal life could not have developed. There would be no clouds, weather, or even sounds, only a deathlike stillness and an endlessly black sky. Without the protection of the atmosphere, the Sun's rays would roast Earth by day. At night, with no blanketing atmosphere, the stored heat would escape into space, dropping the temperature of the planet hundreds of degrees.

Held captive by Earth's gravity, the atmosphere surrounds the planet to a depth of hundreds of miles. However, all but 1 percent of the atmosphere is in a layer about 20 miles deep just above the surface of Earth. It is made up of a mixture of gases and dusts. About 78 percent of it is a gas called nitrogen, which is very important as food for plants. Most of the remaining gas, 21 percent, is oxygen, which all people and animals depend on for life. The remaining 1 percent is made up of a blend of other gases— including carbon dioxide, argon, ozone, and helium—and tiny dust particles. These particles come from ocean salt crystals, bits of rocks and sand, plant pollen, volcanic ash, and even meteor dust.

You may not think of air as matter, as something that can be weighed. In fact, Earth's air weighs billions and billions of tons. Near the surface of the planet, this "air pressure" is greatest. Right now, about 10 tons of air is pressing in on you. Yet, like the fish living near the floor of the ocean, you don't notice this tremendous weight because your body is built to withstand it.

Directions: Answer these questions about Earth's atmosphere.

1. What is the atmosphere? _____

2. Of what is the atmosphere made? _____

3. What is the most abundant gas in the atmosphere? _____

4. Which of the atmosphere's gases is most important to humans and animals?

   _____

5. What is air pressure? _____

Comprehension: Causes/Effects of Weather

The behavior of the atmosphere, which we experience as weather and climate, affects our lives in many important ways. It is the reason no one lives on the South Pole. It controls when a farmer plants the food we will eat, which crops will be planted, and also whether those crops will grow. The weather tells you what clothes to wear and how you will play after school. Weather is the sum of all the conditions of the air that may affect Earth's surface and its living things. These conditions include the temperature, air pressure, wind, and moisture. **Climate** refers to these conditions but generally applies to larger areas and longer periods of time, such as the annual climate of South America rather than today's weather in Oklahoma City.

Climate is influenced by many factors. It depends first and foremost on latitude. Areas nearest the equator are warm and wet, while the poles are cold and relatively dry. The poles also have extreme seasonal changes, while the areas at the middle latitudes have more moderate climates, neither as cold as the poles nor as hot as the equator. Other circumstances may alter this pattern, however. Land near the oceans, for instance, is generally warmer than inland areas.

Elevation also plays a role in climate. For example, despite the fact that Africa's highest mountain, Kilimanjaro, is just south of the equator, its summit is perpetually covered by snow. In general, high land is cooler and wetter than nearby low land.

Directions: Check the answers to these questions about the causes and effects of weather.

1. What is the correct definition for **atmosphere**?

   ☐ the clouds   ☐ the sky   ☐ where weather occurs

2. What is the correct definition for **foremost**?

   ☐ most important   ☐ highest number   ☐ in the front

3. What is the correct definition for **circumstances**?

   ☐ temperatures   ☐ seasons   ☐ conditions

4. What is the correct definition for **elevation**?

   ☐ height above Earth   ☐ nearness to equator   ☐ snow covering

5. What is the correct definition for **perpetually**?

   ☐ occasionally   ☐ rarely   ☐ always

Main Idea/Recalling Details: Weather

People have always searched the sky for clues about upcoming weather. Throughout the ages, farmers and sailors have looked to the winds and clouds for signs of approaching storms. But no real understanding of the weather could be achieved without a scientific study of the atmosphere. Such a study depends on being able to measure certain conditions, including pressure, temperature, and moisture levels.

A true scientific examination of weather, therefore, was not possible until the development of accurate measuring instruments, beginning in the 17th century. Meteorology—the science of studying the atmosphere—was born in 1643 with the invention of the barometer, which measures atmospheric pressure. The liquid-in-glass thermometer, the hygrometer to measure humidity (the amount of moisture in the air), and the weather map also were invented during the 1600s.

With the measurement of these basic elements, scientists began to work out the relationships between these and other atmospheric conditions, such as wind, clouds, and rainfall. Still, their observations failed to show an overall picture of the weather. Such complete weather reporting had to wait two centuries for the rapid transfer of information made possible by the invention of the telegraph during the 1840s.

Today, the forecasts of meteorologists are an international effort. There are thousands of weather stations around the world, both at land and at sea. Upper-level observations are also made by weather balloons and satellites, which continuously send photographs back to Earth. All of this information is relayed to national weather bureaus, where meteorologists plot it on graphs and analyze it. The information is then given to the public through the Internet, newspapers, television, and radio stations.

Directions: Answer these questions about studying the weather.

1. The main idea is:

☐ People have always searched the sky for clues about upcoming weather.
☐ A real understanding of weather depends on measuring conditions such as pressure, temperature, and moisture levels.

2. List three kinds of instruments used to measure atmospheric conditions, and tell what conditions they measure.

   a) _____   _____

   b) _____   _____

   c) _____   _____

3. During what century were many of these measuring instruments invented? _____
4. Name two things used for upper-level observations.

   a) _____   b) _____

Comprehension: Hurricanes

The characteristics of a hurricane are powerful winds, driving rain, and raging seas. Although a storm must have winds blowing at least 74 miles an hour to be classified as a hurricane, it is not unusual to have winds above 150 miles per hour. The entire storm system can be 500 miles in diameter, with lines of clouds that spiral toward a center called the "eye." Within the eye itself, which is about 15 miles across, the air is actually calm and cloudless. But this eye is enclosed by a towering wall of thick clouds where the storm's heaviest rains and highest winds are found.

All hurricanes begin in the warm seas and moist winds of the tropics. They form in either of two narrow bands to the north and south of the equator. For weeks, the blistering sun beats down on the ocean water. Slowly, the air above the sea becomes heated and begins to swirl. More hot, moist air is pulled skyward. Gradually, this circle grows larger and spins faster. As the hot, moist air at the top is cooled, great rain clouds are formed. The storm's fury builds until it moves over land or a cold area of the ocean where its supply of heat and moisture is finally cut off.

Hurricanes that strike North America usually form over the Atlantic Ocean. West coast storms are less dangerous because they tend to head out over the Pacific Ocean rather than toward land. The greatest damage usually comes from the hurricanes that begin in the western Pacific, because they often batter heavily populated regions.

Directions: Answer these questions about hurricanes.

1. What is necessary for a storm to be classified as a hurricane? _____
    _____

2. What is the eye of the hurricane? _____

3. Where do hurricanes come from? _____

4. How does a hurricane finally die down? _____
    _____

5. Why do hurricanes formed in the western Pacific cause the most damage?
    _____

Comprehension: Tornadoes

Tornadoes, which are also called twisters, occur more frequently than hurricanes, but they are smaller storms. The zigzag path of a tornado averages about 16 miles in length and only about a quarter of a mile in width. But the tornado is, pound for pound, the more severe storm. When one touches the ground, it leaves a trail of total destruction.

The winds in a tornado average about 200 miles per hour. At the center of the funnel-shaped cloud of a tornado is a partial vacuum. In combination with the high winds, this is what makes the storm so destructive. Its force is so great that a tornado can drive a piece of straw into a tree. The extremely low atmospheric pressure that accompanies the storm can cause a building to actually explode.

Unlike hurricanes, tornadoes are formed over land. They are most likely to occur over the central plains of the United States, especially in the spring and early summer months. Conditions for a tornado arise when warm, moist air from the south becomes trapped under colder, heavier air from the north. When the surfaces of the two air masses touch, rain clouds form and a thunderstorm begins. At first, only a rounded bulge hangs from the bottom of the cloud. It gradually gets longer until it forms a column reaching toward the ground. The tornado is white from the moisture when it first forms, but it turns black as it sucks up dirt and trash.

Directions: Circle **True** or **False** for these statements about tornadoes.

1. The tornado is a stronger storm than the hurricane.   True   False

2. The path of a tornado usually covers hundreds of miles.   True   False

3. Like the eye of a hurricane, the center of a tornado is calm.   True   False

4. Tornadoes are most likely to occur in the central plains of the
   United States during the spring and early summer months.   True   False

5. High atmospheric pressure usually accompanies a tornado.   True   False

Comprehension: Thunderstorms

With warm weather comes the threat of thunderstorms. The rapid growth of the majestic thunderhead cloud and the damp, cool winds that warn of an approaching storm are familiar in most regions of the world. In fact, it has been estimated that at any given time, 1,800 such storms are in progress around the globe.

As with hurricanes and tornadoes, thunderstorms are formed when a warm, moist air mass meets with a cold air mass. Before long, bolts of lightning streak across the sky, and thunder booms. It is not entirely understood how lightning is formed. It is known that a positive electrical charge builds near the top of the cloud, and a negative charge forms at the bottom. When enough force builds up, a powerful current of electricity zigzags down an electrically charged pathway between the two, causing the flash of lightning.

The clap of thunder you hear after a lightning flash is created by rapidly heated air that expands as the lightning passes through it. The distant rumbling is caused by the thunder's sound waves bouncing back and forth within clouds or between mountains. When thunderstorms rumble through an area, many people begin to worry about tornadoes. But they need to be just as fearful of thunderstorms. In fact, lightning kills more people than any other severe weather condition.

Directions: Answer these questions about thunderstorms.

1. How many thunderstorms are estimated to be occurring at any given time around the world?

    _____

2. When are thunderstorms formed?

    _____

3. What causes thunder?

    _____

4. On average, which causes more deaths, lightning or tornadoes?

    _____

Venn Diagram: Storms

Directions: Complete the Venn diagram below. Think of at least three things to write in the outer parts of each circle and at least three things to write in the intersecting parts.

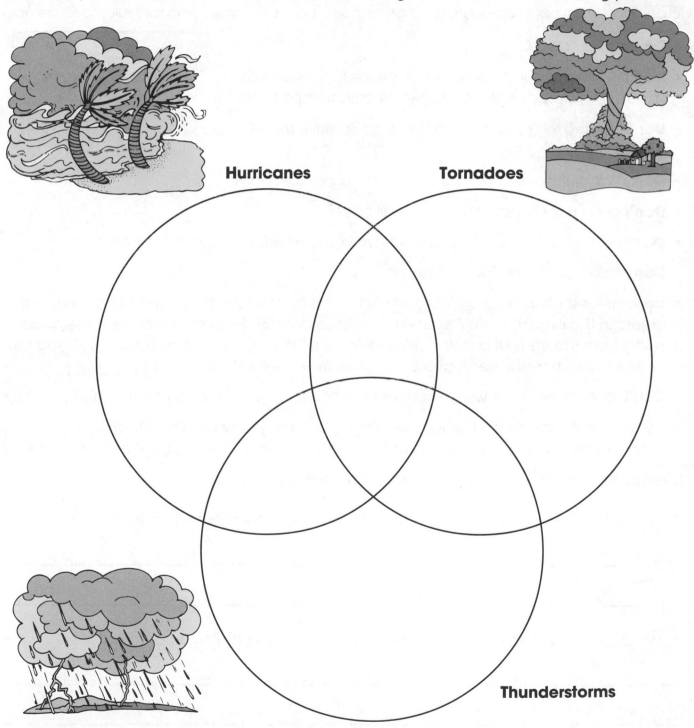

Hurricanes

Tornadoes

Thunderstorms

Recalling Details: Lightning Safety Rules

Lightning causes more fire damage to forests and property than anything else. More importantly, it kills more people than any other weather event. It is important to know what to do—and what not to do—during a thunderstorm. Here are some important rules to remember:

- **Don't** go outdoors.

- **Don't** go near open doors or windows, fireplaces, radiators, stoves, metal pipes, sinks, or plug-in electrical appliances.

- **Don't** use the telephone, as lightning could strike the wires outside. (Cell phones are safe to use.)

- **Don't** handle metal objects, such as fishing poles or golf clubs.

- **Don't** go into the water or ride in small boats.

- **Do** stay in an automobile if you are traveling. Cars offer excellent protection.

- **Don't** take laundry off the clothesline.

- **Do** look for shelter if you are outdoors. If there is no shelter, stay away from the highest object in the area. If there are only a few trees nearby, it is best to crouch in the open, away from the trees at a distance greater than the height of the nearest tree. If you are in an area with many trees, avoid the tallest tree. Look for shorter ones.

- **Don't** take shelter near wire fences or clotheslines, exposed sheds, or on a hilltop.

- If your hair stands on end or your skin tingles, lightning may be about to strike you. Immediately crouch down, put your feet together, and place your hands over your ears.

Directions: Answer these questions about lightning safety rules.

1. Name two things you should avoid if you are looking for shelter outside.

   a)_____

   b)_____

2. What should you do if, during a thunderstorm, your hair stands up or your skin tingles?

   _____

   _____

Main Idea/Comprehension: Rainbows

Although there are some violent, frightening aspects of the weather, there is, considerable beauty, too. The rainbow is one simple, lovely example of nature's atmospheric mysteries.

You usually can see a rainbow when the sun comes out after a rain shower or in the fine spray of a waterfall or fountain. Although sunlight appears to be white, it is actually made up of a mixture of colors—all the colors in the rainbow. We see a rainbow because thousands of tiny raindrops act as mirrors and prisms on the sunlight. Prisms are objects that bend light, splitting it into bands of color.

The bands of color form a perfect semicircle. From the top edge to the bottom, the colors are always in the same order—red, orange, yellow, green, blue, indigo, and violet. The brightness and width of each band may vary from one minute to the next. You also may notice that the sky framed by the rainbow is lighter than the sky above. This is because the light that forms the blue and violet bands is more bent and spread out than the light that forms the top red band.

You will always see morning rainbows in the west, with the sun behind you. Afternoon rainbows, likewise, are always in the east. To see a rainbow, the sun can be no higher than 42 degrees—nearly halfway up the sky. Sometimes, if the sunlight is strong and the water droplets are very small, you can see a double rainbow. This happens because the light is reflected twice in the water droplets. The color bands are fainter and in reverse order in the second band.

Directions: Answer these questions about rainbows.

1. Check the statement that is the main idea.

   ☐   Although there are violent, frightening aspects of weather, there is considerable beauty, too.

   ☐   The rainbow is one simple, lovely example of nature's atmospheric mysteries.

2. What is the correct definition for **semicircle**?

   ☐ colored circle   ☐ diameter of a circle   ☐ half circle

3. What is a prism? _____

4. In which direction would you look to see an afternoon rainbow? _____

Comprehension: Cause and Effect

Directions: Complete the chart by listing the cause and effect of each weather phenomenon.

	Cause	Effect
Thunderstorms		
Hurricanes		
Tornadoes		
Rainbows		
Precipitation		
Drought		

Review

Directions: If necessary, review the section on weather to find the answers to the following questions.

1. Describe Earth's atmosphere. _____

_____

2. The science of studying weather is called _____ .

3. Why is it important for weather forecasting to be an international effort?

_____

_____

_____

4. Define **weather**. _____

_____

5. Name three factors that influence climate.

_____   _____   _____

6. Describe the following weather phenomena.

a. hurricane _____

_____

b. tornado _____

_____

c. thunderstorm _____

_____

Using Prior Knowledge: Sports

Directions: Before reading about sports in the following section, write one or two sentences telling what you know about each sport below.

Wrestling _____

_____

Bowling _____

_____

Volleyball _____

_____

Tennis _____

_____

_____

Boxing _____

_____

Football _____

_____

Softball _____

_____

Field Hockey _____

_____

Comprehension: Wrestling Around the World

In many countries, wrestling is an honored sport. In Iceland, wrestling is called **glima**; in Switzerland, it is called **schweitzer schwingen**; and in Ireland, it is called **cumberland**. In Japan, a form of wrestling called **sumo** began in 23 B.C.

Sumo wrestling is still popular in Japan today. Wrestlers wear the traditional sumo costume of a loincloth—a piece of cloth draped across the hips and bottom—and nothing else. Sumo wrestlers are big men—their average weight is about 300 pounds. Wrestlers compete in small rings with sand floors. The object of the match is to push the opponent out of the ring.

Even in the wrestling ring, however, the Japanese are astonishingly polite. If one wrestler begins to push the other out of the ring, the other may shout, "Matta!" **Matta** is Japanese for "not yet." At this point, the action stops and the wrestlers step out of the ring to take a break. Some wrestling matches in Japan must take a long, long time to complete!

Directions: Answer these questions about wrestling around the world.

1. What is wrestling called in Switzerland? _____

2. In what country is wrestling called **cumberland**?_____

3. What is wrestling called in Iceland? _____

4. In what country is wrestling called **sumo**?_____

5. How much does an average sumo wrestler weigh? _____

6. What does **matta** mean in Japanese?_____

7. What happens if a wrestler shouts, "Matta"? _____

_____

_____

8. In what year did sumo wrestling begin? _____

Comprehension: Tennis, Anyone?

Historians say a form of tennis was played outdoors in England in the 16th century. In France, the game had a much, much earlier start. "Court tennis"—named such because royal courts of kings played it—was played indoors about 1000 A.D. Six hundred years later, indoor tennis was still in full swing. Records show there were 2,500 indoor courts in France at that time.

French tennis players and spectators took the game seriously. In 1780, the surgeon general of the French army recommended the game as one good for the lungs and throat. Why? Because of all the loud screaming and shouting that accompanied French games!

The word **tennis** comes from the French term **tenir**, which means "take heed" or "watch out." That's what the French yelled out centuries ago when they used huge racquets to whack balls over a sagging net. Later, when the game was adopted in England, **tenir** became **tennis**.

Tennis is said to have come to America by way of the island of Bermuda. A young American girl, Mary Outerbridge, played the game when visiting Bermuda in 1873. She brought tennis racquets, balls, and a net home to New York with her. The strange equipment puzzled customs officials (government employees who check travelers' bags to make sure they are not smuggling drugs or other substances). They reluctantly permitted Miss Outerbridge to bring the weird game to America, where it has flourished ever since!

Directions: Answer these questions about tennis.

1. In what year were there 2,500 indoor tennis courts in France? _____

2. In 1780, who recommended tennis as good for the lungs and throat?

_____

3. What does the French word **tenir** mean? _____

_____

4. In what state was tennis first played in America? _____

5. The person who brought tennis to America was

　☐ Marlene Outbridge.　☐ Mary Outbridge.　☐ Mary Outerbridge.

Comprehension: Boxing History

The first known boxers were the ancient Greeks, who "toughened up" young men by making them box with bare fists. Later, a length of leather was wrapped around their hands and forearms to protect them. Although the sport was brutal, in ancient Greece, boxers who killed their opponents received a stiff punishment.

During the Middle Ages—from 500 to 1500 A.D.—boxing fell out of favor. It became popular in England about 100 years later, when the new middle class had the time and money for sports. Boxers would travel to matches held at inns and bars, and their loyal fans would follow. No gloves were used in the early 1600s In England. Instead, like the ancient Greeks, boxers used bare fists and—something new—wrestling holds. Carrier pigeons with messages tied to their bodies were trained to take news of the fights back to the boxers' hometowns.

Because so many people were badly hurt or killed, padded boxing gloves began to be used in the United States around 1880. Boxing became fashionable—and safer. Harvard University offered boxing as an intramural sport in the 1880s. U.S. President Theodore Roosevelt's love of the sport helped to further popularize it. It's said that Roosevelt boxed regularly with a former heavyweight champion named Mike Donovan.

During World War I, boxing was part of the required training for army recruits. The Golden Gloves championship matches for boys, which began in the 1930s, also helped spread the sport's popularity.

Directions: Answer these questions about boxing history.

1. What people were known as the first boxers? _____

2. During what period did boxing fall out of favor? _____

3. What university offered boxing as a sport in the 1880s? _____

4. Which U.S. president enjoyed boxing? _____

5. In England in the 1600s, news about boxing was sent via

☐ telegrams.   ☐ carrier pigeons.   ☐ messengers.

6. The Golden Gloves championships were first offered

☐ in the 1930s.   ☐ during World War I.   ☐ during World War II.

Comprehension: Sports Summaries

Directions: Write a short paragraph summarizing each selection below.

Wrestling Around the World _____

_____

_____

_____

_____

Tennis, Anyone? _____

_____

_____

_____

_____

Boxing History _____

_____

_____

_____

_____

Of the sports listed above, which is your favorite? Why? _____

_____

_____

_____

_____

_____

Main Idea: Bowling Is a Ball

Like tennis and boxing, bowling is also a very old sport. It began in Germany about nine centuries ago. Bowling was first played outdoors with wooden pins and a bowling ball made from a rounded rock.

The first players were church members who bowled with Catholic bishops and priests. Those who bowled a good game were said to be blessed. Those who bowled poorly were believed to be sinners who should improve themselves to improve their games! The name of the game in 11th-century Germany was **Kegelspiel**.

By the late 19th century, bowling was the most popular sport in Germany. A common expression for a person who had died was that he was "bowled out."

The game was introduced to America by way of Holland, where the Dutch had learned bowling from the Germans. Some Dutch citizens brought the game to Manhattan Island in 1623. The first bowling alley—outdoors, of course—opened in New York City more than 100 years later in 1732. Today, bowling is one of the most popular American sports. People who have never put on boxing gloves or raised a tennis racquet have, at one time or another, lifted and rolled a bowling ball.

Directions: Answer these questions about bowling.

1. Circle the main idea:

   Bowling is a very old and popular sport.

   Bad bowlers are sinners who should clean up their acts.

2. Who brought bowling to the United States? _____

3. What was bowling called in Germany? _____

4. What were the first bowling balls made from? _____

5. The first American bowling alley opened in 1732 in what city? _____

6. In 19th-century Germany, what was the meaning of the expression "bowled out"?

   _____

Comprehension: Facts About Football

Like tennis courts, football fields are usually laid out in a north–south fashion so the sun doesn't shine directly into one team's eyes. The field is 120 yards long and $53\frac{1}{3}$ yards wide, with a goalpost at each end that is at least 20 feet high.

Regulation-size footballs are 11 inches long and must weigh at least 14 ounces. The object of the game is for one team of 11 to score more points than the opposing team. There are four ways to score points in football.

A touchdown, worth six points, is scored by carrying the ball across the opponent's goal line or by completing a forward pass in the opponent's end zone. When a team makes a touchdown, it gets the chance to make one or two extra points via a play executed from the 2- or 3-yard line. A field goal, worth three points, is made by kicking the ball from the field over the crossbar of the opponent's goal. A way to earn two points is through a play called a safety.

Football games are 60 minutes long and are divided into four quarters of 15 minutes each. Because of all the commercials and instant replays, televised games seem much longer. For college games, the halftime shows also take a lot of time.

Traditionally, college football games are played on Saturday afternoons, and high school games are played on Friday nights. Professional games are played on Sundays, as well as a few nights throughout the week.

Directions: Answer these questions about football.

1. How long is a regulation football? _____

2. How long is a football field? _____

3. How many players are on a football team? _____

4. A field goal is worth

   ☐ one point.   ☐ two points.   ☐ three points.

5. A touchdown is worth

   ☐ two points.   ☐ three points.   ☐ six points.

6. Football games are _____ minutes long

   with four _____ -minute quarters.

Giving Directions: A Perfect Softball Pitch

A good softball pitcher makes the skill look effortless and graceful. In fact, there are very specific things a softball pitcher must do before, during, and after he or she throws the ball.

Before throwing, the pitcher must have both feet firmly on the ground and be in contact with the pitcher's plate for at least one second. At the beginning of the pitch, the ball must be held in both hands in front of the body. It must be held this way for no longer than 20 seconds. While making the pitch, the pitcher must keep one foot on the ground. Until the ball leaves his or her hands, the pitcher cannot take more than one step toward the batter.

A correct softball pitch looks remarkably like the pitch used to throw horseshoes. As with horseshoes, there is a graceful follow-through with the hand and arm once the ball leaves the pitcher's hand.

There are several types of softball pitches. They include the drop, the slow ball, and the out-curve. The drop is the fastest pitch. The pitcher's hand is behind the ball in this pitch. For the slow ball, the pitcher grips the ball between his or her thumb and little finger. He or she puts the knuckles of the three middle fingers against the ball. When the out-curve ball is thrown, the pitcher thrusts the thumb back and rotates all of his or her fingers out.

Directions: Follow these instructions about softball.

1. Give directions on what to do before pitching a softball. _____

_____

_____

_____

_____

_____

2. Give directions on how to throw a slow ball. _____

_____

_____

3. Give directions on how to throw an out-curve ball. _____

_____

Comprehensive Curriculum - **Grade 6**

Comprehension: Volleyball

Volleyball began in Italy during the Middle Ages and was introduced to Germany in 1893. Germans called the sport **faustball**. Two years later, an American physical education teacher named William Morgan made some changes in **faustball** and brought the new game to Americans as **mintonette**.

In **faustball**, the ball was permitted to bounce twice before being hit back over the net. In **mintonette**, as in modern volleyball, no bounces were allowed. Shortly after Morgan introduced the sport, the director of a YMCA convinced him to change the name to something easier to pronounce. To "volley" a ball means to keep it in the air, and that's what volleyball players try to do.

A volleyball court is 60 feet long by 30 feet wide. It's divided in half by an 8-foot-high net. There are six players on each team, standing three by three across on each side of the net; however, the same person may not hit the ball two times in a row. If the serve is not returned, the team that served gets the point.

The most popular serve is the underhand. The server stands with the left foot forward, right knee bent, weight on the right foot. He or she leans slightly forward. The ball is in the partly extended left hand. The server strikes the ball off the left hand with the right hand. (Left-handers use the opposite hands and feet.) The first team to get 15 points wins the game.

Directions: Answer these questions about volleyball.

1. Circle the main idea:

   Volleyball is a sport that requires a lot of strength.

   Volleyball is a simple game with six players on opposing sides.

2. A valid generalization about volleyball is:

   a. It's safe, requires little equipment, and can be played by all ages.

   b. It's dangerous, difficult to learn, and appeals only to children.

   c. It's dull, slow, and takes players a long time to earn 15 points.

3. Give directions on how to deliver an underhand serve. _____

   _____

   _____

Comprehension: Comparing Sports

Directions: Read each paragraph. Then, answer the questions comparing field hockey, basketball, and softball.

My sister is more interested in sports than I am. Last year, she lettered in field hockey, basketball, and softball. I got my exercise walking to school.

1. What sports did the writer play? _____

My sister's favorite sport is field hockey. Because it requires constant running up and down a field, it provides more exercise than basketball and softball. There's also more danger, because every year someone gets her teeth knocked out with a hockey stick. So far at our school, no one has lost any teeth in basketball or softball.

2. Compared to basketball and softball, field hockey provides one benefit and one danger. Name them.

_____   _____

On the other hand, softball players—especially those who play the outfield—can occasionally take some time to daydream. With an ace strikeout pitcher and batters who can't hit far, outfielders' gloves don't get much of a workout.

3. What sports do not allow time for daydreaming? _____

_____

Write a short paragraph telling which sport you like best and why. _____

_____

_____

_____

_____

_____

_____

_____

Famous Athletes

Athletes are often heroes to young and old alike. Their stories are sometimes about triumph over amazing odds to become one of the best in their sport. Before beginning the section, answer the following questions as a warm-up.

1. What sport most interests you? Why?

_____

_____

2. What sports figure do you most admire? Why?

_____

_____

3. In your opinion, what makes a person a hero?

_____

_____

4. Try to name a sports legend for each of the sports listed below.

Track and field _____

Swimming _____

Boxing _____

Baseball _____

Speed skating _____

Tennis _____

Hitting the Slopes

Directions: Read the selection. Then, answer the questions.

Lindsey Vonn was born to be a skier. She began learning the sport when she was only two years old. Vonn was so talented that her father moved the entire family from Minnesota to Colorado when she was 10. He knew that Colorado was the place to be if Lindsey had a chance of exploring her potential as a skier. Vonn started racing at the age of 7 and won her first competition when she was only 14 years old.

Vonn made her Olympic debut in 2002. Just before the next Olympics In 2006, she was injured. Despite the pain, Vonn was able to ski, and even to place. For the next few years, she worked hard and was prepared for the 2010 Olympics in Vancouver, Canada. Vonn was thrilled to realize a dream: to win a gold medal in the downhill event! In addition, she won a bronze in the Super-G (short for the "super-giant slalom," a downhill event). Lindsey Vonn was becoming known as one of the world's most talented female skiers.

In 2013, Vonn was injured again. This time, her injury resulted in reconstructive knee surgery. Although she skied competitively after her surgery, Vonn's knee continued to give her trouble. It was a hard decision to make, but she knew she'd be unable to compete in the 2014 Winter Olympics. Despite her Injuries, Lindsey Vonn has had an impressive career. In addition to her Olympic medals, she has won almost 60 World Cup victories and inspired female athletes worldwide.

1. Summarize the selection in three sentences.

_____

_____

_____

2. Define the following words:

potential: _____

debut: _____

reconstructive: _____

3. What are four words you could use to describe Lindsey Vonn?

_____ _____ _____ _____

Speed Skating

Directions: Read the selection. Then, answer the questions.

Imagine racing around a rink of glassy ice with only a thin blade of metal supporting you. Now, imagine skating so fast that you set a world record! That's exactly what speed skater Bonnie Blair has done all of her life.

Bonnie started skating before she was walking—on the shoulders of her older brothers and sisters. By the time she was 4, Bonnie was competing. At age 7, Bonnie won the 1971 Illinois state championships and dreamed of becoming an Olympian.

That opportunity soon came. Bonnie competed in the 1988, 1992, and 1994 Olympics. She won a gold medal in the 500-meter race and a bronze medal in the 1,000-meter race in 1988, golds in both the 500- and 1,000-meter races in 1992 and repeated the two golds in 1994. Only two other U.S. women have ever won five gold medals in the Olympics in any sport. Bonnie Blair is truly a champion!

1. Define the following words:

   opportunity: _____

   meter: _____

2. Bonnie Blair competed over a period of six years in the Olympics. What qualities would be necessary to maintain the physical and mental condition to compete for so long?

   _____

   _____

3. Bonnie Blair participated in long-track skating, in which she raced with one other person against a clock for the best time. Do you think this would be easier or more difficult than racing a group to finish first? Why?

   _____

   _____

4. In your opinion, what makes a good athlete?

   _____

   _____

Baseball

Directions: Read the selection. Then, answer the questions.

Babe Ruth was born George Herman Ruth in 1895. His family lived in Baltimore, Maryland, and was quite poor. He overcame poverty to become one of the greatest baseball players of all time.

Babe Ruth's baseball career began with the Baltimore Orioles. He was a pitcher but also a tremendous batter. He later played for the Boston Red Sox and started his home-run hitting fame with 29 home runs in 1919.

In 1920, while playing for the New York Yankees, Babe Ruth hit 54 home runs. He had become very popular with baseball fans of all ages. Amazingly, by 1925, he was making more money than the president of the United States! His home-run record of 60 home runs in a single season went unshattered until Roger Maris broke it in 1961 with 61 home runs.

Babe Ruth retired from baseball in 1935 with a career total of 714 home runs. He died in 1948 at age 53.

1. Summarize the selection in three sentences.

_____

_____

_____

2. In the early 1900s, life expectancy was shorter than it is today. By today's standards, Babe Ruth died at a relatively young age. What factors have contributed to increased life expectancy?

_____

_____

_____

_____

3. Create a time line of Babe Ruth's life beginning with his birth and ending with his death.

├───┤

Swimming

Directions: Read the selection. Then, answer the questions.

In 1968, 18-year-old Mark Spitz boasted that he would win six gold medals at the Olympics being held in Mexico. He won two golds in team relay events. After failing to achieve his goal, Spitz was determined to do better in the 1972 Olympics in Munich.

For the next four years, Mark Spitz trained ferociously. Indeed, at the 1972 Olympics, Spitz amazed the world by breaking all records and winning seven gold medals in seven different events. While doing so, he set new world record times in each event. Mark Spitz had accomplished his goal.

1. What feelings do you think Mark Spitz had after the 1968 Olympics?

_____

_____

_____

2. What do you think is the moral to this story?

_____

_____

_____

3. Many Olympians are as young as Mark Spitz was, and some participate at even younger ages. Write one paragraph detailing the advantages of being a young Olympian and one paragraph detailing the disadvantages.

_____

_____

_____

_____

Boxing

Directions: Read the selection. Then, answer the questions.

Muhammad Ali was born Cassius Clay in Louisville, Kentucky, in 1942. He won the amateur Golden Gloves championship in 1959 and 1960 and went on to become the heavyweight champion of the 1960 Olympics. Four years later, he was champion of the world.

However, Ali's athletic fame came with its share of difficulties. He converted to the religion of Islam and thus changed his name from Cassius Clay to Muhammad Ali. Due to his Islamic beliefs, he refused to comply with the military draft for the Vietnam War. Therefore, he was stripped of his world title and banned from boxing from 1967 to 1970.

Ali regained his title in 1974 and won the world championship again in 1978. This accomplishment made Muhammad Ali the first heavyweight boxer to claim the world championship three times. Most notable about Ali's career is his total 56 wins in the ring with 37 knockouts.

1. Define the following words:

   draft: _____

   banned: _____

   amateur: _____

   notable: _____

   comply: _____

2. Why is it necessary for a country to use the military draft?

   _____

   _____

3. Write a three-sentence summary of the selection.

   _____

   _____

   _____

Tennis

Directions: Read the selection. Then, answer the questions.

Martina Navratilova gained fame as the best women's tennis player of the 1980s. She was born in Czechoslovakia in 1956 and moved to the United States at the age of 19. She became a United States citizen in 1981.

Martina Navratilova excelled in the sport of tennis, but she enjoyed the Wimbledon championship the most. She won the singles finals in 1978, 1979, 1982, 1983, 1984, 1985, 1986, 1987, and 1990.

In 1982, she became the first woman professional tennis player to earn over one million dollars in a single season.

1. What physical characteristics are necessary to excel in the sport of tennis?

_____

_____

_____

2. In your opinion, why would an athlete from another country want to come to the U.S.A. to train and compete?

_____

_____

_____

3. Many athletes find it difficult to adjust to their status as "heroes." What are some possible disadvantages to being an athletic superstar?

_____

_____

_____

_____

_____

_____

Review

Directions: Follow the instructions for each section.

1. On the line below, create a time line of the years of birth for the six athletes discussed in this section.

```
├─────────────────────────────────────────────┤
```

2. What mental and emotional characteristics did all six athletes have in common?

   _____

   _____

   _____

   _____

3. On the line below, create a time line of Muhammad Ali's life.

```
├─────────────────────────────────────────────┤
```

4. Compare and contrast the sports of tennis and baseball in a two-paragraph essay.

   _____

   _____

   _____

   _____

   _____

   _____

Writing: My Sports Hero

Directions: Write a short essay about a man or woman you admire who has excelled in a sport. Make sure to give details about why you admire this person.

_____

_____

_____

_____

_____

_____

_____

_____

_____

Directions: Interview an adult. Ask him or her about a sports figure he or she admired at your age. Write a short paragraph about this person's sports hero.

_____

_____

_____

_____

_____

_____

_____

_____

Using Prior Knowledge: Poetry

Directions: Before reading about poetry in the following section, answer these questions.

1. Have you ever written a poem? If so, was it difficult to do? Why or why not?

_____

_____

_____

2. Write a poem with rhyming verse.

_____

_____

_____

_____

_____

_____

3. Write a poem with unrhymed verse.

_____

_____

_____

_____

_____

Comprehension: Epitaphs

Epitaphs are verses written on tombstones and were very popular in the past. The following epitaphs were written by unknown authors.

On a Man Named Merideth

Here lies one blown out of breath
Who lived a merry life and died a Merideth.

On a Dentist

Stranger, approach this spot with gravity:
John Brown is filling his last cavity.

On Leslie Moore

Here lies what's left
Of Leslie Moore
No Les
No more

Directions: Answer these questions about the epitaphs.

1. What does the phrase "blown out of breath" mean? _____

_____

2. What does the author mean when he says "and died a Merideth"? _____

_____

3. What cavity is John Brown filling? _____

4. Write an epitaph of your own.

_____

_____

_____

_____

_____

Comprehension: "The Ant and the Cricket"

A silly young cricket, who decided to sing
Through the warm sunny months of summer and spring,
Began to complain when he found that at home
His cupboards were empty and winter had come.

At last by starvation the cricket made bold
To hop through the wintertime snow and the cold.
Away he set off to a miserly ant
To see if to keep him alive he would grant
Shelter from rain, a mouthful of grain.
"I wish only to borrow—I'll repay it tomorrow—
If not, I must die of starvation and sorrow!"

Said the ant to the cricket, "It's true I'm your friend,
But we ants never borrow, we ants never lend;
We ants store up crumbs so when winter arrives
We have just enough food to keep ants alive."

Directions: Use context clues to answer these questions about the poem.

1. What is the correct definition of **cupboards**?

   ☐ where books are stored   ☐ where food is stored   ☐ where shoes are stored

2. What is the correct definition of **miserly**?

   ☐ selfish/stingy   ☐ generous/kind   ☐ mean/ugly

3. What is the correct definition of **grant**?

   ☐ to take away   ☐ to belch   ☐ to give

4. In two sentences, describe what the poet is trying to say with this poem.

   _____

   _____

   _____

   _____

Comprehension: "The Elf and the Dormouse"

Under a toadstool
Crept a wee elf
Out of the rain
To shelter himself.

Under the toadstool
Sound asleep
Sat a big dormouse
All in a heap.

Trembled the wee elf
Frightened, and yet
Fearing to fly away
Lest he got wet.

To the next shelter
Maybe a mile!
Sudden the wee elf
Smiled a wee smile,

Tugged 'til the toadstool
Toppled in two,
Holding it over him
Gaily he flew.

Soon he was safe home,
Dry as could be;
Soon woke the dormouse
"Good gracious me!"

"Where is my toadstool?"
Loud he lamented.
And that's when umbrellas
First were invented.

—Oliver Herford

Directions: Use context clues or a dictionary to answer these questions about the poem.

1. This humorous poem tells about what invention? _____

2. What do you think a **dormouse** is? _____

_____

3. What is the correct definition of **lamented**? _____

_____

4. Write a two-verse poem below describing the invention of a useful object.

_____

_____

_____

_____

Comprehension: "The Eagle"

Personification is a figure of speech in which human characteristics are given to an animal or object.

Example: The trees danced in the wind.

Trees do not dance; therefore, the trees are being personified.

He clasps the crag with crooked hands:
Close to the sun in lonely lands,
Ringed with the azure world, he stands.

The wrinkled sea beneath him crawls;
He watches from his mountain walls,
And like a thunderbolt he falls.

—*Alfred, Lord Tennyson*

Directions: Answer these questions about the poem.

1. What is the correct definition of **crag**?_____

_____

2. What is the correct definition of **azure**?_____

3. Which phrases in the poem show personification?_____

_____

4. Explain what one of these phrases actually means. _____

_____

_____

5. What is the author trying to say in the last line of the poem? _____

_____

_____

Comprehension: Proverbs

Proverbs are bits of advice for daily life. The following proverbs were written by Benjamin Franklin in 1732. They were published in *Poor Richard's Almanack*.

1. Keep conscience clear,
   Then never fear.

2. Little strokes
   Fell great oaks.

3. From a slip of foot you may soon recover,
   But a slip of the tongue you may never get over.

4. Doing an injury puts you below your enemy;
   Revenging one makes you but even with him;
   Forgiving it sets you above him.

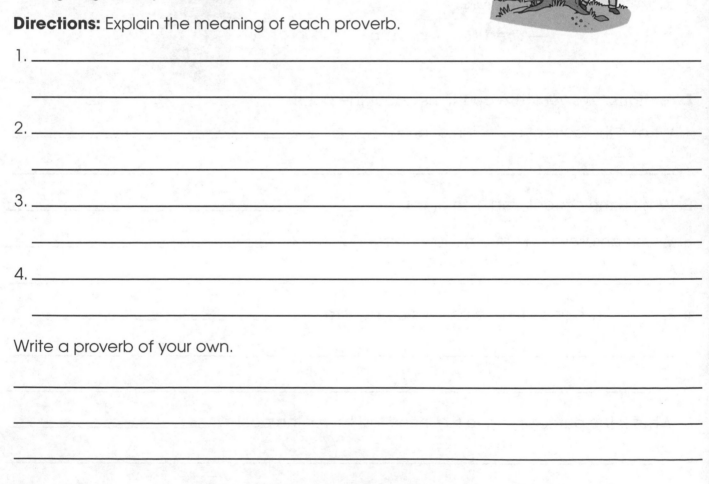

Directions: Explain the meaning of each proverb.

1. _____

   _____

2. _____

   _____

3. _____

   _____

4. _____

   _____

Write a proverb of your own.

_____

_____

_____

_____

Comprehension: Limericks

A **limerick** is a humorous verse consisting of five lines. The first, second, and fifth lines rhyme, and the third and fourth lines rhyme.

Old Man from Peru
There was an old man from Peru,
Who dreamed he was eating his shoe.
In the midst of the night
He awoke in a fright
And—good grief!—it was perfectly true.

Old Man from Darjeeling
There was an old man from Darjeeling,
Who boarded a bus bound for Ealing.
He saw on the door:
"Please don't spit on the floor."
So he stood up and spat on the ceiling.

Directions: Answer these questions about these silly limericks.

1. In "Old Man from Peru," what was perfectly true? _____

_____

2. How did the old man from Peru feel when he awoke? _____

3. In "Old Man from Darjeeling," what is Ealing? _____

4. Did the old man from Darjeeling break any rules? _____

Write your own silly limerick below.

_____

_____

_____

_____

_____

Comprehension: "The Tyger"

Imagery is a picture that comes into the reader's mind when reading certain words.

Tyger! Tyger! burning bright
In the forests of the night,
What immortal hand or eye
Could frame thy fearful symmetry?

In what distant deeps or skies
Burnt the fire of thine eyes?
On what wings dare he aspire?
What the hand dare seize the fire?

And what shoulder, and what art,
Could twist the sinew of thy heart,
And when thy heart began to beat,
What dread hand? and what dread feet?

What the hammer? what the chain?
In what furnace was thy brain?
What the anvil? what dread grasp
Dare its deadly terrors clasp?

When the stars threw down their spears,
And watered heaven with their tears,
Did he smile his work to see?
Did he who made the lamb make thee?

Tyger! Tyger! burning bright
In the forests of the night,
What immortal hand or eye,
Dare frame thy fearful symmetry?

—*William Blake*

Directions: Use context clues or a dictionary to answer these questions about the poem.

1. What is the correct definition of **symmetry**?

_____

_____

2. What is the correct definition of **immortal**?

_____

_____

3. What is the correct definition of **aspire**?

_____

_____

4. What is the correct definition of **sinew**?

_____

_____

5. What is the correct definition of **anvil**?

_____

_____

6. What is some imagery in this poem?

_____

_____

_____

Comprehension: Old Gaelic Lullaby

A **Gaelic lullaby** is an ancient Irish or Scottish song some parents sing as they rock their babies to sleep.

Hush! The waves are rolling in,
White with foam, white with foam,
Father works amid the din,
But baby sleeps at home.

Hush! The winds roar hoarse and deep—
On they come, on they come!
Brother seeks the wandering sheep,
But baby sleeps at home.

Hush! The rain sweeps over the fields,
Where cattle roam, where cattle roam.
Sister goes to seek the cows,
But baby sleeps at home.

Directions: Answer these questions about the Gaelic lullaby.

1. What is Father doing while baby sleeps? _____

_____

2. What is Brother doing? _____

_____

3. What is Sister doing? _____

_____

4. What do we assume Mother is doing? _____

_____

5. Is it quiet or noisy while Father works? ☐ quiet   ☐ noisy

6. Which is not mentioned in the poem?

☐ wind   ☐ sunshine   ☐ waves   ☐ rain

Comprehension: "The Lark and the Wren"

"Goodnight, Sir Wren!" said the little lark.
"The daylight fades; it will soon be dark.
I've sung my hymn to the parting day.
So now I fly to my quiet glen
In yonder meadow—Goodnight, Wren!"

"Goodnight, poor Lark," said the haughty wren,
With a flick of his wing toward his happy friend.
"I also go to my rest profound
But not to sleep on the cold, damp ground.
The fittest place for a bird like me
Is the topmost bough of a tall pine tree."

Directions: Use context clues for these definitions.

1. What is the correct definition of **hymn**?

 ☐ whisper ☐ song ☐ opposite of her

2. What is the correct definition of **yonder**?

 ☐ distant ☐ mountaintop ☐ seaside

3. What is the correct definition of **haughty**?

 ☐ happy ☐ friendly ☐ pompous

4. What is the correct definition of **profound**?

 ☐ restless ☐ deep ☐ uncomfortable

5. What is the correct definition of **bough**?

 ☐ to bend over ☐ tree roots ☐ tree branch

6. Write another verse of the poem.

_____

_____

_____

Nouns

A **noun** names a person, place, thing, or idea. There are several types of nouns.

Examples:
proper nouns: Joe, Jefferson Memorial
common nouns: dog, town
concrete nouns: book, stove
abstract nouns: fear, devotion
collective nouns: audience, flock

A word can be more than one type of noun.

Example: Dog is both a common and a concrete noun.

Directions: Write the type or types of each noun on the lines.

1. desk _____
2. ocean _____
3. love _____
4. cat _____
5. herd _____
6. compassion _____
7. reputation _____
8. eyes _____
9. staff _____
10. day _____
11. Roosevelt Building _____
12. Mr. Timken _____
13. life _____
14. porch _____
15. United States _____

ENGLISH

Metaphor:
Don't be a crab!

Simile:
The wet floor was as slippery as an eel.

Nouns

A **noun** names a person, place, thing, or idea. There are several types of nouns.

Examples:
  proper nouns: Joe, Jefferson Memorial
  common nouns: dog, town
  concrete nouns: book, stove
  abstract nouns: fear, devotion
  collective nouns: audience, flock

A word can be more than one type of noun.

Example: Dog is both a common and a concrete noun.

Directions: Write the type or types of each noun on the lines.

1. desk _____

2. ocean _____

3. love _____

4. cat _____

5. herd _____

6. compassion _____

7. reputation _____

8. eyes _____

9. staff _____

10. day _____

11. Roosevelt Building _____

12. Mr. Timken _____

13. life _____

14. porch _____

15. United States _____

Possessive Nouns

A **possessive** noun owns something. To make a singular noun possessive, add an apostrophe and **s**. **Example:** mayor**'s** campaign

To make a plural noun possessive when it already ends with **s**, add only an apostrophe. **Example:** dog**s'** tails

To make a plural noun possessive when it doesn't end with **s**, add an apostrophe and **s**. **Example:** men**'s** shirts

Directions: Write the correct form of the word for each sentence in the group. Words may be singular, plural, singular possessive, or plural possessive. The first one has been done for you.

teacher   1. How many <u>teachers</u> does your school have?

2. Where Is the <u>teacher's</u> coat?

3. All the <u>teachers'</u> mailboxes are in the school office.

reporter   4. Two _____ were assigned to the story.

5. One _____ car boke down on the way to the scene.

6. The other _____ was riding as a passenger.

7. Both _____ notes ended up missing.

child   8. The _____ are hungry.

9. How much spaghetti can one _____ eat?

10. Put this much on each _____ plate.

11. The _____ spaghetti is ready for them.

mouse   12. Some _____ made a nest under those boards.

13. I can see the _____ hole from here.

14. A baby _____ has wandered away from the nest.

15. The _____ mother is coming to get it.

Verbs

A **verb** is a word that tells what something does or that something exists.

There are two types of verbs: **action** and **state of being**.

Examples:
    Action: run, read, choose, wash, push, cut, drive, laugh, scream, reach
    State of being: feel, sound, taste, stay, look, appear, grow, seem, smell, and forms of **be**

Directions: Write **A** if the verb shows action. Write **S** if it shows state of being.

1. _____ He helped his friend.

2. _____ They appear happy and content.

3. _____ Jordi drives to school each day.

4. _____ The snowfall closed schools everywhere.

5. _____ The dog sniffed at its food.

6. _____ The meat tastes funny.

7. _____ Did you taste the fruit salad?

8. _____ The young boy smelled the flowers.

9. _____ She looked depressed.

10. _____ The coach announced the dates of the scrimmage.

11. _____ The owner of the store stocks all types of sports equipment.

12. _____ He dribbled the ball down the court.

13. _____ Everything seems to be in order.

Verb Tense

Tense is the way a verb is used to express time. To explain what is happening right now, use the **present tense**.

Example: He **is singing** well. He **sings** well.

To explain what has already happened, use the **past tense**.

Example: He **sang** well.

To explain what will happen, use the **future tense**.

Example: He **will sing** well.

Directions: Rewrite each sentence so the verbs are in the same tense. The first one has been done for you.

1. He ran, he jumped, and then he is flying.

   <u>He ran, he jumped, and then he flew.</u>

2. He was crying, and then he will stop.

   _____

3. She feels happy, but she was not sure why.

   _____

4. He is my friend, and so was she.

   _____

5. She bit into the peach and says it is good.

   _____

6. He laughs first and then told us the joke.

   _____

Spelling Different Forms of Verbs

To show that something is happening in the present, we can use the base form of a verb, or we can use **is** or **are** and add **ing** to the verb.

| is/are + verb + ing |
| was/were + verb + ing |

Example: We **run**. We **are running**.

To show that something has already happened, we can add **ed** to many verbs, or we can use **was** or **were** and add **ing** to a verb.

Example: The workers **surveyed** the land. The workers were **surveying** the land.

If a verb ends in **e**, drop the final **e** before adding an ending that begins with a vowel.

Example: She is **driving**. He **restored** the old car.

If a verb ends in **sh** or **ch**, add **es** instead of **s** to change the form.

Example: He furnish**es**. She watch**es**.

Directions: Complete each sentence with the correct form of the verb given. The first one has been done for you.

1. The florist is (have) a sale this week. _____having_____

2. Last night's tornado (destroy) a barn. _____

3. We are (research) the history of our town. _____

4. My mistake was (use) a plural verb instead of a singular one. _____

5. She (act) quickly in yesterday's emergency. _____

6. Our group is (survey) the parents in our community. _____

7. For our last experiment, we (observe) a plant's growth for two weeks. _____

8. A local company already (furnish) all the materials for this project. _____

9. Which dairy (furnish) milk to our cafeteria every day? _____

10. Just (ignore) the mess in here will not help your case. _____

Verb Tense

Directions: Write a sentence using the present tense of each verb.

1. walk _____

_____

2. dream _____

_____

3. achieve _____

_____

Directions: Write a sentence using the past tense of each verb.

4. dance _____

_____

5. study _____

_____

6. hike _____

_____

Directions: Write a sentence using the future tense of each verb.

7. bake _____

_____

8. write _____

_____

9. talk _____

_____

Verb Tense

Verbs can be **present**, **past**, or **past participle**.

Add **d** or **ed** to form the past tense.

Past-participle verbs also use a helping verb, such as **has** or **have**.

Examples:

Present	Past	Past Participle
help	helped	has or have helped
skip	skipped	has or have skipped

Directions: Write the past and past-participle forms of each present tense verb.

Present	Past	Past Participle
1. paint	painted	has (have) painted
2. dream		
3. play		
4. approach		
5. hop		
6. climb		
7. dance		
8. appear		
9. watch		
10. dive		
11. hurry		
12. discover		
13. decorate		
14. close		
15. jump		

Irregular Verb Forms

The past tense of most verbs is formed by adding **ed**. Verbs that do not follow this format are called **irregular verbs**.

The irregular verb chart shows a few of the many verbs with irregular forms.

Irregular Verb Chart

Present Tense	Past Tense	Past Participle
go	went	has, have, or had gone
do	did	has, have, or had done
fly	flew	has, have, or had flown
grow	grew	has, have, or had grown
ride	rode	has, have, or had ridden
see	saw	has, have, or had seen
sing	sang	has, have, or had sung
swim	swam	has, have, or had swum
throw	threw	has, have, or had thrown

The words **had**, **have**, and **has** can be separated from the irregular verb by other words in the sentence.

Directions: Choose the correct verb form from the chart to complete the sentences. The first one has been done for you.

1. The pilot had never before ___*flown*___ that type of plane.

2. She put on her bathing suit and _____ 2 miles.

3. The tall boy had _____ 2 inches over the summer.

4. She insisted she had _____ her homework.

5. He _____ them walking down the street.

6. She _____ the horse around the track.

7. The pitcher has _____ the ball many times.

8. He can _____ safely in the deepest water.

Irregular Verb Forms

Directions: Use the irregular verb chart on the previous page. Write the correct verb form to complete each sentence.

1. Has she ever _____ carrots in her garden?

2. She was so angry she _____ a tantrum.

3. The bird had sometimes _____ from its cage.

4. The cowboy has never _____ that horse before.

5. Will you _____ to the store with me?

6. He said he had often _____ her walking on his street.

7. She insisted she has not _____ taller this year.

8. He _____ briskly across the pool.

9. Have the insects _____ away?

10. Has anyone _____ my sister lately?

11. He hasn't _____ the dishes once this week!

12. Has she been _____ out of the game for cheating?

13. I haven't _____ her yet today.

14. The airplane _____ slowly by the airport.

15. Have you _____ your bike yet this week?

Nouns and Verbs

Some words can be used as both nouns and verbs.

Example:
The **bait** on his hook was a worm.
He couldn't **bait** his hook.

In the first sentence, **bait** is used as a **noun** because it names a thing. In the second sentence, **bait** is used as a **verb** because it shows action.

Directions: Write **noun** or **verb** for the word in bold in each sentence. The first one has been done for you.

verb   1. She **piloted** the small plane across the Pacific Ocean.

_____   2. Does she **water** her garden every night?

_____   3. Did you **rebel** against the rules?

_____   4. Dad will pound the fence **post** into the ground.

_____   5. That was good **thinking**!

_____   6. I **object** to your language!

_____   7. He planned to become a **pilot** after graduation.

_____   8. The teacher will **post** the new school calendar.

_____   9. She was **thinking** of a book she read last week.

_____   10. The **object** of the search was forgotten.

_____   11. She was a **rebel** in high school.

_____   12. Would you like fresh **water** for your tea?

Spelling: Plurals

Is **heros** or **heroes** the correct spelling? Many people aren't sure. These rules have exceptions, but they will help you spell the plural forms of most words that end with **o**.

- If a word ends with a consonant and **o**, add **es**: hero**es**.
- If a word ends with a vowel and **o**, add **s**: radio**s**.

Here are some other spelling rules for plurals:

- If a word ends with **s**, **ss**, **x**, **ch**, or **sh**, add **es**: bus**es**, kiss**es**, tax**es**, peach**es**, wish**es**.
- If a word ends with **f** or **fe**, drop the **f** or **fe** and add **ves**: leaf, leaves; wife, wives.
- Some plurals don't end with **s** or **es**: **geese**, **deer**, **children**.

Directions: Write the plural forms of the words.

1. Our area doesn't often have (tornado). _____

2. How many (radio) does this store sell every month? _____

3. (Radish) are the same color as apples. _____

4. Does this submarine carry (torpedo)? _____

5. Hawaii has a number of active (volcano). _____

6. Did you pack (knife) in the picnic basket? _____

7. We heard (echo) when we shouted in the canyon. _____

8. Where is the list of (address)? _____

9. What will you do when that plant (reach) the ceiling? _____

10. Sometimes my dad (fix) us milkshakes. _____

11. Every night, my sister (wish) on the first star she sees. _____

12. Who (furnish) the school with pencils and paper? _____

13. The author (research) every detail in her books. _____

Spelling: Plurals

Directions: Write the plural form of each word.

1. mother _____
2. ankle _____
3. journey _____
4. ceiling _____
5. governor _____
6. arch _____
7. carnival _____
8. official _____
9. potato _____
10. vacuum _____
11. stereo _____
12. strategy _____
13. column _____
14. architect _____
15. entry _____

16. summary _____
17. issue _____
18. member _____
19. astronomer _____
20. channel _____
21. harmony _____
22. piece _____
23. chicken _____
24. chemical _____
25. journal _____
26. niece _____
27. mayor _____
28. particle _____
29. entrance _____
30. assistant _____

Simple Subjects

The **simple subject** of a sentence tells who or what the sentence is about. It is a noun or a pronoun.

Example: My **mom** is turning forty this year.
　　　　　Mom is the simple subject.

Directions: Circle the simple subject in each sentence.

1. The cat ate all its food.

2. They watched the basketball game.

3. Lucy is going to lunch with her friend.

4. José likes strawberry jam on his toast.

5. The reporter interviewed the victim.

6. She turned down the volume.

7. The farm animals waited to be fed.

8. Can you lift weights?

9. The fan did little to cool the hot room.

10. Thomas Jefferson was one of the founding fathers of our country.

11. I have a lot to do tonight.

12. Will you go to the movie with us?

13. We enjoyed the day at the park.

14. Our pet is a dog.

15. She retrieved her homework from the garbage.

Simple Predicates

The **simple predicate** of a sentence tells what the subject does, is doing, did, or will do. The simple predicate is always a verb.

Example:
    My mom **is turning** forty this year.
    Is turning is the simple predicate.

Directions: Underline the simple predicate in each sentence. Include all helping verbs.

1. I bought school supplies at the mall.

2. The tiger chased its prey.

3. Mark will be arriving shortly.

4. The hamburgers are cooking now.

5. We will attend my sister's wedding.

6. The dental hygienist cleaned my teeth.

7. My socks are hanging on the clothesline.

8. Where are you going?

9. The dog is running toward its owner.

10. Ramos watched the tornado in fear.

11. Please wash the dishes after dinner.

12. My dad cleaned the garage yesterday.

13. We are going hiking at Yellowstone today.

14. The picture shows our entire family at the family picnic.

15. Our coach will give us a pep talk before the game.

Name _____

Parallel Structure

Parts of a sentence are **parallel** when they "match" grammatically and structurally.

Faulty parallelism occurs when the parts of a sentence do not match grammatically and structurally.

For sentences to be parallel, all parts of a sentence—including the verbs, nouns, and phrases—must match. This means that, in most cases, verbs should be in the same tense.

Examples:
   Correct: She liked running, jumping, and swinging outdoors.
   Incorrect: She liked running, jumping, and to swing outdoors.

In the correct sentence, all three of the actions the girl liked to do end in **ing**. In the incorrect sentence, they do not.

Directions: Rewrite the sentences so all elements are parallel. The first one has been done for you.

1. Politicians like making speeches and also to shake hands.

   Politicians like making speeches and shaking hands.

2. He liked singing, acting, and to perform in general.

   _____

3. The soup had carrots, celery, and also has rice.

   _____

4. The drink was cold, frosty, and also is a thirst-quencher.

   _____

5. She was asking when we would arrive, and I told her.

   _____

6. Liz felt like shouting, singing, and to jump.

   _____

Matching Subjects and Verbs

If the subject of a sentence is singular, the verb must be singular. If the subject is plural, the verb must be plural.

Example:
The **dog** with floppy ears **is eating**.
The **dogs** in the yard **are eating**.

Directions: Write the singular or plural form of the subject in each sentence to match the verb.

1. The (yolk) _____ in this egg is bright yellow.

2. The (child) _____ are putting numbers in columns.

3. Both (coach) _____ are resigning at the end of the year.

4. Those three (class) _____ were assigned to the gym.

5. The (lunch) _____ for the children are ready.

6. (Spaghetti) _____ with meatballs is delicious.

7. Where are the (box) _____ of chalk?

8. The (man) _____ in the truck were collecting broken tree limbs.

9. The (rhythm) _____ of that music is exactly right for dancing.

10. Sliced (tomato) _____ on lettuce are good with salmon.

11. The (announcer) _____ on TV was condemning the dictator.

12. Two (woman) _____ are campaigning for mayor of our town.

13. The (group) _____ of travelers was on its way to three foreign countries.

14. The (choir) _____ of thirty children is singing hymns.

15. In spite of the parade, the (hero) _____ were solemn.

Subject/Verb Agreement

Singular subjects require singular verbs. **Plural subjects** require plural verbs. The subject and verb must agree in a sentence.

Example:
   Singular: My dog runs across the field.
   Plural: My dogs run across the field.

Directions: Circle the correct verb in each sentence.

1. Maria (talk/talks) to me each day at lunch.

2. Mom, Dad, and I (is/are) going to the park to play catch.

3. Mr. and Mrs. Ramirez (dance/dances) well together.

4. Astronauts (hope/hopes) for a successful shuttle mission.

5. Trees (prevent/prevents) erosion.

6. The student (is/are) late.

7. She (ask/asks) for directions to the senior high gym.

8. The elephants (plod/plods) across the grassland to the watering hole.

9. My friend's name (is/are) Rebecca.

10. Many people (enjoy/enjoys) orchestra concerts.

11. The pencils (is/are) sharpened.

12. My backpack (hold/holds) a lot of things.

13. The wind (blow/blows) to the south.

14. Sam (collect/collects) butterflies.

15. They (love/loves) fresh strawberries.

Personal Pronouns

Personal pronouns take the place of nouns. They refer to people or things. **I**, **me**, **we**, **she**, **he**, **him**, **her**, **you**, **they**, **them**, **us**, and **it** are personal pronouns.

Directions: Circle the personal pronouns in each sentence.

1. He is a terrific friend.

2. Would you open the door?

3. Jim and I will arrive at ten o'clock.

4. Can you pick me up at the mall after dinner?

5. What did you do yesterday?

6. They are watching the game on television.

7. Jessie's mom took us to the movies.

8. She writes novels.

9. They gave us the refrigerator.

10. Is this the answer she intended to give?

11. What is it?

12. The dog yelped when it saw the cat.

13. I admire him.

14. We parked the bikes by the tree.

15. The ants kept us from enjoying our picnic.

Possessive Pronouns

Possessive pronouns show ownership. **My**, **mine**, **your**, **yours**, **his**, **her**, **hers**, **their**, **theirs**, **our**, **ours**, and **its** are possessive pronouns.

Directions: Circle the possessive pronouns in each sentence.

1. My dogs chase cats continually.

2. Keiko put her sunglasses on the dashboard.

3. His mother and mine are the same age.

4. The cat licked its paw.

5. Their anniversary is February 1.

6. This necklace is yours.

7. We will carry our luggage into the airport.

8. Our parents took us to dinner.

9. My brother broke his leg.

10. Her report card was excellent.

11. Raspberry jam is my favorite.

12. Watch your step!

13. The house on the left is mine.

14. My phone number is unlisted.

15. Our garden is growing out of control.

16. Our pumpkins are ten times larger than theirs.

Interrogative Pronouns

An **interrogative pronoun** asks a question. There are three interrogative pronouns: **who**, **what**, and **which**.

Use **who** when speaking of people.
Use **what** when speaking of things.
Use **which** when speaking of people or things.

Examples:
   Who will go? **What** will you do? **Which** of these is yours?

Who becomes **whom** when it is a direct object or an object of a preposition. The possessive form of **whom** is **whose**.

Examples:
   To **whom** will you write?
   Whose computer is that?

Directions: Write the correct interrogative pronoun.

1. _____ wet raincoat is this?

2. _____ is the president of the United States?

3. _____ is your name?

4. _____ dog made this muddy mess?

5. _____ cat ran away?

6. _____ of you is the culprit?

7. _____ was your grade on the last test?

8. To _____ did you report?

9. _____ do you believe now?

10. _____ is the leader of this English study group?

Name _____

Personal and Possessive Pronouns

Directions: Write personal or possessive pronouns in the blanks to take the place of the words in bold. The first one has been done for you.

___They___   ___him___   1. **Maisie and Marni** told **Trent** they would see him later.

_____ 2. **Spencer** told **Amelia and Jada** good-bye.

_____ 3. **The bike** was parked near **Aaron's** house.

_____ 4. **Maria, Matt, and Greg** claimed the car was new.

_____ 5. The dishes were **the property of Gabriella and Jake**.

_____ 6. Is this **Layla's**?

_____ 7. **Jon** walked near **Jessica and Esau's** house.

_____ 8. **The dog** barked all night long!

_____ 9. **Ana** fell and hurt **Ana's** knee.

_____ 10. **Cory and Devan** gave the dog **the dog's** dinner.

_____ 11. **Tori and I** gave **Brett and Reggie** a ride home.

_____ 12. Do **Josh and Andrea** like cats?

_____ 13. **Sasha and Keesha** gave **Josh and me** a ride home.

_____ 14. Is this sweater **Chloe's**?

_____ 15. The cat meowed because **the cat** was hungry.

Pronoun/Antecedent Agreement

Often, a **pronoun** is used in place of a noun to avoid repeating the noun again in the same sentence. The noun that a pronoun refers to is called its **antecedent**. The word **antecedent** means "going before."

If the noun is singular, the pronoun that takes its place must also be singular. If the noun is plural, the pronoun that takes its place must also be plural. This is called *agreement* between the pronoun and its antecedent.

Examples:
> **Kylie** (singular noun) said **she** (singular pronoun) would dance.
> The **dogs** (plural noun) took **their** (plural pronoun) dishes outside.

When the noun is singular and the gender unknown, it is correct to use **his or her**.

Directions: Rewrite the sentences so the pronouns and nouns agree. The first one has been done for you.

1. Every student opened their book.
   <u>Every student opened his or her book.</u>

2. Has anyone lost their wallet lately?

   _____

3. Somebody found the wallet under their desk.

   _____

4. Someone will have to file their report.

   _____

5. Every dog has their day!

   _____

6. I felt Ted had mine best interests at heart.

   _____

Pronoun/Antecedent Agreement

Directions: Write a pronoun that agrees with the antecedent.

1. Aiden said_____ would go to the store.

2. My friend discovered _____ wallet had been stolen.

3. The cat licked _____ paw.

4. Did any woman here lose _____ necklace?

5. Someone will have to give _____ report.

6. Aliyah wished _____ had not come.

7. All the children decided _____ would attend.

8. My grandmother hurt _____ back while gardening.

9. Jerry, Marco, and I hope _____ win the game.

10. Hailey looked for _____ missing homework.

11. The family had _____ celebration.

12. My dog jumps out of _____ pen.

13. Somebody needs to remove _____ clothes from this chair.

14. Everything has _____ place in Grandma's house.

15. The team will receive _____ uniforms on Monday.

16. Each artist wants _____ painting to win the prize.

Appositives

An **appositive** is a noun or pronoun placed after another noun or pronoun to further identify or rename it. An appositive and the words that go with it are usually set off from the rest of the sentence with commas. Commas are not used if the appositive tells "which one."

Example: Angela's mother, **Ms. Glover**, will visit our school.

Commas are needed because **Ms. Glover** renames Angela's mother.

Example: Angela's neighbor Maggy will visit our school.

Commas are not needed because the appositive "Maggy" tells **which** neighbor.

Directions: Write the appositive in each sentence in the blank. The first one has been done for you.

_____Ava_____ 1. My friend Ava wants a horse.

_____ 2. She subscribes to the magazine Horses.

_____ 3. Her horse is the gelding Brownie.

_____ 4. We rode in her new car, a convertible.

_____ 5. Her gift was jewelry, a bracelet.

_____ 6. Have you met Ms. Abbott, the senator?

_____ 7. My cousin Karl is very shy.

_____ 8. Do you eat the cereal Oaties?

_____ 9. Kiki's cat, Samantha, will eat only tuna.

_____ 10. My last name, Jones, is very common.

Dangling Modifiers

A **dangling modifier** is a word or group of words that does not modify what it is supposed to modify. To correct dangling modifiers, supply the missing words to which the modifiers refer.

Examples:
  Incorrect: While doing the laundry, the dog barked.
  Correct: While I was doing the laundry, the dog barked.

In the **incorrect** sentence, it sounds as though the dog is doing the laundry. In the **correct** sentence, it's clear that **I** is the subject of the sentence.

Directions: Rewrite the sentences to make the subject of the sentence clear and eliminate dangling modifiers. The first one has been done for you.

1. While eating our dinner, the doctor called.

   <u>While we were eating our dinner, the doctor called.</u>

2. Living in Cincinnati, the ball park is nearby.

   _____

3. While watching the movie, the TV screen went blank.

   _____

4. While listening to the concert, the lights went out.

   _____

5. Tossed regularly, anyone can make great salad.

   _____

6. While working, something surprised him.

   _____

   _____

Review

Directions: Write **noun** or **verb** to describe the words in bold.

_____ 1. She is one of the fastest **runners** I've seen.

_____ 2. She is **running** very fast!

_____ 3. She **thought** he was handsome.

_____ 4. Please share your **thoughts** with me.

_____ 5. I will **watch** the volleyball game on video.

_____ 6. The sailor fell asleep during his **watch**.

_____ 7. My grandmother believes my purchase was a real **find**.

_____ 8. I hope to **find** my lost books.

Directions: Rewrite the verb in the correct tense.

_____ 9. She **swim** across the lake in 2 hours.

_____ 10. He has **ride** horses for years.

_____ 11. Have you **saw** my sister?

_____ 12. She **fly** on an airplane last week.

_____ 13. My father had **instruct** me in the language.

_____ 14. I **drive** to the store yesterday.

_____ 15. The movie **begin** late.

_____ 16. Where **do** you go yesterday?

Directions: Circle the pronouns.

17. She and I told them to forget it!

18. They all wondered if her dad would drive his new car.

19. We want our parents to believe us.

20. My picture was taken at her home.

Review

Directions: Rewrite the sentences to correct the faulty parallels.

1. The fresh blueberries were sweet, juicy, and are delicious.

   _____

2. The town was barren, windswept, and is empty.

   _____

3. The dog was black, long-haired, and is quite friendly.

   _____

4. My favorite dinners are macaroni and cheese, spaghetti, and I loved fish.

   _____

Directions: Rewrite the sentences to make the verb tenses consistent.

5. We laughed, cried, and were jumping for joy.

   _____

6. She sang, danced, and was doing somersaults.

   _____

7. The class researched, studied, and were writing their reports.

   _____

8. Orlando and Maya talked about their vacation and share their experiences.

   _____

Directions: Circle the pronouns that agree with their antecedents.

9. She left (her/their) purse at the dance.

10. Each dog wagged (its/their) tail.

11. We walked to (our/he) car.

12. The lion watched (his/its) prey.

Review

Directions: Rewrite the sentences to correct the dangling modifiers.

1. Living nearby, the office was convenient for her.

   _____

2. While doing my homework, the doorbell rang.

   _____

3. Watching over her shoulder, she hurried away.

   _____

4. Drinking from the large mug, he choked.

   _____

Directions: Circle the correct pronouns.

5. She laughed at my brother and (I/me).

6. At dawn, (he and I/him and me) were still talking.

7. Someone left (his or her/their) coat on the floor.

8. Lauren said (her/she) would not be late.

Directions: Circle the appositive.

9. The school nurse, Ms. Franklin, was worried about him.

10. The car, a Volkswagen, was illegally parked.

11. My hero, Babe Ruth, was an outstanding baseball player.

12. Is that car, the plum-colored one, for sale?

13. Will Mr. Zimmer, Todd's father, buy that car?

Name _____

Adjectives

Adjectives describe nouns.

Examples:
 tall girl
 soft voice
 clean hands

Directions: Circle the adjectives. Underline the nouns they describe. Some sentences may have more than one set of adjectives and nouns.

1. The lonely man sat in the dilapidated house.

2. I hope the large crop of grapes will soon ripen.

3. The white boxes house honeybees.

4. My rambunctious puppy knocked over the valuable flower vase.

5. The "unsinkable" *Titanic* sank after striking a gigantic iceberg.

6. His grades showed his tremendous effort.

7. There are many purple flowers in the large arrangement.

8. These sweet peaches are the best I've tasted.

9. The newsletter describes several educational workshops.

10. The rodeo featured professional riders and funny clowns.

11. My evening pottery class is full of very interesting people.

12. My older brother loves his new pickup truck.

13. Amira's family bought a big-screen TV.

Comparing with Adjectives

When adjectives are used to compare two things, **er** is added at the end of the word for most one-syllable words and some two-syllable words.

Example: It is **colder** today than it was yesterday.

With many two-syllable words and all words with three or more syllables, the word **more** is used with the adjective to show comparison.

Example: Dr. X is **more professional** than Dr. Y.

When adjectives are used to compare three or more things, **est** is added at the end of the word for **most** one-syllable words and some two-syllable words.

Example: Today is the **coldest** day of the year.

With many two-syllable words and all words with three or more syllables, **most** is used with the adjective to show comparison.

Example: Dr. X is the **most professional** doctor in town.

When adding **er** or **est** to one-syllable words, these spelling rules apply.
- Double the last consonant if the word has a short vowel before a final consonant: thinner, fatter.
- If a word ends in **y**, change the **y** to **i** before adding **er** or **est**: earliest, prettiest.
- If a word ends in **e**, drop the final **e** before adding **er** or **est**: simpler, simplest.

Directions: Complete these sentences with the correct form of the adjective.

1. This book is (small) _____ than that one.

2. I want the (small) _____ book in the library.

3. My plan is (practical) _____ than yours.

4. My plan is the (practical) _____ one in the class.

5. I wish the change was (gradual) _____ than it is.

6. My sister is the (childish) _____ girl in her day-care group.

7. There must be a (simple) _____ way to do it than that.

8. This is the (simple) _____ way of the four we thought of.

Name _____

Adjectives: Positive, Comparative, and Superlative

There are three degrees of comparison adjectives: **positive**, **comparative**, and **superlative**. The **positive degree** is the adjective itself. The **comparative** and **superlative** degrees are formed by adding **er** and **est**, respectively, to most one-syllable adjectives. The form of the word changes when the adjective is irregular, for example, **good**, **better**, **best**.

Most adjectives of two or more syllables require the words "more" or "most" to form the comparative and superlative degrees.

Examples:

Positive:	big	eager
Comparative:	bigger	more eager
Superlative:	biggest	most eager

Directions: Write the positive, comparative, or superlative forms of these adjectives.

Positive	Comparative	Superlative
1. hard	_____	_____
2. _____	happier	_____
3. _____	_____	most difficult
4. cold	_____	_____
5. _____	easier	_____
6. _____	_____	largest
7. little	_____	_____
8. _____	shinier	_____
9. round	_____	_____
10. _____	_____	most beautiful

Adverbs

Adverbs tell when, where, or how an action occurred.

Examples:
I'll go **tomorrow**. (when)
I sleep **upstairs**. (where)
I screamed **loudly**. (how)

Directions: Circle the adverb, and underline the verb it modifies. Write the question (when, where, or how) the adverb answers.

1. I ran quickly toward the finish line. _____

2. Today, we will receive our report cards. _____

3. He swam smoothly through the pool. _____

4. Many explorers searched endlessly for
   new lands. _____

5. He looked up into the sky. _____

6. My friend drove away in her new car. _____

7. Later, we will search for your missing wallet. _____

8. Most kings rule their kingdoms regally. _____

9. New plants must be watered daily. _____

10. The stream near our house is heavily polluted. _____

11. My baby brother likes to walk backwards
    across his room. _____

Name _____

Adverbs: Positive, Comparative, and Superlative

There are also three degrees of comparison adverbs: **positive**, **comparative**, and **superlative**. They follow the same rules as adjectives.

Example:

Positive:	rapidly	far
Comparative:	more rapidly	farther
Superlative:	most rapidly	farthest

Directions: Write the positive, comparative, or superlative forms of these adverbs.

Positive	Comparative	Superlative
1. easily	_____	_____
2. _____	more quickly	_____
3. _____	_____	most hopefully
4. bravely	_____	_____
5. _____	more strongly	_____
6. near	_____	_____
7. _____	_____	most cleverly
8. _____	more gracefully	_____
9. _____	_____	most humbly
10. excitedly	_____	_____
11. _____	more handsomely	_____
12. slowly	_____	_____

Adjectives and Adverbs

Directions: Write **adjective** or **adverb** in the blanks to describe the words in bold. The first one has been done for you.

___adjective___   1. Her **old** boots were caked with mud.

_____   2. The baby was **cranky**.

_____   3. He took the test **yesterday**.

_____   4. I heard the **funniest** story last week!

_____   5. She left her wet shoes **outside**.

_____   6. Isn't that the **fluffiest** cat you've ever seen?

_____   7. He ran **around** the track twice.

_____   8. Our elderly neighbor seems **lonely**.

_____   9. His **kind** smile lifted my dragging spirits.

_____   10. **Someday**, I'll meet the friend of my dreams!

_____   11. His cat never meows **indoors**.

_____   12. Carlos hung his new shirts **back** in the closet.

_____   13. Put that valuable vase **down** immediately!

_____   14. She is the most **joyful** child!

_____   15. Jonathan's wool sweater is totally **moth-eaten**.

Identifying Sentence Parts

The **subject** tells who or what a sentence is about. Sentences can have more than one subject.

Example: Dogs and **cats** make good pets.

The **predicate** tells what the subject does or that it exists. Predicates can be more than one word. A sentence can have more than one predicate.

Examples: She **was walking**. She **walked** and **ran**.

An **adjective** is a word or group of words that describes the subject or another noun.

Example: The **cheerful yellow** bird with **blue** spots flew across the **flower-covered** meadow.

An **adverb** is a word or group of words that tells how, when, where, or how often.

Example: He sat **there** waiting **quietly**.

Directions: Write **S** for subject, **P** for predicate, **ADJ** for adjective, or **ADV** for adverb above each underlined word or group of words. The first one has been done for you.

    ADJ   S   ADJ   P   ADV
1. A <u>huge</u> <u>dog</u> with <u>long</u> teeth <u>was barking</u> <u>fiercely</u>.

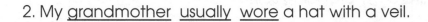

2. My <u>grandmother</u> <u>usually</u> <u>wore</u> a hat with a veil.

3. My <u>niece</u> and her <u>friend</u> <u>are</u> the <u>same</u> height.

4. The <u>lively</u> <u>reindeer</u> <u>danced</u> and <u>pranced</u> <u>briefly</u> on the rooftop.

Directions: Write sentences containing the sentence parts listed. Mark each part even if the verb part gets separated.

  1. Write a question with two subjects, two predicates, and two adjectives:

    _____

  2. Write a statement with one subject, two predicates, and two adjectives:

    _____

Identifying Sentence Parts

Directions: Write **S** for subject, **P** for predicate, **ADJ** for adjective, or **ADV** for adverb above the appropriate words in these sentences.

1. The large cat pounced on the mouse ferociously.

2. Did you remember your homework?

3. My mother is traveling to New York tomorrow.

4. I play basketball on Monday and Friday afternoons.

5. The old, decrepit house sat at the end of the street.

6. Several tiny rabbits nibbled at the grass at the edge of the field.

7. The lovely bride wore a white dress with a long train.

8. We packed the clothes for the donation center in a box.

9. The telephone rang incessantly.

10. The lost child cried helplessly.

11. What will we do with these new puppies?

12. Lauren reads several books each week.

13. The picture hung precariously on the wall.

14. I purchased many new school supplies.

15. Computers have changed the business world.

Comprehensive Curriculum - Grade 6

Prepositions

A **preposition** is a word that comes before a noun or pronoun and shows the relationship of that noun or pronoun to some other word in the sentence.

The **object of a preposition** is the noun or pronoun that follows a preposition and adds to its meaning.

A **prepositional phrase** includes the preposition, the object of the preposition, and all modifiers.

Example:
She gave him a pat **on his back**.
On is the preposition.
Back is the object of the preposition.
His is a possessive pronoun.

Common Prepositions			
about	down	near	through
above	for	of	to
across	from	off	up
at	in	on	with
behind	into	out	within
by	like	past	without

Directions: Underline the prepositional phrases. Circle the prepositions. Some sentences have more than one prepositional phrase. The first one has been done for you.

1. He claimed he felt (at) home only (on) the West Coast.

2. She went up the street and then down the block.

3. The famous poet was near the doorway.

4. The beautiful birthday card was from her father.

5. He left his wallet at home.

6. Her speech was totally without humor.

7. I think he's from New York City.

8. Kari wanted to go with her mother to the mall.

Prepositions

Directions: Complete the sentences by writing objects for the prepositions. The first one has been done for you.

1. He was standing at <u>**the corner of Fifth and Main.**</u> _____

2. She saw her friend across _____

3. Have you ever looked beyond _____

4. His contact lens fell into _____

5. Have you ever gone outside without _____

6. She was anxious for _____

7. Is that dog from _____

8. She was daydreaming and walked past _____

9. The book was hidden behind _____

10. The young couple had fallen in _____

11. She insisted she was through _____

12. He sat down near _____

13. She forgot her umbrella at _____

14. Have you ever thought of _____

15. Henry found his glasses on _____

Object of a Preposition

The **object of a preposition** is the noun or pronoun that follows the preposition and adds to its meaning.

Example:
 Correct: Devan smiled **at** (preposition) **Tori** (noun: object of the preposition) and **me** (pronoun: object of the same preposition.)
 Correct: Devan smiled at Tori. Devan smiled at me. Devan smiled at Tori and me.
 Incorrect: Devan smiled at Tori and I.

Tip: If you are unsure of the correct pronoun to use, pair each pronoun with the verb, and say the phrase out loud to find out which pronoun is correct.

Directions: Write the correct pronouns on the blanks. The first one has been done for you.

_____him_____ 1. It sounded like a good idea to Sadie and (he/him).

_____ 2. I asked Abby if I could attend with (her/she).

_____ 3. To (we/us), holidays are very important.

_____ 4. Between (we/us), we finished the job quickly.

_____ 5. They gave the award to (he and I/him and me).

_____ 6. The party was for my brother and (I/me).

_____ 7. I studied with (he/him).

_____ 8. Tanya and the others arrived after (we/us).

_____ 9. After the zoo, we stopped at the museum with Azim and (her/she).

_____ 10. The chips for (he/him) are in the bag on top of the refrigerator.

Direct Objects

A **direct object** is a noun or pronoun. It answers the question **whom** or **what** after a verb.

Examples:
My mom baked **bread**.
Bread is the direct object. It tells **what** Mom baked.
We saw **Steve**.
Steve is the direct object. It tells **whom** we saw.

Directions: Write a direct object in each sentence.

1. My dog likes _____. WHAT?

2. My favorite drink is _____. WHAT?

3. I saw _____ today. WHOM?

4. The car struck a _____. WHAT?

5. The fan blew _____ through the room. WHAT?

6. I packed a _____ for lunch. WHAT?

7. We watched _____ play basketball. WHOM?

8. I finished my _____. WHAT?

9. The artist sketched the _____. WHAT?

10. He greets _____ at the door. WHOM?

11. The team attended the victory _____. WHAT?

12. The beautician cut my _____. WHAT?

13. Tamika will write _____. WHAT?

Indirect Objects

An **indirect object** is a noun or pronoun that tells **to whom or what** or **for whom or what** the action is performed. An indirect object usually is found between a verb and a direct object.

Example:
I gave **Ellen** my address.
Ellen is the indirect object. It tells **to whom** I gave my address.

Directions: Circle the indirect objects. Underline the direct objects.

1. Emma told Kameko the secret.

2. Advertisers promise consumers the world.

3. The dogs showed me their tricks.

4. Aunt Martha gave Audrey a necklace for her birthday.

5. Ramon brought Mom a bouquet of fresh flowers.

6. I sent my niece a package for Christmas.

7. Mr. Dunbar left his wife a note before leaving.

8. Grandma and Grandpa made their friends dinner.

9. The baby handed her mom a toy.

10. Tierra told Stephanie the recipe for trail mix.

11. We sent Grandma a card.

12. The waiter served us dessert.

13. Mom and Dad sold us the farm.

Joining Sentences

Conjunctions are words that join sentences, words, or ideas. When two sentences are joined with **and**, they are more or less equal.

Example: Julio is coming, **and** he is bringing snacks.

When two sentences are joined with **but**, the second sentence contradicts the first one.

Example: Julio is coming, **but** he will be late.

When two sentences are joined with **or**, they name a choice.

Example: Julio might bring snacks, **or** he might bring lemonade.

When two sentences are joined with **because**, the second one names the reason for the first one.

Example: I'll bring snacks, too, **because** Julio might forget his.

When two sentences are joined with **so**, the second one names a result of the first one.

Example: Julio is bringing snacks, **so** we can eat when he gets here.

Directions: Complete each sentence. The first one has been done for you.

1. We could watch TV, or _we could play a game._ _____

2. I wanted to seize the opportunity, but _____

3. You had better not deceive me, because _____

4. My neighbor was on vacation, so _____

5. Veins take blood back to your heart, and _____

6. You can't always yield to your impulses, because _____

7. I know that is your belief, but _____

8. It could be reindeer on the roof, or _____

9. Brent was determined to achieve his goal, so _____

10. Brittany was proud of her height, because _____

Conjunctions

The conjunctions **and**, **or**, **but**, and **nor** can be used to make a compound subject, a compound predicate, or a compound sentence.

Examples:
   Compound subject: My friend **and** I will go to the mall.
   Compound predicate: We ran **and** jumped in gym class.
   Compound sentence: I am a talented violinist,
                     but my father is better.

Directions: Write two sentences of your own in each section.

Compound subject:

1. _____

   _____

2. _____

   _____

Compound predicate:

1. _____

   _____

2. _____

   _____

Compound sentence:

1. _____

   _____

2. _____

   _____

Review

Directions: Write the missing verb tenses.

Present	Past	Past Participle
1. catch	_____	_____
2. _____	stirred	_____
3. _____	_____	has (have) baked
4. go	_____	_____
5. _____	said	_____

Directions: Circle the simple subject, and underline the simple predicate in each sentence.

6. Maria got sunburned at the beach.

7. The class watched the program.

8. The tomatoes are ripening.

9. We went grocery shopping.

10. The cross country team practiced all summer.

Directions: Write the missing adjective or adverb forms below.

Positive	Comparative	Superlative
11. _____	more friendly	_____
12. small	_____	_____
13. _____	_____	most fun
14. _____	more attractive	_____

Name _____

Review

Directions: Write **adjective** or **adverb** to describe the words in bold.

_____ 1. My **old** piano teacher lives nearby.

_____ 2. My old piano teacher lives **nearby**.

_____ 3. His hair looked **horrible**.

_____ 4. Have you heard this **silly** joke?

_____ 5. **Suddenly**, the door opened.

_____ 6. The **magnificent** lion raised its head.

_____ 7. I accomplished the task **yesterday**.

_____ 8. This party has **delicious** food.

Directions: Circle the prepositions.

9. He went in the door and up the stairs.

10. Is this lovely gift from you?

11. I was all for it, but the decision was beyond my power.

12. His speech dragged on into the night.

13. My great-grandmother's crystal dish is in the curio cabinet.

14. He received a trophy for his accomplishments on the team.

15. The president of the United States is on vacation.

16. Joel wrote an excellent essay about Christopher Columbus.

Cumulative Review

Directions: Identify the part of speech of the words in bold. The first one has been done for you.

<u>preposition</u>

1. The dog ran **across** the field. _____

2. My **parents** allow me to stay up until 10:00 P.M. _____

3. Our cat **is** long-haired. _____

4. Matt will wash the **dirty** dishes. _____

5. Miguel washed the **car** on Saturday. _____

6. The waterfall crashed **over** the cliff. _____

7. What will you give **her**? _____

8. The car **rolled** to a stop. _____

9. He **slowly** finished his homework. _____

10. My **nephew** will be 12 years old on Sunday. _____

11. The news program discussed the **war**. _____

12. Our **family** portrait was taken in the gazebo. _____

13. I **would like** to learn to fly a plane. _____

14. **My** hair needs to be trimmed. _____

15. **Strawberry** jam is her favorite. _____

16. The horse **quickly** galloped across the field. _____

17. **What** will you do next? _____

18. Please stand **and** introduce yourself. _____

19. My neighbor takes **great** pride in her garden. _____

20. She sang **well** tonight. _____

21. My grandmother is from **Trinidad**. _____

Affect and *Effect*

Affect means "to act upon or influence."

Example: Studying will **affect** my test grade.

Effect means "to bring about a result or to accomplish something."

Example: The **effect** of her smile was immediate!

Directions: Write **affect** or **effect** in the blanks to complete these sentences correctly. The first one has been done for you.

__affects__   1. Your behavior (affects/effects) how others feel about you.

_____   2. His (affect/effect) on her was amazing.

_____   3. The (affect/effect) of his jacket was striking.

_____   4. What you say won't (affect/effect) me!

_____   5. There's a relationship between cause and (affect/effect).

_____   6. The (affect/effect) of her behavior was positive.

_____   7. The medicine (affected/effected) my stomach.

_____   8. What was the (affect/effect) of the punishment?

_____   9. Did his behavior (affect/effect) her performance?

_____   10. The cold (affected/effected) her breathing.

_____   11. The (affect/effect) was instantaneous!

_____   12. Your attitude will (affect/effect) your posture.

_____   13. The (affect/effect) on her posture was major.

_____   14. The (affect/effect) of the colored lights was calming.

_____   15. She (affected/effected) his behavior.

Among and *Between*

Among is a preposition that applies to more than two people or things.

Example: The group divided the marbles **among** themselves.

Between is a preposition that applies to only two people or things.

Example: The marbles were divided **between** Jeremy and Sara.

Directions: Write **between** or **among** in the blanks to complete these sentences correctly. The first one has been done for you.

___**between**___ 1. The secret is (between/among) you and Jon.

_____ 2. (Between/Among) the two of them, whom do you think is nicer?

_____ 3. I must choose (between/among) the goldfish, guppies, and tetras.

_____ 4. She threaded her way (between/among) the kids on the playground.

_____ 5. She broke up a fight (between/among) Josh and Sean.

_____ 6. "What's come (between/among) you two?" she asked.

_____ 7. "I'm (between/among) a rock and a hard place," Josh responded.

_____ 8. "He has to choose (between/among) all his friends," Sean added.

_____ 9. "Are you (between/among) his closest friends?" she asked Sean.

_____ 10. "It's (between/among) another boy and me," Sean replied.

_____ 11. "Can't you settle it (between/among) the group?"

_____ 12. "No," said Josh. "This is (between/among) Sean and me."

_____ 13. "I'm not sure he's (between/among) my closest friends."

_____ 14. Sean, Josh, and Andy began to argue (between/among) themselves.

_____ 15. I hope Josh won't have to choose (between/among) the two!

ENGLISH

Name _____

All Together and *Altogether*

All together is a phrase meaning "everyone or everything in the same place."

Example: We put the eggs **all together** in the bowl.

Altogether is an adverb that means "entirely, completely, or in all."

Example: The teacher gave **altogether** too much homework.

THE EGGS ARE
ALL TOGETHER

Directions: Write **altogether** or **all together** in the blanks to complete these sentences correctly. The first one has been done for you.

altogether   1. "You ate (altogether/all together) too much food."

_____   2. The girls sat (altogether/all together) on the bus.

_____   3. (Altogether/All together) now: one, two, three!

_____   4. I am (altogether/all together) out of ideas.

_____   5. We are (altogether/all together) on this project.

_____   6. "You have on (altogether/all together) too much makeup!"

_____   7. They were (altogether/all together) on the same team.

_____   8. (Altogether/All together), we can help stop

_____   pollution (altogether/all together).

_____   9. He was not (altogether/all together) happy with his grades.

_____   10. The kids were (altogether/all together) too loud.

_____   11. (Altogether/All together), the babies cried gustily.

_____   12. She was not (altogether/all together) sure what to do.

_____   13. Let's sing the song (altogether/all together).

_____   14. He was (altogether/all together) too pushy for her taste.

_____   15. (Altogether/All together), the boys yelled the school cheer.

Amount and *Number*

Amount indicates quantity, bulk, or mass.

Example: She carried a large **amount** of money in her purse.

Number indicates units.

Example: What **number** of people volunteered to work?

Directions: Write **amount** or **number** in the blanks to complete these sentences correctly. The first one has been done for you.

number 1. She did not (amount/number) him among her closest friends.

_____ 2. What (amount/number) of food should we order?

_____ 3. The (amount/number) of carrots on her plate was three.

_____ 4. His excuses did not (amount/number) to much.

_____ 5. Her contribution (amounted/numbered) to half the money raised.

_____ 6. The (amount/number) of injured players rose every day.

_____ 7. What a huge (amount/number) of cereal!

_____ 8. The (amount/number) of calories in the diet was low

_____ 9. I can't tell you the (amount/number) of friends she has!

_____ 10. The total (amount/number) of money raised was incredible!

_____ 11. The (amount/number) of gadgets for sale was amazing.

_____ 12. He was startled by the (amount/number) of people present.

_____ 13. He would not do it for any (amount/number) of money.

_____ 14. She offered a great (amount/number) of reasons for her actions.

_____ 15. Can you guess the (amount/number) of beans in the jar?

Irritate and *Aggravate*

Irritate means "to cause impatience, to provoke, or to annoy."

Example: His behavior **irritated** his father.

Aggravate means "to make a condition worse."

Example: Her sunburn was **aggravated** by additional exposure to the sun.

Directions: Write **aggravate** or **irritate** in the blanks to complete these sentences correctly. The first one has been done for you.

aggravated   1. The weeds (aggravated/irritated) his hay fever.

_____ 2. Scratching the bite (aggravated/irritated) his condition.

_____ 3. Her father was (aggravated/irritated) about her low grade in math.

_____ 4. It (aggravated/irritated) him when she switched TV channels.

_____ 5. Are you (aggravated/irritated) when the cat screeches?

_____ 6. Don't (aggravate/irritate) me like that again!

_____ 7. He was in a state of (aggravation/irritation).

_____ 8. Picking at the scab (aggravates/irritates) a sore.

_____ 9. Whistling (aggravates/irritates) the old grump.

_____ 10. She was (aggravated/irritated) when she learned about it.

_____ 11. "Please don't (aggravate/irritate) your mother," Dad warned.

_____ 12. His asthma was (aggravated/irritated) by too much stress.

_____ 13. Sneezing is sure to (aggravate/irritate) his allergies.

_____ 14. Did you do that just to (aggravate/irritate) me?

_____ 15. Her singing always (aggravated/irritated) her brother.

Principal and *Principle*

Principal means "main, leader or chief, or a sum of money that earns interest."

Examples:
The high school **principal** earned interest on the **principal** in his savings account.
The **principal** reason for his savings account was to save for retirement.

Principle means "a truth, law, or a moral outlook that governs the way someone behaves."

Example:
Einstein discovered some fundamental **principles** of science.
Stealing is against her **principles**.

Directions: Write **principle** or **principal** in the blanks to complete these sentences correctly. The first one has been done for you.

___principle___ 1. A (principle/principal) of biology is "the survival of the fittest."

_____ 2. She was a person of strong (principles/principals).

_____ 3. The (principles/principals) sat together at the district conference.

_____ 4. How much of the total in my savings account is (principle/principal)?

_____ 5. His hay fever was the (principle/principal) reason for his sneezing.

_____ 6. It's not the facts that upset me, it's the (principles/principals) of the case.

_____ 7. The jury heard only the (principle/principal) facts.

_____ 8. Our school (principle/principal) is strict but fair.

_____ 9. Spend the interest, but don't touch the (principle/principal).

_____ 10. Helping others is a guiding (principle/principal) of the homeless shelter.

_____ 11. In (principle/principal), we agree; on the facts, we do not.

_____ 12. The (principle/principal) course at dinner was leg of lamb.

_____ 13. Some mathematical (principles/principals) are difficult to understand.

_____ 14. The baby was the (principle/principal) reason for his happiness.

Comprehensive Curriculum - Grade 6

Name _____

Good and *Well*

Good is always an adjective. It is used to modify a noun or pronoun.

Examples:
 We enjoyed the **good** food.
 We had a **good** time yesterday.
 It was **good** to see her again.

Well is used to modify verbs, to describe someone's health, or to describe how someone is dressed.

Examples:
 I feel **well**. He looked **well**.
 He was **well**-dressed for the weather.
 She sang **well**.

Directions: Write **good** or **well** in the blanks to complete these sentences correctly.

1. She performed _____.

2. You look _____ in that color.

3. These apples are _____.

4. He rides his bike _____.

5. She made a _____ attempt to win the race.

6. The man reported that all was _____ in the coal mine.

7. Jonas said, "I feel _____, thank you."

8. The team played _____.

9. Mom fixed a _____ dinner.

10. The teacher wrote, " _____ work!" on top of my paper.

Like and *As*

Like means something is similar or resembles something else, and it describes how things are similar in manner.

Examples:
She could sing **like** an angel.
She looks **like** an angel, too!

As is a conjunction, or joining word, that links two independent clauses in a sentence.

Example: He felt chilly **as** night fell.

Sometimes **as** precedes an independent clause.

Example: As I told you, I will not be at the party.

Directions: Write **like** or **as** in the blanks to complete these sentences correctly. The first one has been done for you.

as 1. He did not behave (like/as) I expected.

_____ 2. She was (like/as) a sister to me.

_____ 3. The puppy acted (like/as) a baby!

_____ 4. (Like/As) I was saying, he will be there at noon.

_____ 5. The storm was 25 miles away, (like/as) he predicted.

_____ 6. He acted exactly (like/as) his father.

_____ 7. The song sounds (like/as) a hit to me!

_____ 8. Grandpa looked (like/as) a much younger man.

_____ 9. (Like/As) I listened to the music, I grew sleepy.

_____ 10. (Like/As) I expected, he showed up late.

_____ 11. She dances (like/as) a ballerina!

_____ 12. (Like/As) she danced, the crowd applauded.

_____ 13. On stage, she looks (like/as) a professional!

_____ 14. (Like/As) I thought, she has taken lessons for years.

Review

Directions: Write the correct word in the blank.

_____ 1. The (affect/effect) of the shot was immediate.

_____ 2. The shot (affected/effected) her allergies.

_____ 3. You have a positive (affect/effect) on me!

_____ 4. I was deeply (affected/effected) by the speech.

_____ 5. The prize was shared (among/between) Malik and Lola.

_____ 6. She was (among/between) the best students in the class.

_____ 7. He felt he was (among/between) friends.

_____ 8. It was hard to choose (among/between) all the gifts.

_____ 9. Does it (irritate/aggravate) you to see people behave rudely?

_____ 10. Does coughing (irritate/aggravate) his sore throat?

_____ 11. He wondered why she was (irritated/aggravated) at him.

_____ 12. The intensity of his (irritation/aggravation) grew each day.

_____ 13. She had a (principal/principle) part in the play.

_____ 14. Beans were the (principal/principle) food in his diet.

_____ 15. She was a woman of strong (principals/principles).

_____ 16. Mr. Larson was their favorite (principal/principle).

_____ 17. The (amount/number) of bananas he ate was incredible.

_____ 18. I wouldn't part with it for any (amount/number) of money.

_____ 19. It happened exactly (like/as) I had predicted!

_____ 20. He sounds almost (like/as) his parents.

Review

Directions: Use these words in sentences of your own.

1. affect _____
_____

2. effect _____
_____

3. among _____
_____

4. between _____
_____

5. irritate _____
_____

6. aggravate _____
_____

7. principal _____
_____

8. principle _____
_____

9. good _____
_____

10. well _____
_____

11. like _____
_____

12. as _____
_____

Name _____

Capitalization

Capitalize . . .
. . . the first word in a sentence.
. . . the first letter of a person's name.
. . . proper nouns, like the names of planets, oceans, and mountain ranges.
. . . titles when used with a person's name, even if abbreviated (Dr., Mr., Lt.).
. . . days of the week and months of the year.
. . . cities, states, and countries.

Directions: Write **C** in the blank if the word or phrase is capitalized correctly. Rewrite the word or phrase if it is incorrect.

1. _____ President Abraham Lincoln _____
2. _____ Larry D. Walters _____
3. _____ saturn _____
4. _____ rosa parks _____
5. _____ August _____
6. _____ professional _____
7. _____ jupiter _____
8. _____ Pacific Ocean _____
9. _____ white house _____
10. _____ pet _____
11. _____ Congress _____
12. _____ Houston _____
13. _____ federal government _____
14. _____ dr. Nina Alvarez _____
15. _____ milwaukee, Wisconsin _____
16. _____ Appalachian mountains _____
17. _____ lake michigan _____
18. _____ Notre Dame College _____
19. _____ department of the Interior _____
20. _____ monday and Tuesday _____

Capitalization

Words that name places, people, months, and landmarks are always capitalized.

Examples:

Sonia Sotomayor	Acme Motor Company
White House	Jefferson Memorial
Fifth Avenue	May, June, July

Directions: Rewrite the sentences using correct capitalization.

1. My family and I visited washington, d.c., in july.

_____

2. We saw the washington monument, the capital building, and the white house.

_____

3. I was very impressed by our visit to the smithsonian institution.

_____

4. Our taxi driver, from the american cab company, showed us around town.

_____

5. We drove down pennsylvania avenue.

_____

6. We were unable to see the president of the united states.

_____

7. However, we did see the first lady.

_____

8. My parents and I decided to visit arlington national cemetery.

_____

Commas

Use **commas** . . .
   . . . after introductory phrases.
   . . . to set off nouns of direct address.
   . . . to set off appositives from the words that go with them.
   . . . to set off words that interrupt the flow of the sentence.
   . . . to separate words or groups of words in a series.

Examples:
   Introductory phrase: Of course, I'd be happy to attend.
   Noun of direct address: Ms. Williams, please sit here.
   To set off appositives: Lee, **the club president**, sat beside me.
   Words interrupting flow: My cousin, **who's 13**, will also be there.
   Words in a series: I ate **popcorn**, **peanuts**, **sunflower seeds**, and **dried berries**.

Directions: Identify how the commas are used in each sentence.
   Write: **I** for introductory phrase
   N for noun of direct address
   A for appositive
   WF for words interrupting flow
   WS for words in a series

_____ 1. Yes, she is my sister.

_____ 2. My teacher, Mr. Hopkins, is very fair.

_____ 3. Her favorite fruits are oranges, plums, and grapes.

_____ 4. The city mayor, Carla Ellison, is quite young.

_____ 5. I will buy bread, milk, fruit, and ice cream.

_____ 6. Her crying, which was quite loud, soon gave me a headache.

_____ 7. Sanjana, please answer the question.

_____ 8. So, do you know her?

_____ 9. Unfortunately, the item is not returnable.

_____ 10. My sister, my cousin, and my friend will accompany me on vacation.

_____ 11. My grandparents, Rose and Bill, are both 57 years old.

Commas

Directions: Use commas to punctuate these sentences correctly.

Commas are important, and you should know when to use them!

COMMAS

1. I'll visit her however not until I'm ready.

2. She ordered coats gloves and a hat from the catalog.

3. Eun-Jung the new girl looked ill at ease.

4. Certainly I'll show Eun-Jung around school.

5. Yes I'll be glad to help her.

6. I paid nevertheless I was unhappy with the price.

7. I bought stamps envelopes and plenty of postcards.

8. No I told you I was not going.

9. The date November 12 was not convenient.

10. Her earache which kept her up all night stopped at dawn.

11. My nephew who loves bike riding will go with us.

12. He'll bring hiking boots a tent and food.

13. The cat a Himalayan was beautiful.

14. The tennis player a professional in every sense signed autographs.

15. No you can't stay out past 10:00 P.M.

Semicolons

A **semicolon** (;) signals a reader to pause longer than for a comma, but not as long as for a period. Semicolons are used between closely related independent clauses not joined by **and**, **or**, **nor**, **for**, **yet**, or **but**.

An **independent clause** contains a complete idea and can stand alone.

Example: Rena was outgoing; her sister was shy.

Directions: Use semicolons to punctuate these sentences correctly. Some sentences require more than one semicolon.

1. Jeff wanted coffee Sophia wanted milk.

2. I thought he was kind she thought he was grouchy.

3. "I came I saw I conquered," wrote Julius Caesar.

4. Harper read books she also read magazines.

5. I wanted a new coat my old one was too small.

6. The airport was fogged-in the planes could not land.

7. Now, he regrets his comments it's too late to retract them.

8. The girls were thrilled their mothers were not.

Directions: Use a semicolon and an independent clause to complete the sentences.

9. She liked him _____

10. I chose a red shirt _____

11. Andrea sang well _____

12. She jumped for joy _____

13. Dancing is good exercise _____

14. The man was kind _____

15. The tire looked flat _____

16. My bike is missing _____

Colons

Use a **colon** . . .
   . . . after the salutation of a business letter.
   . . . between the hour and the minute when showing time.
   . . . between the volume and page number of a periodical.
   . . . between chapters and verses of the Bible.
   . . . before a list of three or more items.
   . . . to introduce a long statement or quotation.

Dear Mr. Ahmad:

I would like to place an order for five of your 1-ton scales. Please contact me concerning price and delivery date.

Sincerely,
Ms. McDonnell

Examples:
Salutation: Dear Madame:
Hour and minute: 8:45 P.M.
Periodical volume and page number: Newsweek 11:32
Bible chapter and verse: John 3:16
Before a list of three or more items: Buy these: fruit, cereal, cheese
To introduce a long statement or quotation: Author Willa Cather said this about experiencing life: "There are only two or three human stories, and they go on repeating themselves as fiercely as if they had never happened before."

Directions: Use colons to punctuate these sentences correctly. Some sentences require more than one colon.

1. At 12 45 the president said this "Where's my lunch?"

2. Don't forget to order these items boots, socks, shoes, and leggings.

3. Ask the librarian for Weekly Reader 3 14.

4. Dear Sir Please send me two copies of your report.

5. Avoid these at all costs bad jokes, bad company, and bad manners.

6. The statement is in either Genesis 1 6 or Exodus 3 2.

7. At 9 15 P.M., she checked in, and at 6 45 A.M., she checked out.

8. I felt all these things at once joy, anger, and sadness.

Dashes

Dashes (—) are used to indicate sudden changes of thought.

Examples:
I want milk—no, make that juice—with my lunch.
Wear your old clothes—new ones would get spoiled.

Directions: If the dash is used correctly in the sentence, write **C** in the blank. If the dash is missing or used incorrectly, write **X** in the blank. The first one has been done for you.

__*C*__ 1. No one—not even my dad—knows about the surprise.

_____ 2. Ask—him—no I will to come to the party.

_____ 3. I'll tell you the answer oh, the phone just rang!

_____ 4. Everyone thought—even her brother—that she looked pretty.

_____ 5. Can you please—oh, forget it!

_____ 6. Just stop it I really mean it!

_____ 7. Tell her that I'll—never mind—I'll tell her myself!

_____ 8. Everyone especially Anna is overwhelmed.

_____ 9. I wish everyone could—forgive me—I'm sorry!

_____ 10. The kids—all six of them—piled into the backseat.

Directions: Write two sentences of your own that include dashes.

11. _____

_____

12. _____

_____

Quotation Marks

Quotation marks are used to enclose a speaker's exact words. Use commas to set off a direct quotation from other words in the sentence.

Examples:
Kira smiled and said, "Quotation marks come in handy."
"Yes," Josh said, "I'll take two."

Directions: If quotation marks and commas are used correctly, write **C** in the blank. If they are used incorrectly, write **X** in the blank. The first one has been done for you.

__C__ 1. "I suppose," Elizabeth remarked, "that you'll be there on time."

_____ 2. "Please let me help! insisted Mark.

_____ 3. I'll be ready in 2 minutes!" her father said.

_____ 4. "Just breathe slowly," the nurse said, "and calm down."

_____ 5. "No one understands me" William whined.

_____ 6. "Would you like more milk?" Jasmine asked politely.

_____ 7. "No thanks, her grandpa replied, "I have plenty."

_____ 8. "What a beautiful morning!" Zola yelled.

_____ 9. "Yes, it certainly is" her mother agreed.

_____ 10. "Whose purse is this?" asked Andrea.

_____ 11. It's mine" said Nadia. "Thank you."

_____ 12. "Can you play the piano?" asked Beatriz.

_____ 13. "Music is my hobby." Jonathan replied.

_____ 14. Great!" yelled Harry. Let's play some tunes."

_____ 15. "I practice a lot," said Jayne proudly.

"This is exactly what I'm saying! You can tell by my quotation marks!"

Quotation Marks

Directions: Use quotation marks and commas to punctuate these sentences correctly.

"Remember: quotation marks are used to enclose a speaker's exact words."

1. No Ms. Elliot replied you may not go.

2. Watch out! yelled the coach.

3. Please bring my coat called Renee.

4. After thinking for a moment, Paul said I don't believe you.

5. Dad said Remember to be home by 9:00 P.M.

6. Finish your projects said the art instructor.

7. Go back instructed Mom and comb your hair.

8. I won't be needing my winter coat anymore replied Mei-ling.

9. He said How did you do that?

10. I stood and said My name is Rosalita.

11. No said Misha I will not attend.

12. Don't forget to put your name on your paper said the teacher.

13. Pay attention, class said our history teacher

14. As I came into the house, Mom called Dinner is almost ready!

15. Jake, come when I call you said Mother.

16. How was your trip to France Mrs. Shaw? asked Grace.

Apostrophes

Use an **apostrophe** (') in a contraction to show that letters have been left out. A **contraction** is a shortened form of two words, usually a pronoun and a verb.

Add an **apostrophe** and **s** to form the **possessive** of singular nouns. **Plural possessives** are formed two ways. If the noun ends in **s**, simply add an apostrophe at the end of the word. If the noun does not end in **s**, add an apostrophe and **s**.

Examples:
   Contraction: He **can't** button his sleeves.
   Singular possessive: The **boy's** sleeves are too short.
   Plural noun ending in s: The **ladies'** voices were pleasant.
   Plural noun not ending in s: The **children's** song was long.

Directions: Use apostrophes to punctuate the sentences correctly. The first one has been done for you.

1. I can't understand that child's game.

2. The farmers wagons were lined up in a row.

3. She didnt like the chairs covers.

4. Our parents beliefs are often our own.

5. Elenas mothers aunt isnt going to visit.

6. Two ladies from work didnt show up.

7. The citizens group wasnt very happy.

8. The colonists demands werent unreasonable.

9. The mothers babies cried at the same time.

10. Our parents generation enjoys music.

Directions: Write two sentences of your own that include apostrophes.

11. _____

   _____

12. _____

   _____

Contractions

Examples:
he will = **he'll**
she is = **she's**
they are = **they're**
can not = **can't**

Contraction Chart

Pronoun		Verb		Contraction
I	+	am	=	I'm
we, you, they	+	are	=	we're, you're, they're
he, she, it	+	is	=	he's, she's, it's
I, we, you, they	+	have	=	I've, we've, you've, they've
I, you, we, she, he, they	+	would	=	I'd, you'd, we'd, she'd, he'd, they'd
I, you, we, she, he, they	+	will	=	I'll, you'll, we'll, she'll, he'll, they'll

Directions: Write a sentence using a contraction. The first one has been done for you.

1. I will _____ I'll see you tomorrow! _____

2. they are _____

3. we have _____

4. she would _____

5. you are _____

6. they will _____

7. she is _____

8. he would _____

9. they are _____

10. I am _____

Singular Possessives

Directions: Write the singular possessive form of each word. Then, add a noun to show possession. The first one has been done for you.

1. spider _spider's web_ _____

2. clock _____

3. car _____

4. book _____

5. Mom _____

6. boat _____

7. table _____

8. baby _____

9. woman _____

10. writer _____

11. mouse _____

12. fan _____

13. lamp _____

14. dog _____

15. boy _____

16. house _____

Plural Possessives

Directions: Write the plural possessive form of each word. Then, add a noun to show possession. The first one has been done for you.

1. kid _____kids' skates_____

2. man _____

3. aunt _____

4. lion _____

5. giraffe _____

6. necklace _____

7. mouse _____

8. team _____

9. clown _____

10. desk _____

11. woman _____

12. worker _____

Directions: Write three sentences of your own that include plural possessives.

13. _____

_____

14. _____

_____

15. _____

_____

Italics

Use **italics** or **underlining** for titles of books, newspapers, plays, magazines, and movies.

Examples:
Book: Have you read *The Humming Room*?
Movie: Did you see *The Muppet Movie*?
Newspaper: I like to read *The New York Times*.
Magazine: Some children read *Sports Illustrated*.
Play: My school is putting on the play *Peter Pan*.

Since we cannot write in italics, we underline words that should be in italics.

Directions: Underline the words that should be in italics. The first one has been done for you.

1. I read about a play titled <u>Cats</u> in <u>The Cleveland Plain Dealer</u>.

2. You can find The New York Times in most libraries.

3. L. M. Montgomery wrote Anne of Green Gables.

4. Parents and Newsweek are both popular magazines.

5. The original Miracle on 34th Street was filmed long ago.

6. Cricket and Ranger Rick are magazines for children.

7. Bon Appetit means "good appetite" and is a cooking magazine.

8. Harper's, The New Yorker, and Vanity Fair are magazines.

9. David Copperfield was written by Charles Dickens.

10. Harriet Beecher Stowe wrote Uncle Tom's Cabin.

11. My cousin has watched The LEGO Movie four times.

12. Jake and Lily is by one of my favorite authors—Jerry Spinelli.

13. The Louisville Courier-Journal is a Kentucky newspaper.

14. American Girl and Boys' Life are magazines for young readers.

15. My whole family loved Disney's nature film Bears.

Complete Sentences

A **complete sentence** has both a simple subject and a simple predicate. It is a complete thought. Sentences that are not complete are called **fragments**.

Example:
   Complete sentence: The wolf howled at the moon.
   Sentence fragment: Howled at the moon.

Directions: Write **C** on the line if the sentence is complete. Write **F** if it is a fragment.

1. _____ The machine is running.

2. _____ What will we do today?

3. _____ Knowing what I do.

4. _____ That statement is true.

5. _____ My parents drove to town.

6. _____ Watching television all afternoon.

7. _____ The storm devastated the town.

8. _____ Our friends can go with us.

9. _____ The palm trees bent in the wind.

10. _____ Spraying the fire all night.

Directions: Rewrite the sentence fragments from above to make them complete sentences.

_____

_____

_____

_____

Run-On Sentences

A **run-on sentence** occurs when two or more sentences are joined together without punctuation or a joining word. Run-on sentences should be divided into two or more separate sentences.

Example:

Run-on sentence: My parents, sister, brother, and I went to the park we saw many animals we had fun.

Correct: My parents, sister, brother, and I went to the park. We saw many animals and had fun.

Directions: Rewrite the run-on sentences correctly.

1. The dog energetically chased the ball I kept throwing him the ball for a half hour.

_____

_____

_____

2. The restaurant served scrambled eggs and bacon for breakfast I had some and they were delicious.

_____

_____

_____

3. The lightning struck close to our house it scared my little brother and my grandmother called to see if we were safe.

_____

_____

_____

_____

_____

Finding Spelling Errors

Name _____

Directions: One word in each sentence below is misspelled. Write the word correctly on the line.

1. Isaiah felt discoraged at the comparison between

   him and his older brother. _____

2. I got inpatient as my curiosity grew. _____

3. She confided that she had not finished the asignment. _____

4. They made the selection after a brief conferrence. _____

5. Obviusly, it's impolite to sneeze on someone. _____

6. This skin cream is practicaly invisible. _____

7. What would prevent you from taking on addtional work? _____

8. I can resite the words to that hymn. _____

9. In a previous columm, the newspaper explained the situation. _____

10. He decieved me so many times that now I distrust him. _____

11. Please have the curtesy to observe the "No Eating" signs. _____

12. The advertisement is so small that it's nearly invisble. _____

13. The best way to communicate is in a face-to-face conservation.

   _____

14. In a cost comparson, salmon is more expensive than tuna. _____

15. Poplarity among friends shouldn't depend on your accomplishments.

   _____

16. Her campaign was quite an acheivement. _____

17. He condemmed it as a poor imitation. _____

Finding Spelling Errors

Directions: Circle all misspelled words. Write the words correctly on the lines at the end of each paragraph. If you need help, consult a dictionary.

Sabrina wanted to aquire a saltwater acquarum. She was worried about the expence, though, so first she did some reseach. She wanted to learn the exxact care saltwater fish need, not just to exsist but to florish. One sorce said she needed to put water in the aquarium and wait 6 weeks before she added the fish. "Good greif!" Sabrina thought. She got a kitten from her nieghbor instead.

_____

_____

_____

One stormy day, Marcel was babysitting his neice. He happened to obsurve that the sky looked darker than norml. At first he ignorred it, but then he noticed a black cloud exxpand and grow in hieght. Then, a tail dropped down from the twisting cloud and siezed a tree! "It's a tornado!" Marcel shouted. "Maybe two tornados! This is an emergensy!" For a breef moment Marcel wished he hadn't shouted, because his niece looked at him with a very frightened expresion. Just then, the cieling began to sag as if it had a heavy wieght on it. "This is an excelent time to visit the basement," he told the little girl as calmy as possible.

_____

_____

Just before Mother's Day, Bethany went to a flourist to buy some flowers for her mother. "Well, what is your reqest?" the clerk asked. "I don't have much money," Bethany told him. "So make up your mind," he said impatiently. "Do you want qualitiy or quanity?" Bethany wondered if he was giving her a quizz. She tried not to sqwirm as he stared down at her. Finally, she said, "I want cortesy," as she headed for the exxit.

_____

_____

_____

Finding Spelling Errors

Directions: Find six errors in each paragraph. Write the words correctly on the lines after each paragraph. Use a dictionary if you need help.

My brother Jim took a math coarse at the high school that was too hard for hymn. My father didn't want him to take it, but Jim said, "Oh, you're just too critcal, Dad. Oviously, you don't think I can do it." Jim ingored Dad. That's norm at our house.

_____

_____

Well, the first day Jim went to the course, he came home with a solem expreion on his face, like a condemed man. "That teacher assined us five pages of homework!" he said. "And two addtional problems that we have to reserch!"

_____

_____

"He sounds like an excelent, profesional teacher," my dad said. "We need more teachers of that qwalitu in our schools." Jim squirmed in his seat. Then, he gradualy started to smile. "Dad, I need some help with a personl problem," he said. "Five pages of problems, right?" Dad asked. Jim smiled and handed Dad his math book. That's tipical at our house, too.

_____

_____

One day, we had a meddical emergensy at home. My sisters' hand got stuck in a basket with a narrow opening, and she couldn't pull it out. I thought she would have to wear the basket on her hand permanentally! First, I tried to stretch and exxpand the baskets opening, but that didn't work.

_____

_____

Then, I smeared a quanity of butter on my sisters hand, and she pulled it right out. I thought she would have the curtesy to thank me, but she just stomped away, still mad. How childsh! Sometimes she seems to think I exxist just to serve her. There are more importanter things in the world than her happiness!

_____

_____

Writing: Four Types of Sentences

There are four main types of sentences: A **statement** tells something. It ends in a period. A **question** asks something. It ends in a question mark. A **command** tells someone to do something. It ends in a period or an exclamation mark. An **exclamation** shows strong feeling or excitement. It ends in an exclamation mark.

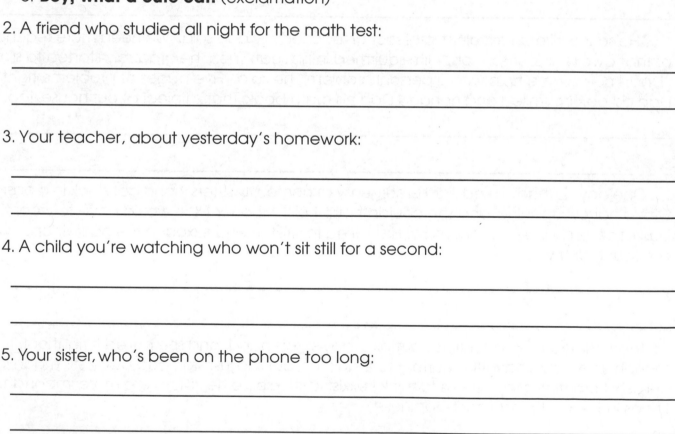

Boy, what a cute cat!

Directions: Write what you would say in each situation. Then, tell whether the sentence you wrote was a statement, question, exclamation, or command. The first one has been done for you.

Write what you might say to:

1. A friend who has a new cat:
   When did you get the new cat? (question)
   or **Boy, what a cute cat!** (exclamation)

2. A friend who studied all night for the math test:

   _____

   _____

3. Your teacher, about yesterday's homework:

   _____

   _____

4. A child you're watching who won't sit still for a second:

   _____

   _____

5. Your sister, who's been on the phone too long:

   _____

   _____

Organizing Paragraphs

A **topic sentence** states the main idea of a paragraph and is usually the first sentence. **Support sentences** follow, providing details about the topic. All sentences in a paragraph should relate to the topic sentence. A paragraph ends with a **conclusion sentence**.

Directions: Rearrange each group of sentences into a paragraph, beginning with the topic sentence. Cross out the sentence in each group that is not related to the topic sentence. Write the new paragraph.

Now, chalk drawings are considered art by themselves. The earliest chalk drawings were found on the walls of caves. Chalk is also used in cement, fertilizer, toothpaste, and makeup. Chalk once was used just to make quick sketches. Chalk has been used for drawing for thousands of years. Then, the artist would paint pictures from the sketches.

_____

_____

_____

_____

Dams also keep young salmon from swimming downriver to the ocean. Most salmon live in the ocean but return to fresh water to lay their eggs and breed. Dams prevent salmon from swimming upriver to their spawning grounds. Pacific salmon die after they spawn the first time. One kind of fish pass is a series of pools of water that lead the salmon over the dams. Dams are threatening salmon by interfering with their spawning. To help with this problem, some dams have special "fish passes" to allow salmon to swim over the dam.

_____

_____

_____

_____

_____

Building Paragraphs

Directions: Read each group of questions and the topic sentence. On another sheet of paper, write support sentences that answer each question. Number your support sentence in order. Make any necessary changes so the sentences fit together in one paragraph. Then, write your paragraph after the topic sentence.

Questions: Why did Noah feel sad?
How did happened to change how he felt?
How does he feel when he comes to school now?

Noah used to look so solemn when he came to school. _____

_____

_____

_____

Questions: Why did Sienna want to go to another country?
Why couldn't she go?
Does she have any plans to change that?

Sienna always wanted to visit a foreign country. _____

_____

_____

_____

Questions: What was Paulo's "new way to fix spaghetti"?
Did anyone else like it?
Did Paulo like it himself?

Paulo thought of a new way to fix spaghetti. _____

_____

_____

_____

Explaining with Examples

Some paragraphs paint word pictures using adjectives, adverbs, similes, and metaphors. Other paragraphs explain by naming examples.

Example:

Babysitting is not an easy way to earn money. For example, the little girl you're watching may be very cranky and cry until her parents come home. Or maybe the family didn't leave any snacks and you have to starve all night. Even worse, the child could fall and get hurt. Then, you have to decide whether you can take care of her yourself or If you need to call for help. No, babysitting isn't easy.

Directions: Write examples for each topic sentence on another sheet of paper. Number them in order to put them in paragraph form. Make any necessary changes so the sentences fit together in one paragraph. Then, write your paragraphs below after the topic sentences.

1. Sometimes, dreams can be scary. _____

_____

_____

_____

_____

_____

_____

2. You can learn a lot by living in a foreign country. _____

_____

_____

_____

_____

_____

_____

Name _____

Creating Word Pictures

Painters create pictures with colors. Writers create pictures with words. Adding adjectives and adverbs and using specific nouns, verbs, similes, and metaphors in sentences help create word pictures.

Notice how much more interesting and informative these two rewritten sentences are.

Original sentence
The animal ate its food.

Rewritten sentences
Like a hungry lion, the starving cocker spaniel wolfed down the entire bowl of food in seconds.

The raccoon delicately washed the berries in the stream before nibbling them slowly, one by one.

Directions: Rewrite each sentence twice, creating two different word pictures.

1. The person built something.

_____

_____

2. The weather was bad.

_____

_____

3. The boy went down the street.

_____

_____

4. The children helped.

_____

_____

Describing People

Often, a writer can show how someone feels by describing how that person looks or what he or she is doing, rather than by using emotion words, like **angry** or **happy**. This is another way to create word pictures.

Directions: Read the phrases below. Write words to describe how you think that person feels.

1. like a tornado, yelling, raised fists _____

2. slumped, walking slowly, head down _____

3. trembling, breathing quickly, like a cornered animal _____

Directions: Write one or two sentences for each phrase without using emotion words.

4. a runner who has just won a race for his or her school _____

_____

_____

5. a sixth grader on the first day in a new school _____

_____

_____

6. a teenager walking down the street and spotting a house on fire _____

_____

_____

7. a scientist who has just discovered a cure for lung cancer _____

_____

_____

8. a kindergarten child being ignored by his or her best friend _____

_____

_____

Describing Events in Order

When we write to explain what happened, we need to describe the events in the same order they occurred. Words and phrases such as **at first**, **then**, **after that**, and **finally** help us relate the order of events.

Directions: Rewrite the paragraph below, putting the topic sentence first and arranging the events in order.

    I got dressed, but I didn't really feel like eating breakfast. By the time I got to school, my head felt hot, so I went to the nurse. This day was terrible from the very beginning. Finally, I ended up where I started—back in my own bed. Then, she sent me home again! I just had some toast and left for school. When I first woke up in the morning, my stomach hurt.

_____

_____

_____

_____

_____

Directions: Follow these steps to write a paragraph about what happened the last time you tried to cook something or the last time you tried to fix something that was broken.

1. Write your first draft on another sheet of paper. Start with a topic sentence.
2. Add support sentences to explain what happened. Include phrases to keep things in order: **at first**, **then**, **after that**, **finally**, **in the middle of it**, **at last**.
3. Read your paragraph out loud to see if it reads smoothly. Make sure the events are in the correct order.
4. Make any needed changes, and then write your paragraph below.

_____

_____

_____

_____

Explaining What Happened

Directions: These pictures tell a story, but they're out of order. Follow these steps to write what happened.

1. On another sheet of paper, write a sentence explaining what is happening in each picture.
2. Put your sentences in order, and write a topic sentence.
3. Read the whole paragraph to yourself. Add words to show the order in which things happened.
4. Include adjectives, adverbs, and a simile or metaphor to make your story more interesting.
5. Write your paragraph below. Be sure to give it a title.

_____

_____

_____

_____

_____

_____

_____

_____

_____

_____

Writing Directions

Directions: must be written clearly. They are easiest to follow when they are in numbered steps. Each step should begin with a verb.

How to Peel a Banana:

1. Hold the banana by the stem end.
2. Find a loose edge of peel at the top.
3. Pull the peel down.
4. Peel the other sections of the banana in the same way.

Directions: Rewrite these directions, number the steps in order, and begin with verbs.

How to Feed a Dog

Finally, call the dog to come and eat. Then, you carry the filled dish to the place where the dog eats. The can or bag should be opened by you. First, clean the dog's food dish with soap and water. Then, get the dog food out of the cupboard. Put the correct amount of food in the dish.

_____

_____

_____

_____

_____

Directions: Follow these steps to write your own directions.

1. On another sheet of paper, draw three symbols, such as a square with a star in one corner and a dot in the center, or a triangle inside a circle with a spiral in the middle. Don't show your drawing to anyone.
2. On a second sheet of paper, write instructions to make the same drawing. Your directions need to be clear, in order, and numbered. Each step needs to begin with a verb.
3. Trade directions (but not pictures) with a partner. See if you can follow each other's directions to make the drawings.
4. Show your partner the drawing you made in step one. Does it look like the one he or she made following your directions? Could you follow your partner's directions? Share what was clear—or not so clear—about each other's instructions.

Review

Directions: Write paragraphs to match the descriptions given. Begin with a topic sentence, and add support sentences that tell the events in order. Write the first draft of your paragraph on another sheet of paper. Read it to yourself, make any necessary changes, and then write it below.

1. Write a short paragraph to explain something that might happen on your way to school.

   _____

   _____

   _____

   _____

   _____

2. Write a paragraph that tells what you usually do during the first hour after you get up on a school day.

   _____

   _____

   _____

   _____

   _____

Directions: Write directions explaining how to brush your teeth. Include at least four steps. Make them as clear as possible. Begin each step with a verb. Write a rough draft on another sheet of paper first.

1. _____

2. _____

3. _____

4. _____

Writing: Stronger Sentences

Sometimes the noun form of a word is not the best way to express an idea. Compare these two sentences:

They made preparations for the party.
They prepared for the party.

The second sentence, using **prepared** as a verb, is shorter and stronger.

Directions: Write one word to replace a whole phrase. Cross out the words you don't need. The first one has been done for you.

1. She ~~made a suggestion~~ that we go on Monday.
   suggested

2. They arranged decorations around the room.

3. Let's make a combination of the two ideas.

4. I have great appreciation for what you did.

5. The buses are acting as transportation for the classes.

6. The group made an exploration of the Arctic Circle.

7. Please make a selection of one quickly.

8. The lake is making a reflection of the trees.

9. The family had a celebration of the holiday.

10. Would you please provide a solution for this problem?

11. Rashid made an imitation of his cat.

12. Please give a definition of that word.

13. I made an examination of the broken bike.

14. Dexter made an invitation for us to join him.

> Write one word to replace a whole phrase.

Writing: Descriptive Sentences

Descriptive sentences make writing more interesting to the reader. This is done by using adjectives, adverbs, prepositional phrases, similes, and metaphors.

Example:
The dog ran down the hill.
The black and white beagle bounded down the steep embankment as though being chased by an invisible dragon.

Directions: Rewrite these sentences so they are more descriptive.

1. Parker likes collecting stamps.

_____

2. Martina drove into town.

_____

3. I enjoy working on the computer.

_____

4. Riverside won the game.

_____

5. Dinner was great.

_____

6. My mom collects antiques.

_____

7. The teacher likes my essay.

_____

8. My brother received a scholarship for college.

_____

Comprehensive Curriculum - Grade 6

Writing: Different Points of View

A **fact** is a statement that can be proved. An **opinion** is what someone thinks or believes.

Directions: Write **F** if the statement is a fact or **O** if it is an opinion.

1. _____ The amusement park near our town just opened last summer.

2. _____ It's the best one in our state.

3. _____ It has a roller coaster that's 300 feet high.

4. _____ You're a chicken if you don't go on it.

Directions: Think about the last movie or TV show you saw. Write one fact and one opinion about it.

OPINION

FACT

Fact: _____

Opinion: _____

In a story, a **point of view** is how one character feels about an event and reacts to it. Different points of view show how characters feel about the same situation.

What if you were at the mall with a friend and saw a shirt you really wanted on sale? You didn't bring enough money, so you borrowed ten dollars from your friend to buy the shirt. Then, you lost the money in the store!

Directions: Write a sentence describing what happened from the point of view of each person named below. Explain how each person felt.

Yourself_____

_____

Your friend _____

_____

The store clerk who watched you look for the money_____

_____

The person who found the money_____

_____

Reading Skills: It's Your Opinion

Your opinion is how you feel or think about something. Although other people may have the same opinion, their reasons will not be exactly the same because of their individuality.

When writing an opinion paragraph, it is important to first state your opinion. Then, in at least three sentences, support your opinion. Finally, end your paragraph by restating your opinion in different words.

Example:

I believe dogs are excellent pets. For thousands of years, dogs have guarded and protected their owners. Dogs are faithful and have been known to save the lives of those they love. Dogs offer unconditional love, as well as company for the quiet times in our lives. For these reasons, I feel that dogs make wonderful pets.

Directions: Write an opinion paragraph on whether you would or would not like to have lived in Colonial America. Be sure to support your opinion with at least three reasons.

_____

_____

_____

_____

_____

_____

_____

Writing Checklist

Reread your paragraph carefully.

☐ My paragraph makes sense.   ☐ I have a good opening and ending.

☐ There are no jumps in ideas.   ☐ I used correct spelling.

☐ I used correct punctuation.   ☐ My paragraph is well-organized.

☐ My paragraph is interesting.

Persuasive Writing

To **persuade** means to convince someone that your opinion is correct. You need to offer reasons, facts, and examples to support your opinion.

Directions: Write two reasons or facts and two examples to persuade someone.

1. Riding a bicycle "no-handed" on a busy street is a bad idea.

    Reasons/Facts: _____

    _____

    Examples: _____

    _____

    _____

2. Taking medicine prescribed by a doctor for someone else is dangerous.

    Reasons/Facts: _____

    _____

    Examples: _____

    _____

    _____

3. Learning to read well will help you in every other subject in school.

    Reasons/Facts: _____

    _____

    Examples: _____

    _____

    _____

Persuasive Writing

When trying to persuade someone, it helps to look at both sides of the issue. If you can understand both sides, you will have a better idea how to convince someone of your point of view.

Directions: Follow these steps to write two persuasive paragraphs about which form of transportation is better: airplanes or cars.

1. On another sheet of paper, list three or four reasons why planes are better and three or four reasons why cars are better.
2. Put each list of reasons in order. Often, persuasive writing is strongest when the best reason is placed last. Readers tend to remember the last reason best.
3. Write topic sentences for each paragraph.
4. Read each paragraph, and make any necessary changes so one sentence leads smoothly to the next.
5. Write your paragraphs below.

Airplanes Are Better Transportation Than Cars _____

_____

_____

_____

_____

Cars Are Better Transportation Than Planes _____

_____

_____

_____

_____

6. Write two more paragraphs on another sheet of paper. Select any topic. Write from both points of view.

Persuasive Writing

Writing is usually more persuasive if written from the reader's point of view.

If you made muffins to sell at a school fair, which of these sentences would you write on your sign?

    I spent a lot of time making these muffins.
    These muffins taste delicious!

If you were writing to ask your school board to start a gymnastics program, which sentence would be more persuasive?

    I really am interested in gymnastics.
    Gymnastics would be good for our school because both boys and girls can participate, and it's a year-round sport we can do in any weather.

In both situations, the second sentence is more persuasive because it is written from the reader's point of view. People care how the muffins taste, not how long it took you to make them. The school board wants to provide activities for all the students, not just you.

Directions: Write **R** if the statement is written from the reader's point of view or **W** if it's written from the writer's point of view.

_____ 1. If you come swimming with me, you'll be able to cool off.

_____ 2. Come swimming with me. I don't want to go alone.

_____ 3. Please write me a letter. I really like to get mail.

_____ 4. Please write me a letter. I want to hear from you.

Directions: Follow these steps to write an invitation on another sheet of paper to persuade people to move to your town or city.

1. Think about reasons someone would want to live in your town. Make a list of all the good things there, like the schools, parks, annual parades, historic buildings, businesses where parents could work, scout groups, Little League, and so on. You might also describe your town's population, transportation, restaurants, celebrations, or even holiday decorations.
2. Now, select three or four items from your list. Write a sentence (or two) about each one from the reader's point of view. For example, instead of writing "Our Little League team won the championship again last year," you could tell the reader, "You could help our Little League team win the championship again this year."
3. Write a topic sentence to begin your invitation, and put your support sentences in order after it.
4. Read your invitation out loud to another person. Make any needed changes, and copy the invitation onto a clean sheet of paper.

Review

Directions: Read the questions. Then, write one or two sentences about the situation from both points of view.

What if your neighbor had a dog that barked all night and kept you awake?

Your point of view: _____

_____

Your neighbor's point of view: _____

_____

What if the school board wanted to begin holding classes every Saturday during the school year?

For Saturday classes: _____

_____

Against Saturday classes: _____

_____

Directions: Rewrite these sentence so they make a stronger statement:

Jacob made a decision to take the test today. _____

_____

Kisha had a dream about the test results. _____

_____

Directions: Write two facts and two opinions about your math class.

Facts: _____

_____

Opinions: _____

_____

Review

Directions: Write a persuasive essay convincing your town that a park is needed for older kids with equipment such as basketball courts, soccer and football fields, and a track. Be sure to end with a convincing statement.

_____

_____

_____

_____

_____

_____

Directions: Write a descriptive paragraph about these topics.

My Pet _____

_____

_____

_____

_____

My Mom _____

_____

_____

_____

_____

Describing Characters

When you write a story, your characters must seem like real people. You need to let your reader know not only how they look but how they act, and how they feel. You could just tell the reader that a character is friendly, scared, or angry, but your story will be more interesting if you show these feelings by the characters' actions.

It started like this. . . .

Example:
Character: A frightened child
Adjectives and adverbs: red-haired, freckled, scared, lost, worried
Simile: as frightened as a mouse cornered by a cat
Action: He peeked between his fingers, but his mother was nowhere in sight.

Directions: Write adjectives, adverbs, similes, and/or metaphors that tell how each character feels. Then, write a sentence that shows how the character feels.

1. an angry woman
   Adjectives and adverbs: _____

   Metaphor or simile: _____

   Sentence: _____

2. a disappointed man
   Adjectives and adverbs: _____

   Metaphor or simile: _____

   Sentence: _____

3. a hungry child
   Adjectives and adverbs: _____

   Metaphor or simile: _____

   Sentence: _____

4. a tired boy
   Adjectives and adverbs: _____

   Metaphor or simile: _____

   Sentence: _____

Setting the Scene

Where and when a story takes place is called the **setting**. As with characters, you can tell about a setting—or you can show what the setting is like. Compare these two pairs of sentences:

The sun was shining.   The bus was crowded.
The glaring sun made my eyes burn.   Paige shouldered her way down the aisle,
                                        searching for an empty seat on the crowded bus.

If you give your readers a clear picture of your story's setting, they'll feel as if they're standing beside your characters. Include words that describe the sights, sounds, smells, feel, and even taste, if appropriate.

Directions: Write at least two sentences for each setting, clearly describing it for your readers.

1. an empty kitchen early in the morning _____

_____

_____

2. a locker room after a basketball game _____

_____

_____

3. a dark living room during a scary TV movie _____

_____

_____

4. a classroom on the first day of school _____

_____

_____

5. a quiet place in the woods _____

_____

_____

Creating a Plot

When you're writing a story, the **plot** is the problem your characters face and how they solve it. It's helpful to write a plot outline or summary before beginning a story.

In the beginning of a story, introduce the characters, setting, and problem.

Example: Oliver and Stella have never met their mother, who lives in another state. They decide they would like very much to meet her. They live with their grandmother and father. On the way home from school, they talk about how they can find and contact her.

In the middle, characters try different ways to solve the problem, usually failing at first.

Example: Oliver and Stella hurry home to ask their grandmother if she can help them find their mother. Their grandmother seems nervous and tells Oliver and Stella to discuss the matter with their father when he gets home from work. When Oliver and Stella's father comes home, they tell him about their plan. Their father is very quiet for several minutes. He says he needs some time to think about it and asks if he can let them know tomorrow. Oliver and Stella can hardly sleep that night. Getting through school the next day is tough as well. After school, Oliver and Stella wait by the window for their father's car to pull in the driveway.

In the end, the characters find a way to solve the problem. Not all stories have happy endings. Sometimes, the characters decide they can live with the situation the way it is.

Example: When their father pulls into the driveway, Oliver and Stella rush out to meet him. Their father hands them airplane tickets. Oliver and Stella hug each other. Then, they hug their father.

Directions: How do you think this story ends? Write a summary for the ending of this story.

_____

_____

_____

_____

_____

_____

Creating a Plot

As you plan your stories, consider these questions.

- Who are the main characters?
- What do they look like?
- Where do they live?
- When do they live?
- What is the problem?
- Why is there a problem?
- How do they solve it?
- How do they feel at first?
- How do they feel at the end?
- Did I leave any loose ends?
- Do I want a surprise ending?

Directions: Write the plot for a story of your own on another sheet of paper. Follow these steps.

1. Select two characters and a setting. Write some descriptive words and phrases you could use.

2. What kinds of problems might the characters face? Jot down your ideas.

3. Select a problem, and think of ways the characters might try to solve it. Number the alternatives in order, with the solution you will use last.

4. Add more details. Then, write a plot outline or summary.

5. Finally, write out the whole story. You can change your plot outline if you think of a better idea. Make your story exciting!

6. Read your story out loud to yourself. Is what happened clear? Make any needed changes, and rewrite your story neatly or type it on the computer and print it out. Be certain your story has a title.

7. Add illustrations or computer graphics to your story if you wish.

Writing Dialogue

Stories are more interesting when characters talk to each other. Conversations help show the characters' feelings and personalities. Compare these two scenes from a story:

Chad asked Angela to help him with his homework. She said she wouldn't, because she was mad at him for ignoring her when he was spending time with friends from his soccer team.

"Angela, would you be a real friend and help me with this math problem?" Chad asked with a big smile.

"I'm awfully busy, Chad," Angela answered without looking up. "Maybe you should ask your soccer friends, since you enjoy talking to them so much."

In the second version, we know Angela is angry, even though the writer didn't use that word. You can show how your characters feel by what they say and how they say it.

When you write dialogue, try to make the words sound natural, the way people really talk. Remember to start a new paragraph every time a different person speaks. Put quotation marks around the words the person says. Commas and periods at the ends of sentences go inside the quotation marks.

Directions: Write dialogue for what each character might say to a classmate in this situation. Show how the character feels without using the word for the feeling. Also, write the reply from the classmate. Use another sheet of paper for your writing.

The teacher explains a new assignment the class will do in groups. The bell rings, and everyone heads for the lunchroom.

1. A discouraged girl who isn't sure she can do the project

2. A self-confident boy who got an A on the last project

3. An impatient girl who has an idea and wants to get started

4. An angry boy who dislikes group projects

5. A bored girl who doesn't care about the project

6. A boy who is worried about a different problem in his life

7. A student who is afraid no one will want him or her for a partner on the project

Writing Dialogue

When it was Megan's turn to present her book report to the class, she dropped all her notecards! Her face turned red, and she wished she was invisible, but all she could do was stand there and say what she could remember without her cards. It was awful!

Directions: Rewrite each paragraph below. Explain the same scenes and feelings using dialogue.

After class, Megan told her friend Ananya she had never been so embarrassed in her life. She saw everyone staring at her, and the teacher looked impatient, but there wasn't anything she could do. Ananya assured Megan that no one disliked her because of what had happened.

_____

_____

_____

When Megan got home, she told her mother about her book report. By then, she felt like crying. Her mother said not to get discouraged. In a couple of days, she would be able to laugh about dropping the cards.

_____

_____

_____

When Megan's older brother Jed came home, he asked her what was wrong. She briefly told him and said she never was going back to school. He started laughing. Megan got mad because she thought he was laughing at her. Then, Jed explained that he had done almost the same thing when he was in sixth grade. He was really embarrassed, too, but not for long.

_____

_____

_____

_____

Writing: Paraphrasing

Paraphrasing means "to restate something in your own words."

Directions: Write the following sentences in your own words. The first one has been done for you.

1. He sat alone and watched movies throughout the cold, rainy night.

   <u>All through the damp, chilly evening, the boy watched television by himself.</u>

2. Many animals such as elephants, zebras, and tigers live in the grasslands.

   _____

   _____

3. In art class, Sarah worked diligently on a clay pitcher, molding and shaping it on the pottery wheel.

   _____

   _____

4. The scientists frantically searched for a cure for the new disease that threatened the entire world population.

   _____

   _____

5. Quietly, the detective crept around the abandoned building, hoping to find the missing man.

   _____

   _____

6. The windmill turned lazily in the afternoon breeze.

   _____

   _____

Writing: Paraphrasing

Directions: Using synonyms and different word order, paraphrase the following paragraphs. The first one has been done for you.

Some of Earth's resources, such as oil and coal, can be used only once. We should always, therefore, be careful how we use them. Some materials that are made from natural resources, including metal, glass, and paper, can be reused. This is called recycling.

Many natural resources, including coal and oil, can be used only one time. For this reason, it is necessary to use them wisely. There are other materials made from resources of the Earth that can be recycled, or used again. Materials that can be recycled include metal, glass, and paper.

Recycling helps to conserve the limited resources of our land. For example, there are only small amounts of gold and silver ores in the earth. If we can recycle these metals, less of the ores need to be mined. While there is much more aluminum ore in the earth, recycling is still important. It takes less fuel energy to recycle aluminum than it does to make the metal from ore. Therefore, recycling aluminum helps to conserve fuel.

_____

_____

_____

_____

It is impossible to get minerals and fossil fuels from the earth without causing damage to its surface. In the past, people did not think much about making these kinds of changes to our planet. They did not think about how these actions might affect the future. As a result, much of the land around mines was left useless and ugly. This is not necessary, because such land can be restored to its former beauty.

_____

_____

_____

_____

Writing: Summarizing

A **summary** is a brief retelling of the main ideas of a reading selection. To summarize, write the author's most important points in your own words.

Directions: Write a two-sentence summary for each paragraph.

The boll weevil is a small beetle that is native to Mexico. It feeds inside the seed pods, or bolls, of cotton plants. The boll weevil crossed into Texas in the late 1800s. It has since spread into most of the cotton-growing areas of the United States. The boll weevil causes hundreds of millions of dollars worth of damage to cotton crops each year.

Summary: _____

_____

_____

Each spring, female boll weevils open the buds of young cotton plants with their snouts. They lay eggs inside the buds, and the eggs soon hatch into wormlike grubs. The grubs feed inside the buds, causing the buds to fall from the plant. They eat their way from one bud to another. Several generations of boll weevils may be produced in a single season.

Summary: _____

_____

_____

The coming of the boll weevil to the United States caused tremendous damage to cotton crops. Yet, there were some good results, too. Farmers were forced to plant other crops. In areas where a variety of crops were raised, the land is in better condition than it would have been if only cotton had been grown.

Summary: _____

_____

_____

Writing: Summarizing a Personal Narrative

Directions: Read the following narrative, and then follow the directions below and on page 333.

My Greatest Fear

I am scared of spiders. I realize this is not a logical fear, but I cannot help myself. I have been frightened by spiders since I was very young. For the following three reasons, spiders will never be pets of mine.

The first reason that I am scared of spiders is their appearance. I do not like their eight wispy, creepy legs. Spiders are never easily seen, but rather dark and unattractive. They are often hairy, and the mere thought of multiple eyeballs gives me shivers.

Spiders are not well-behaved. They are sly and always ready to sneak up on innocent victims. Spiders have habits of scurrying across floors, dropping from ceilings, and dangling from cobwebs. One never knows what to expect from a spider.

Finally, I am scared of spiders due to a "spider experience" as a child. Having just climbed into bed, I noticed a particularly nasty-looking spider on the ceiling over my bed. My father came into dispose of it, and it fell into bed with me. The thought of it crawling over me drove me from the bed shrieking. After that, I checked the ceiling nightly before getting into bed.

Many people love spiders. They are good for the environment and are certainly needed on our planet. However, because of my fear, irrational though it may be, I'd rather just avoid contact with arachnids.

Directions: Write a four-sentence summary of the narrative.

_____

_____

_____

_____

_____

Writing: Summarizing a Personal Narrative

Write the main idea of the second paragraph.

_____

_____

Write the main idea of the third paragraph.

_____

_____

Write the main idea of the fourth paragraph.

_____

_____

Everyone has a fear of something. On another sheet of paper, write a five-paragraph personal narrative about a fear of your own. Use the following guide to help you organize your narrative.

Paragraph 1. State your fear.

Provide background information about fear.

Paragraph 2. State your first reason for fear.

Support this statement with at least three sentences.

Paragraph 3. State your second reason for fear.

Support this statement with at least three sentences.

Paragraph 4. State your third reason for fear.

Support this statement with at least three sentences.

Paragraph 5. Provide a summary of your narrative.

Restate your fear in different words from the opening sentence.

Writing: Outlining

An **outline** is a skeletal description of the main ideas and important details of a reading selection. Making an outline is a good study aid. It is particularly useful when you must write a paper.

Directions: Read the paragraphs, and then complete the outline below.

Weather has a lot to do with where animals live. Cold-blooded animals have body temperatures that change with the temperature of the environment. Cold-blooded animals include snakes, frogs, and lizards. They cannot live anywhere the temperatures stay below freezing for long periods of time. The body temperatures of warm-blooded animals do not depend on the environment. Any animal with hair or fur—including dogs, elephants, and whales—is warm-blooded. Warm-blooded animals can live anywhere in the world where there is enough food to sustain them.

Some warm-blooded animals live where snow covers the ground all winter. These animals have different ways to survive the cold weather. Certain animals store up food to last throughout the snowy season. For example, the tree squirrel may gather nuts to hide in its home. Other animals hibernate in the winter. The ground squirrel, for example, stays in its burrow all winter long, living off the fat reserves in its body.

Title: _____

Main Topic: I. _____

Subtopic: A. Cold-blooded animals' temperatures change with environment.

Detail: 1. _____

Subtopic: B. _____

Detail: 1. They can live anywhere there is food.

Main Topic: II. _____

Subtopic: A. Animals have different ways to survive the cold.

Details: 1. _____

2. _____

Review

Directions: Read the paragraph, and then follow the directions.

According to one estimate, 75 percent of all fresh water on Earth is in the form of ice. The polar regions of Earth are almost completely covered by ice. In some places, the ice is more than 8,000 feet thick. If all of this ice were spread out evenly, Earth would be covered with a 100-foot-thick layer of ice. Although ice is not an important source of fresh water today, it could be in the future. Some people have proposed towing large, floating masses of ice to cities to help keep up with the demand for fresh water.

1. Complete the outline of the paragraph.

Title: _____

Main Topic: I. 75 percent of fresh water on Earth is ice.

Subtopics: A. _____

B. _____

2. Check the most appropriate generalization:

☐ Ice is the most plentiful source of fresh water.

☐ Ice is important to the future.

3. Paraphrase the first sentence by restating it in your own words.

_____

4. Is the author's purpose to inform, entertain, or persuade?

_____

5. Where would you look to find information on the polar ice caps?

_____

Review

Directions: Read the paragraph, and then follow the directions.

Constellations are groups of stars that have been given names. They often represent an animal, person, or object. One of the easiest constellations to identify is the Big Dipper, which is shaped like a spoon. Once the Big Dipper is located, it is easy to see Cassiopeia (a W), the Little Dipper (an upside-down spoon), and the North Star. The North Star's scientific name is Polaris, and it is the last star in the handle of the Little Dipper. Other constellations include Orion the hunter, Gemini the twins, Canis Major the dog, and Pegasus the winged horse. Many ancient cultures, including the Greeks and Native Americans, used the position of the stars to guide them. They also planned daily life activities, such as planting, hunting, and harvesting, by the path the constellations made through the sky. For thousands of years, humans have gazed at the sky, fascinated by the millions of stars and imagining pictures in the night.

The Constellation Orion

1. Complete the outline of the paragraph.

Title: _____

Main Topic: I. _____

Subtopics: A. _____

B. _____

_____

2. In three sentences, summarize the paragraph.

_____

_____

_____

3. What is the author's purpose? _____

4. Under which topics would you look to find more information on constellations?

_____   _____   _____

Review

Directions: Imagine you are making a speech about one of your hobbies. Complete an outline of the speech.

Title: _____

Main Topic: I. _____

Subtopics: A. _____

   B. _____

Who is your audience? _____

Is it appropriately written for that audience? _____

Are you trying to inform, entertain, or persuade? _____

In the space below, write your speech in at least 100 words.

_____

_____

_____

_____

_____

_____

_____

_____

Using the Right Resources

Directions: Decide where you would look to find information on the following topics. All of these resources are available either in print or online form.

- **almanac** — contains tables and charts of statistics and information
- **atlas** — collection of maps
- **dictionary** — contains alphabetical listing of words with their meanings, pronunciations, and origins
- **encyclopedia** — a book, website, or CD-ROM with general information on many subjects
- **library catalog** — library resource showing available books by topic, title or author
- ***Readers' Guide to Periodical Literature*** — an index of articles in magazines and newspapers
- **thesaurus** — contains synonyms and antonyms of words

1. What is the capital of the Netherlands? _____

2. What form of government is practiced there? _____

3. What languages are spoken there? _____

4. What is the meaning of the word **indigenous**? _____

5. Where would you find information on conservation? _____

_____

6. What is a synonym for **catastrophe**? _____

7. Where would you find a description of the play *Cats*? _____

_____

8. Where would you find statistics on the annual rainfall in the Sahara?

_____

9. What is the origin of the word **plentiful**? _____

10. What are antonyms for the word **plentiful**? _____

11. Where would you find statistics for the number of automobiles manufactured in the United States last year? _____

Making Inferences: Reference Sources

Directions: In the box are four different kinds of reference sources. On the line next to each question, write which source you would use to find the information. Some information can be found in more than one reference.

encyclopedia	almanac	dictionary	thesaurus

1. A list of words that mean the same as **strong** _____

2. How much rain fell in Iowa in the year 1992 _____

3. What part of speech the word **porch** is _____

4. How many different types of hummingbirds there are _____

5. Weather patterns in Texas for the last 2 years _____

6. A list of words that mean the opposite of **cold** _____

7. Who invented the telescope _____

8. How to pronounce the word **barometer** _____

9. How many syllables the word **elephant** has _____

10. What the difference is between African and Asian elephants _____

11. The population changes in New York between 1935 and 2015 _____

12. How fast a cheetah can run _____

Conducting Research

Directions: Read the following questions. Use the Internet or library resources to answer them.

1. Choose two figures from history. Research them on www.biography.com. Write two facts you found about each person.

   _____

   _____

2. Use a resource book or online search to find out what Mohs scale of hardness is and what is at the top and bottom of the scale.

   _____

   _____

3. What were the last three winners of the Caldecott Medal for best illustrations in children's books?

   _____

   _____

4. Name three types of butterflies. List the source of your information.

   _____

   _____

5. Visit the site www.libraryspot.com. Write three questions that a classmate could answer by using this site.

   _____

   _____

6. Use a library catalog to search for books about rain forests. List the titles and call numbers of three books you find.

   _____

   _____

Review

Directions: Read the following questions. Use the Internet or library resources to answer them.

1. Use a print or online children's almanac to find two facts about animals or the environment.

_____

_____

2. How tall is the Eiffel Tower? _____

3. List two sources you could use to find current information about the International Space Station.

_____

_____

4. Use a print or online atlas to find out what five South American countries share a border with Bolivia.

_____

Directions: Check the resource you would use to find the following information.

1. How to play checkers ☐ almanac ☐ dictionary ☐ an Internet search

2. An example sentence using the word **breathe**

   ☐ encyclopedia ☐ thesaurus ☐ dictionary

3. How many inches of snow fell in the Colorado Rockies last year

   ☐ an atlas ☐ an Internet search ☐ thesaurus

4. How many syllables are in the word **justification**

   ☐ almanac ☐ thesaurus ☐ dictionary

5. A synonym for **discontent**

   ☐ encyclopedia ☐ almanac ☐ thesaurus

Name _____

Table of Contents

The **table of contents**, located in the front of books or magazines, tells a lot about what is inside.

A table of contents in books lists the headings and page numbers for each chapter. **Chapters** are the parts into which books are divided. Also listed are chapter numbers and the sections and subsections, if any. Look at the sample table of contents below:

Directions: Using the table of contents above, answer the following questions.

1. How many chapters are in this book? _____

2. What chapter contains information about things to plant? _____

3. On what page does information about fences begin? _____

4. What chapter tells you what you can use to help your garden grow better? _____

5. What page tells you how to use fertilizer? _____

6. What page tells you how far apart to plant pumpkin seeds? _____

7. What is on page 11? _____

8. What is on page 4? _____

Table of Contents

The table of contents below is divided into units and sections. **Units** are parts into which a book is divided. **Sections** are segments of each unit.

Table of Contents

Directions: Using the table of contents above, answer the following questions.

1. How many units are in this book? _____

2. Where would you find information about life on Mars? _____

3. Where would you find information about the sun's heat and brightness? _____

4. What is on page 27? _____

5. Orion is a large group of stars, or constellation. Where would you find information about it? _____

6. What is on page 101? _____

7. Where would you find information about the moons of Jupiter? _____

8. How many pages in this book are about Earth? _____

9. How many pages in this book are about Polaris? _____

10. Where would you read about the Big Dipper? _____

Table of Contents

In some magazines, the table of contents lists articles in numerical order. Other magazines' tables of contents are organized by subjects, by columns, and by features. **Subjects** are the topics covered in the articles. A **feature** is a specific kind of article, such as an article about sports or cooking. **Feature** also has another meaning. A regular feature is something that appears in every issue, such as letters to the editor, movie reviews, and sports statistics. Some magazines also call regular features "departments."

Columns are another kind of regular feature published in every issue. Columns are often written by the same person each time. A person who writes a column is called a **columnist**.

Most magazines' tables of contents will also give you an idea of what a story is about. In online magazines, the table of contents often includes links that you can click to jump to a particular page or article.

Kids' Life

Articles

10   Skateboarding in the U.S.A.
       Read about kids from across the country
       and how they make the best of their boards.

12   Summer Camp
       Believe it or not, camp is fun!

20   Battle of Gettysburg
       It was a decisive clash in the American Civil War.

25   Snacks in a Flash
       Look at these treats you can make yourself.

29   Martin Luther King, Jr.
       The man who made people think twice.

Comics

6   Little People
14   Skating Sam
30   Double Trouble

Columns

7   Videos
32   The Great Outdoors
39   Fun and Famous

Departments

34   Your Health
36   Sports
38   Letters to the Editor

Directions: Answer these questions about Kids' Life magazine.

1. On what page does the story about summer camp begin?_____

2. List the titles of the departments in this magazine:

    a) _____   b) _____   c) _____

3. Can you tell what the Battle of Gettysburg is by reading the table of contents?

_____

4. Is there any information in this magazine about in-line skating?_____

Table of Contents

The articles in this magazine are grouped according to subjects.

LIVING
Table of Contents

Exercise	Ride for a while with these experienced cyclists.	13
Discoveries	Walk with a man through the ditches where he discovered dinosaur bones.	27
Happenings	Earth Day becomes important once again.	5
Science	Find out why astronauts like their jobs.	45
Music	Tunes that are sung in the mountains.	33
People	Read about Joe Biden and how he got to be Vice President.	20
	Learn about Jim Henson, the man behind the Muppets.	28
Sports	Why the Cleveland Indians might win the title.	42
History	A look at the lives of soldiers who were at Valley Forge.	39

Departments

Living Well	6	Letters to the Editor	9
Comedy	12	Books	16
Movies	24	Snacks	36

Directions: Answer these questions about *LIVING* magazine.

1. How many departments are in this issue of the magazine? _____

2. Circle the topics that are regular features in *LIVING*.

Books	Dinosaurs	Cleveland Indians	Vice Presidents
Comedy	Living Well	Snacks	Earth Day

3. What page would you look at if you wanted to see reviews of current movies?

_____

4. Is there any information in this magazine about football? _____

5. Who are the two people featured in this issue? _____

6. Is there anything in this issue about cycling? _____

7. Under what heading is it listed? _____

Name _____

Indexes

An **index** is an alphabetical listing of names, topics, and important words. It is found in the back of a book. An index lists every page on which these items appear. For example, in a book about music, dulcimer might be listed this way: Dulcimer 2, 13, 26, 38. Page numbers may also be listed like this: Guitars 18–21. That means that information about guitars begins on page 18 and continues through page 21. **Subject** is the name of the item in an index. **Sub-entry** is a smaller division of the subject. For example, apples would be listed under fruit.

Index

N
Neptune 27
NGC 5128 (galaxy) 39
Novas 32

O
Observatories. *See* El Caracol
Orbits of planets 10
Orion rocket 43

P
Planetoids. *See* Asteroids.
Planet rings
    Jupiter 23
    Saturn 9, 25
    Uranus 26
Planets
    discovered by Greeks 7
    outside the solar system 40
    visible with the naked eye 9

See also planet names.
Pleiades 32
Polaris 35, 36
Pole star. *See* Polaris.
Project Ozma 41

R
Rings. *See* Planet rings.

S
Sagittarius 37
Satellites
    Jupiter 24
    Neptune 27
    Saturn 25
    Uranus 26
    See also Galilean satellites
Saturn 25

Directions: Answer the questions about the index from this book about the solar system.

1. On what pages is there information about Polaris? _____

2. On what pages is information about Saturn's first ring found? _____

3. What is on page 41? _____

4. Where is there information about the pole star? _____

5. What is on page 43? _____

6. On what page would you find information about planets that are visible to the eye? _____

7. On what page would you find information about Jupiter's satellites? _____

Indexes

Some magazines use indexes to guide their readers to information they contain.

Appetizers
Bacon-Wrapped Halibut 92
Scallops with Sorrel and Tomato 116
Shrimp and Basil Beignets 116
Shrimp and Vegetable Spring Rolls with Hoisin and Mustard Sauces 85
Sweet Potato Ribbon Chips 136

Soups
Lemongrass Soup, Hot, with Radishes and Chives 84
Roasted Garlic Soup 22
Vegetable Soup with Creamy Asparagus Flan 154

Salads, Salad Dressings
Arugula Salad with Roasted Beets, Walnuts, and Daikon 158
Chicken, Fennel, Orange, and Olive Salad 24
Jicama Salad 81
Tomato, Onion, and Zucchini Salad 152
Walnut Vinaigrette 158

Directions: Answer the questions about the index from *Bon Appetit* magazine.

1. How many kinds of salad are
   listed in this issue?   _____

2. What is the recipe that contains radishes? _____

3. Name the recipe found on page 24.   _____

4. On what page would you find an
   appetizer that includes scallops?   _____

   What is the name of this recipe?   _____

5. Can you find any listings that
   contain halibut?   _____

6. On what page is a recipe made
   from sweet potatoes?   _____

   What is the name of this recipe?   _____

   For what part of a meal would
   it be served?   _____

Name _____

Review

FARMING
Table of Contents

Directions: Answer the questions about the table of contents from *Farming* magazine.

1. Is there any information about fashion in this magazine? _____

2. Is there any information about computers in this magazine? _____

3. Information about children on farms is probably included in which feature? _____

4. Are there any features about animals in this magazine? _____

Directions: Answer the questions about the index from this book about the world.

1. On what pages would you find information about the Baltic Sea? _____

2. What is listed on pages 2–3? _____

3. Where are the two Colorado Rivers? _____

Review

Directions: Follow the instructions for each section.

1. In your own words, explain why a table of contents is helpful.

   _____

   _____

2. A table of contents is often divided into units and sections.

   What is a unit? _____

   What is a section? _____

3. What is the purpose of breaking a table of contents down into units and sections?

   _____

   _____

4. What is an index?

   _____

   _____

5. What are the differences between a table of contents and an index?

   _____

   _____

   _____

   _____

6. Look at the table of contents in the front of this book. How many pages does the unit on Famous Athletes span?

   _____

Biographical Research

A **biography** is a written history of a person's life. Often, information for a biography can be obtained from an encyclopedia, especially if a person is famous.

Most libraries have a biography section in the nonfiction area of the children's section. In this area, books are usually listed by the last name of the subject of the biography. For example, a biography of Amelia Earhart would appear after one about Mary Cassatt but before one about Bill Gates (Cassatt, Earhart, Gates).

There are also many websites where you can find biographies of athletes, scientists, politicians, artists, inventors, explorers, and so on. Like any other Internet searches, you must be careful to use only reliable, trustworthy sites. Sites such as www.biography.com, www.history.com, www.factmonster.com, and www.kidsclick.org are good places to start. If you ever feel unsure about the reliability of a website, be sure to check with a teacher or parent.

Directions: Answer these questions.

1. You are looking for biographies about the following people. Write the names in the order in which they would appear on the shelf in a library: Nat Turner, Eleanor Roosevelt, Wilma Rudolph, Wilbur Wright, Madeline Albright, and Jonas Salk.

   _____

   _____

   _____

2. Where was Abraham Lincoln born? Use a biographical or online encyclopedia to find the answer.

   _____

3. Look up Anne Lindbergh in a biographical resource and write down the years of her birth and death.

   _____

Biographical Research

Directions: Use the resources suggested on the previous page to research one of the following people. Begin writing your biographical report in the space provided. (If you need more room, use a separate sheet of paper.)

Research Topics:	
Steve Jobs	Barack Obama
Wangari Maathai	Jacques Cousteau
Maya Lin	Malala Yousafzai

_____

_____

_____

_____

_____

_____

_____

_____

_____

_____

_____

Biographical Research

Directions: Conduct research to find one fact about each of the following subjects. Use biographies or biographical encyclopedias you find at the library, online encyclopedias, or biographical Web sites.

1. Sally Ride

   _____

2. Frederick Douglass

   _____

3. Wilson Bentley

   _____

4. Frida Kahlo

   _____

5. Charles Goodyear

   _____

6. Serena Williams

   _____

7. Jeremy Lin

   _____

8. Stephen Hawking

   _____

9. Cynthia Rylant

   _____

Biographical Research

Directions: In the space provided, use print and/or online resources to write a report about one of the people listed below. Use additional paper, if necessary.

Maria Sharapova   Steven Spielberg   Hillary Clinton
John Glenn   Andrew Lloyd Webber   Jodie Foster

_____

_____

_____

_____

_____

_____

_____

_____

_____

_____

_____

_____

_____

_____

_____

_____

Using the Library Catalog

Directions: Use the library catalog entries to answer the questions that follow.

Electric Ben: The Amazing Life and Times of Benjamin Franklin
Byrd, Robert.
Call Number: JB Franklin
New York: Dial Books for Young Readers, 2012.
ISBN: 978-0803737495
Subject: Franklin, Benjamin 1706–1790---Juvenile Literature
        Inventors---United States---Biography---Juvenile Literature
        Statesmen---United States---Biography---Juvenile Literature

1. What is the ISBN for *Electric Ben*? _____

2. How many subjects is the book listed under? _____

3. What is the book's subtitle? _____

4. In what year was *Electric Ben* published? _____

Dogs on Duty : Soldiers' Best Friends on the Battlefield and Beyond
Patent, Dorothy Hinshaw.
Call Number: J355.424
Bloomsbury USA Children's, 2014.
ISBN: 978-0802736505
Subject: Dogs---War Use---Juvenile Literature

5. Who is the author of *Dogs on Duty*? _____

6. What is the book's call number? _____

7. Is this book intended for children or adults? How do you know? _____

_____

8. If you wanted to find more books on this subject, what search could you do in the library catalog?

_____

Using the Library Catalog

A **library catalog** is a digital listing of the materials a library owns. Most libraries offer many search options. The most common ways to search are by title, author, subject, or keyword. If you don't find the book you are looking for at first, you may find it by changing your search. For example, if you can't find a book by title, try doing a keyword search using only one or two main words from the title.

Directions: Use a library catalog to answer the following questions.

1. What are the titles of three books by Roald Dahl?

   _____

2. Write the title of a children's book about volcanoes.

   _____

3. Write the author of one of the books in the Dear America series.

   _____

4. Who wrote the book Ice Island?

   _____

5. In what year was The Voyage of Lucy P. Simmons published?

   _____

6. Who is your favorite author? Write the author's name and the titles of two books he or she has published.

   _____

7. Who illustrated Seababy: A Little Otter Returns Home?

   _____

8. Do a keyword search for children's books about basketball. Write the titles and call numbers of two books that you find in your search results.

   _____

9. In what section of the library would you find Jean Lafitte: The Pirate Who Saved America?

   _____

10. What is the call number of the book The Giant and How He Humbugged America?

   _____

Review

Directions: Write **T** or **F** on the line beside each statement.

_____ 1. A biography of Rosa Parks would come after a biography of Peyton Manning on a library shelf.

_____ 2. A library is the only source of information for biographies.

_____ 3. Most libraries shelve biographies in a separate section than other nonfiction books.

Directions: Write one biographical fact about each of the following people.

1. John F. Kennedy

_____

2. Maya Lin

_____

3. Gustav Klimt

_____

4. Alma Flor Ada

_____

5. Tiger Woods

_____

Directions: Use a library catalog to answer the following questions.

1. Who is the author of *Same Sun Here*? _____

2. What is the ISBN for *What Came from the Stars*? _____

3. Who illustrated *Guys Read: The Sports Pages*? _____

4. Do a subject search for Civil War books. Write the call numbers and titles of two books in your search results.

_____

_____

Poetry

Format:
Line 1: Name
Line 2: Name is a (metaphor)
Line 3: He/she is like (simile)
Line 4: He/she (three action words)
Line 5: He/she (relationship)
Line 6: Name

Example:
Jessica
Jessica is a joy.
She is like a playful puppy.
She tumbles, runs, and laughs.
She's my baby sister!
Jessica

Directions: Build a poem that describes a friend or relative by using similes, metaphors, and other words of your choice. Follow the form of the example poem.

Poetry: Haiku

Haiku is a type of unrhymed Japanese poetry with three lines. The first line has five syllables. The second line has seven syllables. The third line has five syllables.

Example:

Katie

Katie leaps and bounds.
Runs free, full of life and joy.
Companion, friend, dog.

Directions: Write a haiku about a pet and another about a hobby you enjoy. Be sure to write a title on the first line. If you do not have a pet, write about a pet you might like to have.

Pet   _____

_____

_____

_____

_____

Hobby   _____

_____

_____

_____

Poetry: Diamanté

A **diamanté** is a poem in the shape of a diamond. Diamantés have seven lines with this format:

Line 1: one-word noun, opposite of word in line 7
Line 2: two adjectives describing line 1
Line 3: three **ing** or **ed** words about line 1
Line 4: two nouns about line 1 and two nouns about line 7
Line 5: three **ing** or **ed** words about line 7
Line 6: two adjectives describing line 7
Line 7: one word noun, opposite of word in line 1

Example:

child
happy, playful
running, singing, laughing
toys, games, job, family
working, driving, nurturing
responsible, busy
adult

Directions: Write a diamanté of your own.

_____

_____

_____

_____

_____

_____

Writing: Free Verse

Poems that do not rhyme and do not have a regular rhythm are called **free verse**. They often use adjectives, adverbs, similes, and metaphors to create word pictures.

My Old Cat
Curled on my bed at night,
Quietly happy to see me,
Soft, sleepy, relaxed,
A calm island in my life.

Directions: Write your own free verse. Use the guidelines for each poem.

1. Write a two-line free verse poem about a feeling. Compare it to some kind of food. For example, anger could be a tangle of spaghetti. Give your poem a title.

　　　　　　　　 _____

_____

_____

2. Think of how someone you know is like a color—happy like yellow, for example. Write a two-line free verse poem on this topic without naming the person. Don't forget a title.

　　　　　　　　 _____

_____

_____

3. Write a four-line free verse poem, like "My Old Cat," that creates a word picture of a day at school.

　　　　　　　　 _____

_____

_____

_____

_____

Writing: Limericks

A **limerick** is a short, humorous poem. Limericks are five lines long and follow a specific rhyme pattern. Lines 1, 2, and 5 rhyme, and lines 3 and 4 rhyme.

Example:

There once was a young fellow named Fred
Whose big muscles went right to his head.
"I'll make the girls sigh,
'Cause I'm quite a guy!"
But the girls all liked Ted more than Fred!

Directions: Complete the limericks.

1. There was a young lady from Kent

   Whose drawings were quite excellent.

   _____

   _____

   So to the big city she went.

2. I have a pet squirrel named Sonny

   _____

   He ran up a tree

   As far as could be

   _____

3. There once was a boy who yelled, "Fire!"

   _____

   He just did not see

   _____

   _____

Writing: Acrostics

An **acrostic** is a poem that uses the letters of a word to begin each line. Read down, the first letter of each line spells the word. The poem tells something about the word that is spelled out.

Example:

In the grass or underground,
Now and then they fly around.
Slugs and worms and butterflies,
Each has its own shape and size.
Caterpillars, gnats, a bee,
Take them all away from me!

Directions: Write acrostic poems for the words **shoes** and **phone**. Your poems can rhyme or be free verse.

S _____

H _____

O _____

E _____

S _____

P _____

H _____

O _____

N _____

E _____

Directions: Write an acrostic poem for your name or a word of your choice on another sheet of paper. Draw a picture for your poem.

Friendly Letters

Directions: Study the format for writing a letter to a friend. Then, answer the questions.

your return address	4500 Waverly Road Cincinnati, Ohio 45241
date	June 23, 2015
greeting	Dear Josh,
body	How is your summer going? I am enjoying mine so far. I have been swimming twice already this week, and it is only Wednesday! I am glad there is a pool near our house. My parents said that you can stay overnight when your family comes for the 4th of July picnic. Do you want to? We can pitch a tent in the backyard and camp out. It will be a lot of fun! Please write back to let me know if you can stay over on the 4th. I will see you then!
closing **signature**	Your friend, Michael

your return address	Michael Delaney 4500 Waverly Road Cincinnati, Ohio 45241
main address	Josh Sommers 3350 West First Ave. Columbus, OH 43212

1. What words are in the greeting? _____

2. What words are in the closing? _____

3. On what street does the writer live? _____

Friendly Letters

Directions: Follow the format for writing a letter to a friend. Don't forget to address the envelope!

MATH

Place Value

Place value is the position of a digit in a number. A digit's place in a number shows its value. Numbers left of the decimal point represent **whole numbers**. Numbers right of the decimal point represent a part, or fraction, of a whole number. These parts are broken down into tenths, hundredths, thousandths, and so on.

Example:

3,443,221.621

Directions: Write the following number words as numbers.

1. Three million, forty-four thousand, six hundred twenty-one _____

2. One million, seventy-seven _____

3. Nine million, six hundred thousand, one hundred two _____

4. Twenty-nine million, one hundred three thousand, and nine tenths

_____

5. One million, one hundred thousand, one hundred seventy-one, and

thirteen hundredths _____

Directions: In each box, write the corresponding number for each place value.

1. 4,822,000.00   ☐ hundreds

2. 55,907,003.00   ☐ thousands

3. 190,641,225.07   ☐ hundred thousands

4. 247,308,211.59   ☐ tenths

5. 7,594,097.33   ☐ millions

6. 201,480,110.01   ☐ hundred thousands

7. 42,367,109,074.25   ☐ hundredths

Place Value

The chart below shows the place value of each number.

trillions			billions			millions			thousands			ones		
h	t	o	h	t	o	h	t	o	h	t	o	h	t	o
		2	1	4	0	9	0	0	6	8	0	3	5	0

Word form: two trillion, one hundred forty billion, nine hundred million, six hundred eighty thousand, three hundred fifty

Directions: Draw a line to the correct value of each underlined digit. The first one is done for you.

643,000   2 hundred million

13,294,125   9 billion

678,446   40 thousand

389,276   2 thousand

19,000,089,965   2 billion

78,764   1 hundred thousand

612,689   9 thousand

298,154,370   70 thousand

89,256   10 million

1,370   30 million

853,672,175   7 hundred

2,842,751,360   3 hundred

163,456   2 hundred

438,276,587   6 hundred thousand

Expanded Notation

Expanded notation is writing out the value of each digit in a number.

Example:
8,920,077 = 8,000,000 + 900,000 + 20,000 + 70 + 7
Word form: Eight million, nine hundred twenty thousand, seventy-seven

Directions: Write the following numbers using expanded notation.

1. 20,769,033 _____

_____

2. 1,183,541,029 _____

_____

3. 776,003,091 _____

_____

4. 5,920,100,808 _____

_____

5. 14,141,543,760 _____

_____

Directions: Write the following numbers.

1. 700,000 + 900 + 60 + 7 _____

2. 35,000,000 + 600,000 + 400 + 40 + 2 _____

3. 12,000,000 + 700,000 + 60,000 + 4,000 + 10 + 4 _____

4. 80,000,000,000 + 8,000,000,000 + 400,000,000 + 80,000,000 + 10,000 + 400 + 30

_____

5. 4,000,000,000 + 16,000,000 + 30 + 2 _____

Addition and Place Value

Directions: Add the problems below in which the digits with the same place value are lined up correctly. Then, cross out the problems in which the digits are not lined up correctly.

Find each answer in the diagram, and color that section.

yellow	blue	green	pink
638 1,289 + 465 2,392	~~98 324 + 9,756~~	4,326 82 + 699	589 95 + 8,526
579 125 + 244	296 2,183 + 75	93,287 36 + 7,831	51 315 + 7,492
83 1,298 + 62	938 3,297 + 445	1,849 964 + 53	198 72 + 68
987 934 + 3,163	46 390 + 9,785	856 642 + 7,462	591 6,352 + 27
57 7,520 + 463	773 3,118 + 74	64 7,430 + 338	919 52 + 6,835

Name _____

Addition

Directions: Add the following numbers in your head without writing them out.

1. 17 + 33 = _____   2. 35 + 15 = _____   3. 75 + 25 = _____

4. 41 + 25 = _____   5. 27 + 23 = _____   6. 30 + 20 = _____

7. 12 + 18 = _____   8. 43 + 22 = _____   9. 16 + 34 = _____

10. 9 + 11 + 30 = _____   11. 29 + 21 + 40 = _____

12. 14 + 16 + 20 = _____   13. 37 + 13 + 25 = _____

14. 12 + 22 + 36 = _____   15. 19 + 21 + 57 = _____

16. 21 + 24 + 25 = _____   17. 63 + 14 + 11 = _____

18. 33 + 15 + 42 = _____   19. 25 + 15 + 60 = _____

20. 30 + 20 + 10 = _____

Addition Word Problems

Directions: Solve the following addition word problems.

1. 100 students participated in a sports card show in the school gym. Brad brought his entire collection of 2,000 cards to show his friends. He had 700 football cards and 400 basketball cards. If the rest of his cards were baseball cards, how many baseball cards did he bring with him?

_____

2. Refreshments were set up in one area of the gym. Hot pretzels were a dollar, lemonade was 50 cents, fruit was 35 cents, and cookies were a quarter. If you purchased two of each item, how much money would you need?

_____

3. It took each student 30 minutes to set up for the card show and twice as long to put everything away. The show was open for 3 hours. How much time did each student spend on this event?

_____

4. 450 people attended the card show. 55 were mothers of students, 67 were fathers, 23 were grandparents, 8 were aunts and uncles, and the rest were kids. How many kids attended?

_____

5. Of the 100 students who set up displays, most of them sold or traded some of their cards. Jonas sold 75 cards, traded 15 cards, and collected $225. Kevin only sold 15 cards, traded 81 cards, and collected $100. Valentina traded 200 cards, sold 10, and earned $35. Of those listed, how many cards were sold, how many were traded, and how much money was earned?

sold _____   traded _____   earned $ _____

Subtraction

Directions: Subtract the following numbers. When subtracting, begin on the right, especially if you need to regroup and borrow.

549 − 162	823 − 417	370 − 244	648 − 79
700 − 343	475 − 299	603 − 425	354 − 265
1,841 − 952	2,597 − 608	6,832 − 1,774	9,005 − 3,458
23,342 − 9,093	53,790 − 40,813	29,644 − 19,780	35,726 − 16,959
109,432 − 79,145	350,907 − 14,185	217,523 − 44,197	537,411 − 406,514

Subtraction Word Problems

Directions: Solve the following subtraction word problems.

1. Last year, 28,945 people lived in Mike's town. This year, there are 31,889. How many people have moved in? _____

2. Brad earned $227 mowing lawns. He spent $168 on a new easel, paints, and other art supplies. How much money does he have left? _____

3. The school year has 180 days. Carrie has gone to 32 school days so far. How many more days does she have left? _____

4. Xavier wants a skateboard that costs $128. He has saved $47. How much more does he need? _____

5. To get to school, Imani walks 1,275 steps, and Carolyn walks 2,618 steps. How many more steps does Carolyn walk than Imani? _____

6. Sydney has placed 91 of the 389 pieces in a new puzzle she purchased. How many more does she have left to finish? _____

7. From New York, it's 2,823 miles to Los Angeles and 1,327 miles to Miami. How much farther away is Los Angeles? _____

8. Sheila read that a piece of carrot cake has 236 calories, but a piece of apple pie has 427 calories. How many calories will she save by eating the cake instead of the pie? _____

9. Ichiro's summer camp costs $223, while Sam's costs $149. How much more does Tim's camp cost?

   _____

10. Last year, the nation's budget was $45,000,000,000, but the nation spent $52,569,342,000. How much more than its budget did the nation spend?

   _____

Name _____

Multiplication

Directions: Multiply the following numbers. Be sure to keep the numbers aligned, and place a 0 in the ones place when multiplying by the tens digit.

Example:	Correct	Incorrect
	55	55
	x 15	x 15
	275	275
	550	55
	825	330

1. 12
    x 6

2. 44
    x 9

3. 27
    x 7

4. 92
    x 6

5. 85
    x 9

6. 78
    x 24

7. 32
    x 17

8. 19
    x 46

9. 63
    x 12

10. 38
    x 77

11. 125
    x 6

12. 641
    x 25

13. 713
    x 47

14. 586
    x 45

15. 294
    x 79

16. 20 x 4 x 7 = _____

17. 9 x 5 x 11 = _____

18. 16 x 2 x 2 = _____

19. 7 x 6 x 3 = _____

20. 33 x 11 x 3 = _____

21. 2 x 8 x 10 = _____

Division Word Problems

In the example below, 368 is being divided by 4. 4 won't divide into 3, so move over one position, and divide 4 into 36. 4 goes into 36 nine times. Then, multiply 4 x 9 to get 36. Subtract 36 from 36. The answer is 0, less than the divisor, so 9 is the right number. Now bring down the 8, divide 4 into it, and repeat the process.

Example:

$$4\overline{)368} \quad \begin{array}{r} 9 \\ \hline \end{array}$$

$$\begin{array}{r} 9 \\ 4\overline{)368} \\ \underline{36} \\ 0 \end{array} \qquad \begin{array}{r} 92 \\ 4\overline{)368} \\ \underline{36} \\ 08 \\ \underline{8} \\ 0 \end{array}$$

To check your division, multiply 4 x 92 = 368.

Directions: Solve the following division problems. (For some problems, you will also need to add or subtract.)

1. Kristy helped the kindergarten teacher put a total of 192 crayons into 8 boxes. How many crayons did they put into each box? _____

2. The scout troop has to finish a 12-mile hike in 3 hours. How many miles an hour will they have to walk? _____

3. At her slumber party, Makayla had 4 friends and 25 pieces of candy. If she kept 5 pieces and divided the rest among her friends, how many pieces did each friend get? _____

4. Miles's book has 147 pages. He wants to read the same number of pages each day and finish reading the book in 7 days. How many pages should he read each day? _____

5. Brian and 2 friends are going to share 27 marbles. How many will each person get? _____

6. To help the school, 5 parents agreed to sell 485 tickets for a raffle. How many tickets will each person have to sell to do his/her part? _____

7. Jorge is going to weed his neighbor's garden for $3 an hour. How many hours does he have to work to make $72? _____

Equations

In an **equation**, the value on the left of the equal sign must equal the value on the right. Remember the order of operations: solve from left to right, multiply or divide numbers before adding or subtracting, and do the operation inside parentheses first.

Example: 6 + 4 – 2 = 4 x 2
          10 – 2 = 8
             8 = 8

Directions: Write the correct operation signs in the blanks to make accurate equations.

1. (25 _____ 25) _____ 2 = 100 _____ 75

2. (76 _____ 24) _____ 3 = 150 _____ 2

3. 140 _____ 2 _____ 10 = 500 _____ 50 _____ 150

4. 2,100 _____ 2,000 _____ 60 = 80 _____ 2

5. 80 _____ 8 _____ 4 = 160 _____ 160 _____ 160

6. (55 _____ 100) _____ 11 = (1,000 _____ 2) _____ 4

7. 137 _____ 81 _____ 52 = 3 _____ 90

8. 3,000 _____ 10 _____ 10 = (600 _____ 300) _____ 30

9. (720 _____ 20) _____ 4 = 37 _____ 5

10. (457 _____ 43) _____ 500 = (21 _____ 40) x 0

Equations

Directions: Write the correct operation signs in the blanks to make accurate equations.

1. 5 _____ 5 _____ 5 = 3 _____ 5 _____ 0

2. (50 _____ 0) _____ 2 = 25 _____ 2 _____ 2

3. 2 _____ 2 _____ 2 _____ 2 = 2 _____ 2 _____ 4

4. (4 _____ 5) _____ 5 _____ 5 = 2 _____ 3 _____ 5

5. (25 _____ 5) _____ 2 _____ 3 = 3 _____ 6 _____ 2 _____ 5

6. (125 _____ 7) _____ 2 _____ 3 = 100 _____ 2 _____ 4 _____ 70 _____ 10

7. (100 _____ 10) _____ 5 _____ 10 = 10 _____ 5 _____ 100 _____ 10

8. 35 _____ 35 _____ 5 _____ 2 = 5 _____ 3 _____ 2 _____ 5

9. (60 _____ 2) _____ 3 = 3 _____ 3 _____ 3 _____ 0 _____ 15 _____ (5 _____ 15)

10. (120 _____ 4) _____ 7 _____ 3 = (7 _____ 7) _____ (2 _____ 5)

11. (91 _____ 3 _____ 6) _____ 3 = 2 _____ 5 _____ 1 _____ 3 _____ (2 _____ 5)

12. (16 _____ 4) _____ 8 = 5 _____ 5 _____ (3 _____ 3) _____ 6

13. 0 _____ 5 _____ 15 _____ 4 = 3 _____ 3 _____ 3 _____ 8

14. 16 _____ 3 _____ 12 _____ (2 _____ 20) = (2 _____ 2) _____ 6 _____ 10 _____ (2 _____ 7)

15. 21 _____ (3 _____ 3) _____ 3 _____ 1 = 3 _____ 1 _____ 2 _____ 20

Comprehensive Curriculum - **Grade 6**

Rounding and Estimating

Rounding is expressing a number to the nearest whole number, ten, thousand, or other value. **Estimating** is using an approximate number instead of an exact one. When rounding a number, we say a country has 98,000,000 citizens instead of 98,347,425. We can round numbers to the nearest whole number, the nearest hundred, or the nearest million—whatever is appropriate.

Here are the steps: 1) Decide where you want to round the number. 2) If the digit to the right is less than 5, leave the digit at the rounding place unchanged. 3) If the digit to the right is 5 or more, increase the digit at the rounding place by 1.

Examples: 587 rounded to the nearest hundred is 600.
535 rounded to the nearest hundred is 500.
21,897 rounded to the nearest thousand is 22,000.
21,356 rounded to the nearest thousand is 21,000.

When we estimate numbers, we use rounded, approximate numbers instead of exact ones.

Example: A hamburger that costs $1.49 and a drink that costs $0.79 total about $2.30 ($1.50 plus $0.80).

Directions: Use rounding and estimating to find the answers to these questions. You may have to add, subtract, multiply, or divide.

1. Sarita is having a party and wants to fill 11 cups from a 67-ounce bottle of juice. About how many ounces should she pour into each cup? _____

2. Hannah studied 28 minutes every day for 4 days. About how long did she study in all? _____

3. About how much does this lunch cost? $1.19 $ 0.39 $ 0.49 _____

4. The numbers below show how long Frank spent studying last week. Estimate how many minutes he studied for the whole week.
Monday: 23 minutes Tuesday: 37 minutes Wednesday: 38 minutes
Thursday: 12 minutes _____

5. One elephant at the zoo weighs 1,417 pounds, and another one weighs 1,789 pounds. About how much heavier is the second elephant? _____

6. If Jordan studied a total of 122 minutes over 4 days, about how long did he study each day? _____

7. It's 549 miles to Dover and 345 miles to Albany. About how much closer is Albany? _____

Rounding

Directions: Round each number, and then estimate the answer. You can use a calculator to find the exact answer.

Round to the nearest ten.

		Estimate	**Actual Answer**
1.	$86 \div 9 =$		
2.	$237 + 488 =$		
3.	$49 \times 11 =$		
4.	$309 + 412 =$		
5.	$625 - 218 =$		

Round to the nearest hundred.

6.	$790 - 70 =$		
7.	$690 \div 70 =$		
8.	$2,177 - 955 =$		
9.	$4,792 + 3,305 =$		
10.	$5,210 \times 90 =$		

Round to the nearest thousand.

11.	$4,078 + 2,093 =$		
12.	$5,525 - 3,065 =$		
13.	$6,047 \div 2,991 =$		
14.	$1,913 \times 4,216 =$		
15.	$7,227 + 8,449 =$		

Comprehensive Curriculum - **Grade 6**

Decimals

A **decimal** is a number that includes a period called a **decimal point**. The digits to the right of the decimal point are a value less than one.

one whole

one tenth

one hundredth

The place value chart below helps explain decimals.

hundreds	tens	ones	.	tenths	hundredths	thousandths
6	3	2	.	4		
	4	7	.	0	5	
		8	.	0	0	9

A decimal point is read as "and." The first number, 632.4, is read as "six hundred thirty-two and four tenths." The second number, 47.05, is read as "forty-seven and five hundredths." The third number, 8.009, is read as "eight and nine thousandths."

Directions: Write the decimals shown below. Two have been done for you.

1. __1.4__   2. _____   3. _____

4. six and five tenths   __6.5__

5. twenty-two and nine tenths   _____

6. thirty-six and fourteen hundredths   _____

7. forty-seven hundredths   _____

8. one hundred six and four tenths   _____

9. seven and three hundredths   _____

10. one tenth less than 0.6   _____

11. one hundredth less than 0.34   _____

12. one tenth more than 0.2   _____

Adding and Subtracting Decimals

When adding or subtracting decimals, place the decimal points under each other. That way, you add tenths to tenths, for example, not tenths to hundredths. Add or subtract beginning on the right, as usual. Carry or borrow numbers in the same way. Adding 0 to the end of decimals does not change their value, but sometimes makes them easier to add and subtract.

Examples:	39.40	0.064	3.56	6.83
	+ 6.81	+ 0.470	− .09	− 2.14
	46.21	0.534	3.47	4.69

Directions: Solve the following problems.

1. Write each set of numbers in a column and add them.

   a. 2.56 + 0.6 + 76 = _____

   b. 93.5 + 23.06 + 1.45 = _____

   c. 3.23 + 91.34 + 0.85 = _____

2. Write each pair of numbers in a column and subtract them.

   A. 7.89 − 0.56 = _____ B. 34.56 − 6.04 = _____ C. 7.6 − 3.24 = _____

3. In a relay race, Alice ran her part in 23.6 seconds, Xian did hers in 24.7 seconds, and Erin took 20.09 seconds. How many seconds did they take altogether? _____

4. Although Erin ran her part in 20.09 seconds today, yesterday it took her 21.55 seconds. How much faster was she today? _____

5. Add this grocery bill:
   potatoes—$3.49; milk—$2.09; bread—$0.99; apples—$2.30 _____

6. A yellow coat cost $47.59, and a blue coat cost $36.79. How much more did the yellow coat cost? _____

7. A box of Oat Boats cereal has 14.6 ounces. A box of Nut Crunch has 17.85 ounces. How much more cereal is in the Nut Crunch box? _____

8. The Oat Boats cereal has 4.03 ounces of sugar in it. Nut Crunch cereal has only 3.76 ounces. How much more sugar is in a box of Oats Boats? _____

Mulitplying Decimals by Two-Digit Numbers

To multiply by a 2-digit number, just repeat the same steps. In the example below, first multiply 4 times 9, 4 times 5, and 4 times 3. Then, multiply 2 times 9, 2 times 5, and 2 times 3. You may want to place a 0 in the ones place to make sure this answer, 718, is one digit to the left. Now, add 1,436 + 7,180 to get the final answer.

Example:

	359	359	359	359	359	359
	x 24	x 24	x 24	x 24	x 24	x 24
	6	36	1,436	1,436	1,436	1,436
				80	180	7,180
						8,616

When one or both numbers in a multiplication problem have decimals, check to see how many digits are right of the decimal. Then, place the decimal point the same number of places to the left in the answer. Here's how the example above would change if it included decimals:

	35.9	3.59
	x 0.24	x 24
	8.616	86.16

The first example has one digit to the right of the decimal in 35.9 and two more in 0.24, so the decimal point is placed three digits to the left in the answer: 8.616. The second example has two digits to the right of the decimal in 3.59 and none in 24, so the decimal point is placed two digits to the left in the answer: 86.16. (Notice that you do not have to line up the decimals in a multiplication problem.)

Directions: Solve the following problems.

1. Zoe wants to buy 3 T-shirts that cost $15.99 each. How much will they cost altogether? _____

2. Ari is making $8.50 an hour packing groceries. How much will he make in 8 hours? _____

3. Justin made 36 frozen smoothie pops and sold them all at the school carnival for $0.75 each. How much would it cost to buy all 36 of them? _____

4. Last year, the carnival made $467. This year it made 2.3 times as much. How much money did the carnival make this year? _____

5. Troy's car will go 21.8 miles on a gallon of gasoline. His motorcycle will go 1.7 times as far. How far will his motorcycle travel on one gallon of gas? _____

Dividing with Zeros

Sometimes you have a remainder in division problems. You can add a decimal point and zeros to the dividend and keep dividing until you have the answer.

Example:

```
        49
  25 )1,241
      1 00
        241
        225
         16
```

```
        49.64
  25 )1,241.00
      1 00
        241
        225
        160
        150
        100
        100
          0
```

Directions: Solve the following problems.

1. 2) 2.5
2. 4) 115
3. 12) 738
4. 8) 586
5. 25) 3,415

6. Amelia's grandparents sent her a check for $130 to share with her 7 brothers and sisters. How much will each of the 8 children get if the money is divided evenly? _____

7. A vendor had 396 balloons to sell and 16 workers. How many balloons should each worker sell in order to sell out? _____

8. Eight of the workers turned in a total of $754. How much did each worker collect if he or she sold the same number of items? _____

9. A total of 744 tickets were collected from 15 amusement ride operators on the first day of the fair. If each ride required one ticket per person, and they each collected the same number of tickets, how many people rode each ride? _____

    Do you think that was possible? Why? _____

    _____

10. Five people were hired to clean up the area after the fair closed. They turned in a bill for 26 hours of labor. How many hours did each person work? _____

Name _____

Dividing Decimals by Decimals

When a divisor has a decimal, eliminate it before dividing. If there is one digit right of the decimal in the divisor, multiply the divisor and dividend by 10. If there are two digits right of the decimal in the divisor, multiply the divisor and dividend by 100.

Multiply the divisor and dividend by the same number whether or not the dividend has a decimal. The goal is to have a divisor with no decimal.

Examples: $2.3\overline{)89} \times 10 = 23\overline{)890}$ $\qquad$ $4.11\overline{)67.7} \times 100 = 411\overline{)6{,}770}$

$\qquad\qquad$ $4.9\overline{)35.67} \times 10 = 49\overline{)356.7}$ $\qquad$ $0.34\overline{)789} \times 100 = 34\overline{)78{,}900}$

After removing the decimal from the divisor, solve the problem in the usual way.

Directions: Solve the following problems.

1. $3.5\overline{)10.15}$ $\qquad$ 2. $6.7\overline{)415.4}$ $\qquad$ 3. $0.21\overline{)924}$ $\qquad$ 4. $73\overline{)50.37}$

5. If a car travels 1066.8 miles in 16.8 hours, what is the average speed in miles per hour the car travels? _____

6. Mrs. Gutierrez plans to make chili on Friday night. She bought 1.5 lbs. of ground chicken for $8.63. How much does the chicken cost per pound? _____

7. Aiden spent a total of $18.75 on rides at the fair. If each ticket cost $1.25, how many rides did he go on? _____

8. Mr. Washington bought 13.8 gallons of gas for $39.61. What was the price of gas per gallon that day? _____

Decimals and Fractions

A **fraction** is a number that names part of something. The top number in a fraction is called the **numerator**. The bottom number is called the **denominator**. Since a decimal also names part of a whole number, every decimal can also be written as a fraction. For example, 0.1 is read as "one tenth" and can also be written $\frac{1}{10}$. The decimal 0.56 is read as "fifty-six hundredths" and can also be written $\frac{56}{100}$.

Examples:

$$0.7 = \frac{7}{10} \qquad 0.34 = \frac{34}{100} \qquad 0.761 = \frac{761}{1,000} \qquad \frac{5}{10} = 0.5 \qquad \frac{58}{100} = 0.58 \qquad \frac{729}{1,000} = 0.729$$

Even a fraction that doesn't have 10, 100, or 1,000 as the denominator can be written as a decimal. Sometimes you can multiply both the numerator and denominator by a certain number so the denominator is 10, 100, or 1,000. (You can't just multiply the denominator. That would change the amount of the fraction.)

Examples:

$$\frac{3 \times 2 = 6}{5 \times 2 = 10} = 0.6 \qquad\qquad \frac{4 \times 4 = 16}{25 \times 4 = 100} = 0.16$$

Other times, divide the numerator by the denominator.

Examples:

$$\frac{3}{4} = 4\overline{\smash)3.00} = 0.75 \qquad\qquad \frac{5}{8} = 8\overline{\smash)5.000} = 0.625$$

Directions: Follow the instructions below.

1. For each square, write a decimal and a fraction to show the part that is colored. The first one has been done for you.

a.
$$\frac{25}{100}$$
$$0.25$$

b. ____

c. ____

2. Change these decimals to fractions.

a. 0.6 =   b. 0.54 =   c. 0.751 =   d. 0.73 =   e. 0.592 =   f. 0.2 =

3. Change these fractions to decimals. If necessary, round the decimals to the nearest hundredth.

a. $\frac{3}{10}$ =   b. $\frac{89}{100}$ =   c. $\frac{473}{1,000}$ =   d. $\frac{4}{5}$ =   e. $\frac{35}{50}$ =

f. $\frac{7}{9}$ =   g. $\frac{1}{3}$ =   h. $\frac{23}{77}$ =   i. $\frac{12}{63}$ =   j. $\frac{4}{16}$ =

Comprehensive Curriculum - **Grade 6**

Equivalent Fractions and the Lowest Term

Equivalent fractions name the same amount. For example, $\frac{1}{2}$, $\frac{5}{10}$, and $\frac{50}{100}$ are exactly the same amount. They all mean half of something. (And they are all written as the same decimal: 0.5.) To find an equivalent fraction, multiply the numerator and denominator of any fraction by the same number.

Examples: $\frac{3 \times 3}{4 \times 3} = \frac{9 \times 4}{12 \times 4} = \frac{36}{48}$ Thus, $\frac{3}{4}$, $\frac{9}{12}$ and $\frac{36}{48}$ are all equivalent fractions.

Most of the time, we want fractions in their lowest terms. It's easier to work with $\frac{3}{4}$ than $\frac{36}{48}$. To find a fraction's lowest term, instead of multiplying both parts of a fraction by the same number, divide.

Examples: $\frac{36 \div 12}{48 \div 12} = \frac{3}{4}$ The lowest term for $\frac{36}{48}$ is $\frac{3}{4}$.

If the numerator and denominator in a fraction can't be divided by any number, the fraction is in its lowest term. The fractions below are in their lowest terms.

Examples: $\frac{34}{61}$ $\frac{3}{5}$ $\frac{7}{9}$ $\frac{53}{90}$ $\frac{78}{83}$ $\frac{3}{8}$

Directions: Follow the instructions below.

1. Write two equivalent fractions for each fraction. Make sure you multiply the numerator and denominator by the same number. The first one is done for you.

   a. $\frac{1 \times 3}{2 \times 3} = \frac{3}{6}$ $\frac{1 \times 4}{2 \times 4} = \frac{4}{8}$

   b. $\frac{2 \times \underline{\quad}}{3 \times \underline{\quad}} = \frac{\underline{\quad}}{\underline{\quad}}$ $\frac{2 \times \underline{\quad}}{3 \times \underline{\quad}} = \frac{\underline{\quad}}{\underline{\quad}}$

   c. $\frac{3 \times \underline{\quad}}{5 \times \underline{\quad}} = \frac{\underline{\quad}}{\underline{\quad}}$ $\frac{3 \times \underline{\quad}}{5 \times \underline{\quad}} = \frac{\underline{\quad}}{\underline{\quad}}$

   d. $\frac{8 \times \underline{\quad}}{9 \times \underline{\quad}} = \frac{\underline{\quad}}{\underline{\quad}}$ $\frac{8 \times \underline{\quad}}{9 \times \underline{\quad}} = \frac{\underline{\quad}}{\underline{\quad}}$

2. Find the lowest terms for each fraction. Make sure your answers can't be divided by any other numbers. The first one has been done for you.

   a. $\frac{2 \div 2}{36 \div 2} = \frac{1}{18}$

   b. $\frac{12 \div \underline{\quad}}{25 \div \underline{\quad}} = \frac{\underline{\quad}}{\underline{\quad}}$

   c. $\frac{12 \div \underline{\quad}}{16 \div \underline{\quad}} = \frac{\underline{\quad}}{\underline{\quad}}$

   d. $\frac{3 \div \underline{\quad}}{9 \div \underline{\quad}} = \frac{\underline{\quad}}{\underline{\quad}}$

   e. $\frac{25 \div \underline{\quad}}{45 \div \underline{\quad}} = \frac{\underline{\quad}}{\underline{\quad}}$

   f. $\frac{11 \div \underline{\quad}}{44 \div \underline{\quad}} = \frac{\underline{\quad}}{\underline{\quad}}$

Greatest Common Factor

The **greatest common factor (GCF)** is the largest number that will divide evenly into a set of numbers. In the example, both numbers can be divided evenly by 2 and 4; therefore, 4 is the greatest common factor.

Example: 12 and 20   2, 4 (can be divided evenly into both numbers)
                          4 (greatest common factor)

Directions: Circle the greatest common factor for each pair of numbers.

1. 56 and 72	6	10	8	2
2. 45 and 81	7	5	9	3
3. 28 and 49	7	11	4	6
4. 10 and 35	3	5	9	7
5. 42 and 30	4	2	5	6
6. 121 and 33	12	9	4	11
7. 96 and 48	48	15	6	3
8. 12 and 132	2	10	12	9
9. 108 and 27	14	9	3	27
10. 44 and 32	4	6	8	10
11. 16 and 88	12	2	8	5
12. 72 and 144	9	11	7	72

Least Common Multiple

The **least common multiple (LCM)** is the lowest possible multiple any pair of numbers have in common.

> **Examples:** 2 and 4
> The lowest common multiple is 4, because 4 is a multiple for each number and it is the lowest possible.
>
> 6 and 7
> Multiples of 6 are 6, 12, 18, 24, 30, 36, 42.
> Multiples of 7 are 7, 14, 21, 28, 35, 42.
> 42 is the lowest multiple that 6 and 7 have in common.

Directions: Find the least common multiple for each pair of numbers.

1. 7 and 8 = _____

2. 2 and 3 = _____

3. 11 and 4 = _____

4. 5 and 3 = _____

5. 7 and 2 = _____

6. 9 and 4 = _____

7. 2 and 6 = _____

8. 10 and 3 = _____

9. 7 and 5 = _____

10. 9 and 6 = _____

11. 12 and 8 = _____

12. 15 and 3 = _____

Comparing Decimals and Fractions

The symbol **>** means "greater than." The number on its left is greater than that on its right. The symbol **<** means "less than." The number on its left is less than that on its right. An equal sign, **=**, shows the same value on each side.

Directions: Use the sign >, = or < to make each statement true.

1. 0.4 $\bigcirc$ $\dfrac{2}{3}$

2. 1.25 $\bigcirc$ $\dfrac{3}{2}$

3. 0.7 $\bigcirc$ $\dfrac{4}{5}$

4. 0.68 $\bigcirc$ $\dfrac{5}{7}$

5. 0.1 $\bigcirc$ $\dfrac{1}{12}$

6. 0.45 $\bigcirc$ $\dfrac{1}{2}$

7. 0.75 $\bigcirc$ $\dfrac{3}{8}$

8. 0.6 $\bigcirc$ $\dfrac{5}{8}$

9. 0.54 $\bigcirc$ $\dfrac{2}{5}$

10. 0.8 $\bigcirc$ $\dfrac{4}{6}$

11. 0.25 $\bigcirc$ $\dfrac{1}{7}$

12. 1.8 $\bigcirc$ $\dfrac{12}{7}$

13. 0.625 $\bigcirc$ $\dfrac{4}{8}$

14. 0.33 $\bigcirc$ $\dfrac{1}{3}$

15. Jenna looked carefully at the labels on two different types of pretzels. The pretzel rods had $\frac{3}{4}$ pound in the package. The package of mini pretzels claimed it had 0.67 pounds of pretzels inside. Were the pretzel rods <, >, or = to the mini pretzels? _____

Comprehensive Curriculum - **Grade 6**

Mixed Numbers and Improper Fractions

A **mixed number** is a whole number and a fraction, such as $1\frac{3}{4}$. An **improper fraction** has a numerator that is larger than its denominator, such as $\frac{16}{3}$. To write an improper fraction as a mixed number, divide the numerator by the denominator. The quotient becomes the whole number, and the remainder becomes the fraction.

Examples:

$$\frac{16}{3} = 3\overline{)16} = 5\frac{1}{3}$$
$$15$$
$$1$$

$$\frac{28}{5} = 5\overline{)28} = 5\frac{3}{5}$$
$$25$$
$$3$$

To change a mixed number into an improper fraction, multiply the whole number by the denominator and add the numerator.

Examples: $4\frac{1}{3} = 4 \times 3 = 12 + 1 = 13 \quad \frac{13}{3}$

$8\frac{4}{7} = 8 \times 7 = 56 + 4 = 60 \quad \frac{60}{7}$

Directions: Follow the instructions below.

1. Change the improper fractions to mixed numbers, and reduce to lowest terms. Use another sheet of paper if necessary. The first one has been done for you.

a. $\frac{34}{6} = 6\overline{)34} = 5\frac{4}{6} = 5\frac{2}{3}$
$$30$$
$$4$$

b. $\frac{65}{4} =$ c. $\frac{23}{8} =$ d. $\frac{89}{3} =$

e. $\frac{45}{9} =$ f. $\frac{32}{5} =$ g. $\frac{13}{7} =$

h. $\frac{24}{9} =$ i. $\frac{31}{2} =$ j. $\frac{84}{23} =$

2. Change these mixed numbers into improper fractions. The first one has been done for you.

a. $4\frac{6}{7} = 4 \times 7 = 28 + 6 = \frac{34}{7}$ b. $2\frac{1}{9} =$ c. $5\frac{4}{5} =$ d. $12\frac{1}{4} =$

e. $6\frac{7}{8} =$ f. $3\frac{9}{11} =$ g. $8\frac{3}{12} =$ h. $1\frac{6}{14} =$ i. $4\frac{2}{3} =$ j. $9\frac{4}{15} =$

Multiplying Fractions

To multiply two fractions, multiply the numerators, and then multiply the denominators. If necessary, change the answer to its lowest term.

Examples: $\frac{3}{4} \times \frac{2}{3} = \frac{6}{12} = \frac{1}{2}$ $\frac{1}{8} \times \frac{4}{5} = \frac{4}{40} = \frac{1}{10}$

To multiply a whole number by a fraction, first write the whole number as a fraction (with 1 as the denominator). Then, multiply as above. You may need to change an improper fraction to a mixed number.

Examples: $\frac{2}{3} \times \frac{4}{1} = \frac{8}{3} = 2\frac{2}{3}$ $\frac{3}{7} \times \frac{6}{1} = \frac{18}{7} = 2\frac{4}{7}$

Directions: Solve the following problems, writing answers in their lowest terms.

1. $\frac{1}{5} \times \frac{2}{3} =$ 2. $\frac{1}{3} \times \frac{4}{7} =$ 3. $\frac{2}{8} \times 3 =$ 4. $\frac{2}{6} \times \frac{1}{2} =$

5. Tim lost $\frac{1}{8}$ of his marbles. If he had 56 marbles, how many did he lose?   _____

6. Drew is making $\frac{2}{3}$ of a recipe for spaghetti sauce. How much will he need of each ingredient below?

   $1\frac{1}{4}$ cups water = _____   2 cups tomato paste = _____

   $\frac{3}{4}$ teaspoon oregano = _____ $4\frac{1}{2}$ teaspoons salt = _____

7. Carrie bought 2 dozen bagels and asked for $\frac{3}{4}$ of them to be honey grain. How many were honey grain?   _____

8. Sofia let her hair grow 14 inches long and then had $\frac{1}{4}$ of it cut off. How much was cut off?   _____

9. Ethan has finished $\frac{7}{8}$ of 40 math problems. How many has he done?   _____

10. If Jaya's cat eats $\frac{2}{3}$ can of cat food every day, how many cans should Jaya buy for a week?   _____

Name _____

Dividing Fractions

Reciprocals are two fractions that, when multiplied together, make 1. To divide a fraction by a fraction, turn one of the fractions upside down and multiply. The upside-down fraction is a reciprocal of its original fraction. If you multiply a fraction by its reciprocal, you always get 1.

Examples of reciprocals: $\dfrac{2}{3} \times \dfrac{3}{2} = \dfrac{6}{6} = 1$ $\qquad$ $\dfrac{9}{11} \times \dfrac{11}{9} = \dfrac{99}{99} = 1$

Examples of dividing by fractions: $\dfrac{1}{2} \div \dfrac{2}{3} = \dfrac{1}{2} \times \dfrac{3}{2} = \dfrac{3}{4}$ $\qquad$ $\dfrac{2}{5} \div \dfrac{2}{7} = \dfrac{2}{5} \times \dfrac{7}{2} = \dfrac{14}{10} = \dfrac{7}{5} = 1\dfrac{2}{5}$

To divide a whole number by a fraction, first write the whole number as a fraction with a denominator of 1. (Write a mixed number as an improper fraction.) Then, finish the problem as explained above.

Examples: $4 \div \dfrac{2}{6} = \dfrac{4}{1} \times \dfrac{6}{2} = \dfrac{24}{2} = 12$ $\qquad$ $3\dfrac{1}{2} \div \dfrac{2}{5} = \dfrac{7}{2} \times \dfrac{5}{2} = \dfrac{35}{4} = 8\dfrac{3}{4}$

Directions: Solve the following problems, writing answers in their lowest terms. Change any improper fractions to mixed numbers.

1. $\dfrac{1}{3} \div \dfrac{2}{5} =$ $\qquad$ 2. $\dfrac{6}{7} \div \dfrac{1}{3} =$ $\qquad$ 3. $3 \div \dfrac{3}{4} =$ $\qquad$ 4. $\dfrac{1}{4} \div \dfrac{2}{3} =$

5. Judy has 8 candy bars. She wants to give $\frac{1}{3}$ of a candy bar to everyone in her class. Does she have enough for all 24 students? _____

6. A big jar of glue holds $3\frac{1}{2}$ cups. How many little containers that hold $\frac{1}{4}$ cup each can you fill? _____

7. A container holds 27 ounces of frozen yogurt. How many $4\frac{1}{2}$-ounce servings is that? _____

8. It takes $2\frac{1}{2}$ teaspoons of powdered mix to make 1 cup of hot chocolate. How many cups can you make with 45 teaspoons of mix? _____

9. Each cup of hot chocolate also takes $\frac{2}{3}$ cup of milk. How many cups of hot chocolate can you make with 12 cups of milk? _____

Review

Directions: Follow the instructions below.

1. Write each of these decimals as fractions

   a. 0.43 =   b. 0.6 =   c. 0.783 =   d. 0.91 =

2. Write each of these fractions as decimals, rounding them to the nearest hundredth

   a. $\frac{3}{10}$ =   b. $\frac{4}{7}$ =   c. $\frac{3}{9}$ =   d. $\frac{64}{100}$ =

3. Write two equivalent fractions for each of these

   a. $\frac{2}{6}$ =   b. $\frac{1}{4}$ =   c. $\frac{5}{8}$ =

4. Change these fractions into their lowest terms

   a. $\frac{4}{16}$ =   b. $\frac{6}{18}$ =   c. $\frac{5}{90}$ =   d. $\frac{9}{24}$ =

5. Change these improper fractions into mixed numbers

   a. $\frac{30}{9}$ =   b. $\frac{46}{3}$ =   c. $\frac{38}{6}$ =   d. $\frac{18}{4}$ =

6. Change these mixed numbers into improper fractions

   a. $3\frac{1}{6}$ =   b. $7\frac{3}{8}$ =   c. $4\frac{2}{7}$ =   d. $8\frac{1}{9}$ =

7. George has written $1\frac{1}{8}$ pages of a report that is supposed to be $3\frac{1}{2}$ pages long. How much more does he have to write? _____

8. Mira ate $\frac{3}{8}$ of half a pizza. How much of the whole pizza did she eat? _____

9. Alexa's family is driving to Los Angeles. They drove $\frac{1}{6}$ of the way the first day and $\frac{1}{5}$ of the way the second day. How much of the trip have they completed so far? _____

10. Antonio gets $6 a week for his allowance. He saved $\frac{1}{2}$ of it last week and $\frac{1}{3}$ of it this week. How much money did he save in these 2 weeks? _____

11. Of 32 students in one class, $\frac{5}{8}$ have a brother or sister. How many students are only children? _____

12. In one class, $\frac{1}{5}$ of the students were born in January, $\frac{1}{10}$ in February, and $\frac{1}{10}$ in March. How much of the class was born in these 3 months? _____

Comprehensive Curriculum - **Grade 6**

Review

Directions: Follow the instructions below.

Add.

1. $\dfrac{4}{16} + \dfrac{5}{8} =$ 2. $\dfrac{1}{6} + \dfrac{1}{3} =$ 3. $\dfrac{2}{10} + \dfrac{4}{5} =$ 4. $\dfrac{3}{5} + \dfrac{9}{10} =$

Subtract.

1. $\dfrac{15}{9} - \dfrac{2}{3} =$ 2. $\dfrac{3}{4} - \dfrac{3}{8} =$ 3. $\dfrac{4}{7} - \dfrac{2}{14} =$ 4. $\dfrac{3}{5} - \dfrac{1}{10} =$

Multiply.

1. $\dfrac{1}{2} \times \dfrac{4}{16} =$ 2. $\dfrac{1}{3} \times \dfrac{4}{9} =$ 3. $\dfrac{5}{12} \times \dfrac{1}{4} =$ 4. $\dfrac{3}{16} \times \dfrac{3}{4} =$

Divide.

1. $\dfrac{3}{5} \div \dfrac{1}{3} =$ 2. $4 \div \dfrac{1}{2} =$ 3. $\dfrac{1}{4} \div \dfrac{1}{3} =$ 4. $3\dfrac{3}{4} \div \dfrac{1}{3} =$

Write >, <, or = to make the statements true.

1. $0.5 \bigcirc \dfrac{5}{8}$ 2. $0.8 \bigcirc \dfrac{4}{5}$ 3. $0.35 \bigcirc \dfrac{2}{5}$ 4. $1.3 \bigcirc \dfrac{7}{8}$

Trial and Error

Often, the quickest way to solve a problem is to make a logical guess, and test it to see if it works. The first guess, or trial, will probably not be the correct answer—but it should help you figure out a better, more reasonable guess.

Directions: Use trial and error to find the solutions to these problems.

1. Mr. McFerrson is between 30 and 50 years old. The sum of the digits in his age is 11. His age is an even number. How old is Mr. McFerrson?

_____

_____

2. The key for number 5 does not work on Carson's calculator. How can he use his broken calculator to subtract 108 from 351?

_____

_____

3. Tasha likes to swim a certain number of miles each day for 3 days straight. Then, she increases her mileage by 1 for the next 3 days, and so on. Over a 9-day period, Tasha swims a total of 27 miles. She swims equal mileage Monday, Tuesday, and Wednesday. She swims another amount on Thursday, Friday, and Saturday. She swims yet a third amount on Sunday, Monday, and Tuesday. How many miles does Tasha swim each day?

_____ Monday   _____ Tuesday   _____ Wednesday

_____ Thursday   _____ Friday   _____ Saturday

_____ Sunday   _____ Monday   _____ Tuesday

Trial and Error

Directions: Use trial and error to complete each diagram so all the equations work.

Example:

$$\underline{6}, \underline{7} \overset{+}{\longrightarrow} \underline{13}$$
$$\overset{\times}{\longrightarrow} \underline{42}$$

$$\underline{7}, \underline{4} \overset{+}{\longrightarrow} \underline{11}$$
$$\overset{\times}{\longrightarrow} \underline{28}$$

$$\underline{4}, \underline{8} \overset{+}{\longrightarrow} \underline{12}$$
$$\overset{\times}{\longrightarrow} \underline{32}$$

$$\underline{4}, \underline{4} \overset{+}{\longrightarrow} \underline{8}$$
$$\overset{\times}{\longrightarrow} \underline{16}$$

$$\underline{7}, \underline{0} \overset{+}{\longrightarrow} \underline{7}$$
$$\overset{\times}{\longrightarrow} \underline{5}$$

$$\underline{13}, \underline{4} \overset{+}{\longrightarrow} \underline{15}$$
$$\overset{\times}{\longrightarrow} \underline{56}$$

$$\underline{8}, \underline{9} \overset{+}{\longrightarrow} \underline{17}$$
$$\overset{\times}{\longrightarrow} \underline{72}$$

$$\underline{6}, \underline{9} \overset{+}{\longrightarrow} \underline{15}$$
$$\overset{\times}{\longrightarrow} \underline{54}$$

$$\underline{15}, \underline{16} \overset{+}{\longrightarrow} \underline{31}$$
$$\overset{\times}{\longrightarrow} \underline{}$$

$$\underline{5}, \underline{10} \overset{+}{\longrightarrow} \underline{11}$$
$$\overset{\times}{\longrightarrow} \underline{10}$$

$$\underline{100}, \underline{1} \overset{+}{\longrightarrow} \underline{101}$$
$$\overset{\times}{\longrightarrow} \underline{100}$$

Choosing a Method

This table explains different methods of computation that can be used to solve a problem.

Method		
Mental Math	– Calculating in your head.	– Use with small numbers, memorized facts, and multiples of tens, hundreds, thousands, and so on.
Objects/Diagram	– Drawing or using an object to represent the problem.	– Use to model the situation.
Pencil and Paper	– Calculating the answer on paper.	– Use when a calculator is not available and the problem is too difficult to solve mentally.
Calculator	– Using a calculator or computer to find the solution.	– Use with large numbers or for a quick answer.
Trial and Error	– Making a guess at the answer and trying to see if it works.	– Use when unsure what to do or if none of the methods above work.

Directions: Circle the method of computation that seems best for solving each problem. Then, solve the problem.

1. The School Days Fun Fair has 38 booths and 23 games. How many booths and games total are in the fair?

   • Paper and Pencil   Answer: _____

   • Objects/Diagram

2. The lemonade stand was stocked with 230 cups. On the first day, 147 drinks were sold. How many cups were left?

   • Objects/Diagram   Answer: _____

   • Paper and Pencil

3. There are 3 cars in the tram to transport people from the parking lot to the fair. Each car can seat 9 people. How many people can ride the tram at one time?

   • Objects/Diagram   Answer: _____

   • Trial and Error

Choosing a Method

Directions: Write what method you will use for each problem. Then, find the answer.

1. Jenna receives an allowance of $3.50 a week. This week, her mother paid her in nickels, dimes, and quarters. She received more dimes than quarters. How many of each coin did her mom use to pay her?

   Method: _____

   Answer: _____

2. You are buying your lunch at school. There are 4 people in front of you and 7 people behind you. How many people are standing in line? (Hint: it's not 11 people.)

   Method: _____

   Answer: _____

3. A runner can run 1 mile in 12 minutes. He ran for 30 minutes today. How far did he run?

   Method: _____

   Answer: _____

4. A family of four goes out to dinner. They decide to order a 16-piece pizza. Each person likes something different on his or her pizza, but each will eat equal amounts. Maria likes pepperoni and sausage, Tony likes ham and pineapple, Mom likes cheese only, and Dad likes mushrooms. Maria is allergic to mushrooms, so her slices can't be next to Dad's. Mom detests pineapple, so her slices can't be next to Tony's. How will the restaurant arrange their pizza?

   Method: _____

   Answer: _____

5. The Petting Zoo has 72 animals in aquariums, 32 animals in cages, and 57 animals fenced in. How many animals does the Petting Zoo have?

   Method: _____

   Answer: _____

Multi-Step Problems

Some problems take more than one step to solve. First, plan each step needed to find the solution. Then, solve each part to find the answer.

Example: Tickets for a bargain matinee cost $4 for adults and $3 for children. How much would tickets cost for a family of 2 adults and 3 children?

Step 1: Find the cost of the adults' tickets.

Step 2: Find the cost of the children's tickets.

Step 3: Add to find the sum of the tickets.

2 adults	x	$4 each ticket	=	$8 total
3 children	x	$3 each ticket	=	$9 total
$8 adults	+	$9 children	=	$17 total

The tickets cost $17 total.

Directions: Write the operations you will use to solve each problem. Then, find the answer.

1. Arden and her father are riding their bikes 57 miles to Arden's grandma's house. They ride 13 miles and then take a water break. Then, they ride 15 miles to a rest area for a picnic lunch. How many miles do Arden and her father have left to ride after lunch?

   Operations: _____

   Answer: _____

2. A triathlete bikes 15 miles at 20 miles per hour, runs 5 miles at 6 miles per hour, and swims 1 mile at 4 miles per hour. How long does the triathlon take her to complete?

   Operations: _____

   Answer: _____

3. Ray bought strawberries for $1.99, blueberries for $1.40, and 2 pints of raspberries for $1.25 per pint. How much did Ray spend on berries?

   Operations: _____

   Answer: _____

Hidden Questions

When solving a story problem, you may find that some information you want is not stated in the problem. You must ask yourself what information you need and decide how you can use the data in the problem to find this information. The problem contains a hidden question to find before you can solve it.

Example: Chris and his mother are building a birdhouse. He buys 4 pieces of wood for $2.20 each. How much change should he get back from $10?

Step 1: Find the hidden question:
What is the total cost of the wood? $2.20 x 4 = $8.80

Step 2: Use your answer to the hidden
question to solve the problem. $10.00 − $8.80 = $1.20

Directions: Write the hidden questions. Then, solve the problems.

1. Chris used 3 nails to attach each board to the frame. After nailing 6 boards, he had 1 nail left. How many nails did Chris have before he started?

   Hidden Question: _____

   Answer: _____

2. Chris sawed a 72-inch post into 3 pieces. Two of the pieces were each 20 inches long. How long was the third piece?

   Hidden Question: _____

   Answer: _____

3. It took Chris and his mom 15 hours to make a birdhouse. They thought it would take 3 days. How many hours early did they complete the job?

   Hidden Question: _____

   Answer: _____

4. It takes Chris 15 hours to make a birdhouse and 9 hours to make a birdfeeder. He worked for 42 hours and made 1 birdhouse and some birdfeeders. How many birdfeeders did Chris make?

   Hidden Question: _____

   Answer: _____

Logic Problems

Directions: Use the clues below to figure out this logic problem.

Three friends all enjoy sports. Each of their favorite sports involves a ball. Two of these sports are played on courts, and one is played on a field.

- Rachel likes to run and doesn't have to be a good catcher.

- Trinity is a good jumper.

- Betsy is also a good jumper, but she is a good ball handler.

Which sport does each girl play?

Trinity _____

Betsy _____

Rachel _____

A Cool Logic Problem

A family with 5 children went to the frozen-yogurt shop. The children all ordered different flavors.

Directions: Use the clues and the chart to help you write which child ate which flavor of frozen yogurt. Write a dot in the chart for the correct answer. Cross out all the other boxes in that row and column.

- No person had frozen yogurt with the same first initial as his or her name

- Neither of the twins, Corey and Cody, like peanut butter. Corey thinks vanilla is boring.

- The children are the twins, Julia, the brother who got chocolate, and the sister who ate peanut butter.

	Rocky Road	Chocolate Chip	Vanilla	Chocolate	Peanut Butter
Corey					
Cody					
Miranda					
Julia					
Lucas					

Who ate which flavor?

Corey _____

Cody _____

Miranda _____

Julia _____

Lucas _____

Perimeter

The **perimeter** is the distance around a shape formed by straight lines, such as a square or triangle. To find the perimeter of a shape, add the lengths of its sides.

Examples:

8 in.
8 in.

5 in.
4 in.

5 in.
3 in.
4 in.

For the square, add 8 + 8 + 8 + 8 = 32. Or, write a formula using **P** for **perimeter** and **s** for the **sides**: P = 4 x s
P = 4 x 8
P = 32 inches

For the rectangle, add 4 + 5 + 4 + 5 = 18. Or, use a different formula, using **l** for **length** and **w** for **width**. In formulas with parentheses, first do the adding, multiplying, and so on, in the parentheses:

P = (2 x l) + (2 x w)
P = (2 x 5) + (2 x 4)
P = 10 + 8
P = 18

For the triangle, the sides are all different lengths, so the formula doesn't help. Instead, add the sides: 3 + 4 + 5 = 12 inches.

Directions: Find the perimeter of each shape below. Use the formula whenever possible.

10 ft.

8 ft.

6 ft.

3 ft.

11 ft.

4 ft.

1. Find the perimeter of the room pictured at left.   P = _____

2. Brandy plans to frame a picture with a sheet of construction paper. Her picture is 8 in. wide and 13 in. long. She wants the frame to extend 1 in. beyond the picture on all sides. How wide and long should the frame be? What is the perimeter of her picture and of the frame?

Length and width of frame: _____

Perimeter of picture: _____

Perimeter of frame: _____

3. A square has a perimeter of 120 feet. How long is each side?   _____

4. A triangle with equal sides has a perimeter of 96 inches. How long is each side?   _____

5. A rectangle has two sides that are each 14 feet long and a perimeter of 50 feet. How wide is it?   _____

Perimeter

Directions: Find the perimeter of each shape below.

1. $3 \times 4 \times 5 = 60$

3   4

5

P = ___60___

2.

12

2   2

8   2   2   2

2

P = _____

3.

16

16   16

16   16

16   16

16

$\begin{array}{r} 16^4 \\ \times 8 \\ \hline 122 \end{array}$

P = ___122___

4.

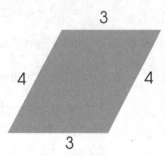

4

4   3

7

P = _____

5.

4

4   4

4

P = ___16___

6.

3

4   4

3

P = _____

7.

4

5

7

9

P = _____

8.

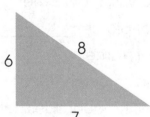

8

6

7

P = _____

Area: Squares and Rectangles

The **area** is the number of square units that covers a certain space. To find the area, multiply the length by the width. The answer is in square units, shown by adding a superscript 2 (^{2}) to the number.

Examples:

 3 in.

 5 in.

8 in.

For the rectangle, use this formula: **A = l x w**
$$A = 8 \times 5$$
$$A = 40 \text{ in.}^2$$

For the square formula, **s** stands for side: **A = s x s** (or s^2)
$$A = 3 \times 3 \text{ (or } 3^2)$$
$$A = 9 \text{ in.}^2$$

Directions: Find the area of each shape below.

7 ft.

12 ft.

1. Find the area of a room that is 12 feet long and 7 feet wide.   A = _____

2. A farmer's field is 32 feet on each side. How many square feet does she have to plow?   _____

3. Kwan's bedroom is 10 feet by 12 feet. How many square feet of carpeting would cover the floor?   _____

4. Two of Kwan's walls are 7.5 feet high and 12 feet long. The other two are the same height and 10 feet long. How many square feet of wallpaper would cover all four walls?

    Square feet for 12-foot wall = _____ x 2 = _____

    Square feet for 10-foot wall = _____ x 2 = _____

5. A clothes shop moved from a store that was 35 by 22 feet to a new location that was 53 by 32 feet. How many more square feet does the store have now?

    Square feet for first location = _____

    Square feet for new location = _____ Difference = _____

6. A school wanted to purchase a climber for the playground. The one they selected would need 98 square feet of space. The only space available on the playground was 12 feet long and 8 feet wide. Will there be enough space for the climber? _____

Area: Triangles

Finding the area of a triangle requires knowing the size of the base and the height. For the triangle formula, use **b** for **base** and **h** for **height**. Multiply ½ times the size of the base, and then multiply by the height. The answer will be in square units.

Example:

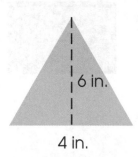

6 in.

4 in.

$A = \frac{1}{2} \times b \times h$

$A = \frac{1}{2} \times 4 \times 6$

$A = 12 \text{ in.}^2$

Directions: Apply the formula to find the area of each triangle below.

1.

5 in.

3 in.

4 in.

A = _____

2.

7 in.

5 in.

A = _____

3.

h = 6 in.

3 in.

A = _____

4.

2 in.

1 in.

A = _____

5. Addison wanted to make a sail for her new boat. The base of the triangular sail would be 7 feet, and the height would be 6 feet. Find the area.

A = _____

Area Challenge

When finding the area of an unusual shape, first try to divide it into squares, rectangles, or triangles. Find the area of each of those parts, and then add your answers together to find the total area of the object.

Directions: Find the area of each shape below.

1.

3 in.   3 in.

4 in. |←—15 in.—→| 4 in.

Total area = _____

2.

6 ft.

5 ft.   7 ft.

4 ft.

Total area = _____

3.

|←— 8 ft. —→|

3 ft.   4 ft.

Total area = _____

4.

6

2

|←— 12 —→|

Total area = _____

5.

4

2

2

4

6

2

Total area = _____ units²

6.
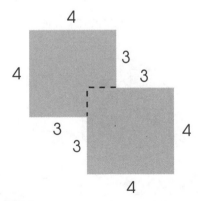

4

3

4   3

3

3

4

3

4

Total area = _____ units²

Volume

Volume is the number of cubic units that fills a space. A **cubic unit** has 6 equal sides, like a child's block. To find the volume (**V**) of something, multiply the length (**l**) by the width (**w**) by the height (**h**), or **V = l x w x h**. The answer will be in cubic units (^{3}). Sometimes it's easier to understand volume if you imagine a figure is made of small cubes.

Example: **V = l x w x h**
V = 4 x 6 x 5
V = 120 in.^{3}

Directions: Solve the following problems.

1. What is the volume of a cube that is 7 inches on each side? _____

2. How many cubic inches of cereal are in a box that is 10 inches long, 6 inches wide, and 4.5 inches high? _____

3. Jeremy made a tower of five blocks that are each 2.5 inches square. How many cubic inches are in his tower? _____

4. How many cubic feet of gravel are in the back of a full dump truck that measures 7 feet wide by 4 feet tall by 16 feet long? _____

5. Will 1,000 cubic inches of dirt fill a flower box that is 32 inches long, 7 inches wide, and 7 inches tall? _____

6. A mouse needs 100 cubic inches of air to live for an hour. Will your pet mouse be okay for an hour in an airtight box that's 4.5 inches wide by 8.25 inches long by 2.5 inches high? _____

7. Find the volume of the figures below. 1 cube = 1 inch^3

A.

V = _____

C.
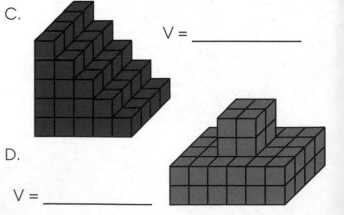
V = _____

B.
V = _____

D.
V = _____

Geometric Patterns

Geometric patterns can be described in several ways. **Similar shapes** have the same shape but in differing sizes. **Congruent shapes** have the same geometric pattern but may be facing in different directions. **Symmetrical shapes** are identical when divided in half.

Directions: Use the terms **similar**, **congruent**, or **symmetrical** to describe the following patterns.

1.

_____

2.

_____

3.

_____

4.

_____

5.

_____

6.

_____

7.

_____

Comprehensive Curriculum - **Grade 6**

Angles

Angles are named according to the number of degrees between the lines. The degrees are measured with a protractor.

Examples:

straight angle
(measures 180°)

right angle
(90°)

acute angle
(less than 90°)

obtuse angle
(more than 90°)

Directions: Study the examples. Then, follow the instructions below.

1. Use a protractor to measure each angle below. Then, write whether it is straight, right, acute, or obtuse.

A.

Degrees: _____

Kind of angle: _____

C.

Degrees: _____

Kind of angle: _____

B.

Degrees: _____

Kind of angle: _____

D.

Degrees: _____

Kind of angle: _____

2. The angles in this figure are named by letters. Write the number of degrees in each angle and whether it is straight, right, acute, or obtuse.

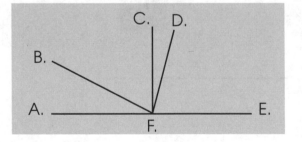

a. Angle AFB   Degrees: _____   Kind of angle: _____

b. Angle AFC   Degrees: _____   Kind of angle: _____

c. Angle AFD   Degrees: _____   Kind of angle: _____

d. Angle AFE   Degrees: _____   Kind of angle: _____

e. Angle BFD   Degrees: _____   Kind of angle: _____

Types of Triangles

The sum of angles in all triangles is 180°. However, triangles come in different shapes. They are categorized by the length of their sides and by their types of angles.

Equilateral:

Three equal sides

Acute:

Three acute angles

Isosceles:

Two equal sides

Right:

One right angle

Scalene:

Zero equal sides

Obtuse:

One obtuse angle

One triangle can be a combination of types, such as isosceles and obtuse.

Directions: Study the examples. Then, complete the exercises below.

1. Read these directions, and color in the correct triangles.

    Color the right scalene triangle blue.
    Color the obtuse scalene triangle red.
    Color the equilateral triangle yellow.
    Color the right isosceles triangle green.
    Color the acute isosceles triangle black.

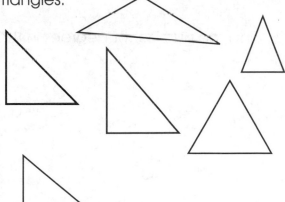

2. Describe each of these triangles in two ways.

    A.

    B.

    _____ _____   _____ _____

3. In the space below, draw the following triangles.

scalene triangle

equilateral triangle

obtuse triangle

Finding Angles

All triangles have three angles. The sum of these angles is 180°. Therefore, if we know the number of degrees in two of the angles, we can add them together and then subtract from 180 to find the size of the third angle.

Directions: Follow the instructions below.

1. Circle the number that shows the third angle of triangles A through F. Then, describe each triangle two ways. The first one has been done for you.

    A. 60°, 60°   45° 50° (60°)   ___equilateral, acute___

    B. 35°, 55°   27° 90° 132°   _____

    C. 30°, 120°   30° 74° 112°   _____

    D. 15°, 78°   65° 87° 98°   _____

    E. 28°, 93°   61° 59° 70°   _____

    F. 12°, 114°   60° 50° 54°   _____

2. Find the number of degrees in the third angle of each triangle below.

    A.

    40°   40°

    _____

    B.

    90°   30°

    _____

    C.

    79°   35°

    _____

    D.

    58°   62°

    _____

    E.

    20°   90°

    _____

    F.

    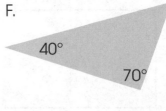
    40°
    70°

    _____

Types of Quadrilaterals

A **quadrilateral** is a shape with four sides and four angles. The sum of angles in all quadrilaterals is 360°. Like triangles, quadrilaterals come in different shapes and are categorized by their sides and their angles.

A **square** has four parallel sides of equal length and four 90° angles.

A **rectangle** has four parallel sides, but only its opposite sides are equal length; it has four 90° angles.

A **parallelogram** has four parallel sides, with the opposite sides of equal length.

A **trapezoid** has two opposite sides that are parallel; its sides may or may not be equal length; its angles may include none, one, or two that are 90°.

Directions: Study the examples. Then, complete the exercises below.

1. Color in the correct quadrilaterals.

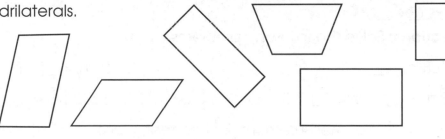

Color two squares blue.   Color two rectangles red.
Color two parallelograms yellow.   Color two trapezoids green.

2. Circle the number that shows the missing angle for each quadrilateral. Then name the possible quadrilaterals that could have those angles.

A. 90°, 90°, 90°	45°	90°	180°	_____
B. 65°, 115°, 65°	65°	90°	115°	_____
C. 90°, 110°, 90°	45°	70°	125°	_____
D. 100°, 80°, 80°	40°	80°	100°	_____
E. 90°, 120°, 50°	50°	75°	100°	_____

Name _____

Length in Customary Units

The **customary system** of measurement is the most widely used in the United States. It measures length in inches, feet, yards, and miles.

Examples:

12 inches (in.) = 1 foot (ft.)
3 ft. (36 in.) = 1 yard (yd.)
5,280 ft. (1,760 yds.) = 1 mile (mi.)

To change to a larger unit, divide. To change to a smaller unit, multiply.

Examples:

To change inches to feet, divide by 12.	24 in. = 2 ft.	27 in. = 2 ft. 3 in.
To change feet to inches, multiply by 12.	3 ft. = 36 in.	4 ft. = 48 in.
To change inches to yards, divide by 36.	108 in. = 3 yd.	80 in. = 2 yd. 8 in.
To change feet to yards, divide by 3.	12 ft. = 4 yd.	11 ft. = 3 yd. 2 ft.

Sometimes in subtraction you have to borrow units.

Examples:

$$3 \text{ ft. } 4 \text{ in.} = 2 \text{ ft. } 16 \text{ in.}$$
$$\underline{- 1 \text{ ft. } 11 \text{ in.}} \quad \underline{- 1 \text{ ft. } 11 \text{ in.}}$$
$$1 \text{ ft. } 5 \text{ in.}$$

$$3 \text{ yd.} = 2 \text{ yd. } 3 \text{ ft.}$$
$$\underline{- 1 \text{ yd. } 2 \text{ ft.}} \quad \underline{- 1 \text{ yd. } 2 \text{ ft.}}$$
$$1 \text{ yd. } 1 \text{ ft.}$$

Directions: Solve the following problems.

1. 108 in. = ____ ft.

2. 68 in. = ____ ft. ____ in.

3. 8 ft. = ____ yd. ____ ft.

4. 3,520 yd. = ____ mi.

5. What form of measurement (inches, feet, yards, or miles) would you use for each item below?

   a. pencil _____   b. vacation trip _____

   c. playground _____   d. wall _____

6. One side of a square box is 2 ft. 4 in. What is the perimeter of the box? _____

7. Jason is 59 in. tall. Kent is 5 ft. 1 in. tall. Who is taller and by how much? _____

8. Kyra bought a doll 2 ft. 8 in. tall for her little sister. She found a box that is 29 in. long. Will the doll fit in that box? _____

9. Dan's dog likes to go out in the backyard, which is 85 ft. wide. The dog's chain is 17 ft. 6 in. long. If Dan attaches one end of the chain to a pole in the middle of the yard, will his dog be able to leave the yard? _____

Weight in Metric Units

A **gram** (**g**) is about 0.035 oz.
A **milligram** (**mg**) is $\frac{1}{1000}$ g or about 0.000035 oz.
A **kilogram** (**kg**) is 1,000 g or about 2.2 lb.
A **metric ton** (**t**) is 1,000 kg or about 1.1 tn.

To change g to mg, multiply by 1,000.
To change g to kg, divide by 1,000.
To change kg to g, multiply by 1,000.
To change t to kg, multiply by 1,000.

Directions: Solve the following problems.

1. 3 kg = _____ g

2. 2 g = _____ mg

3. 145 g = _____ kg

4. 3,000 kg = _____ t

5. _____ g = 450 mg

6. 3.5 t = _____ kg

7. Write the missing units below: g, mg, kg, or t.

    a. A sunflower seed weighs less than 1 _____.

    b. A serving of cereal contains 14 _____ of sugar.

    c. The same serving of cereal has 250 _____ of salt.

    d. A bowling ball weighs about 7 _____.

    e. A whale weighs about 90 _____.

    f. A math textbook weighs about 1 _____.

    g. A safety pin weighs about 1 _____.

    h. An average car weighs about 1 _____.

8. Is 200 g closer to 7 oz. or 70 oz.? _____

9. Is 3 kg closer to 7 lb. or 70 lb.? _____

10. Does a metric ton weigh more or less than a ton
     measured by the customary system? _____

11. How is a kilogram different from a kilometer? _____

12. Which is heavier, 300 g or 1 kg? _____

Capacity in Customary Units

Here are the main ways to measure capacity (how much something will hold) in customary units:

8 fluid ounces (fl. oz.) = 1 cup (c.)
2 c. = 1 pint (pt.)
2 pt. = 1 quart (qt.)
4 qt. = 1 gallon (gal.)

To change ounces to cups, divide by 8.
To change cups to ounces, multiply by 8.
To change cups to pints or pints to quarts, divide by 2.
To change pints to cups or quarts to pints, multiply by 2.

As with measurements of length and weight, you may have to borrow units in subtraction.

Example: 3 gal. 2 qt. =   2 gal. 6 qt.
                  – 1 gal. 3 qt.   – 1 gal. 3 qt.
                      1 gal. 3 qt.

Directions: Solve the following problems.

1. 32 fl. oz. = _____ pt.   2. 4 gal. = _____ pt.   3. _____ c. = 24 fl. oz.

4. 5 pt. = _____ qt.   5. 16 pt. = _____ gal.   6. 3 pt. = _____ fl. oz.

7. A large can of soup contains 19 fl. oz. A serving is about 8 oz. How many cans should you buy if you want to serve 7 people? _____

8. A container of strawberry ice cream holds 36 fl. oz. A container of chocolate ice cream holds 2 pt. Which one has more ice cream? How much more?   _____

9. A day-care worker wants to give 15 children each 6 fl. oz. of milk. How many quarts of milk does she need?   _____

10. This morning, the day-care supervisor bought 3 gal. of milk. The kids drank 2 gal. 3 c. How much milk is left for tomorrow?   _____

11. Harriet bought 3 gal. 2 qt. of paint for her living room. She used 2 gal. 3 qt. How much paint is left over?   _____

12. Yusef's favorite punch takes a pint of raspberry sherbet. If he wants to make $1\frac{1}{2}$ times the recipe, how many fl. oz. of sherbet does he need?   _____

Capacity in Metric Units

A **liter** (**L**) is a little over 1 quart.
A **milliliter** (**mL**) is $\frac{1}{1000}$ of a liter, or about 0.03 oz.
A **kiloliter** (**kL**) is 1,000 liters or about 250 gallons.

Directions: Solve the following problems.

1. 5,000 mL = _____ L

2. 2,000 l = _____ kL

3. 3 L = _____ mL

4. Write the missing unit: L, mL, or kL.

    a. A swimming pool holds about 100 _____ of water.

    b. An eyedropper is marked for 1 and 2 _____.

    c. A pitcher could hold 1 or 2 _____ of juice.

    d. A teaspoon holds about 5 _____ of medicine.

    e. A birdbath might hold 5 _____ of water.

    f. A tablespoon holds about 15 _____ of salt.

    g. A bowl holds about 250 _____ of soup.

    h. We drank about 4 _____ of punch at the party.

5. Which is more, 3 L or a gallon? _____

6. Which is more, 400 mL or 40 oz.? _____

7. Which is more, 1 kL or 500 L? _____

8. Is 4 L closer to a quart or a gallon? _____

9. Is 480 mL closer to 2 cups or 2 pints? _____

10. Is a mL closer to 4 drops or 4 teaspoonsful? _____

11. How many glasses of juice containing 250 mL
each could you pour from a 1-L jug? _____

12. How much water would you need to water an
average-sized lawn, 1 kL or 1 L? _____

Temperature in Customary and Metric Units

The customary system measures temperature in Fahrenheit (F°) degrees.

220
212° boiling
200
180
160
140
120
100
80
60
40 — 32° freezing
20
0
−20

The metric system uses Celsius (C°) degrees.

110
100 — 100° boiling
90
80
60
40
30
20
10
0 — 0° freezing
−10
−20

Directions: Study the thermometers, and answer these questions.

1. Write in the temperature from both systems:

	Fahrenheit	**Celsius**
a. freezing	_____	_____
b. boiling	_____	_____
c. comfortable room temperature	_____	_____

2. Underline the most appropriate temperature for both systems.

   a. a reasonably hot day   34°   54°   84°   10°   20°   35°

   b. a cup of hot chocolate   95°   120°   190°   60°   90°   120°

   c. comfortable water to swim in   55°   75°   95°   10°   25°   40°

3. If the temperature is 35°C, is it summer or winter? _____

4. Would ice cream stay frozen at 35°F? _____

5. Which is colder, −10°C or −10°F? _____

6. Which is warmer, 60°C or 60°F? _____

Review

Directions: Complete the following exercises.

1. 372 in. = _____ yd. _____ ft.

2. 4 km = _____ m

3. 1.25 lb. = _____ oz.

4. 2,000 mg = _____ g

5. 1 qt. = _____ oz.

6. 10,000 mL = _____ L

7. Todd has a board that is 6 ft. 3 in. long. He needs to cut it to 4 ft. 9 in. How much should he cut off? _____

8. In a contest, Lauren threw a ball 12 yd. Jiao threw the ball 500 in. Who threw the farthest? _____

9. Would you measure this workbook in mm or cm? _____

10. Which is heavier, a box of books that weighs 4 lb. 6 oz. or a box of dishes that weighs 80 oz.? _____

11. A 1-lb. package has 10 hot dogs. How many ounces does each hot dog weigh? _____

12. Would the amount of salt (sodium) in 1 oz. of pretzels be 170 g or 170 mg? _____

13. If a family ate half a gallon of frozen yogurt, how many fluid ounces would be left? _____

14. You want to serve 6 fl. oz of fruit juice to each of 16 friends at your party. How many quarts of juice should you buy? _____

15. Would you measure water in a fish pond with L or kL? _____

16. Would popsicles melt at 5°C? _____

17. Would soup be steaming hot at 150°F? _____

Ratios

A **ratio** is a comparison of two quantities. For example, a wall is 96 in. high; a pencil is 8 in. long. By dividing 8 into 96, you find it would take 12 pencils to equal the height of the wall. The ratio, or comparison, of the wall to the pencil can be written three ways: 1 to 12; 1:12; $\frac{1}{12}$. In this example, the ratio of triangles to circles is 4:6. The ratio of triangles to squares is 4:9. The ratio of circles to squares is 6:9. These ratios will stay the same if we divide both numbers in the ratio by the same number.

Examples: $\frac{4 \div 2 = 2}{6 \div 2 = 3}$ $\frac{6 \div 3 = 2}{9 \div 3 = 3}$ (There is no number that will divide into both 4 and 9.)

By reducing 4:6 and 6:9 to their lowest terms, they are the same—2:3. This means that 2:3, 4:6, and 6:9 are all equal ratios. You can also find equal ratios for all three by multiplying both numbers of the ratio by the same number.

Examples: $\frac{4 \times 3 = 12}{6 \times 3 = 18}$ $\frac{6 \times 5 = 30}{9 \times 5 = 45}$ $\frac{4 \times 4 = 16}{9 \times 4 = 36}$

Directions: Solve the following problems.

1. Write two more equal ratios for each of the following by multiplying or dividing both numbers in the ratio by the same number.

    a. $\frac{1}{2}$ $\frac{2}{4}$ $\frac{3}{6}$ _____ _____   b. $\frac{1}{4}$ $\frac{2}{8}$ $\frac{4}{16}$ _____ _____   c. $\frac{8}{24}$ $\frac{1}{3}$ $\frac{3}{9}$ _____ _____

2. Circle the ratios that are equal.

    a. $\frac{1}{6}$ $\frac{3}{6}$ b. $\frac{15}{25}$ $\frac{3}{5}$ c. $\frac{2}{7}$ $\frac{10}{35}$ d. $\frac{2}{3}$ $\frac{6}{10}$

3. Write each ratio three ways.

    a. stars to faces _____

    b. faces to trees _____

    c. stars to all other shapes _____

4. Write two equal ratios (multiplying or dividing) for:

    a. stars to faces _____

    b. faces to trees _____

    c. stars to all other shapes _____

Missing Numbers in Ratios

You can find a missing number (n) in an equal ratio. First, figure out which number has already been multiplied to get the number you know. (In the first example, 3 is multiplied by 3 to get 9; in the second example, 2 is multiplied by 6 to get 12.) Then, multiply the other number in the ratio by the same number (3 and 6 in the examples).

Examples: $\dfrac{3}{4} = \dfrac{9}{n}$ $\dfrac{3}{4} \times \dfrac{3}{3} = \dfrac{9}{12}$ $n = 12$ $\dfrac{1}{2} = \dfrac{n}{12}$ $\dfrac{1}{2} \times \dfrac{6}{6} = \dfrac{6}{12}$ $n = 6$

Directions: Solve the following problems.

1. Find each missing number.

a. $\dfrac{1}{2} = \dfrac{n}{12}$ $n =$ _____

b. $\dfrac{1}{5} = \dfrac{n}{15}$ $n =$ _____

c. $\dfrac{3}{2} = \dfrac{18}{n}$ $n =$ _____

d. $\dfrac{5}{8} = \dfrac{n}{32}$ $n =$ _____

e. $\dfrac{8}{3} = \dfrac{16}{n}$ $n =$ _____

f. $\dfrac{n}{14} = \dfrac{5}{7}$ $n =$ _____

2. If a basketball player makes 9 baskets in 12 tries, what is her ratio of baskets to tries, in lowest terms? _____

3. At the next game, the player has the same ratio of baskets to tries. If she tries 20 times, how many baskets should she make? _____

4. At the third game, she still has the same ratio of baskets to tries. This time she makes 12 baskets. How many times did she probably try? _____

5. If a driver travels 40 miles in an hour, what is his ratio of miles to minutes, in lowest terms? _____

6. At the same speed, how far would the driver travel in 30 minutes? _____

7. At the same speed, how long would it take him to travel 60 miles? _____

Proportions

A **proportion** is a statement that two ratios are equal. To make sure ratios are equal, called a proportion, we multiply the cross products.

Examples of proportions: $\frac{1}{5} = \frac{2}{10}$ $\frac{1}{2} \times \frac{10}{5} = \frac{10}{10}$ $\frac{3}{7} = \frac{15}{35}$ $\frac{3}{7} \times \frac{35}{15} = \frac{105}{105}$

These two ratios are not a proportion: $\frac{4}{3} = \frac{5}{6}$ $\frac{4}{3} \times \frac{6}{5} = \frac{24}{15}$

To find a missing number (n) in a proportion, multiply the cross products and divide.

Examples: $\frac{n}{30} = \frac{1}{6}$ $n \times 6 = 1 \times 30$ $n \times 6 = 30$

$$n = \frac{30}{6}$$
$$n = 5$$

Directions: Solve the following problems.

1. Write = between the ratios if they are a proportion. Write ≠ if they are not a proportion. The first one has been done for you.

   a. $\frac{1}{2}$ $\frac{6}{12}$ b. $\frac{13}{18} \bigcirc \frac{20}{22}$ c. $\frac{2}{6} \bigcirc \frac{5}{15}$ d. $\frac{5}{6} \bigcirc \frac{20}{24}$

2. Find the missing numbers in these proportions.

   a. $\frac{2}{5} = \frac{n}{15}$ $n =$ _____

   b. $\frac{3}{8} = \frac{9}{n}$ $n =$ _____

   c. $\frac{n}{18} = \frac{4}{12}$ $n =$ _____

3. One issue of a magazine costs $2.99, but if you buy a subscription, 12 issues cost $35.88. Is the price at the same proportion?   _____

4. A muffin recipe calls for 3 cups of flour to make 24 muffins. How much flour is needed for 36 muffins?   _____

5. The same recipe requires 4 teaspoons of cinnamon for 36 muffins. How many teaspoons is needed to make 48 muffins? (Answer will include a fraction.)   _____

6. The recipe also calls for 2 cups of sugar for 36 muffins. How much sugar should you use for 48 muffins? (Answer will include a fraction.)   _____

Percents

Percent means "per 100." A percent is a ratio that compares a number with 100. The same number can be written as a decimal and a percent. To change a decimal to a percent, move the decimal point two places to the right and add the % sign. To change a percent to a decimal, drop the % sign and place a decimal point two places to the left.

Examples: $0.25 = 25\%$ $0.1 = 10\%$ $1.456 = 145.6\%$
     $32\% = 0.32$ $99\% = 0.99$ $203\% = 2.03$

A percent or decimal can also be written as a ratio or fraction.

Example: $0.25 = 25\% = \dfrac{25}{100} = \dfrac{1}{4} = 1{:}4$

To change a fraction or ratio to a percent, first change it to a decimal. Divide the numerator by the denominator.

Examples: $\dfrac{1}{3} = 3\overline{\smash{)}1.00}$ $0.33\tfrac{1}{3} = 33\tfrac{1}{3}\%$ $\dfrac{2}{5} = 5\overline{\smash{)}2.0}$ $0.4 = 40\%$

Directions: Solve the following problems.

1. Change the percents to decimals.

   a. $3\% =$ _____   b. $75\% =$ _____   c. $14\% =$ _____   d. $115\% =$ _____

2. Change the decimals and fractions to percents.

   a. $0.56 =$ _____ %   b. $0.03 =$ _____ %   c. $\dfrac{3}{4} =$ _____ %   d. $\dfrac{1}{5} =$ _____ %

3. Change the percents to ratios in their lowest terms. The first one has been done for you.

   a. $75\% =$ ___ $\dfrac{75}{100} = \dfrac{3}{4} = \mathbf{3{:}4}$ ___   b. $40\% =$ _____

   c. $35\% =$ _____   d. $70\% =$ _____

4. The class was 45% girls. What percent was boys?   _____

5. Half the shoes in one store were on sale. What percent of the shoes were their ordinary price?   _____

6. Tierra read 84 pages of a 100-page book. What percent of the book did she read?   _____

Percents

To find the percent of a number, change the percent to a decimal and multiply.

Examples: 45% of $20 = 0.45 x $20 = $9.00
                  125% of 30 = 1.25 x 30 = 37.50

Directions: Solve the following problems. Round the answers to the nearest hundredth where necessary.

1. Find the percent of each number.

   a. 26% of 40 = _____   b. 12% of 329 = _____

   c. 73% of 19 = _____   d. 2% of 24 = _____

2. One family spends 35% of its weekly budget of $375 on food. How much do they spend?

   _____

3. A shirt in a store usually costs $15.99, but today it's on sale for 25% off. The clerk says you will save $4.50. Is that true?

   _____

4. A book that usually costs $12 is on sale for 25% off. How much will it cost?

   _____

5. After you answer 60% of 150 math problems, how many do you have left to do?

   _____

6. A pet store's shipment of tropical fish was delayed. Nearly 40% of the 1,350 fish died. About how many lived?

   _____

7. The shipment had 230 angelfish, which died in the same proportion as the other kinds of fish. About how many angelfish died?

   _____

8. A church youth group was collecting cans of food. Their goal was 1,200 cans, but they exceeded their goal by 25%. How many cans did they collect?

   _____

Probability

Probability is the ratio of favorable outcomes to possible outcomes in an experiment. You can use probability (P) to figure out how likely something is to happen. For example, six picture cards are turned facedown—3 cards have stars, 2 have triangles, and 1 has a circle. What is the probability of picking the circle? Using the formula below, you have a 1 in 6 probability of picking the circle, a 2 in 6 probability of picking a triangle, and a 3 in 6 probability of picking a star.

Example: $P - \dfrac{\text{number of favorable outcomes}}{\text{number of trials}}$ $P = \dfrac{1}{6} = 1{:}6$

Directions: Solve the following problems.

1. A class has 14 girls and 15 boys. If all of their names are put on separate slips in a hat, what is the probability of each person's name being chosen? _____

2. In the same class, what is the probability that a girl's name will be chosen? _____

3. In this class, 3 boys are named Jack. What is the probability that a slip with "Jack" written on it will be chosen? _____

4. A spinner on a board game has the numbers 1–8. What is the probability of spinning and getting a 4? _____

5. A paper bag holds these colors of wooden beads: 4 blue, 5 red, and 6 yellow. If you select a bead without looking, do you have an equal probability of getting each color? _____

6. Using the same bag of beads, what is the probability of reaching in and drawing out a red bead (in lowest terms)? _____

7. In the same bag, what is the probability of not getting a blue bead? _____

8. In a carnival game, plastic ducks have spots. The probability of picking a duck with a yellow spot is 2:15. There is twice as much probability of picking a duck with a red spot. What is the probability of picking a duck with a red spot? _____

9. In this game, all the other ducks have green spots. What is the probability of picking a duck with a green spot (in lowest terms)? _____

Possible Combinations

Today the cafeteria is offering 4 kinds of sandwiches, 3 kinds of drinks, and 2 kinds of fruits. How many possible combinations could you make? To find out, multiply the number of choices together.

Example: 4 x 3 x 2 = 24 possible combinations

Directions: Solve the following problems.

1. If Juan has 3 shirts and 4 pairs of shorts, how many combinations can he make? _____

2. Jamilla can borrow 1 book and 1 magazine at a time from her classroom library. The library has 45 books and 16 magazines. How many combinations are possible? _____

3. Kerry's mother is redecorating the living room. She has narrowed her choices to 6 kinds of wallpaper, 3 shades of paint, and 4 colors of carpeting that all match. How many possible combinations are there? _____

4. Maya has 6 sweaters that she can combine with pants to make 24 outfits. How many pairs of pants does she have? _____

5. Cooper can get to school by walking, taking a bus, riding his bike, or asking his parents for a ride. He can get home the same ways, except his parents aren't available then. How many combinations can he make of ways to get to school and get home? _____

6. Gabby's middle school offers 3 different language classes, 3 art classes, and 2 music classes. If she takes one class in each area, how many possible combinations are there? _____

7. Vikram's school offers 4 language classes, 3 art classes, and some music classes. If Vikram can make 36 possible combinations, how many music classes are there? _____

8. AAA Airlines schedules 12 flights a day from Chicago to Atlanta. Four of those flights go on to Orlando. From the Orlando airport you can take a bus, ride in a taxi, or rent a car to get to Disneyworld. How many different ways are there to get from Chicago to Disneyworld if you make part of your trip on AAA Airlines? _____

Review

Directions: Solve the following problems. Round answers to the nearest hundredth where necessary.

1. Write an equal ratio for each of these:

   a. $\dfrac{1}{7} =$ _____

   b. $\dfrac{5}{8} =$ _____

   c. $\dfrac{15}{3} =$ _____

   d. $\dfrac{6}{24} =$ _____

2. State the ratios below in lowest terms.

   a. cats to bugs = _____

   b. cats to dogs = _____

   c. dogs to all other objects = _____

3. If Shawn drives 45 miles an hour, how far could he go in 40 minutes? _____

4. At the same speed, how many minutes would it take Shawn to drive 120 miles? _____

5. Mr. Herman is building a doghouse in proportion to his family's house. The family's house is 30 ft. high and the doghouse is 5 ft. high. If the family house is 42 ft. wide, how wide should the doghouse be? _____

6. The family house is 24 ft. from front to back. How big should Mr. Herman make the doghouse? _____

7. Change these numbers to percents:

   a. $0.56 =$ _____

   b. $\dfrac{4}{5} =$ _____

   c. $0.04 =$ _____

   d. $\dfrac{3}{8} =$ _____

8. Which is a better deal, a blue bike for $125 at 25% off or a red bike for $130 at 30% off? _____

9. If sales tax is 6%, what would be the total price of the blue bike? _____

10. Richard bought 6 raffle tickets for a free bike. If 462 tickets were sold, what is Richard's probability of winning? _____

11. Lilly bought 48 tickets in the same raffle. What are her chances of winning? _____

Comparing Data

Data is gathered information. The **range** is the difference between the highest and lowest number in a group of numbers. The **median** is the number in the middle when numbers are listed in order. The **mean** is the average of the numbers. We can compare numbers or data by finding the range, median, or mean.

Example: 16, 43, 34, 78, 8, 91, 26

To compare these numbers, we first need to put them in order: 8 16 26 34 43 78 91.
By subtracting the lowest number (8) from the highest one (91), we find the range: 83.
By finding the number that falls in the middle, we have the median: 34 (If no number fell exactly in the middle, we would average the two middle numbers.)
By adding them and dividing by the number of numbers (7), we get the mean: 42.29 (rounded to the nearest hundredth).

Directions: Solve the following problems. Round answers to the nearest hundredth where necessary.

1. Find the range, median, and mean of these numbers: 19, 5, 84, 27, 106, 38, 75.

    Range: _____   Median: _____   Mean: _____

2. Find the range, median, and mean finishing times for 6 runners in a race. Here are their times in seconds: 14.2, 12.9, 13.5, 10.3, 14.8, 14.7.

    Range: _____   Median: _____   Mean: _____

3. If the runner who won the race in 10.3 seconds had run even faster and finished in 7 seconds, would the mean time be higher or lower?   _____

4. If that runner had finished in 7 seconds, what would be the median time?   _____

5. Here are the high temperatures in one city for a week: 65, 72, 68, 74, 81, 68, 85. Find the range, median, and mean temperatures.

    Range: _____   Median: _____   Mean: _____

6. Find the range, median, and mean test scores for this group of students: 41, 32, 45, 36, 48, 38, 37, 42, 39, 36.

    Range: _____   Median: _____   Mean: _____

Tables

Organizing data into tables makes it easier to compare numbers. As evident in the example, putting many numbers in a paragraph is confusing. When the same numbers are organized in a table, you can compare numbers in a glance. Tables can be arranged several ways and still be easy to read and understand.

Example: Money spent on groceries:
Family A: week 1 — $98.50; week 2 — $134.25; week 3 — $142.00; week 4 — $103.50.
Family B: week 1 — $160.25; week 2 — $192.50; week 3 — $171.25; week 4 — $173.50.

	Week 1	Week 2	Week 3	Week 4
Family A	$98.50	$134.25	$142.00	$103.50
Family B	$160.25	$192.50	$171.25	$173.50

Directions: Complete the following exercises.

1. Finish the table below, and then answer the questions.
   Data: Steve weighs 185 lb. and is 6 ft. 2 in. tall. George weighs 218 lb. and is 6 ft. 3 in. tall. Chuck weighs 178 lb. and is 6 ft. 1 in. tall. Henry weighs 166 lb. and is 6 ft. tall.

	Henry	George	Chuck	Steve
Weight				
Height				

   a. Who is tallest? _____   b. Who weighs the least? _____

2. On another sheet of paper, prepare 2 tables comparing the amount of money made by 3 booths at the school carnival this year and last year. In the first table, write the names of the games in the left-hand column (like **Family A** and **Family B** in the example). In the second table (using the same data), write the years in the left-hand column. Here is the data: fish pond—this year $15.60, last year $13.50; bean-bag toss—this year $13.45, last year $10.25; ring toss—this year $23.80, last year $18.80. After you complete both tables, answer the following questions.

   a. Which booth made the most money this year? _____

   b. Which booth made the biggest improvement from last year to this year?

   _____

Bar Graphs

Another way to organize information is a **bar graph**. The bar graph in the example compares the number of students in 4 elementary schools. Each bar stands for 1 school. You can easily see that School A has the most students and School C has the least. The numbers along the left show how many students attend each school.

Example:

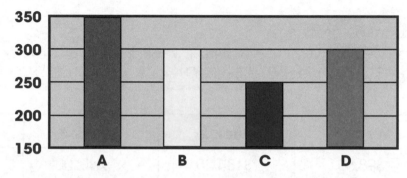

Directions: Complete the following exercises.

1. This bar graph will show how many calories are in 1 serving of 4 kinds of cereal. Draw the bars the correct height, and label each with the name of the cereal. After completing the bar graph, answer the questions. Data: Korn Kernels—150 calories; Oat Floats—160 calories; Rice Puffs—110 calories; Nut Crunch—200 calories.

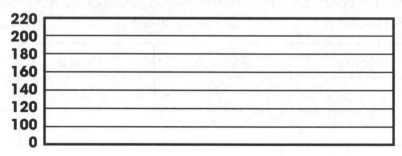

   A. Which cereal is the best to eat if you're trying to lose weight? _____

   B. Which cereal has nearly the same number of calories as Oat Floats?

   _____

2. On another sheet of paper, draw your own graph, showing the number of TV commercials in 1 week for each of the 4 cereals in the graph above. After completing the graph, answer the questions. Data: Oat Floats—27 commercials; Rice Puffs—15; Nut Crunch—35; Korn Kernels—28.

   A. Which cereal is most heavily advertised? _____

   B. What similarities do you notice between the graph of calories and the graph of TV commercials? _____

Picture Graphs

Newspapers and textbooks often use pictures in graphs instead of bars. Each picture stands for a certain number of objects. Half a picture means half the number. The picture graph in the example indicates the number of games each team won. The Astros won 7 games, so they have $3\frac{1}{2}$ balls.

Example:

	Games Won
Astros	⚾ ⚾ ⚾ ⚾
Orioles	⚾ ⚾
Bluebirds	⚾ ⚾ ⚾ ⚾
Sluggers	⚾

(1 ball = 2 games)

Directions: Complete the following exercises.

Finish this picture graph, showing the number of students who have dogs in 4 sixth-grade classes. Draw simple dogs in the graph, letting each drawing stand for 2 dogs.
Data: Class 1—12 dogs; Class 2—16 dogs; Class 3—22 dogs; Class 4—12 dogs.
After completing the graph, answer the questions.

	Dogs Owned by Students
Class 1	
Class 2	
Class 3	
Class 4	

(One dog drawing = 2 students' dogs)

1. Why do you think newspapers use picture graphs? _____

_____

2. Would picture graphs be appropriate to show the exact number of dogs living in America? Why or why not? _____

_____

Line Graphs

Still another way to display information is a line graph. The same data can often be shown in both a bar graph and a line graph. Line graphs are especially useful in showing changes over a period of time.

The line graph in the example shows changes in the number of students enrolled in a school over a 5-year period. Enrollment was highest in 2012 and has decreased gradually each year since then. Notice how labeling the years and enrollment numbers make the graph easy to understand.

Example:

Fall Enrollment at Cedar School

Directions: Complete the following exercises.

1. On another sheet of paper, draw a line graph that displays the growth of a corn plant over a 6-week period. Mark the correct points, using the data below, and connect them with a line. After completing the graph, answer the questions. Data: week 1—3.5 in.; week 2—4.5 in.; week 3—5 in.; week 4—5.5 in.; week 5—5.75 in.; week 6—6 in.

   a. Between which weeks was the growth fastest? _____

   b. Between which weeks was the growth slowest? _____

2. On another sheet of paper, draw a line graph to show how the high temperature varied during one week. Then answer the questions. Data: Sunday—high of 53 degrees; Monday—51; Tuesday—56; Wednesday—60; Thursday—58; Friday—67; Saturday—73. Don't forget to label the numbers.

   a. In general, did the days get warmer or cooler? _____

   b. Do you think this data would have been as clear in a bar graph? _____
      Explain your answer.

      _____

      _____

Circle Graphs

Circle graphs are useful in showing how something is divided into parts. The circle graph in the example shows how Carly spent her $10 allowance. Each section is a fraction of her whole allowance. For example, the movie tickets section is $\frac{1}{2}$ of the circle, showing that she spent $\frac{1}{2}$ of her allowance, $5, on movie tickets.

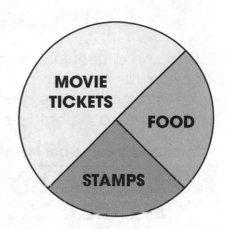

Directions: Complete the following exercises.

1. When the middle school opened last fall, $\frac{1}{2}$ of the students came from East Elementary, $\frac{1}{4}$ came from West Elementary, $\frac{1}{8}$ came from North Elementary, and the remaining students moved into the town from other cities. Make a circle graph showing these proportions. Label each section. Then, answer the questions.

    a. What fraction of students at the new school moved into the area from other cities? _____

    b. If the new middle school has 450 students enrolled, how many used to go to East Elementary?_____

2. This circle graph will show the hair color of 24 students in one class. Divide the circle into 4 sections to show this data: black hair—8 students; brown hair—10 students; blonde hair—4 students; red hair—2 students. (Hint: 8 students are $\frac{8}{24}$ or $\frac{1}{3}$ of the class.) Be sure to label each section by hair color. Then, answer the questions.

    a. Looking at your graph, what fraction of the class is the combined group of blonde- and red-haired students? _____

    b. Which two fractions of hair color combine to total half the class? _____

    _____

Comparing Presentation Methods

Tables and different kinds of graphs have different purposes. Some are more helpful for certain kinds of information. The table and three graphs below all show basically the same information—the amount of money Owen and Leyla made in their lawn-mowing business over a 4-month period.

Combined Income per Month

	Owen	Leyla
June	$34	$36
July	41	35
August	27	28
Sept.	36	40
Totals	$138	$139

Combined Income per Month

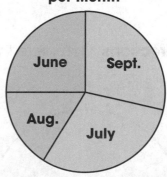

Combined Income per Month

Directions: Study the graphs and table. Then, circle the one that answers each question below.

1. Which one shows the fraction of the total income that Owen and Leyla made in August?

    table   line graph   bar graph   circle graph

2. Which one compares Owen's earnings with Leyla's?

    table   line graph   bar graph   circle graph

3. Which one has the most exact numbers?

    table   line graph   bar graph   circle graph

4. Which one has no numbers?

    table   line graph   bar graph   circle graph

5. Which two best show how Owen and Leyla's income changed from month to month?

    table   line graph   bar graph   circle graph

Graphing Data

Directions: Complete the following exercises.

1. Use the following information to create a bar graph.

Cities	Population (in 1,000s)
Dover	20
Newton Falls	12
Springdale	25
Hampton	17
Riverside	5

2. Study the data, and create a line graph showing the number of baskets Jonah scored during the season.

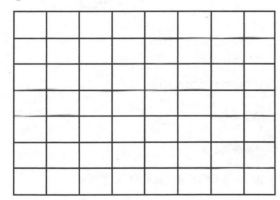

Game 1 — 10
Game 2 — 7
Game 3 — 11
Game 4 — 10
Game 5 — 9
Game 6 — 5
Game 7 — 9

Fill in the blanks.

a. High game: _____

b. Low game: _____

c. Average baskets per game: _____

3. Study the graph, then answer the questions.

a. Which flavor is the most popular? _____

b. Which flavor sold the least? _____

c. What decimal represents the two highest sellers? _____

d. Which flavor had $\frac{1}{10}$ of the sales? _____

Frozen Yogurt Sales

Integers

An **integer** is a whole number above or below 0: −2, −1, 0, +1, +2, and so on. **Opposite integers** are two integers the same distance from 0, but in different directions, such as −2 and +2.

Think of the water level in the picture as 0. The part of the iceberg sticking out of the water is positive. The iceberg has +3 feet above water. The part of the iceberg below the water is negative. The iceberg extends − 9 feet under water.

Numbers greater than 0 are **positive** numbers. Numbers less than 0 are **negative** numbers. Pairs of positive and negative numbers are called **opposite integers**.

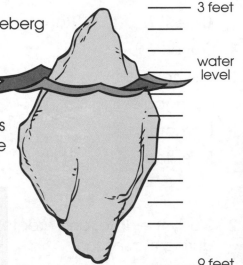

3 feet

water level

9 feet

Examples of opposite integers:
−5 and +5
losing 3 pounds and gaining 3 pounds
earning $12 and spending $12

Directions: Complete the following exercises.

1. Write each of these as an integer. The first one is done for you.

   a. positive 6 = __+6__   b. losing $5 = _____

   c. 5 degrees below 0 = _____   d. receiving $12 = _____

2. Write the **opposite** integer of each of these. The first one is done for you.

   a. negative 4 = __+4__   b. positive 10 = _____

   c. 2 floors below ground level = _____   d. winning a card game by 6 points = _____

3. Write integers to show each idea.

   a. A train that arrives 2 hours after it was scheduled: _____

   b. A package that has 3 fewer cups than it should: _____

   c. A board that's 3 inches too short: _____   d. A golf score 5 over par: _____

   e. A paycheck that doesn't cover $35 of a family's expenses: _____

   f. 30 seconds before a missile launch: _____

   g. A team that won 6 games and lost 2: _____

Comparing Integers

Comparing two integers can be confusing unless you think of them as being on a number line, as shown below. Remember that the integer farther to the right is greater. Thus, +2 is greater than –3, 0 is greater than –4, and –2 is greater than –5.

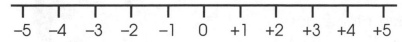

$$-5 \quad -4 \quad -3 \quad -2 \quad -1 \quad 0 \quad +1 \quad +2 \quad +3 \quad +4 \quad +5$$

Directions: Study the number line. Then, complete the following exercises.

1. Write in integers to complete the number line.

$$-5 \quad \underline{} \quad -3 \quad -2 \quad \underline{} \quad 0 \quad +1 \quad \underline{} \quad \underline{} \quad +4 \quad +5$$

2. Write < for "less than" or > for "greater than" to compare the integers. The first one is done for you.

—15°

a. –5 ___<___ +5   b. +3 _____ –3   c. +2 _____ –4

d. –4 _____ –3   e. –1 _____ +3   f. –1 _____ –5

3. Write **T** for true or **F** for false. (All degrees are in Fahrenheit.)

a. +7 degrees is colder than –3 degrees.   _____

b. –14 degrees is colder than –7 degrees.   _____

c. +23 degrees is colder than –44 degrees.   _____

d. –5 degrees is colder than +4 degrees.   _____

4. Draw an **X** by the series of integers that are in order from least to greatest.

_____ +2, +3, –4

_____ –3, 0, +1

_____ –7, –4, –1

_____ –3, –4, –5

Adding Integers

The sum of two positive integers is a positive integer.
    Thus, +4 + +1 = +5.
The sum of two negative integers is a negative integer.
    Thus, −5 + −2 = −7.
The sum of a positive and a negative integer has the
sign of the integer that is farther from 0.
    Thus, −6 + +3 = −3.
The sum of opposite integers is 0.
    Thus, +2 + −2 = 0

Directions: Complete the following exercises.

1. Add these integers.

    a. +2 + +7 = _____   b. −4 + −2 = _____   c. +5 + −3 = _____   d. +4 + −4 = _____

    e. −10 + −2 = _____   f. +6 + −1 = _____   g. +45 + −30 = _____   h. −39 + +26 = _____

2. Write the problems as integers. The first one has been done for you.

    a. One cold morning, the temperature was −14 degrees.
        The afternoon high was 20 degrees warmer. What was the
        high temperature that day?

        −14 + +20 = +6

    b. Another day, the high temperature was 26 degrees,
        but the temperature dropped 35 degrees during the
        night. What was the low that night?

        _____

    c. Valentina's allowance was $10. She paid $7 for a movie
        ticket. How much money did she have left?

        _____

    d. The temperature in a meat freezer was −10 degrees, but
        the power went off and the temperature rose 6 degrees.
        How cold was the freezer then?

        _____

    e. The school carnival took in $235, but it had expenses of $185.
        How much money did the carnival make after paying
        its expenses?

        _____

Subtracting Integers

To subtract an integer, change its sign to the opposite and add it. If you are subtracting a negative integer, make it positive and add it: +4 - -6 = +4 + +6 = +10. If you are subtracting a positive integer, make it negative and add it: +8 - +2 = +8 + -2 = +6.

| More examples: | -5 - -8 = -5 + +8 = +3 |
| | +3 - +7 = +3 + -7 = -4 |

Directions: Complete the following exercises.

1. Before subtracting these integers, rewrite each problem. The first one has been done for you.

   -6 - -8 = ___**-6 + +8 = +2**___   +3 - -4 = _____

   +9 - +3 = _____   -1 - -7 = _____

   +7 - -5 = _____   -4 - +3 = _____

2. Write these problems as integers. The first one is done for you.

   a. The high temperature in the Arctic Circle one day was
      -42 degrees. The low was -67 degrees. What
      was the difference between the two?   **-42 - -67 = -42 + +67 = +25**

   b. At the equator one day, the high temperature was
      +106 degrees. The low was +85 degrees. What
      was the difference between the two?   _____

   c. At George's house one morning, the thermometer showed it was
      +7 degrees. The radio announcer said it was -2 degrees. What is the
      difference between the two temperatures?   _____

   d. What is the difference between a temperature of +11 degrees
      and a wind-chill factor of -15 degrees?   _____

   e. During a dry spell, the level of a river dropped from 3 feet above
      normal to 13 feet below normal. How many
      feet did it drop?   _____

   f. Here are the average temperatures in a meat freezer for four days:
      -12, -11, -14, and -9 degrees. What is the difference between
      the highest and lowest temperature?   _____

Name _____

Plotting Graphs

A graph with horizontal and vertical number lines can show the location of certain points. The horizontal number line is called the **x-axis**, and the vertical number line is called the **y-axis**. Two numbers, called the **x coordinate** and the **y coordinate**, show where a point is on the graph.

The first coordinate, x, tells how many units to the right or left of 0 the point is located. On the example graph, point A is +2, two units to the right of 0.

The second coordinate, y, tells how many units above or below 0 the point is located. On the example, point A is –3, three units below 0.

Thus, the coordinates of A are +2, –3. The coordinates of B are –3, +2. (Notice the order of the coordinates.) The coordinates of C are +3, +1; and D, –2, –2.

Directions: Study the example. Then, answer these questions about the graph below.

1. What towns are at these coordinates?

   +1, +3   _____

   +1, –3   _____

   –4, +1   _____

   –2, –3   _____

   –3, –2   _____

   –3, +3   _____

2. What are the coordinates of these towns?

   Hampton   _____

   Wooster   _____

   Beachwood   _____

   Middletown   _____

   Kirby   _____

   Arbor   _____

Ordered Pairs

Ordered pairs is another term used to describe pairs of integers used to locate points on a graph.

Directions: Complete the following exercises.

1. Place the following points on the graph, using the ordered pairs as data.

+3, +3

−2, +4

+1, −2

+4, −3

−4, −4

+2, +3

−1, +4

2. Create your own set of ordered pairs. Use your home as the center of your coordinates—zero. Let the x-axis serve as East and West. The y-axis will be North and South. Now, select things to plot on your graph—the school, playground, grocery store, a friend's house, and so on.

Place	Ordered pair of coordinates
School	_____
Grocery store	_____
Playground	_____
Friend's house	_____

Review

Directions: Complete the following exercises.

1. Write the **opposite** integers of the following:

    a. 14 degrees above 0 _____

    b. Spending $21 _____

2. Write integers to show these ideas.

    a. 4 seconds after the launch of the space shuttle _____

    b. A lake 3 feet below its usual level _____

    c. 2 days before your birthday _____

3. Write < for "less than" or > for "greater than" to compare these integers.

    −2 __>__ −4   +2 __>__ −3   −1 _____ +1

4. Add the integers.

    −14 + −11 = _____   −6 + +5 = _____   −7 + +7 = _____

5. Subtract the integers.

    −4 − −5 = _____   +3 − −6 = _____   +7 − +2 = _____

6. Write **T** for true or **F** for false.

    a. The x coordinate is on the horizontal number line.   _____

    b. Add the x and y coordinates to find the location of a point.   _____

    c. Always state the x coordinate first.   _____

    d. A y coordinate of +2 would be above the horizontal number line.   _____

    e. An x coordinate of +2 would be to the right of the vertical number line. _____

Acrostic: A poem that uses the letters of a word to begin each line. When read down, the first letter of each line spells the word.

Acute Angle: An angle of less than 90 degrees.

Adverb: A word that tells something about a verb, an adjective, or another adverb. It answers the questions *when*, *where*, or *how*.

Analogy: A comparison showing how two things relate to each other. Example: *Nose* is to *smell* as *tongue* is to *taste* (nose : smell :: tongue : taste).

Angle: The amount of space where two lines meet.

Antecedent: The noun or nouns to which a pronoun refers.

Antonym: A word that means the opposite of another word.

Appositive: A noun or pronoun placed after another noun or pronoun to further identify it.

Area: The number of square units that covers a certain space.

Author's Purpose: The reason why an author writes a particular story or book.

Average: A value that lies within a range of values.

Biographical Dictionary: A book containing histories of people's lives.

Biography: A written history of a person's life.

Cause: The reason something happens.

Chapter: Parts into which some books are divided.

Character: A person in a story.

Classifying: Placing similar things into categories.

Column: A regular feature in a magazine or newspaper, often written by the same person, that states an opinion.

Columnist: A person who writes a column.

Combining Form: A word or word base used in forming words. Example: *tele* in *telephone*.

Command: A sentence telling someone to do something. It ends in a period or exclamation mark.

Comparative Adjectives: Compare two persons, places, things, or ideas.

Comparison: A way to show how things are alike or different.

Complete Sentence: A sentence that has both a simple subject and a simple predicate.

Comprehension: Understanding what is seen, read, or heard.

Conclusion Sentences: End a paragraph. They often restate the main idea.

Congruent Shapes: Identical geometric shapes. They can face in different directions.

Conjunction: A word that joins two or more sentences, words, or ideas.

Connotation: The meaning of a word, including all the emotions associated with it.

Cubic Unit: A unit with six equal sides, like a child's block.

Customary System: Measures length in inches and feet, capacity in cups and pints, weight in ounces and pounds, and temperature in Fahrenheit.

Dangling Modifier: A word, or words, that does not modify what it is meant to modify.

Data: Gathered information (*datum*—singular).

Decimal: A number that includes a period called a decimal point. The digits to the right of the decimal point are a value less than one.

Denominator: The bottom number in a fraction.

Denotation: The literal or dictionary definition of a word.

Dialogue: The words spoken by characters in a story.

Diamanté: A seven-line poem in the shape of a diamond.

Digit: A numeral.

Direct Object: A noun or pronoun that answers "what" or "whom" after the verb.

Dividend: The number to be divided in a division problem.

Divisor: What happens as a result of the cause.

Effect: A syllable at the end of a word that changes its meaning.

Entertain: To hold the attention of or to amuse someone.

Epitaph: A verse written on a tombstone, very popular in the past.

Equation: A number sentence in which the value on the left of the equal sign must equal the value on the right of the equal sign.

Equilateral Triangle: A triangle with three equal sides.

Equivalent Fractions: Fractions that name the same amount, such as $\frac{1}{2}$ and $\frac{5}{10}$.

Estimating: Using an approximate number instead of an exact one.

Exclamation: A sentence that shows strong feeling or excitement. It ends with an exclamation mark.

Expanded Notation: Writing out the value of each digit in a number.

Fact: Information that can be proven to be true. Example: Hawaii is a state.

Faulty Parallelism: When parts of a sentence do not match grammatically or structurally.

Feature: A specific type of article in a magazine or newspaper.

Fraction: A number that names part of something.

Free Verse: Poems that do not rhyme and do not have a regular rhythm.

Future Tense: Explains what will happen.

Gaelic Lullaby: An ancient Irish or Scottish song some parents sing as they rock their babies to sleep.

Generalization: A statement or rule that applies to many situations or examples.

Geometry: The study of lines and angles, the shapes they create, and how they relate to one another.

Giving Directions: Providing clear information explaining how to do or create something.

Greatest Common Factor (GCF): The largest number that will divide evenly into a set of numbers.

Haiku: A Japanese verse of three lines having five, seven, and five syllables each.

Homographs: Words that have the same spelling but different meanings.

Homophones: Words that sound alike but have different spellings and meanings.

Idiom: A phrase that says one thing but actually means something quite different.

Imagery: A picture that comes into the reader's mind when reading certain words.

Improper Fraction: A fraction that has a larger numerator than its denominator.

Independent Clause: Part of a sentence that contains a complete idea. It can stand alone.

Index: An alphabetical listing of names, topics, and important words that is found in the back of a book.

Indirect Object: A noun or pronoun that tells "to whom" or "what" or "for whom" or "what" the action is performed.

Inform: To give factual information.

Integers: Numbers above or below zero: –2, –1, 0, +1, +2, and so on.

Interrogative Pronoun: A pronoun used to ask a question. *Who*, *what*, and *which* are interrogative pronouns.

Irregular Verb: A verb whose past tense is not formed by adding *ed*.

Isosceles Triangle: A triangle with two equal sides.

Least Common Multiple (LCM): The lowest possible multiple any pair of numbers have in common.

Limerick: A humorous verse consisting of five lines with the first, second, and fifth lines rhyming, and the third and fourth lines rhyming.

Main Idea: The most important idea, or main points, in a sentence, paragraph, or story.

Making Inferences: Being able to come to conclusions based on what is suggested in the text.

Magazine: A periodical, regularly printed, containing articles, photographs, advertisements, etc.

Mean: The average of a group of numbers.

Median: The number in the middle when numbers are listed in order.

Metaphor: A figure of speech that directly compares one thing to another. Example: *The grass is a velvet carpet.*

Metric System: Measures length in meters, capacity in liters, mass in grams, and temperature in Celsius.

Mixed Number: A whole number and a fraction, such as $1\frac{1}{2}$.

Negative Numbers: Numbers less than zero.

Noun: A word that names a person, place, thing, or idea.

Numerator: The top number in a fraction.

Object of a Preposition: The noun or pronoun that follows a preposition and adds to its meaning.

Obtuse Angle: An angle of more than 90 degrees.

Opinion: A statement that expresses how someone feels or what he or she thinks about something. It cannot be proven.

Opposite Integers: Two integers the same distance from 0 but in different directions, such as –2 and +2.

Ordered Pairs: Another term used to describe two integers used to locate points on a graph.

Outline: A skeletal description of the main ideas and important details of a reading selection.

Paragraph: A group of sentences that tells about one main idea.

Parallel: Parts of a sentence that match grammatically and structurally.

Parallelogram: Has four parallel sides, with the opposite sides of equal length.

Paraphrase: To restate something in your own words.

Past Tense: Explains what has already happened.

Percent: A kind of ratio that compares a number with 100.

Perimeter: The distance around a shape formed by straight lines, such as a square.

Personal Pronoun: A word that takes the place of a noun. It refers to a person or a thing.

Personification: A figure of speech in which human characteristics are given to an animal or object.

Persuade: To convince someone to believe what is being stated.

Place Value: The position of a digit in a number.

Plot: The problem characters in a story face and how they solve it.

Plural: A word that refers to more than one thing.

Point of View: How a person or character in a story feels about an event and reacts to it.

Positive Adjectives: The adjectives themselves.

Positive Numbers: Numbers greater than zero.

Possessive Noun: A noun that shows ownership. Examples: *Jill's book* or *the women's hair*.

Possessive Pronoun: A pronoun that shows ownership. Examples: *mine, his, hers, yours, its, ours,* and *theirs*.

Predicate: A word, or several words, that tells what the subject does or that it exists.

Prefix: A syllable added to the beginning of a word that changes its meaning.

Preposition: A word that comes before a noun or pronoun and shows the relationship of that noun or pronoun to some other word in the sentence.

Prepositional Phrase: A group of words that includes a preposition, the object of the preposition, and all modifiers.

Present Tense: Explains what is happening now.

Probability: The ratio of favorable outcomes to possible outcomes in an experiment.

Pronoun: A word that takes the place of a noun. Examples: *I, he, she, we, it, you* and *them*.

Proportion: A statement that two ratios are equal.

Proverb: A bit of advice for daily life.

Quadrilateral: A shape with four sides and four angles.

Question: A sentence that asks something. It ends with a question mark.

Quotient: The answer in a division problem.

Range: The difference between the highest and lowest number in a group of numbers.

Ratio: A comparison of two quantities.

Recalling Details: Being able to pick out and remember the who, what, when, where, why, and how of what is read.

Reciprocals: Two fractions that, when multiplied together, make 1, such as $\frac{2}{7}$ and $\frac{7}{2}$.

Rectangle: Has four parallel sides, but only its opposite sides are equal lengths; it has four 90-degree angles.

Right Angle: An angle of 90 degrees.

Root Word: A word that is the common stem from which related words get their meanings.

Rounding: Expressing a number to the nearest whole number, ten, thousand, or other value.

Run-On Sentence: Two or more sentences joined together without punctuation or a joining word.

Scalene Triangle: A triangle with no equal sides.

Scan: To look for certain words in a reading selection to locate facts or answer questions.

Sections: Segments of each unit in a book.

Sentence Fragment: A phrase, not a complete sentence.

Sequencing: Placing items or events in logical order.

Setting: Where and when an event or story takes place.

Similar Shapes: The same geometric shape in differing sizes.

Simile: A figure of speech comparing two things, using the words *like* or *as*. Example: She was as quiet as a mouse.

Simple Predicate: A verb in a sentence telling what the subject does, is doing, did, or will do.

Simple Subject: A noun or pronoun that tells who or what the sentence is about.

Singular: A word that refers to only one thing.

Skim: To read quickly to get a general idea of what a reading selection is about.

Square: Has four parallel sides of equal length and four 90-degree angles.

Statement: A sentence that tells something. It ends with a period.

Straight Angle: An angle of 180 degrees.

Subentry: A smaller division of a subject.

Subject: 1. A word, or several words, that tells who or what a sentence is about; 2. The topic covered or the name of an item in an index; 3. The person in a biography.

Suffix: A syllable added to the end of a word that changes its meaning.

Summary: A brief retelling of the main ideas in a reading selection.

Superlative Adjectives: Compare more than two persons, places, things, or ideas.

Support Sentences: Provide details about the topic.

Syllable: A word or part of a word with only one vowel sound.

Symbolism: The use of something to stand for (symbolize) something else.

Symmetrical Shapes: Shapes that, when divided in half, are identical.

Synonym: A word that means the same or nearly the same as another word.

Table of Contents: A listing of headings and page numbers for chapters or articles located in the front of a book or magazine.

Tense: The way a verb is used to express time.

Topic Sentence: A sentence that states the main idea of a paragraph and is usually the first sentence.

Trapezoid: Has two opposite sides that are parallel; its sides may or may not be of equal lengths.

Units: Parts into which a book is divided.

Using Prior Knowledge: Being able to use what one already knows to find an answer or get information.

Venn Diagram: A diagram used to chart information that shows similarities and differences between two things; used to compare and contrast two things.

Verb: A word in a sentence that tells what something does or that something exists.

Verb Tense: The way a verb expresses time.

Volume: The number of cubic units that fills a space.

X-Axis: The horizontal number line in a plotting graph.

X Coordinate/Y Coordinate: Show where a point is on a plotting graph.

Y-Axis: The vertical number line in a plotting graph.

Spelling: Words with ā

Directions: Write a sentence for each word. Use a dictionary if you are unsure of the meaning of a word.

Answers will vary.

1. favorite
2. gable
3. dangerous
4. patient
5. lakefront
6. statement
7. nation
8. negotiated
9. operate
10. decade

Directions: Write the answers.

11. Which word means "a 10-year period"? **decade**
12. Which word means "a triangle-shaped end of a building's roof"? **gable**
13. Which word means "arbitrated"? **negotiated**

Page 6

Spelling: Words with ē

Directions: Write a sentence for each word. Use a dictionary if you are unsure of the meaning of a word.

Answers will vary.

1. niece
2. meaningful
3. conceited
4. baleen
5. field
6. disease
7. reactivate
8. peony
9. seafaring
10. theme

Directions: Write the answers.

11. Which word is a summer-blooming flower? **peony**
12. Which word is a type of whale? **baleen**
13. Which word is an illness? **disease**

Page 7

Spelling: Words with ī

Directions: Write a sentence for each word. Use a dictionary if you are unsure of the meaning of a word.

Answers will vary.

1. bisect
2. identify
3. frightened
4. glider
5. idol
6. library
7. pipeline
8. hieroglyphic
9. rhinoceros
10. silent

Directions: Write the answers.

11. Which word means "to be scared"? **frightened**
12. Which word means "to divide into two sections"? **bisect**
13. Which word is an animal? **rhinoceros**
14. Which word is a type of ancient writing? **hieroglyphic**

Page 8

Spelling: Words with ō

Directions: Write a sentence for each word. Use a dictionary if you are unsure of the meaning of a word.

Answers will vary.

1. clothing
2. slogan
3. total
4. stethoscope
5. voltage
6. stereo
7. protein
8. negotiate
9. locust
10. locomotive

Directions: Write the answers.

11. Which word is an insect? **locust**
12. Which word means "a train"? **locomotive**
13. Which word means "a listening device to hear the heart"? **stethoscope**
14. Which word means "to bargain"? **negotiate**

Page 9

Spelling: Words with ū

Directions: Write a sentence for each word. Use a dictionary if you are unsure of the meaning of a word.

Answers will vary.

1. universe
2. cruise
3. absolute
4. influence
5. unanimous
6. vacuum
7. putrid
8. incubate
9. peruse
10. numerous

Directions: Write the answers.

11. Which word means "to read carefully"? **peruse**
12. Which word means "everyone is in agreement"? **unanimous**
13. Which word means "a sea voyage taken for pleasure"? **cruise**
14. Which word means "to keep eggs warm until they hatch"? **incubate**

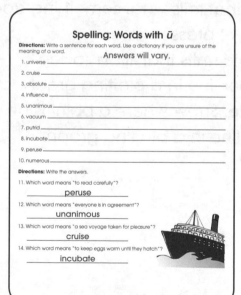

Page 10

Spelling: I Before E, Except After C

Use an **i** before **e**, except after **c**, or when **e** and **i** together sound like long **a**.

Examples:
relieve
deceive
neighbor

Exceptions: weird, foreign, height, seize

Directions: Write **C** in the blank if the word in bold is spelled correctly. Write **X** in the blank if it is spelled incorrectly. The first one has been done for you.

C i before e, except after c, or when sounding like a, as in neighbor and weigh

C 1. They stopped at the crossing for the **freight** train.
X 2. How much does that **wiegh**?
C 3. Did you **believe** his story?
X 4. He **recieved** an A on his paper!
X 5. She said it was the **neighborly** thing to do.
C 6. The guards **seized** the package.
C 7. That movie was **wierd**!
X 8. Her **hieght** is five feet, six inches.
C 9. It's not right to **deceive** others.
X 10. Your answers should be **breif**.
C 11. She felt a lot of **grief** when her dog died.
X 12. He is still **greiving** about his loss.
C 13. Did the police catch the **thief**?
X 14. She was their **cheif** source of information.
C 15. Can you speak a **foreign** language?

Page 11

Spelling: Words with *ie* and *ei*

Many people have trouble remembering when to use **ie** and when to use **ei**. The following rules have many exceptions, but they may be helpful to you.

Rule 1: If the two letters are pronounced like **ē** and are preceded by an **s** sound, use **ei**, as in **receive**.

Rule 2: If the two letters are pronounced like **ē** but are not preceded by an **s** sound, use **ie** as in **believe**.

Rule 3: If the two letters are pronounced like **ā**, use **ei** as in **eight** and **vein**.

Rule 4: If the two letters are pronounced like **ī**, use **ei** in **height**.

The sound **s** could be produced by the letter **s** as in **single** or the letter **c** as in **cease**.

Follow the ei/ie rules!

Directions: Write the words from the box on the lines after the spelling rule that applies.

veil	brief	deceive	belief	niece
reindeer	yield	achieve	height	neighbor
grief	ceiling	weight	vein	seize

Rule 1: __deceive, ceiling, seize__

Rule 2: __brief, belief, niece, yield, achieve, grief__

Rule 3: __veil, reindeer, weight, vein, neighbor__

Rule 4: __height__

Directions: Complete the sentences with words that have the vowel sound shown. Use each word from the box only once.

1. My next-door (ā) __neighbor__ wore a long (ā) __veil__ at her wedding.
2. Will the roof hold the (ā) __weight__ of Santa's (ā) __reindeer__?
3. My nephew and (ē) __niece__ work hard to (ē) __achieve__ their goals.
4. I have a strong (ē) __belief__ they would never (ē) __deceive__ me.
5. For a (ē) __brief__ moment, I thought Will would (ē) __yield__ the game to me.
6. The blood rushed through my (ā) __vein__.
7. What is the (ī) __height__ of this (ē) __ceiling__?

Page 12

Spelling: Words with *ûr* and *ôr*

The difference between **ûr** and **ôr** is clear in the words **fur** and **for**. The **ûr** sound can be spelled **ur** as in **fur**, **our** as in **journal**, **er** as in **her**, and **ear** as in **search**.

The **ôr** sound can be spelled **or** as in **for**, **our** as in **four**, **oar** as in **soar**, and **ore** as in **more**.

Directions: Write the words from the box on the lines to match the sounds.

florist	plural	ignore	courtesy	observe
survey	research	furnish	normal	emergency
tornado	coarse	flourish	source	restore

ûr __plural, courtesy, observe, survey, research, furnish, emergency, flourish__

ôr __florist, ignore, normal, tornado, coarse, source, restore__

Directions: Complete the sentences with words that have the sound shown. Use each word only once.

1. We all get along better when we remember to use (ûr) __courtesy__.
2. My brother likes flowers and wants to be a (ôr) __florist__.
3. What was the (ôr) __source__ of the (ûr) __research__ for your report?
4. He waved at her, but she continued to (ôr) __ignore__ him.
5. For a plural subject, use a (ûr) __plural__ verb.
6. Beneath the dark clouds, a (ôr) __tornado__ formed!
7. Firefighters are used to handling an (ûr) __emergency__.
8. When will they be able to (ûr) __restore__ our electricity?
9. How are you going to (ûr) __furnish__ your apartment?

Page 13

Spelling: Words Beginning with *Sh* and *Th*

Directions: Write a definition for each word. Use a dictionary if you are unsure of the meaning of a word.

th

Answers will vary.

1. shallow: _____
2. thimble: _____
3. shear: _____
4. sheriff: _____
5. thermal: _____
6. throttle: _____
7. shingle: _____
8. shabby: _____
9. thrifty: _____
10. shoreline: _____
11. threaten: _____
12. thyroid: _____

sh

Directions: Use two of the above words in sentences.

13. Answers will vary.
    _____
14. _____
    _____

Page 14

Spelling: Words Beginning with *Ch*

Directions: Write a definition for each word. Use a dictionary if you are unsure of the meaning of a word.

Answers will vary.

1. chimney: _____
2. china: _____
3. cheetah: _____
4. charity: _____
5. channel: _____
6. chandelier: _____
7. challenge: _____
8. chairman: _____
9. champion: _____
10. cheddar: _____
11. chime: _____
12. chisel: _____

Directions: Write the answers.

13. Which word is a tool for shaping wood?
    __chisel__

14. Which word is a type of cheese?
    __cheddar__

15. Which word is an animal?
    __cheetah__

Page 15

Spelling: The Letter *Q*

In English words, the letter **q** is always followed by the letter **u**.

Examples:
question
square
quick

QUARTERS
QUALITY
QUIET

Directions: Write the correct spelling of each word in the blank. The first one has been done for you.

EQUAL
ACQUIRE
EQUATOR

1. qill	quill
2. eqality	equality
3. qarrel	quarrel
4. qarter	quarter
5. qart	quart
6. qibble	quibble
7. qench	quench
8. qeen	queen
9. qip	quip
10. qiz	quiz
11. eqipment	equipment
12. qiet	quiet
13. qite	quite
14. eqity	equity
15. eqator	equator
16. eqivalent	equivalent
17. eqitable	equitable
18. eqestrian	equestrian
19. eqation	equation
20. qantity	quantity

Page 16

Spelling: Words with *kw*, *ks*, and *gz* Sounds

The consonant **q** is always followed by **u** in words and is pronounced **kw**. The letter **x** can be pronounced **ks** as in **mix**. When **x** is followed by a vowel, it is usually pronounced **gz** as in **example**.

Directions: Write the words from the box on the lines to match the sounds shown.

expense	exist	aquarium	acquire	request	exact
expand	exit	quality	excellent	quantity	quiz
exhibit	squirm	expression			

kw __aquarium, acquire, request, quality, quantity, quiz, squirm__

ks __expense, expand, excellent, expression__

gz __exist, exact, exit, exhibit__

Directions: Complete the sentences with words that have the sound shown. Use words from the box only once.

1. We went to the zoo to see the fish (gz) __exhibit__.
2. I didn't know its (gz) __exact__ location, so we followed the map.
3. The zoo plans to (kw) __acquire__ some sharks for its (kw) __aquarium__.
4. Taking care of sharks is a big (ks) __expense__, but a number of people have asked the zoo to (ks) __expand__ its display of fish.
5. These people want a better (kw) __quality__ of fish, not a bigger (kw) __quantity__ of them.
6. I think the zoo already has an (ks) __excellent__ display.
7. Some of its rare fish no longer (gz) __exist__ in the ocean.

Page 17

Spelling: Words with Silent Letters

Some letters in words are not pronounced, like the **b** in **crumb**, the **l** in **yolk**, the **n** in **autumn**, the **g** in **design**, and the **h** in **hour**.

Directions: Write the words from the box on the lines to match the silent letters. Use a dictionary if you are unsure of the meaning or pronunciation of a word.

condemn	yolk	campaign	assign	salmon
hymn	limb	chalk	tomb	foreign
resign	column	spaghetti	rhythm	solemn

n condemn, hymn, column, solemn

l yolk, chalk, salmon

g resign, campaign, assign, foreign

b limb, tomb

h spaghetti, rhythm

Directions: Write words from the box to complete these sentences.

1. What did the teacher (g) **assign** for homework?
2. She put words in a (n) **column** on the board.
3. When she finished writing, her hands were white with (l) **chalk** .
4. The church choir clapped in (h) **rhythm** with the (n) **hymn** .
5. While I was cracking an egg, the (l) **yolk** slipped onto the floor.
6. Did the explorers find anything in the ancient (b) **tomb** ?
7. My favorite dinner of all is (h) **spaghetti** and meatballs.
8. Do not (n) **condemn** me for making one little mistake.

Page 18

Spelling: Words with *ph* or *kn*

The letters **ph** produce the same sound as the letter **f**. When the letters **kn** are together, the **k** is silent.

Directions: Write a definition for each word. Use a dictionary if you are unsure of the meaning of a word. **Answers will vary.**

1. photographer: _____
2. knowledge: _____
3. knee: _____
4. telephone: _____
5. knock: _____
6. phonics: _____
7. physician: _____
8. knife: _____
9. pharmacy: _____
10. knight: _____
11. knit: _____
12. pheasant: _____

Directions: Write the answers.

13. Which word is a place to buy medicine?
   pharmacy
14. Which word is a synonym for **doctor**?
   physician
15. Which word names a bird?
   pheasant

Page 19

Spelling: Words with *gh* or *gn*

Directions: Use the clues and the words in the box to complete the crossword puzzle.

recognize	drought	assign
lightning	night	fought
straight	throughout	

Crossword answers:
- f o u g h t
- a s s i g n
- t h r o u g h o u t
- r e c o g n i z e
- (down) d r o u g h t / s t r a i g h t / l i g h t n i n g / n i g h t

Now Showing / Words with **GH GN**

Across:
3. My siblings and I _____ occasionally while growing up.
5. The teacher will _____ bus seats for the field trip.
7. _____ the storm, the rescue squads worked without stopping.
8. Do you _____ the woman you are meeting for lunch?

Down:
1. The _____ left farmers without crops.
2. My brother has _____ hair, but mine is curly.
4. Tomorrow _____, we will leave for Florida.
6. _____ struck the old barn on Walnut Hill.

Page 20

Root Words

A **root word** is the common stem that gives related words their basic meanings.

Example: Separate is the root word for **separately, separation, inseparable,** and **separator.**

Directions: Identify the root word in each group of words. Look up the meaning of the root word in the dictionary, and write its definition. The first one has been done for you.

1. colorless, colorful, discolor, coloration
   Root word: **color**
   Definition: **any coloring matter, dye, pigment or paint**

2. creator, creation, creating, creative, recreate
   Root word: **create**
   Definition: **to bring into being**

3. remove, movement, movable, immovable, removable
   Root word: **move**
   Definition: **to change the place or position of**

4. contentment, malcontent, discontent, discontentment
   Root word: **content**
   Definition: **happy with what one has**

5. pleasure, displeasure, pleasing, pleasant, unpleasant
   Root word: **please**
   Definition: **to be agreeable to**

6. successor, unsuccessful, successful
   Root word: **success**
   Definition: **a favorable outcome**

Page 21

Greek and Latin Roots

Many word patterns in the English language are combinations of Greek or Latin words. When you know what part of a word means, you may be able to figure out the meaning of the rest of the word. For example, if **cycle** means "circle or wheel" and **bi** means "two," then you can figure out that **bicycle** means "two wheels." **Root words** are the words that longer words are based on. For example, **duct**, which means "to lead," is the root of **conduct** or **induct**. Look at the chart below. It has several root words and their meanings on it.

Root	Meaning	Example	Definition
act	to do	interact	to act with others
aqua	water	aquatint	dyed water
auto	self	automobile	to move oneself
centi	a hundred	centennial	one hundred years

Directions: Look at each word equation below. The meaning of one part is shown in parentheses. Consult the chart of root words to find the meaning of the other part. Write the meaning in the blank. Combine the two meanings. Write the dictionary definition in the space provided. **Possible answers:**

1. react re (again) + act **to do** = **to do again**
   Dictionary definition: To act or do again

2. automatic auto **self** + matic (having a mind) = self having a mind
   Dictionary definition: **self-acting or self-moving**

3. transact trans (across) + act **to do** = **to do across**
   Dictionary definition: **to carry on or conduct business**

4. centimeter centi **a hundred** + meter (meter) = **one hundred meters**
   Dictionary definition: **one-hundredth of a meter**

5. aquanaut aqua **water** + naut (sailor) = **water sailor**
   Dictionary definition: **an underwater explorer**

Page 22

Root Words

Root	Meaning	Example	Definition
cede	to go	supercede	to go beyond
cept	seize	intercept	to seize during
duce	lead	deduce	to find the lead
fer	carry	interfere	to carry into
port	carry	transport	to carry across
spect	to look	inspect	to look in
tain	to hold	obtain	to gain by action
vene	to come	convene	to come to start

Directions: Complete the exercises below. **Possible answers:**

1. precede pre (before) + cede **to go** = **to go before**
   Dictionary definition: to be, go, or come before

2. report re (again) + port **carry** = **carry again**
   Dictionary definition: **to carry and repeat, as in a message**

3. intervene inter (between) + vene **to come** = **to come between**
   Dictionary definition: **to come between**

4. induce in (in) + duce **lead** = **lead in**
   Dictionary definition: **lead by persuasion**

5. retrospect retro (backward) + spect **to look** = **to look backward**
   Dictionary definition: **to look back on past events**

6. refer re (again) + fer **to carry** = **to carry again**
   Dictionary definition: **to hand over for consideration**

7. retain re (again) + tain **to hold** = **to hold again**
   Dictionary definition: **to keep possession of**

8. concept con (with) + cept **seize** = **seized with**
   Dictionary definition: **a general notion or idea**

Page 23

Prefixes (Page 24)

A **prefix** is a syllable added to the beginning of a word to change its meaning. The prefix **re** means "back" or "again," as in **return**. **Pre** means "before," as in **prepare**. **Dis** means "do the opposite," as in **disappear**. **In** and **im** both mean "not," as in **impossible**. (These two prefixes also have other meanings.) **Com** and **con** both mean "with," as in **companion** and **concert**. Use **im** and **com** with words that start with **p**, **b**, or **m**. Use **in** and **con** with words that begin with a vowel or other consonants.

Directions: Match each word from the box to its definition.

disbelieve	recite	connotation	impolite	preview
impatient	distrust	configuration	prevision	incomplete
invisible	dislike	confederate	recover	compassion

1. share another's feelings — compassion
2. not finished — incomplete
3. another meaning — connotation
4. become normal again — recover
5. take away confidence — distrust
6. look to the future — prevision
7. arrangement of parts — configuration
8. say from memory — recite
9. ally — confederate
10. hate — dislike
11. look at — preview
12. rude — impolite
13. in a hurry — impatient
14. doubt — disbelieve
15. not seen — invisible

Directions: Add the rest of the word to each prefix in these sentences. Use words from the box only once. Be sure to use the correct form of the word.

16. When he re**covered** from his cold, Jeff was im**patient** to get back to work.
17. Jonah stared at the ghostly figure with dis**belief** and dis**trust**.
18. I'd like to re**cite** that poem, but my memory of it is in**complete**.
19. She was very im**patient** during the movie pre**view**.

Prefixes (Page 25)

A **prefix** is a syllable added to the beginning of a word that changes its meaning. The prefixes **in, il, ir,** and **im** all mean "not."

Directions: Create new words by adding **in, il, ir,** or **im** to these root words. Use a dictionary to check that the new words are correct. The first one has been done for you.

	Prefix		Root Word		New Word
1.	il	+	logical	=	illogical
2.	il	+	literate	=	illiterate
3.	im	+	patient	=	impatient
4.	im	+	probable	=	improbable
5.	ir	+	reversible	=	irreversible
6.	ir	+	responsible	=	irresponsible
7.	in	+	active	=	inactive
8.	im	+	moral	=	immoral
9.	ir	+	removable	=	irremovable
10.	il	+	legible	=	illegible
11.	im	+	mature	=	immature
12.	im	+	perfect	=	imperfect

Prefixes (Page 26)

The prefixes **un** and **non** also mean "not."

Examples:
Unhappy means "not happy."
Nonproductive means "not productive."

Directions: Divide each word into its prefix and root word. The first one has been done for you.

		Prefix	Root Word
1.	unappreciated	un	appreciate
2.	unlikely	un	like
3.	unkempt	un	keep
4.	untimely	un	time
5.	nonstop	non	stop
6.	nonsense	non	sense
7.	nonprofit	non	profit
8.	nonresident	non	reside

Directions: Use the clues in the first sentence to complete the second sentence with one of the words from the box. The first one has been done for you.

9. She didn't reside at school. She was a **nonresident**.
10. He couldn't stop talking. He talked **nonstop**.
11. The company did not make a profit. It was a **nonprofit** company.
12. She was not talking sense. She was talking **sense**.
13. He visited at a bad time. His visit was **untimely**.
14. No one appreciated his efforts. He felt **unappreciated**.
15. He did not "keep up" his hair. His hair was **unkempt**.
16. She was not likely to come. Her coming was **unlikely**.

Prefixes (Page 27)

The prefixes **co, col, com, con,** and **cor** mean "with" or "together." The prefixes **anti, contra,** and **ob** mean "against."

Directions: Write each word's prefix and root word in the space provided.

Word	Prefix	Root Word
coexist	co	exist
concurrent	con	current
correlate	cor	relate
codependent	co	depend
antigravity	anti	gravity
contraband	contra	band

Directions: Use the words from the chart above to complete the sentences.

1. When airplanes fly very high and then quickly drop down, they cause an **antigravity** effect.
2. Materials that are illegal are called **contraband**.
3. A dog and a cat can **coexist** in the same house if they get along well.
4. Events that happen at the same time are **concurrent**.
5. When two people rely on each other, they are said to be **codependent**.
6. The textbook will **correlate** with the teacher's lectures.

Prefixes (Page 28)

The prefixes **epi, hyper, over,** and **super** mean "above" or "over." The prefixes **under** and **sub** mean "under."

Directions: Write each word's prefix and root word in the space provided.

Word	Prefix	Root Word
hyperactive	hyper	active
overanxious	over	anxious
superimpose	super	impose
epilogue	epi	log
underestimate	under	estimate
subordinate	sub	ordinate

Directions: Use the words above to complete the following sentences.

1. A photographer could **superimpose** one image on top of another.
2. The **epilogue** of the book may tell additional information about the story.
3. All the other children settled down for the night except the boy who was **hyperactive**.
4. He could not sleep because he was **overanxious** about the upcoming trip.
5. The company's president told his **subordinate** to take over some of the responsibilities.
6. Just because you think you are weak, don't **underestimate** how strong you could be.

Numerical Prefixes (Page 29)

Some prefixes are related to numbers. For example, in Latin **uni** means "one." The prefix **mono** means "one" in Greek. The chart below lists prefixes for numbers one through ten from both the Latin and Greek languages.

Number	Latin	Example	Greek	Example
1	uni	university	mon, mono	monopoly
2	du	duplex	di	digress
3	tri	tricycle	tri	trio
4	quad	quadrant	tetra	tetrameter
5	quin	quintuplets	penta	pentagon
6	sex	sexennial	hex	hexagon
7	sept	septuagenarian	hept	heptagon
8	oct	octopus	oct	octagon
9	nov	novena	enne	ennead (group of nine)
10	dec	decade	dec	decimal

Directions: Complete the exercises below.

1. unicycle uni **one** + cycle (wheel) = **one wheel**
   Dictionary definition: **one-wheeled vehicle**
2. monogram mono **one** + gram (writing) = **one writing**
   Dictionary definition: **interlaced initials of a name**
3. sextet sex **six** + tet (group) = **six group**
   Dictionary definition: **a group of six**
4. quadrant quad **four** + rant (part) = **four part**
   Dictionary definition: **one of four parts**
5. decigram dec **ten** + gram (gram) = **ten grams**
   Dictionary definition: **one tenth of a gram**

Comprehensive Curriculum - Grade 6

Review

Roots	Meanings	Prefixes	Meanings
fer	carry	dis	separate
graph	write	epi	upon, above
rupt	break	ex	out
tend	stretch	in	in
vade	go	trans	across

Directions: Complete the exercises below.

1. invade in __in__ + vade __go__ = __go in__

   Dictionary definition: __to intrude upon__

2. disrupt dis __separate__ + rupt __break__ = __separate break__

   Dictionary definition: __to interrupt or disturb__

3. transfer trans __across__ + fer __carry__ = __carry across__

   Dictionary definition: __to carry or remove from one place to another__

4. extend ex __out__ + tend __stretch__ = __stretch out__

   Dictionary definition: __to stretch or draw out__

5. epigraph epi __upon__ + graph __write__ = __upon write__

   Dictionary definition: __an inscription__

Directions: The prefixes **mono** and **uni** both mean "one." Write each word's prefix and root in the space provided.

Word	Prefix	Root
monorhyme	mono	rhyme
monosyllable	mono	syllable
unilingual	uni	lingual
uniparental	uni	parent
unilateral	uni	lateral

Page 30

Suffixes

A **suffix** is a syllable added to the end of a root word that changes its meaning.

When a word ends in silent **e**, keep the **e** before adding a suffix beginning with a consonant.

Example: amuse + ment = amusement

Exception: argue + ment = argument

When a word ends in silent **e**, drop the **e** before adding a suffix beginning with a vowel.

Example: amuse + ing = amusing

Exceptions: hoeing, shoeing, canoeing

Directions: Write **C** on the blank if the word in bold is spelled correctly. Write **X** in the blank if it is spelled incorrectly. The first one has been done for you.

_C_ 1. She was a woman of many **achievements**.

_C_ 2. He hated to hear their **arguments**.

_X_ 3. Do you want to go **canoing**?

_X_ 4. He kept **urgeing** her to eat more dessert.

_C_ 5. She was not good at **deceiving** others.

_C_ 6. He **rarely** skipped lunch.

_X_ 7. Would you repeat that **announcment**?

_C_ 8. Bicycle **safety** was very important to him.

_X_ 9. Their constant **argueing** got on my nerves.

_X_ 10. He found that **shoeing** horses was not easy.

_C_ 11. The sun felt hot as they were **hoeing**.

_X_ 12. She was so **relieveed** that she laughed.

Page 31

Suffixes: Words Ending in Y

If a word ends in a vowel and **y**, keep the **y** when you add a suffix.

Example:
bray + ed = brayed
bray + ing = braying

Exception: lay + ed = laid

If a word ends in a consonant and **y**, change the **y** to **i** when you add a suffix, unless the suffix begins with **i**.

Example:
baby + ed = babied
baby + ing = babying

Directions: Write **C** in the blank if the word in bold is spelled correctly. Write **X** if it is spelled incorrectly. The first one has been done for you.

_C_ 1. She was a good student who did well at her **studies**.

_X_ 2. Will you please stop **babling** him?

_X_ 3. She **layed** her purse on the couch.

_X_ 4. Both the **ferrys** left on schedule.

_C_ 5. Could you repeat what he was **saying**?

_X_ 6. He was **triing** to do his best.

_C_ 7. How many **cherries** are in this pie?

_C_ 8. The cat **stayed** away for two weeks.

_X_ 9. He is **saveing** all his money.

_C_ 10. The lake was **muddier** than I remembered.

_X_ 11. It was the **muddyest** lake I've ever seen!

_C_ 12. Her mother **babied** her when she was sick.

Page 32

Suffixes: Doubling Final Consonants

If a one-syllable word ends in one vowel and consonant, double the last consonant when you add a suffix that begins with a vowel.

Examples: swim + ing = swimming   big + er = bigger

Directions: Add the suffixes to the root words, doubling the final consonants when appropriate. The first one has been done for you.

1. brim	+	ing	=	brimming
2. big	+	est	=	biggest
3. hop	+	ing	=	hopping
4. swim	+	er	=	swimmer
5. thin	+	er	=	thinner
6. spin	+	ing	=	spinning
7. smack	+	ing	=	smacking
8. sink	+	ing	=	sinking
9. win	+	er	=	winner
10. thin	+	est	=	thinnest
11. slim	+	er	=	slimmer
12. slim	+	ing	=	slimming
13. thread	+	ing	=	threading
14. thread	+	er	=	threader
15. win	+	ing	=	winning
16. sing	+	ing	=	singing
17. stop	+	ing	=	stopping
18. thrill	+	ing	=	thrilling
19. drop	+	ed	=	dropped
20. mop	+	ing	=	mopping

Page 33

Suffixes: Doubling Final Consonants

When two-syllable words have the accent on the second syllable and end in a consonant preceded by a vowel, double the final consonant to add a suffix that begins with a vowel.

Examples: occur + ing = occurring   occur + ed = occurred

If the accent shifts to the first syllable when the suffix is added to the two-syllable root word, the final consonant is not doubled.

Example: refer + ence = reference

Directions: Say the words listed to hear where the accent falls when the suffix is added. Then, add the suffix to the root word, doubling the final consonant when appropriate. The first one has been done for you.

1. excel	+	ence	=	excellence
2. infer	+	ing	=	inferring
3. regret	+	able	=	regrettable
4. control	+	able	=	controllable
5. submit	+	ing	=	submitting
6. confer	+	ing	=	conferring
7. refer	+	al	=	referral
8. differ	+	ing	=	differing
9. compel	+	ing	=	compelling
10. commit	+	ed	=	committed
11. regret	+	ing	=	regretting
12. depend	+	able	=	dependable
13. upset	+	ing	=	upsetting
14. propel	+	ing	=	propelling
15. repel	+	ed	=	repelled
16. prefer	+	ing	=	preferring
17. prefer	+	ence	=	preference
18. differ	+	ence	=	difference
19. refer	+	ing	=	referring
20. control	+	ing	=	controlling

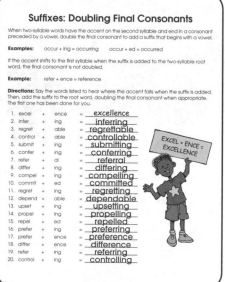

EXCEL + ENCE = EXCELLENCE

Page 34

Suffixes

A **suffix** is a syllable added to the end of a word that changes its meaning. Some suffixes change nouns into adjectives.

Examples: fool — **foolish**   nation — **national**

Other suffixes change adjectives into adverbs.

Examples: foolish — **foolishly**   national — **nationally**

Directions: Match the root words with words from the box.

personal	stylish	obviously	professional
typical	childish	practical	medical
permanently	ticklish	additional	critical
gradually	physical	musical	

1. tickle __ticklish__   6. grade __gradually__   11. type __typical__

2. critic __critical__   7. practice __practical__   12. music __musical__

3. add __additional__   8. physician __physical__   13. style __stylish__

4. person __personal__   9. permanent __permanently__   14. obvious __obviously__

5. child __childish__   10. medic __medical__   15. profess __professional__

Directions: Circle the word or words in each sentence that are a synonym for a word from the box. Write the word from the box on the line. The first one has been done for you.

16. Knowing how to cook is a (useful) skill.   __practical__

17. The lake (slowly) warmed up.   __gradually__

18. (Clearly), I should have stayed on the path.   __obviously__

19. That is a (fashionable) outfit.   __stylish__

20. Wanting your own way all the time is (for little kids).   __childish__

21. Getting lost is (common) for me.   __typical__

22. My grades are a (private) matter.   __personal__

Page 35

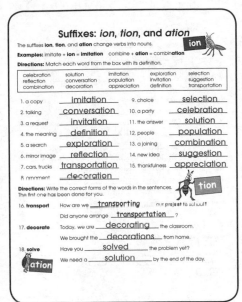

Suffixes: *ion, tion,* and *ation*

The suffixes **ion, tion,** and **ation** change verbs into nouns.

Examples: imitate + **ion** = imitation   combine + **ation** = combination

Directions: Match each word from the box with its definition.

celebration	solution	imitation	exploration	selection
reflection	conversation	population	invitation	suggestion
combination	decoration	appreciation	definition	transportation

1. a copy — imitation
2. talking — conversation
3. a request — invitation
4. the meaning — definition
5. a search — exploration
6. mirror image — reflection
7. cars, trucks — transportation
8. ornament — decoration
9. choice — selection
10. a party — celebration
11. the answer — solution
12. people — population
13. a joining — combination
14. new idea — suggestion
15. thankfulness — appreciation

Directions: Write the correct forms of the words in the sentences. The first one has been done for you.

16. **transport** How are we **transporting** our project to school?
    Did anyone arrange **transportation**?
17. **decorate** Today, we are **decorating** the classroom.
    We brought the **decorations** from home.
18. **solve** Have you **solved** the problem yet?
    We need a **solution** by the end of the day.

Page 36

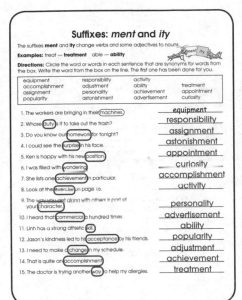

Suffixes: *ment* and *ity*

The suffixes **ment** and **ity** change verbs and some adjectives to nouns.

Examples: treat — **treatment**   able — **ability**

Directions: Circle the word or words in each sentence that are synonyms for words from the box. Write the word from the box on the line. The first one has been done for you.

equipment	responsibility	activity
accomplishment	adjustment	ability
assignment	personality	achievement	treatment
popularity	astonishment	advertisement	appointment	curiosity

1. The workers are bringing in their machines. — equipment
2. Whose duty is it to take out the trash? — responsibility
3. Do you know our homework for tonight? — assignment
4. I could see the surprise in his face. — astonishment
5. Ken is happy with his new position. — appointment
6. I was filled with wondering. — curiosity
7. She lists one achievement in particular. — accomplishment
8. Look at the exercise on page 16. — activity
9. The way you get along with others is part of your character. — personality
10. I heard that commercial a hundred times. — advertisement
11. Linh has a strong athletic skill. — ability
12. Jason's kindness led to his acceptance by his friends. — popularity
13. I need to make a change in my schedule. — adjustment
14. That is quite an accomplishment. — achievement
15. The doctor is trying another way to help my allergies. — treatment

Page 37

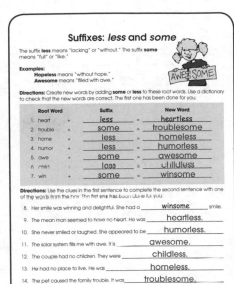

Suffixes: *less* and *some*

The suffix **less** means "lacking" or "without." The suffix **some** means "full" or "like."

Examples:
    Hopeless means "without hope."
    Awesome means "filled with awe."

Directions: Create new words by adding **some** or **less** to these root words. Use a dictionary to check that the new words are correct. The first one has been done for you.

Root Word		Suffix		New Word
1. heart	+	less	=	heartless
2. trouble	+	some	=	troublesome
3. home	+	less	=	homeless
4. humor	+	less	=	humorless
5. awe	+	some	=	awesome
6. child	+	less	=	childless
7. win	+	some	=	winsome

Directions: Use the clues in the first sentence to complete the second sentence with one of the words from the box. The first one has been done for you.

8. Her smile was winning and delightful. She had a **winsome** smile.
9. The mean man seemed to have no heart. He was **heartless.**
10. She never smiled or laughed. She appeared to be **humorless.**
11. The solar system fills me with awe. It is **awesome.**
12. The couple had no children. They were **childless.**
13. He had no place to live. He was **homeless.**
14. The pet caused the family trouble. It was **troublesome.**

Page 38

Suffixes: *ship, ful,* and *ist*

Directions: Write the meaning of each word on the line. Use a dictionary if you are unsure of the meaning of a word.

1. biologist: **Answers will vary.**
2. citizenship:
3. companionship:
4. archaeologist:
5. typist:
6. scholarship:
7. doubtful:
8. hopeful:
9. dictatorship:
10. chemist:
11. principalship:
12. artist:
13. spiteful:
14. professorship:
15. geologist:

Page 39

Suffixes: *ance* and *ence*

Directions: Write words from the box to complete the sentences. Use a dictionary if you are unsure of the meaning of a word.

ance
performance	experience
correspondence	reliance
evidence	sequence
maintenance	absence
dependence	insurance
ence

1. The daycare position required **experience** working with children.
2. During her **absence**, a friend phoned each night with homework assignments.
3. My grandmother is known for her self-**reliance**
4. The alphabet is a **sequence** of 26 letters.
5. A letter to my penpal is called long distance **correspondence**
6. The circus advertised a 2:00 P.M. **performance**
7. Many people have a great **reliance** on calculators for math.
8. Fortunately, most homeowners in the flooded area carried **insurance**
9. The police gathered **evidence** in hopes of solving the burglary.
10. **Maintenance** of football and baseball fields requires much time and effort.

Page 40

Suffixes: *ment, ible,* and *able*

The suffix **ment** means "the act of" or "state of." The suffixes **ible** and **able** mean "able to."

Directions: Create new words by adding **ment, able,** or **ible** to these root words. Use a dictionary to check that the new words are correct. The first one has been done for you.

Root Word		Suffix		New Word
1. rely	+	able	=	reliable
2. retire	+	ment	=	retirement
3. sense	+	ible	=	sensible
4. commit	+	ment	=	commitment
5. repair	+	able	=	repairable
6. love	+	able	=	lovable/loveable
7. quote	+	able	=	quotable
8. honor	+	able	=	honorable

Directions: Use the clues in the first sentence to complete the second sentence with one of the words from the box. The first one has been done for you.

9. Everyone loved her. She was **loveable (also lovable).**
10. He had a lot of sense. He was **sensible.**
11. She committed time to the project. She made a **comitment.**
12. He always did the right thing. His behavior was **honorable.**
13. The tire could not be fixed. It was not **repairable.**
14. They would not buy the car. The car was not **reliable.**
15. He gave the reporter good comments. His comments were **quotable.**
16. She was ready to retire. She looked forward to **retirement.**

Page 41

Comprehensive Curriculum - Grade 6

Review

Directions: Add one of the prefixes, suffixes, or combining forms to a word in the box to complete each sentence. Use the definition in parentheses as a clue.

ian   ous   ship   an   ist   extra   trans   pre   micro   super

| friend | music | geology | sensory | America |
| paid | wave | market | atlantic | danger |

1. The __supermarket__ has a huge selection of fruits and vegetables. (large food store)

2. The first __transatlantic__ flight was a remarkable feat in the history of aviation. (across the Atlantic Ocean)

3. The woman claimed that she knew the future because of her __extrasensory__ capabilities. (beyond the normal senses)

4. When mailing your payment, please use the __prepaid__ envelope. (paid in advance)

5. Mrs. Johnson studied the violin for many years to become the accomplished __musician__ she is today. (person skilled in music)

6. The __microwave__ oven is a modern-day convenience. (operating with extremely small electromagnetic waves)

7. Lightning is the most __dangerous__ part of a storm. (characterized by danger)

8. They raised the __American__ flag over their campground in a gesture of patriotism. (belonging to America)

9. Olivia and I stick together through good times and bad times because we value our __friendship__. (the state of being friends)

10. Dr. Stokes is the finest __geologist__ at the university. (one who is skilled at geology, the study of the earth's crust)

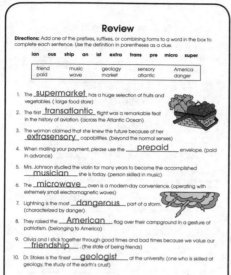

Page 42

Review

Directions: Add suffixes to change these nouns into adjectives.

1. person __able__   music __al__   child __ish__

Directions: Add suffixes to change these adjectives into adverbs.

2. permanent __ly__   obvious __ly__   gradual __ly__

Directions: Add the prefix **pre, un, in, re,** or **con** to each word, and use the word in a sentence.   Sentences will vary.

3. search __research__

4. join __rejoin__

5. compatible __incompatible__

6. wrap __unwrap__

7. school __preschool__

Directions: Add the suffix **ish, ment, ion, ship,** or **ful** to each word, and use the word in a sentence.   Sentences will vary.

8. square __squarish__

9. invent __invention__

10. force __forceful__

11. replace __replacement__

12. chairman __chairmanship__

Directions: Add suffixes to make the noun forms of these verbs.

13. select __selection__   16. imitate __imitation__

14. decorate __decoration__   17. reflect __reflection__

15. invite __invitation__

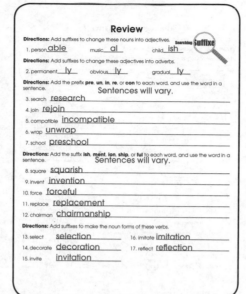

Page 43

Review

Directions: Spell these silent **e** words correctly.

1. achievments __achievements__

2. canoing __canoeing__

3. amuseing __amusing__

4. urgeing __urging__

Directions: Add the suffixes to these words ending in **y,** and spell them correctly.

5. baby + ies = __babies__

6. stay + ed = __stayed__

Directions: Add the suffixes, and spell these two-syllable words correctly.

7. hope + ing = __hoping__

8. stop + ing = __stopping__

Directions: Add the suffixes, and spell these three-syllable words correctly.

9. recur + ing = __recurring__

10. defer + ence = __deference__

Directions: Spell these words correctly by inserting **ie** or **ei.**

11. h __e__ __i__ ght

12. ch __i__ __e__ f

Directions: Circle the **q** words in each row that are spelled correctly.

13. (quip)   qeen   qick   (quit)

14. qestion   (equator)   (quiet)   qart

15. (squirrel)   sqare   (squirm)   sqeak

Page 44

Analyzing Words and Their Parts

A **syllable** is a word or part of a word with only one vowel sound.

Directions: Fill in the missing syllables. Use words from the box. Write the number of syllables after each word. The first one has been done for you.

expense	exist	aquarium	acquire	request
exact	expand	exit	quality	excellent
quiz	quantity	expression	exhibit	squirm

1. ex __cel__ lent (3)   6. ac__quire__ (2)   11. __re__ quest (2)

2. ____ squirm (1)   7. qual__ity__ (3)   12. ex __hib__ it (3)

3. __ex__ act (2)   8. __ex__ it (2)   13. __ex__ pense (2)

4. ____ quiz (1)   9. ex__pres__ sion (3)   14. __ex__ pand (2)

5. aquar __i__ um (4)   10. __ex__ ist (2)   15. quan __ti__ ty (3)

Directions: Write words that rhyme. Use the words in the box.

16. fizz __quiz__   21. it's been sent __excellent__   26. fire __acquire__

17. resist __exist__   22. this is it __exhibit__   27. best __request__

18. fact __exact__   23. made for me __quantity__   28. fit __exit__

19. fence __expense__   24. reflection __expression__

20. sand __expand__   25. worm __squirm__

A **root word** is a common stem that gives related words their basic meaning.

Directions: Write the root word for the bold word in each sentence.

29. I know **exactly** what I want. __exact__

30. Those shoes look **expensive**. __expense__

31. She didn't like my **expression** when I frowned. __express__

32. We went to the train **exhibition** at the park. __exhibit__

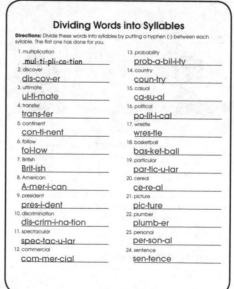

Page 45

Dividing Words into Syllables

Directions: Divide these words into syllables by putting a hyphen (-) between each syllable. The first one has done for you.

1. multiplication
   __mul-ti-pli-ca-tion__

2. discover
   __dis-cov-er__

3. ultimate
   __ul-ti-mate__

4. transfer
   __trans-fer__

5. continent
   __con-ti-nent__

6. follow
   __fol-low__

7. British
   __Brit-ish__

8. American
   __A-mer-i-can__

9. president
   __pres-i-dent__

10. discrimination
    __dis-crim-i-na-tion__

11. spectacular
    __spec-tac-u-lar__

12. commercial
    __com-mer-cial__

13. probability
    __prob-a-bil-i-ty__

14. country
    __coun-try__

15. casual
    __ca-su-al__

16. political
    __po-lit-i-cal__

17. wrestle
    __wres-tle__

18. basketball
    __bas-ket-ball__

19. particular
    __par-tic-u-lar__

20. cereal
    __ce-re-al__

21. picture
    __pic-ture__

22. plumber
    __plumb-er__

23. personal
    __per-son-al__

24. sentence
    __sen-tence__

Page 46

Synonyms

A **synonym** is a word that means the same or nearly the same as another word. **Example: mean** and **cruel**

Directions: Circle the word or group of words in each sentence that is a synonym for a word in the box. Write the synonym from the box on the line. The first one has been done for you.

florist	courtesy	research	emergency	flourish
plural	observe	furnish	tornado	source
ignored	survey	normally	coarse	restore

1. The children seemed to (thrive) in their new school. __flourish__

2. Her (politeness) made me feel welcome. __courtesy__

3. The principal came to (watch) our class. __observe__

4. Are you going to (fix up) that old house? __restore__

5. Six weeks after the (disaster) the neighborhood looked as it usually did. __emergency__

6. What was the (origin) of that rumor? __source__

7. The (cyclone) destroyed two houses. __tornado__

8. She (neglected) her homework. __ignored__

9. The material had a (rough) feel to it. __coarse__

10. Did you fill out the (questionnaire) yet? __survey__

Directions: Select three words from the box below. Write a sentence for each word that shows you understand the meaning of the word.

| plural | flourish | source | restore | observe | furnish | research |

__Sentences will vary.__

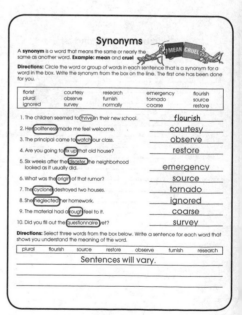

Page 47

Antonyms

An **antonym** is a word that means the opposite of another word.

Example: hopeful and **discouraged**

Directions: Circle the word or group of words in each sentence that is an antonym for a word in the box. Write the antonym from the box on the line.

nuisance	considerate
delicate	frivolous
entrance	shiny
divide	parallel
success	valley

1. It seemed as though we'd never make it to the top of the (butte.) — valley
2. Rosa thought the woman was (rude) to the store clerk. — considerate
3. The two streets run (perpendicular) to each other. — parallel
4. The school carnival was a total (failure) due to the stormy weather. — success
5. Be sure to wash this (sturdy) sweater with other heavy items. — delicate
6. The third-grade class worked hard learning to (multiply). — divide
7. The (exit) was blocked by a table. — entrance
8. The purchase of the coat was quite (practical.) — frivolous
9. The teacher wrote that Colin was a (joy) to have in class. — nuisance
10. The stone in her ring was (dull and cloudy.) — shiny

Page 48

Spelling: Homophones

Homophones are words that sound the same but have different spellings and different meanings.

Examples: night and **knight, fair** and **fare, not** and **knot**

Directions: Complete each sentence with the correct homophone. Then, write a sentence using the other homophone. Use a dictionary if you don't know the meaning of a word. The first one has been done for you.

Sentences will vary.

1. eight / ate — I _ate_ two strawberries.
   Aisha had eight strawberries.
2. vein / vain — Since the newspaper printed his picture, Cam has been self-centered and _vain_.
3. weight / wait — We had to _wait_ a long time for the show to start.
4. weigh / way — He always insists that we do everything his _way_.
5. seize / seas — The explorers charted the _seas_.
6. straight / strait — It is sometimes difficult to draw perfectly _straight_ lines freehand.
7. principle / principal — The _principal_ summoned the student body to the auditorium for a special program.
8. their / they're — I'm sure _they're_ meeting us at the park rather than at home.

Page 49

Vocabulary Building: Homographs

A **homograph** has the same spelling as another word but a different meaning. The two words are often different parts of speech.

Directions: Write the definition from the box for the bold word in each sentence.

con' tract	n.	an agreement to do something
con tract'	v.	to reduce in size, shrink
des' ert	n.	dry land that can support little plant and animal life
de sert'	v.	to abandon
Po' lish	adj.	of or belonging to Poland
pol' ish	v.	to smooth and brighten by rubbing
proj' ect	n.	a proposal or undertaking
pro ject'	v.	to send forth in thoughts or imagination

1. Iron is one of the metals that **contracts** as it cools.
   to reduce in size, shrink
2. You will have to sign a **contract** before I can begin work on your house.
   an agreement to do something
3. The **desert** seems to come to life in the evening when the animals come out in search of food.
   dry land that can support little plant and animal life
4. I hope you will not **desert** your friends now that they really need your support.
   to abandon
5. She will **polish** the stone and then use it to make a necklace.
   to smooth and brighten by rubbing
6. My grandma is going to teach me to make an authentic **Polish** meal this weekend.
   of or belonging to Poland
7. **Project** yourself into the world of tomorrow with this amazing invention!
   to send forth in thoughts or imagination
8. I started this **project** on Monday, but it may be weeks before I finish it.
   a proposal or undertaking

Page 50

Vocabulary Building: Homographs

Directions: After each sentence, write the meaning of the bold word. Write another sentence using a homograph for the word.

Sentences will vary.

1. The owner of the pet store tied a bright red **bow** around the puppies' necks.
   Meaning: a knot tied with a ribbon
   Sentence:
2. Today, fewer pipes are made from **lead**.
   Meaning: a metal
   Sentence:
3. Lia's new house is very **close** to ours.
   Meaning: near
   Sentence:
4. Please **record** the time and day that we finished the project.
   Meaning: write down
   Sentence:
5. It takes only a **minute** to fasten your seatbelt, but it can save your life.
   Meaning: 60 seconds
   Sentence:
6. I cannot **subject** the animal to that kind of treatment.
   Meaning: expose
   Sentence:

Page 51

Multiple Meanings

Directions: Use a dictionary to write the meaning of the bold word in each sentence. Be sure the meaning fits the context of the sentence and the part of speech. The first one has been done for you.

Possible answers:

1. Rosa will **graduate** summa cum laude.
   to receive an academic degree
2. The **graduate** looked for suitable employment.
   one who has graduated
3. The woman balanced her purse on the **counter**.
   a flat surface
4. The boss **countered** the employee's request for a large raise.
   opposed
5. Julio Mentarre will **conduct** the orchestra tonight.
   direct or guide
6. Metal **conducts** electricity.
   conveys or transmits
7. His **conduct** was questionable in that situation.
   action or behavior
8. Please **file** these reports today.
   to put in a useful order
9. The principal asked the students to leave in single **file**.
   a row or line
10. "Please hand me a **file**," said the woodworker to his daughter.
    a tool used for smoothing rough surfaces

Page 52

Vocabulary Building: Multiple Meanings

Directions: Use a dictionary to choose the correct definition for each bold word. The first one has been done for you.

1. My grandfather always has his **spectacles** perched on his nose.
   Meaning: lenses worn in front of the eyes to aid vision
2. The Fourth of July fireworks display was an amazing **spectacle**.
   Meaning: dramatic public display
3. We enjoy a rugged vacation, staying in a hunting **lodge** rather than a hotel.
   Meaning: large rustic cabin for vacationers
4. Don't let the baby have hard candy, because it could **lodge** in his throat.
   Meaning: get stuck
5. Termites will **bore** through the rotten wood in our basement if we don't have it replaced.
   Meaning: make a hole by digging
6. That television show could **bore** even a small child!
   Meaning: to weary by being dull
7. Don't **resort** to lies just to get what you want!
   Meaning: to go back to habitually
8. The **resort** is packed with tourists from May to September each year.
   Meaning: a place providing recreation and entertainment

Page 53

Vocabulary Building: Multiple Meanings

Directions: Read each sentence, then write another sentence using a different meaning for the bold word. **Answers will vary.**

1. The prince will **succeed** his mother as ruler of the country.
2. All through the national anthem, Johnny was singing in the wrong **key**.
3. There has been only a **trace** of rain this month.
4. I can't get involved in a **cause** in which I don't really believe.
5. It is very important to get plenty of **iron** in your diet.
6. A police officer can **issue** a warning to those disturbing the peace.
7. There is a mayoral candidate from each of the major political **parties**.
8. You can take that **stack** of newspapers to be recycled.
9. The judge will likely **sentence** the offender to a year in prison.
10. The lawyer made a **motion** to have the charges dropped.

Page 54

Reading Skills: Classifying

Classifying is placing similar things into categories.
Example: January, May, and **October** can be classified as months.
Directions: Write a category name for each group of words.

1. accordion clarinet trumpet — **instruments**
2. wasp bumblebee mosquito — **insects**
3. antique elderly prehistoric — **synonyms for "old"**
4. chemist astronomer geologist — **scientists**
5. nest cocoon burrow — **animal homes**

Directions: In each row, draw an **X** through the word that does not belong. Then, write a sentence telling why it does not belong.

1. encyclopedia atlas ~~novel~~ dictionary
   A novel is not a reference book.
2. bass ~~otter~~ tuna trout
   An otter is not a fish.
3. sister grandmother niece ~~uncle~~
   An uncle is not a female relative.
4. ~~bark~~ beech dogwood spruce
   Bark is not a type of tree.
5. pebble gravel boulder ~~cement~~
   Cement is not a form of rock.
6. spaniel ~~Siamese~~ collie Doberman
   Siamese is not a dog breed.

Page 55

Reading Skills: Classifying

Directions: In each row, draw an **X** through the word that does not belong. Then, write a word that belongs.

1. monkey lion zebra ~~elephant~~ — **giraffe**
2. daisies roses violets ~~tulips~~ pansies — **sunflowers**
3. ~~paper~~ pencil eraser stapler — **paper clip**
4. sister cousin father aunt ~~friend~~ — **mother**
5. hand mouth ~~nose~~ foot elbow — **nose**
6. ~~shy~~ happy angry sad — **confused**
7. puppy ~~kitten~~ cub lamb — **chick**
8. red blue ~~green~~ yellow purple — **green**
9. Earth Jupiter Saturn Mars ~~Pluto~~ — **Neptune**
10. ~~couch~~ bed desk dresser lamp — **nightstand**

Directions: Name each category above.

1. **African animals** 6. **feelings**
2. **flowers** 7. **baby animals**
3. **school/office supplies** 8. **colors**
4. **relatives** 9. **planets**
5. **body parts** 10. **bedroom furniture**

Page 56

Reading Skills: Classifying

Directions: Write three things that would belong in each category below. The first one has been done for you. **Possible answers:**

1. mammals — whale — horse — elephant
2. rainforest animals — monkey — parrot — snake
3. capital cities — Raleigh — Columbus — Austin
4. oceans — Atlantic — Pacific — Arctic
5. occupations — teacher — photographer — geologist
6. Native American tribes — Cherokee — Iroquois — Wampanoag
7. wars — World War I — Revolutionary War — Vietnam War
8. planets — Mercury — Venus — Mars
9. track and field sports — hurdles — discus — high jump
10. famous Americans — Barack Obama — Georgia O'Keeffe — John Glenn

Page 57

Types of Analogies

An **analogy** shows similarities, or things in common, between a pair of words. The relationships between the words in analogies usually fall into these categories:

1. **Purpose** — One word in the pair shows the **purpose** of the other word (scissors: cut).
2. **Antonyms** — The words are **opposites** (light: dark).
3. **Part/whole** — One word in the pair is a **part**; the other is a **whole** (leg: body).
4. **Action/object** — One word in the pair involves an **action** with or to an **object** (fly: airplane).
5. **Association** — One word in the pair is what you think of or **associate** when you see the other (cow: milk).
6. **Object/location** — One word in the pair tells the **location** of where the other word, an **object**, is found (car: garage).
7. **Cause/effect** — One word in the pair tells the **cause**; the other word shows the **effect** (practice: improvement).
8. **Synonyms** — The words are **synonyms** (small: tiny).

Directions: Write the relationship between the words in each pair. The first two have been done for you.

1. cow: farm — **object/location**
2. toe: foot — **part/whole**
3. watch: TV — **action/object**
4. bank: money — **association**
5. happy: unhappy — **antonyms**
6. listen: radio — **action/object**
7. inning: ballgame — **part/whole**
8. knife: cut — **purpose**
9. safe: dangerous — **antonyms**
10. carrots: soup — **part/whole**

Page 58

Writing Analogies

Once you have determined the relationship between the words in the first pair, the next step is to find a similar relationship between another pair of words.

Examples:
Scissors is to **cut** as **broom** is to **sweep**.
Black is to **white** as **up** is to **down**.

Scissors cut. Brooms sweep. The first analogy shows the purpose of scissors and brooms. In the second example, **up** and **down** are antonyms, as are **black** and **white**.

Directions: Choose the correct word to complete each analogy. The first one has been done for you.

1. **Sky** is to **blue** as **grass** is to
   A. earth B. green C. lawn D. yard — **green**
2. **Snow** is to **winter** as **rain** is to
   A. umbrella B. wet C. slicker D. spring — **spring**
3. **Sun** is to **day** as **moon** is to
   A. dark B. night C. stars D. blackness — **night**
4. **5** is to **10** as **15** is to
   A. 50 B. 25 C. 30 D. 40 — **30**
5. **Collie** is to **dog** as **Siamese** is to
   A. pet B. kitten C. baby D. cat — **cat**
6. **Letter** is to **word** as **note** is to
   A. tuba B. music C. instruments D. singer — **music**
7. **100** is to **10** as **1,000** is to
   A. 10 B. 200 C. 100 D. 10,000 — **100**
8. **Back** is to **rear** as **pit** is to
   A. peach B. hole C. dark D. punishment — **hole**

Page 59

Analogies of Purpose

Directions: Choose the correct word to complete each analogy of purpose. The first one has been done for you.

1. **Knife** is to **cut** as **copy machine** is to
   A. duplicate B. paper C. copies D. office — **duplicate**

2. **Bicycle** is to **ride** as **glass** is to
   A. dishes B. dinner C. drink D. break — **drink**

3. **Hat** is to **cover** as **eraser** is to
   A. chalkboard B. pencil C. mistake D. erase — **erase**

4. **Mystery** is to **clue** as **door** is to
   A. house B. key C. window D. open — **key**

5. **Television** is to **see** as **speaker** is to
   A. sound B. hear C. play D. dance — **hear**

6. **Clock** is to **time** as **ruler** is to
   A. height B. length C. measure D. inches — **measure**

7. **Fry** is to **pan** as **bake** is to
   A. cookies B. dinner C. oven D. baker — **oven**

8. **Bowl** is to **fruit** as **wrapper** is to
   A. present B. candy C. paper D. ribbon — **candy**

Page 60

Antonym Analogies

Directions: Write antonyms for these words. **Possible answers:**

1. run: **walk**
2. start: **finish**
3. laugh: **cry**
4. dependent: **independent**
5. young: **old**
6. North: **South**
7. sink: **float**
8. success: **failure**
9. combine: **separate**
10. innocent: **guilty**
11. polluted: **clean**
12. leader: **follower**
13. future: **born**
14. man: **woman**
15. awake: **asleep**
16. begin: **end**
17. increase: **decrease**
18. reverse: **forward**
19. enlarge: **shrink**
20. East: **West**
21. rural: **urban**
22. amateur: **professional**
23. patient: **impatient**
24. rich: **poor**
25. empty: **full**
26. fancy: **plain**
27. introduction: **conclusion**
28. modern: **old-fashioned**

Directions: Write two antonym analogies of your own.

29. **Answers will vary.**

30. _____

Page 61

Part/Whole Analogies

Directions: Determine whether each analogy is whole to part or part to whole by studying the relationship between the first pair of words. Then, choose the correct word to complete each analogy. The first one has been done for you.

1. **Shoestring** is to **shoe** as **brim** is to
   A. cup B. shade C. hat D. scarf — **hat**

2. **Egg** is to **yolk** as **suit** is to
   A. clothes B. shoes C. business D. jacket — **jacket**

3. **Stanza** is to **poem** as **verse** is to
   A. rhyme B. singing C. song D. music — **song**

4. **Wave** is to **ocean** as **branch** is to
   A. stream B. lawn C. office D. tree — **tree**

5. **Chicken** is to **farm** as **giraffe** is to
   A. animal B. zoo C. tall D. stripes — **zoo**

6. **Finger** is to **nail** as **leg** is to
   A. arm B. torso C. knee D. walk — **knee**

7. **Player** is to **team** as **inch** is to
   A. worm B. measure C. foot D. short — **foot**

8. **Peak** is to **mountain** as **crest** is to
   A. wave B. ocean C. beach D. water — **wave**

Page 62

Action/Object Analogies

Directions: Determine whether each analogy is action/object or object/action by studying the relationship between the first pair of words. Then, choose the correct word to complete each analogy. The first one has been done for you.

1. **Mow** is to **grass** as **shear** is to
   A. cut B. fleece C. sheep D. barber — **sheep**

2. **Rod** is to **fishing** as **oven** is to
   A. police B. crime C. bake D. hunting — **bake**

3. **Ship** is to **captain** as **airplane** is to
   A. fly B. airport C. pilot D. passenger — **pilot**

4. **Car** is to **mechanic** as **body** is to
   A. patient B. doctor C. torso D. hospital — **doctor**

5. **Cheat** is to **exam** as **swindle** is to
   A. criminal B. business C. crook D. crime — **business**

6. **Actor** is to **stage** as **surgeon** is to
   A. patient B. hospital C. operating room D. knife — **operating room**

7. **Ball** is to **throw** as **knife** is to
   A. cut B. spoon C. dinner D. silverware — **cut**

8. **Lawyer** is to **trial** as **surgeon** is to
   A. patient B. hospital C. operation D. operating room — **operation**

Page 63

Analogies of Association

Directions: Choose the correct word to complete each analogy. The first one has been done for you.

1. **Flowers** are to **spring** as **leaves** are to
   A. rakes B. trees C. fall D. green — **fall**

2. **Ham** is to **eggs** as **butter** is to
   A. full B. toast C. breakfast D. spread — **toast**

3. **Bat** is to **swing** as **ball** is to
   A. throw B. dance C. base D. soft — **throw**

4. **Chicken** is to **egg** as **cow** is to
   A. barn B. calf C. milk D. beef — **milk**

5. **Bed** is to **sleep** as **chair** is to
   A. sit B. couch C. relax D. table — **sit**

6. **Cube** is to **square** as **sphere** is to
   A. circle B. triangle C. hemisphere D. spear — **circle**

7. **Kindness** is to **friend** as **cruelty** is to
   A. meanness B. enemy C. war D. unkindness — **enemy**

8. **Pumpkin** is to **pie** as **chocolate** is to
   A. cake B. dark C. taste D. dessert — **cake**

Page 64

Object/Location Analogies

Directions: Write a location word for each object. **Possible answers:**

1. shirt: **closet**
2. milk: **refrigerator**
3. vase: **table**
4. screwdriver: **tool box**
5. cow: **barn**
6. chalkboard: **classroom**
7. shower: **bathroom**
8. cucumbers: **garden**
9. silverware: **drawer**
10. car: **garage**
11. pages: **book**
12. bees: **hive**
13. money: **wallet**
14. salt water: **ocean**
15. dress: **clothing store**
16. ice cream: **freezer**
17. table: **kitchen**
18. medicine: **pharmacy**
19. dog: **kennel**
20. basketball: **gym**
21. bed: **bedroom**
22. roses: **flower garden**
23. dishwasher: **kitchen**
24. toys: **toy chest**
25. cookies: **cookie jar**
26. bird: **tree**
27. seashells: **beach**
28. asteroids: **outer space**

Page 65

Comprehensive Curriculum - Grade 6

Cause/Effect Analogies

Directions: Determine whether the analogy is cause/effect or effect/cause by studying the relationship between the first pair of words. Then, choose the correct word to complete each analogy. The first one has been done for you.

You caused this...and now look at the effect!

1. **Ashes** are to **flame** as darkness is to
   A. light   B. daylight   C. eclipse   D. sun   **eclipse**

2. **Strong** is to **exercising** as elected is to
   A. office   B. senator   C. politician   D. campaigning **campaigning**

3. **Fall** is to **pain** as disobedience is to
   A. punishment   B. morals   C. behavior   D. carelessness **punishment**

4. **Crying** is to **sorrow** as smiling is to
   A. teeth   B. mouth   C. joy   D. friends   **joy**

5. **Germ** is to **disease** as war is to
   A. soldiers   B. enemies   C. destruction   D. tanks   **destruction**

6. **Distracting** is to **noise** as soothing is to
   A. balm   B. warmth   C. hugs   D. music   **music**

7. **Food** is to **nutrition** as light is to
   A. vision   B. darkness   C. sunshine   D. bulb   **vision**

8. **Clouds** are to **rain** as winds are to
   A. springtime   B. hurricanes   C. clouds   D. March   **hurricanes**

Page 66

Synonym Analogies

Directions: Write synonyms for these words. **Possible answers:**

1. miniature: **tiny**
2. wind: **breeze**
3. picture: **photo**
4. quiet: **silent**
5. run: **jog**
6. cloth: **fabric**
7. mean: **unkind**
8. cup: **mug**
9. sweet: **kind**
10. difficult: **challenging**
11. obey: **conform**
12. plenty: **enough**
13. scent: **odor**
14. sudden: **abrupt**
15. gigantic: **huge**
16. rain: **shower**
17. cabinet: **cupboard**
18. loud: **noisy**
19. leap: **jump**
20. jeans: **pants**
21. kind: **considerate**
22. dish: **plate**
23. feline: **cat**
24. simple: **uncomplicated**
25. beautiful: **lovely**
26. scorch: **burn**
27. story: **tale**
28. thaw: **defrost**

Directions: Write two synonym analogies of your own.

29. 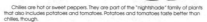 **Answers will vary.**

30. _____

Page 67

Reading Skills: Fact or Opinion?

A **fact** is information that can be proved. An **opinion** is information that tells how someone feels or what he or she thinks about something.

Directions: For each sentence, write **F** for fact or **O** for opinion. The first one has been done for you.

- **F** 1. Each of the countries in South America has its own capital.
- **O** 2. All South Americans are good swimmers.
- **O** 3. People like the climate in Peru better than in Brazil.
- **F** 4. The continent of South America is almost completely surrounded by water.
- **F** 5. The only connection with another continent is a narrow strip of land, called the isthmus of Panama, which links it to North America.
- **F** 6. The Andes Mountains run all the way down the western edge of the continent.
- **F** 7. The Andes are the longest continuous mountain barrier in the world.
- **O** 8. The Andes are the most beautiful mountain range.
- **F** 9. The Amazon River is the second longest river in the world—about 4,000 miles long.
- **F** 10. Half of the people in South America are Brazilians.
- **O** 11. Life in Brazil is better than life in other South American countries.
- **O** 12. Brazil is the best place for South Americans to live.
- **F** 13. Cape Horn is at the southern tip of South America.
- **F** 14. The largest land animal in South America is the tapir, which reaches a length of 6 to 8 feet.

Page 68

Reading Skills: Fact or Opinion?

Directions: Read the paragraphs below. For each numbered sentence, write **F** for fact or **O** for opinion. Write the reason for your answer. The first one has been done for you.

(1) The two greatest poems in the history of the world are the *Iliad* and the *Odyssey*. **(2)** The *Iliad* is the story of the Trojan War; the *Odyssey* tells about the wanderings of the Greek hero Ulysses after the war. **(3)** These poems are so long that they each fill an entire book.

(4) The author of the poems, according to Greek legend, was a blind poet named Homer. **(5)** Almost nothing is known about Homer. **(6)** This indicates to me that it is possible that Homer never existed. **(7)** Maybe Homer existed but didn't write the *Iliad* and the *Odyssey*.

(8) Whether or not there was a Homer does not really matter. We have these wonderful poems, which are still being read more than 2,500 years after they were written.

1. **O** Reason: **This cannot be proven. People have different opinions about which are the greatest poems.**

2. **F** Reason: **explains what the poems are about**

3. **F** Reason: **tells how long the poems are**

4. **F** Reason: **tells a fact about a Greek legend**

5. **F** Reason: **tells that not much is known about Homer**

6. **O** Reason: **not everyone thinks Homer did not exist**

7. **O** Reason: **some people may believe this and some may not**

8. **O** Reason: **some people may not agree with this**

Page 69

Chilies

Directions: Read about chilies. Find the one opinion in each passage, and write it on the lines.

Chilies are hot or sweet peppers. They are part of the "nightshade" family of plants that also includes potatoes and tomatoes. Potatoes and tomatoes taste better than chilies, though.

Opinion: **Potatoes and tomatoes taste better than chilies, though.**

Chilies were originally grown in Central and South America. By the 15th century, Europeans were cooking with them and drying them to use as a spice. European dishes taste better now than they did before chilies were used in them.

Opinion: **European dishes taste better now than they did before chilies were used in them.**

Although it is really a Mexican recipe, every intelligent American loves chili con carne. It is made with spicy meat, beans, and chilies. Today, most Americans call that dish "chili."

Opinion: **Although it is really a Mexican recipe, every intelligent American loves *chili con carne*.**

Some people think that all chilies are hot. Therefore, they never eat any of them. What a silly belief! There are many different kinds of red, yellow, and green chilies. Even red chilies can be sweet.

Opinion: **What a silly belief!**

Page 70

Carol's Country Restaurant

Directions: Write in the corresponding numbered blank below whether each numbered sentence gives a fact or an opinion.

(1) I have visited Carol's Country Restaurant seven times in the past two weeks. **(2)** The meals there are excellent. **(3)** They often feature country dishes such as meatloaf, ham with scalloped potatoes, and fried chicken.

(4) Owner Carol Murphy makes wonderful vegetable soup that includes all home-grown vegetables. **(5)** It's simmered with egg noodles. **(6)** Another of my favorite dishes is Carol's chili. **(7)** I'm sure it is the spiciest chili this side of the Mississippi River. **(8)** Carol says she uses secret ingredients in all her dishes.

(9) Whether ordering a main dish or a dessert, you can't go wrong at Carol's. **(10)** Everything is superb.

(11) Carol's Country Restaurant is on Twig Street in Freeport. **(12)** Prices for main entrees range from $5.95 to $12.95.

1. **fact**
2. **opinion**
3. **fact**
4. **opinion**
5. **fact**
6. **fact**
7. **opinion**
8. **fact**
9. **opinion**
10. **opinion**
11. **fact**
12. **fact**

CAROL'S COUNTRY RESTAURANT
TODAY'S SPECIAL
Carol's Chili

Page 71

Review

Directions: Write 5 sentences that are facts and 5 that are opinions.

Facts: Answers will vary.

1. _____
2. _____
3. _____
4. _____
5. _____

Opinions:

6. _____
7. _____
8. _____
9. _____
10. _____

Page 72

Reading Skills: Cause and Effect

A **cause** is the reason something happens. The **effect** is what happens as the result of the cause.

Directions: Read the paragraphs below. For each numbered sentence, circle the cause or causes, and underline the effect or effects. The first one has been done for you.

(1) All living things in the ocean are endangered by humans polluting the water. Pollution occurs in several ways. One way is the dumping of certain waste materials, such as garbage and sewage, into the ocean. (2) The decaying bacteria that feed on the garbage use up much of the oxygen in the surrounding water, so other creatures in the area often don't get enough.

Other substances, such as radioactive waste material, can also cause pollution. These materials are often placed in the water in securely sealed containers. (3) But after years of being exposed to the ocean water, the containers may begin to leak.

Oil is another major source of concern. (4) Oil is spilled into the ocean when tankers run aground and sink or when oil wells in the ocean cannot be capped. (5) The oil covers the gills of fish and smothers them. (6) Diving birds get the oil on their wings and are unable to fly. (7) When they clean themselves, they are often poisoned by the oil.

Rivers also can contribute to the pollution of oceans. Many rivers receive the runoff water from farmlands. (8) Fertilizers used on the farms may be carried to the ocean, where they cause a great increase in the amount of certain plants. Too much of some plants can actually be poisonous to fish.

Worse yet are the pesticides carried to the ocean. These chemicals slowly build up in shellfish and other small animals. These animals then pass the pesticides on to the larger animals that feed on them. (9) The buildup of these chemicals in the animals can make them ill or harm their young.

Page 73

Reading Skills: Cause and Effect

Directions: Read the following cause-and-effect statements. If you think the cause and effect are properly related, write **true**. If not, explain why not. The first one has been done for you.

1. The best way to make it rain is to wash your car.
   It does not rain every time you wash your car.

2. Getting a haircut really improved Randy's grades.
   Getting a haircut does not improve your grades.

3. Michael got an A in geometry because he spent a lot of time studying.
   true

4. Yesterday, I broke a mirror, and today, I slammed my thumb in the door.
   You don't slam your thumb in a door because you broke a mirror.

5. Natalia isn't allowed to go to the dance tonight because she broke her curfew last weekend.
   true

6. Emily drank a big glass of orange juice, and her headache went away.
   Drinking orange juice doesn't cure headaches.

7. The Akitas had their tree cut down because it had Dutch elm disease.
   true

8. We can't grow vegetables in our backyard because the rabbits keep eating them.
   true

Page 74

Review

Directions: Write **fact** or **opinion** to describe each sentence.

fact	1. Hurricanes are also known as typhoons.
opinion	2. Hurricanes are the worst natural disasters.
fact	3. All hurricanes begin over the ocean near the equator.
opinion	4. All people are concerned about pollution.
opinion	5. Pesticides should never be used.
fact	6. Many colonists died due to lack of food and sickness.
opinion	7. Kites are the best gift to give a child.
fact	8. The names of Columbus's three ships were the *Niña*, the *Pinta*, and the *Santa Maria*.

Directions: If the sentence demonstrates a logical cause and effect relationship, write **yes** on the line. If the sentence is illogical, write **no**.

no	1. I ate fish and got sick, so all fish will make me sick.
yes	2. The farmer began practicing crop rotation, and his crop yield improved.
no	3. I know how to swim, so I cannot possibly drown.
yes	4. While learning to ski, Connor broke his leg.
yes	5. The river overflowed its banks and caused much damage.
no	6. The Cincinnati Reds won 100 games last year, so they probably will this year.
no	7. Because I started using a new toothpaste, I will make more friends.

Page 75

Reading Skills: Personification

When an author gives an object or animal human characteristics, it is called **personification**.

Example: The dragon quickly thought out its next move in the attack on the village.

Thought is a human process and not associated with mythical creatures; therefore, the dragon is personified in that sentence.

Directions: In the following sentences, underline the personification.

1. The cave's gaping mouth led to internal passageways.
2. The tractor sprang to life with a turn of the key.
3. The lights blinked twice and then died.
4. Crops struggled to survive in the blistering heat, hoping for rainfall.
5. The engine of the car coughed and sputtered as if it wanted to breathe but couldn't.
6. The arrow flew through the air, eyeing its target.
7. Snowmen smile from the safety of their yards.
8. Stephanie's doll sipped tea delicately.

Directions: Write a sentence that personifies the following objects.

                 Answers will vary.
1. flower _____
2. stuffed animal _____
3. car _____

Page 76

Reading Skills: Symbolism

Symbolism is the use of something to stand for (symbolize) something else.

Example:

The elderly woman held the pearl necklace in her wrinkled hand and thought back on her life. Many years had gone by since her husband had given her the necklace, as many years as there were pearls. Some of the pearls, she noticed, were darker than others, just as some years in her life had been darker than other years.

The pearl necklace symbolizes the life of the elderly woman. Each pearl stands for a year in her life, and the necklace represents the many years that have passed.

Directions: Write what is being symbolized in the paragraph on the lines below.

The refugees boarded the small ship with high hopes. They had to believe that their destiny was to find the New World and seek shelter there. A few dared to dream of the riches to be found. For them, the boat itself looked like a treasure chest waiting to be discovered.

                 Possible answers:
The boat symbolizes a treasure chest as something that holds riches and excitement for a great future.

For 12-year-old Sam, the basketball court was the best place to be. In Sam's neighborhood, crime ran rampant, and the court was the one safe place for kids like Sam to play. Sam spent most nights there, practicing lay-ups, jump shots, and three-point shots. Sam worked hard because for him it wasn't just a sport, it was a golden key.

Basketball symbolizes a golden key, because if Sam becomes good enough at it, it could be the "key" to getting him into a good school and giving him a good future.

Page 77

Reading Skills: Idioms

An **idiom** is a phrase that says one thing but actually means something quite different.
Example: Now that's *a horse of a different color!* There is not literally a horse of a different color. The idiom means "a different matter altogether."

Directions: Write the letter of the correct meaning for the bold words in each sentence. The first one has been done for you.

a. forgive and make up	**f.** pressed tightly together
b. fact kept secret for fear of disgrace	**g.** relatives and ancestors
c. something that dampens excitement	**h.** rudely ignored
d. get acquainted, become less formal	**i.** excessive paperwork
e. treated like royalty	**j.** people were gossiping

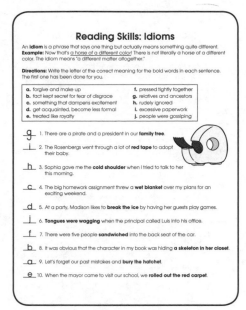

g 1. There are a pirate and a president in our **family tree.**

i 2. The Rosenbergs went through a lot of **red tape** to adopt their baby.

h 3. Sophia gave me the **cold shoulder** when I tried to talk to her this morning.

c 4. The big homework assignment threw a **wet blanket** over my plans for an exciting weekend.

d 5. At a party, Madison likes to **break the ice** by having her guests play games.

j 6. **Tongues were wagging** when the principal called Luis into his office.

f 7. There were five people **sandwiched** into the back seat of the car.

b 8. It was obvious that the character in my book was hiding **a skeleton in her closet.**

a 9. Let's forget our past mistakes and **bury the hatchet.**

e 10. When the mayor came to visit our school, we **rolled out the red carpet.**

Page 78

Reading Skills: Idioms

Directions: Use the following idioms in a sentence of your own. Then, tell what the phrase means in your own words.

Sentences will vary.

1. raining cats and dogs
a. raining very hard
b. _____

2. going to the dogs
a. getting run down or deteriorating
b. _____

3. barking up the wrong tree
a. asking the wrong person or searching in the wrong place
b. _____

4. hit the nail on the head
a. got something exactly right
b. _____

5. went out on a limb
a. took a chance
b. _____

6. all in the same boat
a. all in the same situation
b. _____

7. keep up with the Joneses
a. keeping up with the people around you
b. _____

Page 79

Reading Skills: Denotations and Connotations

Sometimes two words can be similar, yet you would not substitute one for the other because they each suggest different feelings.
Denotation is the literal or dictionary definition of a word.
Connotation is the meaning of a word including all the emotions associated with it. For example, **job** and **chore** are synonyms, but because of their connotations, most people would choose to do a job instead of a chore.

Directions: Circle the word in each group with the most positive connotation.

Example:

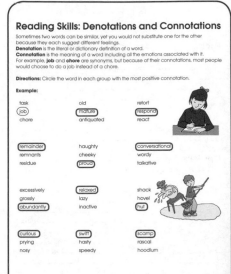

task	old	retort
(job)	(mature)	(respond)
chore	antiquated	react

(remainder)	haughty	(conversational)
remnants	cheeky	wordy
residue	(proud)	talkative

excessively	(relaxed)	shack
grossly	lazy	hovel
(abundantly)	inactive	(hut)

(curious)	(swift)	(scamp)
prying	hasty	rascal
nosy	speedy	hoodlum

Page 80

Reading Skills: Denotations and Connotations

Directions: Replace the bold word in each sentence with a word that has a more positive connotation.

Possible answers:

Example:
shut
He ~~slammed~~ the door when he left.

plentiful
The dog's energy was ~~uncontrollable~~.

disagreement
We hoped to settle our ~~feud~~ peacefully.

corrected
The mother ~~reprimanded~~ the children when people began to look at them.

chatted
The children ~~gossiped~~ at lunchtime.

wrote
The girl ~~scribbled~~ a hasty note to leave behind.

suddenly
Our conversation ended ~~abruptly~~ when the phone rang.

serious
The principal was a ~~severe~~ man.

took
The boy ~~snatched~~ the toy from his baby brother.

declined
The couple ~~rejected~~ their offer of help.

messy
Dad reminded me to clean my ~~disastrous~~ room.

Page 81

Similes and Metaphors

A **simile** compares two unlike things using the word **like** or **as.**

Example: The fog was **like** a blanket around us. The fog was **as** thick **as** a blanket.

A **metaphor** compares two unlike things without using the word **like** or **as.**

Example: The fog was a blanket around us.

"The fog was thick" is not a simile or a metaphor. **Thick** is an adjective. Similes and metaphors compare two unlike things that are both nouns.

Directions: Underline the two things being compared in each sentence. Then, write **S** for simile or **M** for metaphor on the lines.

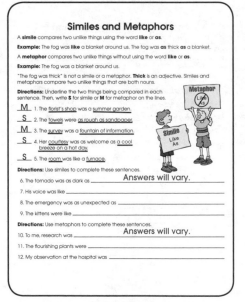

M 1. The florist's shop was a summer garden.

S 2. The towels were as rough as sandpaper.

M 3. The survey was a fountain of information.

S 4. Her courtesy was as welcome as a cool breeze on a hot day.

S 5. The room was like a furnace.

Directions: Use similes to complete these sentences.

Answers will vary.

6. The tornado was as dark as _____

7. His voice was like _____

8. The emergency was as unexpected as _____

9. The kittens were like _____

Directions: Use metaphors to complete these sentences.

Answers will vary.

10. To me, research was _____

11. The flourishing plants were _____

12. My observation at the hospital was _____

Page 82

Vocabulary Building: Similes

A **simile** is a figure of speech comparing two things using **like** or **as.**

Example: The child was as quiet as a mouse.

Directions: Read the following paragraph. Underline the similes.

The kittens were born on a morning as cold as ice. Although it was late spring, the weather hadn't quite warmed up. There were five kittens in the litter, each quite different from its siblings. The oldest was black as deepest night. There was a calico that looked like Grandma's old quilt. One was as orange as a fall pumpkin, and another was orange and white. The runt was a black and gray tiger. She was as little as a baseball and as quick as lightning to fight for food. The kittens will soon become accepted by the other animals as members of the farm.

Directions: Using the following words, create similes of your own.

Example: piano—The piano keys tinkled like a light rain on a tin roof.

Possible answers:

1. fire The fire was as hot as a furnace.

2. thunderstorm The thunderstorm was like an angry old man.

3. ocean The ocean was as blue as the sky.

4. night The night was as black as an underground cave.

5. rainforest The rainforest was like a breath of fresh air.

6. giraffe The giraffe is like a a young sapling.

Page 83

Vocabulary Building: Metaphors

A **metaphor** is a figure of speech that directly compares one thing with another.

Example: As it set, the sun was a glowing orange ball of fire.

The sun is being compared to a glowing orange ball of fire.

<u>sun</u>　　<u>glowing orange ball of fire</u>

Directions: Underline the metaphor in each sentence. Then, write the two things that are being compared on the lines.

1. The ocean, a swirling mass of anger, released its fury on the shore.

<u>the ocean</u>　　<u>a swirling mass of anger</u>

2. He was a top spinning out of control.

<u>He</u>　　<u>a top spinning out of control</u>

3. The heat covered the crowd, a blanket smothering them all.

<u>the heat</u>　　<u>a blanket smothering them all</u>

4. I fed my dog a steak and it was a banquet for her senses.

<u>steak</u>　　<u>a banquet for her senses</u>

5. The flowers in the garden were a stained glass window.

<u>flowers</u>　　<u>a stained glass window</u>

Page 84

Vocabulary Building: Metaphors and Similes

Directions: Underline the metaphors in the following sentences. Then, rewrite each sentence using a simile.

1. She is a playful child, a real kitten!

<u>She is as playful as a kitten.</u>

2. Life today is a merry-go-round.

<u>Life is like a merry-go-round.</u>

3. His emotions were waves washing over him.

<u>His emotions were like waves washing over him.</u>

4. His childhood was an image in a rearview mirror.

<u>His childhood was like an image in a rearview mirror.</u>

Directions: Write the meanings of the following sentences.

1. His mind was as changeable as spring weather. **Possible answers:**

<u>He was likely to change his mind.</u>

2. His demand was like a clap of thunder.

<u>His demand was loud and scary.</u>

3. There was joy written on the children's faces on Christmas morning.

<u>The children's faces had joyful expressions.</u>

Page 85

Reading Skills: Generalizations

A **generalization** is a statement or rule that applies to many situations or examples.

Example: All children get into trouble at one time or another.

Directions: Read each paragraph, and then circle the generalization that best describes the information given.

Although many people think of reptiles as slimy, snakes and other reptiles are covered with scales that are dry to the touch. Scales are outgrowths of the animal's skin. Although in some species they are nearly invisible, in most they form a tile-like covering. The turtle's shell is made up of hardened scales that are fused together. The crocodile has a tough but more flexible covering.

(Every reptile has scales.)
The scales of all reptiles are alike.
There are many different kinds of scales.

The reptile's scales help to protect it from its enemies and conserve moisture in its body. Some kinds of lizards have fan-shaped scales that they can raise up to scare away other animals. The scales also can be used to court a mate. A reptile called a gecko can hang from a ceiling because of specialized scales on its feet. Some desert lizards have other kinds of scales on their feet that allow them to run over the loose sand.

(Scales have many functions.)
Scales scare away other animals.
Scales help reptiles adapt to their environments.

A snake will periodically shed its skin, leaving behind a thin impression of its body—scales and all. A lizard sheds its skin, too, but it tears off in smaller pieces rather than in one big piece. Before a snake begins this process, which is called molting, its eyes cloud over. The snake will go into hiding until they clear. When it comes out again, it brushes against rough surfaces to pull off the old skin.

Snakes go into hiding before they molt.
(Reptiles periodically shed their skin.)
A lizard's skin molts in smaller pieces.

Page 86

Reading Skills: Generalizations

Directions: Identify which statements below are generalizations and which are specific. Write **G** for generalization and **S** for specific.

G　1. We want to have lots of good food for the party.
S　2. Jenna gave me three pink shirts and two pairs of jeans.
G　3. Americans are generous and friendly.
S　4. There are 10 more female teachers than male teachers at our school.
S　5. She wants me to buy watermelon at the grocery store.
G　6. She will never believe anything I say.
S　7. I got poison ivy because I didn't watch out for the foliage on our hike.
G　8. My mom is the best mom in the world.
S　9. I get depressed every time the weather turns bad.
S　10. The team is so good because they work out and practice every day.
G　11. Cats are so bad-tempered.
S　12. My dog has a good temperament because he's had lots of training.
G　13. Our football team is the best this county has ever seen.
S　14. I love the feel of rain on my skin because it's cool.
G　15. That classroom is always out of control.

Page 87

Reading Skills: Skimming and Scanning

Skimming is reading quickly to get a general idea of what a reading selection is about. When skimming, look for headings and key words to give you an overall idea of what you are reading.

Scanning is looking for certain words to find facts or answer questions. When scanning, read or think of questions first.

Directions: Scan the paragraphs below to find the answers to the questions. Then, look for specific words that will help you locate the answers. For example, in the second question, scan for the word **smallest**.

There are many different units to measure time. Probably the smallest unit that you use is the second, and the longest unit is the year. While 100 years seems like a very long time to us, in the history of Earth, it is a smaller amount of time than one second is in a person's entire lifetime.

To describe the history of Earth, scientists use geologic time. Even a million years is a fairly short period of time in geologic time. Some scientists believe that our planet is about 4,600 million years old. Since a thousand million is a billion, Earth is believed to be 4.6 billion years old.

1. What kind of time is used to describe the history of Earth?

<u>geologic time</u>

2. For the average person, what is the smallest unit of time used?

<u>the second</u>

3. In millions of years, how old do some scientists believe Earth is?

<u>4,600 million years</u>

4. How would you express that in billions of years?

<u>4.6 billion years</u>

Page 88

The Author's Purpose

Authors write to entertain, inform, or persuade. To entertain means "to hold the attention of or to amuse someone." A fiction book about outer space entertains its reader, as does a joke book.

To inform means "to give factual information." A cookbook informs the reader of new recipes. A newspaper tells what is happening in the world.

To persuade people means "to convince them." Newspaper editorial writers try to persuade readers to accept their opinions. Doctors write health columns to persuade readers to eat nutritious foods or to exercise regularly.

Directions: Read each of the passages below. Tell whether they entertain, inform, or persuade. (They may do more than one.) Give the reasons why.

George Washington was born in a brick house near the Potomac River in Virginia on February 11, 1732. When he was 11 years old, George went to live with his half-brother, Lawrence, at Mount Vernon. **Possible answers:**

Author's Purpose: <u>inform</u>

Reason: <u>The passage contains facts.</u>

When George Washington was a child, he always measured and counted things. Maybe that is why he became a surveyor when he grew up. Surveyors like to measure and count things, too.

Author's Purpose: <u>inform/persuade</u>

Reason: <u>The passage contains facts and the author's opinion.</u>

George Washington was the best president America has ever had. He led a new nation to independence. He made all the states feel as if they were part of the United States. All presidents should be as involved with the country as George Washington was.

Author's Purpose: <u>persuade</u>

Reason: <u>Most of the sentences are the author's opinion. The author is trying to persuade the reader to agree with his or her point of view.</u>

Page 89

Llamas

Directions: Read each paragraph. Tell whether it informs, entertains, or persuades. One paragraph does more than one. Then, write your reason on the line below.

A llama (LAH'MAH) is a South American animal that is related to the camel. It is raised for its wool. Also, it can carry heavy loads. Some people who live near mountains in the United States train llamas to go on mountain trips. Llamas are sure-footed because they have two long toes and toenails. **Possible answers:**

Author's Purpose: inform

Reason: The passage is factual.

Llamas are the best animals to have if you're planning to backpack in the mountains. They can climb easily and carry your supplies. No one should ever go for a long hiking trip in the mountains without a llama.

Author's Purpose: persuade/inform

Reason: The passage contains facts and the author's opinion.

Llamas can be stubborn animals. Sometimes, they suddenly stop walking for no reason. People have to push them to get them moving again. Stubborn llamas can be frustrating when hiking up a steep mountain.

Author's Purpose: inform

Reason: The passage is mostly factual.

Greg is an 11-year-old boy who raises llamas to climb mountains. One of his llamas is named Dallas. Although there are special saddles for llamas, Greg likes to ride bareback.

Author's Purpose: entertain

Reason: The information is presented to interest/entertain the reader.

Now, use a separate sheet of paper to inform readers about llamas.

Page 90

Roller Coasters

Directions: Read each paragraph, and determine the author's purpose. Then, write down your reason on the line below.

Roller coaster rides are thrilling. The cars chug up the hills and then fly down them. People scream and laugh. They clutch their seats and sometimes raise their arms above their heads. **Possible answers:**

Author's Purpose: inform/entertain

Reason: The passage contains facts, but it is also written in an entertaining way and includes descriptive words.

The first roller coasters were giant slides made of ice in Russia. That was more than 300 years ago! The slides were about 70 feet high, and people had to climb steep ladders to reach their tops. Riders got into carts and slid down very fast. Then, they climbed the ladders again. Early roller coasters were more work than fun.

Author's Purpose: inform

Reason: The passage contains facts about the first roller coasters.

The first roller coaster in America was built in 1884. It cost only a nickel to ride the "Switchback Gravity Pleasure Railway" at Coney Island in New York. Roller coasters did not become very popular until the late 1920s.

Author's Purpose: inform

Reason: The passage contains facts about early roller coasters.

Have you ever ridden a giant roller coaster? Some of the most famous ones in the world include the "Bizarro" at Six Flags New England; the "Intimidator 305" at Kings Dominion in Doswell, Virginia; and the "Millennium Force" at Cedar Point in Sandusky, Ohio. Roller coasters are fun because they have thrilling twists and turns. Some go very high, and some turn upside down. Everyone should go on a roller coaster at least once in his or her life.

Author's Purpose: inform/persuade

Reason: The passage contains facts about roller coasters. It also includes the author's opinion about roller coasters.

Now, use a separate sheet of paper to persuade people to ride roller coasters.

Page 91

Review

Directions: Follow the instructions for each section.

1. Write an informative paragraph about a sport.

Answers will vary.

2. Write an entertaining paragraph about the circus.

3. Write a persuasive paragraph about the desire for a later bedtime.

Page 92

Multiple Choice

Multiple-choice questions are frequently asked on tests. Such questions include three or four possible answers. When answering a multiple-choice question, first read the question carefully. Then, read all the answers that are offered. If you do not know the correct answer, eliminate some of the ones you know are wrong until you have only one left. Remember these points when taking multiple-choice tests:

1. Answers that contain phrases such as **all people, no one,** or **everybody** are probably not correct. For example, a statement such as "all children like candy" is probably not correct because it allows for no exceptions. If there is one child who does not like candy, the statement is not correct. However, if you know that more than one answer is correct and the last choice in the group is "all of the above," then that phrase is probably the correct answer.

2. Answers that contain words you have never seen before probably are not correct. Teachers don't expect you to know material you haven't studied.

3. Answers that are silly usually aren't correct.

4. When two of the answers provided look nearly the same, one of them is probably correct.

5. Always check your answers if there is time.

Directions: Answer the questions about multiple-choice tests.

1. The first thing you should do during a multiple-choice test is _____
read the question carefully

2. When you are reading the possible answers to a multiple-choice question and you know the first one is right, should you immediately mark it without reading the other answers? no
Why or why not? There might be another similar answer that is actually the correct one.

3. Write three phrases that might tell you that an answer is probably not correct.
all people, no one, and everybody

Page 93

True/False

True/false tests include several statements. You must read each one carefully to determine if it is right or wrong. Remember these tips:

1. Watch for one word in the sentence that can change the statement's meaning from true to false or vice versa.

2. Words such as **all, none, everybody,** or **nobody** should alert you that the answer may be false. Using these words means that there are no exceptions.

3. There are usually more true answers on a test than false ones. Therefore, if you have to guess an answer, you have a better chance of answering right by marking it "true."

4. Always check your answers if there is time.

Directions: Answer the questions about true/false tests.

1. List four words that can alert you that a question is false.
all, none, everybody, and nobody

2. One word in a sentence can
change the statement's meaning

3. If you must guess an answer, is it wiser to guess true or false? true

4. True/false tests are made up of several statements

5. Can you do well on a true/false test by only skimming each statement? no

6. If the word **everybody** is in the statement, is the answer probably true or false? false

7. When the word **all** appears in the statement, is the answer probably true or false? false

8. What should you do last when taking a true/false test?
Check your answers if you have time.

Page 94

Fill in the Blank

Fill-in-the-blank tests are more difficult than true/false or multiple-choice tests. However, there may be clues in each sentence that help determine the answer. Look at this example:

The _____ of the United States serves a _____-year term.

Can you tell that the first blank needs a person? (The answer is "president.") The second blank needs a number because it refers to years. ("Four" is the answer.) Think about these other tips for taking fill-in-the-blank tests:

1. Always plan your time wisely. Don't waste too much time on one question. Check the clock or your watch periodically when taking a test.

2. First, read through the entire test. Then, go back to the beginning and answer the questions that you know. Put a small mark beside the questions you are not sure about.

3. Go back to the questions you were not sure of or that you didn't know. Carefully read each one. Think about possible answers. If you think it could be more than one answer, try to eliminate some of the possible answers.

4. Save the most difficult questions to answer last. Don't waste time worrying if you don't know the answer to a question.

5. Sometimes, you should guess at an answer because it may be right. There are some tests, though, that deduct points if your answer is wrong, but not if it is left blank. Make sure you know how the test will be scored.

6. Review your test. Make sure you have correctly read the directions and each question. Check your answers.

Directions: Answer the questions about fill-in-the-blank tests.

1. Fill-in-the-blank tests may have _____ clues _____ in each sentence that help you figure out the answer.

2. Always plan your _____ time _____ wisely when taking a test.

3. Should you try to answer a question as soon as you read it? _____ no _____

4. Should you answer the hard or easy questions first? _____ easy _____

5. If you are not sure of a question, you should make a small mark beside it.

Page 95

Matching

Matching tests have two columns of information. A word or fact from one column matches information in the other. Read these tips to help with matching tests:

1. Look at one question at a time. Start with the first word or phrase in one of the columns. Then, look at the possible answers in the other column until you find the correct one. Then, go to the next word or phrase in the first column. If you don't know the answer to one question, skip it and go back to it later.
2. If there are several words in one column and several definitions in the other column, it is often easier to read the definition first and then find the word that goes with it.
3. Carefully read the directions. Sometimes, one column on a matching test is longer than the other. Find out if there is one answer that won't be used or if an answer in the opposite column can be used twice.
4. Check your answers if there is time.

Directions: Answer the questions about matching tests.

1. Matching tests have how many columns of information? **two**

2. If one column has words in it and the other column has definitions in it, which one should you look at first to make the test easier? **the one with definitions**

3. To eliminate confusion, you should look at **one** question at a time.

4. Do the columns on a matching test always have the same number of things in them? **no**

5. Are there ever items left unmatched on a matching test? **yes**

6. Does it matter if you look at the right or left column of a matching test first? **no**

Page 96

Essays

Essay questions give you a chance to demonstrate what you have learned. They also provide the opportunity to express your opinion. Although many students think essay questions are the most difficult, they can be the most fun. Remember these tips when writing the answer to an essay question:

1. Think about the answer before you write it. Take time to organize your thoughts so that you can better express yourself.
2. Write a few notes or an outline on a piece of scrap paper or on the back of the test. This helps remind you what you want to write.
3. State your answer clearly. Don't forget to use complete sentences.
4. Review the answer before time runs out. Sometimes words are left out. It doesn't take much time to read through your essay to make sure it says what you want it to say.

Directions: Use these essay-writing tips to answer the following question in the space provided.

What is your favorite type of test? Give several reasons why.

Answers will vary.

Page 97

Review

Directions: Complete each question about tests.

1. Four steps for writing an answer for an essay test include:

   a) **Think about your answer before you write it.**

   b) **Write a few notes on scrap paper or the back of the test.**

   c) **State your answer clearly using complete sentences.**

   d) **Review and proofread the answers before time runs out.**

2. In a matching test, it is sometimes easier to read the **definition** and then match it with a word from the opposite column.

3. One column on a **matching test** may be longer than the other.

4. Tests that require you to fill in the blanks may provide **clues** in each statement.

5. Always **check** answers if there is time.

6. Certain words, such as **none** and **all**, should alert you that an answer may be **false**.

7. There are usually, but not always, more **true** statements on a true/false test.

8. If **everybody** or **everything** is used in one of the answers for a **multiple-choice or true/false test**, it is likely that that answer is not right.

9. If two possible answers for a multiple-choice question sound nearly the **same**, one of them is probably correct.

10. If two answers to a multiple-choice question appear to be correct, the answer could be one that says **all of the above**.

Page 98

Comprehension: Ansel Adams

One the world's most well-known photographers is Ansel Adams. You may not recognize his name, but you would probably recognize his photos. Adams was known for his love of nature and his stunning black-and-white landscape photographs. Although photography ended up becoming a passion for Adams, his earlier ambitions were in a completely different area.

Ansel Adams was born in 1902 in California. He was an only child, and he grew up with a rather shy and nervous personality. He did not do particularly well in school. As a result, he learned much on his own and from tutors. As a boy, Adams discovered a love of music. For a number of years, he planned on pursuing a career as a professional pianist.

In addition to his love of piano, Adams was passionate about nature and its preservation. He became involved with the Sierra Club as a teenager. This interest in the environment would last him throughout his life. When Adams was 14, he and his parents took a trip to Yosemite National Park. His parents gave him a Kodak Brownie box camera to use during the trip, and Adams's love of photography was born.

Throughout his life, Adams published a number of books featuring his photos. His pictures of the national parks were among the most famous. Adams lived long before digital cameras were available. He spent many hours in the darkroom, working painstakingly to print an image that matched the one in his mind's eye. Adams died in 1984, but he lives on in his photographs of the natural world he loved so much.

Directions: Answers these questions about Ansel Adams.

1. For what kind of photos was Ansel Adams best known? **black-and-white landscapes**

2. How was Adams's education different from a typical education? **He did a lot of learning on his own and from tutors.**

3. What similarities are there between a career as a photographer and a pianist? **Both careers are in the arts and require creativity.**

4. How was Adams's love of nature reflected in his photography? **He was best known for his photos of the natural world.**

5. Why did Adams's parents give him a camera? **to use during a trip to Yosemite National Park**

Page 100

Comprehension: Photography Terms

Like other good professionals, photographers make their craft look easy. Their skill—like that of the graceful ice skater—comes from years of practice. Where skaters develop a sense of balance, photographers develop an eye for pictures. They can make important technical decisions about photographing, or "shooting," a particular scene in the twinkling of an eye.

It's interesting to know some of the technical language that professional photographers use. "Angle of view" refers to the angle from which a photograph is taken. "Depth of field" is the distance between the nearest point and the farthest point that is in focus in a photo.

"Filling the frame" refers to the amount of space the object being photographed takes up in the picture. A close-up picture of a dog, flower, or person would fill the frame. A far-away picture would not.

Two elements that photographers work with are shutter speed and aperture. Shutter speed refers to how quickly the camera's shutter opens and closes. The longer the shutter stays open, the more light it allows in. The more quickly the shutter opens and closes, the better the photographer can capture an action shot. Shutter speed must work together with the aperture, which is the opening that controls the amount of light passing through the lens. A photographer who learns to properly balance shutter speed and aperture can take wonderful, sharp pictures that skillfully capture his or her subjects.

Directions: Answer these question about photography terms.

1. Name another term for photographing. **shooting**

2. This is the distance between the nearest point and the farthest point that is in focus in a photo. **depth of field**

3. What is aperture? **the opening that controls the amount of light passing through the lens**

4. A close-up picture of someone's face would

   ☐ provide depth of field.   ☐ appear far away.   ☒ fill the frame.

5. Shutter speed and aperture work together.

   ☒ True   ☐ False

Page 101

Comprehension: Photographing Animals

Animals are a favorite subject of many young photographers. Cats, dogs, hamsters, and other pets top the list, followed by zoo animals and the occasional lizard.

Because it's hard to get pets to sit still and "perform on command," some professional photographers refuse to photograph them. There are ways around the problem of short attention spans, however.

One way to get an appealing portrait of a cat or dog is to hold a biscuit or treat above the camera. The animal's longing look toward the food will be captured by the camera as a soulful gaze. Because it's above the camera—out of the camera's range—the treat won't appear in the picture. When you show the picture to your friends afterwards, they will be impressed by your pet's loving expression.

You can also try taking a series of good, quick shots of a pet by simply snapping several pictures right after calling its name. You'll get a different expression from your pet using this technique. Depending on your pet's disposition, the pictures will capture an inquisitive expression or possibly a look of annoyance, especially if you've awakened Rover from a nap!

Taking pictures of zoo animals requires a little more patience. After all, you can't wake up a lion! You may have to wait for a while until the animal does something interesting or moves into a position for you to get a good shot. When photographing zoo animals, don't get too close to the cages, and never tap on the glass or throw things between the bars of a cage. Concentrate on shooting some good pictures, and always respect the animals you are photographing.

Directions: Answer these questions about photographing animals.

1. Why do some professionals dislike photographing animals? **because it is difficult to get them to sit still**

2. Does the author suggest taking a single photo of a pet or several quick photos in a row? Why? **If you take several quick photos in a row, you'll capture different expressions.**

3. To capture a pet's loving expression, hold this out of camera range. **a treat**

4. Compared to taking pictures of pets, what does photographing zoo animals require? **more patience**

Page 102

Generalization: Taking Pictures

A **generalization** is a statement that applies to many different situations.

Directions: Read each passage, and circle the valid generalization.

1. Most people can quickly be taught to use a simple camera. However, it takes time, talent, and a good eye to learn to take professional-quality photographs. Patience is another quality that good photographers must possess. Those who photograph nature often will wait hours to get just the right light or shadow in their pictures.

a. (Anyone can learn to use a camera.)

b. Any patient person can become a good photographer.

c. Good photographers have a good eye for pictures.

2. Photographers such as Diane Arbus, who photographed strange or odd people, also must wait for just the right picture. Many "people photographers" stake out a busy city sidewalk and study faces in the crowd. Then, they must leap up quickly and ask to take a picture or take one without being observed. Either way, it's not an easy task!

a. Staking out a busy sidewalk is a boring task.

b. ("People photographers" must be patient people and good observers.)

c. Taking someone's photo without his or her permission is not a nice thing to do to strangers.

3. Whether the subject is nature or humans, many photographers insist that dawn is the best time to take pictures. The light is clear at this early hour, and mist may still be in the air. The mist gives these early morning photos a haunting, "other world" quality that is very appealing.

a. (Morning mist gives an unusual quality to most outdoor photographs.)

b. Photographers all agree that dawn is the best time to take pictures.

c. Misty light is always important in taking pictures.

Page 103

Generalization: Food Photography

Directions: Read each passage, and circle the valid generalization.

1. Taking good photographs of food is more difficult than it seems. Anyone can snap a photo of a bowl of soup or a basket of apples. The goal is to convey the food's best traits. If the soup is steaming hot and full of chunks of savory veggies, the photo needs to show that to the viewer. If the apples are crisp, sweet, and juicy, the photo should make the viewer want to pick one up and take a bite. A photo taken from a bad angle or with poor lighting won't make food look appealing to anyone.

a. It is not easy to take a photo of a basket of apples.

b. (The goal of food photography is to make the food look appealing to the viewer.)

c. Only professional photographers should take photos of food.

2. Indirect daylight is the best lighting for food photography. Good light is important in making the food look appetizing. Photos of food can often look flat, with a yellowish tone to the picture. The best possible lighting is a shady spot that is surrounded by natural light. Bright, direct sunlight is too harsh. It can create shadows and bleach out bright colors and whites.

a. No one should ever take photos of food on a bright, sunny day.

b. Never use artificial lighting when taking photos of food.

c. (Good lighting, such as indirect daylight, is essential to taking appetizing photos of food.)

3. Using props and styling the food can make a dish look much more attractive. Think of a bowl of chili. Shown on its own, it may not look very appealing. If you were to add a pretty placemat or napkin, the photo would look more interesting. Adding some cheese or a dollop of sour cream to the chili would certainly make the viewer want to dig in! A cutting board, patterned napkins, and garnishes like chopped herbs or cheese can help food look much more appealing in a photo.

a. (Props and food styling can help food appear more appealing in photos.)

b. You should always photograph chili with garnishes.

c. The food is more important than the props and styling in a photograph.

Page 104

Generalization: Choosing a Camera

Photography is an important part of American culture today. Digital cameras have made pictures incredibly easy to take. Many people have phones that can take photos, and it's also easy to share them instantly via the Internet. When it comes to buying a camera, though, there are still many options.

For the casual photographer, a point-and-shoot digital camera is a good choice. This type of camera is easy for almost anyone to use. You don't need to have a great knowledge of how cameras work or the finer points of photography. That's how these cameras got their nickname—all you need to do is point the camera and shoot your picture. The settings are mostly automatic, and the camera makes the decisions for you. Most point-and-shoot cameras allow you to make some adjustments if you like. You can change the setting to do things like take an action shot, photograph fireworks, or take a picture of a sunny day at the beach.

For more serious photographers, a DSLR camera is a likely choice. **DSLR** stands for digital single-lens reflex. A photographer using this type of camera has much more control over the camera's settings. He or she needs to know more about photography in order to manually do what other cameras do automatically. The benefit is that the DSLR photographer can often capture things that a photographer with a point-and-shoot camera cannot. DSLR cameras tend to be quite a bit more expensive than point-and-shoot cameras. In addition, the various lenses are also expensive. Serious photographers accept the added work and expense because they can have so much more control over their photos.

Directions: Answer these questions about choosing a camera.

1. Which generalization is correct?

a. Point-and-shoot cameras cost less than DSLR cameras.

b. (A DSLR camera is a good choice for serious photographers who want to have a lot of control over the photos they take.)

c. Most of the settings are automatic in point-and-shoot cameras.

2. How are point-and-shoot cameras and DSLR cameras different from one another?
   The settings are mostly automatic for point-and-shoot cameras, but the photographer has more control over the settings with a DSLR.

3. If you were to buy a camera, which kind would you choose? Explain why.
   Answers will vary.

Page 105

Review

Directions: Circle the missing word for each sentence.

1. Ansel Adams was known for his beautiful _____ photos.
   a. pianist
   b. amateur
   c. (landscape)

2. The _____ of the camera collects the light rays and draws them together at the center.
   a. shutter
   b. (lens)
   c. aperture

3. The distance between the nearest point and the farthest point in a photo is called the _____.
   a. graphic
   b. shooting
   c. (depth of field)

4. Taking a picture is often referred to as _____.
   a. (shooting)
   b. graphic
   c. speed

5. _____ refers to the angle from which a photograph is taken.
   a. Photos
   b. (Angle of view)
   c. Lens

6. Shutter speed refers to how quickly a camera's shutter _____.
   a. (opens and closes)
   b. flashes
   c. focuses

Page 106

Main Idea/Recalling Details: Kites

Kites are a familiar sight on breezy fall days. They come in a great variety of sizes, colors, and designs. It is not known who invented kites, but kites have been flown since the beginning of recorded history. While today children and adults use them for recreation, throughout history kites have had other uses.

In the United States, kites have been used in weather and other scientific research experiments. Before airplanes and weather balloons, the National Weather Service had kites carry weather instruments as high as 4 miles above Earth. In addition, the United States military used kites for observing the enemy and sending messages between troops.

In other countries, kites had cultural and religious importance. The ancient Chinese flew kites over their homes to drive out evil spirits. The Chinese still enjoy kites so much that one day each year they celebrate Kites' Day.

On some Pacific islands, kites were believed to symbolize both sides of nature—life and death. On some Polynesian islands, kites were used as protection against evil. These kites were often shaped like birds and used as soaring messengers to the heavens. In Hawaii, kites were also used to establish land ownership. A kite was released in the air, and a claim was given for the area where it came down.

Directions: Answer these questions about kites.

1. The main idea is:
   ☐ Kites come in a great variety of sizes, colors, and designs.
   ☒ While today kites are used for recreation, throughout history they have had other uses.

2. Besides recreation, name two ways kites have been used in the United States.
   a) for weather and other scientific research
   b) The military used them for observation and to send messages.

3. What country celebrates a holiday called Kites' Day? China

4. How did Hawaiians use kites to decide land ownership? A kite was released into the air, and a claim was given for the area where it came down.

Page 107

Comprehension: Aerodynamics

Kites are able to fly because of the principle of **aerodynamics**. Aerodynamics is the study of forces that are put into action by moving air. Three main forces work to keep a heavier-than-air kite flying—lift, gravity, and drag.

This is how it works: The flying lines, or strings, are attached to the kite to hold it at a slant. The wind pushes against the underside of the kite. At the same time, the wind rushes around the edges of the kite and "drags" some of the air from the upper side. This creates a partial vacuum there. The push of the air underneath is greater than the push of the air from the top, so the kite is held in the air. An airplane is held in the air in much the same way, except that it must keep moving rapidly to make the pressure above and below its wings different. The wind does this for the kite. In a steady airstream, a kite doesn't move backward or forward. It seems to be unaffected by gravity. This is possible because the lifting force of the wind overcomes the downward force of gravity.

If you have ever ridden a bicycle into a strong wind, you may have felt some of the forces of aerodynamics. If you held your hand out to your side, you could feel the air stream flowing around your hand. With your fingers pointed into the wind and your hand held level, there is little lift or drag. But if you raised your fingers slightly, the wind lifted your hand upwards. Raising your hand higher increases the drag and decreases the lift. Your hand is pushed downward. A kite flying in the sky is subject to these same forces.

Directions: Answer these questions about aerodynamics.

1. What is aerodynamics? the study of forces that are put into action by moving air

2. What three forces are at work to hold a kite in the air?
   a) lift   b) gravity   c) drag

3. An airplane is held in the air in much the same way, except that it must keep moving rapidly to keep the air above and below its wings different.
   (True)   False

Page 108

Comprehension: Getting Your Kite to Fly

There are some basic things to know about kite flying that can help you enjoy the sport more. Here are a few of the most important ones.

First, if you have ever seen someone flying a kite in a movie, you probably saw him or her get the kite off the ground by running into the wind. However, this is not the way to launch a kite. Most beginners will find a "high-start" launch to be the easiest. For a high-start launch, have a friend stand about 100 feet away, facing into the wind. Your friend should face you and hold the kite gently. Place some tension on the flying line by pulling gently on it. With a steady breeze behind you, tug gently on the line, and the kite will rise. If your kite begins to dive, don't panic or pull on the line. Dropping the reel will cause it to spin out of control and could cause someone to be hurt. Simply let the line go slack. This usually will right the kite in midair.

For a kite that is pulling hard away from you, have a friend stand behind you and take up the slack line as you bring it in. Hand over hand, pull down the kite. It is very important to have gloves on to do this, or you may burn or cut your hands. It is recommended that you always wear gloves while kite flying.

When two kite lines get crossed, pulling may cause enough friction to cut one or both of the lines. Instead of pulling, both fliers should walk toward one another until their lines uncross as they pass.

Directions: Circle **True** or **False** for these statements about kite flying.

1. To launch a kite, run into the wind holding the kite behind you. — True **(False)**
2. In a high-start launch, a friend stands about 100 feet away from you, holding the kite. — **(True)** False
3. If your kite begins to dive from the sky, immediately drop the reel. — True **(False)**
4. It is recommended that you always wear gloves when kite flying. — **(True)** False

Page 109

Recalling Details: Kite Safety Rules

Because kite flying is a relaxed, easygoing sport, it is easy to have the mistaken belief that there are no dangers involved. However, like any sport, kite flying must be approached with care. Here are some important safety rules you should always follow while kite flying:

- **Don't** fly a kite in wet or stormy weather or use wet flying line.
- **Don't** fly a kite near electrical power lines, transmission towers, or antennae. If your kite does get caught in one of these, walk away and leave it! If you must get the kite back, contact your local electric company.
- **Don't** use wire for flying line.
- **Don't** use metal for any part of the kite.
- **Don't** fly a kite near a street or in crowded areas.
- **Don't** fly a kite in a field or other area that has rocks or other objects you could trip over.
- **Don't** walk backwards without looking behind you.
- **Don't** fly a kite around trees. (If your kite does happen to get caught in a tree, let the line go slack. Sometimes the wind can work it free.)
- **Don't** fly a kite using unfamiliar equipment. A reel spinning out of control can be quite dangerous.
- **Don't** fly a kite near an airport.
- **Don't** fly a very large kite without proper guidance.
- **Do** wear protective gloves to avoid burns on your hands from rapidly unwinding line.
- **Do** use flying line that has been tested for the type and size of kite you are using.

Directions: Answer these questions about kite safety.

Possible answers:

1. List three things you should never fly a kite around.
   a) __power lines__ b) __a street__ c) __trees__

2. What should you do if your kite gets caught in a tree? _____
   __Let the line go slack to see if the wind can free it.__

3. What material should you never use in any part of your kite? __metal__

Page 110

Recalling Details: Aviation Pioneer

Lawrence Hargrave was born in Middlesex, England, in 1850. When he was a teenager, his family moved to Australia. There, Hargrave went to work for the Australian Steam and Navigation Company, where he spent 5 years gaining practical experience in engineering. He soon became interested in artificial flight.

Hargrave wanted to develop a stable lifting surface that could be used for flying. This goal led to his invention of the box kite, one of the seven basic models. In 1894, he carried out kite experiments along the beaches near his home. One day, in front of onlookers, he was lifted above the beach and out over the sea by four of his box kites. These experiments were very important to the development of air travel, although Hargrave has received little credit for it. In fact, because of his modesty, Hargrave failed to get a patent on his box kite. He spent more than 30 years studying flying, offering many inventions, including a rotary engine.

In 1906, Hargrave began looking for a home for his collection of nearly 200 models of kites and flying machines. After being rejected by several governments, his collection was accepted at a technological museum in Munich, Germany. Unfortunately, many of these models were destroyed during World War I.

Directions: Answer these questions about Lawrence Hargrave.

1. For what kite design was Lawrence Hargrave known? __the box kite__
2. What was Hargrave trying to create when he made this kite?
   __a stable lifting surface that could be used for flying__
3. What was one of the inventions Hargrave contributed to aviation? __the rotary engine__
4. Where was Hargrave's collection of kites and flying machines finally housed?
   __technological museum in Munich, Germany__

Page 111

Main Idea/Recalling Details: A Kite in History

In June 1752, Benjamin Franklin proved that lightning was a type of electricity by flying a kite with a key tied to the bottom of the line during a thunderstorm. Before his experiment, many people thought that lightning was a supernatural power.

After the success of his experiment, Franklin figured that if lightning could be drawn to a kite in a storm, it could be safely redirected into the ground by a metal rod attached to a house. His idea was met with much doubt, but lightning rods were soon seen on buildings in many of the colonies and later in Europe. During the years between 1683 and 1789, studying the universe and laws of nature was of tremendous importance. It was during this Age of Reason, as it was known, that Franklin's kite experiment gained him international fame and respect. He was elected to the Royal Society of London and the French Academy of Sciences, among other honors.

More than 20 years after his bold experiment, American patriots were enduring many hardships in their struggles for freedom from England. The colonial troops had shortages of guns, gunpowder, and food. France was sending supplies but not as much as was needed. Benjamin Franklin was chosen to go to France to persuade the French to aid the American cause. Franklin's reputation as a brilliant scientist earned him a hero's welcome there. The French people were so impressed by him that they wanted to help the colonies, even during a time when they could barely afford it. The supplies sent by the French were instrumental to the colonists in winning the war. And it all started with a kite.

Directions: Answer these questions about Ben Franklin and his historical kite.

1. The main idea is:
   [X] A kite played a role in the American Revolution and gained a spot in history books.
   [ ] Benjamin Franklin proved that lightning was a type of electricity by flying a kite with a key tied to the bottom of the line during a storm.

2. From his kite and key experiment, what did Franklin invent? __the lightning rod__
3. What was the era between 1683 and 1789 known as? __the Age of Reason__
4. Why was Franklin sent to France in 1776? __to persuade the French to aid the American cause__

Page 112

Summarizing: Pioneers

Directions: Think about the lives and accomplishments of Ben Franklin and Lawrence Hargrave. Write one paragraph about each, summarizing what you have learned about these two men. **Answers should include:**

Ben Franklin
1752 kite-and-key experiment
studied universe and laws of nature
ambassador to France
born in Boston in 1706
apprentice printer

Lawrence Hargrave
born in Middlesex, England, in 1850
engineer
invented box kite
used four box kites to lift himself
studied flying for 30 years, creating many inventions

Writing Checklist
Reread your paragraphs carefully.
- [ ] My paragraphs make sense.
- [ ] I used correct punctuation.
- [ ] I have a good opening and ending.
- [ ] I used correct spelling.
- [ ] My paragraphs are well-organized.
- [ ] My paragraphs are interesting.

Page 113

Review

Directions: Number in order the steps for how to launch a kite.

__5__ With a steady breeze behind you, gently pull on the line.
__3__ Have your friend face you and gently hold the kite.
__6__ Your kite will rise.
__2__ Have your friend face into the wind.
__4__ Place some tension on the flying line by pulling on it.
__1__ Have a friend stand about 100 feet away from you.

Directions: Write **true** or **false** for these statements about kite safety.

__true__ 1. You should not use wire for flying line.
__false__ 2. Fly any size kite you wish as long as you have the right flying line.
__true__ 3. If your kite gets caught in a tree, let the line go slack.
__false__ 4. It's okay to fly a kite in the rain.
__true__ 5. You should not fly a kite in crowded areas.
__false__ 6. You can use metal on your kite as long as it's not the flying line itself.
__false__ 7. You don't need to wear gloves unless you're flying a very large kite.
__true__ 8. You should not fly a kite around an airport.
__false__ 9. If your kite gets caught in power lines, just tug the line gently until it works free.
__true__ 10. The best place to fly a kite is in a large field.

Page 114

Comprehension: Colonists Come to America

After Christopher Columbus voyaged to America in 1492, many people wanted to come live in the new land. During the 17th and 18th centuries, a great many Europeans, especially the English, left their countries and settled along the Atlantic Coast of North America between Florida and Canada. Some came to make a better life for themselves. Others, particularly the Pilgrims, the Puritans, and the Quakers, came for religious freedom.

A group of men who wanted gold and other riches from the new land formed the London Company. They asked the king of England for land in America and for permission to found a colony. They founded Jamestown, the first permanent English settlement in America, in 1607. They purchased ships and supplies, and located people who wanted to settle in America.

The voyage to America took about eight weeks and was very dangerous. Often, fierce winds blew the wooden ships off course. Many were wrecked. The ships were crowded and dirty. Frequently, passengers became ill, and some died. Once in America, the early settlers faced even more hardships.

Directions: Answer these questions about the colonists coming to America.

1. How long did it take colonists to travel from England to America? __about 8 weeks__

2. Name three groups that came to America to find religious freedom.

  a) __the Pilgrims__ b) __the Puritans__ c) __the Quakers__

3. Why was the London Company formed? __They wanted to found a colony in America so that they could become rich from the new land.__

4. What was Jamestown? __the first permanent English settlement in America__

5. Why was the voyage to America dangerous? __There were fierce winds, frequent wrecks, and illness.__

Page 115

Recalling Details: Early Colonial Homes

When the first colonists landed in America, they had to find shelter quickly. Their first homes were crude bark and mud huts, log cabins, or dugouts, which were simply caves dug into the hillsides. As soon as possible, the settlers sought to replace these temporary shelters with comfortable houses.

Until the late 17th century, most of the colonial homes were simple in style. Almost all of the New England colonists—those settling in the northern areas of Massachusetts, Connecticut, Rhode Island, and New Hampshire—used wood in building their permanent homes. Some of the buildings had thatched roofs. However, they caught fire easily, and so were replaced by wooden shingles. The outside walls also were covered with wooden shingles to make the homes warmer and less drafty.

In the middle colonies—New York, Pennsylvania, New Jersey, and Delaware—the Dutch and German colonists often made brick or stone homes that were two-and-a-half or three-and-a-half stories high. Many southern colonists—those living in Virginia, Maryland, North Carolina, South Carolina, and Georgia—lived on large farms called plantations. Their homes were usually made of brick.

In the 18th century, some colonists became wealthy enough to replace their simple homes with mansions, often like those being built by the wealthy class in England. They were called Georgian houses because they were popular during the years that Kings George I, George II, and George III ruled England. Most were made of brick. They usually featured columns, ornately carved doors, and elaborate gardens.

Directions: Answer these questions about early colonial homes.

1. What were the earliest homes of the colonists? __bark and mud huts, log cabins, dugouts__

2. What were the advantages of using wooden shingles? __They didn't catch fire as easily as thatched roofs.__

3. What did Dutch and German colonists use to build their homes? __brick and stone__

4. What were Georgian homes? __mansions with columns, ornate doors, and elaborate gardens__

Page 116

Recalling Details: The Colonial Kitchen

The most important room in the home of a colonial family was the kitchen. Sometimes it was the only room in the home. The most important element of the kitchen was the fireplace. Fire was essential to the colonists, and they were careful to keep one burning at all times. Before the man of the house went to bed, he would make sure that the fire was carefully banked so it would burn all night. In the morning, he would blow the glowing embers into flame again with a bellows. If the fire went out, one of the children would be sent to a neighbor's for hot coals. Because there were no matches, it would sometimes take a half hour to light a new fire, using flint, steel, and tinder.

The colonial kitchen, quite naturally, was centered around the fireplace. One or two large iron broilers hung over the hot coals for cooking the family meals. Above the fireplace, a large musket and powder horn were kept for protection in the event of an attack and to hunt deer and other game. Also likely to be found near the fireplace was a butter churn, where cream from the family's cow was beaten until yellow flakes of butter appeared.

The furniture in the kitchen—usually benches, a table, and chairs—were made by the man or men in the family. It was very heavy and not very comfortable. The colonial family owned few eating utensils—no forks and only a few spoons, also made by members of the family. The dishes included pewter plates, trenchers (wooden bowls with handles), and wooden mugs.

Directions: Answer these questions about the colonial kitchen.

1. What was the most important element of the colonial kitchen? __the fireplace__

2. In colonial days, why was it important to keep a fire burning in the fireplace? __There were no matches, and fires were hard to start.__

3. Name two uses of the musket.

  a) __protection__ b) __hunting__

4. Who made most of the furniture in the early colonial home? __the men in the family__

Page 117

Sequencing: Spinning

Most of the colonists could not afford to buy clothes sent over from Europe. Instead, the women and girls, particularly in the New England colonies, spent much time spinning thread and weaving cloth to make their own clothing. They raised sheep for wool and grew flax for linen.

In August, the flax was ready to be harvested and made into linen thread. First, the flax was pulled up and allowed to dry. Then, the men pulled the seed pods from the stalks, bundled the stalks, and soaked them in a stream for about five days. The flax next had to be taken out, cleaned, and dried. To get the linen fibers from the tough bark and heavy wooden core, the stalks had to be pounded and crushed. Finally, the fibers were pulled through the teeth of a brush called a "hatchel" to comb out the short and broken fibers. The long fibers were spun into linen thread on a spinning wheel.

The spinning wheel was low, so a woman sat down to spin. First, she put flax in the hollow end of a slender stick, called the spindle, at one end of the spinning wheel. It was connected by a belt to a big wheel at the other end. The woman turned the wheel by stepping on a pedal. As it turned, the spindle also turned, twisting the flax into thread. The woman constantly dipped her fingers into water to moisten the flax and keep it from breaking. The linen thread came out through a hole in the side of the spindle. It was bleached and put away to be woven into pieces of cloth.

Directions: Number in order the steps to make linen thread from flax.

__7__ The woman sat at the spinning wheel and put flax in the spindle.

__3__ Seed pods were pulled from the stalks; stalks were bundled and soaked.

__1__ In August, the flax was ready to be harvested and made into thread.

__4__ The stalks were pounded and crushed to get the linen fibers.

__11__ The thread was bleached and put away to be woven into cloth.

__5__ The short fibers were separated out with a "hatchel."

__9__ The woman dipped her fingers into water to moisten the flax.

__6__ The long fibers were spun into linen thread on a spinning wheel.

__8__ The woman turned the wheel by stepping on a pedal, twisting the flax into thread.

__2__ The plants were pulled up and allowed to dry.

__10__ The linen thread came out through a hole in the side of the spindle.

Page 118

Recalling Details: Clothing in Colonial Times

The clothing of the colonists varied from the North to the South, accounting for the differences not only in climate, but also in the religions and ancestries of the settlers. The clothes seen most often in the early New England colonies where the Puritans settled were very plain and simple. The materials—wool and linen—were warm and sturdy.

The Puritans had strict rules about clothing. There were no bright colors, jewelry, ruffles, or lace. A Puritan woman wore a long-sleeved gray dress with a big white color, cuffs, apron, and cap. A Puritan man wore long woolen stockings and baggy leather breeches, which were knee-length trousers. Adults and children dressed in the same style of clothing.

In the middle colonies, the clothing ranged from the simple clothing of the Quakers to the colorful, loose-fitting outfits of the Dutch colonists. Dutch women wore more colorful outfits than Puritan women, with many petticoats and fur trim. The men had silver buckles on their shoes and wore big hats decked with curling feathers.

In the southern colonies, where there were no religious restrictions against fancy clothes, wealthy men wore brightly colored breeches and coats of velvet and satin sent from England. The women's gowns also were made of rich materials and were decorated with ruffles, ribbons, and lace. The poorer people wore clothes similar to the simple dress of the New England Puritans.

Directions: Answer these questions about clothing in colonial times.

1. Why did the clothing of the colonists vary from the North to the South? __There were differences in climate, and in the religions and ancestries of the settlers.__

2. Why did the Puritans wear very plain clothing? __The Puritans had strict rules about clothing and didn't wear bright colors, jewelry, ruffles, or lace.__

3. What was the nationality of many settlers in the middle colonies? __Dutch__

4. From what country did wealthy southern colonists obtain their clothing? __England__

Page 119

Recalling Details: Venn Diagrams

A **Venn diagram** is used to chart information that shows similarities and differences between two things. The outer part of each circle shows the differences. The intersecting part of the circles shows the similarities.

Example:

Basketball — Played on a court / Points scored through baskets / Five players on a team

Played with a ball / Two teams / Professional sport

Baseball — Played on a diamond / Points scored through runs / Nine players on a team

Directions: Complete the Venn diagram below. Think of at least three things to write in the outer part of each circle (differences) and at least three things to write in the intersecting part (similarities).

Possible answers:

Colonial Kitchen — • Furniture made by family / • No matches / • Fireplace / • Butter made with churn

• Tables and chairs / • Most important room in house

Your Kitchen — • Furniture bought at store / • Matches / • Oven / • Butter bought at store

Page 120

Comprehension: Colonial Schools

In early colonial days, there were no schools or teachers. Children learned what they could at home from their parents, but often their parents couldn't read or write either. Later, some women in the New England colonies began teaching in their homes. These first schools were known as "dame schools." Often the books used in these schools were not books at all, but rather "hornbooks"—flat, paddle-shaped wooden boards with the alphabet or Lord's Prayer on the front.

In 1647, a law was passed in the New England colonies requiring every town of 50 or more families to establish an elementary school. By the 1700s, one-room log schoolhouses were common. Children of all ages studied together under one strict schoolmaster. They attended school six days a week, from 7:00 or 8:00 in the morning until 4:00 or 5:00 in the afternoon. Their only textbooks were the Bible and the *New England Primer*, which contained the alphabet, spelling words, poems, and questions about the Bible.

Like the New England colonies, the middle colonies also established schools. However, there were few schools in the southern colonies, where most of the people lived on widely separated farms. Wealthy plantation owners hired private teachers from England to teach their children, but the children of poor families received no education.

Directions: Answer these questions about colonial schools.

1. What was a hornbook? **a flat wooden board with the alphabet or Lord's Prayer on the front**

2. What was required by the law passed in the New England colonies in 1647? **Every town with 50 or more families had to establish an elementary school.**

3. During the 1700s, what textbooks were used in the New England schools? **the Bible and the *New England Primer***

4. Why was it hard to establish schools in the southern colonies? **Most people lived on widely separated farms.**

Page 121

Compare/Contrast: Schools

Directions: Think about the differences and similarities between colonial and modern schools. Use the chart below to help organize your ideas. Then, write a paragraph discussing the similarities and a paragraph discussing the differences. The topic sentences have been written for you.

Possible answers:

Similarities	Differences
• studied alphabet, spelling, poems	• one-room log schoolhouses
• one teacher in the room	• six-day school week
	• 8-9 hour school day
	• only two textbooks

There are several similarities between colonial schools and schools today.
Paragraphs will vary.

Although there are similarities between colonial schools and modern schools, there are also many differences.

Page 122

Comprehension: Religion in New England

Many New England colonists had come to America for religious freedom. Religion was very important to them. One of the first buildings erected in any new settlement was a church, or meetinghouse. They were generally in the center of town and were used for public meetings of all kinds. These early meetinghouses were plain, unpainted wood buildings. Later churches were larger and more elaborate. They were usually painted white and had tall, graceful bell towers rising from the roof.

Although they came to America to have freedom of worship, the Puritans thought that everyone in the colonies should worship the same way they did. Because there were so many of them, the Puritans controlled the government in much of New England. They were the only ones allowed to vote, and they passed very strict laws. Lawbreakers received harsh punishments. For example, someone caught lying might be forced to stand in the town square for hours locked in a pillory—wooden boards with holes cut in them for the head and hands. For other minor offenses, the offender was tied to a whipping post and given several lashes with a whip.

Except in cases of extreme illness, everyone in the New England colonies had to attend church on Sunday. The minister stood in a pulpit high above the pews to deliver his sermon, which could last four or five hours. The people sat on hard, straight-backed pews. In the winter, there was no heat, so church members brought foot warmers from home to use during the long services. In many churches, a "tithingman" walked up and down the aisles carrying a long stick. On one end there were feathers attached; the other end had a knob. If anyone dozed off, the tithingman would tickle him or her with the feathers. If this did not rouse the offender, he would thump them soundly with the knob.

Directions: Answer these questions about religion in the colonies.

1. The main idea is:
☒ Many New England colonists had come to America for religious freedom, and religion was very important to them.
☐ One of the first buildings erected in any new settlement was a church.

2. Which religious group exercised a lot of power in the New England colonies? **the Puritans**

3. What was a pillory? **a wooden board with holes cut for the head and hands**

4. What was the only acceptable excuse for missing Sunday church services in the New England colonies? **extreme illness**

5. What was the job of the tithingman? **to keep people awake in church**

Page 123

Writing: Problem and Solution

Directions: Follow the instructions below.

1. Think of a problem the colonial Americans may have encountered. Write a paragraph about this problem. In the paragraph, be sure to state the problem, and then discuss why it would have been a problem for the colonists.
Paragraphs will vary.

2. Think about a solution to the problem above. Write a paragraph outlining your ideas for the solution. Remember to state the solution to the problem and then your ideas to solve the problem.

Page 124

Review

Many great colonists made an impact on American history. Among them was Benjamin Franklin, who left his mark as a printer, author, inventor, scientist and statesman. He has been called "the wisest American."

Franklin was born in Boston in 1706, one of 13 children in a very religious Puritan household. Although he had less than two years of formal education, his tremendous appetite for books served him well. At age 12, he became an apprentice printer at *The New England Courant* and soon began writing articles that poked fun at Boston society.

In 1723, Franklin ran away to Philadelphia, where he started his own newspaper. He was very active in the Philadelphia community. He operated a bookstore and was named postmaster. He also helped to establish a library, a fire company, a college, an insurance company, and a hospital. His well-known *Poor Richard's Almanac* was first printed in 1732.

Over the years, Franklin maintained an interest in science and mechanics, leading to such inventions as a fireplace stove and bifocal lenses. In 1752, he gained world fame with his kite-and-key experiment, which proved that lightning was a form of electricity.

Franklin was an active supporter of the colonies throughout the Revolutionary War. He helped to write and was a signer of the Declaration of Independence in 1776. In his later years, he skillfully represented America in Europe, helping to work out a peace treaty with Great Britain.

Directions: Answer these questions about Benjamin Franklin.

1. The main idea is:
☐ Many great colonists made an impact on American history.
☒ Benjamin Franklin was a great colonist who left his mark as a printer, author, inventor, scientist, and statesman.

2. How did Benjamin Franklin gain world fame? **his kite-and-key experiment**

3. What did Franklin sign and help to write? **the Declaration of Independence**

4. Number in order the following accomplishments of Benjamin Franklin.
6 Served as representative of America in Europe
3 Began printing *Poor Richard's Almanac*
4 Experimented with electricity
2 Started his own newspaper
5 Helped to write and sign the Declaration of Independence
1 Served as apprentice printer at *The New England Courant*

Page 125

Review

Directions: Match each item with its description. If necessary, review the section on colonial times.

a. hornbooks	**j**	year Columbus sailed to America
b. 1647	**m**	schools where New England women taught in their homes
c. pillory	**g**	man who kept worshippers awake during Sunday services
d. Ben Franklin	**l**	plants harvested for linen
e. plantations	**a**	paddle-shaped wooden boards with text on them
f. 1776	**b**	law written in this year required towns of 50 or more to establish a school
g. tithingman	**c**	punishment rack with holes for head and hands
h. spinning wheel	**k**	wooden bowls with handles
i. hatchel	**d**	author of *Poor Richard's Almanac*
j. 1492	**e**	large farms in the South
k. trenchers	**h**	wooden machine used to spin wool or flax into thread
l. flax	**i**	used to comb out the short and broken flax fibers
m. dame schools	**f**	year Declaration of Independence was signed

Page 126

Using Prior Knowledge: Abraham Lincoln and the Civil War

Directions: Before reading about Abraham Lincoln and the Civil War in the following section, answer these questions.

1. The Civil War began because _____ **Answers will vary.**

2. Abraham Lincoln is famous today because _____

3. What brought about the end of slavery in the United States? _____

4. The Gettysburg Address begins with the famous line: "Four score and seven years ago. . . ." What does this mean? _____

5. How did Abraham Lincoln die? _____

Page 127

Main Idea: The Gettysburg Address

On November 19, 1863, President Abraham Lincoln gave a short speech to dedicate a cemetery for Civil War soldiers in Gettysburg, Pennsylvania, where a famous battle was fought. He wrote five drafts of the Gettysburg Address, one of the most stirring speeches of all time.

Four score and seven years ago, our fathers brought forth on this continent a new nation, conceived in liberty, and dedicated to the proposition that all men are created equal.

Now we are engaged in a great civil war, testing whether that nation, or any nation so conceived and so dedicated, can long endure. We are met on a great battlefield of that war. We have come to dedicate a portion of that field as a final resting place for those who here gave their lives that this nation might live. It is altogether fitting and proper that we should do this.

But, in a larger sense, we cannot dedicate—we cannot consecrate—we cannot hallow—this ground. The brave men, living and dead, who struggled here have consecrated it far above our poor power to add or detract. The world will little note nor long remember what we say here, but it can never forget what they did here. It is for us the living, rather, to be dedicated to the unfinished work which they who fought here have thus far so nobly advanced. It is rather for us to be here dedicated to the great task remaining before us—that from these honored dead we take increased devotion to that cause for which they gave their last full measure of devotion—that we here highly resolve that these dead shall not have died in vain—that this nation, under God, shall have a new birth of freedom—and that government of the people, by the people, for the people, shall not perish from this earth.

Directions: Answer the questions about the Gettysburg Address.

1. Circle the main idea:

This speech will be long remembered as a tribute to those who died fighting in the Civil War.

(This speech is to honor the soldiers who gave their lives so that the nation could have freedom for all citizens.)

2. What happened on the ground where the cemetery stood? _____
A great battle was fought, and many lives were lost.

Page 128

Comprehension: The Gettysburg Address

Directions: Use context clues or a dictionary to answer these questions about the Gettysburg Address. **Possible answers:**

1. What is the correct definition of **conceived**? _____
to form an idea

2. What is the correct definition of **consecrate**? _____
bless

3. What is the correct definition of **hallow**? _____
to revere as holy

4. What is the correct definition of **devotion**? _____
dedication to

5. What is the correct definition of **resolve**? _____
end, finish, to find a solution

6. What is the correct definition of **vain**? _____
without cause or reason

7. What is the correct definition of **perish**? _____
to die

8. What is the correct definition of **civil**? _____
relating to a community, country, or civilians

9. In your own words, what point was President Lincoln trying to make? _____
Answers will vary.

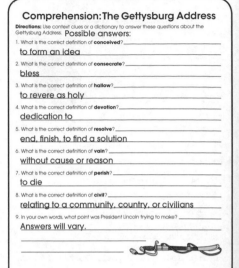

Page 129

Comprehension: The Emancipation Proclamation

On September 22, 1862, a year before delivering the Gettysburg Address, President Lincoln delivered the Emancipation Proclamation, which stated that all slaves in Confederate states should be set free. Since the Confederate states had already seceded (withdrawn) from the Union, they ignored the proclamation. However, the proclamation did strengthen the North's war effort. About 200,000 black men—mostly former slaves—enlisted in the Union Army. Two years later, the 13th Amendment to the Constitution ended slavery in all parts of the United States.

I, Abraham Lincoln, do order and declare that all persons held as slaves within said designated States and parts of States are, and henceforward shall be, free; and that the Executive Government of the United States, including military and naval authorities thereof, shall recognize and maintain the freedom of said persons.

And I hereby enjoin upon the people so declared to be free to abstain from all violence, unless in necessary self-defense; and I recommend to them that, in all cases where allowed, they labor faithfully for reasonable wages.

And I further declare and make known that such persons of suitable condition will be received into the armed forces of the United States to garrison forts, positions, stations, and other places, and to man vessels of all sorts in said service.

(This is not the full text of the Emancipation Proclamation.)

Directions: Answer the questions about the Emancipation Proclamation.

1. How did the Emancipation Proclamation strengthen the North's war effort?
About 200,000 black men enlisted in the Union army.

2. Which came first, the Emancipation Proclamation or the Gettysburg Address?
the Emancipation Proclamation

3. Which amendment to the Constitution grew out of the Emancipation Proclamation?
the 13th amendment

4. **Secede** means to ☐ quit. ☐ fight. ☒ withdraw.

Page 130

Comprehension: The Emancipation Proclamation

Directions: Use context clues or a dictionary to answer these questions about the Emancipation Proclamation.

1. What is the correct definition of **designated**? _____
appointed

2. What is the correct definition of **military**? _____
relating to the armed forces

3. What is the correct definition of **naval**? _____
relating to the navy or warships

4. What is the correct definition of **abstain**? _____
to keep away from or refrain from

5. What is the correct definition of **suitable**? _____
appropriate

6. What is the correct definition of **garrison**? _____
a fort

7. What is the correct definition of **vessels**? _____
ships

8. In your own words, what did the Emancipation Proclamation accomplish? _____
Answers vary.

Page 131

Comprehension: Lincoln and the South

Many people think that Abraham Lincoln publicly came out against slavery from the beginning of his term as president. This is not the case. Whatever his private feelings, he did not criticize slavery publicly. Fearful that the southern states would secede, or leave, the Union, he pledged to respect the southern states' rights to own slaves. He also pledged that the government would respect the southern states' runaway slave laws. These laws required all citizens to return runaway slaves to their masters.

Clearly, Lincoln did not want the country torn apart by a civil war. In the following statement, written in 1861 shortly after he became president, he made it clear that the federal government would do its best to avoid conflict with the southern states.

I hold that, in contemplation of the universal law and the Constitution, the Union of these states is perpetual. . . . No state, upon its own mere motion, can lawfully get out of the Union. . . . I shall take care, as the Constitution itself expressly enjoins upon me, that the laws of the Union be faithfully executed in all the states. . . . The power confided to me will be used to hold, occupy, and possess the property and places belonging to the government, and to collect the duties and imposts. . . .

In your hands, my dissatisfied fellow-countrymen, and not in mine, is the momentous issue of civil war. The government will not assail you. You can have no conflict without yourselves being the aggressors. You have no oath registered in heaven to destroy the government, while I shall have the most solemn one to "preserve, protect, and defend" it.

Directions: Use context clues for these definitions.

1. What is the correct definition of **assail**? **to attack, to confront**

2. What is the correct definition of **enjoin**? **to impose a rule or law**

3. What is the correct definition of **contemplation**? _____
thinking deeply about something

Directions: Answer these questions about Lincoln and the southern states.

4. Lincoln is telling the southern states that the government
☐ does want a war. ☒ doesn't want a war. ☐ will stop a war.

5. As president, Lincoln pledged to "preserve, protect and defend"
☐ slavery. ☐ the northern states. ☒ the Union.

Page 132

Comprehension: Away Down South in Dixie

Although many southerners disapproved of slavery, the pressure to go along with the majority who supported slavery was very strong. Many of those who thought slavery was wrong did not talk about their opinions. It was dangerous to do so!

The main reason the southern states seceded from the Union in 1861 was because they wanted to protect their right to own slaves. They also wanted to increase the number of slaves so they could increase production of cotton and other crops that slaves tended. Many Civil War monuments in the South are dedicated to a war that was described as "just and holy."

"Dixie," a song written in 1859 that is still popular in the South, sums up the attitude of many southerners. As the song lyrics show, southerners' loyalties lay not with the Union representing all the states, but with the South and the southern way of life.

Dixie
I wish I was in Dixie, Hoo-ray! Hoo-ray!
In Dixie land I'll take my stand
To live and die in Dixie.
Away, away, away down south in Dixie!
Away, away, away down south in Dixie!
(This is not the full text of the song.)

Directions: Answer these questions about southerners and "Dixie."

1. Why did southerners who disapproved of slavery keep their opinions to themselves?
   It was dangerous for them to express their opinions.

2. Why did southerners want more slaves?
   to increase production of cotton and other crops

3. What are the words on some southern Civil War monuments?
   "just and holy"

4. What "stand" is referred to in "Dixie"?
   ☒ stand for slavery   ☐ stand against slavery   ☐ stand for cotton

Page 133

Fact and Opinion

Directions: Read each sentence. Then, draw an **X** in the box to tell whether it is a fact or opinion.

1. "Dixie" is a beautiful song! — ☐ Fact ☒ Opinion

2. It was written in 1859 by a man named Daniel Emmett, who died in 1904. — ☒ Fact ☐ Opinion

3. The song became a rallying cry for southerners, because it showed where their loyalties were. — ☒ Fact ☐ Opinion

4. I think their loyalty to slavery was absolutely wrong! — ☐ Fact ☒ Opinion

5. These four states where people owned slaves did not secede from the Union: Delaware, Maryland, Kentucky, and Missouri. — ☒ Fact ☐ Opinion

6. The people in these states certainly made the right moral choice. — ☐ Fact ☒ Opinion

7. The ownership of one human being by another is absolutely and totally wrong under any circumstances. — ☐ Fact ☒ Opinion

8. In the states that did not secede from the Union, some people fought for the Union, and others fought for the Confederacy of Southern States. — ☒ Fact ☐ Opinion

9. Sometimes brothers fought against brothers on opposite sides of the war. — ☒ Fact ☐ Opinion

10. What a horrible situation to be in! — ☐ Fact ☒ Opinion

Page 134

Recalling Details: The Civil War

Although they were outnumbered, most southerners were convinced they could win the Civil War. The white population of the southern states that had seceded from the Union was 5.5 million. The population was 18.9 million in the 19 states that stayed with the Union. Despite these odds, southerners felt history was on their side.

After all, the colonists had been the underdogs against the British and had won the War of Independence. Europeans also felt that Lincoln could not force the South to rejoin the Union. The United Netherlands had successfully seceded from Spain. Greece had seceded from Turkey. Europeans were laying odds that two countries would take the place of what had once been the United States.

Directions: Answer these questions, and complete the puzzle about the Civil War.

1. What was the difference in population between the Union and the Confederate states?
   13.4 million

2. Circle the main idea:
   [Although they were outnumbered, many people here and abroad felt the South wouldn't win the Civil War.]

   Because they were outnumbered, southerners knew that winning the Civil War was a long shot.

Across:
3. They won the War of Independence against England.
5. Did Europeans believe the South would win the war?
6. ___teen states belonged to the Union.

Down:
1. Slave owners lived in this area of the country.
2. The president during the Civil War
4. To withdraw from the Union

Crossword: colonists, south, lincoln, yes, nine

Page 135

Recalling Details: Abraham Lincoln

Directions: Complete the following exercises.

1. Describe two accomplishments of Abraham Lincoln.
   Answers will vary.

2. Complete the time line by writing and illustrating the events.

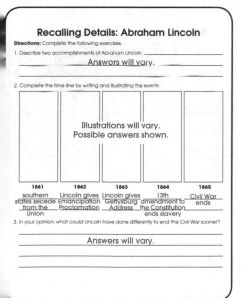

Illustrations will vary. Possible answers shown.

1861	1862	1863	1864	1865
southern states secede from the Union	Lincoln gives Emancipation Proclamation	Lincoln gives Gettysburg Address	13th amendment to the Constitution ends slavery	Civil War ends

3. In your opinion, what could Lincoln have done differently to end the Civil War sooner?
   Answers will vary.

Page 136

Fact and Opinion

Directions: Read each sentence. Then, draw an **X** in the box to tell whether it is a fact or an opinion.

1. Lincoln warned the southern states that they could not legally leave the Union. — ☒ Fact ☐ Opinion

2. I believe Lincoln thought the northern states were the best because they did not have slaves. — ☐ Fact ☒ Opinion

3. I think Lincoln did the right thing, don't you? — ☐ Fact ☒ Opinion

4. The issues that sparked the Civil War were complicated and difficult ones. — ☒ Fact ☐ Opinion

5. It would take a historian to really understand them! — ☐ Fact ☒ Opinion

6. The "dissatisfied fellow-countrymen" Lincoln refers to in his statement lived in the southern states. — ☒ Fact ☐ Opinion

7. As president, Lincoln took an oath to "preserve, protect, and defend" the Union, which included all the states. — ☒ Fact ☐ Opinion

8. Lincoln did his personal best to hold the country together, but it didn't do one bit of good. — ☐ Fact ☒ Opinion

9. The Confederate States of America had already been organized in February 1861, a month before Lincoln was sworn in as president. — ☒ Fact ☐ Opinion

10. Poor Abraham Lincoln—what a crummy start to his presidency! — ☐ Fact ☒ Opinion

Page 137

Using Prior Knowledge: Anthems and Songs

Directions: Before reading about anthems and songs in the following section, answer these questions.

1. How do national anthems help pull a country together?
   Answers will vary.

2. Describe what you know about how and why "The Star-Spangled Banner" was written.

3. What is your favorite anthem or song?

4. What images do the words of your favorite anthem or song bring to mind? Why do you like it?

Page 138

Comprehension: Our National Anthem

Written in 1814 by Francis Scott Key, our American national anthem is stirring, beautiful, and difficult to sing. Key wrote the song while aboard a ship off the coast of Maryland, where one long night he watched the gunfire from a British attack on America's Fort McHenry. The following morning, he wrote "The Star-Spangled Banner" when, to his great joy, he saw the American flag still flying over the fort—a sign that the Americans had not lost the battle.

The Star-Spangled Banner
Oh say, can you see, by the dawn's early light,
What so proudly we hail'd at the twilight's last gleaming?
Whose broad stripes and bright stars, thro' the perilous fight,
O'er the ramparts we watch'd were so gallantly streaming?
And the rockets' red glare, the bombs bursting in air,
Gave proof thro' the night that our flag was still there.
Oh say, does that star-spangled banner yet wave
O'er the land of the free and the home of the brave?

Oh, the shore dimly seen thro' the mists of the deep,
Where the foe's haughty host in dread silence reposes,
What is that which the breeze, o'er the towering steep,
As it fitfully blows, half conceals, half discloses?
Now it catches the gleam of the morning's first beam,
In full glory reflected, now shines on the stream:
'Tis the star-spangled banner: O, long may it wave
O'er the land of the free and the home of the brave!

Directions: Answer these questions about the first two verses of "The Star-Spangled Banner."

1. Who wrote "The Star-Spangled Banner"? __Francis Scott Key__
2. What is "The Star-Spangled Banner"? __the American National Anthem__
3. In what year was the song written? __1814__
4. At what time of day was the song written? __in the morning__
5. Tell what is meant by the lines " . . . the rockets' red glare, the bombs bursting in air/Gave proof through the night that our flag was still there." __He would see the U.S. flag flying by the light of the rockets and bombs.__

Page 139

Comprehension: "The Star-Spangled Banner"

Directions: Use context clues or a dictionary to answer these questions about "The Star-Spangled Banner."

1. What is the correct definition of **spangled**? __shining or glittering__
2. What is the correct definition of **twilight**? __early evening, dusk__
3. What is the correct definition of **ramparts**? __walls of a fort__
4. What is the correct definition of **gallantly**? __bravely, proudly__
5. What is the correct definition of **haughty**? __proud__
6. What is the correct definition of **reposes**? __rests, sleeps__
7. Why do you think United States citizens only sing the first verse of "The Star-Spangled Banner"? __Answers will vary.__
8. What war was being fought when this song was written? __the War of 1812__
9. Have you ever heard the second verse of "The Star-Spangled Banner"? Knowing the tune, can you sing the second verse? __Answers will vary.__

Page 140

Comprehension: "America the Beautiful"

Written in 1895 by Katherine Lee Bates, "America the Beautiful" is another very popular patriotic song. It is so popular, in fact, that some people would like to see it replace "The Star-Spangled Banner" as the United States' national anthem. Ms. Bates was inspired to write the song while visiting Colorado, where she was struck by the splendor of the mountains. Today, "America the Beautiful" remains a tribute to our country's natural beauty.

America the Beautiful
Oh beautiful for spacious skies,
For amber waves of grain,
For purple mountains majesties
Above the fruited plain!
America! America!
God shed His grace on thee,
And crown thy good
With brotherhood
From sea to shining sea!

Directions: Use context clues or a dictionary to answer these questions about "America the Beautiful."

1. What is the correct definition of **tribute**? __something that shows respect, gratitude, or affection__
2. What is the correct definition of **amber**? __dark yellow-gold__
   What other word might you use for **amber** in the song? __golden__
3. What is the singular form of **majesties**? What does it mean in the song? __majesty; beautiful, glorious sights__
4. "From sea to shining sea" means the oceans to the east and west of the United States. What are their names? __Atlantic__ __Pacific__
5. Do you think "America the Beautiful" should be our national anthem? Why or why not? __Answers will vary.__

Page 141

Comprehension: Civil War Marching Song

When soldiers march, they sometimes sing a song to help them keep in step. One of the most famous marching songs of the Civil War was the "Battle Hymn of the Republic," written in 1861 by Julia Ward Howe. Mrs. Howe wrote the song after visiting a Union army camp in the North. The words are about how God is on the side of the soldiers.

Battle Hymn of the Republic
Mine eyes have seen the glory of the coming of the Lord,
He is trampling out the vintage where the grapes of wrath are stored,
He has loosed the fateful lightning of his terrible swift sword,
His truth is marching on.

Glory, glory hallelujah! Glory, glory hallelujah!
Glory, glory hallelujah! His truth is marching on.

I have seen him in the watchfires of a hundred circling camps,
I have builded him an altar in the evening dews and damps,
I can read his righteous sentence by the dim and flaring lamps,
His day is marching on.

Glory, glory hallelujah! Glory, glory hallelujah!
Glory, glory hallelujah! His truth is marching on.

Directions: Answer these questions about the "Battle Hymn of the Republic."

1. Who wrote the "Battle Hymn of the Republic"? __Julia Ward Howe__
2. When was the song written? __1861__
3. What war was in progress at the time? __the Civil War__
4. Why did soldiers sing while they marched? __to help them keep in step__
5. What marches on along with the soldiers? __God__
6. What did the soldiers sing about building in the evening? __an altar__

Page 142

Review

National anthems, work songs, and marching songs share some common characteristics. Perhaps the most important characteristic is that the words strike an emotional response in singers and listeners alike.

Have you ever sung "The Star-Spangled Banner" at a baseball game or other large public event? The next time you do, look around as you sing. You will see that Americans from all walks of life and all races sing the song proudly. The words to the national anthem help create a feeling of unity among people who may not have much in common. The same is true of the national anthems of France, England, and other countries.

Another characteristic of these types of songs is that the words are simple, the message is clear, and the tune should be easy to carry. This is not always true, of course. Many people's voices crack during the high notes of "The Star-Spangled Banner." But attempts to change the national anthem to "America the Beautiful" or another song with a simpler tune have always met with dismal failure. It may be hard to sing, but most Americans wouldn't trade it for any other tune. It's a long-held American tradition, and nearly everyone knows the words. Americans love what this song stands for. They are proud to live in a country that is the "land of the free."

Directions: Answer these questions about the characteristics of national anthems, work songs, and marching songs.

1. Explain what goes into writing a good national anthem. __They must strike an emotional response, create a feeling of unity, and have simple words and a melody.__
2. What does our national anthem help do? __It helps create a feeling of unity among people.__
3. What happens each time someone tries to change the national anthem to "America the Beautiful" or another song? __They are met with failure.__
4. Why do people stick with "The Star-Spangled Banner" as our national anthem? __It's traditional and most people know the words.__

Page 143

Recalling Details: The Island Continent

Australia is the only country that fills an entire continent. It is the smallest continent in the world but the sixth largest country. Australia, called the island continent, is totally surrounded by water—the Indian Ocean on the west and south, the Pacific Ocean on the east, and the Arafura Sea, which is formed by these two oceans coming together, to the north.

The island continent is, in large part, a very dry, flat land. Yet it supports a magnificent and unusual collection of wildlife. Because of its remoteness, Australia is home to plants and animals that are not found anywhere else in the world. Besides the well-known kangaroo and koala, the strange animals of the continent include the wombat, dingo, kookaburra, emu, and, perhaps the strangest of all, the duckbill platypus.

There are many physical features of Australia that also are unique, including the central part of the country known as the Outback, which consists of three main deserts—the Great Sandy, the Gibson, and the Great Victoria. Because much of the country is desert, more than half of all Australians live in large, modern cities along the coast. There are also many people living in the small towns on the edge of the Outback, where there is plenty of grass for raising sheep and cattle. In fact, there are about five times as many sheep in Australia as there are people!

Directions: Answer these questions about Australia.

1. What are the three large bodies of water that surround Australia?
   a) __the Indian Ocean__ b) __the Pacific Ocean__ c) __the Arafura Sea__
2. Besides the kangaroo and the koala, name three other unusual animals found only in Australia. **Possible answers:**
   a) __wombat__ b) __dingo__ c) __emu__
3. What three deserts make up the Outback?
   a) __the Great Sandy__ b) __the Gibson__ c) __the Great Victoria__

Page 144

Comprehension: The Aborigines

The native, or earliest known, people of Australia are the Aborigines (ab-ur-U-uh-neez). They arrived on the continent from Asia more than 20,000 years ago. Before the Europeans began settling in Australia during the early 1800s, there were about 300,000 Aborigines. But the new settlers brought diseases that killed many of these native people. Today, there are only about 125,000 Aborigines living in Australia, many of whom now live in the cities.

The way of life of the Aborigines, who still live like their ancestors, is closely related to nature. They live as hunters and gatherers and do not produce crops or raise livestock. The Aborigines have no permanent settlements, but they have small camps near watering places. Because they live off the land, they must frequently move about in search of food. They have few belongings and little or no clothing.

Some tribes of Aborigines, especially those who live in the desert, may move 100 times in a year. They might move more than 1,000 miles on foot during that time. These tribes set up temporary homes, such as tents made of bark and igloo-like structures made of grass.

The Aborigines have no written language, but they have developed a system of hand signals. These are used during hunting when silence is necessary and during their elaborate religious ceremonies when talking is forbidden.

Directions: Circle **True** or **False** for these statements about Aborigines.

1. The Aborigines came from Europe to settle in Australia. — True (**False**)
2. The Aborigines live as hunters and gatherers rather than as farmers. — (**True**) False
3. The tribes move about often to find jobs. — True (**False**)
4. The people move often to help them raise their livestock. — True (**False**)
5. Aborigine tribes always move 200 times a year. — True (**False**)

Page 145

Main Idea/Comprehension: The Boomerang

The Aborigines have developed a few tools and weapons, including spears, flint knives, and the boomerang. The boomerang comes in different shapes and has many uses. This curved throwing stick is used for hunting, playing, digging, cutting, and even making music.

You may have seen a boomerang that, when thrown, returns to the thrower. This type of boomerang is sometimes used in duck hunting, but it is most often used as a toy and for sporting contests. It is lightweight—about three-fourths of a pound—and has a big curve in it. However, the boomerang used by the Aborigines for hunting is much heavier and is nearly straight. It does not return to its thrower.

Because of its sharp edges, the boomerang makes a good knife for skinning animals. The Aborigines also use boomerangs as digging sticks, to sharpen stone blades, to start fires, and as swords and clubs in fighting. Boomerangs sometimes are used to make music—two clapped together provide rhythmic background for dances. Some make musical sounds when they are pulled across one another.

To throw a boomerang, the thrower grasps it at one end and holds it behind his head. He throws it overhanded, adding a sharp flick of the wrist at the last moment. It is thrown into the wind to make it come back. A skillful thrower can do many tricks with his boomerang. He can make it spin in several circles, or make a figure eight in the air. He can even make it bounce on the ground several times before it soars into the air and returns.

Directions: Answer these questions about boomerangs.

1. The main idea is:
   ☐ The Aborigines have developed a few tools and weapons, including spears, flint knives, and the boomerang.
    The boomerang comes in different shapes and has many uses.
2. To make it return, the thrower tosses the boomerang
    into the wind.   ☐ against the wind.   Possible answers:
3. List three uses for the boomerang.
   a) _hunting_
   b) _playing_
   c) _digging_

Page 146

Comprehension: The Kangaroo

Many animals found in Australia are not found anywhere else in the world. Because the island continent was separated from the rest of the world for many years, these animals developed in different ways. Many of the animals in Australia are marsupials. Marsupials are animals whose babies are born underdeveloped and are then carried in a pouch on the mother's body until they are able to care for themselves. The kangaroo is perhaps the best known of the marsupials.

There are 45 kinds of kangaroos, and they come in a variety of sizes. The smallest is the musky rat kangaroo, which is about a foot long, including its hairless tail. It weighs only a pound. The largest is the gray kangaroo, which is more than 9 feet long, counting its tail, and can weigh 200 pounds. When moving quickly, a kangaroo can leap 25 feet and move at 30 miles an hour!

A baby kangaroo, called a joey, is totally helpless at birth. It is only three-quarters of an inch long and weighs a fraction of an ounce. The newly born joey immediately crawls into its mother's pouch and remains there until it is old enough to be independent—which can be as long as eight months.

Kangaroos eat grasses and plants. They can cause problems for farmers and ranchers in Australia because they compete with cattle for pastures. During a drought, kangaroos may invade ranches and even airports looking for food.

Directions: Answer these questions about kangaroos.

1. What are marsupials? _Marsupials are animals whose babies are born underdeveloped and are carried in the mother's pouch until they can care for themselves._
2. What is the smallest kangaroo? _the musky rat kangaroo_
3. What is a baby kangaroo called? _a joey_
4. Why did Australian animals develop differently from other animals? _The island was separated from the rest of the world for many years, so these animals developed in different ways._

Page 147

Comprehension: The Koala

The koala lives in eastern Australia in the eucalyptus (you-ca-LIP-tes) forests. These slow, gentle animals hide by day, usually sleeping in the trees. They come out at night to eat. Koalas eat only certain types of eucalyptus leaves. Their entire way of life centers on this unique diet. The koala's digestive system is specially adapted for eating eucalyptus leaves. In fact, to other animals, these leaves are poisonous!

The wooly, round-eared koala looks like a cuddly teddy bear, but it is not related to any bear. It is a marsupial like the kangaroo. And, like the joey, a baby koala requires a lot of care. It will remain constantly in its mother's pouch until it is six months old. After that, a baby koala will ride piggyback on its mother for another month or two, even though it is nearly as big as she is. Koalas have few babies—only one every other year. While in her pouch, the baby koala lives on its mother's milk. After it is big enough to be on its own, the koala will almost never drink anything again.

Oddly, the mother koala's pouch is backwards—the opening is at the bottom. This leads scientists to believe that the koala once lived on the ground and walked on all fours. But at some point, the koala became a tree dweller. This makes an upside-down pouch very awkward! The babies keep from falling to the ground by holding on tightly with their mouths. The mother koala has developed strong muscles around the rim of her pouch that also help to hold the baby in.

Directions: Answer these questions about koalas.

1. What is the correct definition for **eucalyptus**?
   ☐ enormous   a type of tree   ☐ rain
2. What is the correct definition for **digestive**?
   ☒ the process in which food is absorbed in the body
   ☐ the process of finding food
   ☐ the process of tasting
3. What is the correct definition for **dweller**?
   ☐ one who climbs   ☐ one who eats   ☒ one who lives in

Page 148

Comprehension: The Wombat

Another animal unique to Australia is the wombat. The wombat has characteristics in common with other animals. Like the koala, the wombat is also a marsupial with a backwards pouch. The pouch is more practical for the wombat, which lives on the ground rather than in trees. The wombat walks on all fours, so the baby is in less danger of falling out.

The wombat resembles a beaver without a tail. With its strong claws, it is an expert digger. It makes long tunnels beneath cliffs and boulders in which it sleeps all day. At night, it comes out to look for food. It has strong, beaver-like teeth to chew through the various plant roots it eats. A wombat's teeth have no roots, like a rodent's. Its teeth keep growing from the inside as they are worn down from the outside.

The wombat, which can be up to 4 feet long and weighs 60 pounds when full grown, eats only grass, plants, and roots. It is a shy, quiet, and gentle animal that would never attack. But when angered, it has a strong bite and very sharp teeth! And, while wombats don't eat or attack other animals, the many deep burrows they dig to sleep in are often dangerous to the other animals living nearby.

Directions: Answer these questions about the wombat.

1. How is the wombat similar to the koala? _It is a marsupial with a backwards pouch._
2. How is the wombat similar to the beaver? _It has strong claws to dig and strong teeth to chew through plants._
3. How is the wombat similar to a rodent? _Its teeth have no roots but keep growing from the inside as they are worn down from the outside._

Page 149

Comprehension: The Duckbill Platypus

Australia's duckbill platypus is a most unusual animal. It is very strange-looking and has caused a lot of confusion for people studying it. For many years, even scientists did not know how to classify it. The platypus has webbed feet and a bill like a duck. But it doesn't have wings, has fur instead of feathers, and has four legs instead of two. The baby platypus gets milk from its mother, like a mammal, but it is hatched from a tough-skinned egg, like a reptile. A platypus also is a poisonous spur on each of its back legs that is like the tip of a viper's fangs. Scientists have put the platypus—along with another strange animal from Australia called the spiny anteater—in a special class of mammal called "monotremes."

The platypus has an amazing appetite! It has been estimated that a full-grown platypus eats about 1,200 earthworms, 50 crayfish, and numerous tadpoles and insects every day. The platypus is an excellent swimmer and diver. It dives under the water of a stream and searches the muddy bottom for food.

A mother platypus lays one or two eggs, which are very small—only about an inch long—and leathery in appearance. During the seven to 14 days it takes for the eggs to hatch, the mother never leaves them, not even to eat. The tiny platypus, which is only a half-inch long, cuts its way out of the shell with a sharp point on its bill. This point is known as an "egg tooth," and it will fall off soon after birth. (Many reptiles and birds have egg teeth, but they are unknown in other mammals.) By the time it is 4 months old, the baby platypus is about a foot long—half its adult size—and is learning how to swim and hunt.

Directions: Answer these questions about the duckbill platypus.

1. In what way is a duckbill platypus like other mammals? _It gets milk from its mother._
2. In what way is it like a reptile? _It hatches from an egg._
3. What other animal is in the class of mammal called "monotremes"? _the spiny anteater_
4. What makes up the diet of a platypus? _earthworms, crayfish, tadpoles, and insects_
5. On what other animals would you see an "egg tooth"? _on many reptiles and birds_

Page 150

Recalling Details: Animals of Australia

Directions: Complete the chart with information from the selection on Australian animals.

	Gray Kangaroo	Koala	Wombat	Platypus
What are the animal's physical characteristics?	9 feet long 200 pounds marsupial good leaper fast mover	wooly round-eared marsupial good climber	marsupial walks on all fours strong claws and teeth up to 4 feet long 60 pounds	webbed feet duck-like bill fur, four legs hatches from egg poisonous spur 2 feet long good swimmer
What is the animal's habitat?	farmland of Australia	eucalyptus forests of eastern Australia	tunnels beneath cliffs and boulders	streams with muddy bottoms
What does the animal eat?	grasses, plants	eucalyptus leaves	grasses, plants, roots	earthworms, crayfish, tadpoles, insects

Page 151

Main Idea/Recalling Details: Land Down Under

Australia and New Zealand are often referred to as the "land down under." The name, made popular by American soldiers stationed there during World War II, grew out of the idea that these two countries are opposite or below Europe on the globe. While Australia and New Zealand are often linked, they are individual countries, separated by more than 1,000 miles of ocean.

Their landscapes are quite different. New Zealand is made up of two main islands, North and South Island, which are nearly covered by snowy mountains. One of the most unusual and beautiful areas of New Zealand is the volcanic region around Lake Taupo on North Island. There, you will see boiling springs, pools of steaming mud, hot-water geysers, small lakes with beds of brightly colored rocks, and waterfalls. While most of the people of New Zealand live and work in the industrialized cities, dairy farming is most important to the country's economy. New Zealanders eat a great deal of meat and butter, and they sell huge amounts to other countries.

As in Australia, many of the customs in New Zealand would be familiar to a traveler from America because the two countries were settled by British settlers hundreds of years ago. However, the native islanders have descended from Asian ancestors, so the remnants of ancient Eastern practices exist alongside the European way of life.

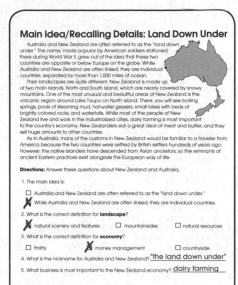

Directions: Answer these questions about New Zealand and Australia.

1. The main idea is:
   - ☐ Australia and New Zealand are often referred to as the "land down under."
   - ☒ While Australia and New Zealand are often linked, they are individual countries.

2. What is the correct definition for **landscape**?
   - ☒ natural scenery and features ☐ mountainsides ☐ natural resources

3. What is the correct definition for **economy**?
   - ☐ thrifty ☒ money management ☐ countryside

4. What is the nickname for Australia and New Zealand? <u>"the land down under"</u>

5. What business is most important to the New Zealand economy? <u>dairy farming</u>

Page 152

Venn Diagrams: Australia and New Zealand

Directions: Although Australia and New Zealand are close geographically to each other, they have many differences. After reading the selection, "Land Down Under," complete the following Venn diagram.

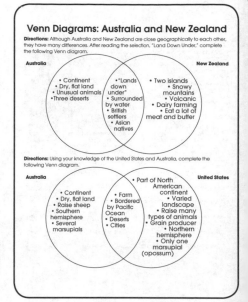

Australia — New Zealand

- Continent
- Dry, flat land
- Unusual animals
- Three deserts

- "Lands down under"
- Surrounded by water
- British settlers
- Asian natives

- Two islands
- Snowy mountains
- Volcanic
- Dairy farming
- Eat a lot of meat and butter

Directions: Using your knowledge of the United States and Australia, complete the following Venn diagram.

Australia — United States

- Continent
- Dry, flat land
- Raise sheep
- Southern hemisphere
- Several marsupials

- Farm
- Bordered by Pacific Ocean
- Deserts
- Cities

- Part of North American continent
- Varied landscape
- Raise many types of animals
- Grain producer
- Northern hemisphere
- Only one marsupial (opossum)

Page 153

Review

Directions: Write **T** for true and **F** for false.

1. <u>F</u> Australia and New Zealand are similar in landscape.
2. <u>T</u> Australia is home to the duckbill platypus.
3. <u>T</u> The wombat resembles a beaver without a tail.
4. <u>T</u> The platypus is a special mammal called a monotreme.
5. <u>T</u> A kangaroo is a marsupial.
6. <u>F</u> Baby kangaroos are independent at birth.
7. <u>F</u> Koalas are related to bears.
8. <u>T</u> Female koalas and kangaroos both have pouches.
9. <u>F</u> Koalas eat all types of leaves.
10. <u>T</u> There are over 40 kinds of kangaroos.
11. <u>T</u> The Australian Outback is located in the central part of the country.
12. <u>T</u> Australia is known for its great number of sheep.
13. <u>T</u> Aborigines arrived in Australia over 20,000 years ago.
14. <u>F</u> Aborigines live in one central place.

Page 154

Using Prior Knowledge: World Cities

Directions: Before reading about world cities in the following section, write one or two sentences telling what you know about each city below. **Answers will vary.**

London, England

Berlin, Germany

Sydney, Australia

Cairo, Egypt

Washington, D.C., United States

Ottawa, Canada

Page 155

Creative Writing: London

- London is the capital of England.
- Over 8 million people live in London.
- Among cities its size, London is the greenest city in the world.
- London is one of Europe's largest seaports.
- London has many historic sites, including Westminster Abbey, Houses of Parliament, Big Ben, and Buckingham Palace.
- Buckingham Palace is the residence of the queen of England, Queen Elizabeth II.

Directions: Using the above information, create a tourist article describing London. Do some research, and add other interesting information. **Answers will vary.**

When you think of England, what comes to mind?

Would you like to visit London? Why or why not?

Page 156

Creative Writing: Berlin

- Berlin is the capital of Germany.
- The population of Berlin is over 3.5 million people.
- Berlin's Inland Harbor is connected to the Baltic Sea.
- Germany was once divided into East and West Germany after World War II. East Germany was Communist, and West Germany was a democracy.
- Berlin has more museums (175) than rainy days per year.
- Interesting sites in Berlin include the Brandenburg Gate, the State Opera House, Tiergarten Park, and the Philharmonic Concert Hall.

Directions: Using the above information, create a tourist article describing Berlin. Do some research, and add other interesting information.

Answers will vary.

When you think of Germany, what comes to mind?

Would you like to visit Berlin? Why or why not?

Page 157

Making Inferences: Sydney

- Sydney is the capital of New South Wales, Australia.
- Manufacturing is a strong industry in Sydney. The city is also the headquarters of many large companies.
- Sydney is the major port of southeastern Australia.
- Sydney is Australia's largest city.
- The discovery of gold in 1851 increased Sydney's population. The population today is over 4.5 million people.
- Interesting sites in Sydney include the Sydney Opera House, the Sydney Harbour Bridge, and the Australia Square Tower.

Directions: Answer these questions about Sydney.

1. Why is manufacturing a strong industry in Sydney, as well as other major cities?

It is the headquarters of many large companies, a major port, and the largest city.

2. Gold was discovered in Australia in what year? 1851

3. What two states in the United States were given by gold diggers at about the same time?

California and Alaska

4. When you think of Australia, what comes to mind?

Answers will vary.

5. Would you like to visit Sydney? Why or why not?

Answers will vary.

Page 158

Making Inferences: Cairo

- Cairo is the capital of Egypt.
- Cairo is the largest city of not only Egypt but also the Middle East.
- The population of Cairo is almost 8 million people.
- Cairo is the cultural center for the Islamic religion.
- Cairo is a major industrial site for Egypt.
- Cairo is a port on the Nile River near the head of the Nile delta.
- Interesting sites include the Egyptian Museum, the Sphinx, the pyramids, and the City of the Dead.

Directions: Answer these questions about Cairo.

1. All the major cities discussed so far, including Cairo, have a seaport. Historically speaking, what is the importance of having access to the sea?

Answers will vary.

2. Cairo has a population of almost 8 million people. What are three problems that could arise from having such a large population?

a)

b)

c)

3. Would you like to visit Cairo? Why or why not?

Page 159

Creative Writing: Washington, D.C.

- Washington, D.C., is the capital of the United States.
- The population of Washington, D.C., is over 600,000 people in the city itself. Many people who work in Washington, D.C., reside in suburbs of the city in Virginia and Maryland. The population of the Washington, D.C. metropolitan area is 5.4 million.
- It's no surprise that the federal government is one of the largest employers in Washington, D.C.
- The Potomac and Anacostia rivers join in Washington, D.C.
- Interesting sites include the White House, the Vietnam Veterans Memorial, the Lincoln Memorial, the Washington Monument, and the United States Capitol Building.

Directions: Using the above information, create a tourist article describing Washington, D.C. Do some research, and add other interesting information.

Answers will vary.

When you think of Washington, D.C., what comes to mind?

Would you like to visit Washington, D.C.? Why or why not?

Page 160

Making Inferences: Ottawa

- Ottawa is the capital of Canada and is located in Ontario.
- The federal government employs most people in the city. Manufacturing is another large employer.
- The Rideau Canal connects Ottawa to Lake Ontario.
- The population of Ottawa is over 850,000 people.
- Points of interest include the Peace Tower, Parliament Buildings, the Royal Canadian Mint, and the Canadian Museum of Nature.

Directions: Answer these questions about Ottawa.

1. Who employs the most people in Ottawa, Canada? the federal government

2. What body of water connects Ottawa to Lake Ontario? the Rideau Canal

3. In order from largest to smallest, list the six cities you have read about and their populations.

London	over 8 million
Cairo	almost 8 million
Sydney	4.5 million
Berlin	3.5 million
Ottawa	850,000
Washington D.C.	600,000

4. Canada is the United States' neighbor to the north. What problems could arise due to a shared border?

Answers will vary.

Page 161

Review

Directions: Using page 162 as a guide, complete the Venn diagram comparing Washington, D.C., and London, England. Then, write a two-paragraph compare/contrast essay.

Washington, D.C.   Both   London, England

Answers will vary.

Compare/Contrast Essay

Essays will vary.

Page 163

Review

Directions: Using page 162 as a guide, complete the Venn diagram comparing Sydney, Australia, and Cairo, Egypt. Then, write a two-paragraph compare/contrast essay.

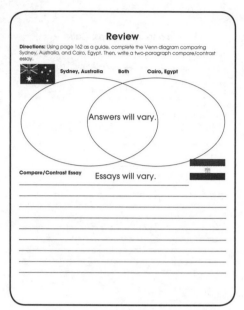

Sydney, Australia   Both   Cairo, Egypt

Answers will vary.

Compare/Contrast Essay

Essays will vary.

Page 164

Using Prior Knowledge: Dinosaurs

Everyone is intrigued by dinosaurs. Their size, ferocity, and sudden disappearance have fueled scientific investigations for well over a century.

Directions: Before reading about dinosaurs in the following section, answer these questions.

1. Describe what you know about meat-eating dinosaurs.

Answers will vary.

2. Describe what you know about plant-eating dinosaurs.

3. Which dinosaur most intrigues you? Why?

Page 165

Main Idea: Small Dinosaurs

When most people think of dinosaurs, they visualize enormous creatures. Actually, there were many species of small dinosaurs—some were only the size of chickens.

Like the larger dinosaurs, the Latin names of the smaller ones usually describe the creature. A small but fast species of dinosaur was Saltopus, which means "leaping foot." An adult Saltopus weighed only about 2 pounds and grew to be approximately 2 feet long. Fossils of this dinosaur, which lived about 200 million years ago, have been found only in Scotland.

Another small dinosaur with an interesting name was Compsognathus, which means "pretty jaw." About the same length as Saltopus, Compsognathus weighed about three times more. It's unlikely that these two species knew one another, since Compsognathus remains have been found only in France and Germany.

A small dinosaur whose remains have been found in southern Africa is Lesothosaurus, which means "Lesotho lizard." This lizard-like dinosaur was named only partly for its appearance. The first half of its name is based on the place its remains were found— Lesotho, in southern Africa.

Directions: Answer these questions about small dinosaurs.

1. Circle the main idea:

People who think dinosaurs were big are completely wrong.

(There are several species of small dinosaurs, some weighing only 2 pounds.)

2. How much did Saltopus weigh? about 2 pounds

3. Which dinosaur's name means "pretty jaw"? Compsognathus

Page 166

Comprehension: Dinosaur History

Dinosaurs are so popular today that it's hard to imagine this not always being the case. The fact is, no one had any idea that dinosaurs ever existed until about 150 years ago.

In 1841, a British scientist named Richard Owen coined the term **Dinosauria** to describe several sets of recently discovered large fossil bones. **Dinosauria** is Latin for "terrible lizards," and even though some dinosaurs were similar to lizards, modern science now also links dinosaurs to birds. Today's birds are thought to be the closest relatives to the dinosaurs.

Like birds, most dinosaurs had fairly long legs that extended straight down from beneath their bodies. Because of their long legs, many dinosaurs were able to move fast. They were also able to balance themselves well. Long-legged dinosaurs, such as Iguanodon, needed balance to walk upright.

Iguanodon walked on its long hind legs and used its stubby front legs as arms. On the end of its arms were five hoof-like fingers, one of which functioned as a thumb. Because it had no front teeth for tearing meat, scientists believe Iguanodon was a plant eater. Its large, flat back teeth were useful for grinding tender plants before swallowing them.

Directions: Answer these questions about the history of dinosaurs.

1. How were dinosaurs like today's birds? Most had fairly long, straight legs that extended straight down beneath their bodies.

2. This man coined the term **Dinosauria**.

☐ Owen Richards   ☐ Richard Owens   ☒ Richard Owen

3. Which of these did Iguanodon not have?

☐ short front legs   ☒ front teeth   ☐ back teeth

4. List other ways you can think of that dinosaurs and birds are alike.

Answers will vary.

Page 167

Recalling Details: Dinosaur Puzzler

Directions: Use the facts you have learned about dinosaurs to complete the puzzle.

Across:
5. This dinosaur had five hoof-like fingers on its short front legs.
6. Dinosaurs with flat back teeth were ___ eaters.
9. Because of where their legs were positioned, dinosaurs had good ___.

Down:
1. Most dinosaurs had ___ legs.
2. The word **Dinosauria** means "terrible ___."
3. A bone that has been preserved for many years
4. Dinosaurs were not always as ___ as they are now.
7. Iguanodons walked on their ___ legs.
8. Richard ___ coined the term **Dinosauria**.
9. Dinosaurs are closely related to today's ___.

Crossword:
- p o p u l a r (down)
- i z a r d s (down)
- i g u a n o d o n (across)
- p l a n t (across)
- f o s s i l (down)
- l o n g (down)
- h i n d (down)
- O w (down)
- b a l a n c e (across)
- p p p p (down)

Page 168

Comprehension: Tyrannosaurus Rex

One of the largest meat-eating animal ever to roam Earth was Tyrannosaurus Rex. **Rex** is Latin for "king," and because of its size, Tyrannosaurus certainly was at the top of the dinosaur heap. With a length of 46 feet and a weight of 7 tons, there's no doubt this dinosaur commanded respect!

Unlike smaller dinosaurs, Tyrannosaurus wasn't tremendously fast on its huge feet. It could stroll along at a walking speed of 2 to 3 miles an hour. Not bad, considering Tyrannosaurus was pulling along a body that weighed 14,000 pounds! Like other dinosaurs, Tyrannosaurus walked upright, probably balancing its 16-foot-long head by lifting its massive tail.

Compared to the rest of its body, Tyrannosaurus's front claws were tiny. Scientists aren't really sure what the claws were for, although it seems likely that they may have been used for holding food. In that case, Tyrannosaurus would have had to lower its massive head down to its short claws to take anything in its mouth. Maybe it just used the claws to scratch nearby itches!

Because of their low metabolism, dinosaurs did not require a lot of food for survival. Scientists speculate that Tyrannosaurus ate off the same huge piece of meat—usually the carcass of another dinosaur—for several weeks. What do you suppose Tyrannosaurus did the rest of the time?

Directions: Answer these questions about Tyrannosaurus Rex.

1. Why was this dinosaur called "Rex"? Rex means "king." Tyrannosaurus was large and fierce, so it "ruled" over other dinosaurs.

2. For what might Tyrannosaurus Rex have used its claws? to hold food

3. How long was Tyrannosaurus Rex? about 46 feet

4. Tyrannosaurus weighed

☐ 10,000 lbs.   ☐ 12,000 lbs.   ☒ 14,000 lbs.

5. Tyrannosaurus ate

☐ plants.   ☒ other dinosaurs.   ☐ birds.

Page 169

Generalization: Dinosaur Characteristics

Directions: Read each passage, and circle the valid generalization.

1. Not surprisingly, Tyrannosaurus had huge teeth in its mammoth head. They were 6 inches long! Because it was a meat eater, Tyrannosaurus's teeth were sharp. They looked like spikes! In comparison, the long-necked, plant-eating Mamenchisaurus had a tiny head and small, flat teeth.

a. Scientists can't figure out why some dinosaurs had huge teeth.

b. Tyrannosaurus was probably scarier looking than Mamenchisaurus.

c. Sharp teeth would have helped Mamenchisaurus chew better.

2. Dinosaurs' names often reflect their size or some other physical trait. For example, Compsognathus means "pretty jaw." Saltopus means "leaping foot." Lesothosaurus means "lizard from Lesotho."

a. Of the three species, Lesothosaurus was probably the fastest.

b. Of the three species, Compsognathus was probably the fastest.

c. Of the three species, Saltopus was probably the fastest.

3. Edmontosaurus, a huge 3-ton dinosaur, had 1,000 teeth! The teeth were cemented into chewing pads in the back of Edmontosaurus's mouth. Unlike the sharp teeth of the meat-eating Tyrannosaurus, this dinosaur's teeth were flat.

a. Edmontosaurus did not eat meat.

b. Edmontosaurus did not eat plants.

c. Edmontosaurus moved very fast.

Page 170

Comprehension: Dinosaur Fossils

Imagine putting together the world's largest jigsaw puzzle. That is what scientists who reassemble the fossil bones of dinosaurs must do to find out what the creatures looked like. Fossilized bones are imbedded, or stuck, in solid rock, so scientists must first get the bones out of the rocks without breaking or otherwise damaging them. This task requires enormous patience.

In addition to hammers, drills, and chisels, sound waves are used to break up the rock. The drills, which are similar to high-speed dental drills, cut through the rock very quickly. As the bones are removed, scientists begin trying to figure out how they attach to one another. Sometimes the dinosaur's skeleton was preserved just as it was when it died. This, of course, shows scientists exactly how to reassemble it. Other times, parts of bone are missing. It then becomes a guessing game to decide what goes where.

When scientists discover dinosaur fossils, it is called a "find." A particularly exciting find in 1978 occurred in Montana when, for the first time, fossilized dinosaur eggs, babies, and several nests were found. The species of dinosaur in this exciting find was Maiasaura, which means "good mother lizard." From the size of the nest, which was 23 feet, scientists speculated that the adult female Maiasaura was about the same size.

Unlike birds' nests, dinosaur nests were not made of sticks and straw. Instead, since they were land animals, nests were made of dirt hollowed out into a bowl shape. The Maiasaura's nest was 3 feet deep and held about 20 eggs.

Directions: Answer these questions about dinosaur fossils.

1. Name four tools used to remove dinosaur bones from rock. _____
   hammers, drills, chisels, sound waves

2. What do scientists do with the bones they remove?
   They try to reassemble them.

3. The type of dinosaur fossils found in Montana in 1978 were
   ☐ Mayiasaura. ☐ Maisaura. ☒ Maiasaura.

4. When scientists discover dinosaur fossils, it is called a
   ☐ found. ☒ find. ☐ nest.

Page 171

Generalization: Plant-Eating Dinosaurs

Directions: Read each passage, and circle the valid generalization.

1. Many of the plant-eating dinosaurs belonged to a common species called Sauropods. Most Sauropods were very large. They had peg-shaped teeth, and they formed herds to search for food. They used their long necks to reach the top branches of trees, where the most tender leaves grew.

a. Their size, teeth, and long necks made Sauropods perfectly suited to their environment.

b. The Sauropods' peg-like teeth were not well suited to eating meat.

c. Vegetarian dinosaurs needed short necks and sharp teeth to survive.

2. Sauropods were not the only dinosaurs that traveled in herds. Sets of different-sized fossilized dinosaur footprints discovered in Texas show that other types of dinosaurs also traveled together. The footprints—23 sets of them—were of another plant-eating dinosaur, the Apatosaurus.

a. All dinosaurs traveled in herds because they needed companionship.

b. It appears that some plant-eating dinosaurs traveled in herds.

c. Traveling in herds offered dinosaurs protection and friendship.

3. Not all plant-eating dinosaurs were huge. The Hypsilophodon was only about 6½ feet tall. It stood on its two back legs and, because of its smaller size, probably ran away from danger.

a. The Hypsilophodon didn't stand a chance against bigger dinosaurs.

b. The Hypsilophodon could not eat from the tops of tall trees.

c. The Hypsilophodon was cowardly and always ran from danger.

Page 172

Comprehension: Dinosaur Tracks

Some scientists refer to dinosaurs' fossilized tracks as "footprints in time." The tracks that survived in Texas for 120 million years had been made in sand or mud. These large footprints were of the Apatosaurus. The footprints were more than 3 feet across!

Although Apatosaurus had a long, heavy tail, there is no sign that the tail hit the ground along with the feet. Scientists speculate that the place where the tracks were found was once a riverbed, and that Apatosaurus's tail floated in the water and thus left no tracks. Another theory is that the dinosaur always carried its tail out behind it. This second theory is not as popular, because scientists say it's unlikely the dinosaur would consistently carry its long, heavy tail off the ground. When Apatosaurus rested, for example, the tail would have left its mark.

Besides Texas, fossilized tracks have been found in England, Canada, Australia, and Brazil. Some tracks have also been found in New England. The tracks discovered in Canada were quite a find! They showed a pattern made by 10 species of dinosaurs. In all, about 1,700 fossilized footprints were discovered. Maybe the scientists uncovered what millions of years ago was a dinosaur playground!

Directions: Answer these questions about dinosaur tracks.

1. Circle the main idea:

Fossilized dinosaur tracks provide scientists with information from which to draw conclusions about dinosaur size and behavior.

Fossilized dinosaur tracks are not very useful because so few have been found in the United States.

2. Explain how a dinosaur might have crossed a river without its tail leaving a track.
   The tail may have floated in the water.

3. Name five countries where dinosaur tracks have been found. **United States, England, Canada, Australia, and Brazil**

4. Circle the valid generalization about dinosaur tracks.

a. The fact that 10 species of tracks were found together proves dinosaurs were friends with others outside their groups.

b. The fact that 10 species of tracks were found together means the dinosaurs probably gathered in that spot for water or food.

Page 173

Review

Directions: Reread the following selections. Then, write the main idea of each.

Small Dinosaurs _____ **Answers will vary.**
_____
_____

Dinosaur History _____
_____
_____

Tyrannosaurus Rex _____
_____
_____

Dinosaur Fossils _____
_____
_____

Dinosaur Tracks _____
_____
_____

Page 174

The Solar System

This section is about our solar system. It includes the sun, comparisons among the planets, each planet's physical characteristics, and each planet's moons. Before beginning this section, try to answer the following questions.

1. Name the eight planets of the solar system in order beginning with the planet closest to the sun.
   a. **Mercury** b. **Venus** c. **Earth**
   d. **Mars** e. **Jupiter** f. **Saturn**
   g. **Uranus** h. **Neptune**

2. Write a distinguishing characteristic for each planet listed below.
   Earth **supports life and civilization**
   Jupiter **the largest planet**
   Saturn **has rings**
   Mars **known as the "red planet"**

3. The study of the solar system, stars, and outer space is called
   astronomy

4. The **Sun** is the center of the solar system and is a star.

5. Which planet is similar in size to Earth? **Venus**

6. Humans have landed on which outer space object? **the moon**

7. Have humans landed on any planets? Why or why not? _____
   No. Possible answer: Either they are too far away, or they are inhospitable to humans.

Page 175

The Sun

Directions: Read the selection. Then, answer the questions.

The Sun is the center of our solar system. It is a star that seems massive to those on Earth but is dwarfed in comparison to other giant stars farther out in the universe. It rotates on its axis just like Earth. The Sun is made up of heated gases, and it releases heat and light energy. The part of the Sun we see is called the photosphere. The chromosphere is the colored ring of gases surrounding the Sun. Solar flares often shoot out from the Sun's surface for thousands of miles. Without the Sun's warmth, life on Earth would cease to exist.

1. Define the following words.

axis: __an imaginary line around which a body rotates__

universe: __all known celestial materials__

dwarfed: __made to seem smaller__

cease: __to stop__

2. What effect could a solar flare have on Earth?
__It could disrupt radio signals.__

3. Does the Sun revolve or rotate? __rotate__

4. Why isn't the Sun visible at night? __It faces the other side of Earth.__

5. Why is it important never to look directly at the Sun?
__Its rays can burn our eyes.__

Page 176

Mercury

Directions: Read the selection. Then, answer the questions.

The planet Mercury is named for the Roman god Mercury who was the messenger of the gods. Ancient Greek astronomers named the heavenly bodies "planets," which means "wanderers." Mercury is the planet closest to the Sun and also the smallest of the inner planets. Because of its proximity to the Sun (nearly 36 million miles), its surface is extraordinarily hot. Mercury's solid surface is covered with craters. It rotates on its axis once every 59 days. One year on Mercury lasts 88 Earth days. Mercury has no moons or rings and has virtually no atmosphere.

1. Define the following words:

astronomer: __Someone who studies the universe outside the Earth's atmosphere__

proximity: __nearness__

atmosphere: __the gaseous envelope surrounding Earth (or any celestial body)__

crater: __an impression formed by the impact of a meteorite__

2. Could life survive on Mercury? Why or why not?
__No, the surface is far too hot for life to exist there.__

3. Write a three-sentence summary of the selection above.
__Possible answer: The planet Mercury, named after the Roman god Mercury, is the smallest inner planet and is closest to the Sun. It has no moons, rings, or atmosphere. It is too hot to support life.__

4. Mercury's period of revolution is 88 days. How many months would that be?
__almost three months__

Page 177

Venus

Directions: Read the selection. Then, answer the questions.

Located over 67 million miles from the Sun, Venus is an incredibly hot planet. Venus is named for the Roman goddess of love and beauty. Temperatures can reach 470 degrees Celsius. Venus is close in size to Earth and is often referred to as Earth's twin. Space probes and unmanned crafts have landed on Venus and found Venus to be dust-covered and very windy. Because Venus is very bright, it is often thought of as a star. Venus has no moons or rings. Its period of rotation is 243 days, and it revolves once around the Sun in 225 days.

1. Create a Venn diagram comparing Mercury and Venus.
Mercury __Possible answer:__ Venus

- Rotates every 59 days
- Revolves around the Sun every 88 days
- Many craters

- Has no moons or rings
- Very hot

- Earth's "twin"
- Rotates every 243 days
- Revolves around the Sun every 225 days
- Very windy and dusty
- Venus is next to Earth

2. Write a three-sentence summary about Venus.
__Answers will vary.__

3. Approximately how far is Venus from Mercury? __31 million miles__

4. If you were to design a spacecraft capable of landing on Venus, what might it require?
__Answers will vary.__

Page 178

Earth

Directions: Read the selection. Then, answer the questions.

Earth is the only planet with known life forms. It revolves around the Sun every 365¼ days. One rotation takes 24 hours to complete. Earth has seasons due to the tilt of its axis and its revolution. Rotation causes night and day. Earth is almost 93 million miles away from the Sun. Its surface is three-fourths water and one-fourth land mass. Earth is surrounded by gases called the atmosphere, which allows life to survive. Earth has one moon that has been explored many times.

1. Define the following word.

mass: __how dense something is; the matter a body possesses__

2. Approximately how far is Earth from Venus?
__26 million miles__

3. Approximately how far is Earth from Mercury?
__57 million miles__

4. What factors allow life to exist on Earth?
__Its atmosphere and its distance from the Sun (which helps temperatures)__

5. What causes the seasons?
__The tilt of Earth's axis and its revolution cause the seasons.__

6. What differences are there between Earth and the planets Mercury and Venus?
__Possible answer: Earth's atmosphere and cooler surface support life. Mercury and Venus are much hotter. Earth has a moon, while Mercury and Venus do not.__

Page 179

Mars

Directions: Read the selection. Then, answer the questions.

Mars is named for the god of war. It is the fourth of the inner planets. Mars is called the Red Planet and has polar caps, craters, and evidence of ancient volcanoes. Recently, space probes have landed there and given scientists information about its surface. The red color is produced by the reaction of iron-rich minerals to soil and water, which scientists believe happened long ago. Mars rotates on its axis every 24 hours, 37 minutes and is 142 million miles from the Sun. Its period of revolution is 687 days. Mars has two moons, Phobos and Deimos. Mars's identifying feature is the volcano Olympus Mons. Its temperature varies, but averages ~50 degrees Celsius.

1. Define the following words.

polar: __the ends of a planet's axis__

mineral: __an inorganic substance occurring in nature__

2. Name two distinguishing characteristics of Mars.
__Possible answers: Mars is red, and it has a volcano named Olympus Mons.__

3. Could life survive on Mars? Why or why not?
__Possible answer: No, life could not survive on Mars because the average temperature is extremely cold.__

4. For years, people have been interested in the possibility of Martian life. What special characteristics would allow life on Mars have?
__Answers will vary.__

Page 180

Jupiter

Directions: Read the selection. Then, answer the questions.

The planet Jupiter is the largest planet of our solar system and is named for the king of the gods. Its distinguishing feature is the Great Red Spot, which changes occasionally in both color and brightness. Jupiter has a thin ring and at least 67 moons. Jupiter is the first of the outer planets, separated from the inner planets by an asteroid belt. It is almost 500 million miles from the Sun and takes nearly 12 years to complete a revolution around the Sun. It rotates on its axis in approximately 10 hours. Jupiter does not have a solid surface but rather a surface of gaseous clouds.

1. Define the following words.

asteroid: __any small body that revolves around the Sun in orbit__

gaseous: __containing gas__

2. Approximately how far is Jupiter from Earth?
__407 million miles__

3. Name three characteristics of Jupiter.
__Possible answer: Jupiter is the largest planet in our solar system. Its distinguishing feature is the Great Red Spot. It also has a thin ring and at least 67 moons.__

4. Write a three-sentence summary about Jupiter.
__Answers will vary.__

5. What separates the inner and outer planets?
__an asteroid belt__

6. Why do you think ancient astronomers chose to name Jupiter after the king of the gods?
__because it is the largest planet__

Page 181

Saturn

Directions: Read the selection. Then, answer the questions.

Saturn's rings were first discovered in 1610. Scientists now know that Saturn has over 1,000 rings of varying color. Not only do the rings rotate at different speeds but also in varying patterns. Saturn has at least 53 moons. It is almost 900 million miles from the Sun and is the second largest planet of our solar system. Saturn rotates on its axis once in just under 11 hours. Saturn is named for the god of agriculture and harvest.

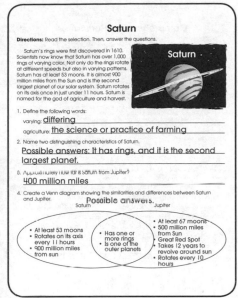
Saturn

1. Define the following words:

varying: **differing**

agriculture: **the science or practice of farming**

2. Name two distinguishing characteristics of Saturn.

Possible answers: It has rings, and it is the second largest planet.

3. Approximately how far is Saturn from Jupiter?

400 million miles

4. Create a Venn diagram showing the similarities and differences between Saturn and Jupiter.

Possible answers.

Saturn / Jupiter

- At least 53 moons
- Rotates on its axis every 11 hours
- 900 million miles from sun

- Has one or more rings
- Is one of the outer planets

- At least 67 moons
- 500 million miles from Sun
- Great Red Spot
- Takes 12 years to revolve around sun
- Rotates every 10 hours

Page 182

Uranus and Neptune

Directions: Read the selection. Then, answer the questions.

Because of their immense distance from Earth, it is difficult to study Uranus and Neptune. Uranus is named for the god of the skies, and Neptune is named for the god of the sea.

Uranus rotates on its side, thus making its rings spin vertically rather than horizontally. It has 27 moons and is almost 2 billion miles from the Sun. It rotates on its axis once every 17.25 hours and revolves around the Sun every 84 years. Uranus was the first planet discovered by telescope.

Neptune is similar in size and color to Uranus. It is almost 3 billion miles from the Sun and takes approximately 164 years to orbit it. Neptune has 14 moons and also has rings. It takes a little over 16 hours to make one rotation on its axis. Neptune is known for its large, windy storms. One massive storm, known as the Great Dark Spot, lasted for five years!

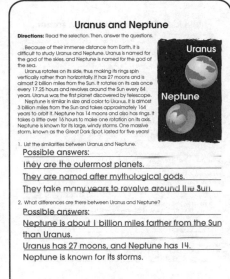
Uranus

Neptune

1. List the similarities between Uranus and Neptune.

Possible answers:

They are the outermost planets.

They are named after mythological gods.

They take many years to revolve around the Sun.

2. What differences are there between Uranus and Neptune?

Possible answers:

Neptune is about 1 billion miles farther from the Sun than Uranus.

Uranus has 27 moons, and Neptune has 14.

Neptune is known for its storms.

Page 183

Uranus and Neptune

Directions: Use the lists you created on page 183 to create a Venn diagram showing the similarities and differences between Uranus and Neptune.

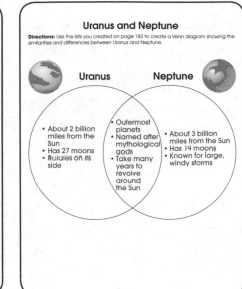

Uranus / Neptune

- About 2 billion miles from the Sun
- Has 27 moons
- Rotates on its side

- Outermost planets
- Named after mythological gods
- Take many years to revolve around the Sun

- About 3 billion miles from the Sun
- Has 14 moons
- Known for large, windy storms

Page 184

Review

Directions: Follow the instructions for each question.

1. List the four inner planets.

Mercury   Venus   Earth   Mars

2. List the four outer planets.

Jupiter   Saturn   Uranus   Neptune

3. What separates the inner and outer planets?

an asteroid belt

4. Name a distinguishing feature of each planet.

Mercury: **the closest planet to the Sun**

Venus: **Earth's "twin" in the solar system**

Earth: **supports life**

Mars: **the red planet**

Jupiter: **the largest planet**

Saturn: **has many rings**

Uranus: **rotates on its side**

Neptune: **farthest from the Sun and the smallest planet**

5. List the planets in order from most moons to least.

a) **Jupiter (at least 67 moons)**   e) **Mars (2 moons)**

b) **Saturn (at least 53 moons)**   f) **Earth (1 moon)**

c) **Uranus (27 moons)**   g) **Venus (0 moons)**

d) **Neptune (14 moons)**   h) **Mercury (0 moons)**

Page 185

Review

6. Which planets have rings?

Jupiter, Saturn, Uranus, and Neptune

7. If you were in charge of the space program, what would your priorities be? Why?

Answers will vary.

8. Draw a diagram of the planets and the Sun. Be sure to depict color and the following diameter sizes.

Mercury — 3,031 mi.   Venus — 7,521 mi.   Earth — 7,926 mi.

Mars — 4,217 mi.   Jupiter — 88,730 mi.   Saturn — 74,900 mi.

Uranus — 31,763 mi.   Neptune — 30,775 mi.

Neptune Uranus Saturn Jupiter Mars Earth Venus Mercury Sun

Page 186

Recalling Details: Earth's Atmosphere

The most important reason that life can exist on Earth is its atmosphere—the air around us. Without it, plant and animal life could not have developed. There would be no clouds, weather, or even sounds, only a deathlike stillness and an endlessly black sky. Without the protection of the atmosphere, the Sun's rays would roast Earth by day. At night, with no blanketing atmosphere, the stored heat would escape into space, dropping the temperature of the planet hundreds of degrees.

Held captive by Earth's gravity, the atmosphere surrounds the planet to a depth of hundreds of miles. However, all but 1 percent of the atmosphere is in a layer about 20 miles deep just above the surface of Earth. It is made up of a mixture of gases and dusts. About 78 percent of it is a gas called nitrogen, which is very important as food for plants. Most of the remaining gas, 21 percent, is oxygen, which all people and animals depend on for life. The remaining 1 percent is made up of a blend of other gases—including carbon dioxide, argon, ozone, and helium—and tiny dust particles. These particles come from ocean salt crystals, bits of rocks and sand, plant pollen, volcanic ash, and even meteor dust.

You may not think of air as matter, as something that can be weighed. In fact, Earth's air weighs billions and billions of tons. Near the surface of the planet, this "air pressure" is greatest. Right now, about 10 tons of air is pressing in on you. Yet, like the fish living near the floor of the ocean, you don't notice this tremendous weight because your body is built to withstand it.

Directions: Answer these questions about Earth's atmosphere.

1. What is the atmosphere? **the air around us**

2. Of what is the atmosphere made? **nitrogen, oxygen, other gases, and dust particles**

3. What is the most abundant gas in the atmosphere? **nitrogen**

4. Which of the atmosphere's gases is most important to humans and animals?

oxygen

5. What is air pressure? **the weight of the air on Earth**

Page 187

Comprehension: Causes/Effects of Weather

The behavior of the atmosphere, which we experience as weather and climate, affects our lives in many important ways. It is the reason no one lives on the South Pole. It controls when a farmer plants the food we will eat, which crops will be planted, and also whether those crops will grow. The weather tells you what clothes to wear and how you will play after school. Weather is the sum of all the conditions of the air that may affect Earth's surface and its living things. These conditions include the temperature, air pressure, wind, and moisture. **Climate** refers to these conditions but generally applies to larger areas and longer periods of time, such as the annual climate of South America rather than today's weather in Oklahoma City.

Climate is influenced by many factors. It depends first and foremost on latitude. Areas nearest the equator are warm and wet, while the poles are cold and relatively dry. The poles also have extreme seasonal changes, while the areas at the middle latitudes have more moderate climates, neither as cold as the poles nor as hot as the equator. Other circumstances may alter this pattern, however. Land near the oceans, for instance, is generally warmer than inland areas.

Elevation also plays a role in climate. For example, despite the fact that Africa's highest mountain, Kilimanjaro, is just south of the equator, its summit is perpetually covered by snow. In general, high land is cooler and wetter than nearby low land.

Directions: Check the answers to these questions about the causes and effects of weather.

1. What is the correct definition for **atmosphere**?
   ☐ the clouds ☐ the sky ☒ where weather occurs

2. What is the correct definition for **foremost**?
   ☒ most important ☐ highest number ☐ in the front

3. What is the correct definition for **circumstances**?
   ☐ temperatures ☐ seasons ☒ conditions

4. What is the correct definition for **elevation**?
   ☒ height above Earth ☐ nearness to equator ☐ snow covering

5. What is the correct definition for **perpetually**?
   ☐ occasionally ☐ rarely ☒ always

Page 188

Main Idea/Recalling Details: Weather

People have always searched the sky for clues about upcoming weather. Throughout the ages, farmers and sailors have looked to the winds and clouds for signs of approaching storms. But no real understanding of the weather could be achieved without a scientific study of the atmosphere. Such a study depends on being able to measure certain conditions, including pressure, temperature, and moisture levels.

A true scientific examination of weather, therefore, was not possible until the development of accurate measuring instruments, beginning in the 17th century. Meteorology—the science of studying the atmosphere—was born in 1643 with the invention of the barometer, which measures atmospheric pressure. The liquid-in-glass thermometer, the hygrometer to measure humidity (the amount of moisture in the air), and the weather map also were invented during the 1600s.

With the measurement of these basic elements, scientists began to work out the relationships between these and other atmospheric conditions, such as wind, clouds, and rainfall. Still, their observations failed to show an overall picture of the weather. Such complete weather reporting had to wait two centuries for the rapid transfer of information made possible by the invention of the telegraph during the 1840s.

Today, the forecasts of meteorologists are an international effort. There are thousands of weather stations around the world, both at land and at sea. Upper-level observations are also made by weather balloons and satellites, which continuously send photographs back to Earth. All of this information is relayed to national weather bureaus, where meteorologists plot it on graphs and analyze it. The information is then given to the public through the internet, newspapers, television, and radio stations.

Directions: Answer these questions about studying the weather.

1. The main idea is:
   ☐ People have always searched the sky for clues about upcoming weather.
   ☒ A real understanding of weather depends on measuring conditions such as pressure, temperature, and moisture levels.

2. List three kinds of instruments used to measure atmospheric conditions, and tell what conditions they measure.
   a) barometer — atmospheric pressure
   b) hygrometer — humidity
   c) liquid-in-glass thermometer — temperature

3. During what century were many of these measuring instruments invented? 17th

4. Name two things used for upper-level observations.
   a) weather balloons b) satellites

Page 189

Comprehension: Hurricanes

The characteristics of a hurricane are powerful winds, driving rain, and raging seas. Although a storm must have winds blowing at least 74 miles an hour to be classified as a hurricane, it is not unusual for hurricanes to have winds above 150 miles per hour. The entire storm system can be 500 miles in diameter, with lines of clouds that spiral toward a center called the "eye." Within the eye itself, which is about 15 miles across, the air is actually calm and cloudless. But this eye is enclosed by a towering wall of thick clouds where the storm's heaviest rains and highest winds are found.

All hurricanes begin in the warm seas and moist winds of the tropics. They form in either of two narrow bands to the north and south of the equator. For weeks, the blistering sun beats down on the ocean water. Slowly, the air above the sea becomes heated and begins to swirl. More hot, moist air is pulled skyward. Gradually, this circle grows larger and spins faster. As the hot, moist air at the top is cooled, great rain clouds are formed. The storm's fury builds until it moves over land or a cold area of the ocean where its supply of heat and moisture is finally cut off.

Hurricanes that strike North America usually form over the Atlantic Ocean. West coast storms are less dangerous because they tend to head out over the Pacific Ocean rather than toward land. The greatest damage usually comes from the hurricanes that begin in the western Pacific, because they often batter heavily populated regions.

Directions: Answer these questions about hurricanes.

1. What is necessary for a storm to be classified as a hurricane? winds blowing at least 74 miles an hour

2. What is the eye of the hurricane? the center of the hurricane

3. Where do hurricanes come from? the warm seas and moist winds of the tropics

4. How does a hurricane finally die down? It moves over land or a cold area of the ocean where its supply of heat and moisture is cut off.

5. Why do hurricanes formed in the western Pacific cause the most damage? They often batter heavily populated regions.

Page 190

Comprehension: Tornadoes

Tornadoes, which are also called twisters, occur more frequently than hurricanes, but they are smaller storms. The zigzag path of a tornado averages about 16 miles in length and only about a quarter of a mile in width. But the tornado is, pound for pound, the more severe storm. When one touches the ground, it leaves a trail of total destruction.

The winds in a tornado average about 200 miles per hour. At the center of the funnel-shaped cloud of a tornado is a partial vacuum. In combination with the high winds, this is what makes the storm so destructive. Its force is so great that a tornado can drive a piece of straw into a tree. The extremely low atmospheric pressure that accompanies the storm can cause a building to actually explode.

Unlike hurricanes, tornadoes are formed over land. They are most likely to occur over the central plains of the United States, especially in the spring and early summer months. Conditions for a tornado arise when warm, moist air from the south becomes trapped under colder, heavier air from the north. When the surfaces of the two air masses touch, rain clouds form and a thunderstorm begins. At first, only a rounded bulge hangs from the bottom of the cloud. It gradually gets longer until it forms a column reaching toward the ground. The tornado is white from the moisture when it first forms, but it turns black as it sucks up dirt and trash.

Directions: Circle **True** or **False** for these statements about tornadoes.

1. The tornado is a stronger storm than the hurricane. **True** False
2. The path of a tornado usually covers hundreds of miles. True **False**
3. Like the eye of a hurricane, the center of a tornado is calm. True **False**
4. Tornadoes are most likely to occur in the central plains of the United States during the spring and early summer months. **True** False
5. High atmospheric pressure usually accompanies a tornado. True **False**

Page 191

Comprehension: Thunderstorms

With warm weather comes the threat of thunderstorms. The rapid growth of the majestic thunderhead cloud and the damp, cool breath that warn of an approaching storm are familiar in most regions of the world. In fact, it has been estimated that at any given time, 1,800 such storms are in progress around the globe.

As with hurricanes and tornadoes, thunderstorms are formed when a warm, moist air mass meets with a cold air mass. Before long, bolts of lightning streak across the sky, and thunder booms. It is not entirely understood how lightning is formed. It is known that a positive electrical charge builds near the top of the cloud, and a negative charge forms at the bottom. When enough force builds up, a powerful current of electricity zigzags down an electrically charged pathway between the two, causing the flash of lightning.

The clap of thunder you hear after a lightning flash is created by rapidly heated air that expands as the lightning passes through it. The distant rumbling is caused by the thunder's sound waves bouncing back and forth within clouds or between mountains. When thunderstorms rumble through an area, many people begin to worry about tornadoes. But they need to be just as fearful of thunderstorms. In fact, lightning kills more people than any other severe weather condition.

Directions: Answer these questions about thunderstorms.

1. How many thunderstorms are estimated to be occurring at any given time around the world? 1,800

2. When are thunderstorms formed? when a warm, moist air mass meets with a cold air mass

3. What causes lightning? rapidly heated air that expands as lightning passes through it

4. On average, which causes more deaths, lightning or tornadoes? lightning

Page 192

Venn Diagram: Storms

Directions: Complete the Venn diagram below. Think of at least three things to write in the outer parts of each circle and at least three things to write in the intersecting parts.

Possible answers:

Hurricanes
- Occur most often off Atlantic Ocean
- Formed over warm seas
- "Eye" in center is peaceful

Tornadoes
- Occur most often in central plains of U.S.
- Funnel cloud
- Vacuum in center is destructive

Hurricanes ∩ Tornadoes: Strong winds

Center (all): Rain, Warm, moist air

Tornadoes ∩ Thunderstorms: Occur in spring and summer

Thunderstorms
- Occur anywhere in U.S.
- Thunder and lightning
- Lightning is the deadliest severe weather condition

Page 193

Recalling Details: Lightning Safety Rules

Lightning causes more fire damage to forests and property than anything else. More importantly, it kills more people than any other weather event. It is important to know what to do—and what not to do—during a thunderstorm. Here are some important rules to remember:

- **Don't** go outdoors.
- **Don't** go near open doors or windows, fireplaces, radiators, stoves, metal pipes, sinks, or plug-in electrical appliances.
- **Don't** use the telephone, as lightning could strike the wires outside. (Cell phones are safe to use.)
- **Don't** handle metal objects, such as fishing poles or golf clubs.
- **Don't** go into the water or ride in small boats.
- **Do** stay in an automobile if you are traveling. Cars offer excellent protection.
- **Don't** take laundry off the clothesline.
- **Do** look for shelter if you are outdoors. If there is no shelter, stay away from the highest object in the area. If there are only a few trees nearby, it is best to crouch in the open, away from the trees at a distance greater than the height of the nearest tree. If you are in an area with many trees, avoid the tallest tree. Look for shorter ones.
- **Don't** take shelter near wire fences or clotheslines, exposed sheds, or on a hilltop.
- If your hair stands on end or your skin tingles, lightning may be about to strike you. Immediately crouch down, put your feet together, and place your hands over your ears.

Directions: Answer these questions about lightning safety rules.

Possible answers:
1. Name two things you should avoid if you are looking for shelter outside.
   a) wire fences
   b) exposed sheds

2. What should you do if, during a thunderstorm, your hair stands up or your skin tingles?
Crouch down, put your feet together, and place your hands over your ears.

Page 194

Main Idea/Comprehension: Rainbows

Although there are some violent, frightening aspects of the weather, there is, considerable beauty, too. The rainbow is one simple, lovely example of nature's atmospheric mysteries.

You usually can see a rainbow when the sun comes out after a rain shower or in the fine spray of a waterfall or fountain. Although sunlight appears to be white, it is actually made up of a mixture of colors—all the colors in the rainbow. We see a rainbow because thousands of tiny raindrops act as mirrors and prisms on the sunlight. Prisms are objects that bend light, splitting it into bands of color.

The bands of color form a perfect semicircle. From the top edge to the bottom, the colors are always in the same order—red, orange, yellow, green, blue, indigo, and violet. The brightness and width of each band may vary from one minute to the next. You also may notice that the sky framed by the rainbow is lighter than the sky above. This is because the light that forms the blue and violet bands is more bent and spread out than the light that forms the top red band.

You will always see morning rainbows in the west, with the sun behind you. Afternoon rainbows, likewise, are always in the east. To see a rainbow, the sun can be no higher than 42 degrees—nearly halfway up the sky. Sometimes, if the sunlight is strong and the water droplets are very small, you can see a double rainbow. This happens because the light is reflected twice in the water droplets. The color bands are fainter and in reverse order in the second band.

Directions: Answer these questions about rainbows.

1. Check the statement that is the main idea.
   ☐ Although there are violent, frightening aspects of weather, there is considerable beauty, too.
   ☒ The rainbow is one simple, lovely example of nature's atmospheric mysteries.

2. What is the correct definition for **semicircle**?
   ☐ colored circle   ☐ diameter of a circle   ☒ half circle

3. What is a prism? an object that bends light and splits it into bands of color

4. In which direction would you look to see an afternoon rainbow? east

Page 195

Comprehension: Cause and Effect

Directions: Complete the chart by listing the cause and effect of each weather phenomenon.

	Cause	Effect
Thunderstorms	warm, moist air mass collides with cold air mass	lightning, thunder, rain
Hurricanes	air above the sea heats and swirls; hot, moist air is pulled up and spins faster	rain clouds form; spiraling wind
Tornadoes	warm, moist air gets trapped under cold, heavy air	rain clouds form; thunderstorms occur; tornado develops
Rainbows	sun comes out after rain	raindrops reflect sun's light like mirrors and act like prisms, bending light into bands of color
Precipitation	warm, moist air; low pressure system	rain
Drought	lack of rain and dew	dry earth, loss of livestock, dust bowl conditions

Page 196

Review

Directions: If necessary, review the section on weather to find the answers to the following questions.

1. Describe Earth's atmosphere. a mixture of gases and dusts that surrounds Earth at a depth of 100 miles

2. The science of studying weather is called meteorology

3. Why is it important for weather forecasting to be an international effort?
Possible answer: As more people travel, knowledge of weather in other countries becomes important. It is also important to track weather systems.

4. Define **weather**. the sum of all the conditions of the air that may affect Earth's surface and its living things

5. Name three factors that influence climate.
   latitude   elevation   proximity to ocean

6. Describe the following weather phenomena.
   a. hurricane powerful winds, driving rain, and raging seas
   b. tornado warm, moist winds trapped under cold, heavy air, which results in a funnel cloud
   c. thunderstorm warm, moist air meets a cold air mass, which results in rain, thunder, and lightning

Page 197

Using Prior Knowledge: Sports

Directions: Before reading about sports in the following section, write one or two sentences telling what you know about each sport below.

Wrestling ___ Answers will vary. ___

Rowing _____

Volleyball _____

Tennis _____
_____
_____

Boxing _____

Football _____

Softball _____

Field Hockey _____

Page 198

Comprehension: Wrestling Around the World

In many countries, wrestling is an honored sport. In Iceland, wrestling is called **glima**; in Switzerland, it is called **schweitzer schwingen**; and in Ireland, it is called **cumberland**. In Japan, a form of wrestling called **sumo** began in 23 B.C.

Sumo wrestling is still popular in Japan today. Wrestlers wear the traditional sumo costume of a loincloth—a piece of cloth draped across the hips and bottom—and nothing else. Sumo wrestlers are big men—their average weight is about 300 pounds. Wrestlers compete in small rings with sand floors. The object of the match is to push the opponent out of the ring.

Even in the wrestling ring, however, the Japanese are astonishingly polite. If one wrestler begins to push the other out of the ring, the other may shout, "Matta!" **Matta** is Japanese for "not yet." At this point, the action stops and the wrestlers step out of the ring to take a break. Some wrestling matches in Japan must take a long, long time to complete!

Directions: Answer these questions about wrestling around the world.

1. What is wrestling called in Switzerland? schweitzer schwingen

2. In what country is wrestling called **cumberland**? Ireland

3. What is wrestling called in Iceland? glima

4. In what country is wrestling called **sumo**? Japan

5. How much does an average sumo wrestler weigh? about 300 pounds

6. What does **matta** mean in Japanese? "not yet"

7. What happens if a wrestler shouts, "Matta"?
The action stops, and the wrestlers step out of the ring to take a break.

8. In what year did sumo wrestling begin? 23 B.C.

Page 199

Comprehensive Curriculum - Grade 6

ANSWER KEY

Comprehension: Tennis, Anyone?

Historians say a form of tennis was played outdoors in England in the 16th century. In France, the game had a much, much earlier start. "Court tennis"—named such because royal courts of kings played it—was played indoors about 1000 A.D. Six hundred years later, indoor tennis was still in full swing. Records show there were 2,500 indoor tennis courts in France at that time.

French tennis players and spectators took the game seriously. In 1780, the surgeon general of the French army recommended the game as one good for the lungs and throat. Why? Because of all the loud screaming and shouting that accompanied French games!

The word **tennis** comes from the French term **tenir**, which means "take heed" or "watch out." That's what the French yelled out centuries ago when they used huge racquets to whack balls over a sagging net. Later, when the game was adopted in England, **tenir** became **tennis**.

Tennis is said to have come to America by way of the island of Bermuda. A young American girl, Mary Outerbridge, played the game when visiting Bermuda in 1873. She brought tennis racquets, balls, and a net home to New York with her. The strange equipment puzzled customs officials (government employees who check travelers' bags to make sure they are not smuggling drugs or other substances). They reluctantly permitted Miss Outerbridge to bring the weird game to America, where it has flourished ever since!

Directions: Answer these questions about tennis.

1. In what year were there 2,500 indoor tennis courts in France? **1600**

2. In 1780, who recommended tennis as good for the lungs and throat?
the surgeon general of the French army

3. What does the French word **tenir** mean?
"take heed" or "watch out"

4. In what state was tennis first played in America? **New York**

5. The person who brought tennis to America was
☐ Marlene Outbridge. ☐ Mary Outbridge. ☒ Mary Outerbridge.

Page 200

Comprehension: Boxing History

The first known boxers were the ancient Greeks, who "toughened up" young men by making them box with bare fists. Later, a length of leather was wrapped around their hands and forearms to protect them. Although the sport was brutal, in ancient Greece, boxers who killed their opponents received a stiff punishment.

During the Middle Ages—from 500 to 1500 A.D.—boxing fell out of favor. It became popular in England about 100 years later, when the new middle class had the time and money for sports. Boxers would travel to matches held at inns and bars, and their loyal fans would follow. No gloves were used in the early 1600s in England. Instead, like the ancient Greeks, boxers used bare fists—something new—wrestling holds. Carrier pigeons with messages tied to their bodies were trained to take news of the fights back to the boxers' hometowns.

Because so many people were badly hurt or killed, padded boxing gloves began to be used in the United States around 1880. Boxing became fashionable—and safer. Harvard University offered boxing as an intramural sport in the 1880s. U.S. President Theodore Roosevelt's love of the sport helped to further popularize it. It's said that Roosevelt boxed regularly with a former heavyweight champion named Mike Donovan.

During World War I, boxing was part of the required training for army recruits. The Golden Gloves championship matches for boys, which began in the 1930s, also helped spread the sport's popularity.

Directions: Answer these questions about boxing history.

1. What people were known as the first boxers? **the ancient Greeks**
2. During what period did boxing fall out of favor? **during the Middle Ages**
3. What university offered boxing as a sport in the 1880s? **Harvard University**
4. Which U.S. president enjoyed boxing? **Theodore Roosevelt**
5. In England in the 1600s, news about boxing was sent via
☐ telegrams. ☒ carrier pigeons. ☐ messengers.
6. The Golden Gloves championships were first offered
☒ in the 1930s. ☐ during World War I. ☐ during World War II.

Page 201

Comprehension: Sports Summaries

Directions: Write a short paragraph summarizing each selection below.

Wrestling Around the World _____ Answers will vary.

_____

Tennis, Anyone? _____
_____
_____

Boxing History _____
_____
_____

Of the sports listed above, which is your favorite? Why? ____
_____
_____
_____
_____

Page 202

Main Idea: Bowling Is a Ball

Like tennis and boxing, bowling is also a very old sport. It began in Germany about nine centuries ago. Bowling was first played outdoors with wooden pins and a bowling ball made from a rounded rock.

The first players were church members who bowled with Catholic bishops and priests. Those who bowled a good game were said to be blessed. Those who bowled poorly were believed to have sinned and should improve themselves to improve their games! The name of the game in 11th-century Germany was **Kegelspiel**.

By the late 19th century, bowling was the most popular sport in Germany. A common expression for a person who had died was that he was "bowled out."

The game was introduced to America by way of Holland, where the Dutch had learned bowling from the Germans. Some Dutch citizens brought the game to Manhattan Island in 1623. The first bowling alley—outdoors, of course—opened in New York City more than 100 years later in 1732. Today, bowling is one of the most popular American sports. People who have never put on boxing gloves or raised a tennis racquet have, at one time or another, lifted and rolled a bowling ball.

Directions: Answer these questions about bowling.

1. Circle the main idea:
[Bowling is a very old and popular sport.]
Bad bowlers are sinners who should clean up their acts.

2. Who brought bowling to the United States? **the Dutch**
3. What was bowling called in Germany? **Kegelspiel**
4. What were the first bowling balls made from? **a rounded rock**
5. The first American bowling alley opened in 1732 in what city? **New York City**
6. In 19th-century Germany, what was the meaning of the expression "bowled out"?
a person who had died

Page 203

Comprehension: Facts About Football

Like tennis courts, football fields are usually laid out in a north-south fashion so the sun doesn't shine directly into one team's eyes. The field is 120 yards long and 53⅓ yards wide, with a goalpost at each end that is at least 20 feet high.

Regulation-size footballs are 11 inches long and must weigh at least 14 ounces. The object of the game is for one team of 11 to score more points than the opposing team. There are four ways to score points in football.

A touchdown, worth six points, is scored by carrying the ball across the opponent's goal line or by completing a forward pass in the opponent's end zone. When a team makes a touchdown, it gets the chance to make one or two extra points via a play executed from the 2- or 3-yard line. A field goal, worth three points, is made by kicking the ball from the field over the crossbar of the opponent's goal. A way to earn two points is through a play called a safety.

Football games are 60 minutes long and are divided into four quarters of 15 minutes each. Because of all the commercials and instant replays, televised games seem much longer. For college games, the halftime shows also take a lot of time.

Traditionally, college football games are played on Saturday afternoons, and high school games are played on Friday nights. Professional games are played on Sundays, as well as a few nights throughout the week.

Directions: Answer these questions about football.

1. How long is a regulation football? **11 inches long**
2. How long is a football field? **120 yards long**
3. How many players are on a football team? **11 players**
4. A field goal is worth
☐ one point. ☐ two points. ☒ three points.
5. A touchdown is worth
☐ two points. ☐ three points. ☒ six points.
6. Football games are **60** minutes long
with four **15** -minute quarters.

Page 204

Giving Directions: A Perfect Softball Pitch

A good softball pitcher makes the skill look effortless and graceful. In fact, there are very specific things a softball pitcher must do before, during, and after he or she throws the ball.

Before throwing, the pitcher must have both feet firmly on the ground and be in contact with the pitcher's plate for at least one second. At the beginning of the pitch, the ball must be held in both hands in front of the body. It must be held this way for no longer than 20 seconds. While making the pitch, the pitcher must keep one foot on the ground. Until the ball leaves his or her hands, the pitcher cannot take more than one step toward the batter.

A correct softball pitch looks remarkably like the pitch used to throw horseshoes. As with horseshoes, there is a graceful follow-through with the hand and arm once the ball leaves the pitcher's hand.

There are several types of softball pitches. They include the drop, the slow ball, and the out-curve. The drop is the fastest pitch. The pitcher's hand is behind the ball in this pitch. For the slow ball, the pitcher grips the ball between his or her thumb and little finger. He or she puts the knuckles of the three middle fingers against the ball. When the out-curve ball is thrown, the pitcher thrusts the thumb back and rotates all of his or her fingers out.

Directions: Follow these instructions about softball.

1. Give directions on what to do before pitching a softball.
Place both feet firmly on the ground. Be in contact with the pitcher's plate for at least 1 second. Hold the ball in both hands for no more than 20 seconds.

2. Give directions on how to throw a slow ball. **Grip the ball between the thumb and little fingers with the knuckles of the three middle fingers against the ball.**

3. Give directions on how to throw an out-curve ball. **Thrust the thumb back, and rotate all fingers out.**

Page 205

Comprehensive Curriculum - Grade 6

490

Comprehension: Volleyball

Volleyball began in Italy during the Middle Ages and was introduced to Germany in 1893. Germans called the sport **faustball**. Two years later, an American physical education teacher named William Morgan made some changes in **faustball** and brought the new game to Americans as **mintonette**.

In **faustball**, the ball was permitted to bounce twice before being hit back over the net. In **mintonette**, as in modern volleyball, no bounces were allowed. Shortly after Morgan introduced the sport, the director of a YMCA convinced him to change the name to something easier to pronounce. To "volley" a ball means to keep it in the air, and that's what volleyball players try to do.

A volleyball court is 60 feet long by 30 feet wide. It's divided in half by an 8-foot-high net. There are six players on each team, standing three by three across on each side of the net; however, the same person may not hit the ball two times in a row. If the serve is not returned, the team that served gets the point.

The most popular serve is the underhand. The server stands with the left foot forward, right knee bent, weight on the right foot. He or she leans slightly forward. The ball is in the partly extended left hand. The server strikes the ball off the left hand with the right hand. (Left-handers use the opposite hands and feet.) The first team to get 15 points wins the game.

Directions: Answer these questions about volleyball.

1. Circle the main idea:

Volleyball is a sport that requires a lot of strength.

(Volleyball is a simple game with six players on opposing sides)

2. A valid generalization about volleyball is:

a. It's safe, requires little equipment, and can be played by all ages.

b. It's dangerous, difficult to learn, and appeals only to children.

c. It's dull, slow, and takes players a long time to earn 15 points.

3. Give directions on how to deliver an underhand serve.

Stand with the left foot forward, right knee bent, and weight on the right foot. Lean forward slightly, and strike the ball off the left hand with the right hand.

Page 206

Comprehension: Comparing Sports

Directions: Read each paragraph. Then, answer the questions comparing field hockey, basketball, and softball.

My sister is more interested in sports than I am. Last year, she lettered in field hockey, basketball, and softball. I got my exercise walking to school.

1. What sports did the writer play? none

My sister's favorite sport is field hockey. Because it requires constant running up and down a field, it provides more exercise than basketball and softball. There's also more danger, because every year someone gets her teeth knocked out with a hockey stick. So far at our school, no one has lost any teeth in basketball or softball.

2. Compared to basketball and softball, field hockey provides one benefit and one danger. Name them.

It provides more exercise. Every year someone gets her teeth knocked out.

On the other hand, softball players—especially those who play the outfield—can occasionally take some time to daydream. With an ace strikeout pitcher and batters who can't hit far, outfielders' gloves don't get much of a workout.

3. What sports do not allow time for daydreaming?

field hockey and basketball

Write a short paragraph telling which sport you like best and why.

Answers will vary.

Page 207

Famous Athletes

Athletes are often heroes to young and old alike. Their stories are sometimes about triumph over amazing odds to become one of the best in their sport. Before beginning the section, answer the following questions as a warm-up.

1. What sport most interests you? Why?

Answers will vary.

2. What sports figure do you most admire? Why?

3. In your opinion, what makes a person a hero?

4. Try to name a sports legend for each of the sports listed below.

Track and field

Swimming

Boxing

Baseball

Speed skating

Tennis

Page 208

Hitting the Slopes

Directions: Read the selection. Then, answer the questions.

Lindsey Vonn was born to be a skier. She began learning the sport when she was only two years old. Vonn was so talented that her father moved the entire family from Minnesota to Colorado when she was 10. He knew that Colorado was the place to be if Lindsey had a chance of exploring her potential as a skier. Vonn started racing at the age of 7 and won her first competition when she was only 14 years old.

Vonn made her Olympic debut in 2002. Just before the next Olympics in 2006, she was injured. Despite the pain, Vonn was able to ski, and even to place. For the next few years, she worked hard and was prepared for the 2010 Olympics in Vancouver, Canada. Vonn was thrilled to realize a dream: to win a gold medal in the downhill event! In addition, she won a bronze in the Super-G (short for the "super-giant slalom," a downhill event). Lindsey Vonn was becoming known as one of the world's most talented female skiers.

In 2013, Vonn was injured again. This time, her injury resulted in reconstructive knee surgery. Although she skied competitively after her surgery, Vonn's knee continued to give her trouble. It was a hard decision to make, but she knew she'd be unable to compete in the 2014 Winter Olympics. Despite her injuries, Lindsey Vonn has had an impressive career. In addition to her Olympic medals, she has won almost 60 World Cup victories and inspired female athletes worldwide.

1. Summarize the selection in three sentences.

Answers will vary.

2. Define the following words:

potential: a quality that can be developed into something better

debut: a first appearance

reconstructive: rebuilding or reassembling

3. What are four words you could use to describe Lindsey Vonn? Possible answers:

hardworking   dedicated   talented   competitive

Page 209

Speed Skating

Directions: Read the selection. Then, answer the questions.

Imagine racing around a rink of glassy ice with only a thin blade of metal supporting you. Now, imagine skating so fast that you set a world record! That's exactly what speed skater Bonnie Blair has done all of her life.

Bonnie started skating before she was walking—on the shoulders of her older brothers and sisters. By the time she was 4, Bonnie was competing. At age 7, Bonnie won the 1971 Illinois state championships and dreamed of becoming an Olympian.

That opportunity soon came. Bonnie competed in the 1988, 1992, and 1994 Olympics. She won a gold medal in the 500-meter race and a bronze medal in the 1,000-meter race in 1988, golds in both the 500- and 1,000-meter races in 1992 and repeated the two golds in 1994. Only two other U.S. women have ever won five gold medals in the Olympics in any sport. Bonnie Blair is truly a champion!

1. Define the following words:

opportunity: a favorable combination of circumstances, time and place

meter: the basic metric unit of length (equals 39.37 inches)

2. Bonnie Blair competed over a period of six years in the Olympics. What qualities would be necessary to maintain the physical and mental condition to compete for so long?

Answers will vary.

3. Bonnie Blair participated in long-track skating, in which she raced with one other person against a clock for the best time. Do you think this would be easier or more difficult than racing a group to finish first? Why?

Answers will vary.

4. In your opinion, what makes a good athlete?

Answers will vary.

Page 210

Baseball

Directions: Read the selection. Then, answer the questions.

Babe Ruth was born George Herman Ruth in 1895. His family lived in Baltimore, Maryland, and was quite poor. He overcame poverty to become one of the greatest baseball players of all time.

Babe Ruth's baseball career began with the Baltimore Orioles. He was a pitcher but also a tremendous batter. He later played for the Boston Red Sox and started his home-run hitting fame with 29 home runs in 1919.

In 1920, while playing for the New York Yankees, Babe Ruth hit 54 home runs. He had become very popular with baseball fans of all ages. Amazingly, by 1925, he was making more money than the president of the United States! His home-run record of 60 home runs in a single season went unshattered until Roger Maris broke it in 1961 with 61 home runs.

Babe Ruth retired from baseball in 1935 with a career total of 714 home runs. He died in 1948 at age 53.

1. Summarize the selection in three sentences.

Answers will vary.

2. In the early 1900s, life expectancy was shorter than it is today. By today's standards, Babe Ruth died at a relatively young age. What factors have contributed to increased life expectancy?

Possible answers: better medical care, people are more educated about self-care, the invention of new medicines, better medical facilities

3. Create a time line of Babe Ruth's life beginning with his birth and ending with his death.

1895	1919	1920	1935	1948
Babe Ruth born	Babe Ruth hit 29 home runs with Boston Red Sox.	Babe Ruth hit 54 home runs with N.Y. Yankees	Babe Ruth retired with 714 home runs	Babe Ruth died

Page 211

Swimming

Directions: Read the selection. Then, answer the questions.

In 1968, 18-year-old Mark Spitz boasted that he would win six gold medals at the Olympics being held in Mexico. He won two golds in team relay events. After failing to achieve his goal, Spitz was determined to do better in the 1972 Olympics in Munich.

For the next four years, Mark Spitz trained ferociously. Indeed, at the 1972 Olympics, Spitz amazed the world by breaking all records and winning seven gold medals in seven different events. While doing so, he set new world record times in each event. Mark Spitz had accomplished his goal.

1. What feelings do you think Mark Spitz had after the 1968 Olympics?
Answers will vary.

2. What do you think is the moral to this story?

3. Many Olympians are as young as Mark Spitz was, and some participate at even younger ages. Write one paragraph detailing the advantages of being a young Olympian and one paragraph detailing the disadvantages.

Page 212

Boxing

Directions: Read the selection. Then, answer the questions.

Muhammad Ali was born Cassius Clay in Louisville, Kentucky, in 1942. He won the amateur Golden Gloves championship in 1959 and 1960 and went on to become the heavyweight champion of the 1960 Olympics. Four years later, he was champion of the world.

However, Ali's athletic fame came with its share of difficulties. He converted to the religion of Islam and thus changed his name from Cassius Clay to Muhammad Ali. Due to his Islamic beliefs, he refused to comply with the military draft for the Vietnam War. Therefore, he was stripped of his world title and banned from boxing from 1967 to 1970.

Ali regained his title in 1974 and won the world championship again in 1978. This accomplishment made Muhammad Ali the first heavyweight boxer to claim the world championship three times. Most notable about Ali's career is his total 56 wins in the ring with 37 knockouts.

1. Define the following words:
draft: to select, usually forcing someone to do something
banned: forbidden
amateur: a non-professional who engages in his/her pursuit for pleasure
notable: worthy of notice
comply: to go along with

2. Why is it necessary for a country to use the military draft?
Answers will vary.

3. Write a three-sentence summary of the selection.
Answers will vary.

Page 213

Tennis

Directions: Read the selection. Then, answer the questions.

Martina Navratilova gained fame as the best women's tennis player of the 1980s. She was born in Czechoslovakia in 1956 and moved to the United States at the age of 19. She became a United States citizen in 1981.

Martina Navratilova excelled in the sport of tennis, but she enjoyed the Wimbledon championship the most. She won the singles finals in 1978, 1979, 1982, 1983, 1984, 1985, 1986, 1987, and 1990.

In 1982, she became the first woman professional tennis player to earn over one million dollars in a single season.

1. What physical characteristics are necessary to excel in the sport of tennis?
Answers will vary.

2. In your opinion, why would an athlete from another country want to come to the U.S.A. to train and compete?

3. Many athletes find it difficult to adjust to their status as "heroes." What are some possible disadvantages to being an athletic superstar?

Page 214

Review

Directions: Follow the instructions for each section.

1. On the line below, create a time line of the years of birth for the six athletes discussed in this section.

| 1895 Babe Ruth | 1942 Cassius Clay | 1950 Mark Spitz | 1956 Martina Navratilova | 1964 Bonnie Blair | 1984 Lindsey Vonn |

2. What mental and emotional characteristics did all six athletes have in common?
Answers will vary.

3. On the line below, create a time line of Muhammad Ali's life.

| 1942 | M.A. won Golden Gloves Championship 1959 | M.A. won Olympics 1960 | 1964 | Heavyweight champion of the world | M.A. banned from boxing and stripped of world title 1967 | 1970 |

4. Compare and contrast the sports of tennis and baseball in a two-paragraph essay.
Answers will vary.

Page 215

Writing: My Sports Hero

Directions: Write a short essay about a man or woman you admire who has excelled in a sport. Make sure to give details about why you admire this person.
Answers will vary.

Directions: Interview an adult. Ask him or her about a sports figure he or she admired at your age. Write a short paragraph about this person's sports hero.

Page 216

Using Prior Knowledge: Poetry

Directions: Before reading about poetry in the following section, answer these questions.

1. Have you ever written a poem? If so, was it difficult to do? Why or why not?
Answers will vary.

2. Write a poem with rhyming verse.

3. Write a poem with unrhymed verse.

Page 217

Comprehension: Epitaphs

Epitaphs are verses written on tombstones and were very popular in the past. The following epitaphs were written by unknown authors.

On a Man Named Merideth
Here lies one blown out of breath
Who lived a merry life and died a Merideth.

On a Dentist
Stranger, approach this spot with gravity;
John Brown is filling his last cavity.

On Leslie Moore
Here lies what's left
Of Leslie Moore
No Les
No more

R I P
Here he rests
in eternal slumber.
In his coffin
six feet under.

Directions: Answer these questions about the epitaphs.

1. What does the phrase "blown out of breath" mean? _____
dead—no longer breathing

2. What does the author mean when he says "and died a Merideth"?
This is a play on words –the person's name and "merry death."

3. What cavity is John Brown filling? the grave

4. Write an epitaph of your own.
Answers will vary.

Page 218

Comprehension: "The Ant and the Cricket"

A silly young cricket, who decided to sing
Through the warm sunny months of summer and spring,
Began to complain when he found that at home
His cupboards were empty and winter had come.

At last by starvation the cricket made bold
To hop through the wintertime snow and the cold.
Away he set off to a miserly ant
To see if to keep him alive he would grant
Shelter from rain, a mouthful of grain.
"I wish only to borrow—I'll repay it tomorrow—
If not, I must die of starvation and sorrow!"

Said the ant to the cricket, "It's true I'm your friend,
But we ants never borrow, we ants never lend;
We ants store up crumbs so when winter arrives
We have just enough food to keep ants alive."

Directions: Use context clues to answer these questions about the poem.

1. What is the correct definition of **cupboards**?

☐ where books are stored ☒ where food is stored ☐ where shoes are stored

2. What is the correct definition of **miserly**?

☒ selfish/stingy ☐ generous/kind ☐ mean/ugly

3. What is the correct definition of **grant**?

☐ to take away ☐ to belch ☒ to give

4. In two sentences, describe what the poet is trying to say with this poem.
Answers will vary.

Page 219

Comprehension: "The Elf and the Dormouse"

Under a toadstool
Crept a wee elf
Out of the rain
To shelter himself.

Under the toadstool
Sound asleep
Sat a big dormouse
All in a heap.

Trembled the wee elf
Frightened, and yet
Fearing to fly away
Lest he got wet.

To the next shelter
Maybe a mile!
Sudden the wee elf
Smiled a wee smile,

Tugged 'til the toadstool
Toppled in two,
Holding it over him
Gaily he flew.

Soon he was safe home,
Dry as could be;
Soon woke the dormouse
"Good gracious me!"

"Where is my toadstool?"
Loud he lamented.
And that's when umbrellas
First were invented.

—Oliver Herford

Directions: Use context clues or a dictionary to answer these questions about the poem.

1. This humorous poem tells about what invention? umbrellas

2. What do you think a **dormouse** is? a small mouse

3. What is the correct definition of **lamented**? said sadly

4. Write a two-verse poem below describing the invention of a useful object.
Answers will vary.

Page 220

Comprehension: "The Eagle"

Personification is a figure of speech in which human characteristics are given to an animal or object.

Example: The trees danced in the wind

Trees do not dance; therefore, the trees are being personified.

He clasps the crag with crooked hands;
Close to the sun in lonely lands,
Ringed with the azure world, he stands.

The wrinkled sea beneath him crawls;
He watches from his mountain walls,
And like a thunderbolt he falls.

—Alfred, Lord Tennyson

Directions: Answer these questions about the poem.

1. What is the correct definition of **crag**? a steep, rugged, rocky cliff

2. What is the correct definition of **azure**? blue

3. Which phrases in the poem show personification?
crooked hands, wrinkled sea . . . crawls, he stands

4. Explain what one of these phrases actually means.
Answers will vary.

5. What is the author trying to say in the last line of the poem?
The eagle is powerful and swoops down from the sky very quickly.

Page 221

Comprehension: Proverbs

Proverbs are bits of advice for daily life. The following proverbs were written by Benjamin Franklin in 1732. They were published in Poor Richard's Almanack.

1. Keep conscience clear,
Then never fear.

2. Little strokes
Fell great oaks.

3. From a slip of foot you may soon recover,
But a slip of the tongue you may never get over.

4. Doing an injury puts you below your enemy;
Revenging one makes you but even with him;
Forgiving it sets you above him.

Directions: Explain the meaning of each proverb.
Possible answers:

1. You don't have to worry if you do nothing wrong.

2. Persistence can accomplish great deeds. Break large jobs into smaller ones.

3. If you say the wrong thing at the wrong time, it may change your life.

4. If you hurt someone, you are less of a person. If you seek revenge, you are as bad as your enemy. If you forgive, you are a better person.

Write a proverb of your own.
Answers will vary.

Page 222

Comprehension: Limericks

A **limerick** is a humorous verse consisting of five lines. The first, second, and fifth lines rhyme, and the third and fourth lines rhyme.

Old Man from Peru
There was an old man from Peru,
Who dreamed he was eating his shoe.
In the midst of the night
He awoke in a fright
And—good grief!—it was perfectly true.

Old Man from Darjeeling
There was an old man from Darjeeling,
Who boarded a bus bound for Ealing.
He saw on the door:
"Please don't spit on the floor."
So he stood up and spat on the ceiling.

Directions: Answer these questions about these silly limericks.

1. In "Old Man from Peru," what was perfectly true? _____
He was eating his shoe.

2. How did the old man from Peru feel when he awoke? He was frightened.

3. In "Old Man from Darjeeling," what is Ealing? a city/town

4. Did the old man from Darjeeling break any rules? no

Write your own silly limerick below.
Answers will vary.

Page 223

Comprehension: "The Tyger"

Imagery is a picture that comes into the reader's mind when reading certain words.

Tyger! Tyger! burning bright
In the forests of the night,
What immortal hand or eye
Could frame thy fearful symmetry?

In what distant deeps or skies
Burnt the fire of thine eyes?
On what wings dare he aspire?
What the hand dare seize the fire?

And what shoulder, and what art,
Could twist the sinew of thy heart,
And when thy heart began to beat,
What dread hand? and what dread feet?

What the hammer? what the chain?
In what furnace was thy brain?
What the anvil? what dread grasp
Dare its deadly terrors clasp?

When the stars threw down their spears,
And watered heaven with their tears,
Did he smile his work to see?
Did he who made the lamb make thee?

Tyger! Tyger! burning bright
In the forests of the night,
What immortal hand or eye,
Dare frame thy fearful symmetry?

—William Blake

Directions: Use context clues or a dictionary to answer these questions about the poem.

1. What is the correct definition of **symmetry**?
in balance—one side the same as the other

2. What is the correct definition of **immortal**?
eternal, undying

3. What is the correct definition of **aspire**?
to be eager to achieve

4. What is the correct definition of **sinew**?
physical strength or tendon

5. What is the correct definition of **anvil**?
an iron blacksmiths use to hammer metal upon

6. What is some imagery in this poem?
Answers will vary.

Page 224

Comprehension: Old Gaelic Lullaby

A **Gaelic lullaby** is an ancient Irish or Scottish song some parents sing as they rock their babies to sleep.

Hush! The waves are rolling in,
White with foam, white with foam,
Father works amid the din,
But baby sleeps at home.

Hush! The winds roar hoarse and deep—
On they come, on they come!
Brother seeks the wandering sheep,
But baby sleeps at home.

Hush! The rain sweeps over the fields,
Where cattle roam, where cattle roam,
Sister goes to seek the cows,
But baby sleeps at home.

Directions: Answer these questions about the Gaelic lullaby.

1. What is Father doing while baby sleeps? Father is working.

2. What is Brother doing? Brother is looking for the wandering sheep.

3. What is Sister doing? Sister goes to look for the cows.

4. What do we assume Mother is doing? Answers will vary.

5. Is it quiet or noisy while Father works? ☐ quiet ☒ noisy

6. Which is not mentioned in the poem?
☐ wind ☒ sunshine ☐ waves ☐ rain

Page 225

Comprehension: "The Lark and the Wren"

"Goodnight, Sir Wren!" said the little lark.
"The daylight fades; it will soon be dark.
I've sung my hymn to the parting day,
So now I fly to my quiet glen
In yonder meadow—Goodnight, Wren!"

"Goodnight, poor Lark," said the haughty wren,
With a flick of his wing toward his happy friend.
"I also go to my rest profound
But not to sleep on the cold, damp ground.
The fittest place for a bird like me
Is the topmost bough of a tall pine tree."

Directions: Use context clues for these definitions.

1. What is the correct definition of **hymn**?
☐ whisper ☒ song ☐ opposite of her

2. What is the correct definition of **yonder**?
☒ distant ☐ mountaintop ☐ seaside

3. What is the correct definition of **haughty**?
☐ happy ☐ friendly ☒ pompous

4. What is the correct definition of **profound**?
☐ restless ☒ deep ☐ uncomfortable

5. What is the correct definition of **bough**?
☐ to bend over ☐ tree roots ☒ tree branch

6. Write another verse of the poem. Answers will vary.

Page 226

Nouns

A **noun** names a person, place, thing, or idea. There are several types of nouns.

Examples:
proper nouns: Joe, Jefferson Memorial
common nouns: dog, town
concrete nouns: book, stove
abstract nouns: fear, devotion
collective nouns: audience, flock

A word can be more than one type of noun.

Example: Dog is both a common and a concrete noun.

Directions: Write the type or types of each noun on the lines.

1. desk common, concrete
2. ocean common, concrete
3. love common, abstract
4. cat common, concrete
5. herd common, concrete, collective
6. compassion common, abstract
7. reputation common, abstract
8. eyes common, concrete
9. staff common, concrete, collective
10. day common, concrete
11. Roosevelt Building proper, concrete
12. Mr. Timken proper, concrete
13. life common, abstract
14. porch common, concrete
15. United States proper, concrete or abstract

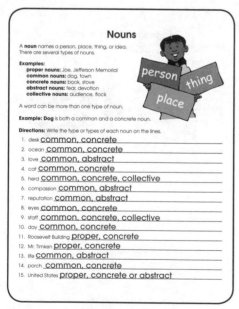

Page 228

Possessive Nouns

A **possessive** noun owns something. To make a singular noun possessive, add an apostrophe and **s**. **Example:** mayor**'s** campaign

To make a plural noun possessive when it already ends with **s**, add only an apostrophe. **Example:** dogs**'** tails

To make a plural noun possessive when it doesn't end with **s**, add an apostrophe and **s**. **Example:** men**'s** shirts

Directions: Write the correct form of the word for each sentence in the group. Words may be singular, plural, singular possessive, or plural possessive. The first one has been done for you.

teacher
1. How many teachers does your school have?
2. Where is the teacher's coat?
3. All the teachers' mailboxes are in the school office.

reporter
4. Two reporters were assigned to the story.
5. One reporter's car boke down on the way to the scene.
6. The other reporter was riding as a passenger.
7. Both reporters' notes ended up missing.

child
8. The children are hungry.
9. How much spaghetti can one child eat?
10. Put this much on each child's plate.
11. The children's spaghetti is ready for them.

mouse
12. Some mice made a nest under those boards.
13. I can see the mouse's or mice's hole from here.
14. A baby mouse has wandered away from the nest.
15. The mouse's mother is coming to get it.

Page 229

Verbs

A **verb** is a word that tells what something does or that something exists.

There are two types of verbs: **action** and **state of being**.

Examples:
Action: run, read, choose, wash, push, cut, drive, laugh, scream, reach
State of being: feel, sound, taste, stay, look, appear, grow, seem, smell, and forms of **be**

Directions: Write **A** if the verb shows action. Write **S** if it shows state of being.

1. A He helped his friend.
2. S They appear happy and content.
3. A Jordi drives to school each day.
4. A The snowfall closed schools everywhere.
5. A The dog sniffed at its food.
6. S The meat tastes funny.
7. A Did you taste the fruit salad?
8. A The young boy smelled the flowers.
9. S She looked depressed.
10. A The coach announced the dates of the scrimmage.
11. A The owner of the store stocks all types of sports equipment.
12. A He dribbled the ball down the court.
13. S Everything seems to be in order.

Page 230

Verb Tense

Tense is the way a verb is used to express time. To explain what is happening right now, use the **present tense**.

Example: He **is singing** well. He **sings** well.

To explain what has already happened, use the **past tense**.

Example: He **sang** well.

To explain what will happen, use the **future tense**.

Example: He **will sing** well.

Directions: Rewrite each sentence so the verbs are in the same tense. The first one has been done for you.

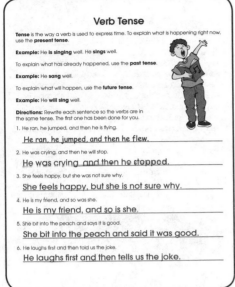

1. He ran, he jumped, and then he is flying.

   He ran, he jumped, and then he flew.

2. He was crying, and then he will stop.

   He was crying and then he stopped.

3. She feels happy, but she is not sure why.

   She feels happy, but she is not sure why.

4. He is my friend, and so was she.

   He is my friend, and so is she.

5. She bit into the peach and says it is good.

   She bit into the peach and said it was good.

6. He laughs first and then told us the joke.

   He laughs first and then tells us the joke.

Page 231

Spelling Different Forms of Verbs

is/are + verb + ing
was/were + verb + ing

To show that something is happening in the present, we can use the base form of a verb, or we can use **is** or **are** and add **ing** to the verb.

Example: We **run**. We **are running**.

To show that something has already happened, we can add **ed** to many verbs, or we can use **was** or **were** and add **ing** to a verb.

Example: The workers **surveyed** the land. The workers **surveying** the land.

If a verb ends in **e**, drop the final **e** before adding an ending that begins with a vowel.

Example: She is **driving**. He **restored** the old car.

If a verb ends in **sh** or **ch**, add **es** instead of **s** to change the form.

Example: He **furnishes**. She **watches**.

Directions: Complete each sentence with the correct form of the verb given. The first one has been done for you.

1. The florist is (have) a sale this week. having
2. Last night's tornado (destroy) a barn. destroyed
3. We are (research) the history of our town. researching
4. My mistake was (use) a plural verb instead of a singular one. using
5. She (act) quickly in yesterday's emergency. acted
6. Our group is (survey) the parents in our community. surveying
7. For our last experiment, we (observe) a plant's growth for two weeks. observed
8. A local company already (furnish) all the materials for this project. furnished
9. Which dairy (furnish) milk to our cafeteria every day? furnishes
10. Just (ignore) the mess in here will not help your case. ignoring

Page 232

Verb Tense
Answers will vary.

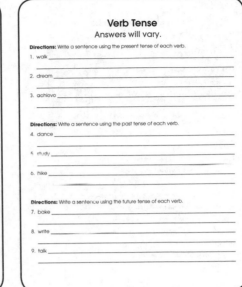

Directions: Write a sentence using the present tense of each verb.

1. walk
2. dream
3. achieve

Directions: Write a sentence using the past tense of each verb.

4. dance
5. study
6. hike

Directions: Write a sentence using the future tense of each verb.

7. bake
8. write
9. talk

Page 233

Verb Tense

Verbs can be **present**, **past**, or **past participle**.

Add **d** or **ed** to form the past tense.

Past-participle verbs also use a helping verb, such as **has** or **have**.

Examples:

Present	Past	Past Participle
help	helped	has or have helped
skip	skipped	has or have skipped

Directions: Write the past and past-participle forms of each present tense verb.

Present	Past	Past Participle
1. paint	painted	has (have) painted
2. dream	dreamed	has (have) dreamed
3. play	played	has (have) played
4. approach	approached	has (have) approached
5. hop	hopped	has (have) hopped
6. climb	climbed	has (have) climbed
7. dance	danced	has (have) danced
8. appear	appeared	has (have) appeared
9. watch	watched	has (have) watched
10. dive	dove/dived	has (have) dived
11. hurry	hurried	has (have) hurried
12. discover	discovered	has (have) discovered
13. decorate	decorated	has (have) decorated
14. close	closed	has (have) closed
15. jump	jumped	has (have) jumped

Page 234

Irregular Verb Forms

The past tense of most verbs is formed by adding **ed**. Verbs that do not follow this format are called **irregular verbs**.

The irregular verb chart shows a few of the many verbs with irregular forms.

Irregular Verb Chart

Present Tense	Past Tense	Past Participle
go	went	has, have, or had gone
do	did	has, have, or had done
fly	flew	has, have, or had flown
grow	grew	has, have, or had grown
ride	rode	has, have, or had ridden
see	saw	has, have, or had seen
sing	sang	has, have, or had sung
swim	swam	has, have, or had swum
throw	threw	has, have, or had thrown

The words **had**, **have**, and **has** can be separated from the irregular verb by other words in the sentence.

Directions: Choose the correct verb form from the chart to complete the sentences. The first one has been done for you.

1. The pilot had never before __flown__ that type of plane.
2. She put on her bathing suit and __swam__ 2 miles.
3. The tall boy had __grown__ 2 inches over the summer.
4. She insisted she had __done__ her homework.
5. He __saw__ them walking down the street.
6. She __rode__ the horse around the track.
7. The pitcher has __thrown__ the ball many times.
8. He can __swim__ safely in the deepest water.

Page 235

Irregular Verb Forms

Directions: Use the irregular verb chart on the previous page. Write the correct verb form to complete each sentence.

1. Has she ever __grown__ carrots in her garden?
2. She was so angry she __threw__ a tantrum.
3. The bird had sometimes __flown__ from its cage.
4. The cowboy has never __ridden__ that horse before.
5. Will you __go__ to the store with me?
6. He said he had often __seen__ her walking on his street.
7. She insisted she has not __grown__ taller this year.
8. He __swam__ briskly across the pool.
9. Have the insects __flown__ away?
10. Has anyone __seen__ my sister lately?
11. He hasn't __done__ the dishes once this week!
12. Has she been __thrown__ out of the game for cheating?
13. I haven't __seen__ her yet today.
14. The airplane __flew__ slowly by the airport.
15. Have you __ridden__ your bike yet this week?

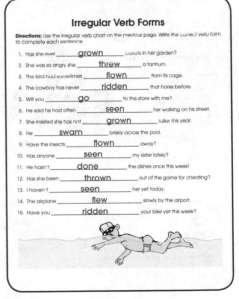

Page 236

Nouns and Verbs

Some words can be used as both nouns and verbs.

Example:
The **bait** on his hook was a worm.
He couldn't **bait** his hook.

In the first sentence, **bait** is used as a **noun** because it names a thing. In the second sentence, **bait** is used as a **verb** because it shows action.

Directions: Write **noun** or **verb** for the word in bold in each sentence. The first one has been done for you.

verb 1. She **piloted** the small plane across the Pacific Ocean.

verb 2. Does she **water** her garden every night?

verb 3. Did you **rebel** against the rules?

noun 4. Dad will pound the fence **post** into the ground.

noun 5. That was good **thinking**!

verb 6. I **object** to your language!

noun 7. He planned to become a **pilot** after graduation.

verb 8. The teacher will **post** the new school calendar.

verb 9. She was **thinking** of a book she read last week.

noun 10. The **object** of the search was forgotten.

noun 11. She was a **rebel** in high school.

noun 12. Would you like fresh **water** for your tea?

Page 237

Spelling: Plurals

Is **heros** or **heroes** the correct spelling? Many people aren't sure. These rules have exceptions, but they will help you spell the plural forms of most words that end with **o**.
• If a word ends with a consonant and **o**, add **es**: heroes.
• If a word ends with a vowel and **o**, add **s**: radios.

Here are some other spelling rules for plurals:
• If a word ends with **s, ss, x, ch,** or **sh**, add **es**: buses, kisses, taxes, peaches, wishes.
• If a word ends with **f** or **fe**, drop the **f** or **fe** and add **ves**: leaf, leaves; wife, wives.
• Some plurals don't end with **s** or **es**: geese, deer, children.

Directions: Write the plural forms of the words.

1. Our area doesn't often have (tornado). tornadoes

2. How many (radio) does this store sell every month? radios

3. (Radish) are the same color as apples. Radishes

4. Does this submarine carry (torpedo)? torpedoes

5. Hawaii has a number of active (volcano). volcanoes

6. Did you pack (knife) in the picnic basket? knives

7. We heard (echo) when we shouted in the canyon. echoes

8. Where is the list of (address)? addresses

9. What will you do when that plant (reach) the ceiling? reaches

10. Sometimes my dad (fix) us milkshakes. fixes

11. Every night, my sister (wish) on the first star she sees. wishes

12. Who (furnish) the school with pencils and paper? furnishes

13. The author (research) every detail in her books. researches

Page 238

Spelling: Plurals

Directions: Write the plural form of each word.

1. mother — mothers
2. ankle — ankles
3. journey — journeys
4. ceiling — ceilings
5. governor — governors
6. arch — arches
7. carnival — carnivals
8. official — officials
9. potato — potatoes
10. vacuum — vacuums
11. stereo — stereos
12. strategy — strategies
13. column — columns
14. architect — architects
15. entry — entries
16. summary — summaries
17. issue — issues
18. member — members
19. astronomer — astronomers
20. channel — channels
21. harmony — harmonies
22. piece — pieces
23. chicken — chickens
24. chemical — chemicals
25. journal — journals
26. niece — nieces
27. mayor — mayors
28. particle — particles
29. entrance — entrances
30. assistant — assistants

Page 239

Simple Subjects

The **simple subject** of a sentence tells who or what the sentence is about. It is a noun or a pronoun.

Example: My mom is turning forty this year.
Mom is the simple subject.

Directions: Circle the simple subject in each sentence.

1. The **cat** ate all its food.
2. **They** watched the basketball game.
3. **Lucy** is going to lunch with her friend.
4. **Jose** likes strawberry jam on his toast.
5. The **reporter** interviewed the victim.
6. **She** turned down the volume.
7. The farm **animals** waited to be fed.
8. Can **you** lift weights?
9. The **fan** did little to cool the hot room.
10. **Thomas Jefferson** was one of the founding fathers of our country.
11. **I** have a lot to do tonight.
12. Will **you** go to the movie with us?
13. **We** enjoyed the day at the park.
14. Our **pet** is a dog.
15. **She** retrieved her homework from the garbage.

Page 240

Simple Predicates

The **simple predicate** of a sentence tells what the subject does, is doing, did, or will do. The simple predicate is always a verb.

Example:
My mom **is turning** forty this year.
Is turning is the simple predicate.

Directions: Underline the simple predicate in each sentence. Include all helping verbs.

1. I <u>bought</u> school supplies at the mall.
2. The tiger <u>chased</u> its prey.
3. Mark <u>will be arriving</u> shortly.
4. The hamburgers <u>are cooking</u> now.
5. We <u>will attend</u> my sister's wedding.
6. The dental hygienist <u>cleaned</u> my teeth.
7. My socks <u>are hanging</u> on the clothesline.
8. Where <u>are</u> you going?
9. The dog <u>is running</u> toward its owner.
10. Ramos <u>watched</u> the tornado in fear.
11. Please <u>wash</u> the dishes after dinner.
12. My dad <u>cleaned</u> the garage yesterday.
13. We <u>are going</u> hiking at Yellowstone today.
14. The picture <u>shows</u> our entire family at the family picnic.
15. Our coach <u>will give</u> us a pep talk before the game.

PREDICATES

Page 241

Parallel Structure

Parts of a sentence are **parallel** when they "match" grammatically and structurally.

Faulty parallelism occurs when the parts of a sentence do not match grammatically and structurally.

For sentences to be parallel, all parts of a sentence—including the verbs, nouns, and phrases—must match. This means that, in most cases, verbs should be in the same tense.

Examples:
Correct: She liked running, jumping, and swinging outdoors.
Incorrect: She liked running, jumping, and to swing outdoors.

In the correct sentence, all three of the actions the girl liked to do end in **ing**. In the incorrect sentence, they do not.

Directions: Rewrite the sentences so all elements are parallel. The first one has been done for you.

1. Politicians like making speeches and also to shake hands.
   Politicians like making speeches and shaking hands.

2. He liked singing, acting, and to perform in general.
   He liked singing, acting, and performing in general.

3. The soup had carrots, celery, and also has rice.
   The soup had carrots, celery, and rice.

4. The drink was cold, frosty, and also is a thirst-quencher.
   The drink was cold, frosty, and thirst-quenching.

5. She was asking when we would arrive, and I told her.
   She asked when we would arrive, and I told her.

6. Liz felt like shouting, singing, and to jump.
   Liz felt like shouting, singing, and jumping.

Page 242

Matching Subjects and Verbs

If the subject of a sentence is singular, the verb must be singular. If the subject is plural, the verb must be plural.

Example:
The **dog** with floppy ears **is eating**.
The **dogs** in the yard **are eating**.

Directions: Write the singular or plural form of the subject in each sentence to match the verb.

1. The (yolk) __yolk__ in this egg is bright yellow.
2. The (child) __children__ are putting numbers in columns.
3. Both (coach) __coaches__ are resigning at the end of the year.
4. Those three (class) __classes__ were assigned to the gym.
5. The (lunch) __lunches__ for the children are ready.
6. (Spaghetti) __Spaghetti__ with meatballs is delicious.
7. Where are the (box) __boxes__ of chalk?
8. The (man) __men__ in the truck were collecting broken tree limbs.
9. The (rhythm) __rhythm__ of that music is exactly right for dancing.
10. Sliced (tomato) __tomatoes__ on lettuce are good with salmon.
11. The (announcer) __announcer__ on TV was condemning the dictator.
12. Two (woman) __women__ are campaigning for mayor of our town.
13. The (group) __group__ of travelers was on its way to three foreign countries.
14. The (choir) __choir__ of thirty children is singing hymns.
15. In spite of the parade, the (hero) __heroes__ were solemn.

Page 243

Subject/Verb Agreement

Singular subjects require singular verbs. **Plural subjects** require plural verbs. The subject and verb must agree in a sentence.

Example:
Singular: My dog runs across the field.
Plural: My dogs run across the field.

Directions: Circle the correct verb in each sentence.

1. Maria (talk/**talks**) to me each day at lunch.
2. Mom, Dad, and I (is/**are**) going to the park to play catch.
3. Mr. and Mrs. Ramirez (**dance**/dances) well together.
4. Astronauts (**hope**/hopes) for a successful shuttle mission.
5. Trees (**prevent**/prevents) erosion.
6. The student (**is**/are) late.
7. She (ask/**asks**) for directions to the senior high gym.
8. The elephants (**plod**/plods) across the grassland to the watering hole.
9. My friend's name (**is**/are) Rebecca.
10. Many people (**enjoy**/enjoys) orchestra concerts.
11. The pencils (is/**are**) sharpened.
12. My backpack (hold/**holds**) a lot of things.
13. The wind (blow/**blows**) to the south.
14. Sam (collect/**collects**) butterflies.
15. They (**love**/loves) fresh strawberries.

Page 244

Personal Pronouns

Personal pronouns take the place of nouns. They refer to people or things. **I, me, we, she, he, him, her, you, they, them, us,** and **it** are personal pronouns.

Directions: Circle the personal pronouns in each sentence.

1. **He** is a terrific friend.
2. Would **you** open the door?
3. Jim and **I** will arrive at ten o'clock.
4. Can **you** pick **me** up at the mall after dinner?
5. What did **you** do yesterday?
6. **They** are watching the game on television.
7. Jessie's mom took **us** to the movies.
8. **She** writes novels.
9. **They** gave **us** the refrigerator.
10. Is this the answer **she** intended to give?
11. What is **it**?
12. The dog yelped when **it** saw the cat.
13. **I** admire **him**.
14. **We** parked the bikes by the tree.
15. The ants kept **us** from enjoying our picnic.

Page 245

Possessive Pronouns

Possessive pronouns show ownership. **My, mine, your, yours, his, her, hers, their, theirs, our, ours,** and **its** are possessive pronouns.

Directions: Circle the possessive pronouns in each sentence.

1. **My** dogs chase cats continually.
2. Keiko put **her** sunglasses on the dashboard.
3. **His** mother and **mine** are the same age.
4. The cat licked **its** paw.
5. **Their** anniversary is February 1.
6. This necklace is **yours**.
7. We will carry **our** luggage into the airport.
8. **Our** parents took us to dinner.
9. **My** brother broke **his** leg.
10. **Her** report card was excellent.
11. Raspberry jam is **my** favorite.
12. Watch **your** step!
13. The house on the left is **mine**.
14. **My** phone number is unlisted.
15. **Our** garden is growing out of control.
16. **Our** pumpkins are ten times larger than **theirs**.

Page 246

Interrogative Pronouns

An **interrogative pronoun** asks a question. There are three interrogative pronouns: **who, what,** and **which**.

Use **who** when speaking of people.
Use **what** when speaking of things.
Use **which** when speaking of people or things.

Examples:
Who will go? **What** will you do? **Which** of these is yours?

Who becomes **whom** when it is a direct object or an object of a preposition. The possessive form of **whom** is **whose**.

Examples:
To **whom** will you write?
Whose computer is that?

Directions: Write the correct interrogative pronoun.

1. __Whose__ wet raincoat is this?
2. __Who__ is the president of the United States?
3. __What__ is your name?
4. __Which/Whose__ dog made this muddy mess?
5. __Which/Whose__ cat ran away?
6. __Which__ of you is the culprit?
7. __What__ was your grade on the last test?
8. To __whom__ did you report?
9. __Whom__ do you believe now?
10. __Who__ is the leader of this English study group?

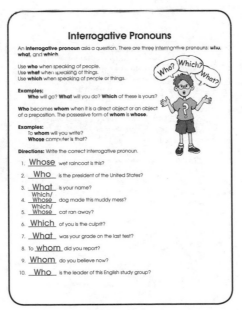

Page 247

Personal and Possessive Pronouns

Directions: Write personal or possessive pronouns in the blanks to take the place of the words in bold. The first one has been done for you.

__They, him__ 1.	**Maisie and Marni** told **Trent** they would see **him** later.
__He, them__ 2.	**Spencer** told **Amelia and Jada** good-bye.
__It, his__ 3.	**The bike** was parked near **Aaron's** house.
__They__ 4.	**Maria, Matt, and Greg** claimed the car was new.
__theirs__ 5.	The dishes were **the property of Gabriella and Jake**.
__hers__ 6.	Is this **Layla's**?
__He, their__ 7.	**Jon** walked near **Jessica and Esau's** house.
__It__ 8.	**The dog** barked all night long!
__She, her__ 9.	**Ana** fell and hurt **Ana's** knee.
__They, its__ 10.	**Cory and Devan** gave the dog **the dog's** dinner.
__We, them__ 11.	**Tori and I** gave **Brett and Reggie** a ride home.
__they__ 12.	Do **Josh and Andrea** like cats?
__They, us__ 13.	**Sasha and Keesha** gave **Josh and me** a ride home.
__hers__ 14.	Is this sweater **Chloe's**?
__it__ 15.	The cat meowed because **the cat** was hungry.

Page 248

Comprehensive Curriculum - Grade 6

Pronoun/Antecedent Agreement

Often, a **pronoun** is used in place of a noun to avoid repeating the noun again in the same sentence. The noun that a pronoun refers to is called its **antecedent**. The word **antecedent** means "going before."

If the noun is singular, the pronoun that takes its place must also be singular. If the noun is plural, the pronoun that takes its place must also be plural. This is called agreement between the pronoun and its antecedent.

Examples:
Kylie (singular noun) said **she** (singular pronoun) would dance.
The **dogs** (plural noun) took **their** (plural pronoun) dishes outside.

When the noun is singular and the gender unknown, it is correct to use **his or her.**

Directions: Rewrite the sentences so the pronouns and nouns agree. The first one has been done for you.

1. Every student opened their book.
   Every student opened his or her book.
2. Has anyone lost their wallet lately?
   Has anyone lost his or her wallet lately?
3. Somebody found the wallet under their desk.
   Somebody found the wallet under his or her desk.
4. Someone will have to file their report.
   Someone will have to file his or her report.
5. Every dog has their day!
   Every dog has its day!
6. I felt Ted had mine best interests at heart.
   I felt Ted had my best interests at heart.

Page 249

Pronoun/Antecedent Agreement

Directions: Write a pronoun that agrees with the antecedent.

1. Aiden said ___he___ would go to the store.
2. My friend discovered ___his or her___ wallet had been stolen.
3. The cat licked ___its___ paw.
4. Did any woman here lose ___her___ necklace?
5. Someone will have to give ___his or her___ report.
6. Aliyah wished ___she___ had not come.
7. All the children decided ___they___ would attend.
8. My grandmother hurt ___her___ back while gardening.
9. Jerry, Marco, and I hope ___we___ win the game.
10. Hailey looked for ___her___ missing homework.
11. The family had ___its___ celebration.
12. My dog jumps out of ___its___ pen.
13. Somebody needs to remove ___his or her___ clothes from this chair.
14. Everything has ___its___ place in Grandma's house.
15. The team will receive ___its___ uniforms on Monday.
16. Each artist wants ___his or her___ painting to win the prize.

Page 250

Appositives

An **appositive** is a noun or pronoun placed after another noun or pronoun to further identify or rename it. An appositive and the words that go with it are usually set off from the rest of the sentence with commas. Commas are not used if the appositive tells "which one."

Example: Angela's mother, **Ms. Glover**, will visit our school.

Commas are needed because **Ms. Glover** renames Angela's mother.

Example: Angela's neighbor Maggy will visit our school.

Commas are not needed because the appositive "Maggy" tells **which** neighbor.

Directions: Write the appositive in each sentence in the blank. The first one has been done for you.

___Ava___ 1. My friend Ava wants a horse.
___Horses___ 2. She subscribes to the magazine Horses.
___Brownie___ 3. Her horse is the gelding Brownie.
___a convertible___ 4. We rode in her new car, a convertible.
___a bracelet___ 5. Her gift was jewelry, a bracelet.
___the senator___ 6. Have you met Ms. Abbott, the senator?
___Karl___ 7. My cousin Karl is very shy.
___Oaties___ 8. Do you eat the cereal Oaties?
___Samantha___ 9. Kiki's cat, Samantha, will eat only tuna.
___Jones___ 10. My last name, Jones, is very common.

Page 251

Dangling Modifiers

A **dangling modifier** is a word or group of words that does not modify what it is supposed to modify. To correct dangling modifiers, supply the missing words to which the modifiers refer.

Examples:
Incorrect: While doing the laundry, the dog barked.
Correct: While I was doing the laundry, the dog barked.

In the **incorrect** sentence, it sounds as though the dog is doing the laundry. In the **correct** sentence, it's clear that **I** is the subject of the sentence.

Directions: Rewrite the sentences to make the subject of the sentence clear and eliminate dangling modifiers. The first one has been done for you.

1. While eating our dinner, the doctor called.
   While we were eating our dinner, the doctor called.
2. Living in Cincinnati, the ball park is nearby.
   I live in Cincinnati, and the ball park is nearby.
3. While watching the movie, the TV screen went blank.
   While we were watching the movie, the TV screen went blank.
4. While listening to the concert, the lights went out.
   While we were listening to the concert, the lights went out.
5. Tossed regularly, anyone can make great salad.
   Anyone can make a great salad if it is tossed regularly.
6. While working, something surprised him.
   While he was working, something surprised him.

Page 252

Review

Directions: Write **noun** or **verb** to describe the words in bold.

___noun___ 1. She is one of the fastest **runners** I've seen.
___verb___ 2. She is **running** very fast!
___verb___ 3. She **thought** he was handsome.
___noun___ 4. Please share your **thoughts** with me.
___verb___ 5. I will **watch** the volleyball game on video.
___noun___ 6. The sailor fell asleep during his **watch**.
___noun___ 7. My grandmother believes my purchase was a real **find**.
___verb___ 8. I hope to **find** my lost books.

Directions: Rewrite the verb in the correct tense.

___swam___ 9. She **swim** across the lake in 2 hours.
___ridden___ 10. He has **ride** horses for years.
___seen___ 11. Have you **saw** my sister?
___flew___ 12. She **fly** on an airplane last week.
___instructed___ 13. My father had **instruct** me in the language.
___drove___ 14. I **drive** to the store yesterday.
___began___ 15. The movie **begin** late.
___did___ 16. Where **do** you go yesterday?

Directions: Circle the pronouns.

17. She and I told them to forget it.
18. They all wondered if her dad would drive his new car.
19. We want our parents to believe us.
20. My picture was taken at her home.

Page 253

Review

Directions: Rewrite the sentences to correct the faulty parallels.

1. The fresh blueberries were sweet, juicy, and are delicious.
   The fresh blueberries were sweet, juicy, and delicious.
2. The town was barren, windswept, and is empty.
   The town was barren, windswept, and empty.
3. The dog was black, long-haired, and is quite friendly.
   The dog was black, long-haired, and quite friendly.
4. My favorite dinners are macaroni and cheese, spaghetti, and I loved fish.
   My favorite dinners are macaroni and cheese, spaghetti, and fish.

Directions: Rewrite the sentences to make the verb tenses consistent.

5. We laughed, cried, and were jumping for joy.
   We laughed, cried, and jumped for joy.
6. She sang, danced, and was doing somersaults.
   She sang, danced, and did somersaults.
7. The class researched, studied, and were writing their reports.
   The class researched, studied, and wrote their reports.
8. Orlando and Maya talked about their vacation and share their experiences.
   Orlando and Maya talked about their vacation and shared their experiences.

Directions: Circle the pronouns that agree with their antecedents.

9. She left her/their purse at the dance.
10. Each dog wagged its/their tail.
11. We walked to our/the car.
12. The lion watched his/its prey.

Page 254

Review

Directions: Rewrite the sentences to correct the dangling modifiers.

1. Living nearby, the office was convenient for her.

   She was living nearby, so the office was convenient for her.

2. While doing my homework, the doorbell rang.

   While I was doing my homework, the doorbell rang.

3. Watching over her shoulder, she hurried away.

   She watched over her shoulder as she hurried away.

4. Drinking from the large mug, he choked.

   While he was drinking from the large mug, he choked.

Directions: Circle the correct pronouns.

5. She laughed at my brother and (I, me).

6. Al Juwir, (he and I, him and me) were still talking.

7. Someone left (his or her, their) coat on the floor.

8. Lauren said (her, she) would not be late.

Directions: Circle the appositive.

9. The school nurse, Ms. Franklin, was worried about him.

10. The car, a Volkswagen, was illegally parked.

11. My hero, Babe Ruth, was an outstanding baseball player.

12. Is that car, the plum-colored one, for sale?

13. Will Mr. Zimmer, Todd's father, buy that car?

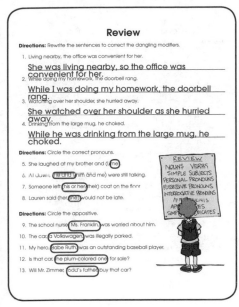

Page 255

Adjectives

Adjectives describe nouns.

Examples:
   tall girl
   soft voice
   clean hands

Directions: Circle the adjectives. Underline the nouns they describe. Some sentences may have more than one set of adjectives and nouns.

1. The lonely man sat in the dilapidated house.

2. I hope the large crop of grapes will soon ripen.

3. The white boxes house honeybees.

4. My rambunctious puppy knocked over the valuable flower vase.

5. The unsinkable Titanic sank after striking a gigantic iceberg.

6. His grades showed his tremendous effort.

7. There are many purple towers in the large arrangement.

8. These sweet peaches are the best I've tasted.

9. The newsletter describes several educational workshops.

10. The rodeo featured professional riders and funny clowns.

11. My evening pottery class is full of very interesting people.

12. My older brother loves his new pickup truck.

13. Amira's family bought a big-screen TV.

Page 256

Comparing with Adjectives

When adjectives are used to compare two things, **er** is added at the end of the word for most one-syllable words and some two-syllable words.

Example: It is **colder** today than it was yesterday.

With many two-syllable words and all words with three or more syllables, the word **more** is used with the adjective to show comparison.

Example: Dr. X is **more professional** than Dr. Y.

When adjectives are used to compare three or more things, **est** is added at the end of the word for most one-syllable words and some two-syllable words.

Example: Today is the **coldest** day of the year.

With many two-syllable words and all words with three or more syllables, **most** is used with the adjective to show comparison.

Example: Dr. X is the **most professional** doctor in town.

When adding **er** or **est** to one-syllable words, these spelling rules apply.
   • Double the last consonant if the word has a short vowel before a final consonant: thinner, fattest.
   • If a word ends in **y**, change the **y** to **i** before adding **er** or **est**: earliest, prettiest.
   • If a word ends in **e**, drop the final **e** before adding **er** or **est**: simpler, simplest.

Directions: Complete these sentences with the correct form of the adjective.

1. This book is (small) __smaller__ than that one.

2. I want the (small) __smallest__ book in the library.

3. My plan is (practical) __more practical__ than yours.

4. My plan is the (practical) __most practical__ one in the class.

5. I wish the change was (gradual) __more gradual__ than it is.

6. My sister is (childish) __most childish__ girl in her day-care group.

7. There must be a (simple) __simpler__ way to do it than that.

8. This is the (simple) __simplest__ way of the four we thought of.

Page 257

Adjectives: Positive, Comparative, and Superlative

There are three degrees of comparison adjectives: **positive, comparative**, and **superlative**. The **positive degree** is the adjective itself. The **comparative** and **superlative** degrees are formed by adding **er** and **est**, respectively, to most one-syllable adjectives. The form of the word changes when the adjective is irregular, for example, **good, better, best**.

Most adjectives of two or more syllables require the words "more" or "most" to form the comparative and superlative degrees.

Examples:

	Positive	Comparative	Superlative
Positive:	big	eager	
Comparative:	bigger	more eager	
Superlative:	biggest	most eager	

Directions: Write the positive, comparative, or superlative forms of these adjectives.

	Positive	Comparative	Superlative
1.	hard	harder	hardest
2.	happy	happier	happiest
3.	difficult	more difficult	most difficult
4.	cold	colder	coldest
5.	easy	easier	easiest
6.	large	larger	largest
7.	little	littler	littlest
8.	shiny	shinier	shiniest
9.	round	rounder	roundest
10.	beautiful	more beautiful	most beautiful

Page 258

Adverbs

Adverbs tell when, where, or how an action occurred.

Examples:
   I'll go **tomorrow**. (when)
   I sleep **upstairs**. (where)
   I screamed **loudly**. (how)

When? Where? How?

Directions: Circle the adverb, and underline the verb it modifies. Write the question (when, where, or how) the adverb answers.

1. I ran quickly toward the finish line. ___how___

2. Today we will receive our report cards. ___when___

3. He swam smoothly through the pool. ___how___

4. Many explorers searched endlessly for new lands. ___how or when___

5. He looked up into the sky. ___where___

6. My friend drove away in her new car. ___where___

7. Later, we will search for your missing wallet. ___when___

8. Most kings rule their kingdoms regally. ___how___

9. New plants must be watered daily. ___when___

10. The stream near our house is heavily polluted. ___how___

11. My baby brother likes to walk backwards across his room. ___how___

Page 259

Adverbs: Positive, Comparative, and Superlative

There are also three degrees of comparison adverbs: **positive, comparative**, and **superlative**. They follow the same rules as adjectives.

Example:

	Positive	Comparative	Superlative
Positive:	rapidly	far	
Comparative:	more rapidly	farther	
Superlative:	most rapidly	farthest	

Directions: Write the positive, comparative, or superlative forms of these adverbs.

	Positive	Comparative	Superlative
1.	easily	more easily	most easily
2.	quickly	more quickly	most quickly
3.	hopefully	more hopefully	most hopefully
4.	bravely	more bravely	most bravely
5.	strongly	more strongly	most strongly
6.	near	nearer	nearest
7.	cleverly	more cleverly	most cleverly
8.	gracefully	more gracefully	most gracefully
9.	humbly	more humbly	most humbly
10.	excitedly	more excitedly	most excitedly
11.	handsomely	more handsomely	most handsomely
12.	slowly	more slowly	most slowly

Page 260

Adjectives and Adverbs

Directions: Write **adjective** or **adverb** in the blanks to describe the words in bold. The first one has been done for you.

adjective 1. Her **old** boots were caked with mud.

adjective 2. The baby was **cranky**.

adverb 3. He took the test **yesterday**.

adjective 4. I heard the **funniest** story last week!

adverb 5. She left her wet shoes **outside**.

adjective 6. Isn't that the **fluffiest** cat you've ever seen?

adverb 7. He ran **around** the track twice.

adjective 8. Our elderly neighbor seems **lonely**.

adjective 9. His **kind** smile lifted my dragging spirits.

adverb 10. **Someday**, I'll meet the friend of my dreams!

adverb 11. His cat never meows **indoors**.

adverb 12. Carlos hung his new shirts **back** in the closet.

adverb 13. Put that valuable vase **down** immediately!

adjective 14. She is the most **joyful** child!

adjective 15. Jonathan's wool sweater is totally **moth-eaten**.

Page 261

Identifying Sentence Parts

The **subject** tells who or what a sentence is about. Sentences can have more than one subject.

Example: Dogs and **cats** make good pets.

The **predicate** tells what the subject does or that it exists. Predicates can be more than one word. A sentence can have more than one predicate.

Examples: She **was walking**. She **walked** and **ran**.

An **adjective** is a word or group of words that describes the subject or another noun.

Example: The **cheerful yellow** bird with **blue** spots flew across the **flower-covered** meadow.

An **adverb** is a word or group of words that tells how, when, where, or how often.

Example: He sat **there** waiting **quietly**.

Directions: Write **S** for subject, **P** for predicate, **ADJ** for adjective, or **ADV** for adverb above each underlined word or group of words. The first one has been done for you.

ADJ S ADJ P ADV
1. A huge dog with long teeth was barking fiercely.

S ADV P
2. My grandmother usually wore a hat with a veil.

S S P ADJ
3. My niece and her friend are the same height.

ADJ S P ADV
4. The lively reindeer danced and pranced briefly on the rooftop.

Directions: Write sentences containing the sentence parts listed. Mark each part even if the verb part gets separated. **Possible answers:**

1. Write a question with two subjects, two predicates, and two adjectives:

   When will the yellow daisies and purple irises sprout and bloom?

2. Write a statement with one subject, two predicates, and two adjectives:

   The enormous mountain blocked the hot sun and made a shady spot for our picnic.

Page 262

Identifying Sentence Parts

Directions: Write **S** for subject, **P** for predicate, **ADJ** for adjective, or **ADV** for adverb above the appropriate words in these sentences.

ADJ S P ADV
1. The large cat pounced on the mouse ferociously.

P S P
2. Did you remember your homework?

S P ADV
3. My mother is traveling to New York tomorrow.

S P ADJ ADJ
4. I play basketball on Monday and Friday afternoons.

ADJ S P
5. The old decrepit house sat at the end of the street.

ADJ S P
6. Several tiny rabbits nibbled at the grass at the edge of the field.

ADJ S P ADJ ADJ
7. The lovely bride wore a white dress with a long train.

S P ADJ
8. We packed the clothes for the donation center in a box.

S P ADV
9. The telephone rang incessantly.

ADJ S P ADV
10. The lost child cried helplessly.

P S P ADJ ADJ
11. What will we do with these new puppies?

S P ADJ ADV
12. Lauren reads several books each week.

S P ADV
13. The picture hung precariously on the wall.

S P ADJ
14. I purchased many new school supplies.

S P ADJ
15. Computers have changed the business world.

Page 263

Prepositions

A **preposition** is a word that comes before a noun or pronoun and shows the relationship of that noun or pronoun to some other word in the sentence.

The **object of a preposition** is the noun or pronoun that follows a preposition and adds to its meaning.

A **prepositional phrase** includes the preposition, the object of the preposition, and all modifiers.

Example:
She gave him a pat **on his back**.
On is the preposition.
Back is the object of the preposition.
His is a possessive pronoun.

Common Prepositions

about	down	near	through
above	for	of	to
across	from	off	up
at	in	on	with
behind	into	out	within
by	like	past	without

Directions: Underline the prepositional phrases. Circle the prepositions. Some sentences have more than one prepositional phrase. The first one has been done for you.

1. He claimed he felt (at) home only (on) the West Coast.
2. She went (up) the street and then (down) the block.
3. The famous poet was (near) the doorway.
4. The beautiful birthday card was (from) her father.
5. He left his wallet (at) home.
6. Her speech was totally (without) humor.
7. I think he's (from) New York City.
8. Karl wanted to go (with) her mother (to) the mall.

Page 264

Prepositions

Directions: Complete the sentences by writing objects for the prepositions. The first one has been done for you.

Answers will vary.
Possible answers shown.

1. He was standing at **the corner of Fifth and Main.**
2. She saw her friend across **the street.**
3. Have you ever looked beyond **the index.**
4. His contact lens fell into **the sink.**
5. Have you ever gone outside without **a raincoat?**
6. She was anxious for **the test to begin.**
7. Is that dog from **the pound?**
8. She was daydreaming and walked past **the store.**
9. The book was hidden behind **the bookcase.**
10. The young couple had fallen in **the lake.**
11. She insisted she was through **the hardest part.**
12. He sat down near **the window.**
13. She forgot her umbrella at **the library.**
14. Have you ever thought of **how you will get home?**
15. Henry found his glasses on **the top of the refrigerator.**

Page 265

Object of a Preposition

The **object of a preposition** is the noun or pronoun that follows the preposition and adds to its meaning.

Example:
Correct: Devan smiled **at** (preposition) **Tori** (noun: object of the preposition) and **me** (pronoun: object of the same preposition.)
Correct: Devan smiled at Tori. Devan smiled at me. Devan smiled at Tori and me.
Incorrect: Devan smiled at Tori and I.

Tip: If you are unsure of the correct pronoun to use, pair each pronoun with the verb, and say the phrase out loud to find out which pronoun is correct.

Directions: Write the correct pronouns on the blanks. The first one has been done for you.

him 1. It sounded like a good idea to Sadie and (he/him).

her 2. I asked Abby if I could attend with (her/she).

_us_ 3. To (we/us), holidays are very important.

_us_ 4. Between (we/us), we finished the job quickly.

him and me 5. They gave the award to (he and I/him and me).

_me_ 6. The party was for my brother and (I/me).

him 7. I studied with (he/him).

_us_ 8. Tanya and the others arrived after (we/us).

her 9. After the zoo, we stopped at the museum with Azim and (her/she).

him 10. The chips for (he/him) are in the bag on top of the refrigerator.

Page 266

Direct Objects

A **direct object** is a noun or pronoun. It answers the question **whom** or **what** after a verb.

Answers will vary. Possible answers shown.

Examples:
My mom baked **bread**.
Bread is the direct object. It tells **what** Mom baked.
We saw **Steve**.
Steve is the direct object. It tells **whom** we saw.

Directions: Write a direct object in each sentence.

1. My dog likes _ice cream_. WHAT?
2. My favorite drink is _hot chocolate_. WHAT?
3. I saw _a clown_ today. WHOM?
4. The car struck a _fire hydrant_. WHAT?
5. The fan blew _bits of paper_ through the room. WHAT?
6. I packed a _sandwich_ for lunch. WHAT?
7. We watched _the team_ play basketball. WHOM?
8. I finished my _homework_. WHAT?
9. The artist sketched the _bowl of fruit_. WHAT?
10. He greets _his cat_ at the door. WHOM?
11. The team attended the victory _party_. WHAT?
12. The beautician cut my _hair_. WHAT?
13. Tamika will write _a novel_. WHAT?

Page 267

Indirect Objects

An **indirect object** is a noun or pronoun that tells **to whom** or **what** or **for whom** or **what** the action is performed. An indirect object usually is found between a verb and a direct object.

Example:
I gave **Ellen** my address.
Ellen is the indirect object. It tells **to whom** I gave my address.

Directions: Circle the indirect objects. Underline the direct objects.

1. Emma told *Kameko* the secret.
2. Advertisers promise *consumers* the world.
3. The dogs showed *me* their tricks.
4. Aunt Martha gave *Audrey* a necklace for her birthday.
5. Ramon brought *Mom* a bouquet of fresh flowers.
6. I sent my *niece* a package for Christmas.
7. Mr. Dunbar left his *wife* a note before leaving.
8. Grandma and Grandpa made their *friends* dinner.
9. The baby handed her *mom* a toy.
10. Tierra told *Stephanie* the recipe for trail mix.
11. We sent *Grandma* a card.
12. The waiter served *us* dessert.
13. Mom and Dad sold *us* the farm.

For me? For you!

Page 268

Joining Sentences

Conjunctions are words that join sentences, words, or ideas. When two sentences are joined with **and**, they are more or less equal.

Example: Julio is coming, **and** he is bringing snacks.

When two sentences are joined with **but**, the second sentence contradicts the first one.

Example: Julio is coming, **but** he will be late.

When two sentences are joined with **or**, they name a choice.

Example: Julio might bring snacks, **or** he might bring lemonade.

When two sentences are joined with **because**, the second one names the reason for the first one.

Answers will vary. Possible answers shown.

Example: I'll bring snacks, too, **because** Julio might forget his.

When two sentences are joined with **so**, the second one names a result of the first one.

Example: Julio is bringing snacks, **so** we can eat when he gets here.

Directions: Complete each sentence. The first one has been done for you.

1. We could watch TV, or _we could play a game._
2. I wanted to seize the opportunity, but _I acted too late._
3. You had better not deceive me, because _I will tell Grandma._
4. My neighbor was on vacation, so _I took care of his cats._
5. Veins take blood back to your heart, and _your lungs add oxygen to your blood._
6. You can't always yield to your impulses, because _they may get you in trouble._
7. I know that is your belief, but _I have a different belief._
8. It could be reindeer on the roof, or _it could be sleet._
9. Brent was determined to achieve his goal, so _he worked hard for two weeks._
10. Brittany was proud of her height, because _she was tall like her mother._

Page 269

Conjunctions

The conjunctions **and**, **or**, **but**, and **nor** can be used to make a compound subject, a compound predicate, or a compound sentence.

Examples:
Compound subject: My friend **and** I will go to the mall.
Compound predicate: We ran **and** jumped in gym class.
Compound sentence: I am a talented violinist, **but** my father is better.

Me AND You

Directions: Write two sentences of your own in each section.
Answers will vary. Possible answers shown.

Compound subject:
1. Ava and Marnie played chess after school.
2. The rangers and the students hiked to the top of the mountain.

Compound predicate:
1. My uncle served in the navy and sailed around the world.
2. The squirrel ran up the tree and chattered at the dog.

Compound sentence:
1. I wanted to see the movie, but my parents would not let me.
2. The chicks pecked at the ground, and the duckling waded in the water.

Page 270

Review

Directions: Write the missing verb tenses.

Present	Past	Past Participle
1. catch	caught	has (have) caught
2. stir	stirred	has (have) stirred
3. bake	baked	has (have) baked
4. go	went	has (have) gone
5. say	said	has (have) said

Directions: Circle the simple subject, and underline the simple predicate in each sentence.

6. Maria got sunburned at the beach.
7. The class watched the program.
8. The tomatoes are ripening.
9. We went grocery shopping.
10. The cross country team practiced all summer.

Directions: Write the missing adjective or adverb forms below.

Positive	Comparative	Superlative
11. friendly	more friendly	most friendly
12. small	smaller	smallest
13. fun	more fun	most fun
14. attractive	more attractive	most attractive

Page 271

Review

Directions: Write **adjective** or **adverb** to describe the words in bold.

adjective 1. My **old** piano teacher lives nearby.
adverb 2. My old piano teacher lives **nearby**.
adjective 3. His hair looked **horrible**.
adjective 4. Have you heard this **silly** joke?
adverb 5. **Suddenly**, the door opened.
adjective 6. The **magnificent** lion raised its head.
adverb 7. I accomplished the task **yesterday**.
adjective 8. This party has **delicious** food.

Directions: Circle the prepositions.

9. He went *in* the door and *up* the stairs.
10. Is this lovely gift *from* you?
11. I was all for it, but the decision was *beyond* my power.
12. His speech dragged *on* *into* the night.
13. My great-grandmother's crystal dish is *in* the curio cabinet.
14. He received a trophy *for* his accomplishments *on* the team.
15. The president *of* the United States is *on* vacation.
16. Joel wrote an excellent essay *about* Christopher Columbus.

Page 272

Comprehensive Curriculum - Grade 6

Cumulative Review

Directions: Identify the part of speech of the words in bold.
The first one has been done for you.

1. The dog ran **across** the field. — preposition
2. My **parents** allow me to stay up until 10:00 P.M. — noun as subject
3. Our cat **is** long-haired. — verb
4. Matt will wash the **dirty** dishes. — adjective
5. Miguel washed the **car** on Saturday. — noun as direct object
6. The waterfall crashed **over** the cliff. — preposition
7. What will you give **her**? — personal pronoun
8. The car **rolled** to a stop. — verb
9. He **slowly** finished his homework. — adverb
10. My **nephew** will be 12 years old on Sunday. — noun as subject
11. The news program discussed the **war**. — noun as direct object
12. Our **family** portrait was taken in the gazebo. — adjective
13. I **would** like to learn to fly a plane. — verb
14. **My** hair needs to be trimmed. — possessive pronoun
15. **Strawberry** jam is her favorite. — adjective
16. The horse **quickly** galloped across the field. — adverb
17. **What** will you do next? — interrogative pronoun
18. Please stand **and** introduce yourself. — conjunction
19. My neighbor takes **great** pride in her garden. — adjective
20. She sang **well** tonight. — adverb
21. My grandmother is from **Trinidad**. — noun as object of preposition

Page 273

Affect and Effect

Affect means "to act upon or influence."

Example: Studying will **affect** my test grade.

Effect means "to bring about a result or to accomplish something."

Example: The **effect** of her smile was immediate!

Directions: Write **affect** or **effect** in the blanks to complete these sentences correctly. The first one has been done for you.

1. affects — Your behavior (affects/effects) how others feel about you.
2. effect — His (affect/effect) on her was amazing.
3. effect — The (affect/effect) of his jacket was striking.
4. affect — What you say won't (affect/effect) me!
5. effect — There's a relationship between cause and (affect/effect).
6. effect — The (affect/effect) of her behavior was positive.
7. affected — The medicine (affected/effected) my stomach.
8. effect — What was the (affect/effect) of the punishment?
9. affect — Did his behavior (affect/effect) her performance?
10. affected — The cold (affected/effected) her breathing.
11. effect — The (affect/effect) was instantaneous!
12. affect — Your attitude will (affect/effect) your posture.
13. effect — The (affect/effect) on her posture was major.
14. effect — The (affect/effect) of the colored lights was calming.
15. affected — She (affected/effected) his behavior.

Page 274

Among and Between

Among is a preposition that applies to more than two people or things.

Example: The group divided the marbles **among** themselves.

Between is a preposition that applies to only two people or things.

Example: The marbles were divided **between** Jeremy and Sara.

Directions: Write **between** or **among** in the blanks to complete these sentences correctly. The first one has been done for you.

1. between — The secret is (between/among) you and Jon.
2. Between — (Between/Among) the two of them, whom do you think is nicer?
3. among — I must choose (between/among) the goldfish, guppies, and tetras.
4. among — She threaded her way (between/among) the kids on the playground.
5. between — She broke up a fight (between/among) Josh and Sean.
6. between — "What's come (between/among) you two?" she asked.
7. between — "I'm (between/among) a rock and a hard place," Josh responded.
8. among — "He has to choose (between/among) all his friends," Sean added.
9. among — "Are you (between/among) his closest friends?" she asked Sean.
10. between — "It's (between/among) another boy and me," Sean replied.
11. among — "Can't you settle it (between/among) the group?"
12. between — "No," said Josh. "This is (between/among) Sean and me."
13. among — "I'm not sure he's (between/among) my closest friends."
14. among — Sean, Josh, and Andy began to argue (between/among) themselves.
15. between — I hope Josh won't have to choose (between/among) the two!

Page 275

All Together and Altogether

All together is a phrase meaning "everyone or everything in the same place."

Example: We put the eggs **all together** in the bowl.

Altogether is an adverb that means "entirely, completely, or in all."

Example: The teacher gave **altogether** too much homework.

Directions: Write **altogether** or **all together** in the blanks to complete these sentences correctly. The first one has been done for you.

1. altogether — "You ate (altogether/all together) too much food."
2. all together — The girls sat (altogether/all together) on the bus.
3. All together — (Altogether/All together) now: one, two, three!
4. altogether — I am (altogether/all together) out of ideas.
5. all together — We are (altogether/all together) on this project.
6. altogether — "You have on (altogether/all together) too much makeup!"
7. all together — They were (altogether/all together) on the same team.
8. All together — (Altogether/All together), we can help stop pollution (altogether/all together).
9. altogether — He was not (altogether/all together) happy with his grades.
10. altogether — The kids were (altogether/all together) too loud.
11. All together — (Altogether/All together), the babies cried gustily.
12. altogether — She was not (altogether/all together) sure what to do.
13. all together — Let's sing the song (altogether/all together).
14. altogether — He was (altogether/all together) too pushy for her taste.
15. All together — (Altogether/All together), the boys yelled the school cheer.

Page 276

Amount and Number

Amount indicates quantity, bulk, or mass.

Example: She carried a large **amount** of money in her purse.

Number indicates units.

Example: What **number** of people volunteered to work?

Directions: Write **amount** or **number** in the blanks to complete these sentences correctly. The first one has been done for you.

1. number — She did not (amount/number) him among her closest friends.
2. amount — What (amount/number) of food should we order?
3. number — The (amount/number) of carrots on her plate was three.
4. amount — His excuses did not (amount/number) to much.
5. amounted — Her contribution (amounted/numbered) to half the money raised.
6. number — The (amount/number) of injured players rose every day.
7. amount — What a huge (amount/number) of cereal!
8. number — The (amount/number) of calories in the diet was low.
9. number — I can't tell you the (amount/number) of friends she has!
10. amount — The total (amount/number) of money raised was incredible!
11. number — The (amount/number) of gadgets for sale was amazing.
12. number — He was startled by the (amount/number) of people present.
13. amount — He would not do it for any (amount/number) of money.
14. number — She offered a great (amount/number) of reasons for her actions.
15. number — Can you guess the (amount/number) of beans in the jar?

Page 277

Irritate and Aggravate

Irritate means "to cause impatience, to provoke, or to annoy."

Example: His behavior **irritated** his father.

Aggravate means "to make a condition worse."

Example: Her sunburn was **aggravated** by additional exposure to the sun.

Directions: Write **aggravate** or **irritate** in the blanks to complete these sentences correctly. The first one has been done for you.

1. aggravated — The weeds (aggravated/irritated) his hay fever.
2. aggravated — Scratching the bite (aggravated/irritated) his condition.
3. irritated — Her father was (aggravated/irritated) about her low grade in math.
4. irritated — It (aggravated/irritated) him when she switched TV channels.
5. irritated — Are you (aggravated/irritated) when the cat screeches?
6. irritate — Don't (aggravate/irritate) me like that again!
7. irritation — He was in a state of (aggravation/irritation).
8. aggravates — Picking at the scab (aggravates/irritates) a sore.
9. irritates — Whistling (aggravates/irritates) the old grump.
10. irritated — She was (aggravated/irritated) when she learned about it.
11. irritate — "Please don't (aggravate/irritate) your mother," Dad warned.
12. aggravated — His asthma was (aggravated/irritated) by too much stress.
13. aggravate — Sneezing is sure to (aggravate/irritate) his allergies.
14. irritate — Did you do that just to (aggravate/irritate) me?
15. irritated — Her singing always (aggravated/irritated) her brother.

Page 278

Principal and Principle

Principal means "main, leader or chief, or a sum of money that earns interest."

Examples:
The high school **principal** earned interest on the **principal** in his savings account.
The **principal** reason for his savings account was to save for retirement.

Principle means "a truth, law, or a moral outlook that governs the way someone behaves."

Example:
Einstein discovered some fundamental **principles** of science.
Stealing is against her **principles**.

Directions: Write **principle** or **principal** in the blanks to complete these sentences correctly. The first one has been done for you.

principle	1. A (principle/principal) of biology is "the survival of the fittest."
principles	2. She was a person of strong (principles/principals).
principals	3. The (principles/principals) sat together at the district conference.
principal	4. How much of the total in my savings account is (principle/principal)?
principal	5. His hay fever was the (principle/principal) reason for his sneezing.
principles	6. It's not the facts that upset me, it's the (principles/principals) of the case.
principal	7. The jury heard only the (principle/principal) facts.
principal	8. Our school (principle/principal) is strict but fair.
principal	9. Spend the interest, but don't touch the (principle/principal).
principle	10. Helping others is a guiding (principle/principal) of the homeless shelter.
principle	11. In (principle/principal), we agree; on the facts, we do not.
principal	12. The (principle/principal) course at dinner was leg of lamb.
principles	13. Some mathematical (principles/principals) are difficult to understand.
principal	14. The baby was the (principle/principal) reason for his happiness.

Page 279

Good and Well

Good is always an adjective. It is used to modify a noun or pronoun.

Examples:
We enjoyed the **good** food.
We had a **good** time yesterday.
It was **good** to see her again.

Well is used to modify verbs, to describe someone's health, or to describe how someone is dressed.

Examples:
I feel **well**. He looked **well**.
He was **well**-dressed for the weather.
She sang **well**.

Directions: Write **good** or **well** in the blanks to complete these sentences correctly.

1. She performed **well**.
2. You look **good** in that color.
3. These apples are **good**.
4. He rides his bike **well**.
5. She made a **good** attempt to win the race.
6. The man reported that all was **well** in the coal mine.
7. Jonas said, "I feel **well**, thank you."
8. The team played **well**.
9. Mom fixed a **good** dinner.
10. The teacher wrote, "**Good** work!" on top of my paper.

Page 280

Like and As

Like means something is similar or resembles something else, and it describes how things are similar in manner.

Examples:
She could sing **like** an angel.
She looks **like** an angel, too!

As is a conjunction, or joining word, that links two independent clauses in a sentence.

Example: He felt chilly **as** night fell.

Sometimes **as** precedes an independent clause.

Example: **As** I told you, I will not be at the party.

Directions: Write **like** or **as** in the blanks to complete these sentences correctly. The first one has been done for you.

as	1. He did not behave (like/as) I expected.
like	2. She was (like/as) a sister to me.
like	3. The puppy acted (like/as) a baby!
As	4. (Like/As) I was saying, he will be there at noon.
as	5. The storm was 25 miles away, (like/as) he predicted.
like	6. He acted exactly (like/as) his father.
like	7. The song sounds (like/as) a hit to me!
like	8. Grandpa looked (like/as) a much younger man.
As	9. (Like/As) I listened to the music, I grew sleepy.
As	10. (Like/As) I expected, he showed up late.
like	11. She dances (like/as) a ballerina!
As	12. (Like/As) she danced, the crowd applauded.
like	13. On stage, she looks (like/as) a professional!
As	14. (Like/As) I thought, she has taken lessons for years.

Page 281

Review

Directions: Write the correct word in the blank.

effect	1. The (affect/effect) of the shot was immediate.
affected	2. The shot (affected/effected) her allergies.
effect	3. You have a positive (affect/effect) on me!
affected	4. I was deeply (affected/effected) by the speech.
between	5. The prize was shared (among/between) Malik and Lola.
among	6. She was (among/between) the best students in the class.
among	7. He felt he was (among/between) friends.
among	8. It was hard to choose (among/between) all the gifts.
irritate	9. Does it (irritate/aggravate) you to see people behave rudely?
aggravate	10. Does coughing (irritate/aggravate) his sore throat?
irritated	11. He wondered why she was (irritated/aggravated) at him.
irritation	12. The intensity of his (irritation/aggravation) grew each day.
principal	13. She had a (principal/principle) part in the play.
principal	14. Beans were the (principal/principle) food in his diet.
principles	15. She was a woman of strong (principals/principles).
principal	16. Mr. Larson was their favorite (principal/principle).
number	17. The (amount/number) of bananas he ate was incredible.
amount	18. I wouldn't part with it for any (amount/number) of money.
as	19. It happened exactly (like/as) I had predicted!
like	20. He sounds almost (like/as) his parents.

Page 282

Review

Directions: Use these words in sentences of your own.

1. affect **Answers will vary.**
2. effect
3. among
4. between
5. irritate
6. aggravate
7. principal
8. principle
9. good
10. well
11. like
12. as

Page 283

Capitalization

Capitalize:
...the first word in a sentence.
...the first letter of a person's name.
...proper nouns, like the names of planets, oceans, and mountain ranges.
...titles when used with a person's name, even if abbreviated (Dr., Mr., Lt.).
...days of the week and months of the year.
...cities, states, and countries.

Directions: Write **C** in the blank if the word or phrase is capitalized correctly. Rewrite the word or phrase if it is incorrect.

1.	C	President Abraham Lincoln
2.	C	Larry D. Walters
3.		saturn **Saturn**
4.		rosa parks **Rosa Parks**
5.	C	August
6.	C	professional
7.		jupiter **Jupiter**
8.	C	Pacific Ocean
9.		white house **White House**
10.	C	pet
11.	C	Congress
12.	C	Houston
13.	C	federal government
14.		dr. Nina Alvarez **Dr. Nina Alvarez**
15.		milwaukee, Wisconsin **Milwaukee, Wisconsin**
16.		Appalachian mountains **Appalachian Mountains**
17.		lake michigan **Lake Michigan**
18.	C	Notre Dame College
19.		department of the Interior **Department of the Interior**
20.		monday and Tuesday **Monday and Tuesday**

Page 285

Capitalization

Words that name places, people, months, and landmarks are always capitalized.

Examples:
Sonia Sotomayor — Acme Motor Company
White House — Jefferson Memorial
Fifth Avenue — May, June, July

Directions: Rewrite the sentences using correct capitalization.

1. My family and I visited washington, d.c., in july.
   My family and I visited Washington, D.C., in July.

2. We saw the washington monument, the capital building, and the white house.
   We saw the Washington Monument, the Capital Building, and the White House.

3. I was very impressed by our visit to the smithsonian institution.
   I was very impressed by our visit to the Smithsonian Institution.

4. Our taxi driver, from the american cab company, showed us around town.
   Our taxi driver, from the American Cab Company, showed us around town.

5. We drove down pennsylvania avenue.
   We drove down Pennsylvania Avenue.

6. We were unable to see the president of the united states.
   We were unable to see the President of the United States.

7. However, we did see the first lady.
   However, we did see the First Lady.

8. My parents and I decided to visit arlington national cemetery.
   My parents and I decided to visit Arlington National Cemetery.

Page 286

Commas

Use **commas** . . .
 . . . after introductory phrases.
 . . . to set off nouns of direct address.
 . . . to set off appositives from the words that go with them.
 . . . to set off words that interrupt the flow of the sentence.
 . . . to separate words or groups of words in a series.

Examples:
Introductory phrase: Of course, I'd be happy to attend.
Noun of direct address: Ms. Williams, please sit here.
To set off appositives: Lee, **the club president,** sat beside me.
Words interrupting flow: My cousin, **who's 13,** will also be there.
Words in a series: I ate **popcorn, peanuts, sunflower seeds,** and **dried berries.**

Directions: Identify how the commas are used in each sentence.
Write: **I** for introductory phrase
N for noun of direct address
A for appositive
WF for words interrupting flow
WS for words in a series

I 1. Yes, she is my sister.
A 2. My teacher, Mr. Hopkins, is very fair.
WS 3. Her favorite fruits are oranges, plums, and grapes.
A 4. The city mayor, Carla Ellison, is quite young.
WS 5. I will buy bread, milk, fruit, and ice cream.
WF 6. Her crying, which was quite loud, soon gave me a headache.
N 7. Sanjana, please answer the question.
I 8. So, do you know her?
I 9. Unfortunately, the item is not returnable.
WS 10. My sister, my cousin, and my friend will accompany me on vacation.
A 11. My grandparents, Rose and Bill, are both 57 years old.

Page 287

Commas

Directions: Use commas to punctuate these sentences correctly.

1. I'll visit her, however, not until I'm ready.
2. She ordered coats, gloves, and a hat from the catalog.
3. Eun-Jung, the new girl, looked ill at ease.
4. Certainly, I'll show Eun-Jung around school.
5. Yes, I'll be glad to help her.
6. I paid, nevertheless, I was unhappy with the price.
7. I bought stamps, envelopes, and plenty of postcards.
8. No, I told you I was not going.
9. The date, November 12, was not convenient.
10. Her earache, which kept her up all night, stopped at dawn.
11. My nephew, who loves bike riding, will go with us.
12. He'll bring hiking boots, a tent, and food.
13. The cat, a Himalayan, was beautiful.
14. The tennis player, a professional in every sense, signed autographs.
15. No, you can't stay out past 10:00 P.M.

Page 288

Semicolons

A **semicolon** (;) signals a reader to pause longer than for a comma, but not as long as for a period. Semicolons are used between closely related independent clauses not joined by **and, or, nor, for, yet,** or **but.**

An **independent clause** contains a complete idea and can stand alone.

Example: Rena was outgoing; her sister was shy.

Directions: Use semicolons to punctuate these sentences correctly. Some sentences require more than one semicolon.

1. Jeff wanted coffee; Sophia wanted milk.
2. I thought he was kind; she thought he was grouchy.
3. "I came; I saw; I conquered," wrote Julius Caesar.
4. Harper read books; she also read magazines.
5. I wanted a new coat; my old one was too small.
6. The airport was fogged-in; the planes could not land.
7. Now, he regrets his comments; it's too late to retract them.
8. The girls were thrilled; their mothers were not.

Directions: Use a semicolon and an independent clause to complete the sentences.
Answers will vary. Possible answers shown.

9. She liked him; she wished they were friends.
10. I chose a red shirt; he chose a green shirt.
11. Andrea sang well; her parents were impressed.
12. She jumped for joy; the team had won.
13. Dancing is good exercise; I do it at least once a day.
14. The man was kind; his children loved him.
15. The tire looked flat; we did not buy the car.
16. My bike is missing; I feel sad.

Page 289

Colons

Use a **colon** . . .
 . . . after the salutation of a business letter.
 . . . between the hour and the minute when showing time.
 . . . between the volume and page number of a periodical.
 . . . between chapters and verses of the Bible.
 . . . before a list of three or more items.
 . . . to introduce a long statement or quotation.

Examples:
Salutation: Dear Madame:
Hour and minute: 8:45 P.M.
Periodical volume and page number: Newsweek 11:32
Bible chapter and verse: John 3:16
Before a list of three or more items: Buy these: fruit, cereal, cheese
To introduce a long statement or quotation: Author Willa Cather said this about experiencing life: "There are only two or three human stories, and they go on repeating themselves as fiercely as if they had never happened before."

Dear Mr. Ahmad:
I would like to place an order for five of your 1-ton scales. Please contact me concerning price and delivery date.
Sincerely,
Ms. McDonnell

Directions: Use colons to punctuate these sentences correctly. Some sentences require more than one colon.

1. At 12:45 the president said this: "Where's my lunch?"
2. Don't forget to order these items: boots, socks, shoes, and leggings.
3. Ask the librarian for Weekly Reader 3:14.
4. Dear Sir: Please send me two copies of your report.
5. Avoid these at all costs: bad jokes, bad company, and bad manners.
6. The statement is in either Genesis 1:6 or Exodus 3:2.
7. At 9:15 P.M., she checked in, and at 6:45 A.M., she checked out.
8. I felt all these things at once: joy, anger, and sadness.

Page 290

Dashes

Dashes (—) are used to indicate sudden changes of thought.

Examples:
I want milk—no, make that juice—with my lunch.
Wear your old clothes—new ones would get spoiled.

Directions: If the dash is used correctly in the sentence, write **C** in the blank. If the dash is missing or used incorrectly, write **X** in the blank. The first one has been done for you.

C 1. No one—not even my dad—knows about the surprise.
X 2. Ask—him—no I will to come to the party.
X 3. I'll tell you the answer oh, the phone just rang!
C 4. Everyone thought—even her brother—that she looked pretty.
C 5. Can you please—oh, forget it!
X 6. Just stop it I really mean it!
C 7. Tell her that I'll—never mind—I'll tell her myself!
X 8. Everyone especially Anna is overwhelmed.
X 9. I wish everyone could—forgive me—I'm sorry!
C 10. The kids—all six of them—piled into the backseat.

Directions: Write two sentences of your own that include dashes.

11. Answers will vary.
12.

Page 291

Quotation Marks

Quotation marks are used to enclose a speaker's exact words. Use commas to set off a direct quotation from other words in the sentence.

Examples:
Kira smiled and said, "Quotation marks come in handy."
"Yes," Josh said, "I'll take two."

Directions: If quotation marks and commas are used correctly, write **C** in the blank. If they are used incorrectly, write **X** in the blank. The first one has been done for you.

_C_ 1. "I suppose," Elizabeth remarked, "that you'll be there on time."
_X_ 2. "Please let me help! Insisted Mark.
_X_ 3. I'll be ready in 2 minutes!" her father said.
_C_ 4. "Just breathe slowly," the nurse said, "and calm down."
_X_ 5. "No one understands me" William whined.
_C_ 6. "Would you like more milk?" Jasmine asked politely.
_X_ 7. "No thanks, her grandpa replied. "I have plenty."
_C_ 8. "What a beautiful morning!" Zola yelled.
_X_ 9. "Yes, it certainly is" her mother agreed.
_C_ 10. "Whose purse is this?" asked Andrea.
_X_ 11. It's mine" said Nadia. "Thank you."
_C_ 12. "Can you play the piano?" asked Beatriz.
_X_ 13. "Music is my hobby." Jonathan replied.
_X_ 14. Great!" yelled Harry. Let's play some tunes."
_C_ 15. "I practice a lot," said Jayne proudly.

"This is exactly what I'm saying! You can tell by my quotation marks!"

Page 292

Quotation Marks

Directions: Use quotation marks and commas to punctuate these sentences correctly.

"Remember: quotation marks are used to enclose a speaker's exact words."

1. "No," Ms. Elliot replied, "you may not go."
2. "Watch out!" yelled the coach.
3. "Please bring my coat," called Renee.
4. After thinking for a moment, Paul said, "I don't believe you!"
5. Dad said, "Remember to be home by 9:00 P.M."
6. "Finish your projects," said the art instructor.
7. "Go back," instructed Mom, "and comb your hair."
8. "I won't be needing my winter coat anymore," replied Mei-linn.
9. He said, "How did you do that?"
10. I stood and said, "My name is Rosalita."
11. "No," said Misha, "I will not attend."
12. "Don't forget to put your name on your paper," said the teacher.
13. "Pay attention, class!" said our history teacher.
14. As I came into the house, Mom called, "Dinner is almost ready!"
15. "Jake, come when I call you," said Mother.
16. "How was your trip to France, Mrs. Shaw?" asked Grace.

Page 293

Apostrophes

Use an **apostrophe** (') in a contraction to show that letters have been left out. A **contraction** is a shortened form of two words, usually a pronoun and a verb.

Add an **apostrophe** and **s** to form the **possessive** of singular nouns. **Plural possessives** are formed two ways. If the noun ends in **s**, simply add an apostrophe at the end of the word. If the noun does not end in **s**, add an apostrophe and **s**.

Examples:
Contraction: He **can't** button his sleeves.
Singular possessive: The **boy's** sleeves are too short.
Plural noun ending in s: The **ladies'** voices were pleasant.
Plural noun not ending in s: The **children's** song was long.

Directions: Use apostrophes to punctuate the sentences correctly. The first one has been done for you.

1. I can't understand that child's game.
2. The farmers' wagons were lined up in a row.
3. She didn't like the sheet covers.
4. Our parents' beliefs are often our own.
5. Elena's mother's aunt isn't going to visit.
6. Two ladies from work didn't show up.
7. The citizens' group wasn't very happy.
8. The colonists' demands weren't unreasonable.
9. The mothers' babies cried at the same time.
10. Our parents' generation enjoys music.

Use John's pencil!

I can't. The lead's broken.

Directions: Write two sentences of your own that include apostrophes.

11. _____ Answers will vary. _____
12. _____

Page 294

Contractions

Examples:
he will = **he'll**
she is = **she's**
they are = **they're**
can not = **can't**

Contraction Chart

Pronoun		Verb	Contraction
I	+	am	I'm
we, you, they	+	are	we're, you're, they're
he, she, it	+	is	he's, she's, it's
I, we, you	+	have	I've, we've, you've, they've
I, you, we, she, he, they	+	would	I'd, you'd, we'd, she'd, he'd, they'd
I, you, we, she, he, they	+	will	I'll, you'll, we'll, she'll, he'll, they'll

Answers will vary. Possible answers shown.

Directions: Write a sentence using a contraction. The first one has been done for you.

1. I will _____ I'll see you tomorrow!
2. they are _____ They're going to the park.
3. we have _____ We've been waiting for two hours!
4. she would _____ She'd like to go to the store with you.
5. you are _____ You're responsible for the fish tank.
6. they will _____ They'll finish the work later today.
7. she is _____ She's a good friend of mine.
8. he would _____ He'd better follow the rules.
9. they are _____ They're going to be surprised.
10. I am _____ I'm ready for my swim lesson.

Page 295

Singular Possessives

Directions: Write the singular possessive form of each word. Then, add a noun to show possession. The first one has been done for you.

Answers will vary. Possible answers shown.

1. spider _spider's web_
2. clock _clock's hands_
3. car _car's wheel_
4. book _book's pages_
5. Mom _Mom's hair_
6. boat _boat's rudder_
7. table _table's legs_
8. baby _baby's bottle_
9. woman _woman's coat_
10. writer _writer's talent_
11. mouse _mouse's tail_
12. fan _fan's dedication_
13. lamp _lamp's light_
14. dog _dog's collar_
15. boy _boy's name_
16. house _house's roof_

Page 296

Plural Possessives

Directions: Write the plural possessive form of each word. Then, add a noun to show possession. The first one has been done for you.

Answers will vary. Possible answers shown.

1. kid _kids' skates_
2. man _men's shoes_
3. aunt _aunts' husbands_
4. lion _lions' homes_
5. giraffe _giraffes' necks_
6. necklace _necklaces' prices_
7. mouse _mice's feet_
8. team _teams' players_
9. clown _clowns' car_
10. desk _desks' legs_
11. woman _women's store_
12. worker _workers' hardhats_

Directions: Write three sentences of your own that include plural possessives.

13. _____ Answers will vary. _____
14. _____
15. _____

Page 297

Comprehensive Curriculum - Grade 6

Italics

Use **italics** or **underlining** for titles of books, newspapers, plays, magazines, and movies.

Examples:
Book: Have you read The Humming Room?
Movie: Did you see The Muppet Movie?
Newspaper: I like to read The New York Times.
Magazine: Some children read Sports Illustrated.
Play: My school is putting on the play Peter Pan.

Since we cannot write in italics, we underline words that should be in italics.

Directions: Underline the words that should be in italics. The first one has been done for you.

1. I read about a play titled <u>Cats</u> in <u>The Cleveland Plain Dealer</u>.
2. You can find <u>The New York Times</u> in most libraries.
3. L. M. Montgomery wrote <u>Anne of Green Gables</u>.
4. <u>Parents</u> and <u>Newsweek</u> are both popular magazines.
5. The original <u>Miracle on 34th Street</u> was filmed long ago.
6. <u>Cricket</u> and <u>Ranger Rick</u> are magazines for children.
7. <u>Bon Appetit</u> means "good appetite" and is a cooking magazine.
8. <u>Harper's</u>, <u>The New Yorker</u>, and <u>Vanity Fair</u> are magazines.
9. <u>David Copperfield</u> was written by Charles Dickens.
10. Harriet Beecher Stowe wrote <u>Uncle Tom's Cabin</u>.
11. My cousin has watched <u>The LEGO Movie</u> four times.
12. Jake and Lily is by one of my favorite authors—Jerry Spinelli.
13. <u>The Louisville Courier-Journal</u> is a Kentucky newspaper.
14. <u>American Girl</u> and <u>Boys' Life</u> are magazines for young readers.
15. My whole family loved Disney's nature film <u>Bears</u>.

Page 298

Complete Sentences

A **complete sentence** has both a simple subject and a simple predicate. It is a complete thought. Sentences that are not complete are called **fragments**.

Example:
Complete sentence: The wolf howled at the moon.
Sentence fragment: Howled at the moon.

Directions: Write C on the line if the sentence is complete. Write F if it is a fragment.

1. **C** The machine is running.
2. **C** What will we do today?
3. **F** Knowing what I do.
4. **C** That statement is true.
5. **C** My parents drove to town.
6. **F** Watching television all afternoon.
7. **C** The storm devastated the town.
8. **C** Our friends can go with us.
9. **C** The palm trees bent in the wind.
10. **F** Spraying the fire all night.

Answers will vary. Possible answers shown.
Directions: Rewrite the sentence fragments from above to make them complete sentences.
Knowing what I do now, I would not try to talk to him.
Watching television all afternoon makes me feel sleepy.
The firemen were exhausted after spraying the fire all night.

Page 299

Run-On Sentences

A **run-on sentence** occurs when two or more sentences are joined together without punctuation or a joining word. Run-on sentences should be divided into two or more separate sentences.

Example:
Run-on sentence: My parents, sister, brother, and I went to the park we saw many animals we had fun.
Correct: My parents, sister, brother, and I went to the park. We saw many animals and had fun.

Directions: Rewrite the run-on sentences correctly.

1. The dog energetically chased the ball I kept throwing him the ball for a half hour.
The dog energetically chased the ball. I kept throwing him the ball for a half hour.

2. The restaurant served scrambled eggs and bacon for breakfast I had some and they were delicious.
The restaurant served scrambled eggs and bacon for breakfast. I had some, and they were delicious.

3. The lightning struck close to our house it scared my little brother and my grandmother called to see if we were safe.
The lightning struck close to our house. It scared my little brother, and my grandmother called to see if we were safe.

Page 300

Finding Spelling Errors

Directions: One word in each sentence below is misspelled. Write the word correctly on the line.

1. Isaiah felt discoraged at the comparison between him and his older brother. **discouraged**
2. I got inpatient as my curiosity grew. **impatient**
3. She confided that she had not finished the asignment. **assignment**
4. They made the selection after a brief conferrence. **conference**
5. Obviusly, it's impolite to sneeze on someone. **Obviously**
6. This skin cream is practicaly invisible. **practically**
7. What would prevent you from taking on addtional work? **additional**
8. I can resite the words to that hymn. **recite**
9. In a previous colum, the newspaper explained the situation. **column**
10. He decieved me so many times that now I distrust him. **deceived**
11. Please have the curtesy to observe the "No Eating" signs. **courtesy**
12. The advertisement is so small that it's nearly invisable. **invisible**
13. The best way to communicate is in a face-to-face conservation. **conversation**
14. In a cost comparson, salmon is more expensive than tuna. **comparison**
15. Poplarity among friends shouldn't depend on your accomplishments. **Popularity**
16. Her campaign was quite an achievment. **achievement**
17. He condemed it as a poor imitation. **condemned**

Page 301

Finding Spelling Errors

Directions: Circle all misspelled words. Write the words correctly on the lines at the end of each paragraph. If you need help, consult a dictionary.

Sabrina wanted to *aquire* a saltwater *aquarium*. She was worried about the *expence*, though, so first she did some *research*. She wanted to learn the *exact* care saltwater fish need, not just to *exist* but to *florish*. One *sorce* said she needed to put water in the aquarium and wait 6 weeks before she added the fish. "Good *greif*," Sabrina thought. She got a kitten from her *neighbor* instead.

acquire, aquarium, expense, research, exact, exist, flourish, source, grief, neighbor

One stormy day, Marcel was babysitting his *neice*. He happened to *obsurve* that the sky looked darker than *norml*. At first he *ignorred* it, but then he noticed a black cloud *expand* and grow in *hieght*. Then, a tail dropped down from the twisting cloud and *sezed* a tree! "It's a tornado!" Marcel shouted. "Maybe two *tornadoes*. This is an *emergensy*!" For a *breif* moment Marcel wished he hadn't shouted, because his niece looked at him with a very frightened *expression*. Just then, the *cieling* began to sag as if it had a heavy *wieght* on it. "This is an *excelent* time to visit the basement," he told the little girl as calmly as possible.

niece, observe, normal, ignored, expand, height, seized, tornadoes, emergency, brief, expression, ceiling, weight, excellent

Just before Mother's Day, Bethany went to a *florist* to buy some flowers for her mother. "Well, what is your *requst*?" the clerk asked. "I don't have much money," Bethany told him. "So make up your mind," he said impatiently. "Do you want *quallity* or *quanity*?" Bethany wondered if he was giving her a *quizz*. She tried not to *squirm* as he stared down at her. Finally, she said, "I want *curtesy*," as she headed for the *exxit*.

florist, request, quality, quantity, quiz, squirm, courtesy, exit

Page 302

Finding Spelling Errors

Directions: Find six errors in each paragraph. Write the words correctly on the lines after each paragraph. Use a dictionary if you need help.

My brother Jim took a math *corse* at the high school that was too hard for *hym*. My father didn't want him to take it, but Jim said, "Oh, you're just too *critcal*! Dad! *Obviosly* you don't think I can do it." Jim *ignored* Dad. That's *norml* at our house.

course, him, critical, Obviously, ignored, normal

Well, the first day Jim went to the course, he came home with a *solem expreion* on his face, like a *condemed* man. "That teacher *assined* us five pages of homework!" he said. "And two *comlicated* problems that we have to *reserch*."

solemn, expression, condemned, assigned, additional, research

"He sounds like an *excelent professinal* teacher," my dad said. "We need more teachers of that *qwalitii* in our schools." Jim squirmed in his seat. Then, he *gradualy* started to smile. "Dad, I need some help with a *persnal* problem," he said. "Five pages of problems, right?" Dad asked. Jim smiled and handed Dad his math book. That's *tipical* at our house, too.

excellent, professional, quality, gradually, personal, typical

One day, we had a *medicial emergeny* at home. My *sisters* hand got stuck in a basket with a narrow opening, and she couldn't pull it out. I thought she would have to wear the basket on her hand *permanently*! First, I tried to stretch and *expand* the *baskets* opening, but that didn't work.

medical, emergency, sister's, permanently, expand, basket's

Then, I smeared a *smanll* of butter on my *sisters* hand, and she pulled it right out. I thought she would have the *curtesy* to thank me, but she just stomped away, still mad. How *childsh*! Sometimes she seems to think *exiss* just to serve her. There are more *importante* things in the world than her happiness!

quantity, sister's, courtesy, childish, exist, important

Page 303

Writing: Four Types of Sentences

There are four main types of sentences: A **statement** tells something. It ends in a period. A **question** asks something. It ends in a question mark. A **command** tells someone to do something. It ends in a period or an exclamation mark. An **exclamation** shows strong feeling or excitement. It ends in an exclamation mark.

Boy, what a cute cat!

Directions: Write what you would say in each situation. Then, tell whether the sentence you wrote was a statement, question, exclamation, or command. The first one has been done for you.

Write what you might say to:

1. A friend who has a new cat:
   When did you get the new cat? (question)
   or **Boy, what a cute cat!** (exclamation)

2. A friend who studied all night for the math test:

   <u>Answers will vary.</u>

3. Your teacher, about yesterday's homework:

4. A child you're watching who won't sit still for a second:

5. Your sister, who's been on the phone too long:

Page 304

Organizing Paragraphs

A **topic sentence** states the main idea of a paragraph and is usually the first sentence. **Support sentences** follow, providing details about the topic. All sentences in a paragraph should relate to the topic sentence. A paragraph ends with a **conclusion sentence**.

Directions: Rearrange each group of sentences into a paragraph, beginning with the topic sentence. Cross out the sentence in each group that is not related to the topic sentence. Write the new paragraph.

Now, chalk drawings are considered art by themselves. The earliest chalk drawings were found on the walls of caves. Chalk is also used in cement, fertilizer, toothpaste, and makeup. Chalk once was used just to make quick sketches. Chalk has been used for drawing for thousands of years. Then, the artist would paint pictures from the sketches.

Chalk has been used for drawing for thousands of years. The earliest chalk drawings were found on the walls of caves. Chalk once was used just to make quick sketches. Then, the artist would paint pictures from the sketches. Now, chalk drawings are considered art by themselves.

Dams also keep young salmon from swimming downriver to the ocean. Most salmon live in the ocean but return to fresh water to lay their eggs and breed. Dams prevent salmon from swimming upriver to their spawning grounds. Pacific salmon die after they spawn the first time. One kind of fish pass is a series of pools of water that lead the salmon over the dams. Dams are threatening salmon by interfering with their spawning. To help with this problem, some dams have special "fish passes" to allow salmon to swim over the dam.

Dams are threatening salmon by interfering with their spawning. Most salmon live in the ocean but return to fresh water to lay their eggs and breed. Dams prevent salmon from swimming upriver to their spawning grounds. Dams also keep young salmon from swimming downriver to the ocean. To help with this problem, some dams have special "fish passes" to allow salmon to swim over the dam. One kind of fish pass is a series of pools of water that lead the salmon over the dams.

Page 305

Building Paragraphs

Directions: Read each group of questions and the topic sentence. On another sheet of paper, write support sentences that answer each question. Number your support sentences in order. Make any necessary changes so the sentences fit together in one paragraph. Then, write your paragraph after the topic sentence.

Questions: Why did Noah feel sad?
What happened to change how he felt?
How does he feel when he comes to school now?

Noah used to look so solemn when he came to school. _____
_____ <u>Answers will vary.</u>

Questions: Why did Sienna want to go to another country?
Why couldn't she go?
Does she have any plans to change that?

Sienna always wanted to visit a foreign country. _____

Questions: What was Paulo's "new way to fix spaghetti"?
Did anyone else like it?
Did Paulo like it himself?

Paulo thought of a new way to fix spaghetti. _____

Page 306

Explaining with Examples

Some paragraphs paint word pictures using adjectives, adverbs, similes, and metaphors. Other paragraphs explain by naming examples.

Example:
Babysitting is not an easy way to earn money. For example, the little girl you're watching may be very cranky and cry until her parents come home. Or maybe the family didn't leave any snacks and you have to starve all night. Even worse, the child could fall and get hurt. Then, you have to decide whether you can take care of her yourself or if you need to call for help. No, babysitting isn't easy.

Directions: Write examples for each topic sentence on another sheet of paper. Number them in order to put them in paragraph form. Make any necessary changes so the sentences fit together in one paragraph. Then, write your paragraphs below after the topic sentences.
<u>Answers will vary.</u>

1. Sometimes, dreams can be scary. _____

2. You can learn a lot by living in a foreign country. _____

Page 307

Creating Word Pictures

Painters create pictures with colors. Writers create pictures with words. Adding adjectives and adverbs and using specific nouns, verbs, similes, and metaphors in sentences help create word pictures.

Notice how much more interesting and informative these two rewritten sentences are.

Original sentence
The animal ate its food.

Rewritten sentences
Like a hungry lion, the starving cocker spaniel wolfed down the entire bowl of food in seconds.

The raccoon delicately washed the berries in the stream before nibbling them slowly, one by one.

Nouns · Similes · Verbs · Metaphors · Words

Directions: Rewrite each sentence twice, creating two different word pictures.

1. The person built something.
   <u>Answers will vary.</u>

2. The weather was bad.

3. The boy went down the street.

4. The children helped.

Page 308

Describing People

Often, a writer can show how someone feels by describing how that person looks or what he or she is doing, rather than by using emotion words, like **angry** or **happy**. This is another way to create word pictures.

Directions: Read the phrases below. Write words to describe how you think that person feels.

1. like a tornado, yelling, raised fists <u>angry</u>
2. slumped, walking slowly, head down <u>depressed</u>
3. trembling, breathing quickly, like a cornered animal <u>scared</u>

Directions: Write one or two sentences for each phrase without using emotion words.

4. a runner who has just won a race for his or her school _____
   <u>Answers will vary.</u>

5. a sixth grader on the first day in a new school _____

6. a teenager walking down the street and spotting a house on fire _____

7. a scientist who has just discovered a cure for lung cancer _____

8. a kindergarten child being ignored by his or her best friend _____

Page 309

Describing Events in Order

When we write to explain what happened, we need to describe the events in the same order they occurred. Words and phrases such as **at first, then, after that,** and **finally** help us relate the order of events.

Directions: Rewrite the paragraph below, putting the topic sentence first and arranging the events in order.

I got dressed, but I didn't really feel like eating breakfast. By the time I got to school, my head felt hot, so I went to the nurse. This day was terrible from the very beginning. Finally, I ended up where I started—back in my own bed. Then, she sent me home again! I just had some toast and left for school. When I first woke up in the morning, my stomach hurt.

This day was terrible from the very beginning. When I first woke up in the morning, my stomach hurt. I got dressed, but I didn't really feel like eating breakfast. I just had some toast and left for school. By the time I got to school, my head felt hot, so I went to the nurse. Then, she sent me home again! Finally, I ended up where I started—back in my own bed.

Directions: Follow these steps to write a paragraph about what happened the last time you tried to cook something or the last time you tried to fix something that was broken.

1. Write your first draft on another sheet of paper. Start with a topic sentence.
2. Add support sentences to explain what happened. Include phrases to keep things in order: **at first, then, after that, finally, in the middle of it, at last.**
3. Read your paragraph out loud to see if it reads smoothly. Make sure the events are in the correct order.
4. Make any needed changes, and then write your paragraph below.

Paragraphs will vary.

Page 310

Explaining What Happened

Directions: These pictures tell a story, but they're out of order. Follow these steps to write what happened.

1. On another sheet of paper, write a sentence explaining what is happening in each picture.
2. Put your sentences in order, and write a topic sentence.
3. Read the whole paragraph to yourself. Add words to show the order in which things happened.
4. Include adjectives, adverbs, and a simile or metaphor to make your story more interesting.
5. Write your paragraph below. Be sure to give it a title.

Paragraphs will vary.

Page 311

Writing Directions

Directions: must be written clearly. They are easiest to follow when they are in numbered steps. Each step should begin with a verb.

How to Peel a Banana:
1. Hold the banana by the stem end.
2. Find a loose edge of peel at the top.
3. Pull the peel down.
4. Peel the other sections of the banana in the same way.

Directions: Rewrite these directions, number the steps in order, and begin with verbs.

How to Feed a Dog
Finally, call the dog to come and eat. Then, you carry the filled dish to the place where the dog eats. The can or bag should be opened by you. First, clean the dog's food dish with soap and water. Then, get the dog food out of the cupboard. Put the correct amount of food in the dish.

1. Clean the dog's food dish with soap and water.
2. Get the dog food out of the cupboard.
3. Open the can or bag.
4. Put the correct amount of food in the dish.
5. Carry the filled dish to the place where the dog eats.
6. Call the dog to come and eat.

Directions: Follow these steps to write your own directions.

1. On another sheet of paper, draw three symbols, such as a square with a star in one corner and a dot in the center, or a triangle inside a circle with a spiral in the middle. Don't show your drawing to anyone.
2. On a second sheet of paper, write instructions to make the same drawing. Your directions need to be clear, in order, and numbered. Each step needs to begin with a verb.
3. Trade directions (but not pictures) with a partner. See if you can follow each other's directions to make the drawings.
4. Show your partner the drawing you made in step one. Does it look like the one he or she made following your directions? Could you follow your partner's directions? Share what was clear—or not so clear—about each other's instructions.

Page 312

Review

Directions: Write paragraphs to match the descriptions given. Begin with a topic sentence, and add support sentences that tell the events in order. Write the first draft of your paragraph on another sheet of paper. Read it to yourself, make any necessary changes, and then write it below.

1. Write a short paragraph to explain something that might happen on your way to school.

Answers will vary.

2. Write a paragraph that tells what you usually do during the first hour after you get up on a school day.

Directions: Write directions explaining how to brush your teeth. Include at least four steps. Make them as clear as possible. Begin each step with a verb. Write a rough draft on another sheet of paper first.

1. _____
2. _____
3. _____
4. _____

Page 313

Writing: Stronger Sentences

Sometimes the noun form of a word is not the best way to express an idea. Compare these two sentences:

They made preparations for the party.
They prepared for the party.

The second sentence, using **prepared** as a verb, is shorter and stronger.

Directions: Write one word to replace a whole phrase. Cross out the words you don't need. The first one has been done for you.

suggested
1. She ~~made a suggestion~~ that we go on Monday.
decorated
2. They ~~arranged decorations around~~ the room.
combine
3. Let's ~~make a combination of the~~ two ideas.
appreciate
4. I ~~have great appreciation for~~ what you did.
transport
5. The buses ~~are acting as transportation for~~ the classes.
explored
6. The group ~~made an exploration of~~ the Arctic Circle.
select
7. Please ~~make a selection of~~ one quickly.
reflects
8. The lake ~~is making a reflection of~~ the trees.
celebrated
9. The family ~~had a celebration of~~ the holiday.
solve
10. Would you please ~~provide a solution for~~ this problem?
imitated
11. Rashid ~~made an imitation of~~ his cat.
define
12. Please ~~give a definition of~~ that word.
examined
13. I ~~made an examination of~~ the broken bike.
invited
14. Dexter ~~made an invitation for~~ us to join him.

Write one word to replace a whole phrase.

Page 314

Writing: Descriptive Sentences

Descriptive sentences make writing more interesting to the reader. This is done by using adjectives, adverbs, prepositional phrases, similes, and metaphors.

Example:
The dog ran down the hill.
The black and white beagle bounded down the steep embankment as though being chased by an invisible dragon.

Directions: Rewrite these sentences so they are more descriptive.

1. Parker likes collecting stamps.

Answers will vary.

2. Martina drove into town.

3. I enjoy working on the computer.

4. Riverside won the game.

5. Dinner was great.

6. My mom collects antiques.

7. The teacher likes my essay.

8. My brother received a scholarship for college.

Page 315

Writing: Different Points of View

A **fact** is a statement that can be proved. An **opinion** is what someone thinks or believes.

Directions: Write **F** if the statement is a fact or **O** if it is an opinion.

1. _F_ The amusement park near our town just opened last summer.
2. _O_ It's the best one in our state.
3. _F_ It has a roller coaster that's 300 feet high.
4. _O_ You're a chicken if you don't go on it.

Directions: Think about the last movie or TV show you saw. Write one fact and one opinion about it.

Fact: _____ Answers will vary. _____

Opinion: _____

In a story, a **point of view** is how one character feels about an event and reacts to it. Different points of view show how characters feel about the same situation.

What if you were at the mall with a friend and saw a shirt you really wanted on sale? You didn't bring enough money, so you borrowed ten dollars from your friend to buy the shirt. Then, you lost the money in the store!

Directions: Write a sentence describing what happened from the point of view of each person named below. Explain how each person felt.

Yourself _____ Answers will vary. _____

Your friend _____

The store clerk who watched you look for the money _____

The person who found the money _____

Page 316

Reading Skills: It's Your Opinion

Your opinion is how you feel or think about something. Although other people may have the same opinion, their reasons will not be exactly the same because of their individuality.

When writing an opinion paragraph, it is important to first state your opinion. Then, in at least three sentences, support your opinion. Finally, end your paragraph by restating your opinion in different words.

Example:
I believe dogs are excellent pets. For thousands of years, dogs have guarded and protected their owners. Dogs are faithful and have been known to save the lives of those they love. Dogs offer unconditional love, as well as company for the quiet times in our lives. For those reasons, I feel that dogs make wonderful pets.

Directions: Write an opinion paragraph on whether you would or would not like to have lived in Colonial America. Be sure to support your opinion with at least three reasons.

Answers will vary.

_____
_____
_____
_____
_____

Writing Checklist
Reread your paragraph carefully.
- ☐ My paragraph makes sense.
- ☐ There are no jumps in ideas.
- ☐ I used correct punctuation.
- ☐ I have a good opening and ending.
- ☐ I used correct spelling.
- ☐ My paragraph is well-organized.
- ☐ My paragraph is interesting.

Page 317

Persuasive Writing

To **persuade** means to convince someone that your opinion is correct. You need to offer reasons, facts, and examples to support your opinion.

Directions: Write two reasons or facts and two examples to persuade someone.

1. Riding a bicycle "no-handed" on a busy street is a bad idea.
   Reasons/Facts: _____ Answers will vary. _____
   _____
   Examples: _____
   _____

2. Taking medicine prescribed by a doctor for someone else is dangerous.
   Reasons/Facts: _____
   _____
   Examples: _____
   _____

3. Learning to read well will help you in every other subject in school.
   Reasons/Facts: _____
   _____
   Examples: _____
   _____

Page 318

Persuasive Writing

When trying to persuade someone, it helps to look at both sides of the issue. If you can understand both sides, you will have a better idea how to convince someone of your point of view.

Directions: Follow these steps to write two persuasive paragraphs about which form of transportation is better: airplanes or cars.

1. On another sheet of paper, list three or four reasons why planes are better and three or four reasons why cars are better.
2. Put each list of reasons in order. Often, persuasive writing is strongest when the best reason is placed last. Readers tend to remember the last reason best.
3. Write topic sentences for each paragraph.
4. Read each paragraph, and make any necessary changes so one sentence leads smoothly to the next.
5. Write your paragraphs below.

Answers will vary.

Airplanes Are Better Transportation Than Cars _____
_____
_____
_____
_____

Cars Are Better Transportation Than Planes _____
_____
_____
_____

6. Write two more paragraphs on another sheet of paper. Select any topic. Write from both points of view.

Page 319

Persuasive Writing

Writing is usually more persuasive if written from the reader's point of view.

If you made muffins to sell at a school fair, which of these sentences would you write on your sign?
I spent a lot of time making these muffins.
These muffins taste delicious!

If you were writing to ask your school board to start a gymnastics program, which sentence would be more persuasive?
I really am interested in gymnastics.
Gymnastics would be good for our school because both boys and girls can participate, and it's a year-round sport we can do in any weather.

In both situations, the second sentence is more persuasive because it is written from the reader's point of view. People care how the muffins taste, not how long it took you to make them. The school board wants to provide activities for all the students, not just you.

Directions: Write **R** if the statement is written from the reader's point of view or **W** if it's written from the writer's point of view.

_R_ 1. If you come swimming with me, you'll be able to cool off.
_W_ 2. Come swimming with me. I don't want to go alone.
_W_ 3. Please write me a letter! I really like to get mail.
_R_ 4. Please write me a letter. I want to hear from you.

Directions: Follow these steps to write an invitation on another sheet of paper to persuade people to move to your town or city.

1. Think about reasons someone would want to live in your town. Make a list of all the good things there, like the schools, parks, annual parades, historic buildings, businesses where parents could work, scout groups, Little League, and so on. You might also describe your town's population, transportation, restaurants, celebrations, or even holiday decorations.
2. Now, select three or four items from your list. Write a sentence (or two) about each one from the reader's point of view. For example, instead of writing "Our Little League team won the championship again last year," you could tell the reader, "You could help our Little League team win the championship again this year."
3. Write a topic sentence to begin your invitation, and put your support sentences in order after it.
4. Read your invitation out loud to another person. Make any needed changes, and copy the invitation onto a clean sheet of paper.

Page 320

Review

Directions: Read the questions. Then, write one or two sentences about the situation from both points of view.

What if your neighbor had a dog that barked all night and kept you awake?
Your point of view: _____ Answers will vary. _____

Your neighbor's point of view: _____

What if the school board wanted to begin holding classes every Saturday during the school year?
For Saturday classes: _____

Against Saturday classes: _____

Directions: Rewrite these sentence so they make a stronger statement:

Jacob made a decision to take the test today. _____

Kisha had a dream about the test results. _____

Directions: Write two facts and two opinions about your math class.

Facts: _____
_____

Opinions: _____
_____

Page 321

Review

Directions: Write a persuasive essay convincing your town that a park is needed for older kids with equipment such as basketball courts, soccer and football fields, and a track. Be sure to end with a convincing statement.

Paragraphs will vary.

Directions: Write a descriptive paragraph about these topics.

My Pet

My Mom

Page 322

Describing Characters

When you write a story, your characters must seem like real people. You need to let your reader know not only how they look but how they act, and how they feel. You could just tell the reader that a character is friendly, scared, or angry, but your story will be more interesting if you show these feelings by the characters' actions.

Example:
Character: A frightened child
Adjectives and adverbs: red-haired, freckled, scared, lost, worried
Simile: as frightened as a mouse cornered by a cat
Action: He peeked between his fingers, but his mother was nowhere in sight.

Directions: Write adjectives, adverbs, similes, and/or metaphors that tell how each character feels. Then, write a sentence that shows how the character feels.

Answers will vary.

1. an angry woman
Adjectives and adverbs:
Metaphor or simile:
Sentence:

2. a disappointed man
Adjectives and adverbs:
Metaphor or simile:
Sentence:

3. a hungry child
Adjectives and adverbs:
Metaphor or simile:
Sentence:

4. a tired boy
Adjectives and adverbs:
Metaphor or simile:
Sentence:

Page 323

Setting the Scene

Where and when a story takes place is called the **setting**. As with characters, you can tell about a setting—or you can show what the setting is like. Compare these two pairs of sentences:

The sun was shining.
The glaring sun made my eyes burn.

The bus was crowded.
Paige shouldered her way down the aisle, searching for an empty seat on the crowded bus.

If you give your readers a clear picture of your story's setting, they'll feel as if they're standing beside your characters. Include words that describe the sights, sounds, smells, feel, and even taste, if appropriate.

Directions: Write at least two sentences for each setting, clearly describing it for your readers.

Answers will vary.

1. an empty kitchen early in the morning

2. a locker room after a basketball game

3. a dark living room during a scary TV movie

4. a classroom on the first day of school

5. a quiet place in the woods

Page 324

Creating a Plot

When you're writing a story, the **plot** is the problem your characters face and how they solve it. It's helpful to write a plot outline or summary before beginning a story.

In the beginning of a story, introduce the characters, setting, and problem.

Example: Oliver and Stella have never met their mother, who lives in another state. They decide they would like very much to meet her. They live with their grandmother and father. On the way home from school, they talk about how they can find and contact her.

In the middle, characters try different ways to solve the problem, usually failing at first.

Example: Oliver and Stella hurry home to ask their grandmother if she can help them find their mother. Their grandmother seems nervous and tells Oliver and Stella to discuss the matter with their father when he gets home from work. When Oliver and Stella's father comes home, they tell him about their plan. Their father is very quiet for several minutes. He says he needs some time to think about it and asks if he can let them know tomorrow. Oliver and Stella can hardly sleep that night. Getting through school the next day is tough as well. After school, Oliver and Stella wait by the window for their father's car to pull in the driveway.

In the end, the characters find a way to solve the problem. Not all stories have happy endings. Sometimes, the characters decide they can live with the situation the way it is.

Example: When their father pulls into the driveway, Oliver and Stella rush out to meet him. Their father hands them airplane tickets. Oliver and Stella hug each other. Then, they hug their father.

Directions: How do you think this story ends? Write a summary for the ending of this story.

Answers will vary.

Page 325

Writing Dialogue

When it was Megan's turn to present her book report to the class, she dropped all her notecards! Her face turned red, and she wished she was invisible, but all she could do was stand there and say what she could remember without her cards. It was awful!

Directions: Rewrite each paragraph below. Explain the same scenes and feelings using dialogue.

After class, Megan told her friend Ananya she had never been so embarrassed in her life. She saw everyone staring at her, and the teacher looked impatient, but there wasn't anything she could do. Sara assured Megan that no one disliked her because of what had happened.

Answers will vary.

When Megan got home, she told her mother about her book report. By then, she felt like crying. Her mother said not to get discouraged. In a couple of days, she would be able to laugh about dropping the cards.

When Megan's older brother Jed came home, he asked her what was wrong. She briefly told him and said she never was going back to school. He started laughing. Megan got mad because she thought he was laughing at her. Then, Jed explained that he had done almost the same thing when he was in sixth grade. He was really embarrassed, too, but not for long.

Page 328

Writing: Paraphrasing

Paraphrasing means "to restate something in your own words."

Directions: Write the following sentences in your own words. The first one has been done for you.

Answers will vary.

1. He sat alone and watched movies throughout the cold, rainy night.

   All through the damp, chilly evening, the boy watched television by himself.

2. Many animals such as elephants, zebras, and tigers live in the grasslands.

3. In art class, Sarah worked diligently on a clay pitcher, molding and shaping it on the pottery wheel.

4. The scientists frantically searched for a cure for the new disease that threatened the entire world population.

5. Quietly, the detective crept around the abandoned building, hoping to find the missing man.

6. The windmill turned lazily in the afternoon breeze.

Page 329

Writing: Paraphrasing

Directions: Using synonyms and different word order, paraphrase the following paragraphs. The first one has been done for you.

Some of Earth's resources, such as oil and coal, can be used only once. We should always, therefore, be careful how we use them. Some materials that are made from natural resources, including metal, glass, and paper, can be reused. This is called recycling.

Many natural resources, including coal and oil, can be used only one time. For this reason, it is necessary to use them wisely. There are other materials made from resources of the Earth that can be recycled, or used again. Materials that can be recycled include metal, glass, and paper.

Recycling helps to conserve the limited resources of our land. For example, there are only small amounts of gold and silver ores in the earth. If we can recycle these metals, less of the ores need to be mined. While there is much more aluminum ore in the earth, recycling is still important. It takes less fuel energy to recycle aluminum than it does to make the metal from ore. Therefore, recycling aluminum helps to conserve fuel.

Paragraphs will vary.

It is impossible to get minerals and fossil fuels from the earth without causing damage to its surface. In the past, people did not think much about making these kinds of changes to our planet. They did not think about how these actions might affect the future. As a result, much of the land around mines was left useless and ugly. This is not necessary, because such land can be restored to its former beauty.

Page 330

Writing: Summarizing

A **summary** is a brief retelling of the main ideas of a reading selection. To summarize, write the author's most important points in your own words.

Directions: Write a two-sentence summary for each paragraph.

The boll weevil is a small beetle that is native to Mexico. It feeds inside the seed pods, or bolls, of cotton plants. The boll weevil crossed into Texas in the late 1800s. It has since spread into most of the cotton-growing areas of the United States. The boll weevil causes hundreds of millions of dollars worth of damage to cotton crops each year.

Summary: **Answers will vary.**

Each spring, female boll weevils open the buds of young cotton plants with their snouts. They lay eggs inside the buds, and the eggs soon hatch into wormlike grubs. The grubs feed inside the buds, causing the buds to fall from the plant. They eat their way from one bud to another. Several generations of boll weevils may be produced in a single season.

Summary: _____

The coming of the boll weevil to the United States caused tremendous damage to cotton crops. Yet, there were some good results, too. Farmers were forced to plant other crops. In areas where a variety of crops were raised, the land is in better condition than it would have been if only cotton had been grown.

Summary: _____

Page 331

Writing: Summarizing a Personal Narrative

Directions: Read the following narrative, and then follow the directions below and on page 333.

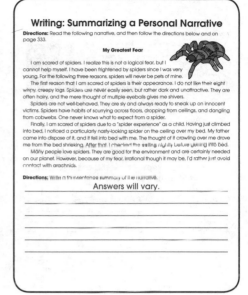

My Greatest Fear

I am scared of spiders. I realize this is not a logical fear, but I cannot help myself. I have been frightened by spiders since I was very young. For the following three reasons, spiders will never be pets of mine.

The first reason that I am scared of spiders is their appearance. I do not like their eight wispy, creepy legs. Spiders are never easily seen, but rather dark and unattractive. They are often hairy, and the mere thought of multiple eyeballs gives me shivers.

Spiders are not well-behaved. They are sly and always ready to sneak up on innocent victims. Spiders have habits of scurrying across floors, dropping from ceilings, and dangling from cobwebs. One never knows what to expect from a spider.

Finally, I am scared of spiders due to a "spider experience" as a child. Having just climbed into bed, I noticed a particularly nasty-looking spider on the ceiling over my bed. My father came into dispose of it, and it fell into bed with me. The thought of it crawling over me drove me from the bed shrieking. After that, I checked the ceiling nightly before getting into bed.

Many people love spiders. They are good for the environment and are certainly needed on our planet. However, because of my fear, irrational though it may be, I'd rather just avoid contact with arachnids.

Directions: Write a four-sentence summary of the narrative.

Answers will vary.

Page 332

Writing: Summarizing a Personal Narrative

Write the main idea of the second paragraph.

The author doesn't like spiders because of their appearance.

Write the main idea of the third paragraph.

The author doesn't like spiders because they are not well-behaved.

Write the main idea of the fourth paragraph.

The author doesn't like spiders because of an experience as a child.

Everyone has a fear of something. On another sheet of paper, write a five-paragraph personal narrative about a fear of your own. Use the following guide to help you organize your narrative.

Paragraph 1. State your fear.

Provide background information about fear.

Paragraph 2. State your first reason for fear.

Support this statement with at least three sentences.

Paragraph 3. State your second reason for fear.

Support this statement with at least three sentences.

Paragraph 4. State your third reason for fear.

Support this statement with at least three sentences.

Paragraph 5. Provide a summary of your narrative.

Restate your fear in different words from the opening sentence.

Page 333

Writing: Outlining

An **outline** is a skeletal description of the main ideas and important details of a reading selection. Making an outline is a good study aid. It is particularly useful when you must write a paper.

Directions: Read the paragraphs, and then complete the outline below.

Weather has a lot to do with where animals live. Cold-blooded animals have body temperatures that change with the temperature of the environment. Cold-blooded animals include snakes, frogs, and lizards. They cannot live anywhere the temperatures stay below freezing for long periods of time. The body temperatures of warm-blooded animals do not depend on the environment. Any animal with hair or fur—including dogs, elephants, and whales—is warm-blooded. Warm-blooded animals can live anywhere in the world where there is enough food to sustain them.

Some warm-blooded animals live where snow covers the ground all winter. These animals have different ways to survive the cold weather. Certain animals store up food to last throughout the snowy season. For example, the tree squirrel may gather nuts to hide in its home. Other animals hibernate in the winter. The ground squirrel, for example, stays in its

Answers may vary. Possible answers shown.

Title: **Animal Habitats**

Main Topic: I. **Weather has a lot to do with where animals live.**

Subtopic: A. Cold-blooded animals' temperatures change with environment.

Detail: 1. **They cannot live anywhere it stays below freezing too long.**

Subtopic: B. **Warm-blooded animals' temperatures do not depend on the environment.**

Detail: 1. They can live anywhere there is food.

Main Topic: II. **Some warm-blooded animals can live in the snow all winter.**

Subtopic: A. Animals have different ways to survive the cold.

Details: 1. **Some animals store food for the winter.**

2. **Some animals hibernate in the winter.**

Page 334

Review

Directions: Read the paragraph, and then follow the directions.

According to one estimate, 75 percent of all fresh water on Earth is in the form of ice. The polar regions of earth are almost completely covered by ice. In some places, the ice is more than 8,000 feet thick. If all of this ice were spread out evenly, Earth would be covered with a 100-foot thick layer of ice. Although ice is not an important source of fresh water today, it could be in the future. Some people have proposed towing large, floating masses of ice to cities to help keep up with the demand for fresh water.

1. Complete the outline of the paragraph.

Answers may vary. Possible answers shown.

Title: **Using Ice for Fresh Water**

Main Topic: I. 75 percent of fresh water on Earth is ice.

Subtopics: A. **The polar regions have the largest source of ice.**

B. **Ice could be an important source of fresh water in the future.**

2. Check the most appropriate generalization.

☒ Ice is the most plentiful source of fresh water.

☐ Ice is important to the future.

3. Paraphrase the first sentence by restating it in your own words.

Answers will vary.

4. Is the author's purpose to inform, entertain, or persuade?

to inform

5. Where would you look to find information on the polar ice caps?

an encyclopedia and/or an almanac

Page 335

Review

Directions: Read the paragraph, and then follow the directions.

Constellations are groups of stars that have been given names. They often represent an animal, person, or object. One of the easiest constellations to identify is the Big Dipper, which is shaped like a spoon. Once the Big Dipper is located, it is easy to see Cassiopeia (a W), the Little Dipper (an upside-down spoon), and the North Star. The North Star's scientific name is Polaris, and it is the last star in the handle of the Little Dipper. Other constellations include Orion the hunter, Gemini the twins, Canis Major the dog, and Pegasus the winged horse. Many ancient cultures, including the Greeks and Native Americans, used the position of the stars to guide them. They also planned daily life activities, such as planting, hunting, and harvesting, by the path the constellations made through the sky. For thousands of years, humans have gazed at the sky, fascinated by the millions of stars and imagining pictures in the night.

The Constellation Orion

Answers may vary.
1. Complete the outline of the paragraph. **Possible answers shown.**

Title: Constellations
Main Topic: I. Constellations are groups of stars that represent something.
Subtopics: A. How to locate a few of the constellations
B. The meanings of constellations to ancient Greeks and Native Americans

2. In three sentences, summarize the paragraph.
Answers will vary.

3. What is the author's purpose? to inform
4. Under which topics would you look to find more information on constellations?
Possible answers shown.
astronomy   Greek mythology   Native American legends

Page 336

Review

Directions: Imagine you are making a speech about one of your hobbies. Complete an outline of the speech.
Answers will vary.

Title:
Main Topic: I.
Subtopics: A.
B.
Who is your audience?
Is it appropriately written for that audience?
Are you trying to inform, entertain, or persuade?
In the space below, write your speech in at least 100 words.

Page 337

Using the Right Resources

Directions: Decide where you would look to find information on the following topics. All of these resources are available either in print or online form.

- **almanac** — contains tables and charts of statistics and information
- **atlas** — collection of maps
- **dictionary** — contains alphabetical listing of words with their meanings, pronunciations, and origins
- **encyclopedia** — a book, website, or CD-ROM with general information on many subjects
- **library catalog** — library resource showing available books by topic, title or author
- **Readers' Guide to Periodical Literature** — an index of articles in magazines and newspapers
- **thesaurus** — contains synonyms and antonyms of words

Answers may vary. Possible answers shown.
1. What is the capital of the Netherlands? atlas, encyclopedia
2. What form of government is practiced there? almanac, encyclopedia
3. What languages are spoken there? almanac, encyclopedia
4. What is the meaning of the word **indigenous**? dictionary, thesaurus
5. Where would you find information on conservation? library catalog, Readers' Guide to Periodical Literature, encyclopedia
6. What is a synonym for **catastrophe**? dictionary, thesaurus
7. Where would you find a description of the play Cats? Readers' Guide to Periodical Literature, encyclopedia
8. Where would you find statistics on the annual rainfall in the Sahara? almanac, encyclopedia
9. What is the origin of the word **plentiful**? dictionary
10. What are antonyms for the word **plentiful**? dictionary, thesaurus
11. Where would you find statistics for the number of automobiles manufactured in the United States last year? almanac, encyclopedia

Page 338

Making Inferences: Reference Sources

Directions: In the box are four different kinds of reference sources. On the line next to each question, write which source you would use to find the information. Some information can be found in more than one reference.

encyclopedia	almanac	dictionary	thesaurus

1. A list of words that mean the same as **strong** — thesaurus
2. How much rain fell in Iowa in the year 1992 — almanac
3. What part of speech the word **porch** is — dictionary
4. How many different types of hummingbirds there are — encyclopedia
5. Weather patterns in Texas for the last 2 years — almanac
6. A list of words that mean the opposite of **cold** — thesaurus
7. Who invented the telescope — encyclopedia
8. How to pronounce the word **barometer** — dictionary
9. How many syllables the word **elephant** has — thesaurus
10. What the difference is between African and Asian elephants — encyclopedia
11. The population changes in New York between 1935 and 2015 — almanac
12. How fast a cheetah can run — encyclopedia

Page 339

Conducting Research

Directions: Read the following questions. Use the Internet or library resources to answer them.

1. Choose two figures from history. Research them on www.biography.com. Write two facts you found about each person.
Answers will vary.

2. Use a resource book or online search to find out what Mohs scale of hardness is and what is at the top and bottom of the scale.

3. What were the last three winners of the Caldecott Medal for best illustrations in children's books?

4. Name three types of butterflies. List the source of your information.

5. Visit the site www.libraryspot.com. Write three questions that a classmate could answer by using this site.

6. Use a library catalog to search for books about rain forests. List the titles and call numbers of three books you find.

Page 340

Review

Directions: Read the following questions. Use the Internet or library resources to answer them.

1. Use a print or online children's almanac to find two facts about animals or the environment.
Answers will vary.

2. How tall is the Eiffel Tower?
3. List two sources you could use to find current information about the International Space Station.

4. Use a print or online atlas to find out what five South American countries share a border with Bolivia.

Directions: Check the resource you would use to find the following information.

1. How to play checkers ☐ almanac ☐ dictionary ☒ an Internet search
2. An example sentence using the word **breathe**
☐ encyclopedia ☐ thesaurus ☒ dictionary
3. How many inches of snow fell in the Colorado Rockies last year
☐ an atlas ☒ an Internet search ☐ thesaurus
4. How many syllables are in the word **justification**
☐ almanac ☐ thesaurus ☒ dictionary
5. A synonym for **discontent**
☐ encyclopedia ☐ almanac ☒ thesaurus

Page 341

Table of Contents

The **table of contents**, located in the front of books or magazines, tells a lot about what is inside.

A table of contents in books lists the headings and page numbers for each chapter. **Chapters** are the parts into which books are divided. Also listed are chapter numbers and the sections and subsections, if any. Look at the sample table of contents below:

Contents

Directions: Using the table of contents above, answer the following questions.

1. How many chapters are in this book? **3**
2. What chapter contains information about things to plant? **2**
3. On what page does information about fences begin? **5**
4. What chapter tells you what you can use to help your garden grow better? **3**
5. What page tells you how to use fertilizer? **19**
6. What page tells you how far apart to plant pumpkin seeds? **14**
7. What is on page 11? **information about tomatoes**
8. What is on page 4? **information about garden locations**

Page 342

Table of Contents

The table of contents below is divided into units and sections. **Units** are parts into which a book is divided. **Sections** are segments of each unit.

Table of Contents

Directions: Using the table of contents above, answer the following questions.

1. How many units are in this book? **4**
2. Where would you find information about life on Mars? **pages 32-38**
3. Where would you find information about the sun's heat and brightness? **Unit 1**
4. What is on page 27? **information about Earth**
5. Orion is a large group of stars, or constellation. Where would you find information about it? **page 74**
6. What is on page 101? **information about comets**
7. Where would you find information about the moons of Jupiter? **pages 39-48**
8. How many pages in this book are about Earth? **5**
9. How many pages in this book are about Polaris? **3**
10. Where would you read about the Big Dipper? **pages 67-68**

Page 343

Table of Contents

In some magazines, the table of contents lists articles in numerical order. Other magazines' tables of contents are organized by subjects, by columns, and by features. **Subjects** are the topics covered in the articles. A **feature** is a specific kind of article, such as an article about sports or cooking. **Feature** also has another meaning. A regular feature is something that appears in every issue, such as letters to the editor, movie reviews, and sports statistics. Some magazines also call regular features "departments." **Columns** are another kind of regular feature published in every issue. A person who writes a column is called a **columnist**.

Most magazines' tables of contents will also give you an idea of what a story is about. In online magazines, the table of contents often includes links that you can click to jump to a particular page or article.

Kids' Life

Directions: Answer these questions about Kids' Life magazine.

1. On what page does the story about summer camp begin? **12**
2. List the titles of the departments in this magazine.
  a) **Your Health**   b) **Sports**   c) **Letters to the Editor**
3. Can you tell what the Battle of Gettysburg is by reading the table of contents? **Yes (battle in the American Civil War)**
4. Is there any information in this magazine about in-line skating? **No**

Page 344

Table of Contents

The articles in this magazine are grouped according to subjects.

LIVING
Table of Contents

Directions: Answer these questions about LIVING magazine.

1. How many departments are in this issue of the magazine? **6**
2. Circle the topics that are regular features in LIVING.
  (Books)   Dinosaurs   Cleveland Indians   Vice Presidents
  (Comedy)   (Living Well)   (Snacks)   Earth Day
3. What page would you look at if you wanted to see reviews of current movies? **24**
4. Is there any information in this magazine about football? **No**
5. Who are the two people featured in this issue? **Joe Biden and Jim Henson**
6. Is there anything in this issue about cycling? **Yes**
7. Under what heading is it listed? **Exercise**

Page 345

Indexes

An **index** is an alphabetical listing of names, topics, and important words. It is found in the back of a book. An index lists every page on which these items appear. For example, in a book about music, dulcimer might be listed this way: Dulcimer 2, 13, 26, 38. Page numbers may also be listed like this: Guitars 18–21. That means that information about guitars begins on page 18 and continues through page 21. **Subject** is the name of the item in an index. **Sub-entry** is a smaller division of the subject. For example, apples would be listed under fruit.

Index

Directions: Answer the questions about the index from this book about the solar system.

1. On what pages is there information about Polaris? **35 and 36**
2. On what pages is information about Saturn's first ring found? **9 and 25**
3. What is on page 41? **information about Project Ozma**
4. Where is there information about the pole star? **pages 35 and 36**
5. What is on page 43? **information about the *Orion* rocket**
6. On what page would you find information about planets that are visible to the eye? **9**
7. On what page would you find information about Jupiter's satellites? **24**

Page 346

Indexes

Some magazines use indexes to guide their readers to information they contain.

Directions: Answer the questions about the index from Bon Appetit magazine.

1. How many kinds of salad are listed in this issue? **4**
2. What is the recipe that contains radishes? **Lemongrass Soup**
3. Name the recipe found on page 24. **Chicken, Fennel, Orange, and Olive Salad**
4. On what page would you find an appetizer that includes scallops? **116**
  What is the name of this recipe? **Scallops with Sorrel and Tomato**
5. Can you find any listings that contain halibut? **Yes**
6. On what page is a recipe made from sweet potatoes? **136**
  What is the name of this recipe? **Sweet Potato Ribbon Chips**
  For what part of a meal would it be served? **Appetizer**

Page 347

Review

FARMING
Table of Contents

9   Farmers of the Midwest — Read about small farmers still trying to survive in the business.

15   Farmers' Markets — Some farmers take their goods to town and sell them to the city folk.

26   Hay: The Cheapest Way — New technology helps produce bales of hay quicker and cheaper than in the past.

36   The Farm Family — Farming is a way of life, and everybody helps!

Departments

Letters to the Editor 5
Finances 7
High Tech 13
Haymaker 27

INDEX

Africa 6
Alabama 49
Alps 21, 25
Antarctica 10-12
Antarctica Circle 8-10
Arctic 12-14
Arctic Circle 14
Arctic Ocean 15
Asia 37
Athens 33
Atlantic Ocean 11

Baltic Sea 15, 30
Baltimore 51
Black Sea 37
Bombay 39
Brazil 59
British Isles 19
Buffalo 52
Bug River 31

Cadiz 27
California 48
Cambridge 19
Cape of Good Hope 49
China 11, 41
Colorado River, Argentina 61
Colorado River, U.S.A. 62
Continents 2-3
Cuba 55

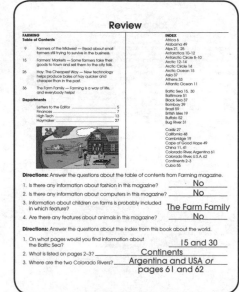

Directions: Answer the questions about the table of contents from *Farming* magazine.

1. Is there any information about fashion in this magazine? **No**
2. Is there any information about computers in this magazine? **No**
3. Information about children on farms is probably included in which feature? **The Farm Family**
4. Are there any features about animals in this magazine? **No**

Directions: Answer the questions about the index from this book about the world.

1. On what pages would you find information about the Baltic Sea? **15 and 30**
2. What is listed on pages 2–3? **Continents**
3. Where are the two Colorado Rivers? **Argentina and USA** *or* **pages 61 and 62**

Page 348

Review

Directions: Follow the instructions for each section.
Answers may vary. Possible answers shown.

1. In your own words, explain why a table of contents is helpful.
   Answers will vary.

2. A table of contents is often divided into units and sections.
   What is a unit? **one part into which a book has been divided**
   What is a section? **a smaller part of a unit**

3. What is the purpose of breaking a table of contents down into units and sections?
   It helps make information in the book easier to find.

4. What is an index?
   An index is an alphabetical listing of names, topics and important words. It is found in the back of a book.

5. What are the differences between a table of contents and an index?
   The information contained in each may differ slightly. Indexes are organized alphabetically, and tables of contents are organized according to subject, column, or feature in numerical order. The table of contents is in front, the index, the back.

6. Look at the table of contents in the front of this book. How many pages does the unit on Famous Athletes span?
   9 pages

Page 349

Biographical Research

A **biography** is a written history of a person's life. Often, information for a biography can be obtained from an encyclopedia, especially if a person is famous.

Most libraries have a biography section in the nonfiction area of the children's section. In this area, books are usually listed by the last name of the subject of the biography. For example, a biography of Amelia Earhart would appear after one about Mary Cassatt but before one about Bill Gates (Cassatt, Earhart, Gates).

There are also many websites where you can find biographies of athletes, scientists, politicians, artists, inventors, explorers, and so on. Like any other Internet searches, you must be careful to use only reliable, trustworthy sites. Sites such as www.biography.com, www.history.com, www.factmonster.com, and www.kidsclick.org are good places to start. If you ever feel unsure about the reliability of a website, be sure to check with a teacher or parent.

Directions: Answer these questions.

1. You are looking for biographies about the following people. Write the names in the order in which they would appear on the shelf in a library: Nat Turner, Eleanor Roosevelt, Wilma Rudolph, Wilbur Wright, Madeline Albright, and Jonas Salk.
   Madeline Albright, Eleanor Roosevelt, Wilma Rudolph, Jonas Salk, Nat Turner, Wilbur Wright

2. Where was Abraham Lincoln born? Use a biographical or online encyclopedia to find the answer.
   Hodgenville, Kentucky

3. Look up Anne Lindbergh in a biographical resource and write down the years of her birth and death.
   1906-2001

Page 350

Biographical Research

Directions: Use the resources suggested on the previous page to research one of the following people. Begin writing your biographical report in the space provided. (If you need more room, use a separate sheet of paper.)

Research Topics:	
Steve Jobs	Barack Obama
Wangari Maathai	Jacques Cousteau
Maya Lin	Malala Yousafzai

Answers will vary.

Page 351

Biographical Research

Directions: Conduct research to find one fact about each of the following subjects. Use biographies or biographical encyclopedias you find at the library, online encyclopedias, or biographical Web sites.

Answers will vary.

1. Sally Ride
2. Frederick Douglass
3. Wilson Bentley
4. Frida Kahlo
5. Charles Goodyear
6. Serena Williams
7. Jeremy Lin
8. Stephen Hawking
9. Cynthia Rylant

Page 352

Biographical Research

Directions: In the space provided, use print and/or online resources to write a report about one of the people listed below. Use additional paper, if necessary.

Maria Sharapova   Steven Spielberg   Hillary Clinton
John Glenn   Andrew Lloyd Webber   Jodie Foster

Answers will vary.

Page 353

Using the Library Catalog

Directions: Use the library catalog entries to answer the questions that follow.

Electric Ben: The Amazing Life and Times of Benjamin Franklin
Byrd, Robert.
Call Number: JB Franklin
New York: Dial Books for Young Readers, 2012.
ISBN: 978-0803737495
Subject: Franklin, Benjamin 1706–1790—Juvenile Literature
Inventors—United States—Biography—Juvenile Literature
Statesmen—United States—Biography—Juvenile Literature

1. What is the ISBN for Electric Ben? __978-0803737495__
2. How many subjects is the book listed under? __3__
3. What is the book's subtitle? __The Amazing Life and Times of Benjamin Franklin__
4. In what year was Electric Ben published? __2012__

Dogs on Duty: Soldiers' Best Friends on the Battlefield and Beyond
Patent, Dorothy Hinshaw.
Call Number: J355.424
Bloomsbury USA Children's, 2014.
ISBN: 978-0802736505
Subject: Dogs—War Use—Juvenile Literature

5. Who is the author of Dogs on Duty? __Dorothy Hinshaw Patent__
6. What is the book's call number? __J355.424__
7. Is this book intended for children or adults? How do you know? __Children: the subject Dogs is listed under Juvenile Literature__
8. If you wanted to find more books on this subject, what search could you do in the library catalog? __Dogs, War Use__

Page 354

Using the Library Catalog

A **library catalog** is a digital listing of the materials a library owns. Most libraries offer many search options. The most common ways to search are by title, author, subject, or keyword. If you don't find the book you are looking for at first, you may find it by changing your search. For example, if you can't find a book by title, try doing a keyword search using only one or two main words from the title.

Directions: Use a library catalog to answer the following questions.

1. What are the titles of three books by Roald Dahl? __Answers will vary.__
2. Write the title of a children's book about volcanoes. __Answers will vary.__
3. Write the author of one of the books in the Dear America series. __Answers will vary.__
4. Who wrote the book Ice Island? __Sherry Shahan__
5. In what year was The Voyage of Lucy P. Simmons published? __2012__
6. Who is your favorite author? Write the author's name and the titles of two books he or she has published. __Answers will vary.__
7. Who illustrated Scout: A Little Otter Returns Home? __Jon Van Zyle__
8. Do a keyword search for children's books about basketball. Write the titles and call numbers of two books that you find in your search results. __Answers will vary.__
9. In what section of the library would you find Jean Lafitte: The Pirate Who Saved America? __biography__
10. What is the call number of the book The Giant and How He Humbugged America? __J 974.765 MURP__

Page 355

Review

Directions: Write **T** or **F** on the line beside each statement.

__T__ 1. A biography of Rosa Parks would come after a biography of Peyton Manning on a library shelf.
__F__ 2. A library is the only source of information for biographies.
__T__ 3. Most libraries shelve biographies in a separate section than other nonfiction books.

Directions: Write one biographical fact about each of the following people.

1. John F. Kennedy   Answers will vary.
2. Maya Lin
3. Gustav Klimt
4. Alma Flor Ada
5. Tiger Woods

Directions: Use a library catalog to answer the following questions.

1. Who is the author of Same Sun Here? __Silas House and Neela Vaswani__
2. What is the ISBN for What Came from the Stars? __0544336364 or 978-0544336360__
3. Who illustrated Guys Read: The Sports Pages? __Dan Santat__
4. Do a subject search for Civil War books. Write the call numbers and titles of two books in your search results. __Answers will vary.__

Page 356

Poetry

Format:
Line 1: Name
Line 2: Name is a (metaphor)
Line 3: He/she is like a (simile)
Line 4: He/she (three action words)
Line 5: He/she (relationship)
Line 6: Name

Example:
Jessica
Jessica is a joy.
She is like a playful puppy.
She tumbles, runs, and laughs.
She's my baby sister!
Jessica

Directions: Build a poem that describes a friend or relative by using similes, metaphors, and other words of your choice. Follow the form of the example poem.

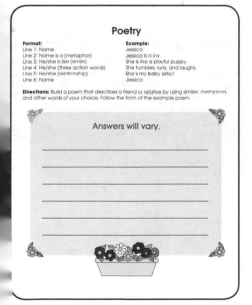

Answers will vary.

Page 357

Poetry: Haiku

Haiku is a type of unrhymed Japanese poetry with three lines. The first line has five syllables. The second line has seven syllables. The third line has five syllables.

Example:

Katie
Katie leaps and bounds.
Runs free, full of life and joy.
Companion, friend, dog.

Directions: Write a haiku about a pet and another about a hobby you enjoy. Be sure to write a title on the first line. If you do not have a pet, write about a pet you might like to have.

Answers will vary.

Pet

Hobby

Page 358

Poetry: Diamanté

A **diamanté** is a poem in the shape of a diamond. Diamantés have seven lines with this format:

Line 1: one-word noun, opposite of word in line 7
Line 2: two adjectives describing line 1
Line 3: three ing or ed words about line 1
Line 4: two nouns about line 1 and two nouns about line 7
Line 5: three ing or ed words about line 7
Line 6: two adjectives describing line 7
Line 7: one word noun, opposite of word in line 1

Example:

child
happy, playful
running, singing, laughing
toys, games, job, family
working, driving, nurturing
responsible, busy
adult

Directions: Write a diamanté of your own.

Answers will vary.

Page 359

Writing: Free Verse

Poems that do not rhyme and do not have a regular rhythm are called **free verse**. They often use adjectives, adverbs, similes, and metaphors to create word pictures.

My Old Cat
Curled on my bed at night,
Quietly happy to see me,
Soft, sleepy, relaxed,
A calm island in my life.

Directions: Write your own free verse. Use the guidelines for each poem.

1. Write a two-line free verse poem about a feeling. Compare it to some kind of food. For example, anger could be a tangle of spaghetti. Give your poem a title.

Answers will vary.

2. Think of how someone you know is like a color—happy like yellow, for example. Write a two-line free verse poem on this topic without naming the person. Don't forget a title.

3. Write a four-line free verse poem, like "My Old Cat," that creates a word picture of a day at school.

Page 360

Writing: Limericks

A **limerick** is a short, humorous poem. Limericks are five lines long and follow a specific rhyme pattern. Lines 1, 2, and 5 rhyme, and lines 3 and 4 rhyme.

Example:
There once was a young fellow named Fred
Whose big muscles went right to his head.
"I'll make the girls sigh,
'Cause I'm quite a guy!"
But the girls all liked Ted more than Fred!

Directions: Complete the limericks.

1. There was a young lady from Kent

Whose drawings were quite excellent.

Answers will vary.

So to the big city she went.

2. I have a pet squirrel named Sonny

He ran up a tree

As far as could be

3. There once was a boy who yelled, "Fire!"

He just did not see

Page 361

Writing: Acrostics

An **acrostic** is a poem that uses the letters of a word to begin each line. Read down, the first letter of each line spells the word. The poem tells something about the word that is spelled out.

Example:
In the grass or underground,
Now and then they fly around.
Slugs and worms and butterflies,
Each has its own shape and size.
Caterpillars, gnats, a bee,
Take them all away from me!

Directions: Write acrostic poems for the words **shoes** and **phone**. Your poems can rhyme or be free verse.

Answers will vary.

S _____
H _____
O _____
E _____
S _____

P _____
H _____
O _____
N _____
E _____

Directions: Write an acrostic poem for your name or a word of your choice on another sheet of paper. Draw a picture for your poem.

Page 362

Friendly Letters

Directions: Study the format for writing a letter to a friend. Then, answer the questions.

your return address — 4500 Waverly Road
Cincinnati, Ohio 45241
date — June 23, 2015
greeting — Dear Josh,
body —
How is your summer going? I am enjoying mine so far. I have been swimming twice already this week, and it is only Wednesday! I am glad there is a pool near our house.
My parents said that you can stay overnight when your family comes for the 4th of July picnic. Do you want to? We can pitch a tent in the backyard and camp out. It will be a lot of fun!
Please write back to let me know if you can stay over on the 4th. I will see you then!
closing — Your friend,
signature — Michael

your return address — Michael Delaney
4500 Waverly Road
Cincinnati, Ohio 45241

main address — Josh Sommers
3350 West First Ave.
Columbus, OH 43212

1. What words are in the greeting? **Dear Josh**
2. What words are in the closing? **Your friend**
3. On what street does the writer live? **Waverly Road**

Page 363

Friendly Letters

Directions: Follow the format for writing a letter to a friend. Don't forget to address the envelope!

Answers will vary.

Page 364

Place Value

Place value is the position of a digit in a number. A digit's place in a number shows its value. Numbers left of the decimal point represent **whole numbers**. Numbers right of the decimal point represent a part, or fraction, of a whole number. These parts are broken down into tenths, hundredths, thousandths, and so on.

Example:
3,443,221.621

millions	hundred thousands	ten thousands	thousands	hundreds	tens	ones	tenths	hundredths	thousandths
3	4	4	3	2	2	1	6	2	1
Whole Numbers							Fractions		

Directions: Write the following number words as numbers.

1. Three million, forty-four thousand, six hundred twenty-one __3,044,621__
2. One million, seventy-seven __1,000,077__
3. Nine million, six hundred thousand, one hundred two __9,600,102__
4. Twenty-nine million, one hundred three thousand, and nine tenths __29,103,000.9__
5. One million, one hundred thousand, one hundred seventy-one, and thirteen hundredths __1,100,171.13__

Directions: In each box, write the corresponding number for each place value.

1. 4,822,000.00 — [0] hundreds
2. 55,907,003.00 — [7] thousands
3. 190,641,225.07 — [6] hundred thousands
4. 247,308,211.59 — [5] tenths
5. 7,594,097.33 — [7] millions
6. 201,480,110.01 — [4] hundred thousands
7. 42,367,109,074.25 — [5] hundredths

Page 366

Place Value

The chart below shows the place value of each number.

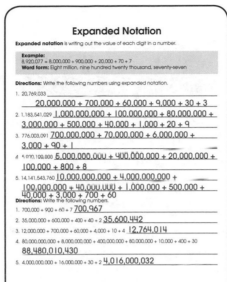

trillions			billions			millions			thousands			ones		
h	t	o	h	t	o	h	t	o	h	t	o	h	t	o
		2		1	4	0	9	0	0	6	8	0	3	5	0

Word form: two trillion, one hundred forty billion, nine hundred million, six hundred eighty thousand, three hundred fifty

Directions: Draw a line to the correct value of each underlined digit. The first one is done for you.

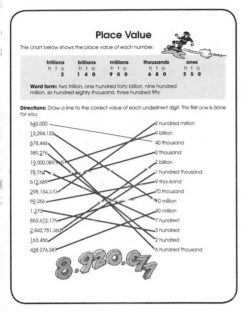

643,000 → 2 hundred million
13,294,125 → 9 billion
678,446 → 40 thousand
389,276 → 2 thousand
19,000,089,945 → 2 billion
78,764 → 1 hundred thousand
612,689 → 9 thousand
298,154,370 → 70 thousand
89,256 → 40 million
1,370 → 30 million
853,672,175 → 7 hundred
2,842,751,360 → 3 hundred
163,456 → 2 hundred
438,276,587 → 6 hundred thousand

Page 367

Expanded Notation

Expanded notation is writing out the value of each digit in a number.

Example:
8,920,077 = 8,000,000 + 900,000 + 20,000 + 70 + 7
Word form: Eight million, nine hundred twenty thousand, seventy-seven

Directions: Write the following numbers using expanded notation.

1. 20,769,033
   20,000,000 + 700,000 + 60,000 + 9,000 + 30 + 3
2. 1,183,541,029 1,000,000,000 + 100,000,000 + 80,000,000 + 3,000,000 + 500,000 + 40,000 + 1,000 + 20 + 9
3. 776,003,091 700,000,000 + 70,000,000 + 6,000,000 + 3,000 + 90 + 1
4. 5,920,100,808 5,000,000,000 + 400,000,000 + 20,000,000 + 100,000 + 800 + 8
5. 14,141,543,760 10,000,000,000 + 4,000,000,000 + 100,000,000 + 40,000,000 + 1,000,000 + 500,000 + 40,000 + 3,000 + 700 + 60

Directions: Write the following numbers.

1. 700,000 + 900 + 60 + 7 700,967
2. 35,000,000 + 600,000 + 400 + 40 + 2 35,600,442
3. 12,000,000 + 700,000 + 60,000 + 4,000 + 10 + 4 12,764,014
4. 80,000,000,000 + 8,000,000,000 + 400,000,000 + 80,000,000 + 10,000 + 400 + 30 88,480,010,430
5. 4,000,000,000 + 16,000,000 + 30 + 2 4,016,000,032

Page 368

Addition and Place Value

Directions: Add the problems below in which the digits with the same place value are lined up correctly. Then, cross out the problems in which the digits are not lined up correctly.

Find each answer in the diagram, and color that section.

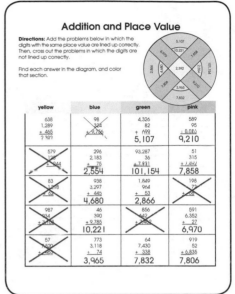

yellow	blue	green	pink
638 1,289 + 465 2,392	98 324 + 9,750	4,326 82 + 699 5,107	589 95 + 1,050 9,210
579 128 + 844	296 2,183 + 75 2,554	93,287 36 + 7,831 101,154	51 315 + 1,492 7,858
83 1,278 + 64	938 3,297 + 445 4,680	1,849 964 + 53 2,866	198 72 + 408
987 234 + 9,782	46 390 + 9,785 10,221	856 642 + 2,404	591 6,352 + 27 6,970
57 290 + 463	773 3,118 + 74	64 7,430 + 338 7,832	919 52 + 6,835 7,806

Page 369

Addition

Directions: Add the following numbers in your head without writing them out.

1. 17 + 33 = 50
2. 35 + 15 = 50
3. 75 + 25 = 100
4. 41 + 25 = 66
5. 27 + 23 = 50
6. 30 + 20 = 50
7. 12 + 18 = 30
8. 43 + 22 = 65
9. 16 + 34 = 50
10. 9 + 11 + 30 = 50
11. 29 + 21 + 40 = 90
12. 14 + 16 + 20 = 50
13. 37 + 13 + 25 = 75
14. 12 + 22 + 36 = 70
15. 19 + 21 + 57 = 97
16. 21 + 24 + 25 = 70
17. 63 + 14 + 11 = 88
18. 33 + 15 + 42 = 90
19. 25 + 15 + 60 = 100
20. 30 + 20 + 10 = 60

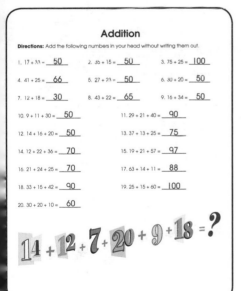

14 + 12 + 7 + 20 + 9 + 18 = ?

Page 370

Addition Word Problems

Directions: Solve the following addition word problems.

1. 100 students participated in a sports card show in the school gym. Brad brought his entire collection of 2,000 cards to show his friends. He had 700 football cards and 400 basketball cards. If the rest of his cards were baseball cards, how many baseball cards did he bring with him?

   900 baseball cards

2. Refreshments were set up in one area of the gym. Hot pretzels were a dollar, lemonade was 50 cents, fruit was 35 cents, and cookies were a quarter. If you purchased two of each item, how much money would you need?

   $4.20

3. It took each student 30 minutes to set up for the card show and twice as long to put everything away. The show was open for 3 hours. How much time did each student spend on this event?

   4 1/2 hours

4. 450 people attended the card show. 55 were mothers of students, 67 were fathers, 23 were grandparents, 8 were aunts and uncles, and the rest were kids. How many kids attended?

   297 kids

5. Of the 100 students who set up displays, most of them sold or traded some of their cards. Jonas sold 75 cards, traded 15 cards, and collected $225. Kevin only sold 15 cards, traded 81 cards, and collected $100. Valentina traded 200 cards, sold 10, and earned $35. Of those listed, how many cards were sold, how many were traded, and how much money was earned?

   sold **100**   traded **296**   earned $ **360**

Page 371

Subtraction

Directions: Subtract the following numbers. When subtracting, begin on the right, especially if you need to regroup and borrow.

549 - 162 387	823 - 417 406	370 - 244 126	648 - 79 569
700 - 343 357	475 - 299 176	603 - 425 178	354 - 265 89
1,841 - 952 889	2,597 - 608 1,989	6,832 - 1,774 5,058	9,005 - 3,458 5,547
23,342 - 9,093 14,249	53,790 - 40,813 12,977	29,644 - 19,780 9,864	35,726 - 16,959 18,767
109,432 - 79,145 30,287	350,907 - 14,185 336,722	217,523 - 44,197 173,326	537,411 - 406,514 130,897

Page 372

Comprehensive Curriculum - Grade 6

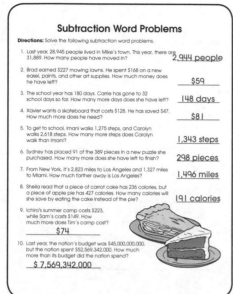

Subtraction Word Problems

Directions: Solve the following subtraction word problems.

1. Last year, 28,945 people lived in Mike's town. This year, there are 31,889. How many people have moved in? — **2,944 people**

2. Brad earned $227 mowing lawns. He spent $168 on a new easel, paints, and other art supplies. How much money does he have left? — **$59**

3. The school year has 180 days. Carrie has gone to 32 school days so far. How many more days does she have left? — **148 days**

4. Xavier wants a skateboard that costs $128. He has saved $47. How much more does he need? — **$81**

5. To get to school, Imani walks 1,275 steps, and Carolyn walks 2,618 steps. How many more steps does Carolyn walk than Imani? — **1,343 steps**

6. Sydney has placed 91 of the 389 pieces in a new puzzle she purchased. How many more does she have left to finish? — **298 pieces**

7. From New York, it's 2,823 miles to Los Angeles and 1,327 miles to Miami. How much farther away is Los Angeles? — **1,496 miles**

8. Sheila read that a piece of carrot cake has 236 calories, but a piece of apple pie has 427 calories. How many calories will she save by eating the cake instead of the pie? — **191 calories**

9. Ichiro's summer camp costs $223, while Sam's costs $149. How much more does Tim's camp cost? — **$74**

10. Last year, the nation's budget was $45,000,000,000, but the nation spent $52,569,342,000. How much more than its budget did the nation spend? — **$ 7,569,342,000**

Page 373

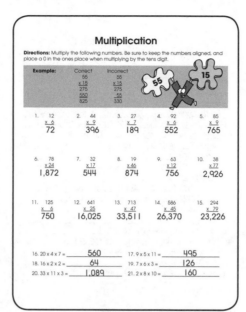

Multiplication

Directions: Multiply the following numbers. Be sure to keep the numbers aligned, and place a 0 in the ones place when multiplying by the tens digit.

Example:

Correct	Incorrect
55	55
x 15	x 15
275	275
550	55
825	330

1. 12 × 6 = **72**
2. 44 × 9 = **396**
3. 27 × 7 = **189**
4. 92 × 6 = **552**
5. 85 × 9 = **765**

6. 78 × 24 = **1,872**
7. 32 × 17 = **544**
8. 19 × 46 = **874**
9. 63 × 12 = **756**
10. 38 × 77 = **2,926**

11. 125 × 6 = **750**
12. 641 × 25 = **16,025**
13. 713 × 47 = **33,511**
14. 586 × 45 = **26,370**
15. 294 × 79 = **23,226**

16. 20 x 4 x 7 = **560**
17. 9 x 5 x 11 = **495**
18. 16 x 2 x 2 = **64**
19. 7 x 6 x 3 = **126**
20. 33 x 11 x 3 = **1,089**
21. 2 x 8 x 10 = **160**

Page 374

Multiplying with Zeros

Directions: Multiply the following numbers. If a number ends with zero, you can eliminate it while calculating the rest of the answer. Then, count how many zeros you took off, and add them to your answer.

Example:

550	Take off 2 zeros	500	Take off 2 zeros
x 50		x 5	
27,500	Add on 2 zeros	2,500	Add on 2 zeros

1. 300 × 6 = **1,800**
2. 400 × 7 = **2,800**
3. 620 × 5 = **3,100**
4. 290 × 7 = **2,030**

5. 142 × 20 = **2,840**
6. 505 × 50 = **25,250**
7. 340 × 70 = **23,800**
8. 600 × 60 = **36,000**

9. 550 × 380 = **209,000**
10. 290 × 150 = **43,500**
11. 2,040 × 360 = **734,400**
12. 8,800 × 200 = **1,760,000**

13. Bruce traveled 600 miles each day of a 10-day trip. How far did he go during the entire trip? — **6,000 miles**

14. 30 children each sold 20 items for the school fundraiser. Each child earned $100 for the school. How much money did the school collect? — **$3,000**

15. 10 x 40 x 2 = **800**
16. 30 x 30 x 10 = **9,000**
17. 100 x 60 x 10 = **60,000**
18. 500 x 11 x 2 = **11,000**
19. 9 x 10 x 10 = **900**
20. 7,000 x 20 x 10 = **1,400,000**

Page 375

Division

In a division problem, the **dividend** is the number to be divided, the **divisor** is the number used to divide, and the **quotient** is the answer. To check your work, multiply your answer times the divisor, and you should get the dividend.

Example:

```
          130 ← quotient      Check:   130 ← quotient
divisor→ 4 520 ← dividend             x   4 ← divisor
          4                           520 ← dividend
          12
          12
          00
```

Directions: Solve the following division problems.

1. 3)546 = **182**
2. 5)720 = **144**
3. 2)458 = **229**
4. 4)796 = **199**
5. 7)896 = **128**

6. 4)128 = **32**
7. 4)376 = **94**
8. 5)225 = **45**
9. 3)684 = **228**
10. 6)924 = **154**

11. 25)475 = **19**
12. 16)768 = **48**
13. 14)840 = **60**
14. 22)418 = **19**
15. 21)693 = **33**

Directions: Solve these division problems in your head. Challenge yourself for speed and accuracy.

1. 22 ÷ 2 = **11**
2. 15 ÷ 3 = **5**
3. 72 ÷ 9 = **8**
4. 36 ÷ 4 = **9**
5. 27 ÷ 9 = **3**
6. 56 ÷ 8 = **7**
7. 81 ÷ 9 = **9**
8. 42 ÷ 6 = **7**
9. 63 ÷ 9 = **7**
10. 60 ÷ 5 = **12**
11. 70 ÷ 10 = **7**
12. 98 ÷ 7 = **14**
13. 55 ÷ 5 = **11**
14. 64 ÷ 8 = **8**
15. 84 ÷ 3 = **28**

Page 376

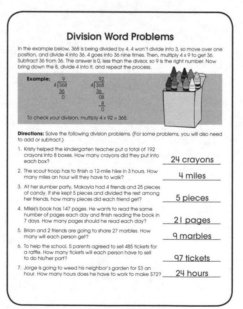

Division Word Problems

In the example below, 368 is being divided by 4. 4 won't divide into 3, so move over one position, and divide 4 into 36. 4 goes into 36 nine times. Then, multiply 4 x 9 to get 36. Subtract 36 from 36. The answer is 0, less than the divisor, so 9 is the right number. Now bring down the 8, divide 4 into it, and repeat the process.

Example:

```
     9           92
4)368       4)368
  36          36
   0          08
               8
               0
```

To check your division, multiply 4 x 92 = 368.

Directions: Solve the following division problems. (For some problems, you will also need to add or subtract.)

1. Kristy helped the kindergarten teacher put a total of 192 crayons into 8 boxes. How many crayons did they put into each box? — **24 crayons**

2. The scout troop has to finish a 12-mile hike in 3 hours. How many miles an hour will they have to walk? — **4 miles**

3. At her slumber party, Makayla had 4 friends and 25 pieces of candy. If she kept 5 pieces and divided the rest among her friends, how many pieces did each friend get? — **5 pieces**

4. Miles's book has 147 pages. He wants to read the same number of pages each day and finish reading the book in 7 days. How many pages should he read each day? — **21 pages**

5. Brian and 2 friends are going to share 27 marbles. How many will each person get? — **9 marbles**

6. To help the school, 5 parents agreed to sell 485 tickets for a raffle. How many tickets will each person have to sell to do his/her part? — **97 tickets**

7. Jorge is going to weed his neighbor's garden for $3 an hour. How many hours does he have to work to make $72? — **24 hours**

Page 377

Equations

In an **equation**, the value on the left of the equal sign must equal the value on the right. Remember the order of operations: solve from left to right, multiply or divide numbers before adding or subtracting, and do the operation inside parentheses first.

Example:

```
6 + 4 - 2 = 4 x 2
   10 - 2 = 8
        8 = 8
```

Directions: Write the correct operation signs in the blanks to make accurate equations.

1. (25 **+** 25) **÷** 2 = 100 **−** 75
2. (76 **+** 24) **×** 3 = 150 **×** 2
3. 140 **÷** 2 **×** 10 = 500 **+** 50 **+** 150
4. 2,100 **−** 2,000 **+** 60 = 80 **×** 2
5. 80 **×** 8 **÷** 4 = 160 **+** 160 **−** 160
6. (55 **×** 100) **÷** 11 = (1,000 **×** 2) **÷** 4
7. 137 **+** 81 **+** 52 = 3 **×** 90
8. 3,000 **÷** 10 **−** 10 = (600 **+** 300) **÷** 30
9. (720 **+** 20) **÷** 37 **×** 5
10. (457 **+** 43) **−** 500 = (21 **+** 40) x 0

Page 378

Equations

Directions: Write the correct operation signs in the blanks to make accurate equations.

1. 5 __+__ 5 __+__ 3 = 3 __×__ 5 __+__ 0
2. (50 __+__ 0) __×__ 2 = 25 __×__ 2 __×__ 2
3. 2 __×__ 2 __×__ 2 __×__ 2 = 2 __×__ 2 __×__ 4
4. (4 __×__ 5) __+__ 5 __+__ 5 = 2 __×__ 3 __×__ 5
5. 5 __+__ 5 __+__ 5 __+__ 5 = 3 __×__ 5 __+__ 2 __×__ 5
6. (125 __×__ 7) __+__ 2 __+__ 3 = 100 __×__ 2 __×__ 4 __+__ 70 __×__ 10
7. (100 __×__ 10) __×__ 5 __+__ 10 = 10 __×__ 5 __×__ 100 __+__ 10
8. 35 __+__ 35 __+__ 5 __×__ 2 = 5 __×__ 3 __×__ 2 __×__ 5
9. (60 __÷__ 2) __×__ 3 = 3 __×__ 3 __×__ 3 __×__ 0 + 15 __+__ (5 __×__ 15)
10. (120 __×__ 4) __+__ 7 __×__ 3 = 7 __×__ (7 __×__ 7) __×__ (2 __×__ 5)
11. (91 __+__ 3 __+__ 6) __×__ 3 = 2 __×__ 5 __×__ 1 __×__ 3 __×__ (2 __×__ 5)
12. (16 __×__ 4) __−__ 8 = 5 __+__ 5 __×__ (3 __×__ 3) __+__ 4
13. 0 __×__ 5 + 16 __−__ 4 = 3 __−__ 3 __÷__ 3 + 8
14. 16 __×__ 3 + 12 = (2 __×__ 20) = (2 __×__ 2) __×__ 6 __+__ 10 __−__ (7 __×__ 7)
15. 21 __+__ (3 __×__ 3) __−__ 3 = 1 __×__ 3 __×__ 1 __+__ 20

Rounding and Estimating

Rounding is expressing a number to the nearest whole number, ten, thousand, or other value.
Estimating is using an approximate number instead of an exact one. When rounding a number, you might say a country has 98,000,000 citizens instead of 98,347,425. We can round numbers to the nearest whole number, the nearest hundred, or the nearest million—whatever is appropriate.

Here are the steps: 1) Decide where you want to round the number. 2) If the digit to the right is less than 5, leave the digit at the rounding place unchanged. 3) If the digit to the right is 5 or more, increase the digit at the rounding place by 1.

> **Examples:** 587 rounded to the nearest hundred is 600.
> 535 rounded to the nearest hundred is 500.
> 21,897 rounded to the nearest thousand is 22,000.
> 21,356 rounded to the nearest thousand is 21,000.
>
> When we estimate numbers, we use rounded, approximate numbers instead of exact ones.
>
> **Example:** A hamburger that costs $1.49 and a drink that costs $0.79 total about $2.30 ($1.50 plus $0.80).

Directions: Use rounding and estimating to find the answers to these questions. You may have to add, subtract, multiply, or divide.

1. Sarita is having a party and wants to fill 11 cups from a 67-ounce bottle of juice. About how many ounces should she pour into each cup? __6 ounces__
2. Hannah studied 28 minutes every day for 4 days. About how long did she study in all? __120 minutes__
3. About how much does this lunch cost? $1.19 $0.39 $0.49 __$2.00__
4. The numbers below show how long Frank spent studying last week. Estimate how many minutes he studied for the whole week.
Monday: 23 minutes Tuesday: 37 minutes Wednesday: 38 minutes
Thursday: 12 minutes __110 minutes__
5. One elephant at the zoo weighs 1,417 pounds, and another one weighs 1,789 pounds. About how much heavier is the second elephant? __400 pounds__
6. If Jordan studied a total of 122 minutes over 4 days, about how long did he study each day? __30 minutes__
7. It's 549 miles to Dover and 345 miles to Albany. About how much closer is Albany? __200 miles__

Rounding

Directions: Round each number, and then estimate the answer. You can use a calculator to find the exact answer.

Round to the nearest ten.	Estimate	Actual Answer
1. 86 ÷ 9 =	9	9.56
2. 237 + 488 =	730	725
3. 49 × 11 =	500	539
4. 309 + 412 =	720	721
5. 625 − 218 =	410	407
Round to the nearest hundred.		
6. 790 − 70 =	700	720
7. 690 ÷ 70 =	7	9.86
8. 2,177 + 33 =	1,200	1,222
9. 4,792 + 3,305 =	8,100	8,097
10. 5,210 × 90 =	520,000	468,900
Round to the nearest thousand.		
11. 4,078 + 2,093 =	6,000	6,171
12. 5,525 − 3,065 =	3,000	2,460
13. 6,047 ÷ 2,991 =	2	2.02
14. 1,913 × 4,216 =	8,000,000	8,065,208
15. 7,227 + 8,449 =	15,000	15,676

Decimals

A **decimal** is a number that includes a period called a **decimal point**. The digits to the right of the decimal point are a value less than one.

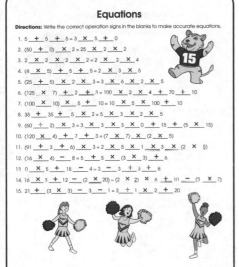

one whole   one tenth   one hundredth

The place value chart below helps explain decimals.

hundreds	tens	ones	tenths	hundredths	thousandths
6	3	2	. 4		
4	7	. 0	5		
	8	. 0	0	9	

A decimal point is read as "and." The first number, 632.4, is read as "six hundred thirty-two and four tenths." The second number, 47.05, is read as "forty-seven and five hundredths." The third number, 8.009, is read as "eight and nine thousandths."

Directions: Write the decimals shown below. Two have been done for you.

1. __1.4__   2. __1.16__   3. __1.78__

4. six and five tenths __6.5__
5. twenty-two and nine tenths __22.9__
6. thirty-six and fourteen hundredths __36.14__
7. forty-seven hundredths __0.47__
8. one hundred six and four tenths __106.4__
9. seven and three hundredths __7.03__
10. one tenth less than 0.6 __0.5__
11. one hundredth less than 0.34 __0.33__
12. one tenth more than 0.2 __0.3__

Adding and Subtracting Decimals

When adding or subtracting decimals, place the decimal points under each other. That way, you add tenths to tenths, for example, not tenths to hundredths. Add or subtract beginning on the right, as usual. Carry or borrow numbers in the same way. Adding 0 to the end of decimals does not change their value, but sometimes makes them easier to add and subtract.

> **Examples:**
> 39.40
> + 6.81
> 46.21
>
> 0.064
> + 0.470
> 0.534
>
> 3.56
> − .09
> 3.47
>
> 6.83
> − 2.14
> 4.69

Directions: Solve the following problems.

1. Write each set of numbers in a column and add them.
a. 2.56 + 0.6 + 76 = __79.16__
b. 93.5 + 23.06 + 1.45 = __118.01__
c. 3.23 + 91.34 + 0.85 = __95.42__
2. Write each pair of numbers in a column and subtract them.
A. 7.89 − 0.56 = __7.33__   B. 34.56 − 6.04 = __28.52__   C. 7.6 − 3.24 = __4.36__
3. In a relay race, Alice ran her part in 23.6 seconds, Xian did hers in 24.7 seconds, and Erin took 20.09 seconds. How many seconds did they take altogether? __68.39 seconds__
4. Although Erin ran her part in 20.09 seconds today, yesterday it took her 21.55 seconds. How much faster was she today? __1.46 seconds__
5. Add this grocery bill:
potatoes—$3.49; milk—$2.09; bread—$0.99; apples—$2.30 __$8.87__
6. A yellow coat cost $47.59, and a blue coat cost $36.79. How much more did the yellow coat cost? __$10.80__
7. A box of Oat Boats cereal has 14.6 ounces. A box of Nut Crunch has 17.85 ounces. How much more cereal is in the Nut Crunch box? __3.25 ounces__
8. The Oat Boats cereal has 4.03 ounces of sugar in it. Nut Crunch cereal has only 3.76 ounces. How much more sugar is in a box of Oats Boats? __0.27 ounces__

Mulitplying Decimals by Two-Digit Numbers

To multiply by a 2-digit number, just repeat the same steps. In the example below, first multiply 4 times 9, 4 times 5, and 4 times 3. Then, multiply 2 times 9, 2 times 5, and 2 times 3. You may want to place a 0 in the ones place to make sure this answer, 718, is one digit to the left. Now, add 1,436 + 7,180 to get the final answer.

> **Example:**
> 359
> × 24
> 6
>
> 359
> × 24
> 36
>
> 359
> × 24
> 1,436
>
> 359
> × 24
> 1,436
>
> 359
> × 24
> 1,436
> 80
> 180
>
> 359
> × 24
> 1,436
> 7,180
> 8,616

When one or both numbers in a multiplication problem have decimals, check to see how many digits are right of the decimal. Then, place the decimal point the same number of places to the left in the answer. Here's how the example above would change if it included decimals:

> 35.9
> × 0.24
> 8.616
>
> 3.59
> × 24
> 86.16

The first example has one digit to the right of the decimal in 35.9 and two more in 0.24, so the decimal point is placed three digits to the left in the answer: 8.616. The second example has two digits to the right of the decimal in 3.59 and none in 24, so the decimal point is placed two digits to the left in the answer: 86.16. (Notice that you do not have to line up the decimals in a multiplication problem.)

Directions: Solve the following problems.

1. Zoe wants to buy 3 T-shirts that cost $15.99 each. How much will they cost altogether? __$47.97__
2. Ari is making $8.50 an hour packing groceries. How much will he make in 8 hours? __$68__
3. Justin made 36 frozen smoothie pops and sold them all at the school carnival for $0.75 each. How much would it cost to buy all 36 of them? __$27__
4. Last year, the carnival made $467. This year it made 2.3 times as much. How much money did the carnival make this year? __$1,074.10__
5. Troy's car will go 21.8 miles on a gallon of gasoline. His motorcycle will go 1.7 times as far. How far will his motorcycle travel on one gallon of gas? __37.06 miles__

Multiplying Decimals

In some problems, you may need to add zeros in order to place the decimal point correctly.

Examples:	0.34	0.0067	0.046
	x 0.08	x 4	x 0.07
	0.0272	0.0268	0.003222

Directions: Solve the following problems.

1. 0.15
x 0.02
0.003

2. 0.67
x 0.08
0.0536

3. 7.3
x 0.06
0.438

4. 3.59
x 0.08
0.2872

5. 0.061
x 0.014
0.000854

6. 7.10
x 0.042
0.2982

7. 5.05
x 0.08
0.404

8. 8.75
x 0.067
0.58625

9. 0.0647
x 0.3
0.01941

10. 3.62
x 0.003
0.01086

11. 1.07
x 0.05
0.0535

12. 3.03
x 0.07
0.2121

13. 0.02
x 0.02
0.0004

14. 0.501
x 0.03
0.01503

15. 0.321
x 0.09
0.02889

16. The players and coaches gathered for refreshments after the soccer game. Of the 30 people there, 0.50 of them had energy drinks, 0.20 of them had fruit juice, and 0.30 of them had water. How many people had each type of drink?

energy drink **15**
fruit juice **6**
water **9**

Page 385

Dividing Decimals by Two-Digit Numbers

Dividing by a 2-digit divisor (34 in the example below) is very similar to dividing by a 1-digit divisor. In this example, 34 will divide into 78 twice. Then, multiply 34 x 2 to get 68. Subtract 68 from 78. The answer is 10, which is smaller than the divisor, so 2 was the right number. Now, bring down the next 8. 34 goes into 108 three times. Continue dividing as with a 1-digit divisor.

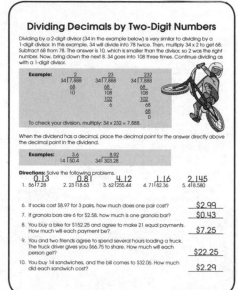

To check your division, multiply: 34 x 232 = 7,888.

When the dividend has a decimal, place the decimal point for the answer directly above the decimal point in the dividend.

Examples:	3.6	8.92
	14⟌50.4	34⟌303.28

Directions: Solve the following problems.

1. 56⟌7.28 **0.13**
2. 23⟌18.63 **0.81**
3. 62⟌255.44 **4.12**
4. 71⟌82.36 **1.16**
5. 4⟌8.580 **2.145**

6. If socks cost $8.97 for 3 pairs, how much does one pair cost? **$2.99**

7. If granola bars are 6 for $2.58, how much is one granola bar? **$0.43**

8. You buy a bike for $152.25 and agree to make 21 equal payments. How much will each payment be? **$7.25**

9. You and two friends agree to spend several hours loading a truck. The truck driver gives you $66.75 to share. How much will each person get? **$22.25**

10. You buy 14 sandwiches, and the bill comes to $32.06. How much did each sandwich cost? **$2.29**

Page 386

Dividing with Zeros

Sometimes you have a remainder in division problems. You can add a decimal point and zeros to the dividend and keep dividing until you have the answer.

Example:	49	49.64
	25⟌1,241	25⟌1,241.00
	100	100
	241	241
	225	225
	16	160
		150
		100
		100
		0

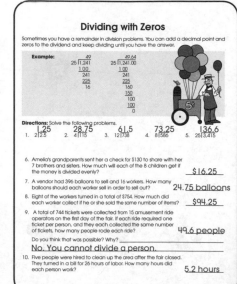

Directions: Solve the following problems.

1. 2⟌2.5 **1.25**
2. 4⟌115 **28.75**
3. 12⟌738 **61.5**
4. 8⟌586 **73.25**
5. 25⟌3.415 **136.6**

6. Amelia's grandparents sent her a check for $130 to share with her 7 brothers and sisters. How much will each of the 8 children get if the money is divided evenly? **$16.25**

7. A vendor had 396 balloons to sell and 16 workers. How many balloons should each worker sell in order to sell out? **24.75 balloons**

8. Eight of the workers turned in a total of $754. How much did each worker collect if he or she sold the same number of items? **$94.25**

9. A total of 744 tickets were collected from 15 amusement ride operators on the first day of the fair. If each ride required one ticket per person, and they each collected the same number of tickets, how many people rode each ride? **49.6 people**

Do you think that was possible? Why? **No. You cannot divide a person.**

10. Five people were hired to clean up the area after the fair closed. They turned in a bill for 26 hours of labor. How many hours did each person work? **5.2 hours**

Page 387

Dividing Decimals by Decimals

When a divisor has a decimal, eliminate it before dividing. If there is one digit right of the decimal in the divisor, multiply the divisor and dividend by 10. If there are two digits right of the decimal in the divisor, multiply the divisor and dividend by 100.

Multiply the divisor and dividend by the same number whether or not the dividend has a decimal. The goal is to have a divisor with no decimal.

Examples:	2.3⟌89 x 10 = 23⟌890	4.11⟌67.7 x 100 = 411⟌6,770
	4.9⟌35.67 x 10 = 49⟌356.7	0.34⟌789 x 100 = 34⟌78,900

After removing the decimal from the divisor, solve the problem in the usual way.

Directions: Solve the following problems.

1. 3.5⟌10.15 **2.9**
2. 6.7⟌415.4 **62**
3. 0.21⟌924 **4,400**
4. 73⟌50.37 **0.69**

5. If a car travels 1066.8 miles in 16.8 hours, what is the average speed in miles per hour the car travels? **63.5 m.p.h.**

6. Mrs. Gutierrez plans to make chili on Friday night. She bought 1.5 lbs. of ground chicken for $8.63. How much does the chicken cost per pound? **$5.75 per pound**

7. Aiden spent a total of $18.75 on rides at the fair. If each ticket cost $1.25, how many rides did he go on? **15 rides**

8. Mr. Washington bought 13.8 gallons of gas for $39.61. What was the price of gas per gallon that day? **$2.87**

Page 388

Decimals and Fractions

A **fraction** is a number that names part of something. The top number in a fraction is called the **numerator**. The bottom number is called the **denominator**. Since a decimal also names part of a whole number, every decimal can also be written as a fraction. For example, 0.1 is read as "one tenth" and can also be written $\frac{1}{10}$. The decimal 0.56 is read as "fifty-six hundredths" and can also be written $\frac{56}{100}$.

$0.7 = \frac{7}{10}$	$0.34 = \frac{34}{100}$	$0.761 = \frac{761}{1,000}$	$\frac{5}{10} = 0.5$	$\frac{58}{100} = 0.58$	$\frac{729}{1,000} = 0.729$

Even a fraction that doesn't have 10, 100, or 1,000 as the denominator can be written as a decimal. Sometimes you can multiply both the numerator and denominator by a certain number so the denominator is 10, 100, or 1,000. (You can't just multiply the denominator. That would change the amount of the fraction.)

Examples:	$\frac{3}{5} \times \frac{2}{2} = \frac{6}{10} = 0.6$	$\frac{4}{25} \times \frac{4}{4} = \frac{16}{100} = 0.16$

Other times, divide the numerator by the denominator.

Examples:	$\frac{3}{4} = 4⟌\frac{0.75}{3.00} = 0.75$	$\frac{5}{8} = 8⟌\frac{0.625}{5.000} = 0.625$

Directions: Follow the instructions below.

1. For each square, write a decimal and a fraction to show the part that is colored. The first one has been done for you.

a. $\frac{25}{100}$ / 0.25
b. $\frac{60}{100}$ / 0.6
c. $\frac{32}{100}$ / 0.32

2. Change these decimals to fractions.
a. $0.6 = \frac{6}{10}$ b. $0.54 = \frac{54}{100}$ c. $0.751 = \frac{751}{1,000}$ d. $0.73 = \frac{73}{100}$ e. $0.592 = \frac{592}{1,000}$ f. $0.2 = \frac{2}{10}$

3. Change these fractions to decimals. If necessary, round the decimals to the nearest hundredth.
a. $\frac{3}{10} = 0.3$ b. $\frac{89}{100} = 0.89$ c. $\frac{473}{1,000} = 0.473$ d. $\frac{4}{5} = 0.8$ e. $\frac{35}{50} = 0.7$
f. $\frac{7}{9} = 0.78$ g. $\frac{1}{3} = 0.33$ h. $\frac{23}{77} = 0.30$ i. $\frac{12}{63} = 0.19$ j. $\frac{4}{16} = 0.25$

Page 389

Equivalent Fractions and the Lowest Term

Equivalent fractions name the same amount. For example, $\frac{1}{2}$, $\frac{4}{8}$, and $\frac{18}{36}$ are exactly the same amount. They all mean half of something. (And they are all written as the same decimal: 0.5.) To find an equivalent fraction, multiply the numerator and denominator of any fraction by the same number.

Examples:	$\frac{3 \times 3}{4 \times 3} = \frac{9 \times 4}{12 \times 4} = \frac{36}{48}$	Thus, $\frac{3}{4}$, $\frac{9}{12}$, and $\frac{36}{48}$ are all equivalent fractions.

Most of the time, we want fractions in their lowest terms. It's easier to work with $\frac{3}{4}$ than $\frac{36}{48}$. To find a fraction's lowest terms, instead of multiplying both parts of a fraction by the same number, divide.

Examples:	$\frac{36 \div 12}{48 \div 12} = \frac{3}{4}$ The lowest term for $\frac{36}{48}$ is $\frac{3}{4}$.

If the numerator and denominator in a fraction can't be divided by any number, the fraction is in its lowest term. The fractions below are in their lowest terms.

Examples:	$\frac{34}{61}$	$\frac{3}{7}$	$\frac{7}{90}$	$\frac{53}{83}$	$\frac{78}{83}$	$\frac{3}{8}$

Directions: Follow the instructions below.

Answers may vary. Possible answers shown.

1. Write two equivalent fractions for each fraction. Make sure you multiply the numerator and denominator by the same number. The first one is done for you.

a. $\frac{1 \times 3}{2 \times 3} = \frac{3}{6}$ $\frac{1 \times 4}{2 \times 4} = \frac{4}{8}$
b. $\frac{3 \times 2}{3 \times 2} = \frac{6}{6}$ $\frac{2 \times 3}{3 \times 3} = \frac{6}{9}$
c. $\frac{3 \times 2}{5 \times 2} = \frac{6}{10}$ $\frac{3 \times 3}{5 \times 3} = \frac{9}{15}$
d. $\frac{8 \times 2}{9 \times 2} = \frac{16}{18}$ $\frac{8 \times 3}{9 \times 3} = \frac{24}{27}$

2. Find the lowest terms for each fraction. Make sure your answers can't be divided by any other numbers. The first one is done for you.

a. $\frac{2 \div 2}{36 \div 2} = \frac{1}{18}$
b. $\frac{12 \div 1}{25 \div 1} = \frac{12}{25}$
c. $\frac{12 \div 4}{16 \div 4} = \frac{3}{4}$
d. $\frac{3 \div 3}{9 \div 3} = \frac{1}{3}$
e. $\frac{25 \div 5}{45 \div 5} = \frac{5}{9}$
f. $\frac{11 \div 11}{44 \div 11} = \frac{1}{4}$

Page 390

Greatest Common Factor

The **greatest common factor (GCF)** is the largest number that will divide evenly into a set of numbers. In the example, both numbers can be divided evenly by 2 and 4; therefore, 4 is the greatest common factor.

Example: 12 and 20   2, 4 (can be divided evenly into both numbers)
4 (greatest common factor)

Directions: Circle the greatest common factor for each pair of numbers.

1. 56 and 72	6	10	**8**	2
2. 45 and 81	7	5	**9**	3
3. 28 and 49	**7**	11	4	6
4. 10 and 35	3	**5**	9	7
5. 42 and 30	4	2	5	**6**
6. 121 and 33	12	9	4	**11**
7. 96 and 48	**48**	15	6	4
8. 12 and 132	2	10	**12**	9
9. 108 and 27	14	9	3	**27**
10. 44 and 82	**4**	6	8	10
11. 16 and 88	12	2	**8**	5
12. 72 and 144	9	11	7	**72**

Page 391

Least Common Multiple

The **least common multiple (LCM)** is the lowest possible multiple any pair of numbers have in common.

Examples: 2 and 4
The lowest common multiple is 4, because 4 is a multiple for each number and it is the lowest possible.

6 and 7
Multiples of 6 are 6, 12, 18, 24, 30, 36, 42.
Multiples of 7 are 7, 14, 21, 28, 35, 42.
42 is the lowest multiple that 6 and 7 have in common.

Directions: Find the least common multiple for each pair of numbers.

1. 7 and 8 = 56
2. 2 and 3 = 6
3. 11 and 4 = 44
4. 5 and 3 = 15
5. 7 and 2 = 14
6. 9 and 4 = 36
7. 2 and 6 = 6
8. 10 and 3 = 30
9. 7 and 5 = 35
10. 9 and 6 = 18
11. 12 and 8 = 24
12. 15 and 3 = 15

Page 392

Comparing Decimals and Fractions

The symbol > means "greater than." The number on its left is greater than that on its right. The symbol < means "less than." The number on its left is less than that on its right. An equal sign, =, shows the same value on each side.

Directions: Use the sign >, = or < to make each statement true.

1. 0.4 **<** $\frac{2}{3}$
2. 1.25 **<** $\frac{3}{2}$
3. 0.7 **<** $\frac{4}{5}$
4. 0.68 **<** $\frac{5}{7}$
5. 0.1 **>** $\frac{1}{12}$
6. 0.45 **<** $\frac{1}{2}$
7. 0.75 **>** $\frac{3}{5}$
8. 0.6 **<** $\frac{5}{8}$
9. 0.54 **>** $\frac{2}{5}$
10. 0.8 **>** $\frac{4}{6}$
11. 0.25 **>** $\frac{1}{7}$
12. 1.8 **>** $\frac{12}{7}$
13. 0.625 **>** $\frac{4}{8}$
14. 0.33 **<** $\frac{1}{3}$

15. Jenna looked carefully at the labels on two different types of pretzels. The pretzel rods had $\frac{3}{4}$ pound in the package. The package of mini pretzels claimed it had 0.67 pounds of pretzels inside. Were the pretzel rods <, >, or = to the mini pretzels?

$\frac{3}{4}$ > 0.67

Page 393

Mixed Numbers and Improper Fractions

A **mixed number** is a whole number and a fraction, such as $1\frac{1}{2}$. An **improper fraction** has a numerator that is larger than its denominator, such as $\frac{9}{7}$. To write an improper fraction as a mixed number, divide the numerator by the denominator. The quotient becomes the whole number, and the remainder becomes the fraction.

Examples:
$\frac{16}{3} = 3)\overline{16} = 5\frac{1}{3}$
$\frac{28}{5} = 5)\overline{28} = 5\frac{3}{5}$

To change a mixed number into an improper fraction, multiply the whole number by the denominator and add the numerator.

Examples:
$4\frac{1}{3} = 4 \times 3 = 12 + 1 = 13 \quad \frac{13}{3}$
$8\frac{4}{7} = 8 \times 7 = 56 + 4 = 60 \quad \frac{60}{7}$

Directions: Follow the instructions below.

1. Change the improper fractions to mixed numbers, and reduce to lowest terms. Use another sheet of paper if necessary. The first one has been done for you.

a. $\frac{34}{6} = 6)\overline{34} = 5\frac{4}{6} = 5\frac{2}{3}$

b. $\frac{65}{4} = 16\frac{1}{4}$ c. $\frac{23}{8} = 2\frac{7}{8}$ d. $\frac{89}{3} = 29\frac{2}{3}$

e. $\frac{45}{9} = 5$ f. $\frac{32}{5} = 6\frac{2}{5}$ g. $\frac{13}{6} = 1\frac{6}{7}$

h. $\frac{24}{9} = 2\frac{2}{3}$ i. $\frac{31}{2} = 15\frac{1}{2}$ j. $\frac{84}{23} = 3\frac{15}{23}$

2. Change these mixed numbers into improper fractions. The first one has been done for you.

a. $4\frac{6}{7} = 4 \times 7 = 28 + 6 = \frac{34}{7}$ b. $2\frac{1}{9} = \frac{19}{9}$ c. $5\frac{4}{5} = \frac{29}{5}$ d. $12\frac{1}{4} = \frac{49}{4}$

e. $6\frac{7}{8} = \frac{55}{8}$ f. $3\frac{9}{11} = \frac{42}{11}$ g. $8\frac{3}{12} = \frac{99}{12}$ h. $1\frac{6}{14} = \frac{20}{14}$ i. $4\frac{2}{3} = \frac{14}{3}$ j. $9\frac{4}{15} = \frac{139}{15}$

Page 394

Adding Fractions

When adding fractions, if the denominators are the same, simply add the numerators. When the result is an improper fraction, change it to a mixed number.

Examples: $\frac{3}{5} + \frac{1}{5} = \frac{4}{5}$ $\frac{3}{9} + \frac{7}{9} = \frac{10}{9} = 1\frac{1}{9}$

If the denominators of fractions are different, change them so they are the same. To do this, find equivalent fractions. In the first example below, $\frac{1}{4}$ and $\frac{1}{8}$ have different denominators, so change $\frac{1}{4}$ to the equivalent fraction $\frac{2}{8}$. Then, add the numerators. In the second example, $\frac{5}{7}$ and $\frac{2}{3}$ also have different denominators. Find a denominator both 7 and 3 divide into. The lowest number they both divide into is 21. Multiply the numerator and denominator of $\frac{5}{7}$ by 3 to get the equivalent fraction $\frac{15}{21}$. Then, multiply the numerator and denominator of $\frac{2}{3}$ by 7 to get the equivalent fraction $\frac{14}{21}$.

Examples:
$\frac{1 \times 2 = 2}{4 \times 2 = 8}$
$\frac{2}{8}$
$+\frac{3}{8}$
$\frac{5}{8}$

$\frac{5 \times 3 = 16}{7 \times 3 = 21}$
$\frac{2 \times 7 = 14}{3 \times 7 = 21}$
$\frac{20}{21} = 1\frac{8}{21}$

Directions: Solve the following problems. Find equivalent fractions when necessary.

1. $\frac{3}{5} + \frac{1}{5} = \frac{4}{5}$
2. $\frac{7}{8} + \frac{2}{16} = \frac{16}{16} = 1$
3. $\frac{1}{9} + \frac{2}{3} = \frac{7}{9}$
4. $\frac{1}{2} + \frac{1}{3} = \frac{6}{6} = 1$
5. $\frac{2}{15} + \frac{1}{5} = \frac{5}{15} = \frac{1}{3}$

6. Cora is making some soup. She needs $\frac{1}{2}$ cup diced yellow onion and $\frac{1}{4}$ cup chopped green onion. How much onion does she need altogether? $\frac{3}{4}$ cup

7. Henry is painting a wall. Yesterday, he painted $\frac{1}{3}$ of it. Today, he painted $\frac{1}{4}$ of it. How much has he painted altogether? $\frac{7}{12}$

8. Zahra ate $\frac{1}{6}$ of a pie. Her father ate $\frac{1}{4}$ of it. How much did they eat altogether? $\frac{5}{12}$

Page 395

Subtracting Fractions

Subtracting fractions is very similar to adding them. In that the denominators must be the same. If the denominators are different, use equivalent fractions.

Examples:
$\frac{2 \times 8 = 16}{5 \times 8 = 40}$
$\frac{1 \times 5 = 5}{8 \times 5 = 40}$
$\frac{11}{40}$

Adding and subtracting mixed numbers are also similar. Often, though, change the mixed numbers to improper fractions. If the denominators are different, use equivalent fractions.

Examples:
$2\frac{3}{5} = \frac{13}{5}$
$-1\frac{4}{5} = \frac{9}{5}$
$\frac{4}{5}$

$3\frac{3}{14} = \frac{45}{14}$
$-2\frac{1}{7} = \frac{15}{7} \times \frac{2}{2} = \frac{30}{14}$
$\frac{15}{14} = 1\frac{1}{14}$

Directions: Solve the following problems. Use equivalent fractions and improper fractions where necessary.

1. $\frac{6}{7} - \frac{5}{7} = \frac{1}{7}$
2. $1\frac{2}{9} - \frac{4}{9} = \frac{7}{9}$
3. $2\frac{3}{6} - \frac{3}{4} = \frac{51}{30} = 1\frac{7}{30}$
4. $\frac{3}{4} - \frac{1}{4} = \frac{1}{2}$
5. $2\frac{1}{3} - \frac{3}{4} = \frac{19}{12} = 1\frac{7}{12}$

6. Leah promised to weed the flower garden for $1\frac{1}{2}$ hours this morning. So far she has pulled weeds for $\frac{3}{4}$ of an hour. How much longer does she have to work? $\frac{3}{4}$ hour

7. Vijay started out with $1\frac{1}{4}$ gallons of paint. He used $\frac{3}{8}$ gallon of the paint on his boat. How much paint is left? $\frac{7}{8}$ gallon

8. A certain movie lasts $2\frac{1}{3}$ hours. Tess has already watched it for $1\frac{1}{2}$ hours. How much longer is the movie? $\frac{5}{6}$ hours

9. Nico didn't finish $\frac{1}{3}$ of the math problems on a test. He made mistakes on $\frac{1}{8}$ of the problems. The rest he answered correctly. What fraction of the problems did he answer correctly? $\frac{17}{24}$

Page 396

Comprehensive Curriculum - Grade 6

Multiplying Fractions

To multiply two fractions, multiply the numerators, and then multiply the denominators. If necessary, change the answer to its lowest term.

Examples: $\frac{3}{4} \times \frac{2}{3} = \frac{6}{12} = \frac{1}{2}$ $\frac{1}{8} \times \frac{4}{5} = \frac{4}{40} = \frac{1}{10}$

To multiply a whole number by a fraction, first write the whole number as a fraction (with 1 as the denominator). Then, multiply as above. You may need to change an improper fraction to a mixed number.

Examples: $\frac{2}{3} \times \frac{4}{1} = \frac{8}{3} = 2\frac{2}{3}$ $\frac{3}{7} \times \frac{6}{1} = \frac{18}{7} = 2\frac{4}{7}$

Directions: Solve the following problems, writing answers in their lowest terms.

1. $\frac{1}{5} \times \frac{2}{3} = \frac{2}{15}$ 2. $\frac{1}{3} \times \frac{4}{7} = \frac{4}{21}$ 3. $\frac{3}{8} \times \frac{3}{2} = \frac{9}{16} = \frac{3}{8}$ 4. $\frac{2}{6} \times \frac{1}{2} = \frac{2}{12} = \frac{1}{6}$

5. Tim lost $\frac{1}{8}$ of his marbles. If he had 56 marbles, how many did he lose? __7 marbles__

6. Drew is making $\frac{2}{3}$ of a recipe for spaghetti sauce. How much will he need of each ingredient below?
   1$\frac{1}{4}$ cups water = __$\frac{5}{6}$ cups__   2 cups tomato paste = __1$\frac{1}{3}$ cups__
   $\frac{1}{2}$ teaspoon oregano = __$\frac{1}{2}$ teaspoon__   4$\frac{1}{2}$ teaspoons salt = __3 teaspoons__

7. Carrie bought 2 dozen bagels and asked for $\frac{3}{4}$ of them to be honey grain. How many were honey grain? __18 bagels__

8. Sofia let her hair grow 14 inches long and then had $\frac{1}{4}$ of it cut off. How much was cut off? __3$\frac{1}{2}$ inches__

9. Ethan has finished $\frac{7}{8}$ of 40 math problems. How many has he done? __35 problems__

10. If Jaya's cat eats $\frac{2}{3}$ can of cat food every day, how many cans should Jaya buy for a week? __4$\frac{2}{3}$ cans, or 5 cans__

Page 397

Dividing Fractions

Reciprocals are two fractions that, when multiplied together make 1. To divide a fraction by a fraction, turn one of the fractions upside down and multiply. The upside-down fraction is a reciprocal of its original fraction. If you multiply a fraction by its reciprocal, you always get 1.

Examples of reciprocals: $\frac{2}{3} \times \frac{3}{2} = \frac{6}{6} = 1$ $\frac{9}{11} \times \frac{11}{9} = \frac{99}{99} = 1$

Examples of dividing by fractions: $\frac{1}{2} \div \frac{2}{3} = \frac{1}{2} \times \frac{3}{2} = \frac{3}{4}$ $\frac{2}{5} \div \frac{2}{7} = \frac{2}{5} \times \frac{7}{2} = \frac{14}{10} = 1\frac{2}{5}$

To divide a whole number by a fraction, first write the whole number as a fraction with a denominator of 1. (Write a mixed number as an improper fraction.) Then, finish the problem as explained above.

Examples: $4 \div \frac{1}{3} = \frac{4}{1} \times \frac{6}{2} = \frac{24}{2} = 12$ $3\frac{1}{2} \div \frac{2}{7} = \frac{7}{2} \times \frac{7}{2} = \frac{35}{4} = 8\frac{3}{4}$

Directions: Solve the following problems, writing answers in their lowest terms. Change any improper fractions to mixed numbers.

1. $\frac{1}{3} \div \frac{2}{5} = \frac{5}{6}$ 2. $\frac{2}{7} \div \frac{1}{3} = \frac{18}{7} = 2\frac{4}{7}$ 3. $3 \div \frac{3}{4} = \frac{12}{3} = 4$ 4. $\frac{1}{4} \div \frac{2}{3} = \frac{3}{8}$

5. Judy has 8 candy bars. She wants to give $\frac{1}{3}$ of a candy bar to everyone in her class. Does she have enough for all 24 students? __Yes__

6. A big jar of glue holds 3$\frac{1}{2}$ cups. How many little containers that hold $\frac{1}{4}$ cup each can you fill? __14 containers__

7. A container holds 27 ounces of frozen yogurt. How many 4$\frac{1}{2}$-ounce servings is that? __6 servings__

8. It takes 2$\frac{1}{4}$ teaspoons of powdered mix to make 1 cup of hot chocolate. How many cups can you make with 45 teaspoons of mix? __18 cups__

9. Each cup of hot chocolate also takes $\frac{2}{3}$ cup of milk. How many cups of hot chocolate can you make with 12 cups of milk? __18 cups__

Page 398

Review

Directions: Follow the instructions below.

1. Write each of these decimals as fractions.
   a. $0.43 = \frac{43}{100}$ b. $0.6 = \frac{6}{10}$ c. $0.783 = \frac{783}{1,000}$ d. $0.91 = \frac{91}{100}$

2. Write each of these fractions as decimals, rounding them to the nearest hundredth.
   a. $\frac{3}{10} = 0.3$ b. $\frac{4}{7} = 0.57$ c. $\frac{3}{9} = 0.33$ d. $\frac{64}{100} = 0.64$

3. Write two equivalent fractions for each of these
   a. $\frac{2}{6} = \frac{6}{18}, \frac{4}{12}$ b. $\frac{1}{4} = \frac{2}{8}, \frac{4}{16}$ c. $\frac{5}{8} = \frac{10}{16}, \frac{15}{24}$

4. Change these fractions into their lowest terms
   a. $\frac{4}{16} = \frac{1}{4}$ b. $\frac{6}{18} = \frac{1}{3}$ c. $\frac{5}{90} = \frac{1}{18}$ d. $\frac{9}{24} = \frac{3}{8}$

5. Change these improper fractions into mixed numbers
   a. $\frac{30}{9} = 3\frac{1}{3}$ b. $\frac{46}{3} = 15\frac{1}{3}$ c. $\frac{38}{6} = 6\frac{1}{3}$ d. $\frac{18}{4} = 4\frac{1}{2}$

6. Change these mixed numbers into improper fractions
   a. $3\frac{1}{6} = \frac{19}{6}$ b. $7\frac{3}{8} = \frac{59}{8}$ c. $4\frac{2}{7} = \frac{30}{7}$ d. $8\frac{1}{9} = \frac{73}{9}$

7. George has written 1$\frac{1}{8}$ pages of a report that is supposed to be 3$\frac{1}{2}$ pages long. How much more does he have to write? __2$\frac{3}{8}$ pages__

8. Mira ate $\frac{3}{8}$ of half a pizza. How much of the whole pizza did she eat? __$\frac{3}{16}$__

9. Alexa's family is driving to Los Angeles. They drove $\frac{1}{5}$ of the way the first day and $\frac{1}{6}$ of the way the second day. How much of the trip have they completed so far? __$\frac{11}{30}$__

10. Antonio gets $6 a week for his allowance. He saved $\frac{1}{3}$ of it last week and $\frac{1}{2}$ of it this week. How much money did he save in these 2 weeks? __$5__

11. Of 32 students in one class, $\frac{5}{8}$ have a brother or sister. How many students are only children? __12 students__

12. In one class, $\frac{1}{4}$ of the students were born in January, $\frac{1}{10}$ in February, and $\frac{1}{20}$ in March. How much of the class was born in these 3 months? __$\frac{2}{5}$__

Page 399

Review

Directions: Follow the instructions below.

Add.
1. $\frac{4}{16} + \frac{5}{8} = \frac{14}{16} = \frac{7}{8}$ 2. $\frac{1}{6} + \frac{1}{3} = \frac{3}{6} = \frac{1}{2}$ 3. $\frac{2}{10} + \frac{4}{5} = \frac{10}{10} = 1$ 4. $\frac{3}{5} + \frac{9}{10} = \frac{15}{10} = 1\frac{1}{2}$

Subtract.
1. $\frac{15}{9} - \frac{2}{3} = \frac{9}{9} = 1$ 2. $\frac{3}{4} - \frac{3}{8} = \frac{3}{8}$ 3. $\frac{4}{7} - \frac{2}{14} = \frac{6}{14} = \frac{3}{7}$ 4. $\frac{3}{5} - \frac{5}{10} = \frac{5}{10} = \frac{1}{2}$

Multiply.
1. $\frac{1}{2} \times \frac{4}{16} = \frac{4}{32} = \frac{1}{8}$ 2. $\frac{1}{3} \times \frac{4}{9} = \frac{4}{27}$ 3. $\frac{5}{12} \times \frac{1}{4} = \frac{5}{48}$ 4. $\frac{3}{16} \times \frac{3}{4} = \frac{9}{64}$

Divide.
1. $\frac{3}{5} \div \frac{1}{3} = \frac{9}{5} = 1\frac{4}{5}$ 2. $4 \div \frac{1}{2} = \frac{8}{1} = 8$ 3. $\frac{1}{4} \div \frac{1}{3} = \frac{3}{4}$ 4. $3\frac{3}{4} \div \frac{1}{3} = \frac{45}{4} = 11\frac{1}{4}$

Write >, <, or = to make the statements true.

1. 0.5 $<$ $\frac{5}{8}$ 2. 0.8 $=$ $\frac{4}{5}$ 3. 0.35 $<$ $\frac{2}{5}$ 4. 1.3 $>$ $\frac{7}{8}$

Page 400

Trial and Error

Often, the quickest way to solve a problem is to make a logical guess, and test it to see if it works. The first guess, or trial, will probably not be the correct answer—but it should help you figure out a better, more reasonable guess.

Directions: Use trial and error to find the solutions to these problems.

1. Mr. McFerrson is between 30 and 50 years old. The sum of the digits in his age is 11. His age is an even number. How old is Mr. McFerrson?
   __He is 38 years old.__

2. The key for number 5 does not work on Carson's calculator. How can he use his broken calculator to subtract 108 from 351?
   __Possible answer: Add 10 to each number, and then subtract 118 from 361 to find the answer: 243.__

3. Tasha likes to swim a certain number of miles each day for 3 days straight. Then, she increases her mileage by 1 for the next 3 days, and so on. Over a 9-day period, Tasha swims a total of 27 miles. She swims equal mileage Monday, Tuesday, and Wednesday. She swims another amount on Thursday, Friday, and Saturday. She swims yet a third amount on Sunday, Monday, and Tuesday. How many miles does Tasha swim each day?

   __2__ Monday   __2__ Tuesday   __2__ Wednesday
   __3__ Thursday   __3__ Friday   __3__ Saturday
   __4__ Sunday   __4__ Monday   __4__ Tuesday

Page 401

Trial and Error

Directions: Use trial and error to complete each diagram so all the equations work.

Example:

$6 , 7 \begin{array}{c} + \\ \times \end{array} \begin{array}{c} 13 \\ 42 \end{array}$

$7 , 4 \begin{array}{c} + \\ \times \end{array} \begin{array}{c} 11 \\ 28 \end{array}$ $4 , 8 \begin{array}{c} + \\ \times \end{array} \begin{array}{c} 12 \\ 32 \end{array}$

$4 , 4 \begin{array}{c} + \\ \times \end{array} \begin{array}{c} 8 \\ 16 \end{array}$ $7 , 0 \begin{array}{c} + \\ \times \end{array} \begin{array}{c} 7 \\ 0 \end{array}$

$7 , 8 \begin{array}{c} + \\ \times \end{array} \begin{array}{c} 15 \\ 56 \end{array}$ $8 , 9 \begin{array}{c} + \\ \times \end{array} \begin{array}{c} 17 \\ 72 \end{array}$

$6 , 9 \begin{array}{c} + \\ \times \end{array} \begin{array}{c} 15 \\ 54 \end{array}$ $15 , 16 \begin{array}{c} + \\ \times \end{array} \begin{array}{c} 31 \\ 240 \end{array}$

$10 , 1 \begin{array}{c} + \\ \times \end{array} \begin{array}{c} 11 \\ 10 \end{array}$ $100 , 1 \begin{array}{c} + \\ \times \end{array} \begin{array}{c} 101 \\ 100 \end{array}$

Page 402

Choosing a Method

This table explains different methods of computation that can be used to solve a problem.

Method		
Mental Math	– Calculating in your head.	– Use with small numbers, memorized facts, and multiples of tens, hundreds, thousands, and so on.
Objects/Diagram	– Drawing or using an object to represent the problem.	– Use to model the situation.
Pencil and Paper	– Calculating the answer on paper.	– Use when a calculator is not available and the problem is too difficult to solve mentally.
Calculator	– Using a calculator or computer to find the solution.	– Use with large numbers or for a quick answer.
Trial and Error	– Making a guess at the answer and trying to see if it works.	– Use when unsure what to do or if none of the methods above work.

Directions: Circle the method of computation that seems best for solving each problem. Then, solve the problem.

1. The School Days Fun Fair has 38 booths and 23 games. How many booths and games total are in the fair?
   - (Paper and Pencil)   Answer: __61__
   - Objects/Diagram

2. The lemonade stand was stocked with 230 cups. On the first day, 147 drinks were sold. How many cups were left?
   - Objects/Diagram   Answer: __83__
   - (Paper and Pencil)

3. There are 3 cars in the tram to transport people from the parking lot to the fair. Each car can seat 9 people. How many people can ride the tram at one time?
   - (Objects/Diagram)   Answer: __27__
   - Trial and Error

Page 403

Choosing a Method

Directions: Write what method you will use for each problem. Then, find the answer.
Answers may vary. Possible answers shown.

1. Jenna receives an allowance of $3.50 a week. This week, her mother paid her in nickels, dimes, and quarters. She received more dimes than quarters. How many of each coin did her mom use to pay her?
   Method: __Trial and Error__
   Answer: __8 quarters, 13 dimes, 4 nickels__

2. You are buying your lunch at school. There are 4 people in front of you and 7 people behind you. How many people are standing in line? (Hint: it's not 11 people.)
   Method: __Mental Math__
   Answer: __12 people__

3. A runner can run 1 mile in 12 minutes. He ran for 30 minutes today. How far did he run?
   Method: __Calculator/Pencil and Paper__
   Answer: __2.5 miles__

4. A family of four goes out to dinner. They decide to order a 16-piece pizza. Each person likes something different on his or her pizza, but each will eat equal amounts. Maria likes pepperoni and sausage. Tony likes ham and pineapple. Mom likes cheese only, and Dad likes mushrooms. Maria is allergic to mushrooms, so her slices can't be next to Dad's. Mom detests pineapple, so her slices can't be next to Tony's. How will the restaurant arrange their pizza?
   Method: __Objects/Diagram__
   Answer: __starting at top of pizza: Dad's, Mom's, Maria's, Tony's__

5. The Petting Zoo has 72 animals in aquariums, 32 animals in cages, and 57 animals fenced in. How many animals does the Petting Zoo have?
   Method: __Calculator/Pencil and Paper__
   Answer: __161 animals__

Page 404

Multi-Step Problems

Some problems take more than one step to solve. First, plan each step needed to find the solution. Then, solve each part to find the answer.

Example: Tickets for a bargain matinee cost $4 for adults and $3 for children. How much would tickets cost for a family of 2 adults and 3 children?

Step 1: Find the cost of the adults' tickets.
Step 2: Find the cost of the children's tickets.
Step 3: Add to find the sum of the tickets.

2 adults	x	$4 each ticket	=	$8 total
3 children	x	$3 each ticket	=	$9 total
$8 adults	+	$9 children	=	$17 total

The tickets cost $17 total.

Directions: Write the operations you will use to solve each problem. Then, find the answer.

1. Arden and her father are riding their bikes 57 miles to Arden's grandma's house. They ride 13 miles and then take a water break. Then, they ride 15 miles to a rest area for a picnic lunch. How many miles do Arden and her father have left to ride after lunch?
   Operations: __1. Add the miles they've gone; 2. Subtract from total miles__
   Answer: __29 miles__

2. A triathlete bikes 15 miles at 20 miles per hour, runs 5 miles at 6 miles per hour, and swims 1 mile at 4 miles per hour. How long does the triathlon take her to complete?
   Operations: __1. Devise a formula: number of miles divided by mph = time. 2. Add the time totals. 3. Convert to hours.__
   Answer: __approximately 1 hour and 50 minutes__

3. Ray bought strawberries for $1.99, blueberries for $1.40, and 2 pints of raspberries for $1.25 per pint. How much did Ray spend on berries?
   Operations: __1. Find total cost of raspberries; 2. Add to the cost of blueberries and strawberries__
   Answer: __$5.89__

Page 405

Hidden Questions

When solving a story problem, you may find that some information you want is not stated in the problem. You must ask yourself what information you need and decide how you can use the data in the problem to find it. This information, the problem contains a hidden question to find before you can solve it.

Example: Chris and his mother are building a birdhouse. He buys 4 pieces of wood for $2.20 each. How much change should he get back from $10?

Step 1: Find the hidden question.
What is the total cost of the wood? $2.20 x 4 = $8.80

Step 2: Use your answer to the hidden question to solve the problem. $10.00 - $8.80 = $1.20

Directions: Write the hidden questions. Then, solve the problems.

1. Chris used 3 nails to attach each board to the frame. After nailing 6 boards, he had 1 nail left. How many nails did Chris have before he started?
   Hidden Question: __How many nails had he used?__
   Answer: __19 nails__

2. Chris sawed a 72-inch post into 3 pieces. Two of the pieces were each 20 inches long. How long was the third piece?
   Hidden Question: __How long were the two pieces total?__
   Answer: __32 inches__

3. It took Chris and his mom 15 hours to make a birdhouse. They thought it would take 3 days. How many hours early did they complete the job?
   Hidden Question: __How many hours are in 3 days?__
   Answer: __57 hours__

4. It takes Chris 15 hours to make a birdhouse and 9 hours to make a birdfeeder. He worked for 42 hours and made 1 birdhouse and some birdfeeders. How many birdfeeders did Chris make?
   Hidden Question: __How much time total did he spend on birdfeeders?__
   Answer: __3 birdfeeders__

Page 406

Logic Problems

Directions: Use the clues below to figure out this logic problem.

Three friends all enjoy sports. Each of their favorite sports involves a ball. Two of these sports are played on courts, and one is played on a field.

- Rachel likes to run and doesn't have to be a good catcher.
- Trinity is a good jumper.
- Betsy is also a good jumper, but she is a good ball handler.

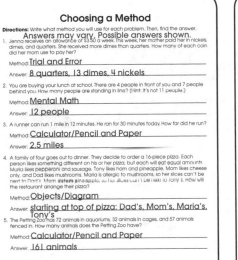

Which sport does each girl play?

Trinity   __Volleyball__
Betsy   __Basketball__
Rachel   __Soccer__

Page 407

A Cool Logic Problem

A family with 5 children went to the frozen-yogurt shop. The children all ordered different flavors.

Directions: Use the clues and the chart to help you write which child ate which flavor of frozen yogurt. Write a dot in the chart for the correct answer. Cross out all the other boxes in that row and column.

- No person had frozen yogurt with the same first initial as his or her name.
- Neither of the twins, Corey and Cody, like peanut butter. Corey thinks vanilla is boring.
- The children are the twins, Julia, the brother who got chocolate, and the sister who ate peanut butter.

	Rocky Road	Chocolate Chip	Vanilla	Chocolate	Peanut Butter
Corey	●	X	X	X	X
Cody	X	X	●	X	X
Miranda	X	X	X	X	●
Julia	X	●	X	X	X
Lucas	X	X	X	●	X

Who ate which flavor?

Corey   __Rocky Road__
Cody   __Vanilla__
Miranda __Peanut Butter__
Julia   __Chocolate Chip__
Lucas   __Chocolate__

Page 408

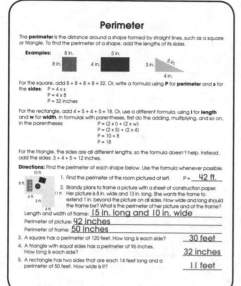

Perimeter

The **perimeter** is the distance around a shape formed by straight lines, such as a square or triangle. To find the perimeter of a shape, add the lengths of its sides.

Examples:

For the square, add $8 + 8 + 8 + 8 = 32$. Or, write a formula using **P** for perimeter and **s** for the **sides**:
$P = 4 \times s$
$P = 4 \times 8$
$P = 32$ inches

For the rectangle, add $4 + 5 + 4 + 5 = 18$. Or, use a different formula, using **l** for **length** and **w** for **width**. In formulas with parentheses, first do the adding, multiplying, and so on, in the parentheses:
$P = (2 \times l) + (2 \times w)$
$P = (2 \times 5) + (2 \times 4)$
$P = 10 + 8$
$P = 18$

For the triangle, the sides are all different lengths, so the formula doesn't help. Instead, add the sides: $3 + 4 + 5 = 12$ inches.

Directions: Find the perimeter of each shape below. Use the formula whenever possible.

1. Find the perimeter of the room pictured at left. $P = $ __42 ft.__

2. Brandy plans to frame a picture with a sheet of construction paper. Her picture is 8 in. wide and 13 in. long. She wants the frame to extend 1 in. beyond the picture on all sides. How wide and long should the frame be? What is the perimeter of her picture and of the frame?
Length and width of frame: __15 in. long and 10 in. wide__
Perimeter of picture: __42 inches__
Perimeter of frame: __50 inches__

3. A square has a perimeter of 120 feet. How long is each side? __30 feet__

4. A triangle with equal sides has a perimeter of 96 inches. How long is each side? __32 inches__

5. A rectangle has two sides that are each 14 feet long and a perimeter of 50 feet. How wide is it? __11 feet__

Page 409

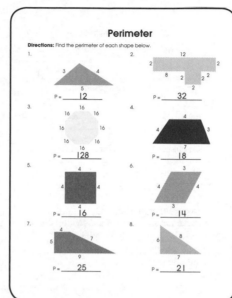

Perimeter

Directions: Find the perimeter of each shape below.

1. $P = $ __12__
2. $P = $ __32__
3. $P = $ __128__
4. $P = $ __18__
5. $P = $ __16__
6. $P = $ __14__
7. $P = $ __25__
8. $P = $ __21__

Page 410

Area: Squares and Rectangles

The **area** is the number of square units that covers a certain space. To find the area, multiply the length by the width. The answer is in square units, shown by adding a superscript 2 (^{2}) to the number.

Examples:

For the rectangle, use this formula: $A = l \times w$
$A = 8 \times 5$
$A = 40$ in.^{2}

For the square formula, **s** stands for side: $A = s \times s$ (or s^2)
$A = 3 \times 3$ (or 3^2)
$A = 9$ in.^{2}

Directions: Find the area of each shape below.

1. Find the area of a room that is 12 feet long and 7 feet wide. $A = $ __84 ft.^{2}__

2. A farmer's field is 32 feet on each side. How many square feet does she have to plow? __1,024 ft.^{2}__

3. Kwan's bedroom is 10 feet by 12 feet. How many square feet of carpeting would cover the floor? __120 ft.^{2}__

4. Two of Kwan's walls are 7.5 feet high and 12 feet long. The other two are the same height and 10 feet long. How many square feet of wallpaper would cover all four walls?
Square feet for 12-foot wall = __90 ft.^{2}__ × 2 = __180 ft.^{2}__
Square feet for 10-foot wall = __75 ft.^{2}__ × 2 = __150 ft.^{2}__

5. A clothes shop moved from a store that was 35 by 22 feet to a new location that was 53 by 32 feet. How many more square feet does the store have now?
Square feet for first location = __770 ft.^{2}__
Square feet for new location = __1,696 ft.^{2}__ Difference = __926 ft.^{2}__

6. A school wanted to purchase a climber for the playground. The one they selected would need 98 square feet of space. The only space available on the playground was 12 feet long and 8 feet wide. Will there be enough space for the climber? __No__

Page 411

Area: Triangles

Finding the area of a triangle requires knowing the size of the base and the height. For the triangle formula, use **b** for **base** and **h** for **height**. Multiply $\frac{1}{2}$ times the size of the base, and then multiply by the height. The answer will be in square units.

Example:
$A = \frac{1}{2} \times b \times h$
$A = \frac{1}{2} \times 4 \times 6$
$A = 12$ in.^{2}

Directions: Apply the formula to find the area of each triangle below.

1. $A = $ __6 in.^{2}__
2. $A = $ __17.5 in.^{2}__
3. $A = $ __9 in.^{2}__
4. $A = $ __1 in.^{2}__

5. Addison wanted to make a sail for her new boat. The base of the triangular sail would be 7 feet, and the height would be 6 feet. Find the area.
$A = $ __21 ft.^{2}__

Page 412

Area Challenge

When finding the area of an unusual shape, first try to divide it into squares, rectangles, or triangles. Find the area of each of those parts, and then add your answers together to find the total area of the object.

Directions: Find the area of each shape below.

1. Total area = __69 in.^{2}__
2. Total area = __34 ft.^{2}__
3. Total area = __38 ft.^{2}__
4. Total area = __18 units^2__
5. Total area = __32__ units^2
6. Total area = __31__ units^2

Page 413

Volume

Volume is the number of cubic units that fills a space. A **cubic unit** has 6 equal sides, like a child's block. To find the volume (**V**) of something, multiply the length (**l**) by the width (**w**) by the height (**h**), or $V = l \times w \times h$. The answer will be in cubic units (^{3}). Sometimes it's easier to understand volume if you imagine a figure is made of small cubes.

Example: $V = l \times w \times h$
$V = 4 \times 6 \times 5$
$V = 120$ in.^{3}

Directions: Solve the following problems.

1. What is the volume of a cube that is 7 inches on each side? __343 in.^{3}__

2. How many cubic inches of cereal are in a box that is 10 inches long, 6 inches wide, and 4.5 inches high? __270 in.^{3}__

3. Jeremy made a tower of five blocks that are each 2.5 inches square. How many cubic inches are in his tower? __78.125 in.^{3}__

4. How many cubic feet of gravel are in the back of a full dump truck that measures 7 feet wide by 4 feet tall by 16 feet long? __448 ft.^{3}__

5. Will 1,000 cubic inches of dirt fill a flower box that is 32 inches long, 7 inches wide, and 7 inches tall? __No__

6. A mouse needs 100 cubic inches of air to live for an hour. Will your pet mouse be okay for an hour in an airtight box that's 4.5 inches wide by 8.25 inches long by 2.5 inches high? __No__

7. Find the volume of the figures below. 1 cube = 1 inch^3
A. $V = $ __14 in.^{3}__
B. $V = $ __26 in.^{3}__
C. $V = $ __60 in.^{3}__
D. $V = $ __56 in.^{3}__

Page 414

Geometric Patterns

Geometric patterns can be described in several ways. **Similar shapes** have the same shape but in differing sizes. **Congruent shapes** have the same geometric pattern but may be facing in different directions. **Symmetrical shapes** are identical when divided in half.

Directions: Use the terms **similar**, **congruent**, or **symmetrical** to describe the following patterns.

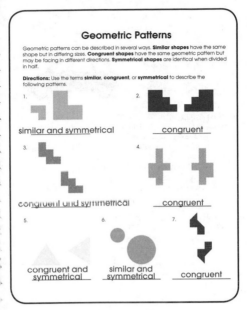

1. similar and symmetrical
2. congruent
3. congruent and symmetrical
4. congruent
5. congruent and symmetrical
6. similar and symmetrical
7. congruent

Page 415

Angles

Angles are named according to the number of degrees between the lines. The degrees are measured with a protractor.

Examples:

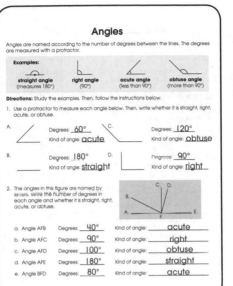

straight angle (measures 180°)   right angle (90°)   acute angle (less than 90°)   obtuse angle (more than 90°)

Directions: Study the examples. Then, follow the instructions below.

1. Use a protractor to measure each angle below. Then, write whether it is straight, right, acute, or obtuse.

A. Degrees: 60° Kind of angle: acute
C. Degrees: 120° Kind of angle: obtuse
B. Degrees: 180° Kind of angle: straight
D. Degrees: 90° Kind of angle: right

2. The angles in this figure are named by letters. Write the number of degrees in each angle and whether it is straight, right, acute, or obtuse.

a. Angle AFB Degrees: 40° Kind of angle: acute
b. Angle AFC Degrees: 90° Kind of angle: right
c. Angle AFD Degrees: 100° Kind of angle: obtuse
d. Angle AFE Degrees: 180° Kind of angle: straight
e. Angle BFD Degrees: 80° Kind of angle: acute

Page 416

Types of Triangles

The sum of angles in all triangles is 180°. However, triangles come in different shapes. They are categorized by the length of their sides and by their types of angles.

Equilateral: Three equal sides
Acute: Three acute angles
Isosceles: Two equal sides
Right: One right angle
Scalene: Zero equal sides
Obtuse: One obtuse angle

One triangle can be a combination of types, such as isosceles and obtuse.

Directions: Study the examples. Then, complete the exercises below

1. Read these directions, and color in the correct triangles
   Color the right scalene triangle blue.
   Color the obtuse scalene triangle red.
   Color the equilateral triangle yellow.
   Color the right isosceles triangle green.
   Color the acute isosceles triangle black.

2. Describe each of these triangles in two ways.
   A. acute equilateral
   B. scalene right

3. In the space below, draw the following triangles.
   scalene triangle   equilateral triangle   obtuse triangle

Page 417

Finding Angles

All triangles have three angles. The sum of these angles is 180°. Therefore, if we know the number of degrees in two of the angles, we can add them together and then subtract from 180 to find the size of the third angle.

Directions: Follow the instructions below.

1. Circle the number that shows the third angle of triangles A through F. Then, describe each triangle two ways. The first one has been done for you.

A. 60°, 60° 45° 50° (60°) equilateral, acute
B. 35°, 55° 27° (90°) 132° scalene, right
C. 30°, 120° (30°) 74° 112° isosceles, obtuse
D. 15°, 78° 65° (87°) 98° scalene, acute
E. 28°, 93° 61° (59°) 70° scalene, obtuse
F. 12°, 114° 60° 50° (54°) scalene, obtuse

2. Find the number of degrees in the third angle of each triangle below.

A. 40° 40° 100°
B. 90° 30° 60°
C. 79° 35° 66°
D. 58° 62° 60°
E. 20° 90° 70°
F. 40° 70° 70°

Page 418

Types of Quadrilaterals

A **quadrilateral** is a shape with four sides and four angles. The sum of angles in all quadrilaterals is 360°. Like triangles, quadrilaterals come in different shapes and are categorized by their sides and their angles.

A **square** has four parallel sides of equal length and four 90° angles.

A **rectangle** has four parallel sides, but only its opposite sides are equal length; it has four 90° angles.

A **parallelogram** has four parallel sides, with the opposite sides of equal length.

A **trapezoid** has two opposite sides that are parallel; its sides may or may not be equal length; its angles may include none, one, or two that are 90°.

Directions: Study the examples. Then, complete the exercises below.

1. Color in the correct quadrilaterals.
   Color two squares blue.   Color two rectangles red.
   Color two parallelograms yellow.   Color two trapezoids green.

2. Circle the number that shows the missing angle for each quadrilateral. Then name the possible quadrilaterals that could have those angles.

A. 90°, 90°, 90° 45° (90°) 180° rectangle, square
B. 65°, 115°, 65° 65° 90° (115°) parallelogram, trapezoid
C. 90°, 110°, 90° 45° (70°) 125° trapezoid
D. 100°, 80°, 80° 40° 80° (100°) parallelogram, trapezoid
E. 90°, 120°, 50° 50° 75° (100°) trapezoid

Page 419

Length in Customary Units

The **customary system** of measurement is the most widely used in the United States. It measures length in inches, feet, yards, and miles.

Examples:
12 inches (in.) = 1 foot (ft.)
3 ft. (36 in.) = 1 yard (yd.)
5,280 ft. (1,760 yds.) = 1 mile (mi.)

To change to a larger unit, divide. To change to a smaller unit, multiply.

Examples:
To change inches to feet, divide by 12. 24 in. = 2 ft. 27 in. = 2 ft. 3 in.
To change feet to inches, multiply by 12. 3 ft. = 36 in. 4 ft. = 48 in.
To change inches to yards, divide by 36. 108 in. = 3 yd. 80 in. = 2 yd. 8 in.
To change feet to yards, divide by 3. 12 ft. = 4 yd. 11 ft. = 3 yd. 2 ft.

Sometimes in subtraction you have to borrow units.

Examples: 3 ft. 4 in. = 2 ft. 16 in.   3 yd. = 2 yd. 3 ft.
-1 ft. 11 in. -1 ft. 11 in.   -1 yd. 2 ft. -1 yd. 2 ft.
1 ft. 5 in.   1 yd. 1 ft.

Directions: Solve the following problems.

1. 108 in. = 9 ft.
2. 68 in. = 5 ft. 8 in.
3. 8 ft. = 2 yd. 2 ft.
4. 3,520 yd. = 2 mi.

5. What form of measurement (inches, feet, yards, or miles) would you use for each item below?
   a. pencil inches   b. vacation trip miles
   c. playground yards or feet   d. wall feet or yards

6. One side of a square box is 2 ft. 4 in. What is the perimeter of the box? 9 ft. 4 in.

7. Jason is 59 in. tall. Kent is 5 ft. 1 in. tall. Who is taller and by how much? Kent, 2 in.

8. Kyra bought a doll 2 ft. 8 in. tall for her little sister. She found a box that is 29 in. long. Will the doll fit in that box? No

9. Dan's dog likes to go out in the backyard, which is 85 ft. wide. The dog's chain is 17 ft. 6 in. long. If Dan attaches one end of the chain to a pole in the middle of the yard, will his dog be able to leave the yard? No

Page 420

Length in Metric Units

The **metric system** measures length in meters, centimeters, millimeters, and kilometers.

Examples:
A **meter (m)** is about 40 inches or 3.3 feet.
A **centimeter (cm)** is 1/100 of a meter or 0.4 inches.
A **millimeter (mm)** is 1/1000 of a meter or 0.04 inches.
A **kilometer (km)** is 1,000 meters or 0.6 miles.

As before, divide to find a larger unit, and multiply to find a smaller unit.

Examples:
To change cm to mm, multiply by 10.
To change cm to meters, divide by 100.
To change mm to meters, divide by 1,000.
To change km to meters, multiply by 1,000.

Directions: Solve the following problems.

1. 600 cm = __6__ m   2. 12 cm = __120__ mm   3. 47 m = __4,700__ cm   4. 3 km = __3,000__ m

5. In the sentences below, write the missing unit: m, cm, mm, or km.

   a. A fingernail is about 1 __mm__ thick.
   b. An average car is about 5 __m__ long.
   c. Someone could walk 1 __km__ in 10 minutes.
   d. A finger is about 7 __cm__ long.
   e. A street could be 3 __km__ long.
   f. The Earth is about 40,000 __km__ around at the equator.
   g. A pencil is about 17 __cm__ long.
   h. A noodle is about 4 __mm__ wide.
   i. A teacher's desk is about 1 __m__ wide.

6. A nickel is about 1 mm thick. How many nickels would be in a stack 1 cm high? __10__
7. Is something 25 cm long closer to 10 inches or 10 feet? __10 inches__
8. Is something 18 mm wide closer to 0.7 inch or 7 inches? __0.7 inch__
9. Would you get more exercise running 4 km or 500 m? __4 km__
10. Which is taller, something 40 m or 350 cm? __40 m__

Page 421

Weight in Customary Units

Here are the main ways to measure weight in customary units:

16 ounces (oz.) = 1 pound (lb.)
2,000 lb. = 1 ton (tn.)
To change ounces to pounds, divide by 16.
To change pounds to ounces, multiply by 16.

As with measurements of length, you may have to borrow units in subtraction.

Example: 4 lb. 5 oz. = 3 lb. 21 oz.
          − 2 lb. 10 oz. − 2 lb. 10 oz.
                        1 lb. 11 oz.

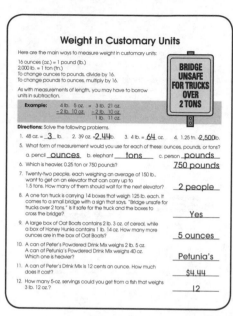

Directions: Solve the following problems.

1. 48 oz. = __3__ lb.   2. 39 oz. = __2.44__ lb.   3. 4 lb. = __64__ oz.   4. 1.25 tn. = __2,500__ lb.
5. What form of measurement would you use for each of these: ounces, pounds, or tons?

   a. pencil __ounces__   b. elephant __tons__   c. person __pounds__

6. Which is heavier, 0.25 ton or 750 pounds? __750 pounds__
7. Twenty-two people, each weighing an average of 150 lb., want to get on an elevator that can carry up to 1.5 tons. How many of them should wait for the next elevator? __2 people__
8. A one ton truck is carrying 14 boxes that weigh 125 lb. each. It comes to a small bridge with a sign that says, "Bridge unsafe for trucks over 2 tons." Is it safe for the truck and the boxes to cross the bridge? __Yes__
9. A large box of Oat Boats contains 2 lb. 3 oz. of cereal, while a box of Honey Hunks contains 1 lb. 14 oz. How many more ounces are in the box of Oat Boats? __5 ounces__
10. A can of Peter's Powdered Drink Mix weighs 2 lb. 5 oz. A can of Petunia's Powdered Drink Mix weighs 40 oz. Which one is heavier? __Petunia's__
11. A can of Peter's Drink Mix is 12 cents an ounce. How much does it cost? __$4.44__
12. How many 5-oz. servings could you get from a fish that weighs 3 lb. 12 oz.? __12__

Page 422

Weight in Metric Units

A **gram (g)** is about 0.035 oz.
A **milligram (mg)** is 1/1000 g or about 0.000035 oz.
A **kilogram (kg)** is 1,000 g or about 2.2 lb.
A **metric ton (t)** is 1,000 kg or about 1.1 tn.

To change g to mg, multiply by 1,000.
To change g to kg, divide by 1,000.
To change kg to g, multiply by 1,000.
To change t to kg, multiply by 1,000.

Directions: Solve the following problems.

1. 3 kg = __3,000__ g   2. 2 g = __2,000__ mg   3. 145 g = __0.145__ kg
4. 3,000 kg = __3__ t   5. 0.45 g = 450 mg   6. 3.5 t = __3,500__ kg

7. Write the missing unit below: g, mg, kg, or t.

   a. A sunflower seed weighs less than 1 __g__.
   b. A serving of cereal contains 14 __g__ of sugar.
   c. The same serving of cereal has 250 __mg__ of salt.
   d. A bowling ball weighs about 7 __kg__.
   e. A whale weighs about 90 __t__.
   f. A math textbook weighs about 1 __kg__.
   g. A safety pin weighs about 1 __g__.
   h. An average car weighs about 1 __t__.

8. Is 200 g closer to 7 oz. or 70 oz.? __7 oz.__
9. Is 3 kg closer to 7 lb. or 70 lb.? __7 lbs.__
10. Does a metric ton weigh more or less than a ton measured by the customary system? __more__
11. How is a kilogram different from a kilometer? __A kilogram measure weight; a kilometer measures distance.__
12. Which is heavier, 300 g or 1 kg? __1 kg__

Page 423

Capacity in Customary Units

Here are the main ways to measure capacity (how much something will hold) in customary units:

8 fluid ounces (fl. oz.) = 1 cup (c.)
2 c. = 1 pint (pt.)
2 pt. = 1 quart (qt.)
4 qt. = 1 gallon (gal.)

To change ounces to cups, divide by 8.
To change cups to ounces, multiply by 8.
To change cups to pints or pints to quarts, divide by 2.
To change pints to cups or quarts to pints, multiply by 2.

As with measurements of length and weight, you may have to borrow units in subtraction.

Example: 3 gal. 2 qt. = 2 gal. 6 qt.
          − 1 gal. 3 qt.   − 1 gal. 3 qt.
                          1 gal. 3 qt.

Directions: Solve the following problems.

1. 32 fl. oz. = __2__ c.   2. 4 gal. = __32__ pt.   3. __3__ c. = 24 fl. oz.
4. 5 pt. = __2.5__ qt.   5. 16 pt. = __2__ gal.   6. 3 pt. = __48__ fl. oz.
7. A large can of soup contains 19 fl. oz. A serving is about 8 oz. How many cans should you buy if you want to serve 7 people? __3 cans__
8. A container of strawberry ice cream holds 36 fl. oz. A container of chocolate ice cream holds 2 pt. Which one has more ice cream? How much more? __strawberry; 4 fl. oz.__
9. A day-care worker wants to give 15 children each 6 fl. oz. of milk. How many quarts of milk does she need? __3 qt.__
10. This morning, the day-care supervisor bought 3 gal. of milk. The kids drank 2 gal. 3 c. How much milk is left for tomorrow? __13 cups__
11. Harriet bought 3 gal. 2 qt. of paint for her living room. She used 2 gal. 3 qt. How much paint is left over? __3 qt.__
12. Yusef's favorite punch takes a pint of raspberry sherbet. If he wants to make 1½ times the recipe, how many fl. oz. of sherbet does he need? __24 fl. oz.__

Page 424

Capacity in Metric Units

A **liter (L)** is a little over 1 quart.
A **milliliter (mL)** is 1/1000 of a liter, or about 0.03 oz.
A **kiloliter (kL)** is 1,000 liters or about 250 gallons.

Directions: Solve the following problems.

1. 5,000 mL = __5__ L
2. 2,000 L = __2__ kL
3. 3 L = __3,000__ mL
4. Write the missing unit: L, mL, or kL.

   a. A swimming pool holds about 100 __kL__ of water.
   b. An eyedropper is marked for 1 and 2 __mL__.
   c. A pitcher could hold 1 or 2 __L__ of juice.
   d. A teaspoon holds about 5 __mL__ of medicine.
   e. A birdbath might hold 5 __L__ of water.
   f. A tablespoon holds about 15 __mL__ of salt.
   g. A bowl holds about 250 __mL__ of soup.
   h. We drank about 4 __L__ of punch at the party.

5. Which is more, 3 L or a gallon? __gallon__
6. Which is more, 400 mL or 40 oz.? __40 oz.__
7. Which is more, 1 kL or 500 L? __1 kL__
8. Is 4 L closer to a quart or a gallon? __gallon__
9. Is 480 mL closer to 2 cups or 2 pints? __2 cups__
10. Is a mL closer to 4 drops or 4 teaspoonsful? __4 drops__
11. How many glasses of juice containing 250 mL each could you pour from a 1-L jug? __4 glasses__
12. How much water would you need to water an average-sized lawn, 1 kL or 1 L? __1 kL__

Page 425

Temperature in Customary and Metric Units

The customary system measures temperature in Fahrenheit (F°) degrees.

The metric system uses Celsius (C°) degrees.

Directions: Study the thermometers, and answer these questions.

1. Write in the temperature from both systems.

	Fahrenheit	Celsius
a. freezing	32°	0°
b. boiling	212°	100°
c. comfortable room temperature	Answers will vary.	

2. Underline the most appropriate temperature for both systems.

   a. a reasonably hot day   34° 54° __84__   10° 20° __35°__
   b. a cup of hot chocolate   __95°__ 120° 190°   __60°__ 90° 120°
   c. comfortable water to swim in   55° __75°__ 95°   10° __25°__ 40°

3. If the temperature is 35°C, is it summer or winter? __summer__
4. Would ice cream stay frozen at 35°F? __No__
5. Which is colder, -10°C or -10°F? __-10° F__
6. Which is warmer, 60°C or 60°F? __60° C__

Page 426

Review

Directions: Complete the following exercises.

1. 372 in. = __10__ yd. __1__ ft.
2. 4 km = __4,000__ m
3. 1.25 lb. = __20__ oz.
4. 2,000 mg = __2__ g
5. 1 qt. = __32__ oz.
6. 10,000 mL = __10__ L
7. Todd has a board that is 6 ft. 3 in. long. He needs to cut it to 4 ft. 9 in. How much should he cut off? __18 in. (1 ft. 6 in.)__
8. In a contest, Lauren threw a ball 12 yd. Jiao threw the ball 500 in. Who threw the farthest? __Jiao__
9. Would you measure this workbook in mm or cm? __cm__
10. Which is heavier, a box of books that weighs 4 lb. 6 oz. or a box of dishes that weighs 80 oz.? __box of dishes__
11. A 1-lb. package has 10 hot dogs. How many ounces does each hot dog weigh? __1.6 oz.__
12. Would the amount of salt (sodium) in 1 oz. of pretzels be 170 g or 170 mg? __170 mg__
13. If a family ate half a gallon of frozen yogurt, how many fluid ounces would be left? __64 fl. oz.__
14. You want to serve 6 fl. oz. of fruit juice to each of 16 friends at your party. How many quarts of juice should you buy? __3 qt.__
15. Would you measure water in a fish pond with L or kL? __kL__
16. Would popsicles melt at 5°C? __Yes__
17. Would soup be steaming hot at 150°F? __Yes__

Page 427

Ratios

A **ratio** is a comparison of two quantities. For example, a wall is 96 in. high; a pencil is 8 in. long. By dividing 8 into 96, you find it would take 12 pencils to equal the height of the wall. The ratio, or comparison, of the wall to the pencil can be written three ways:
1 to 12; 1:12; 1/12. In this example, the ratio of triangles to circles is 4:6. The ratio of triangles to squares is 4:9. The ratio of circles to squares is 6:9. These ratios stay the same if we divide both numbers in the ratio by the same number.

Examples: 4÷2 = 2, 6÷3 = 2, (There is no number that will divide into both 4 and 9.)
4÷2 = 2/3; 6÷3 = 2/3

By reducing 4:6 and 6:9 to their lowest terms, they are the same—2:3. This means that 2:3, 4:6, and 6:9 are all equal ratios. You can also find equal ratios for all three by multiplying both numbers of the ratio by the same number.

Examples: 4×3 = 12/6×3 = 18; 6×5 = 30/9×5 = 45; 4×4 = 16/9×4 = 36

Directions: Solve the following problems.

1. Write two more equal ratios for each of the following by multiplying or dividing both numbers in the ratio by the same number.
   a. 1/2, 3/4, 6/8, __4/8__, __5/10__
   b. 1/4, 3/8, 2/6, __5/20__, __3/12__
   c. 8/24, 1/3, 3/9, __2/6__, __4/12__

2. Circle the ratios that are equal.
   a. 1/6, 3/6
   b. 15/25, 10/35 (circled)
   c. 2/7, 10/35 (circled)
   d. 2/3, 6/10

3. Write each ratio three ways.
   a. stars to faces __3 to 7; 3:7; 3/7__
   b. faces to trees __7 to 5; 7:5; 7/5__
   c. stars to all other shapes __3 to 12; 3:12; 3/12__

4. Write two equal ratios (multiplying or dividing) for:
   a. stars to faces __6/14; 14__
   b. faces to trees __14/10; 14__
   c. stars to all other shapes __6/24; 3/12__

Page 428

Missing Numbers in Ratios

You can find a missing number (n) in an equal ratio. First, figure out which number has already been multiplied to get the number you know. (In the first example, 3 is multiplied by 3 to get 9; in the second example, 2 is multiplied by 6 to get 12.) Then, multiply the other number in the ratio by the same number (3 and 6 in the examples).

Examples: 3/4 = 9/n, 3/4 × 3/3 = 9/12, n = 12, 1/2 = n/12, 1/2 × 6/6 = 6/12, n = 6

Directions: Solve the following problems.

1. Find each missing number.
   a. 1/2 = n/12, n = __6__
   b. 1/5 = n/15, n = __3__
   c. 3/2 = 18/n, n = __12__
   d. 5/8 = n/32, n = __20__
   e. 8/3 = 16/n, n = __6__
   f. n/14 = 5/7, n = __10__

2. If a basketball player makes 9 baskets in 12 tries, what is her ratio of baskets to tries, in lowest terms? __3:4__
3. At the next game, the player has the same ratio of baskets to tries. If she tries 20 times, how many baskets should she make? __15 baskets__
4. At the third game, she still has the same ratio of baskets to tries. This time she makes 12 baskets. How many times did she probably try? __16 times__
5. If a driver travels 40 miles in an hour, what is his ratio of miles to minutes, in lowest terms? __2:3__
6. At the same speed, how far would the driver travel in 30 minutes? __20 miles__
7. At the same speed, how long would it take him to travel 60 miles? __1 hr. 30 min.__

Page 429

Proportions

A **proportion** is a statement that two ratios are equal. To make sure ratios are equal, called a proportion, we multiply the cross products.

Examples of proportions: 1/5 = 2/10, 1/5 = 10/10, 3/7 = 15/35, 3/16 = 35/100... 105/100

These two ratios are not a proportion: 4/3 = 6/5, 4/5 × 6/5 = 24/15

To find a missing number (n) in a proportion, multiply the cross products and divide.

Examples: n/30 = 1/6, n × 6 = 1 × 30, n = 30/6, n = 5

Directions: Solve the following problems.

1. Write = between the ratios if they are a proportion. Write ≠ if they are not a proportion. The first one has been done for you.
   a. 1/2 (=) 6/12
   b. 13/18 (≠) 20/22
   c. 2/6 (=) 5/15
   d. 5/6 (=) 20/24
2. Find the missing numbers in these proportions.
   a. 2/5 = n/15, n = __6__
   b. 3/8 = 9/n, n = __24__
   c. n/18 = 4/12, n = __6__
3. One issue of a magazine costs $2.99, but if you buy a subscription, 12 issues cost $35.88. Is the price at the same proportion? __Yes__
4. A muffin recipe calls for 3 cups of flour to make 24 muffins. How much flour is needed for 36 muffins? __4.5 cups__
5. The same recipe requires 4 teaspoons of cinnamon for 36 muffins. How many teaspoons is needed to make 48 muffins? (Answer will include a fraction.) __5 1/3 teaspoons__
6. The recipe also calls for 2 cups of sugar for 36 muffins. How much sugar should you use for 48 muffins? (Answer will include a fraction.) __5 2/3 cups__

Page 430

Percents

Percent means "per 100." A percent is a ratio that compares a number with 100. The same number can be written as a decimal and a percent. To change a decimal to a percent, move the decimal point two places to the right and add the % sign. To change a percent to a decimal, drop the % sign and place a decimal point two places to the left.

Examples: 0.25 = 25%, 0.1 = 10%, 1.456 = 145.6%, 32% = 0.32, 99% = 0.99, 203% = 2.03

A percent or decimal can also be written as a ratio or fraction.

Example: 0.25 = 25% = 25/100 = 1/4 = 1:4

To change a fraction or ratio to a percent, first change it to a decimal. Divide the numerator by the denominator.

Examples: 1/3 = 3|1.00 (0.33⅓ = 33⅓%), 2/5 = 5|2.0 (0.4 = 40%)

Directions: Solve the following problems.

1. Change the percents to decimals.
   a. 3% = __0.03__
   b. 75% = __0.75__
   c. 14% = __0.14__
   d. 115% = __1.15__
2. Change the decimals and fractions to percents.
   a. 0.56 = __56__ %
   b. 0.03 = __3__ %
   c. 3/4 = __75__ %
   d. 1/5 = __20__ %
3. Change the percents to ratios in their lowest terms. The first one has been done for you.
   a. 75% = 75/100 = 3/4 = 3:4
   b. 40% = 40/100 = 2/5 = 2:5
   c. 35% = 35/100 = 7/20 = 7:20
   d. 70% = 70/100 = 7/10 = 7:10
4. The class was 45% girls. What percent was boys? __55%__
5. Half the shoes in one store were on sale. What percent of the shoes were their ordinary price? __50%__
6. Tierra read 84 pages of a 100-page book. What percent of the book did she read? __84%__

Page 431

Percents

To find the percent of a number, change the percent to a decimal and multiply.

Examples: 45% of $20 = 0.45 × $20 = $9.00, 126% of 30 = 1.26 × 30 = 37.50

Directions: Solve the following problems. Round the answers to the nearest hundredth where necessary.

1. Find the percent of each number.
   a. 26% of 40 = __10.4__
   b. 12% of 329 = __39.48__
   c. 73% of 19 = __13.87__
   d. 2% of 24 = __0.48__
2. One family spends 35% of its weekly budget of $375 on food. How much do they spend? __$131.25__
3. A shirt in a store usually costs $15.99, but today it's on sale for 25% off. The clerk says you will save $4.50. Is that true? __No__
4. A book that usually costs $12 is on sale for 25% off. How much will it cost? __$9.00__
5. After you answer 60% of 150 math problems, how many do you have left to do? __60__
6. A pet store's shipment of tropical fish was delayed. Nearly 40% of the 1,350 fish died. About how many lived? __810__
7. The shipment had 230 angelfish, which died in the same proportion as the other kinds of fish. About how many angelfish died? __92__
8. A church youth group was collecting cans of food. Their goal was 1,200 cans, but they exceeded their goal by 25%. How many cans did they collect? __1,500__

Page 432

Probability

Probability is the ratio of favorable outcomes to possible outcomes in an experiment. You can use probability (P) to figure out how likely something is to happen. For example, six picture cards are turned facedown—3 cards have stars, 2 have triangles, and 1 has a circle. What is the probability of picking the circle? Using the formula below, you have a 1 in 6 probability of picking the circle, a 2 in 6 probability of picking a triangle, and a 3 in 6 probability of picking a star.

Example: P = number of favorable outcomes   P = $\frac{1}{6}$ = 1:6
number of trials

Directions: Solve the following problems.

1. A class has 14 girls and 15 boys. If all of their names are put on separate slips in a hat, what is the probability of each person's name being chosen? — **1:29**

2. In the same class, what is the probability that a girl's name will be chosen? — **14:29**

3. In this class, 3 boys are named Jack. What is the probability that a slip with "Jack" written on it will be chosen? — **3:29**

4. A spinner on a board game has the numbers 1–8. What is the probability of spinning and getting a 4? — **1:8**

5. A paper bag holds these colors of wooden beads: 4 blue, 5 red, and 6 yellow. If you select a bead without looking, do you have an equal probability of getting each color? — **No**

6. Using the same bag of beads, what is the probability of reaching in and drawing out a red bead (in lowest terms)? — **1:3**

7. In the same bag, what is the probability of not getting a blue bead? — **11:15**

8. In a carnival game, plastic ducks have spots. The probability of picking a duck with a yellow spot is 2:15. There is twice as much probability of picking a duck with a red spot. What is the probability of picking a duck with a red spot? — **4:15**

9. In this game, all the other ducks have green spots. What is the probability of picking a duck with a green spot? (in lowest terms)? — **3:5**

Page 433

Possible Combinations

Today the cafeteria is offering 4 kinds of sandwiches, 3 kinds of drinks, and 2 kinds of fruits. How many possible combinations could you make? To find out, multiply the number of choices together.

Example: 4 x 3 x 2 = 24 possible combinations

Directions: Solve the following problems.

1. If Juan has 3 shirts and 4 pairs of shorts, how many combinations can he make? — **12**

2. Jamilla can borrow 1 book and 1 magazine at a time from her classroom library. The library has 45 books and 16 magazines. How many combinations are possible? — **720**

3. Kerry's mother is redecorating the living room. She has narrowed her choices to 6 kinds of wallpaper, 3 shades of paint, and 4 colors of carpeting that all match. How many possible combinations are there? — **72**

4. Maya has 6 sweaters that she can combine with pants to make 24 outfits. How many pairs of pants does she have? — **4**

5. Cooper can get to school by walking, taking a bus, riding his bike, or asking his parents for a ride. He can get home the same ways, except his parents aren't available then. How many combinations can he make of ways to get to school and get home? — **12**

6. Gabby's middle school offers 3 different language classes, 3 art classes, and 2 music classes. If she takes one class in each area, how many possible combinations are there? — **18**

7. Vikram's school offers 4 language classes, 3 art classes, and some music classes. If Vikram can make 36 possible combinations, how many music classes are there? — **3**

8. AAA Airlines schedules 12 flights a day from Chicago to Atlanta. Four of those flights go on to Orlando. From the Orlando airport you can take a bus, ride in a taxi, or rent a car to get to Disneyworld. How many different ways are there to get from Chicago to Disneyworld if you make part of your trip on AAA Airlines? — **12**

Page 434

Review

Directions: Solve the following problems. Round answers to the nearest hundredth where necessary.

1. Write an equal ratio for each of these:
   a. $\frac{1}{7} = \frac{2}{14}$ b. $\frac{5}{8} = \frac{10}{16}$ c. $\frac{15}{3} = \frac{30}{6}$ d. $\frac{6}{24} = \frac{12}{48}$

2. State the ratios below in lowest terms.
   a. cats to bugs = **2:3**
   b. cats to dogs = **4:5**
   c. dogs to all other objects = **1:2**

3. If Shawn drives 45 miles an hour, how far could he go in 40 minutes? **30 miles**

4. At the same speed, how many minutes would it take Shawn to drive 120 miles? **2 hours and 40 minutes**

5. Mr. Herman is building a doghouse in proportion to his family's house. The family's house is 30 ft. high and the doghouse is 5 ft. high. If the family house is 42 ft. wide, how wide should the doghouse be? **7 ft.**

6. The family house is 24 ft. from front to back. How big should Mr. Herman make the doghouse? **4 ft.**

7. Change these numbers to percents:
   a. 0.56 = **56%**   b. $\frac{4}{5}$ = **80%**   c. 0.04 = **4%**   d. $\frac{3}{8}$ = **37.5%**

8. Which is a better deal, a blue bike for $125 at 25% off or a red bike for $130 at 30% off? **red bike**

9. If sales tax is 6%, what would be the total price of the blue bike? **$96.46**

10. Richard bought 6 raffle tickets for a free bike. If 462 tickets were sold, what is Richard's probability of winning? **6:462 = 1:77**

11. Lilly bought 48 tickets in the same raffle. What are her chances of winning? **48:462 = 8:77**

Page 435

Comparing Data

Data is gathered information. The **range** is the difference between the highest and lowest number in a group of numbers. The **median** is the number in the middle when numbers are listed in order. The **mean** is the average of the numbers. We can compare numbers or data by finding the range, median, or mean.

Example: 16, 43, 34, 78, 8, 91, 26

To compare these numbers, we first need to put them in order: 8 16 26 34 43 78 91. By subtracting the lowest number (8) from the highest one (91), we find the range: 83. By finding the number that falls in the middle, we have the median: 34 (If no number fell exactly in the middle, we would average the two middle numbers.) By adding them and dividing by the number of numbers (7), we get the mean: 42.29 (rounded to the nearest hundredth).

Directions: Solve the following problems. Round answers to the nearest hundredth where necessary.

1. Find the range, median, and mean of these numbers: 19, 5, 84, 27, 106, 38, 75.
   Range: **101**   Median: **38**   Mean: **50.57**

2. Find the range, median, and mean finishing times for 6 runners in a race. Here are their times in seconds: 14.2, 12.9, 13.5, 10.3, 14.8, 14.7.
   Range: **4.5**   Median: **13.85**   Mean: **13.4**

3. If the runner who won the race in 10.3 seconds had run even faster and finished in 7 seconds, would the mean time be higher or lower? **Lower**

4. If that runner had finished in 7 seconds, what would be the median time? **13.85**

5. Here are the high temperatures in one city for a week: 65, 72, 68, 74, 81, 68, 85. Find the range, median, and mean temperatures.
   Range: **20**   Median: **72**   Mean: **73.29**

6. Find the range, median, and mean test scores for this group of students: 41, 32, 45, 36, 48, 38, 37, 42, 39, 36.
   Range: **16**   Median: **38.5**   Mean: **39.4**

Page 436

Tables

Organizing data into tables makes it easier to compare numbers. As evident in the example, putting many numbers in a paragraph is confusing. When the same numbers are organized in a table, you can compare numbers in a glance. Tables can be arranged several ways and still be easy to read and understand.

Example: Money spent on groceries:
Family A: week 1 — $98.50; week 2 — $134.25; week 3 — $142.00; week 4 — $103.50.
Family B: week 1 — $160.25; week 2 — $192.50; week 3 — $171.25; week 4 — $173.50.

	Week 1	Week 2	Week 3	Week 4
Family A	$98.50	$134.25	$142.00	$103.50
Family B	$160.25	$192.50	$171.25	$173.50

Directions: Complete the following exercises.

1. Finish the table below, and then answer the questions.
Data: Steve weighs 185 lb. and is 6 ft. 2 in. tall. George weighs 218 lb. and is 6 ft. 3 in. tall. Chuck weighs 178 lb. and is 6 ft. 1 in. tall. Henry weighs 166 lb. and is 6 ft. tall.

	Henry	George	Chuck	Steve
Weight	166 lb.	218 lb.	178 lb.	185 lb.
Height	6 ft.	6 ft. 3 in.	6 ft. 1 in.	6 ft. 2 in.

a. Who is tallest? **George**   b. Who weighs the least? **Henry**

2. On another sheet of paper, prepare 2 tables comparing the amount of money made by 3 booths at the school carnival this year and last year. In the first table, write the names of the games in the left-hand column (like **Family A** and **Family B** in the example). In the second table (using the same data), write the years in the left-hand column. Here is the data: fish pond—this year $15.60, last year $13.50; bean-bag toss—this year $13.45, last year $10.25; ring toss—this year $23.80, last year $18.80. After you complete both tables, answer the following questions.

a. Which booth made the most money this year? **ring toss**

b. Which booth made the biggest improvement from last year to this year? **ring toss**

Page 437

Bar Graphs

Another way to organize information is a **bar graph**. The bar graph in the example compares the number of students in 4 elementary schools. Each bar stands for 1 school. You can easily see that School A has the most students and School C has the least. The numbers along the left show how many students attend each school.

Example:

Directions: Complete the following exercises.

1. This bar graph will show how many calories are in 1 serving of 4 kinds of cereal. Draw the bars the correct height, and label each with the name of the cereal. After completing the bar graph, answer the questions. Data: Korn Kernels—150 calories; Oat Floats—160 calories; Rice Puffs—110 calories; Nut Crunch—200 calories.

A. Which cereal is the best to eat if you're trying to lose weight? **Rice Puffs**

B. Which cereal has nearly the same number of calories as Oat Floats? **Korn Kernels**

2. On another sheet of paper, draw your own graph, showing the number of TV commercials in 1 week for each of the 4 cereals in the graph above. After completing the graph, answer the questions. Data: Oat Floats—27 commercials; Rice Puffs—15; Nut Crunch—35; Korn Kernels—28.

A. Which cereal is most heavily advertised? **Nut Crunch**

B. What similarities do you notice between the graph of calories and the graph of TV commercials? **Nut Crunch is the highest in sugar and advertising.**

Page 438

Picture Graphs

Newspapers and textbooks often use pictures in graphs instead of bars. Each picture stands for a certain number of objects. Half a picture means half the number. The picture graph in the example indicates the number of games each team won. The Astros won 7 games, so they have 3½ balls.

Example:

Games Won				
Astros				
Orioles				
Bluebirds				
Sluggers				

(1 ball = 2 games)

Directions: Complete the following exercises.

Finish this picture graph, showing the number of students who have dogs in 4 sixth-grade classes. Draw simple dogs in the graph, letting each drawing stand for 2 dogs. Data: Class 1—12 dogs; Class 2—16 dogs; Class 3—?? dogs; Class 4—12 dogs. After completing the graph, answer the questions.

Dogs Owned by Students	
Class 1	
Class 2	
Class 3	
Class 4	

(One dog drawing = 2 students' dogs)

1. Why do you think newspapers use picture graphs? **Answers will vary. It simplifies information and is easier to read.**

2. Would picture graphs be appropriate to show the exact number of dogs living in America? Why or why not? **No. There are too many dogs.**

Page 439

Line Graphs

Still another way to display information is a line graph. The same data can often be shown in both a bar graph and a line graph. Line graphs are especially useful in showing changes over a period of time.

The line graph in the example shows changes in the number of students enrolled in a school over a 5-year period. Enrollment was highest in 2012 and has decreased gradually each year since then. Notice how labeling the years and enrollment numbers make the graph easy to understand.

Example:

Fall Enrollment at Cedar School

Directions: Complete the following exercises.

1. On another sheet of paper, draw a line graph that displays the growth of a corn plant over a 6-week period. Mark the correct points, using the data below, and connect them with a line. After completing the graph, answer the questions. Data: week 1—3.5 in.; week 2—4.5 in.; week 3—5 in.; week 4—5.5 in.; week 5—5.75 in.; week 6—6 in.

   a. Between which weeks was the growth fastest? **Weeks 1 and 2**

   b. Between which weeks was the growth slowest? **Weeks 4 and 5; Weeks 5 and 6**

2. On another sheet of paper, draw a line graph to show how the high temperature varied during one week. Then answer the questions. Data: Sunday—high of 53 degrees; Monday—51; Tuesday—56; Wednesday—60; Thursday—58; Friday—67; Saturday—73. Don't forget to label the numbers.

   a. In general, did the days get warmer or cooler? **Warmer**

   b. Do you think this data would have been as clear in a bar graph? **No** Explain your answer. **Line graphs show a trend up and down across the graph.**

Page 440

Circle Graphs

Circle graphs are useful in showing how something is divided into parts. The circle graph in the example shows how Carly spent her $10 allowance. Each section is a fraction of her whole allowance. For example, the movie tickets section is ⅓ of the circle, showing that she spent ⅓ of her allowance, $5, on movie tickets.

MOVIE TICKETS / FOOD / STAMPS

Directions: Complete the following exercises.

East Elementary / West Elementary / other / North Elementary

1. When the middle school opened last fall, ½ of the students came from East Elementary, ¼ came from West Elementary, ⅛ came from North Elementary, and the remaining students moved into the town from other cities. Make a circle graph showing these proportions. Label each section. Then, answer the questions.

   a. What fraction of students at the new school moved into the area from other cities? **1/8**

   b. If the new middle school has 450 students enrolled, how many used to go to East Elementary? **225 students**

2. This circle graph will show the hair color of 24 students in one class. Divide the circle into 4 sections to show this data: black hair—8 students; brown hair—10 students; blonde hair—4 students; red hair—2 students. (Hint: 8 students are ⅓ or ⅓ of the class.) Be sure to label each section by hair color. Then, answer the questions.

blonde / red / black / brown

   a. Looking at your graph, what fraction of the class is the combined group of blonde- and red-haired students? **6/24 = 1/4**

   b. Which two fractions of hair color combine to total half the class? **red and brown or black and blonde**

Page 441

Comparing Presentation Methods

Tables and different kinds of graphs have different purposes. Some are more helpful for certain kinds of information. The table and three graphs below all show basically the same information—the amount of money Owen and Leyla made in their lawn-mowing business over a 4-month period.

Combined Income per Month

	Owen	Leyla
June	$34	$36
July	41	35
August	27	28
Sept.	36	40
Totals	$138	$139

Combined Income per Month

Directions: Study the graphs and table. Then, circle the one that answers each question below.

1. Which one shows the fraction of the total income that Owen and Leyla made in August?
   table   line graph   bar graph   **(circle graph)**

2. Which one compares Owen's earnings with Leyla's?
   (table)   line graph   bar graph   circle graph

3. Which one has the most exact numbers?
   (table)   line graph   bar graph   circle graph

4. Which one has no numbers?
   table   line graph   bar graph   **(circle graph)**

5. Which two best show how Owen and Leyla's income changed from month to month?
   table   **(line graph)**   **(bar graph)**   circle graph

Page 442

Graphing Data

Directions: Complete the following exercises.

1. Use the following information to create a bar graph.

Cities	Population (in 1,000s)
Dover	20
Newton Falls	12
Springdale	25
Hampton	17
Riverside	5

Dover NF SD Hamp. RS

2. Study the data, and create a line graph showing the number of baskets Jonah scored during the season.

Game 1 — 10	Fill in the blanks.	
Game 2 — 7	a. High game: **3**	
Game 3 — 11		
Game 4 — 10	b. Low game: **6**	
Game 5 — 9		
Game 6 — 5	c. Average baskets per game: **8.7**	
Game 7 — 9		

3. Study the graph, then answer the questions.

Chocolate 50% / Vanilla 10% / Strawberry 25% / Blue Moon / Frozen Yogurt Sales

   a. Which flavor is the most popular? **chocolate**

   b. Which flavor sold the least? **Blue Moon**

   c. What decimal represents the two highest sellers? **0.75**

   d. Which flavor had ⅒ of the sales? **vanilla**

Page 443

Integers

An **integer** is a whole number above or below 0: -2, -1, 0, +1, +2, and so on. **Opposite integers** are two integers the same distance from 0, but in different directions, such as -2 and +2.

Think of the water level in the picture as 0. The part of the iceberg sticking out of the water is positive. The iceberg has +3 feet above water. The part of the iceberg below the water is negative. The iceberg extends -9 feet under water.

Numbers greater than 0 are **positive** numbers. Numbers less than 0 are **negative** numbers. Pairs of positive and negative numbers are called **opposite integers**.

3 feet / water level / 9 feet

Examples of opposite integers:
-5 and +5
losing 3 pounds and gaining 3 pounds
earning $12 and spending $12

Directions: Complete the following exercises.

1. Write each of these as an integer. The first one is done for you.
   a. positive 6 = **+6**   b. losing $5 = **-$5**
   c. 5 degrees below 0 = **-5**   d. receiving $12 = **+$12**

2. Write the **opposite** integer of each of these. The first one is done for you.
   a. negative 4 = **+4**   b. positive 10 = **-10**
   c. 2 floors below ground level = **+2**   d. winning a card game by 6 points = **-6**

3. Write integers to show each idea.
   a. A train that arrives 2 hours after it was scheduled: **+2**
   b. A package that has 3 fewer cups than it should: **-3**
   c. A board that's 3 inches too short: **-3**   d. A golf score 5 over par: **+5**
   e. A paycheck that doesn't cover $35 of a family's expenses: **-$35**
   f. 30 seconds before a missile launch: **-$30**
   g. A team that won 6 games and lost 2: **+4**

Page 444

Comparing Integers

Comparing two integers can be confusing unless you think of them as being on a number line, as shown below. Remember that the integer farther to the right is greater. Thus, +2 is greater than –3, 0 is greater than –4, and –2 is greater than –5.

$$-5 \quad -4 \quad -3 \quad -2 \quad -1 \quad 0 \quad +1 \quad +2 \quad +3 \quad +4 \quad +5$$

Directions: Study the number line. Then, complete the following exercises.

1. Write in integers to complete the number line.

$$-5 \quad \_\_ \quad -3 \quad -2 \quad \_\_ \quad 0 \quad +1 \quad \_\_ \quad \_\_ \quad +4 \quad +5$$

2. Write < for "less than" or > for "greater than" to compare the integers. The first one is done for you.

   a. –5 **<** +5   b. +3 **>** –3   c. +2 **>** –4
   d. –4 **<** –3   e. –1 **<** +3   f. –1 **>** –5

3. Write **T** for true or **F** for false. (All degrees are in Fahrenheit.)

   a. +7 degrees is colder than –3 degrees. ____ **F**
   b. –14 degrees is colder than –7 degrees. ____ **T**
   c. +23 degrees is colder than –44 degrees. ____ **F**
   d. –5 degrees is colder than +4 degrees. ____ **T**

4. Draw an **X** by the series of integers that are in order from least to greatest.

   ____ +2, +3, –4
   X –3, 0, +1
   X –7, –4, –1
   ____ –3, –4, –5

Page 445

Adding Integers

The sum of two positive integers is a positive integer.
   Thus, +4 + +1 = +5.
The sum of two negative integers is a negative integer.
   Thus, –5 + –2 = –7.
The sum of a positive and a negative integer has the sign of the integer that is farther from 0.
   Thus, –6 + +3 = –3.
The sum of opposite integers is 0.
   Thus, +2 + –2 = 0.

Directions: Complete the following exercises.

1. Add these integers.

   a. +2 + +7 = **+9**   b. –4 + –2 = **–6**   c. +5 + –3 = **+2**   d. +4 + –4 = **0**
   e. –10 + –2 = **–12**   f. +6 + –1 = **+5**   g. +45 + –30 = **+15**   h. –39 + +26 = **–13**

2. Write the problems as integers. The first one has been done for you.

   a. One cold morning, the temperature was –14 degrees. The afternoon high was 20 degrees warmer. What was the high temperature that day?
   –14 + +20 = +6

   b. Another day, the high temperature was 26 degrees, but the temperature dropped 35 degrees during the night. What was the low that night?
   +26 + –35 = –9

   c. Valentina's allowance was $10. She paid $7 for a movie ticket. How much money did she have left?
   +$10 + –$7 = +$3

   d. The temperature in a meat freezer was –10 degrees, but the power went off and the temperature rose 6 degrees. How cold was the freezer then?
   –10 + +6 = –4

   e. The school carnival took in $235, but it had expenses of $185. How much money did the carnival make after paying its expenses?
   +$235 + –$185 = +$50

Page 446

Subtracting Integers

To subtract an integer, change its sign to the opposite and add it. If you are subtracting a negative integer, make it positive and add it: +4 – –6 = +4 + +6 = +10. If you are subtracting a positive integer, make it negative and add it: +8 – +2 = +8 + –2 = +6.

> **More examples:**   –5 – –8 = –5 + +8 = +3
> +3 – +7 = +3 + –7 = –4

Directions: Complete the following exercises.

1. Before subtracting these integers, rewrite each problem. The first one has been done for you.

   –6 – –8 = **–6 + +8 = +2**   +3 – –4 = **+3 + +4 = +7**
   +9 – +3 = **+9 + –3 = +6**   –1 – +7 = **–1 + +7 = +6**
   +7 – +5 = **+7 + +5 = +12**   –4 – +3 = **–4 + –3 = –7**

2. Write these problems as integers. The first one is done for you.

   a. The high temperature in the Arctic Circle one day was –42 degrees. The low was –67 degrees. What was the difference between the two?
   –42 – –67 = –42 + +67 = +25

   b. At the equator one day, the high temperature was +106 degrees. The low was +85 degrees. What was the difference between the two?
   +106 – +85 = +106 + –85 = +21

   c. At George's house one morning, the thermometer showed it was +7 degrees. The radio announcer said it was –2 degrees. What is the difference between the two temperatures?
   +7 – –2 = +7 + +2 = +9

   d. What is the difference between a temperature of +11 degrees and a wind-chill factor of –15 degrees?
   +11 – –15 = +11 + +15 = +26

   e. During a dry spell, the level of a river dropped from 3 feet above normal to 13 feet below normal. How many feet did it drop?
   +3 – –13 = +3 + +13 = +16

   f. Here are the average temperatures in a meat freezer for four days: –12, –11, –14, and –9 degrees. What is the difference between the highest and lowest temperature?
   –14 – –9 = –14 + +9 = –5

Page 447

Plotting Graphs

A graph with horizontal and vertical number lines can show the location of certain points. The horizontal number line is called the **x-axis**, and the vertical number line is called the **y-axis**. Two numbers, called the **x coordinate** and the **y coordinate**, show where a point is on the graph.

The first coordinate, x, tells how many units to the right or left of 0 the point is located. On the example graph, point A is +2, two units to the right of 0.

The second coordinate, y, tells how many units above or below 0 the point is located. On the example, point A is –3, three units below 0.

Thus, the coordinates of A are +2, –3. The coordinates of B are –3, +2. (Notice the order of the coordinates.) The coordinates of C are +3, +1; and D, –2, –2.

Directions: Study the example. Then, answer these questions about the graph below.

1. What towns are at these coordinates?

   +1, +3   **Patterson**
   +1, –3   **Harlow**
   –4, +1   **Stewart**
   –2, –3   **Clinton**
   –3, –2   **Weston**
   –3, +3   **Hillsville**

2. What are the coordinates of these towns?

   Hampton   **–2, +1**
   Wooster   **+3, +2**
   Beachwood **+2, –4**
   Middletown **+1, –1**
   Kirby   **–4, –1**
   Arbor   **+3, –2**

Page 448

Ordered Pairs

Ordered pairs is another term used to describe pairs of integers used to locate points on a graph.

Directions: Complete the following exercises.

1. Place the following points on the graph, using the ordered pairs as data.

   +3, +3
   –2, +4
   +1, –2
   +4, –4
   –4, –4
   +2, +3
   –1, +4

2. Create your own set of ordered pairs. Use your home as the center of your coordinates—zero. Let the x-axis serve as East and West. The y-axis will be North and South. Now, select things to plot on your graph—the school, playground, grocery store, a friend's house, and so on.

   Answers will vary.

Place	Ordered pair of coordinates
School	_____
Grocery store	_____
Playground	_____
Friend's house	_____

Page 449

Review

Directions: Complete the following exercises.

1. Write the **opposite** integers of the following:

   a. 14 degrees above 0 **–14**
   b. Spending $21 **+$21**

2. Write integers to show these ideas.

   a. 4 seconds after the launch of the space shuttle **+4**
   b. A lake 3 feet below its usual level **–3**
   c. 2 days before your birthday **–2**

3. Write < for "less than" or > for "greater than" to compare these integers.

   –2 **>** –4   +2 **>** –3   –1 **<** +1

4. Add the integers.

   –14 + –11 = **–25**   –6 + +5 = **–1**   –7 + +7 = **0**

5. Subtract the integers.

   –4 – –5 = **+1**   +3 – –6 = **+9**   +7 – +2 = **+5**

6. Write **T** for true or **F** for false.

   a. The x coordinate is on the horizontal number line. ____ **T**
   b. Add the x and y coordinates to find the location of a point. ____ **F**
   c. Always state the x coordinate first. ____ **T**
   d. A y coordinate of +2 would be above the horizontal number line. ____ **T**
   e. An x coordinate of +2 would be to the right of the vertical number line. ____ **T**

Page 450

Author's Purpose

Books, magazines, and websites all have specific purposes for their existence. While your child is reading or watching television, ask her to tell the purpose of the story, show, news segment, or commercial. Discriminating among authors' purposes makes for a more informed citizen and consumer.

Cause and Effect

Invite your child to read the newspaper front page, circling the causes of an event and underlining the effects. You can also have your child read an article on an online news site and tell you the causes and effects she reads about. Have your child write cause-and-effect statements for her daily activities. For example: I hit the snooze button on my alarm clock, so I was late for school. I practiced fielding ground balls over the weekend, so I did much better at baseball practice.

Classifying

Give your child several category names, and invite her to provide examples. For example: Modes of Transportation—car, train, bicycle, airplane, wheelchair, horse and buggy. See how many examples she can come up with for each category. Then, provide your child with several examples, and ask her to name the category. For example: sugar, candy, honey, fruit—Sweet Things.

Comprehension

As you read with your child, encourage her to create a mental image of what is happening. This will help your child recall the story using the mind's eye as well as the ear. Discuss details of the story. Ask your child about the sequence of events. Ask her to retell the story, noting details from the beginning, middle, and end.

Invite your child to write a different ending or new chapter to a story. If your child can do this in a logical manner, she has grasped the plot or ideas presented.

Ask your child questions about the story before you begin reading. For example: What do you think the illustration on the book cover means? Will this be an adventure story? A true story? What do you think the title means? What do you think will happen to (character's name)?

Your child is now reading chapter books. These books have very few pictures. Check your child's comprehension by having her draw pictures representing the action or the problem for each chapter. Before starting each new chapter, ask your child to predict what will happen.

TEACHING SUGGESTIONS

Decimals

Have your child use money to understand the concept of decimals as part of a whole. Use dollar bills and a variety of coins. Ask your child to find various fractions, or parts, of a dollar. You and your child can write out money problems for each other to figure out. Also, use money as a cross-reference with fractions. Example: 25 cents is 0.25 of a dollar .25 cents is also $\frac{25}{100}$ of a dollar.

Estimating

Take your child to the grocery store with you. While shopping, ask him to compare the prices of similar items of varying sizes and determine which is the better bargain. Invite your child to look at labels, pointing out that many are listed with customary and metric measurements. Ask him to estimate the total cost of the items by rounding numbers and averaging. Tell your child how much money you have to spend, and ask him to estimate the amount of change you should receive.

Take the family out to dinner, and have your child estimate the bill and calculate the appropriate amount to leave for a tip.

Take your child to a shopping mall in which several stores are having sales. Ask your child to estimate how much 40%, 25%, or 15% off an item would be, and so on. Then, calculate the sale price.

Fact/Opinion

Use the editorial section of a newspaper or magazine. Have your child read an article or letter and classify each sentence as either fact or opinion.

Many advertisements are confusing or misleading. Teach your child that everything in an ad may not be factual. Much of the appeal of ads is opinion. Cut out ads from magazines and newspapers, view or read them using online sources, and listen to them on television and radio. Help your child sort through the information. Ask him to point out the parts that are facts and those that are opinions. By realizing the difference and separating the two, your child will be able to make better judgments about which products to buy.

Fractions

Cut up fruits, vegetables, and other foods to help your child with the concept of fractions. Example: 8 sections of one whole orange, 1/8, 8/8; 2 halves of an apple, 1/2, 2/2; 6 pieces of pizza, 1/6, 6/6.

Your child can also use toy blocks in sets of 10, with a total of 100. Place the blocks on the floor, and explain that this represents one whole. Select different fractions for your child to find.

Geometry

Have your child cut out geometric shapes from cereal boxes, wallpaper scraps, construction paper, and so on. Invite him to create unique designs, and discuss the differences and similarities among the shapes.

Invite the whole family to join in measuring activities. See how quickly each family member can find the perimeter and area of his or her bedroom. Then, figure out the volumes. Invite your child to figure out how many square feet of living space are in your home, and how much space is used as storage areas.

Design a flower bed, or plant a vegetable garden. Ask your child to figure the dimensions needed for each plant, what percentage of the garden will be used for flowers, the ratio of edible plants to flowering plants, whether you will plant in straight lines or in geometric patterns, and so on.

Giving Directions

Ask your child if she has ever tried to assemble a game, toy, or other item and had difficulty following the directions. Invite your child to write more specific, easier-to-understand directions for any of those with which she had trouble. Once she has rewritten the directions, read them together. Do the directions make more sense?

Show your child the importance of giving clear directions by preparing a simple recipe together. Point out how the steps must be followed in order. Then, invite her to write a simple recipe for you to follow. Encourage your child to include all the necessary steps, andthen see if you can create the recipe from her directions.

Graphing

With your child, collect data of birds, insects, flowers, and plants that you see in your backyard. Do this on several different occasions, and then find the ratio between the sets of data.

Invite your child to make charts of games, books, or music owned by different family members. Any topic will work! Arrange the data into charts or line graphs.

Have your child record the ages of all the family members, including grandparents, aunts, uncles, and cousins. Then, have her calculate the mean age of the family. Point out to your child how this differs from the median age, using the same set of numbers.

TEACHING SUGGESTIONS

Homophone Challenge

Homophones are words that are pronounced the same but are spelled differently and have different meanings, like **pear** and **pair**. Challenge your child to a contest to see who can write the most homophones.

Main Idea

Show your child that the chapters or units in her textbooks are grouped according to the main idea: The Human Body, Space, and so on.

Invite your child to group things into categories to see if the concept, or main idea, is understood. Examples: wild animals, sports played outside, board games, books about famous American women.

Ask your child questions while reading together, such as, "What is the most important thing the author is saying in this paragraph?" or "Can you tell what the author means in this sentence?"

Making Inferences

Guide your child to figure out what an author means, even when it is not directly stated in the writing. Practice by describing a situation to your child and having her tell you what is happening. Start out with simple situations, and then move on to more complicated situations.

Poetry

Share your favorite poems with your child. Borrow books of poetry from the library to read together. Make up poems together, taking turns with every other line. There are many different types of poetry besides haiku, diamanté, and descriptive poetry. Try different poetry styles with your child.

Metaphor and Simile Poems: Have your child use metaphors and similes to create poetry. Poems can rhyme, but it's not necessary.

Example: Metaphor
The clouds in the sky,
Are popcorn rolling by.

Example: Simile
Elephants' noses
Are like firemen's hoses.
They squirt and they shower,
With plenty of power.

Let your child illustrate her poems for greater visual effect or write her best poems with glittery pens on fancy paper. Poetry can be printed in fancy type on the computer with graphics added. Frame the best ones, and hang them for all to enjoy.

Verb Poems: Many action words can be arranged on paper so the shape represents the action. Encourage your child to create his own action verb poems.

Example: ping ping ping ping; p$_o$^{u}r$_i$^{n}g

Limericks: Limericks are short, funny, five-line poems. The first, second, and fifth lines rhyme. The second and third lines rhyme as well. Edward Lear (1812–1888) first popularized limericks. Read the example below and other limericks out loud together.

Example: There is a fat cat in my town
               Whose fur is all spotted with brown;
               He spends his days,
               In a variety of ways,
               Strolling in the park with a clown.

Have your child use this sentence as the first line and complete the limerick. Then, have him write another one of his own.

               There was an old horse from Bellaire

Tanka: Tanka is an extension of haiku. Tankas complete the poet's thoughts by adding two extra lines at the end of seven syllables each. Remember, haiku has three lines of five, seven, and five syllables, respectively.

Example: Snow is falling down.
               Crystals collect on the ground.
               Winter has arrived.
               Snowmen will soon decorate
               The yards of children in town.

Have your child begin by composing a haiku. Then, have him add two additional lines to make the poem a tanka.

Changing Prose to Poetry

Often, colorful writing in essays, narratives, speeches, and advertisements can be easily transformed into poetry. Read the example with your child. Then, look for other topics, and create your own poem together.Example: HOUSE FOR SALE: This lovely home is situated on rolling ground in the country. Horses frolic in the pasture by day and retire to a well-kept barn at night. Lush forests surround the estate and offer plentiful wildlife along the winding paths.

Poem: I would love to live in a house,
Surrounded by nature and silence.
I would ride my horse through the woods,
And enjoy the sights and sounds of the forest.
I dream of being at peace,
Relaxed and carefree.
Alone in my beautiful house,
Surrounded by nature and silence.

Point of View

Learning to look at issues from more than one point of view can help your child see both sides. Read editorials in your local newspaper together. Discuss whose point of view is stated. Ask your child to present an opposing point of view to the one read. Even if he agrees with the writer, it is good practice. If you and your child feel strongly about an issue, write an editorial together and send it to your local newspaper. Remember to add reasons, facts, and examples to your editorial.

Problem Solving/Logic Problems

As you go about your daily business, point out the problem solving to be done. Have your child help you work through the problems, whether they are while cooking, fixing something, or creating a budget. He may help you map out the order for going around town to shop, taking your children to activities, doing your banking, and so on.

There are also books, websites, and magazines with word problems, such as crossword puzzles, logic problems, and diagramming logic puzzles. If your child enjoys the logic problems in this book, he may enjoy flexing his mind with one of these during leisure time.

Proofreading

The first draft of a story, whether handwritten or typed on a computer, should be one in which the writer doesn't worry about mechanics. She needs to create the characters, the setting, and the plot. Most stories take several revisions before they are finished. When the story is completed, you can guide your child in proofreading before making a final copy.

Help your child proofread other letters and reports she writes. Proofreading consists of checking for grammatical errors, misspellings, punctuation mistakes, and capitalization errors, and substituting synonyms for overused words. Using a spell-checking program on a computer is helpful, but it will not find and correct every error.

Make the corrections together until your child is able to handle proofreading on her own. Ask your child to help you check your written work, like memos, letters, and reports. This gives your child more practice and could be quite helpful to you.

Reading Extensions
Colonial America

Have your child research famous colonial women, such as Betsy Ross, Pocahontas, and Sacajawea. Write an informational paragraph about each woman's accomplishments. Invite your child to read more about the Puritans and the Quakers, and then complete a Venn diagram comparing the two groups.

Have your child make a time line of important Colonial American events. She can include events such as the arrival at Plymouth Rock, the first Thanksgiving, the Revolutionary War, and the signing of the Declaration of Independence.

Weather

Collect the daily newspaper weather map for a week, or print out a weather report from the Internet. Have you child go on a scavenger hunt for information such as Yesterday's High, Tomorrow's Forecast, Temperature in Paris, Pollen Count, and Pollution Index.

Give your child weather math problems to solve, such as computing the average daily temperature forecast for a week, or changing the high and low temperatures for the week from Fahrenheit to Celsius.

Invite your child to research earthquakes and compare them to weather phenomena such as tornadoes, hurricanes, and thunderstorms. Which is the most devastating force of nature? Compare damage in casualties and dollar amounts for each for a 10-year period in the United States. Ask your child to record her findings.

Australia

Ask your child to find a picture of the Australian flag and compare it to the United States flag. How are the flags alike? Different? What symbols are on the flags, and what do they represent? Invite your child to write a brief paragraph comparing and contrasting the two flags.

Have your child research the number of sheep in Australia versus the number of people. Have her create bar and circle graphs showing this information.

Invite your child to do additional research on the Aborigine culture. What is their diet? What traditions do they have? What dangers do they face in the future?

Have your child create a habitat display on an Australian animal. Divide a poster board into four equal sections. In the top left section, have her write an informational report about the animal. In the top right, have her make a web of animals to whom it is related. In the bottom left, have your child write a poem about the animal. Finally, in the last section, your child can draw the animal.

Kites

Invite your child to read more about Benjamin Franklin's kite and key experiment; then, write a one-paragraph informational essay about what was discovered. How was this discovery later applied in the world of science?

Have your child research different types of kites, including box kites, stunt kites, flat kites, and sled kites. Have your child describe what makes the kites alike and what makes them different.

Many kite terms are also weather terms. Encourage your child to find the definitions for the following words: **drag**, **lift**, **turbulence**, **upwind**, **wind speed**, and **downwind**. Ask your child to explain how these terms apply to kite flying. Or better yet, take your child out to fly a kite, and ask him to use these terms in the process!

Recalling Details

Write main ideas on index cards, such as "summer vacation." Then, ask your child to write several details about the idea, such as "no school," "playing with friends," "camping," "riding bikes," and so on.

Write a simple sentence for your child. Example: *The cat ran down the street.* Show your child how adding details makes the sentence more interesting. Example: *The fluffy white cat ran quickly down the noisy street.*

Ask him to add details to several simple sentences. Point out that these details are describing words, or adjectives.

Research/Locating Information

Have your child choose a topic that interests him. Help your child brainstorm a project he could do to find and present information about that topic. The project may include a written report, a speech, a demonstration, a model, a web page, an interview, etc. Help your child map out a "plan of attack" in obtaining, organizing, and presenting the information.

If there's not enough information about the chosen topic, help your child brainstorm again about researchable topics. Or, if there is too much information, you may need to help your child focus on a subtopic to research.

Then, allow your child to research and organize data independently. Check to make sure he is finding the needed information and is organizing it for easy use later. Make as many of the following resources available to your child as possible: newspapers, the Internet, encyclopedias, dictionaries, topical magazines, or journals. Your local public library should have all these resources available to you.

Have your child talk to his teacher about sharing the information/project with the rest of the class or turning it in for extra credit.

Summarizing Plots

The plot is the action in a story. To summarize a plot, tell about the most important parts in order. After your child finishes reading a book or watching a video, ask him to summarize the plot for you and make a recommendation whether he thinks you would enjoy it too.

Tests

Have your child create his own test using any or all of the formats covered in this book. Have him look at past tests to analyze what he might do differently on the next one. There are practice tests for many of the national standardized tests. If your child's school does not have access to them, they can give you a way to contact a company directly.

Using a Dictionary/Vocabulary Building

Encourage your child to learn the spelling and definitions of new words. Select a word of the day, and write it on a sheet of paper. Have your child look up the word and use it in a sentence. At the end of each week, review the new words for the week.

Another way to learn new words is to ask your child to open a dictionary at random and begin reading the words on that page. Stop at the first new word. Learn how to pronounce it and use it in a sentence.

Have your child think of synonyms for words he may overuse. For example: Cold can be replaced with **frosty**, **icy**, **freezing**, **chilly**, **cool**, and so on.

Word Origins

Help your child research your family name and your family tree. When and how did your ancestors arrive in America? Have any changes been made to the spelling of your surname?

Invite your child to find words that originate from Native American words. The states of Florida, Ohio, and New Jersey have many towns and lakes with Native American origins. Ask your child to trace the names to a specific tribe.

Guide your child to see that, although Latin is not a spoken language, many of the words in the English language are derived from Latin words. For example, the words **amiable**, **fictitious**, **liquid**, **major**, **omit**, and **poet** all have Latin origins. Invite your child to trace these and other words to the Latin words from which they are derived.

Writing

Read the editorial section of your local newspaper with your child. This section includes opinion essays. Invite your child to write a sample letter to the editor describing something about which she feels strongly. If it is currently relevant in your community, help her send it to the paper.

Have your child keep a daily journal during a vacation. She can record sights, sounds, and smells; favorite destinations; and so on. Collect and read brochures about various places and activities. At the end of the vacation, have your child reread her journal and write a short essay about vacation highlights.

Writing Directions

Being able to write and give clear directions is a useful skill for everyone. Encourage your child to practice writing directions for various tasks, like painting a room or planting a garden. Remind your child to think about what steps need to be done, in what order they should be done, and what equipment or tools are needed.

Directions from one location to another also need to be very clear. Ask your child to give the exact directions from your home to the library, post office, mall, or other location. Watch for vague words or phrases, like "turn by the yellow house" or "go past the blue car." Travel to that destination together following the directions exactly. Did you make it?

Before your child begins a task, ask her to write each step in order. Then, ask her to follow the directions exactly as written. This is the best way to determine if any steps or information have been omitted. Have her go back and add any missing information or clarify any steps that are unclear.

Writing an Invitation

An invitation needs to include the time, date, and place for an event; the reason for the invitation; and whether the receiver should indicate her ability to attend (RSVP).

Invitations may be written in paragraph form, but it is often much easier to follow the example to the right.
Let your child create an invitation for your next birthday bash or other get-together. She can decorate the cards by hand, or use a computer to create an original card. Be sure to include all relevant information.

> You're Invited!
> We're having a party for Mom and Dad's
> 50thAnniversary!
> Date: September 10, 2015
> Time: 5:00 P.M.–9:00 P.M.
> Place: McFrange Party Center
> RSVP: Mary at 555-1234
> by September 1, 2015
>
> Dinner will be served promptly at 5:30 P.M. No gifts please.

Writing a Thank-You Note

Saying thank you in writing is a good habit for children to learn. Children should write thank-you notes, not only for gifts, but also for thoughtful actions, like an invitation from a friend's parents or dinner or an overnight visit.

Help your child use proper form when composing a thank-you note, even though it may be informal in nature or sent via email.

> December 28, 2015
>
> Dear Grandma,
>
> I received your package in the mail yesterday. I love the quilt you made for my new bedroom. It will match perfectly. I have decorated my room with wildlife, and your choice of the Canadian goose is perfect. Thank you for thinking of me.
>
> Love,
> Zach

INDEX

Comprehensive Curriculum - Grade 6

INDEX